# DICTIONARY
# OF THE BRITISH ENGLISH
# SPELLING SYSTEM

# Dictionary of the British English Spelling System

*Greg Brooks*

*Emeritus Professor of Education, University of Sheffield*

OpenBook Publishers

http://www.openbookpublishers.com

© 2015 Greg Brooks
Version 1.1. Minor edits made July 2017

This work is licensed under a Creative Commons Attribution 4.0 International license (CC BY 4.0). This license allows you to share, copy, distribute and transmit the work; to adapt the work and to make commercial use of the work providing attribution is made to the author (but not in any way that suggests that he endorses you or your use of the work). Attribution should include the following information:

Brooks, Greg, *Dictionary of the British English Spelling System*. Cambridge, UK: Open Book Publishers, 2015. http://dx.doi.org/10.11647/OBP.0053

In order to access detailed and updated information on the license, please visit http://www.openbookpublishers.com/product/325#copyright

Further details about CC BY licenses are available at http://creativecommons.org/licenses/by/4.0

All the external links were active on the 19/07/2017 unless otherwise stated.

Digital material and resources associated with this volume are available at http://www.openbookpublishers.com/product/325#resources

ISBN Paperback: 978-1-78374-107-6
ISBN Hardback: 978-1-78374-108-3
ISBN Digital (PDF): 978-1-78374-109-0
ISBN Digital ebook (epub): 978-1-78374-110-6
ISBN Digital ebook (mobi): 978-1-78374-111-3
DOI: 10.11647/OBP.0053

Cover image: *Spiegel* by Jaume Plensa (2010). http://commons.wikimedia.org/wiki/Category:Yorkshire_Sculpture_Park#mediaviewer/File:YSP_11.jpg

All paper used by Open Book Publishers is SFI (Sustainable Forestry Initiative), and PEFC (Programme for the Endorsement of Forest Certification Schemes) Certified.

Printed in the United Kingdom and United States by Lightning Source
for Open Book Publishers (Cambridge, UK)

*To Maxine Burton,
for being such a patient and reliable native-speaker informant,
and for tolerating my obsession for so long.*

# Contents

| | |
|---|---|
| List of tables | xvii |
| About the author | xxi |
| Acknowledgments | xxiii |
| A 40-year gestation | xxv |
| How to use this book | xxix |

| | |
|---|---|
| 1 Introduction | 1 |
|    1.1 Context | 1 |
|    1.2 Aims | 2 |
|    1.3 Some terminology | 3 |
|    1.4 Phonemes | 4 |
|    1.5 Long and short vowels | 5 |
|    1.6 Graphemes | 5 |
|    1.7 Consonant clusters and 'blends' | 6 |
|    1.8 Split digraphs and 'magic <e>' | 6 |
|    1.9 Stem words and derived forms | 7 |
|    1.10 Positions within words | 7 |
|    1.11 Open and closed syllables | 9 |
|    1.12 '2-phoneme graphemes' | 9 |
|    1.13 'Regular' correspondences | 10 |
| 2 The phonemes of spoken English | 13 |
|    2.1 Choosing an accent to analyse | 13 |
|    2.2 How many phonemes? | 13 |
|    2.3 The consonant phonemes of Received Pronunciation | 14 |
|    2.4 The vowel phonemes of Received Pronunciation | 16 |
|    2.5 Polysyllabic words and word stress | 18 |

| | | |
|---|---|---|
| 3 | The phoneme-grapheme correspondences of English, 1: Consonants | 19 |
| | 3.1 The general picture: the regular spellings of English consonant phonemes | 19 |
| | 3.2 Order of description | 21 |
| | 3.3 Frequencies | 22 |
| | 3.4 The main system and the rest | 23 |
| | 3.5 Consonants with doubled spellings which are rare in one-syllable words: /b d g m n p t/, plus /r/ | 24 |
| |     3.5.1 /b/ as in *by* | 24 |
| |     3.5.2 /d/ as in *dye* | 25 |
| |     3.5.3 /g/ as in *goo* | 27 |
| |     3.5.4 /m/ as in *my* | 29 |
| |     3.5.5 /n/ as in *nigh* | 32 |
| |     3.5.6 /p/ as in *pie* | 34 |
| |     3.5.7 /t/ as in *tie* | 35 |
| |     3.5.8 /r/ as in *rye* | 39 |
| | 3.6 /r/-linking | 41 |
| | 3.7 Consonants with doubled spellings which are regular at the end of one-syllable words after a short vowel spelt with one letter: /k tʃ f dʒ l s v z/ | 47 |
| |     3.7.1 /k/ as in *coo* | 47 |
| |     3.7.2 /tʃ/ as in *chew* | 55 |
| |     3.7.3 /f/ as in *few* | 59 |
| |     3.7.4 /dʒ/ as in *jaw* | 62 |
| |     3.7.5 /l/ as in *law* | 66 |
| |     3.7.6 /s/ as in *sue* | 69 |
| |     3.7.7 /v/ as in *view* | 78 |
| |     3.7.8 /z/ as in *zoo* | 81 |
| | 3.8 Consonants without doubled spellings: /h ŋ ʃ ʒ θ ð w j/ | 86 |
| |     3.8.1 /h/ as in *who* | 86 |
| |     3.8.2 /ŋ/ as in *ring* | 87 |
| |     3.8.3 /ʃ/ as in *fission* | 89 |
| |     3.8.4 /ʒ/ as in *vision* | 94 |

| | |
|---|---|
| 3.8.5 /θ/ as in *thigh* | 96 |
| 3.8.6 /ð/ as in *thy* | 97 |
| 3.8.7 /w/ as in *well* | 98 |
| 3.8.8 /j/ as in *yell, union* | 103 |

**4 How do you know when to write a consonant letter double?** 109

4.1 The easy bits — 109

 4.1.1 Consonant letters are never doubled at the beginning of a word — 109

 4.1.2 Some consonant letters are never or almost never written double: <h, j, q, v, w, x, y> — 110

 4.1.3 Doubled consonant letters are very rare after long vowels and diphthongs — 110

4.2 The main consonant-doubling rule (Part 1 of 'double, drop or swop' – see sections 6.4–5) — 111

4.3 Other hints for writing a consonant letter double — 115

 4.3.1 Where the two parts of a compound word, or an affix and a stem, have adjacent identical consonant letters, the consonant letter is written double — 115

 4.3.2 Monosyllabic content words with /VC/ structure have a double consonant letter: the Three-Letter Rule — 116

 4.3.3 Consonant phonemes /b d f g k p t z/ are almost always spelt with double letters before final /əl/ spelt <-le> where the immediately preceding vowel phoneme is short, stressed and spelt with a single letter — 118

 4.3.4 More generally, consonant letters are mostly written double in the middle of two-syllable words where the immediately preceding vowel phoneme is short and written with a single letter — 120

 4.3.5 At the end of one-syllable words where the preceding vowel phoneme is short and spelt with a single letter the following consonant phonemes are mostly written double: /k tʃ f dʒ l s z v/ — 123

4.4 Hints for *not* writing consonant letters double 123
    4.4.1 At the end of one-syllable words where the preceding vowel phoneme is short and spelt with a single letter the following consonant phonemes are mostly written single: /b d g m n p t/ 123
    4.4.2 When do you not write consonant phonemes /b d f g k p t z/ with double letters before final /əl/ spelt <-le>? 124
    4.4.3 Digression: When do you not spell final /əl/ as <-le>? 125
    4.4.4 When do you not write doublable consonant letters double in the middle of two-syllable words (other than those ending in /əl/)? 128
    4.4.5 The third syllable from the end of a word rarely ends in a doubled consonant letter 128
    4.4.6 Doubled consonant letters are very rare immediately before the endings <-ic(al), -id, -it, -ule> 130
    4.4.7 When do you reduce <ll> to <l>? 131
4.5 Learn the rest 132
4.6 Consolation prizes 132
    4.6.1 Consonant letters are never written triple 132
    4.6.2 Final <CC> + <e> 133

5 The phoneme-grapheme correspondences of English, 2: Vowels 135
5.1 The general picture: the principal spellings of English vowel phonemes 135
5.2 Order of description 138
5.3 The main system and the rest 139
5.4 Short pure vowels: /æ e ɪ ɒ ʌ ʊ ə/ 139
    5.4.1 /æ/ as in *ash* 139
    5.4.2 /e/ as in *end* 140
    5.4.3 /ɪ/ as in *ink* 142
    5.4.4 /ɒ/ as in *ox* 148
    5.4.5 /ʌ/ as in *up* 150

|  |  |  |
|---|---|---|
| | 5.4.6 /ʊ/ as in *pull* | 151 |
| | 5.4.7 /ə/ (the schwa vowel) as in the first sound in *about* | 153 |
| 5.5 | Long pure vowels (other than /iː, uː/): /ɑː ɜː ɔː/ | 167 |
| | 5.5.1 /ɑː/ as in *aardvark* | 167 |
| | 5.5.2 /ɜː/ as in *earl* | 170 |
| | 5.5.3 /ɔː/ as in *awe* | 173 |
| 5.6 | Diphthongs (other than /eɪ, aɪ, əʊ/): /ɔɪ aʊ eə ɪə ʊə/ | 179 |
| | 5.6.1 /ɔɪ/ as in *oyster* | 179 |
| | 5.6.2 /aʊ/ as in *ouch* | 180 |
| | 5.6.3 /eə/ as in *air* | 181 |
| | 5.6.4 /ɪə/ as in *ear* | 185 |
| | 5.6.5 /ʊə/ as in *rural* | 188 |
| 5.7 | Letter-name vowels: /eɪ iː aɪ əʊ juː/, plus /uː/ | 191 |
| | 5.7.1 /eɪ/ as in *aim* | 191 |
| | 5.7.2 /iː/ as in *eel* | 196 |
| | 5.7.3 /aɪ/ as in *ice* | 205 |
| | 5.7.4 /əʊ/ as in *oath* | 210 |
| | 5.7.5 /juː/ as in *union* | 214 |
| | 5.7.6 /uː/ as in *ooze* | 216 |
| 6 Some spelling rules for vowels | | 221 |
| | 6.1 '<i> before <e> except after <c>' | 221 |
| | 6.2 'To spell the names of letters <a, i, o, u> in one-syllable words ending with a single consonant phoneme, write the vowel-name letter and the consonant letter and magic <e>' | 222 |
| | 6.3 'In non-final syllables of stem words, spell letter-name vowels with their name letters' | 223 |
| | 6.4 <e>-deletion (Part 2 of 'double, drop or swop') | 226 |
| | 6.5 <y>-replacement (Part 3 of 'double, drop or swop') | 229 |
| | 6.6 <ie>-replacement, <y>-deletion and <e>-insertion | 231 |
| | 6.7 <-able/-ible> | 232 |
| | 6.8 <- ant/-ent, -ance/-ence, -ancy/-ency> | 233 |

| | | |
|---|---|---|
| | 6.9 Using related forms to spell schwa | 234 |
| | 6.10 Elided vowels | 237 |
| 7 | Special processes | 245 |
| | 7.1 Dual-functioning | 245 |
| |     7.1.1 Letter \<e\> | 245 |
| |     7.1.2 Letter \<r\> | 246 |
| |     7.1.3 Letter \<w\> | 247 |
| |     7.1.4 Letter \<y\> | 248 |
| | 7.2 Surfacing sounds | 248 |
| |     7.2.1 Sounds which surface in stem-initial position | 248 |
| |     7.2.2 Sounds which surface in medial position | 249 |
| |     7.2.3 Sounds which surface in stem-final position | 250 |
| 8 | The graphemes of written English | 253 |
| | 8.1 Choosing a written variety to analyse | 253 |
| | 8.2 How many graphemes, and how many correspondences? | 253 |
| | 8.3 The graphemes of the main system and the rest | 262 |
| 9 | The grapheme-phoneme correspondences of English, 1: Graphemes beginning with consonant letters | 267 |
| | 9.0 Unwritten consonant phonemes | 267 |
| | 9.1 General introduction to the grapheme-phoneme correspondences | 267 |
| | 9.2 When is a digraph not a digraph? | 269 |
| | 9.3 Frequencies | 270 |
| | 9.4 The general picture: the regular pronunciations of English graphemes beginning with consonant letters | 271 |
| | 9.5 Order of description | 277 |
| | 9.6 \<b, bb\> | 278 |
| | 9.7 \<c\> | 279 |
| | 9.8 \<ce\> | 282 |
| | 9.9 \<ch\> | 283 |

| | |
|---|---|
| 9.10 &lt;ci&gt; | 286 |
| 9.11 &lt;ck&gt; | 287 |
| 9.12 &lt;d, dd&gt; | 287 |
| 9.13 &lt;dg, dge&gt; | 289 |
| 9.14 &lt;f, ff&gt; | 289 |
| 9.15 &lt;g, gg&gt; | 290 |
| 9.16 &lt;ge&gt; | 295 |
| 9.17 &lt;h&gt; | 296 |
| 9.18 &lt;j&gt; | 297 |
| 9.19 &lt;k&gt; | 298 |
| 9.20 &lt;l, ll&gt; | 299 |
| 9.21 &lt;le&gt; | 300 |
| 9.22 &lt;m, mm&gt; | 301 |
| 9.23 &lt;n, nn&gt; | 303 |
| 9.24 &lt;ng&gt; | 306 |
| 9.25 &lt;p, pp&gt; | 308 |
| 9.26 &lt;ph&gt; | 309 |
| 9.27 &lt;q&gt; | 310 |
| 9.28 &lt;r, rr&gt; | 312 |
| 9.29 &lt;s, ss&gt; | 313 |
| 9.30 &lt;se&gt; | 319 |
| 9.31 &lt;sh&gt; | 321 |
| 9.32 &lt;si&gt; | 322 |
| 9.33 &lt;ssi&gt; | 323 |
| 9.34 &lt;t, tt&gt; | 324 |
| 9.35 &lt;tch&gt; | 329 |
| 9.36 &lt;th&gt; | 329 |
| 9.37 &lt;ti&gt; | 331 |
| 9.38 &lt;v&gt; | 332 |
| 9.39 &lt;ve&gt; | 333 |
| 9.40 &lt;w&gt; | 334 |
| 9.41 &lt;wh&gt; | 335 |
| 9.42 &lt;x&gt; | 336 |

| | | |
|---|---|---|
| 9.43 | <z, zz> | 338 |
| 9.44 | Some useful generalisations about graphemes beginning with consonant letters | 339 |

**10 The grapheme–phoneme correspondences of English, 2: Graphemes beginning with vowel letters** — 343

| | | |
|---|---|---|
| 10.1 | The general picture: the regular pronunciations of English graphemes beginning with vowel letters | 343 |
| 10.2 | Order of description | 346 |
| 10.3 | <a> | 347 |
| 10.4 | <a.e> | 356 |
| 10.5 | <ai> | 360 |
| 10.6 | <air> | 361 |
| 10.7 | <ar> | 362 |
| 10.8 | <are> | 364 |
| 10.9 | <au> | 364 |
| 10.10 | <aw> | 366 |
| 10.11 | <ay> | 366 |
| 10.12 | <e> | 367 |
| 10.13 | <ea> | 378 |
| 10.14 | <ear> | 379 |
| 10.15 | <ed> | 380 |
| 10.16 | <ee> | 382 |
| 10.17 | <e.e> | 383 |
| 10.18 | <eer> | 384 |
| 10.19 | <er> | 384 |
| 10.20 | <ere> | 386 |
| 10.21 | <ew> | 387 |
| 10.22 | <i> | 388 |
| 10.23 | <ie> | 396 |
| 10.24 | <i.e> | 397 |
| 10.25 | <igh> | 400 |
| 10.26 | <ir> | 401 |

| | |
|---|---|
| 10.27 <o> | 402 |
| 10.28 <o.e> | 408 |
| 10.29 <oi> | 410 |
| 10.30 <oo> | 411 |
| 10.31 <or> | 413 |
| 10.32 <ore> | 414 |
| 10.33 <ou> | 415 |
| 10.34 <ow> | 418 |
| 10.35 <oy> | 419 |
| 10.36 <u> | 420 |
| 10.37 <ue> | 426 |
| 10.38 <u.e> | 427 |
| 10.39 <ur> | 428 |
| 10.40 <y> | 431 |
| 10.41 Correspondences of <a, e, i, o, u, y> (±word-final <e>) in content words with no other vowel letters (monosyllables) | 436 |
| 10.42 Correspondences of <a, e, i, o, u, y> in words with at least one later vowel letter other than 'silent' <e> (polysyllables) | 439 |
| 10.43 Consolation prize? | 445 |
| 11 Evaluating some pronunciation rules for vowel graphemes | 447 |
| 11.1 Some history | 447 |
| 11.2 'When there are two vowels side by side, the long sound of the first one is heard and the second is usually silent.' Often popularly stated as: 'When two vowels go walking, the first does the talking.' | 448 |
| 11.3 'When a written word has only one vowel letter, and that letter is followed by at least one consonant letter other than <r, w, y>, the vowel has its usual short pronunciation.' | 451 |
| 11.4 'When a final <e> is preceded by a consonant letter other than <r, w, x, y> and that consonant is preceded by a single vowel letter, the final <e> is silent and the other vowel letter has its letter-name ('long') sound.' | 452 |

11.5 'When <a> follows <qu, w, wh> and is not followed by <r>, or by any consonant letter plus <e>, it is pronounced /ɒ/.'   454

11.6 'When <y> is the final letter in a word, it always has a vowel sound, either alone or in combination with a preceding <a, e, o>.'   455

| | |
|---|---|
| Appendix A: Assumptions and technicalities | 457 |
|    A.1 Citation forms | 457 |
|    A.2 Phonemes | 457 |
|    A.3 Syllables | 458 |
|    A.4 Graphemes | 459 |
|    A.5 Every letter belongs to a grapheme (almost) | 460 |
|    A.6 Split digraphs | 461 |
|    A.7 Rhymes and phonograms (and rimes) | 466 |
|    A.8 Dual-functioning | 469 |
|    A.9 Graphemes containing apostrophes | 470 |
|    A.10 Word stress | 471 |
| Appendix B: Pedagogically selected lists of phoneme-grapheme and grapheme-phoneme correspondences | 477 |
| References | 487 |

# List of tables

2.1 The International Phonetic Alphabet symbols for the 24 consonant phonemes of the Received Pronunciation accent of English    15

2.2 The International Phonetic Alphabet symbols for the 20 vowel phonemes of the Received Pronunciation accent of English, plus /juː/    16

3.1 Main correspndences of the 11 consonant phonemes with variable spellings, by position in the word    20

3.2 Full list of /r/-linking categories    42

3.3 The distribution of <c, ck, k, x> in spellings of /k, ks/    54

3.4 The distribution of <c, s, ss> in initial and medial spellings of /s/ other than in /ks/    74

3.5 The distribution of <c, ce, s, se, ss> in stem-final spellings of /s/ other than in /ks/ (also excluding grammatical suffixes)    76

3.6 The distribution of <ti, ce, ci, si, ssi> as spellings of medial /ʃ/    93

3.7 Examples of /w/ represented or not between a stem word ending in /(j)uː, əʊ, aʊ/ and a suffix beginning with a vowel phoneme    102

3.8 Examples of /j/ represented or not between a stem word ending in /aɪ, eɪ, ɔɪ, iː/ and a suffix beginning with a vowel phoneme    107

4.1 Single and double consonant spellings after short and long vowels    111

4.2 Non-equivalence of sets of consonant phonemes spelt double in two circumstances    120

| | | |
|---|---|---|
| 4.3 | Examples and exceptions of the rule that two-syllable words have medial consonant letters written double after a short vowel phoneme written with a single letter | 121 |
| 4.4 | Some cases where stem words ending in /əl/ do or do not retain /ə/ before a suffix beginning with a vowel phoneme | 127 |
| 4.5 | Examples of the rule that the third syllable from the end of a word rarely ends in a doubled consonant letter, with exceptions not arising from affixation | 128 |
| 5.1 | Main spellings of the 20 vowel phonemes, plus /juː/, by word position | 136 |
| 5.2 | Spellings of /ɒ/ as <a> after /w/ | 149 |
| 5.3 | Spellings of /ɔː/ as <ar> after /w/ | 175 |
| 5.4 | <au, aw, or, ore> as spellings of /ɔː/ | 176 |
| 5.5 | Spellings of /ɪə/ in medial and final positions | 187 |
| 5.6 | <ea, ee, e.e, ie, i.e> as spellings of /iː/ in closed final syllables | 202 |
| 5.7 | Spellings of /əʊ/ in final syllables | 212 |
| 8.1 | All the consonant graphemes of written English, by RP phoneme | 255 |
| 8.2 | All the vowel graphemes of written English, by RP phoneme, plus /juː/ | 259 |
| 8.3 | Alphabetical list of the 89 graphemes of the main system | 264 |
| 8.4 | Alphabetical list of the other 195 graphemes | 265 |
| 9.1 | 21 main-system consonant graphemes with only one pronunciation each | 272 |
| 9.2 | 20 main-system consonant graphemes with only one frequent pronunciation each | 273 |
| 9.3 | Nine main-system consonant graphemes with two regular pronunciations each | 274 |
| 9.4 | Main-system graphemes beginning with consonant letters, by main- system and minor correspondences and numbers of Oddities | 275 |
| 9.5 | Medial <s> pronounced /z/, with sub-exceptions pronounced /s/ and sub-sub-exceptions pronounced /z/ | 315 |
| 9.6 | /s, z/ as pronunciations of word-final <se> | 320 |

10.1 Main-system graphemes beginning with vowel letters, by main- 344
system and minor correspondences and numbers of oddities
10.2 Regular correspondences of <a, e, i, o, u, y> (±word-final 437
<e>) in monosyllabic content words
10.3 Open monosyllables with a single vowel letter 438
10.4 Short and long pronunciations of single-letter vowel graphemes 439
before single and double consonant spellings

11.1 'When two vowels go walking, the first does the talking' 450
11.2 Pronunciations of vowel letters in words with a single, non- 451
final vowel letter followed by at least one consonant letter other
than <r, w, y>
11.3 Reliability of rules for split digraphs or 'magic <e>' where the 453
intervening letter is not <r, w, x, y>

B.1 The phoneme-grapheme correspondences of British English 477
spelling, by RP phoneme, 1: Consonants
B.2 The phoneme-grapheme correspondences of British English 479
spelling, by RP phoneme, 2: Vowels
B.3 The phoneme-grapheme correspondences of British English 480
spelling, 3: 2-phoneme sequences frequently spelt with single
graphemes
B.4 The grapheme-phoneme correspondences of British English 481
spelling, 1: Single graphemes frequently pronounced as
2-phoneme sequences
B.5 The grapheme-phoneme correspondences of British English 481
spelling, 2: Major correspondences for consonant graphemes
B.6 The grapheme-phoneme correspondences of British English 483
spelling, 3: Minor correspondences for consonant graphemes
B.7 The grapheme-phoneme correspondences of British English 484
spelling, 4: Major correspondences for vowel graphemes
B.8 The grapheme-phoneme correspondences of British English 485
spelling, 5: Minor correspondences for vowel graphemes

# About the author

Greg Brooks is Emeritus Professor of Education, University of Sheffield, where he held a personal chair in 2002-07. He had previously worked at the National Foundation for Educational Research for 20 years, and before that taught for various periods in France, Kenya, Essex and Northern Ireland. He has been engaged in virtually full-time educational research since 1977, almost all of it concerned with literacy and/or the phonological aspects of language – phonological coding in silent reading, speaking and listening abilities, adult and family literacy, phonics and its phonetic underpinnings, literacy interventions for children and young people, trends in literacy and numeracy attainment over time, and of course spelling. He is a former President, and Honorary Life Member, of the UK Literacy Association, and a member of the Reading Hall of Fame. In 2011-12 he was one of the 10 expert members of the European Union High Level Group of Experts on Literacy, and in 2015 is Chairperson of the Federation of European Literacy Associations, and a member of the management board of the European Literacy Policy Network.

# Acknowledgments

My special thanks (for the reasons, see the following section) go to:
- Tom Gorman, who deflected me from this quest in 1976 in favour of my doctoral subject
- Roger Beard, who set me on it again, and
- John Mountford, who went off on a different one.

Special thanks also to Ros Fisher, who provided the anecdote in section 3.7.2.

I am indebted to several people's previous efforts, especially their copious word-lists: Kenneth Albrow, Masha Bell, Vivian Cook, A.C. Gimson, Alan Cruttenden, W.R. Lee, John Mountford, Andrew Rollings, Axel Wijk, the now anonymous authors of *The Spelling Rulebook*, and above all Edward Carney, whose frequencies for phoneme-grapheme correspondences also feature regularly in chapters 3 and 5.

Ivair Gontijo kindly engaged in discussion by email from California about his and his wife Possi's grapheme-phoneme database, which provided the basis for the frequencies cited in chapters 9 and 10.

A paper given by Irina F. Shcherbakova (then of the Moscow Reading Centre) at the 11th European Conference on Reading in Stavanger, Norway, in 1999 (Shcherbakova, 1999) contained an analysis of the pronunciation of vowel letters in English monosyllables which I have expanded into Table 10.2. Her colleague Natalia N. Smetannikova told me in 2014 that she and others had been using Irina's 11 Tables of phoneme-grapheme and grapheme-phoneme correspondences in teaching English for 40 years - see next page for a parallel.

For two further acknowledgments see the beginning of section 4.2.

# A 40-year gestation

In 1972-73 I took the MA in Applied Linguistics course at the University of Essex. A year or two later, reflecting on that course and hoping to do a doctorate, I identified two possible topics: an attempt to specify the relationships between the graphemes of written English and the phonemes of spoken English as a set of TG (transformational-generative) rewrite rules (this being my preference), and phonological coding in silent reading.

In 1976 I visited the University of Essex to consult Tom Gorman on those topics. He advised strongly against my grapheme-phoneme idea ('It would require a large computer and a lot of programming', he said, accurately, in terms of the machines available then), and strongly in favour of the phonological one, which became the subject of my PhD at the University of Leeds (Brooks, 1985), on which I worked full-time in 1977-80, then in my spare time.

Meanwhile Tom had become head of a department at NFER, which I joined at the beginning of 1981. I was still interested in my grapheme-phoneme idea, but able to work on it only sporadically, even after completing my doctorate. Then in early 1989 the Director of NFER, Clare Burstall, passed on a query from Keith Joseph (who had been Secretary of State for Education and Science, 1981-86): 'He asked whether information was available on the book or books most commonly used in Initial Teacher Education in courses relating to the teaching of reading' (Gorman, 1989: 3). In his report Tom cited Christopher Brumfit (1988) who, in a 'study of the teaching of language in teacher education in the UK ... note[d] a lack of books explicitly on the description of language' (Gorman, 1989: 3), and Tom himself concluded that predominant approaches to the teaching of reading at the time 'underplay the amount of knowledge teachers need to have about the sound system and the written system of English in order to intervene strategically to assist children to understand the relationship between these' (Gorman, 1989: 7).

In 1991 the Secretary of State for Education and Science, Ken Clarke, asked the Council for the Accreditation of Teacher Education (CATE) to undertake a much larger, systematic enquiry into the preparation of teachers to teach reading. As part of this the DES commissioned a team at NFER to conduct the research that CATE would need. We produced both a summary report (Brooks et al., 1991) which formed Part B of the official report (CATE, 1992), and a volume containing our working papers (Brooks et al., 1992). In the summary report (p.13) we repeated Tom Gorman's 'underplay' statement (above), and concluded it still held; and bemoaned (pp.11-12) the absence of any teaching of the phonetics needed to underpin accurate teaching of phonics. In the Working Papers volume, specifically in our analysis of the ITE institutions' reading lists (p.41), we said: 'No books dealing in any detail with the complex relationships between the writing system (the orthography) and the sound system (the phonology) of English ... are to be found among the 30 most common reference books.'

The last point was picked up by Roger Beard of the University of Leeds, who saw that there was a gap in the literature, not because there were no relevant books – see those by Albrow, Gimson (early editions), Venezky and Wijk in the references – but because they were all far too technical. He was then a commissioning editor of books on language and literacy, and invited me to Leeds to discuss what a book 'dealing with the complex relationships between the orthography and the phonology of English' should contain, and who might write it. We agreed that it should cover comprehensively both grapheme–phoneme and phoneme–grapheme relationships, and provide information of use to teachers. I was too busy to write it, but Roger already had John Mountford in mind. John's book (Mountford, 1998) took a while to appear, and even in early drafts was clearly rather different from the book Roger and I had envisaged. So I began to work in earnest on my own.

The need for 'a large computer and a lot of programming' that Tom Gorman had once warned me about was obviated by the work of others who had those resources: first for frequencies of phoneme–grapheme correspondences by Carney (1994), and later for frequencies of grapheme–phoneme correspondences by Gontijo et al. (2003). (Carney's book also contained grapheme–phoneme frequencies, but in a form unsuited to my purposes.) However, the more I delved into the intricacies of English spelling, the larger my comprehensive lists and analyses became – hence the size of this book.

Along the way a teacher-friendlier spin-off was possible. When Laura Huxford and Jenny Chew were drafting the *Letters and Sounds* materials (D*f*ES, 2007), they consulted me on details of correspondences (both directions), and I provided them with handy phonics-friendly tables of the main ones which (slightly modified) appeared in *Letters and Sounds*. In 2008 I also provided them to Roger Beard, who was then chairing a panel evaluating phonics schemes. He has commented (personal communication, 2013) that they 'proved to be succinct, easily accessible and linguistically accurate'. Further versions appear in Appendix B here.

However, the battle to convince policy-makers and others of the need for teachers to understand the phonetic underpinnings of phonics has yet to be won. When I was on the Rose Committee, Maxine Burton and I submitted a paper (Burton and Brooks, 2005) to the committee putting the case for using the International Phonetic Alphabet (IPA) in teaching teachers about phonics, but this was ignored, as was my attempt to convince Laura and Jenny to use IPA symbols (rather than those of their own devising) in *Letters and Sounds*. I have argued that case into an apparent wilderness again (Brooks, 2007, 2011), but Maxine's book *Phonetics for Phonics* (Burton, 2011), which also contains the eight tables of correspondences included here in Appendix B, appears to be having some impact. We will fight on, and I hope the uncompromising use of IPA in this book will support that.

# How to use this book

To find an explanation of International Phonetic Alphabet (IPA) symbols, see chapter 2.

To look up the various ways a consonant phoneme is spelt, find its entry in chapter 3.

To look up the various ways a vowel phoneme is spelt, find its entry in chapter 5.

To look up the various ways a grapheme beginning with a consonant letter is pronounced, find its entry in chapter 9.

To look up the various ways a grapheme beginning with a vowel letter is pronounced, find its entry in chapter 10.

To find full lists and numbers of graphemes and phoneme–grapheme correspondences, see chapter 8.

To find lists of the major grapheme–phoneme correspondences, see Table 9.4 in chapter 9 and Table 10.1 in chapter 10.

For teacher-friendlier lists of both kinds of correspondence, see Appendix B.

Rules and hints for writing consonant letters double are in chapter 4.

Some spelling rules for vowel phonemes are in chapter 6.

Chapter 11 evaluates a few pronunciation rules for vowel graphemes.

For discussion of assumptions and technicalities see Appendix A.

To find discussions of individual words, search for them in the online version, as follows:
- Find the book at http://www.openbookpublishers.com/product/325
- Click on 'READ THE HTML'.
- In the 'Search this book' box enter the word you're interested in.
- If this fails to produce even one Google search result, sorry, the word isn't in the book.

- But if a Google search result does come up, click on it to bring up the relevant chapter, then press Control+F, enter the word you're interested in and press Return. Happy browsing!

**Caveat emptor**: Here are some things this book is **not** about (see also the penultimate paragraph of section 1.2):

- It has very little to say about the teaching of spelling – for a handy online guide to that and to the anlaysis of spelling errors, see http://spellingmeshguide.pbworks.com/?_ci=15968.HqTypA-2
- It does not attempt to teach the technicalities of phonetics or phonology – for those see Cruttenden (2014) and Roach (2009);
- Because the range of accents with which English is spoken is so vast, attempting to relate English spelling to all of them would produce an encyclopedia, hence this book focuses solely on the British Received Pronunciation accent (and British spelling). Should I live long enough, I may try to produce a parallel volume on the General American accent (and US spelling);
- It does not attempt to relate the description of the spelling system to psycholinguistic theories about the processes involved in reading and spelling (e.g. 'dual-route theory') – for all of that I recommend Snowling and Hulme (2005);
- It does not tackle in any detail the question of how to tell from the written forms of English words which of their spoken counterparts' syllables are stressed and which are not – but for some reflections on this see section A.10 in Appendix A.

To hear the phonemes of English pronounced in context with an RP accent, try this British Library website: http://www.bl.uk/learning/langlit/sounds/case-studies/received-pronunciation

For very user- and teacher-friendly guidance on spelling, *Jazzy Spelling Secrets: Teacher's Toolkit*, shortly to be published by Jaz Ampaw-Farr of Which Phonics Ltd, sign up to her website: http://whichphonics.co.uk

# 1. Introduction

## 1.1 Context

English spelling is notoriously complicated and difficult to learn, and is correctly described as much less regular and predictable than any other alphabetic orthography. The 40+ distinctive speech sounds (phonemes) of the spoken language are represented by a multiplicity of letters and letter-combinations (graphemes) in the written language; correspondingly, many graphemes have more than one pronunciation. This is because English has absorbed words from many other languages (especially French, Latin and classical Greek) into its Germanic base, and mainly taken over spellings or transliterations of those words without adapting them to the original system. Two recent books (Crystal, 2012; Upward and Davidson, 2011) tell this story with wit and insight.

However, there is more regularity in the English spelling system than is generally appreciated. This book, based on a very detailed analysis of the relationships between the phonemes and graphemes of British English, provides a thorough account of the whole complex system. It does so by describing how phonemes relate to graphemes, and vice versa. It is intended to be an authoritative reference guide for all those with a professional interest in English spelling, including and especially those who devise materials for teaching it, whatever their students' age and whether their own or their students' mother tongue is English or not. It may be particularly useful to those wishing to produce well-designed materials for teaching initial literacy via phonics (for guidance on the phonetics which should underpin accurate phonics teaching see Burton, 2011), or for teaching English as a foreign or second language, and to teacher trainers.

The book is intended mainly as a work of reference rather than theory. However, all works of reference are based on some theory or other, whether or not explicitly stated for readers, and even if not consciously known to the writer. For the assumptions I have made and for discussion of technical issues, see Appendix A.

## 1.2 Aims

My aims are to set out:
1) the distinctive speech sounds (phonemes) of spoken English
2) the letters and letter-combinations (graphemes, spelling choices) of written English
3) how the phonemes of spoken English relate to the graphemes of written English
4) the mirror-image of that, that is, how the graphemes of written English relate to the phonemes of spoken English
5) some guidance on the patterning of those relationships.

The core of the book is the chapters in which I set out the relationships (correspondences) between phonemes and graphemes:

|  | Phoneme-grapheme correspondences | Grapheme-phoneme correspondences |
|---|---|---|
| **Consonants** | Chapter 3 | Chapter 9 |
| **Vowels** | Chapter 5 | Chapter 10 |

Although chapters 9 and 10 are concerned with how the **graphemes** of English are pronounced, those seeking guidance on how to pronounce (including where to stress) whole English **words**, given only their written form, should instead consult a pronouncing dictionary in which the International Phonetic Alphabet is used, e.g. the *Cambridge English Pronouncing Dictionary, 18th Edition* (Cambridge: Cambridge University Press, 2011). The phonetic transcription system used in this book (see chapter 2) is identical to the system used in that dictionary. A useful guide for those who are uncertain whether, for example, an English word beginning with a 'yuh'-sound begins with the letter <y> or the letter <u> is the ACE (Aurally Coded English) Spelling Dictionary by David Moseley (1998).

I make only a few suggestions in this book about how to **teach** English spelling – my aim is mainly to set out my analysis of the system. However, some findings may have pedagogical applications – see especially chapter 11, section A.7 in Appendix A, and Appendix B. I also make no attempt to justify English spelling or summarise its history (see again Crystal, 2012; Upward and Davidson, 2011), and make only a very few remarks on changes that might be helpful. For a few other things which this book does not attempt to do see p.xii.

My analysis is confined to the main vocabulary of English – I almost entirely omit the extra complexities of spellings which occur only in personal, place- and brand-names (though I mention a few where they parallel rare spellings in ordinary words; see also section A.5 in Appendix A), archaic or obsolete words, words which occur in non-standard dialects of English but not in Standard English, culinary terms with spelling patterns which occur in no other word, words known only to Scrabble addicts, and new spellings in text messaging. And there are intricacies which I have glossed over or passed over in silence – if you want to go further consult one or more of the books listed in the references.

# 1.3 Some terminology

Some familiarity with linguistic and grammatical terminology is assumed, e.g. 'indefinite article', 'noun', 'adjective', 'verb', 'adverb', 'content word', 'function word', 'singular', 'plural', 'third person', 'present', 'past', 'tense', 'participle', 'possessive', 'bound forms', 'affix', 'prefix', 'suffix', 'syllable', 'penultimate', 'antepenultimate'. Some terms, however, are used in different senses by different writers and/or are less familiar – most of those I find indispensable are explained in the remaining sections of this chapter (and various others in sections 2.3, 2.5, 3.6, 5.5.3, 6.4–6, 6.10, 7.1, 7.2).

Throughout the book,
- I refer to the distinctive speech sounds of spoken English as 'phonemes' and show them between forward slashes; for example, /b/ is the first phoneme in the word *bad*;
- I refer to the spelling choices of written English as 'graphemes' and show them between angled brackets; for example, <p> is the first grapheme in the word *pad*; and
- I refer to the relationships between phonemes and graphemes (in both directions) as 'correspondences'.

An asterisk before a word indicates that the word is misspelt, e.g. *accomodation, *hastle, *occured.

## 1.4 Phonemes

Phonemes are distinctive speech sounds, that is, they make a difference to the meanings of words. For example, the difference between /b/ and /p/ makes the difference in meaning between *bad* and *pad*. (There is of course much more to this – for some discussion, see Appendix A, section A.2).

In English, phonemes fall into two main categories, consonants and vowels. These terms may well be familiar to you as categories of **letters**, but the very familiarity of these labels for letters may cause confusion when thinking about **phonemes**. For one thing, there are many more phonemes in spoken English (44 or thereabouts) than there are letters in the English version of the Roman alphabet (26). For another, some graphemes are used to represent both consonant and vowel phonemes – the most familiar example being the letter <y>.

To phoneticians, the difference between consonant and vowel **phonemes** is that consonants require some obstruction of the airflow between lungs and lips, whereas vowels do not. For technical details on this see Peter Roach (2009) *English Phonetics and Phonology*, Fourth edition, Cambridge: Cambridge University Press. However, for practical purposes a test for distinguishing between consonant and vowel phonemes which works for English is that the indefinite article, when immediately followed by a word which begins with a consonant phoneme, takes its *a* form, but when immediately followed by a word which begins with a vowel phoneme takes its *an* form. So *hand*, *union* and *one-off* begin with consonant phonemes, but *hour*, *umbrella* and *on-off* begin with vowel phonemes.

Vowel phonemes can consist of one or two sounds. Those which consist of one sound are pure vowels, and those which consist of two sounds are diphthongs. When you pronounce a pure vowel, your jaw, lips, etc., remain relatively stationary; when you pronounce a diphthong, they move. Try saying the words *awe* (which consists in speech of one pure vowel) and then *owe* (which consists in speech of a diphthong), and feel the difference.

(For long and short vowels see sections 1.5 and 2.4).

In contrast, most consonant phonemes consist of only one sound, though they can of course occur in clusters, for example at the beginning and end of *strengths*. The only consonant phonemes in English which consist of two sounds are those at the beginning of *chew* and *jaw* – see the complex symbols for these phonemes in Table 2.1 in chapter 2.

(For consonant clusters and blends see section 1.7).

## 1.5 Long and short vowels

To many teachers, a short vowel is a **sound** related within the teaching approach known as phonics to one of the **letters** <a, e, i, o, u>, and a long vowel is a different sound related within phonics to one of the same five letters. In this book the terms 'short vowel' and 'long vowel' are not used in this way, but in the senses they have in phonetics. To phoneticians, a short vowel is a **phoneme** that takes only a few milliseconds to pronounce, and a long vowel is a **phoneme** that takes rather longer to pronounce. Both are pure vowels in the sense defined in section 1.4, and both categories are listed and exemplified in section 2.4, where it is shown that the English accent on which this book is based has seven short pure vowel phonemes and five long pure vowel phonemes.

Five of the short pure vowels are indeed the sounds associated with the letters <a, e, i, o, u> in phonics teaching, but there are two more short vowels in the phonetic sense: the sound represented by letter <u> in *put*, and the sound represented by letter <a> in *about*. And of the five so-called long vowels associated with the letters <a, e, i, o, u> in phonics teaching, only the name of letter <e> is a long pure vowel in the phonetic sense; three are diphthongs (the names of <a, i, o>), and the name of <u> is a sequence of two phonemes, the sound of letter <y> when it begins a word followed by the sound of the exclamation 'Oo!'.

However, the sounds which are the names of the letters <a, e, i, o, u>, plus the phoneme whose sound is 'oo' (phonetic symbol /uː/), do have some useful spelling properties as a set. I make use of this fact in chapters 5 and 6, where you will find them grouped together as the 'letter-name vowels plus /uː/'. See also section 1.10 below.

## 1.6 Graphemes

I define graphemes as single letters or letter-combinations that represent phonemes. (Again, there is more to it than this – for some discussion, see Appendix A, section A.4).

Graphemes come in various sizes, from one to four letters. I call graphemes consisting of one, two and three letters 'single-letter graphemes', 'digraphs' and 'trigraphs' respectively. Where it is necessary to mention four-letter graphemes (of which there are 19, in my analysis – see Tables 8.1-2), for example <ough> representing a single phoneme as in *through*,

I call them 'four-letter graphemes' (and not 'tetragraphs' or 'quadgraphs'). Graphemes of all four sizes are used in English to spell both consonant and vowel phonemes.

## 1.7 Consonant clusters and 'blends'

As already illustrated with the word *strengths*, consonant phonemes (and letters) can occur in groups. Many teachers use the term 'blend' for such groups, but I have observed that it is often used to cover not only **groups** of consonant phonemes or letters, but also digraphs and trigraphs representing **single** consonant phonemes – which can and does create two sources of confusion. First, using 'blend' in this way means that letters and sounds are being muddled up; it is a central tenet of my approach that graphemes and phonemes must be carefully distinguished.

Secondly, it encourages some teachers to think that 'blends' need to be taught as units, rather than as sequences of letters and phonemes. For example, it makes more sense to teach <bl> at the beginning of the word *blend* itself as two units, <b> pronounced /b/ and <l> pronounced /l/ (segmentation, in the terminology of synthetic phonics), and then merge them into /bl/ (blending (!), again in the terminology of synthetic phonics, where this term is entirely appropriate). For both analytical and teaching purposes the two categories of clusters and multi-letter graphemes are best kept apart. I therefore stick with the term 'clusters' for groups of consonant phonemes or letters, and avoid the term 'blend' completely.

## 1.8 Split digraphs and 'magic <e>'

In English spelling there are six digraphs which are not written continuously but are interrupted by a consonant letter (or occasionally two consonant letters or a consonant letter plus <u>). These digraphs have one of the letters <a, e, i, o, u, y> as the first letter and <e> as the second letter, and in most cases that <e> marks the first vowel letter as having what teachers call its 'long' sound (if we accept, which never seems to be pointed out, that the 'long' sound of <y> when used as a vowel letter is the same as that of <i>). For example, in *bite* the 'eye' sound is represented by the letters <i, e> even though they are separated by the <t>. I call digraphs which consist of two separated letters 'split digraphs'. To symbolise split digraphs I write the two relevant letters with a dot between them; for example, the split digraph representing the 'eye' sound in *bite* is written as <i.e>. In my analysis, the full set of split digraphs is <a.e, e.e, i.e, o.e, u.e, y.e>. I have not found it necessary to posit more complicated graphemes such as <ae.e> ('split trigraphs'?) – see section A.6 in Appendix A.

Split digraphs occur only towards the end of written stem words. They have no place in conventional alphabetical order, so when I need to include them in alphabetical lists, I place them immediately after the digraph consisting of the same two letters but not split, for example <a.e> comes after <ae> (or sometimes where the unsplit digraph would be, if it happens not to be needed in a particular list).

(I also posit four graphemes containing apostrophes: <e'er, e're, ey're, ou're> – these I place in lists as if the apostrophe were a 27th letter of the alphabet. See section A.9 in Appendix A).

Many teachers refer to the split digraph use of <e> as 'magic <e>'. While this seems perfectly valid pedagogically (and I use the expression occasionally in this book), I mostly use the term 'split digraph' because not all occurrences of the split digraphs contain 'magic <e>' in the sense that the other vowel letter has its usual 'long' pronunciation. (See the entries for <a.e, e.e, i.e, o.e, u.e, y.e> in chapter 10, sections 10.4/17/24/28/38/40).

For a more technical discussion of split digraphs see section A.6 in Appendix A, and for a pedagogical discussion of 'magic <e>' rules see section 11.4.

## 1.9 Stem words and derived forms

Stem words are those which are indivisible into parts which still have independent meaning; derived forms are all other words, i.e. those which contain either a stem word and one or more prefixes or suffixes, and/or two (or more) stem words combined into a compound word. This book is mainly concerned with stem words, but some sections apply specifically to derived forms (e.g. section 4.2 on the rule for doubling stem-final consonant letters before suffixes beginning with a vowel letter). I try throughout to indicate where rules or correspondences differ between stem words and derived forms, sometimes in separate lists, sometimes by using brackets round prefixes and suffixes; and I often refer to derived forms as 'derivatives'.

## 1.10 Positions within words

Many correspondences are specific to particular positions in words, some to the beginnings of words ('word-initial position'), some to the middle of words ('medial position'), some to the ends of words ('word-final position'). In chapters 3-7, that is, all the chapters concerned with the sound-to-symbol direction, I have tried to be consistent in using 'initial', 'medial' and 'final' only in terms of **phonemes** (or, where specifically indicated, syllables – see third and fourth paragraphs below). For example, the phoneme /j/ (the sound of letter <y> at the beginning of a word) is in word-initial position in both *yell* and *union*.

Word-final position applies to consonant phonemes even when the letters representing them occur within split digraphs, e.g. the /t/ phoneme in *bite* is in word-final position even though the letter <t> is not. Correspondingly, vowel phonemes and diphthongs spelt by the split digraphs are never word-final – as I've just implied with the example of *bite*, there is always a consonant phoneme after the vowel phoneme or diphthong, even though the letter <e> is at the end of the **written** word. In section 5.5.3 (only) I also refer to 'pre-final' position, that is, the phoneme immediately preceding the last phoneme in a word.

In chapters 3-7 I frequently use the term 'word-final position' to mean the end of stem words. For instance, when I say that the grapheme <sh> is the regular spelling of the 'sh' phoneme in word-final position I include its occurrences in both *fish* and *fishing*. Even more generally, when I say that a particular correspondence occurs in a stem word, this also applies to words derived from it, unless otherwise stated.

Other correspondences are specific to particular syllables in words; some are specific to monosyllabic words and the final syllables of polysyllabic words – I call these collectively 'final syllables' – and others to syllables before the last one in words of more than one syllable ('non-final syllables'). In sections 10.27 and 10.36 I also distinguish between penultimate and antepenultimate syllables, that is, those immediately before the final syllable and immediately before that in words with enough syllables; and in section 10.42 antepenultimate syllables reappear, along with the fourth syllable from the end of a word.

The largest set of exceptions to analysing phoneme-grapheme correspondences according to intial, medial and stem-final **phonemic** positions within words relates to the letter-name vowels, plus /uː/. As will be shown in section 5.1, these need instead to be analysed according to final v. non-final syllables.

Some authors use the terms 'polysyllables' and 'polysyllabic words' to refer to words of three or more syllables, and therefore distinguish systematically between monosyllables, disyllables (two-syllable words) and polysyllables. However, in my analysis I have mainly found it unnecessary to distinguish between disyllables and longer words, and therefore use the terms 'polysyllables' and 'polysyllabic words' to refer to words of **two or more** syllables. On the few occasions when a process operates specifically in words of two syllables (see especially the second part of the main consonant-doubling rule, section 4.2) I refer to them as two-syllable words, and similarly for longer words.

In chapters 9 and 10, which deal with the grapheme-phoneme direction, the meanings of 'initial', 'medial' and 'final' referring to positions in words necessarily change: there they refer to positions in **written** words. So, for instance, there the 'magic <e>' in split digraphs is described as being in word-final position, and consonant letters enclosed within split digraphs are in medial position.

## 1.11 Open and closed syllables

Many vowel correspondences differ between open and closed syllables. Open syllables end in a vowel phoneme; closed syllables end in a consonant phoneme. The distinction is clearest in monosyllabic words; for example, *go* is an open syllable, *goat* is a closed syllable.

For more on syllables in general, see section A.3 in Appendix A.

## 1.12 '2-phoneme graphemes'

In English spelling, the letter <x> frequently spells /ks/, which is a sequence of two phonemes, /k/ and /s/. An example is the word *box*. So when <x> spells /ks/ I call it a '2-phoneme grapheme'. (Carney, 1994: 107-8 has a rather different approach to 'two-phoneme strings'.) My analysis has uncovered 36 of these in all (see Tables 8.1-2).

When dealing with phoneme-grapheme correspondences in chapters 3 and 5, I mention each 2-phoneme grapheme in two places, one for each of the phonemes it spells. For example, you will find <x> spelling /ks/ under both /k/ and /s/ (sections 3.7.1, 3.7.6). However, in chapters 9 and 10, which deal with grapheme-phoneme correspondences, each multi-phoneme grapheme is mentioned in only one place, under its leading letter.

One of the 2-phoneme graphemes - <u> spelling /juː/ (the sound of the whole words *ewe, yew, you* and the name of the letter <u>) - is so frequent that I have infringed my otherwise strictly phonemic analysis to accord the 2-phoneme sequence /juː/ special status as a quasi-phoneme that is important enough to have its own entry – see Table 2.2 and section 5.7.5 – as does Carney (1994: 200-2).

Two of the 2-phoneme graphemes also function as 3-phoneme graphemes: <x> spelling /eks/ in *X(-ray)*, etc., and <oir> spelling /waɪə/ (the pronunciation of the whole word *wire*) only in *choir*. Logically, therefore, each of these is dealt with in several places in chapters 3 and 5 (but in chapters 9 and 10, only once, under <x> and <o> respectively).

For what I have called '2-phoneme graphemes' Haas (1970: 49, 70) suggested the term 'diphone', to parallel 'digraph' – but it never caught on (though 'diphone' is used in phonetics to mean a sequence of two sounds or the transition between them). If it had caught on, my identification of 3-phoneme graphemes would logically have required coining 'triphone' (which also exists in phonetics and means 'a sequence of three phonemes'). I have stuck with my terminology.

## 1.13 'Regular' correspondences

I refer to many correspondences as 'regular'. This does not mean that they apply always and without exception. Very few spelling correspondences in English have no exceptions. (At least in the main system – many minor correspondences have no exceptions, but are very restricted in scope. One example is the grapheme <aigh>, which is always pronounced like the name of letter <a> – but since it occurs only in the word *straight*, this is not much help.) So I use the word 'regular' to mean 'predominant', the major tendency.

Where lesser generalisations are possible I try to state only those that are helpful. For instance, Carney (1994: 185), in the course of analysing the correspondences of the vowel phoneme /ɔː/ (the sound of the word *awe*) shows that only spellings with <or> occur before four particular consonants or consonant clusters, and that spellings with <or> never occur before six others. But these generalisations only cover just over 30 words, so I have ignored them. For a contrast, see Table 3.5, where I organise spellings of word-final /s/ as in *hiss* into 11 subcategories – justified by the very large number of words with this final consonant phoneme and relatively small amounts of overlap between the subcategories.

Also, some words which seem quite irregular in the phoneme–grapheme (spelling) direction are less so in the grapheme–phoneme (reading aloud) direction, for example *ocean*. This is partly irregular in the phoneme–grapheme direction: every other word which ends in the sound of the word *ocean* is spelt <-otion>, so in *ocean* the spellings of the 'sh' phoneme as <ce> and the following schwa vowel (see chapter 2) as <a> are unusual in this context. However, in the grapheme–phoneme direction *ocean* is entirely regular: all words ending in <-cean> have the stress on the preceding vowel, which has its letter-name pronunciation, 'Oh' in this case, and the <-cean> ending, though rare, is always pronounced roughly like the word *shun*.

On the other hand, when I speak of 'regular verbs' the word 'regular' has its usual sense – these are the verbs (the great majority) that form both past tense and past participle (in writing) by adding <-ed> (see sections 3.5.2, 3.5.7, 5.4.3 and 10.15 for the phonetic equivalents). Some oddities can be noted here: the past tense and participle forms of the verbs *lay, pay* are pronounced regularly as /leɪd, peɪd/ but are spelt irregularly: *laid, paid* (regular spellings would be \**layed*, \**payed* – which do appear occasionally – see sections 3.7.1, 5.7.1 and 6.5). Similarly, regular spellings of the adverbs *daily* (also an adjective), *gaily* would be \**dayly*, \**gayly* (see again section 6.5). Conversely, there is one plural noun with a regular spelling but an irregular pronunciation: *houses*, which is pronounced /ˈhaʊzɪz/ with irregular change of the stem-final consonant from /s/ to /z/ (if its pronunciation were regular it would be /ˈhaʊsɪz/ 'haussiz').

But those quirks are tiny compared to the overall irregularities in the relationships between pronunciation and spelling. For many languages the complete set of both phoneme–grapheme and grapheme–phoneme correspondences could be set out on one page. The complexities of English spelling, especially of vowels, which entail that this book is so large are a measure of the task facing learners who wish to write correctly-spelt English and (try to) derive accurate pronunciations of English words from their written forms.

# 2. The phonemes of spoken English

## 2.1 Choosing an accent to analyse

English is spoken with many accents, and the number of phonemes, and the exact sounds of many of them, vary across accents. In order to list phonemes, therefore, I first had to choose an accent to base my list on. Because this book deals with British spelling, the accent I have chosen is the British accent known to many linguists as 'Received Pronunciation' (RP). Recently some linguists have re-named it 'Southern British Standard' (SBS), or 'Standard Southern British', or even 'General British' (Cruttenden, 2014), but I have retained the term RP because it is more widely known. The French textbook of English from which I learnt phonetic transcription (see below) in 1963 called it the accent 'des milieux cultivés du sud-est anglais', but that was too narrow a definition; though it is particularly prevalent in educated circles in the South-East of England, people from all over Britain have this accent, and their regional origins are therefore difficult to deduce from their accent.

## 2.2 How many phonemes?

**In RP there are 44 phonemes. Of these, 24 are consonant phonemes, and 20 are vowel phonemes.**

From the fact that there are many more phonemes in RP than the 26 letters of the English alphabet, it is fairly clear that some phonemes have no predominant one-letter spelling. But for the purposes of this book a single way of representing each phoneme is needed. To do this, I use the symbols of the International Phonetic Alphabet (IPA). You will need to learn to read this system fluently in order to be able to use the rest of this book. Many words in this book are written in IPA alongside the conventional spelling, so that you can do some incidental learning as you read. The symbols for consonant phonemes are easier to learn (because most are ordinary letters, though some have unfamiliar values), so I start with them.

For some purposes it is important to distinguish between voiceless consonant phonemes – those pronounced without vibrating the vocal cords – and voiced consonant phonemes – the rest. Those which are voiceless are so labelled in Table 2.1, and various sub-systems which rely on this distinction are discussed under /d, t/ in sections 3.5.2 and 3.5.7, under /ɪ/ in section 5.4.3, and also in sections 3.7.8, 5.7.2 and 7.2.3.

There is little difference in the number or pronunciation of the consonant phonemes across much of the English-speaking world, and much less variation than in the vowel phonemes – in fact, differences in vowel phonemes almost entirely define the differences between accents. However, two consonant phonemes which do not occur in RP (and are therefore not counted in my analyses of correspondences) but do occur in many Scots accents are mentioned in a few places:

- the voiceless counterpart of /w/, which is usually spelt <wh>, sounds roughly like 'hw', and is symbolised /ʍ/; examples would be *which*, *when*
- the throat-clearing sound which is spelt <ch> in some Scottish words, e.g. *dreich*, *loch*, *Sassenach*, and German names like *Schumacher* (or <gh> in some Irish words, e.g. *lough*, or <kh> in transcriptions of some Russian names, e.g. *Mikhail*), and is symbolised /x/ – on no account to be confused with letter <x>, but I have not included this correspondence in my analysis because /x/ is not a phoneme of RP. See Notes to sections 9.9/15/19 and 10.33.

# 2.3 The consonant phonemes of Received Pronunciation

Table 2.1 presents the IPA symbols for the 24 consonant phonemes of RP.

TABLE 2.1: THE INTERNATIONAL PHONETIC ALPHABET SYMBOLS FOR THE 24 CONSONANT PHONEMES OF THE RECEIVED PRONUNCIATION ACCENT OF ENGLISH.

| | | | | |
|---|---|---|---|---|
| Consonant phonemes with doubled spellings* which are rare in one-syllable words | | | | |
| /b/ | as in the first sound of | by | /baɪ/ | |
| /d/ | as in the first sound of | dye | /daɪ/ | |
| /g/ | as in the first sound of | goo | /guː/ | |
| /m/ | as in the first sound of | my | /maɪ/ | |
| /n/ | as in the first sound of | nigh | /naɪ/ | |
| /p/ | as in the first sound of | pie | /paɪ/ | voiceless |
| /t/ | as in the first sound of | tie | /taɪ/ | voiceless |
| /r/ | as in the first sound of | rye | /raɪ/ | |
| Consonant phonemes with doubled spellings* which are regular at the end of one-syllable words after a short vowel phoneme spelt with one letter | | | | |
| /k/ | as in the first sound of | coo | /kuː/ | voiceless |
| /tʃ/ | as in the first sound of | chew | /tʃuː/ | voiceless |
| /f/ | as in the first sound of | few | /fjuː/ | |
| /dʒ/ | as in the first sound of | jaw | /dʒɔː/ | |
| /l/ | as in the first sound of | law | /lɔː/ | |
| /s/ | as in the first sound of | sue | /suː/ | voiceless |
| /v/ | as in the first sound of | view | /vjuː/ | |
| /z/ | as in the first sound of | zoo | /zuː/ | |
| Consonant phonemes without doubled spellings | | | | |
| /h/ | as in the first sound of | who | /huː/ | |
| /ŋ/ | as in the **last** sound of | ring | /rɪŋ/ | |
| /ʃ/ | as in the **third** sound of | fission | /ˈfɪʃən/ | voiceless |
| /ʒ/ | as in the **third** sound of | vision | /ˈvɪʒən/ | |
| /θ/ | as in the first sound of | thigh | /θaɪ/ | voiceless |
| /ð/ | as in the first sound of | thy | /ðaɪ/ | |
| /w/ | as in the first sound of | well | /wel/ | |
| /j/ | as in the first sound of | yell, union | /jel, ˈjuːnjən/ | |

\* For doubled spellings see section 3.2 and much of chapter 4.

## 2.4 The vowel phonemes of Received Pronunciation

Table 2.2 presents the IPA symbols for the 20 vowel phonemes of RP and, as mentioned in section 1.12, the 2-phoneme sequence /juː/.

TABLE 2.2: THE INTERNATIONAL PHONETIC ALPHABET SYMBOLS FOR THE 20 VOWEL PHONEMES OF THE RECEIVED PRONUNCIATION ACCENT OF ENGLISH, PLUS /juː/.

| | | | |
|---|---|---|---|
| Short pure vowels | | | |
| /æ/ | as in the first sound of | ant | /ænt/ |
| /e/ | as in the first sound of | end | /end/ |
| /ɪ/ | as in the first sound of | ink | /ɪŋk/ |
| /ɒ/ | as in the first sound of | ox | /ɒks/ |
| /ʌ/ | as in the first sound of | up | /ʌp/ |
| /ʊ/ | as in the **second** sound of | pull | /pʊl/ |
| /ə/ (schwa) | as in the first sound of | about | /əˈbaʊt/ |
| Long pure vowels | | | |
| /ɑː/ | as in the first sound of | aardvark | /ˈɑːdvɑːk/ |
| /ɜː/ | as in the first sound of | earl | /ɜːl/ |
| /ɔː/ | as in the **whole** sound of | awe | /ɔː/ |
| /uː/ | as in the first sound of | ooze | /uːz/ |
| /iː/ * | as in the first sound of | eel | /iːl/ |
| Special 2-phoneme sequence | | | |
| /juː/ * | as in the first **two** sounds of | union | /ˈjuːnjən/ |
| Diphthongs | | | |
| /eɪ/ * | as in the first sound of | aim | /eɪm/ |
| /aɪ/ * | as in the first sound of | ice | /aɪs/ |
| /əʊ/ * | as in the first sound of | oath | /əʊθ/ |
| /aʊ/ | as in the first sound of | ouch | /aʊtʃ/ |
| /ɔɪ/ | as in the first sound of | oyster | /ˈɔɪstə/ |
| /eə/ | as in the **whole** sound of | air | /eə/ |
| /ɪə/ | as in the **whole** sound of | ear | /ɪə/ |
| /ʊə/ | as in the **second** sound of | rural | /ˈrʊərəl/ |

\* These four vowel phonemes and /juː/ are the 'letter-name' vowels – see sections 5.1, 5.7, 6.2 and 6.3. Phoneme /uː/ also belongs with them.

The last short pure vowel listed in Table 2.2, the /ə/ phoneme, is heard in the first syllable of *about* /əˈbaʊt/ and the second syllable of *oyster* /ˈɔɪstə/. It is the least distinctive phoneme in English – think how little effort is needed to say it. However, that does not mean it is unimportant, because it has three special characteristics:

- in RP it occurs only in **un**stressed syllables, and (almost) never in stressed syllables (except that RP-speakers now increasingly pronounce *because* as /bɪˈkəz/ rather than /bɪˈkɒz/). In occurring only in unstressed syllables /ə/ is unique among English vowel phonemes (but note that this applies only to English – in many other languages /ə/ occurs in both stressed and unstressed syllables);
- in (my analysis/version of) RP it is the only short vowel phoneme which occurs word-finally;
- it is the most frequent phoneme of all in spoken English, in every accent, because a high proportion of unstressed syllables contain it. In RP, for example, it constitutes about 10% of running speech.

Also uniquely, this phoneme has a special name (derived from Hebrew): schwa, or the schwa vowel.

As stated in section 1.2, the phonetic symbols used in this book are identical to those used in the 18th (2011) edition of the *Cambridge English Pronouncing Dictionary*. They are also identical to those used in most of the eight editions of *Gimson's Pronunciation of English*, including the 7th. However, as this book was nearing publication, my attention was drawn to the fact that, in the latest (eighth) edition of *Gimson's Pronunciation of English* (Cruttenden, 2014), Cruttenden has introduced two changes:

- for the 'short a' sound, listed above as '/æ/ as in the first sound of *ant*', he now uses plain /a/ (for the reasons for this see his page xvii);
- for /eə/ as in the **whole** sound of *air* he now uses /ɛː/, on the grounds that this phoneme, in the mouths of most speakers of 'General British' (≈ RP), is no longer a diphthong but a long pure vowel.

One of the current editors of the *Cambridge English Pronouncing Dictionary*, Prof. Jane Setters of the University of Reading, kindly told me that, although she and her fellow editors are aware of these changes and use them in their teaching, they do not propose to introduce them into the *Dictionary*. Since I wish this this book to parallel the *Dictionary* I have not adopted them either.

## 2.5 Polysyllabic words and word stress

In all English words of two or more syllables, one of the syllables is spoken with heavier emphasis than the rest. For example:
- *oyster* is stressed on the first syllable
- *about* is stressed on the second syllable.

In IPA transcriptions the stressed syllable is marked with a small vertical notch placed **in front of** it: /ˈɔɪstə, əˈbaʊt/. Analysing and marking word stress is not just an exercise; many phoneme–grapheme and grapheme–phoneme correspondences apply only in words of more than one syllable, some only in stressed syllables, others only in unstressed syllables. The clearest example is the occurrence of /ə/ only in unstressed syllables. Occasionally for simplicity I use an acute accent on the ordinary spelling of a word to indicate stress, e.g. *aríthmetic* (noun), *arithmétic* (adjective).

The question of predicting from the written form of polysyllabic words where the stress falls on them is attempted, and largely failed, in section A.10 in Appendix A.

# 3. The phoneme-grapheme correspondences of English, 1: Consonants

## 3.1 The general picture: the regular spellings of English consonant phonemes

This chapter can be summed up by saying that 13 of the 24 consonant phonemes of RP have highly regular spellings (though for two of these, /w, ŋ/, positional constraints have to be stated), while the other 11 have to be analysed according to position in the word.

So, the 11 consonant phonemes /b d g h m n p r t θ ð/ are regularly spelt <b d g h m n p r t th th> respectively; /w/ (which occurs only before vowel phonemes and therefore does not occur word-finally) is regularly spelt <w> initially, <u> medially (but see the note below Table 3.1); and /ŋ/ (which occurs only after short vowel phonemes and therefore does not occur initially) is regularly spelt <n> before /k, g/, however spelt, otherwise <ng>.

The main regularities for the other 11 consonant phonemes are summarised in Table 3.1, by position in the word. For seven phonemes final position has to be subdivided, and final /s, k/ have a further sub-subdivision. The entries for /dʒ, s, k/ blur the distinction between phonemes and graphemes in defining word positions – for more detail on these phonemes' complicated correspondences, and for the 2-phoneme grapheme <x>, see sections 3.7.1, 3.7.4 and 3.7.6 and Tables 3.3 and 3.4.

TABLE 3.1: MAIN CORRESPONDENCES OF THE 11 CONSONANT PHONEMES WITH VARIABLE SPELLINGS, BY POSITION IN THE WORD.

| Phoneme | Position in word | | |
|---|---|---|---|
| | Initial | Medial | Final |
| /ʃ/ | sh | ti | sh |
| /f/ | f | f | ff |
| /v/ | v | v | ve |
| /j/ within /juː/ | See Table 5.1 | | |
| /j/ elsewhere | y | i * | (does not occur) |
| | | | in monosyllables after a short vowel spelt with one letter | otherwise |
| /l/ | l | l | ll | L |
| /tʃ/ | ch but <t> before /uː/ | t | tch | ch |
| /ʒ/ | (rare) | si | (does not occur) | ge |
| /z/ | z | s | zz | s |
| /dʒ/ | j | <g> before <e, i, y>, otherwise <j> | dge | ge |
| /s/ | s | s | ss | in other monosyllables <ce>; in polysyllables <s> |
| /k/ | c but <k> before <e, i, y> | c | ck | in other monosyllables <k>; in polysyllables <c> |

\* N.B. Many occurrences of medial /j/ (and some of medial /w/) are actually **not** represented in the spelling at all – see sections 3.8.7–8.

## 3.2 Order of description

In sections 3.5, 3.7 and 3.8 I set out the consonantal phoneme-grapheme correspondences of English, under the consonant phonemes listed in the order in which they appear in Table 2.1 in chapter 2.

The consonant phonemes fall into two main categories, those which have a doubled spelling, such as <bb> for /b/ in *rabbit*, and those which do not. Within those which do have a doubled spelling there is a further important distinction, between those whose doubled spellings are rare in one-syllable words and those whose doubled spellings are regular at the end of one-syllable words after a short vowel phoneme spelt with one letter (Crystal, 2012, especially chapters 7 and 8, explains how this division goes back many centuries). Sections 3.5 and 3.7 cover these two categories of consonant phonemes with doubled spellings, and section 3.8 those which do not have a doubled spelling.

This trichotomy (the Greek etymology of this word officially means 'cutting into three', but unofficially could also mean 'haircut' – how neat is it that the word meaning 'cutting into three' could also mean 'splitting hairs'?) does not quite accommodate /r/. It does have a doubled spelling (<rr>) and therefore does not belong in section 3.8 (phonemes without a doubled spelling). But /r/ does not occur word-finally in RP, so is not even a candidate for section 3.7 (phonemes whose doubled spellings are regular at the end of one-syllable words after a short vowel phoneme spelt with one letter). Yet /r/ spelt <rr> is not just rare in one-syllable words – it is non-existent – so it might seem not to fit into section 3.5 (phonemes whose doubled spellings are rare in one-syllable words) either. However, section 3.5 is where I have put it, on the grounds that (a) there are some medial examples of /r/ spelt <rr>, e.g. *error*; (b) many other examples of /r/ spelt <rr> arise from suffixation, e.g. *preferring, referral*; (c) in these respects /r/ is similar to the other phonemes in section 3.5.

Within each group I list the phonemes in alphabetical order of the letter(s) comprising their basic spellings, except that in section 3.5 /r/ is dealt with after /t/; /r/ is dealt with last because that leads on naturally to the treatment in section 3.6 of a special process involving /r/, namely /r/-linking, hence the interruption in the order of sections.

Under each consonant phoneme I deal with the spellings in this order:
1) The basic grapheme. In my opinion, each of the 24 consonant phonemes of English has a basic grapheme, the one that seems most natural as its spelling. The identification of <si> as the basic grapheme for /ʒ/

may seem curious – but this is the least frequent phoneme in English speech and <si> is its most frequent spelling. As you will see from the percentages at the beginning of each section, the basic grapheme is also, in 20 cases, the most frequent spelling of that phoneme – the exceptions are /z, dʒ, ʃ, j/.
2) Other graphemes which are used for the phoneme with reasonable frequency. By reasonable frequency I mean at least 5 per cent of the occurrences of the phoneme in running text.
3) The doubled spelling, if the phoneme has one – 16 of the 24 consonant phonemes do (indeed, a few have more than one). Most doubled consonant spellings consist of the basic single-letter grapheme written twice, but some have a different pattern. Most of the doubled spellings are quite rare in stem words. For some guidance on when to spell a consonant double see chapter 4. None of the doubled spellings of English consonant phonemes ever occur in word-initial position (with the two exceptions noted under /l/ in sections 3.7.5 and 4.1), so word-initial position is not mentioned in the entries about doubled spellings in this chapter (except under /l/).
4) The doubled spelling plus final <e>, if the phoneme has such a spelling.
5) Oddities, graphemes which are used to spell that phoneme only rarely.
6) Any 2-phoneme graphemes in which the phoneme is represented. Almost all the 2-phoneme graphemes are also Oddities, but a few belong to the main system (see section 3.4) and are included there.
7) Any 3-phoneme grapheme in which the phoneme is represented. Both 3-phoneme graphemes are definitely Oddities.

Some entries end with Notes, and a few have Tables.

## 3.3 Frequencies

Under most phonemes I give the frequency of occurrence of each major grapheme as a spelling of the phoneme, using the information in Edward Carney's massive study *A Survey of English Spelling* (1994). He gives two frequencies for most phoneme-grapheme correspondences:
- text frequency, that is, the frequency with which the correspondence occurs when you count all the correspondences in a large set of pieces of continuous prose, but discounting derived forms of stem words, e.g. past tenses, and all function words, e.g. *of, is, there, where*. Because Carney lemmatised his corpus (that is, reduced all the words to stem forms), his text frequencies for doubled consonants are probably systematically underestimated, since large numbers of

occurrences of doubled consonant letters arise from suffixation – see sections 4.2 and 4.3.1;
- lexical frequency, that is, the frequency with which the correspondence occurs when you count all and only the correspondences in a dictionary.

Usually the two frequencies are similar, but where a particular correspondence occurs in only a few words but those words are very common, the text frequency will be high and the lexical frequency low (and vice versa where a correspondence occurs in many words but those words are rare). For this chapter and chapter 5 I've used only Carney's text frequencies since those (mainly) represent what readers encounter. However, my lists of examples range far and wide within English vocabulary, and take in words which are so rare that they certainly did not contribute to Carney's text frequencies. An odd category here is words in which /ɪə/ is spelt <ier> – this category is never mentioned by Carney; presumably no such words turned up in the corpus he compiled and analysed.

I give no frequencies for doubled spellings plus final <e> since these are all rare, and in most cases the frequencies for the Oddities are lumped together.

## 3.4 The main system and the rest

Under each phoneme I separate the correspondences with graphemes into what I consider to be the main system and the rest (this distinction is very similar to that between major and minor units postulated by Venezky, 1970: 52–55). The correspondences which I include in the main system are those which seem to me to operate as part of larger regularities, even though pretty rarely as absolute rules. For the consonant phonemes the larger regularities comprise the basic correspondences, the correspondences which have reasonable frequency as I've defined it above, and the doubled spellings, but not the doubled spellings plus <e>, the 2-and 3-phoneme graphemes (except a few 2-phoneme graphemes which are of reasonably high frequency), or the Oddities. In this chapter (and in chapters 5, 9 and 10) correspondences which have reasonable frequency are shown in 9-point type, the rest in smaller 7.5-point type.

Three quite rare correspondences are, however, included in the main system – /k/ spelt <q>, /ʒ/ spelt <ge>, and /uː/ spelt <ue>. For /k/ spelt <q> this is because <q> would otherwise not appear in the main system at all, but <q> is a grapheme of written English and therefore has to be included; also, the 2-phoneme sequence /kw/ is mainly spelt <qu>. /ʒ/ spelt <ge> is needed to complete the pattern of correspondences in word-final position – see Table 3.1. And although /uː/ spelt <ue> is very rare, I found it necessary to include it in the main system because the mirror-image correspondence (<ue> pronounced /uː/) is one of only two frequent correspondence of <ue> – see section 10.37.

## 3.5 Consonants with doubled spellings which are rare in one-syllable words: /b d g m n p t/, plus /r/

For the incluson of /r/ in this section see section 3.2.

Despite their rarity in stem words, the doubled spellings of these consonant phonemes arise very frequently from suffixation, e.g. *rubbed, budding, begged, skimmed, skinned, hopped, pitted, preferring* (see sections 4.2 and 4.3.1).

### 3.5.1 /b/ as in *by*

**THE MAIN SYSTEM**

*Basic grapheme*                 <b>    98%   e.g. *rabid*

*Other frequent graphemes* (none)

*Doubled spelling*             <bb>   <1%   medially, regular before final /əl/ spelt <-le> after a short vowel spelt with a single letter, e.g. *babble* – see section 4.3.3; there are also independent medial examples, e.g. *abbey, abbot, bobbin, cabbage, dibber, hobbit, hobby, hubbub, rabbi, rabbit, ribbon, rubber, rubbish, Sabbath, shibboleth, stubborn* – see sections 4.3.4 and 4.4.5–6; word-finally, only in *ebb* – see section 4.3.2

*The phoneme-grapheme correspondences, 1: Consonants* 25

### THE REST

| | | | |
|---|---|---|---|
| *Doubled spelling* + <e> | | | (does not occur) |
| *Oddities* | | | 1% in total |
| | <bh> | | only in *abhor* and its derivatives *abhorred*, *abhorrent*, plus *bhaji*, *bhang(ra)*, *bhindi*, *Bhutan* and a few other rare words from the Indian sub-continent. <b, h> are usually separate graphemes at a morpheme boundary, as in *clubhouse*, *subheading* |
| | <bu> | | only in *build*, *buoy*, *buy*. See Notes |
| | <pb> | | only in the compound words *cupboard*, *raspberry*, plus *Campbell* |
| *2-phoneme graphemes* | (none) | | |

### NOTES

For the compound words *gooseberry* /ˈgʊzbriː/), *raspberry* /ˈrɑːzbriː/), *strawberry* /ˈstrɔːbriː/) see section 6.10.

I analyse <bu> in *build*, *buoy*, *buy* as a grapheme spelling /b/ because this is more economical than adding /ɪ/ spelt <ui>, /ɔɪ/ spelt <uoy> and /aɪ/ spelt <uy> to the list of graphemes; cf. <gu> under /g/, section 3.5.3, and <cu> under /k/, section 3.7.1.

## 3.5.2 /d/ as in *dye*

### THE MAIN SYSTEM

| | | | |
|---|---|---|---|
| *Basic grapheme* | <d> | 98% | e.g. *bud* |
| *Other frequent grapheme* | <ed> | | (not counted in percentages) See Note |
| *Doubled spelling* | <dd> | 2% | medially, regular before final /əl/ spelt <-le> after a short vowel spelt with one letter, e.g. *griddle* – see section 4.3.3; other medial examples include *addictive*, *additive*, *adduce*, *bladder*, |

*buddy, cheddar, fodder, judder, ladder, midden, rudder, ruddy, shoddy, sodden, sudden, teddy, toddy, widdershins* – see sections 4.3.4 and 4.4.5-6; perhaps also the compound word *granddad*, but see section 4.4.7; word-finally, only in *add, odd, rudd, Sudd* – on *add, odd* see section 4.3.2

## THE REST

| | | |
|---|---|---|
| *Doubled spelling* + <e> | | (does not occur) |
| *Oddities* | | <1% in total |
| | <bd> | only in *bdellium* |
| | <ddh> | only in *Buddha* and derivatives, *saddhu* |
| | <de> | only in *aide, blende, blonde, horde* and *(for)bade* pronounced /(fə')bæd/ (also pronounced /(fə')beɪd/ with <d> alone spelling /d/ and <a.e> spelling /eɪ/). The <e> in *blonde* marks it French-style as feminine (masculine: *blond*) |
| | <dh> | only in a few loanwords and names from the Indian subcontinent, e.g. *dhobi, dhoti, dhow, Gandhi, jodhpurs, sandhi, Sindh* |
| *2-phoneme graphemes* | (none) | |

## NOTE

/d/ is almost always spelt <ed> in past forms of regular verbs ending in a voiced consonant other than /d/ or a vowel, e.g. *ebbed, flowed*. The only exceptions are *laid, paid* which would (if they were spelt regularly) be *layed, *payed – cf. *delayed, played* and sections 5.7.1 and 6.5. See also the entry for <ed> in chapter 10, section 10.15.

# 3.5.3 /g/ as in *goo*

### THE MAIN SYSTEM

| | | | |
|---|---|---|---|
| *Basic grapheme* | <g> | 92% | e.g. *beg* |
| *Other frequent graphemes* | (none) | | |
| *Doubled spelling* | <gg> | 2% | medially, regular before final /əl/ spelt <-le> after a short vowel spelt with one letter, e.g. *muggle* – see section 4.3.3; other medial examples include *aggressive, beggar, dagger, doggerel, haggis, jagged, maggot, nugget, ragged, rugged, rugger, sluggish, trigger* – see sections 4.3.4 and 4.4.5–6; word-finally, only in *egg* – see section 4.3.2 |

### THE REST

| | | | |
|---|---|---|---|
| *Doubled spelling + <e>* | | | (does not occur) |
| *Oddities* | | | 2% in total |
| | <ckgu> | | only in *blackguard* /ˈblægəd, ˈblægɑːd/ |
| | <gh> | | word-final only in *ugh*; otherwise only in *afghan, aghast, burgher, ghastly, ghat, ghee, gherkin, ghetto, ghillie* (also spelt *gillie*), *ghost, ghoul, ogham, sorghum* and a few more rare words |
| | <gu> | | word-initially, only in *guarantee, guard, guerrilla, guess, guest, guide, guild, guilder, guile, guillemot, guillotine, guilt, guinea, guise, guitar, guy* and a few more rare words; |

medially, only in *baguette, beguine, dengue, disguise, languor* (the <u> surfaces as /w/ in *languid, languish* – see section 7.2) and suffixed forms of a few words in next category, e.g. *cataloguing*; phonemically word-final only in *brogue, drogue, fatigue, fugue, intrigue, plague, rogue, vague, vogue* and a few more rare words where the final written <e> is part of a split digraph with the vowel letter preceding the <g> – see also next paragraph, and Notes

<gue>   only word-final and only in *analogue, catalogue, colleague, decalogue, demagogue, dialogue, eclogue, epilogue, ideologue, league, monologue, morgue, pedagogue, prologue, prorogue, synagogue*. In some of the words ending <-ogue> US spelling has <-og>, which is simpler in the stem forms but means that in, e.g., *cataloging* the first <g> (less regularly) spells /g/ before <i>, a problem which the spelling with <u> avoids. The only word in which final <g, u, e> are all separate graphemes is *segue* /ˈsegweɪ/

*2-phoneme graphemes*   For all of these see Notes

/gz/   4%

(1) spelt <x>   only in some polysyllabic words of Latin origin, namely *anxiety* pronounced /æŋˈgzaɪjɪtiː/ (also pronounced /æŋˈzaɪjɪtiː/), *auxiliary, exact, exaggerate, exalt, exam(ine), example, exasperate, executive, executor, exemplar, exemplify, exempt, exert, exigency, exiguous, exile, exist, exonerate, exorbitant, exordium, exuberant, exude, exult*, plus *exotic* from Greek and a few more rare words; also in *Alexandra, Alexander* and becoming frequent in *exit* pronounced /ˈegzɪt/ (also pronounced /ˈeksɪt/). For *anxiety* see also under /ŋ/ in section 3.8.2

(2) spelt <xh> only in about 7 polysyllabic words of Latin origin: *exhaust(ion), exhibit, exhilarat-e/ion, exhort, exhume* – but in some derivatives <xh> spells /eks/, e.g. *exhibition, exhortation, exhumation*

/gʒ/ spelt <x> only in *luxuriance, luxuriant, luxuriate, luxurious*

## NOTES

In *blackguard* (also spelt *blaggard*), *guarantee, guard* the <u> is technically redundant because <ckg, g> would spell (and be pronounced) /g/ without it. But in all the other words with <gu> the <u> has to be there in order to prevent the <g> appearing to spell (and be pronounced) /dʒ/. It's because *guild, guy* must be analysed this way that I analyse *build, buy* (and by extension *buoy*) as having /b/ spelt <bu> (see section 3.5.1, and cf. <cu> under /k/, section 3.7.1).

The regular 2-grapheme spelling of /gz/ is <gs>, e.g. *dogs*. The sequence <gz> seems to occur only in *zigzag*.

The 2-phoneme sequence /gʒ/ seems to occur only in the four words listed above and to have no 2-grapheme spelling.

The 2-phoneme sequence /gw/ is almost always spelt <gu>, e.g. in *anguish, distinguish, extinguish, guacamole, guano, guava, iguana, language, languish, linguist, penguin, sanguine, segue, unguent.* Exception: *wigwam*. The converse does not hold – most occurrences of <gu> are pronounced either as /g/ or as 2 phonemes (/g/ plus a vocalic pronunciation of <u>) – see section 9.15.

For <go> in *allegory, category* see section 6.10.

## 3.5.4 /m/ as in *my*

### THE MAIN SYSTEM

*Basic grapheme*        <m>    96%    e.g. *sum*
*Other frequent graphemes* (none)

| | | |
|---|---|---|
| *Doubled spelling* | <mm> 3% | medially, does NOT occur before final /əl/ spelt <-le>; medial examples include *comma, commune, cummerbund, hammock, hummock, immense, plummet, rummage, slummock, summit* and some derived forms, e.g. *dia/pro-grammatic, immodest* – see sections 4.3.4 and 4.4.5–6; never word-final |

## THE REST

| | | |
|---|---|---|
| *Doubled spelling + <e>* | <mme> | now only in *oriflamme* and (non-computer) *programme* since *gram* and its derivatives are no longer spelt *\*gramme*, etc. |
| *Oddities (all word-final only)* | | <1% in total |
| | <gm> | only in *apophthegm, diaphragm, epiphragm, paradigm, phlegm, syntagm*. /g/ surfaces in some derivatives: *paradigmatic, phlegmatic, syntagma(tic)* – see section 7.2 |
| | <mb> | only in *dithyramb, lamb; climb, limb; aplomb, bomb, catacomb, comb, coomb, coxcomb, coulomb, hecatomb, rhomb, tomb, womb; crumb, dumb, numb, plumb, rhumb, succumb, thumb* and a few more very rare words. /b/ surfaces in some derivatives: *dithyrambic, bombard(ier), bombast(ic), rhomb-ic/us, crumble* and supposedly, according to some authorities, in *thimble* – see section 7.2 |
| | <mbe> | only in *buncombe* ('nonsense'; also spelt *bunkum*), *co(o)mbe* ('short valley'; also spelt *coomb*); and contrast *flambe* /ˈflɒmbeɪ/, where <m, b, e> are all separate graphemes |

*The phoneme-grapheme correspondences, 1: Consonants*

|  |  |  |
|---|---|---|
|  | \<me\> | never initial; mainly word-final and there only in *become, come, some, welcome* and the adjectival suffix /səm/ spelt \<-some\>, e.g. *handsome* (contrast *hansom*); medially only in *camera, emerald, omelette, ramekin* pronounced /'ræmkɪn/ (also pronounced /'ræmɪkɪn/) – see section 6.10 – and *Thames* |
|  | \<mn\> | only in *autumn, column, condemn, contemn, damn, hymn, limn, solemn*. /n/ surfaces in some derivatives: *autumnal, columnar, columnist, condemnation, contemner, damnable, damnation, hymnal, solemnity* – see section 7.2 |
|  | \<nd\> | only in *sandwich* pronounced /'sæmwɪdʒ/ (also has a 'regular' spelling pronunciation /'sændwɪtʃ/) |
| 2-phoneme grapheme | /əm/ spelt \<m\> | only word-final, e.g. *chasm, enthusiasm, orgasm, phantasm, pleonasm, sarcasm, spasm*, several words ending in *-plasm* (e.g. *ectoplasm*), *chrism, prism, schism* and all the many derived forms ending in *-ism, macrocosm, microcosm, abysm, aneurysm* (also spelt *aneurism*), *cataclysm, paroxysm, algorithm, rhythm* and a few other very rare words; also in *film* pronounced /'fɪləm/ in some Irish accents. See Note |

*NOTE*

In all but the last three of the words just listed with word-final /əm/ spelt \<-m\> the preceding phoneme is /z/ spelt \<s\>, so the regular spelling of word-final /zəm/ is \<-sm\> (only exception: *bosom*). This is one of only a handful of cases where the spelling of a final syllable is more predictable as a whole than from its separate phonemes, which here would predict (for example) *chusam, *prisom, etc. However, word-final /əm/ with other preceding phonemes has various 2-grapheme spellings in, e.g., *alyssum, balsam, besom, fathom* (but contrast the 1-grapheme spelling in *algorithm, rhythm*), *gypsum, hansom, lissom, opossum, ransom, transom* and all the adjectives ending \<-some\>.

## 3.5.5 /n/ as in *nigh*

### THE MAIN SYSTEM

| | | | |
|---|---|---|---|
| Basic grapheme | <n> | 97% | e.g. *tin* |
| Other frequent graphemes | (none) | | |
| Doubled spelling | <nn> | <1% | medially, does NOT occur before final /əl/ spelt <-le>; medial examples include *anneal, annual, annul, biennale, binnacle, Britannic, cannibal, chardonnay, cinnabar, cinnamon, ennui, innocent, punnet, tannic, tinnitus, tintinnabulation, zinnia* – see sections 4.3.4 and 4.4.5–6; word-finally, only in *Ann, djinn, Finn, inn* – on *Ann, inn* see section 4.3.2 |

### THE REST

| | | | |
|---|---|---|---|
| Doubled spelling + <e> | <nne> | | only word-final and only in *Anne, cayenne, comedienne, cretonne, doyenne, tonne* and a few other rare words |
| Oddities | | | 3% in total |
| | <dne> | | only in *Wednesday* |
| | <gn> | | word-initially, only in *gnarl, gnash, gnat, gnaw, gneiss, gnome, gnosis, Gnostic* and *gnu* analysed as /n/ spelt <gn> plus /juː/ spelt <u>; medially, only in *cognisance* (also pronounced with /gn/), *physiognomy, recognise* pronounced /ˈrekənaɪz/ (usually pronounced /ˈrekəgnaɪz/); word-finally, only in *align, arraign, assign, benign, campaign, coign, condign, consign, deign, design, ensign, feign, foreign, impugn* and a few other very rare words in *-pugn, malign, reign, resign, sign, sovereign, thegn*; also phonemically word-final in *champagne, cologne* where the final written <e> is part of a split digraph with the letter before the <g> spelling a diphthong. /g/ surfaces in some derivatives: *agnostic, diagnosis, prognosis, malignant, pugnacious, repugnant, assignation, designation, resignation, signal, signature* – see section 7.2 |

# The phoneme-grapheme correspondences, 1: Consonants

| | |
|---|---|
| \<gne\> | only word-final and only in *cockaigne, epergne, frankalmoigne* /kəˈkeɪn, ɪˈpɜːn, ˈfræŋkælmɔɪn/ |
| \<kn\> | 1% never word-final; medially, only in *acknowledge, knick-knack*; otherwise only word-initial and only in *knack(er(s)), knap, knave, knead, knee, knell, knew, knick(er(s)), knickerbocker, knick-knack, knife, knight, knit, knob, knobbly, knock, knoll, knot, know(ledge), knuckle* and a few more very rare words |
| \<mn\> | only word-initial and only in *mnemonic, mnemonist*. /m/ surfaces in *amnesia, amnesty* - see section 7.2 |
| \<nd\> | only in *grandfather, Grandma* (hence the frequent misspelling *\*Granma* - cf. section 4.4.7 on *Gran(d)dad*), *handsome* (cf. *hansom* (*cab*)), *landscape* |
| \<ne\> | non-finally, only in *vineyard* (and even there it's stem-final), *vulnerable* pronounced /ˈvʌlnrəbəl/ - see also Notes and section 6.10 (I refuse to analyse the alternative pronunciation /ˈvʌnrəbəl/ with loss of the first /l/ because it would add an otherwise not-needed grapheme \<lne\> to the inventory); otherwise only word-final and only in about 35 words, namely *borne, bourne, bowline, Catherine, clandestine* pronounced /klænˈdestɪn/ (also pronounced /ˈklændəstaɪn/), *cocaine, compline, crinoline, demesne, (pre)destine, determine, discipline, engine, ermine, examine, famine, feminine, genuine, gone, groyne, heroine, hurricane* pronounced /ˈhʌrɪkən/ (also pronounced /ˈhʌrɪkeɪn/), *illumine, intestine, jasmine, marline, masculine, medicine, migraine, moraine, none, peregrine, ptomaine, saccharine, sanguine, scone* pronounced /skɒn/ (also pronounced /skəʊn/), *shone, urine, vaseline, wolverine*. In all these words the \<e\> is phonographically redundant, in that its removal would not affect the pronunciation. However, without \<e\> *done, none* would become *don* and the prefix *non-* (and changing their spellings to *dun, nun* would cause other confusions). Also, the \<e\> keeps *borne, heroine* visually distinct from *born, heroin* |
| \<ng\> | only in *length, lengthen, strength, strengthen* pronounced /lenθ, ˈlenθən, strenθ, ˈstrenθən/. See also under /k, ŋ/, sections 3.7.1, 3.8.2 |
| \<nt\> | only in *croissant, denouement, rapprochement* |

|  |  |  |
|---|---|---|
|  | <nw> | only in *gunwale* |
|  | <pn> | only word-initial and only in words derived from Greek πνεῦμα *pneuma* ('breath') or πνεύμων *pneumon* ('lung'), e.g. *pneumatic, pneumonia* |
| *2-phoneme graphemes* | /ən/ spelt <n> | only in *Haydn* (I mention him in memory of Chris Upward of the Simplified Spelling Society) and most contractions of *not* with auxiliary verbs, i.e. *isn't, wasn't, haven't, hasn't, hadn't, doesn't, didn't, mayn't, mightn't, mustn't, couldn't, shouldn't, wouldn't, oughtn't, usedn't,* some of which are rare to the point of disuse, plus *durstn't,* which is regional/comic; in all of these except mayn't the preceding phoneme is a consonant. Other contractions of not with auxiliary verbs (*ain't, aren't, can't, daren't, don't, shan't, weren't, won't*), i.e. all those with a preceding vowel phoneme (except *mayn't*) are monosyllabic (though some Scots say /ˈdeərənt/ with a preceding consonant and linking /r/ and therefore two syllables). Curiously, *innit*, being a contraction of *isn't it*, reduces *isn't* to a single syllable. See Notes |
|  | /nj/ spelt <gn> | see under /j/, section 3.8.8 |

## NOTES

/ən/ has several 2-grapheme spellings, e.g. in *cotton, ruffian, written*.

For <ne> in *confectionery, generative, stationery, vulnerable* see section 6.10.

## 3.5.6 /p/ as in *pie*

### THE MAIN SYSTEM

| | | | |
|---|---|---|---|
| *Basic grapheme* | <p> | 95% | e.g. *apt* |
| *Other frequent graphemes* | (none) | | |
| *Doubled spelling* | <pp> | 5% | medially, regular before final /əl/ spelt <-le> after a short vowel spelt with one letter, e.g. *apple*: other medial examples |

include *apply, apprehend, cappuccino, dapper, frippery, hippodrome, hippopotamus, guppy, opponent, oppose, opposite, scupper, supper, supply, support* – see sections 4.3.4 and 4.4.5–6; word-finally, only in *Lapp*

## THE REST

| | | |
|---|---|---|
| *Doubled spelling + <e>* | <ppe> | only in *grippe, steppe* |
| *Oddities* | | <1% in total |
| | <b> | only in *presbyterian* pronounced /prespɪˈtɪəriːjən/ (also pronounced /prezbɪˈtɪəriːjən/) |
| | <bp> | only in *subpoena* /səˈpiːnə/ |
| | <gh> | only in misspelling of *hiccup* as *hiccough |
| | <pe> | only in *canteloupe, troupe,* plus *opera* in rapid speech – for <pe> in *opera* see section 6.10 |
| | <ph> | only in *diphtheria, diphthong, naphtha, ophthalmic* and *shepherd*. The first four also have pronunciations with /f/ – e.g. /ˈdɪfθɒŋ/ versus /ˈdɪpθɒŋ/ |
| *2-phoneme graphemes* | (none) | |

## 3.5.7 /t/ as in *tie*

### THE MAIN SYSTEM

| | | | |
|---|---|---|---|
| *Basic grapheme* | <t> | 96% | e.g. *rat* |
| *Other frequent grapheme* | <ed> | | (not counted in percentages) See Notes |
| *Doubled spelling* | <tt> | 3% | medially, regular before final /əl/ spelt <-le> after a short vowel spelt with one letter, e.g. *rattle*; other medial examples include *attention, attract, attribute,* |

*battalion, battery, butter, button, buttress, chitterlings, falsetto, glutton, jitter(s), mattress, rattan, smattering, tattoo, tittup* – see sections 4.3.4 and 4.4.5-6; word-finally, only in *bott, boycott, butt, matt, mitt, mutt, nett, putt, watt*. See also Notes

## THE REST

| | | |
|---|---|---|
| Doubled spelling + <e> | <tte> | only word-final and only in about 23 stem words, namely *baguette, brunette, cassette, coquette, corvette, croquette, epaulette, etiquette, garrotte, gavotte, gazette, maisonette, omelette, oubliette, palette, pipette, pirouette, roulette, serviette, silhouette, toilette, vignette, vinaigrette*, and a few derived forms, e.g. *cigarette, launderette, rosette, statuette, suffragette*, and some other rare words. In *latte* <tt, e> represent separate phonemes, as do <u.e, tt> in *butte* |
| Oddities | | 1% in total |
| | <bt> | only in *debt, doubt, subtle*. /b/ surfaces in *debit, indubitable, subtility* – see section 7.2 |
| | <ct> | only in *Connecticut, indict, victualler, victuals*. /k/ surfaces in *indiction* – see section 7.2 |
| | <dt> | only in *veldt* |
| | <phth> | only in *phthisic, phthisis* pronounced /ˈtaɪsɪk, ˈtaɪsɪs/ |
| | <pt> | only in *Deptford, ptarmigan, pterodactyl* (Greek, = 'wing finger'), *pterosaur* (Greek, = 'wing lizard'), *Ptolem-y/aic, ptomaine, receipt* and a few more very rare words. /p/ surfaces in *archaeopteryx, helicopter* (Greek, = 'ancient wing, spiral wing'), *reception, receptive* – see section 7.2 |
| | <te> | mainly word-final and in that position in at least 120 words, namely<br>– *ate* pronounced /et/ (also pronounced /eɪt/, which requires a different analysis: /t/ spelt <t> and /eɪ/ spelt <a.e>), *Bacchante, composite, compote, confidante, debutante, definite, detente, dirigiste, enceinte, entente, entracte, exquisite, favourite, granite, hypocrite, infinite, minute* |

('sixtieth of an hour'), *opposite, perquisite, plebiscite, pointe, requisite, riposte, route, svelte* – about 30 nouns/adjectives in /ət/ spelt <-ate> where the verbs with the same spelling are pronounced with /eɪt/, e.g. *advocate, affiliate, aggregate, alternate* (here with also a difference in stress and vowel pattern: noun/ adjective pronounced /ɔːlˈtɜːnət/, verb pronounced /ˈɔːltəneɪt/), *animate, appropriate, approximate, articulate, associate, certificate, consummate* (here with also a difference in stress and vowel pattern: adjective pronounced /kənˈsʌmət/, verb pronounced /ˈkɒnsjəmeɪt/), *coordinate, curate* (here with also a difference in meaning and stress: noun ('junior cleric') pronounced /ˈkjʊərət/, verb ('mount an exhibition') pronounced /kjʊəˈreɪt/), *degenerate, delegate, deliberate* (here with also a difference in syllable structure: adjective /dɪˈlɪbrət/ with three syllables and an elided vowel – see section 6.10; verb /dɪˈlɪbəreɪt/ with four syllables), *designate, desolate, duplicate, elaborate, estimate, expatriate, graduate, initiate, intimate, legitimate, moderate, pontificate* (here with unrelated (?) meanings: noun ('pope's reign') pronounced /pɒnˈtɪfɪkət/, verb ('speak pompously') pronounced /pɒnˈtɪfɪkeɪt/), *precipitate* (but here only the adjective has /ət/; the noun as well as the verb has /eɪt/), *predicate, separate* (here too with a difference in syllable structure: adjective /ˈseprət/ with two syllables and an elided vowel – see section 6.10; verb /ˈsepəreɪt/ with three syllables), *subordinate, syndicate, triplicate*. In the verbs and the many other nouns and adjectives with this ending pronounced /eɪt/, the <e> is part of the split digraph <a.e> spelling /eɪ/ and the /t/ is spelt solely by the <t>
– a further set of at least 60 nouns/adjectives (some of which are derived forms) in /ət/ spelt <-ate> with no identically-spelt verb, e.g. *accurate, adequate, agate, appellate, celibate, chocolate, climate, collegiate, conglomerate, (in)considerate, consulate, delicate, desperate, (in)determinate, directorate, disconsolate, doctorate, electorate, episcopate, extortionate, fortunate, illegitimate, immaculate, immediate,*

inanimate, in(sub)ordinate, inspectorate, intricate, inviolate, (bacca)laureate, legate, (il)literate, novitiate, obdurate, palate, particulate, (com/dis-)passionate, private, profligate, proletariate (also spelt proletariat), (dis)proportionate, protectorate, proximate, roseate, senate, surrogate, (in)temperate, triumvirate, ultimate, (in)vertebrate (a few of these words do have related but not identically-spelt verb forms with <-ate> pronounced /eɪt/: animate, legitimate, mediate, subordinate, violate)
– possibly just one word where both noun and verb have <-ate> pronounced /ət/: pirate
– <te> spelling /t/ also occurs medially in a few words in rapid speech, e.g. interest, literacy, literal, literary, literature, sweetener, veterinary – see section 6.10

In all cases where /ət/ is spelt <-ate> the <e> is phonographically redundant (that is, it does not indicate a 'long' pronunciation of the preceding vowel letter and could therefore be omitted from the spelling without altering the pronunciation; hence I have not analysed such words as having /ə/ spelt <a.e> and /t/ spelt <t>), but in two cases it makes the words visually distinct from words without the <e> and with an unrelated meaning: point, rout.

Carney does not recognise <te> as a spelling of /t/ and this probably means that percentages for my analysis would be slightly different from his

| | | |
|---|---|---|
| | <th> | only in Thai, thali, Thame, Thames, Therese, Thomas, thyme, Wrotham /ˈruːtəm/ |
| | <tw> | only in two and derivatives, e.g. twopence, twopenny. /w/ surfaces in between, betwixt, twain, twelfth, twelve, twenty, twice, twilight, twilit, twin – see section 7.2 |
| 2-phoneme graphemes | /tθ/ spelt <th> | only in eighth. See section 4.4.7 |
| | /ts/ | |
| | (1) spelt <z> | only in Alzheimer's, bilharzia, Nazi (but Churchill said /ˈnaːziː/), scherzo, schizo(-) |
| | (2) spelt <zz> | only in intermezzo, paparazzi, pizza, pizzicato |

*The phoneme-grapheme correspondences, 1: Consonants* 39

### NOTES

/t/ is always spelt <ed> in past forms of regular verbs ending in a voiceless consonant other than /t/, e.g. *walked*. See also the entry for <ed>, section 10.15.

/ts/ also has 2-grapheme spellings, the regular one being <ts>, plus the Oddity <tz> – for the latter see under /s/, section 3.7.6.

## 3.5.8 /r/ as in *rye*

Occurs only before a vowel phoneme (in RP).

### THE MAIN SYSTEM

| | | | |
|---|---|---|---|
| *Basic grapheme* | <r> | 94% | e.g. *very* |
| *Other frequent graphemes* | (none) | | |
| *Doubled spelling* | <rr> | 4% | medially, does NOT occur before final /əl/ spelt <-le> and arises mainly from suffixation (see Notes), but there are some independent examples, e.g. *arroyo, barrow, berry, borrow, burrow, carrot, derrick, garrotte, guerrilla, herring, horrid, hurry, lorry, mirror, (to)morrow, parrot, porridge, scurrilous, serrate, sorry, squirrel, stirrup, terrine, warrant, wherry, worrit, worry* – see sections 4.3.4 and 4.4.5–6; never word-final as a separate grapheme – see Notes |

### THE REST

| | | |
|---|---|---|
| *Doubled spelling + <e>* | | (does not occur as a spelling of /r/ – but see Notes) |
| *Oddities* | | 2% in total |
| | <re> | only in *forehead* pronounced /ˈfɒrɪd/ |

| | | |
|---|---|---|
| | <rh> | only word-initial and only in a few words mainly of Greek origin, namely *rhapsody* and several other words beginning *rhapsod-*, *rhea*, *rheme*, *rhesus*, *rhetor(ic)*, *rheum(ati-c/sm)*, *rhinestone*, *rhinoceros* and several other words beginning *rhin(o)-*, *rhizome* and several other words beginning *rhizo-*, *rhododendron* and several other words beginning *rhodo-*, *rhodium*, *rhomb-ic/us*, the Greek letter name *rho*, *rhotic*, *rhubarb*, *rhyme*, *rhythm* and a few other rare words |
| | <rrh> | only medial and only in a few words of Greek origin, namely *amenorrhoea*, *arrhythmia*, *cirrhosis*, *diarrhoea*, *gonorrhoea*, *haemorrhage*, *haemorrhoid*, *lactorrhoea*, *logorrhoea*, *pyorrhoea*, *pyrrhic*. N.B. In *catarrh*, *myrrh* the <rrh> is not a separate grapheme – see Notes (but in *catarrhal* /r/-linking occurs – see section 3.6) |
| | <wr> | except in *awry*, only in initial position and only in *wrap*, *wrasse*, *wreck*, *wren*, *wrench*, *wrest(le)*, *wretch(ed)*, *wriggle*, *wring*, *wrinkle*, *wrist*, *write*, *wrong*, *Wrotham* /ˈruːtəm/, *wrought*, *wry* and a few more rare words |
| 2-phoneme graphemes | (none) | |

## NOTES

The only stem words in which final <-rr, -rre, -rrh> occur are *carr*, *charr*, *parr*, *err*, *chirr*, *shirr*, *skirr*, *whirr*, *burr*, *purr*, *barre*, *bizarre*, *parterre*; *catarrh*, *myrrh*. Because there is no /r/ phoneme in these words (in RP), these letters do not form separate graphemes but are part of the trigraphs or four-letter graphemes <arr, err, irr, urr, arre, erre, arrh, yrrh> spelling variously /ɑː, ɜː, eə/ – see the entries for those phonemes in sections 5.5.1, 5.5.2 and 5.6.3 and, for some suffixed forms, the next section. For *err* see also section 4.3.2.

In words like *preferring*, *referral*, the <rr> is due purely to a spelling rule involving the suffix – see the next section and section 4.2. In such words the letters <err> spell the vowel /ɜː/ and the <rr> also spells the linking /r/ consonant – for /r/-linking see section 3.6, and for dual-functioning section 7.1. But in *berry*, *errant*, *guerrilla*, *herring*, *wherry*, *abhorrent*, *demurral*, *garrotte*, <e, o, u, a> spell /e, ɒ, ʌ, ə/ and the <rr> simply spells /r/ without influencing the pronunciation of the vowel; similarly in the other words listed above as having independently-occurring medial <rr>.

## 3.6 /r/-linking

Although word-final /r/ does not occur in RP when words are pronounced in isolation, words which end in letter <r> after a vowel letter retain the possibility of a /r/ phoneme surfacing when a suffix or the next word begins with a vowel phoneme. For example, I pronounce the phrase *dearer and dearer* with three /r/ sounds, corresponding to the first three occurrences of the letter <r>: /ˈdɪərərənˈdɪərə/. For more phonological detail see Cruttenden (2014: 224, 315-7).

Many people call this phenomenon '<r>-linking', using the name of the **letter** <r>. I prefer to call it '/r/-linking', using (in speech) the sound of, or (in writing) the symbol for, the **phoneme** /r/ because that is what the link consists of in speech. Moreover, various other graphemes which can spell /r/ allow /r/-linking - see, for example, <rrh> in *catarrhal* in the entry for /r/ just above. /r/-linking is one of four special processes which I have identified as operating in English spelling (for the others see section 6.10 and chapter 7).

In Table 3.2 I have assembled all the examples of /r/-linking mentioned in this book.

NOTES TO TABLE 3.2: FULL LIST OF /r/-LINKING CATEGORIES.

In some cases the pre-linking 'phoneme' is actually a 2-phoneme sequence.

In a few categories where, before linking, the last phoneme of the stem is /ə/ spelt <er, or>, /ə/ is deleted in speech and <e, o> in writing, and the <r> is left to spell /r/. This process needs to be distinguished from vowel elision (see section 6.10), where a vowel letter is written even though there is no vowel phoneme at that point in the spoken word.

Where <e>-deletion (see section 6.4) occurs, I analyse the phoneme before the linking /r/ (provided it has not been deleted or elided) as spelt by the pre-linking grapheme minus <e>, even when that phoneme has changed.

Except where stated:
1) stress placement and the phoneme before the linking /r/ remain unchanged;
2) the /r/-linking grapheme continues to function as part of the spelling of the preceding phoneme (dual-functioning - see section 7.1), even when that phoneme has changed and/or <e>-deletion has occurred. This principle is adopted in order to avoid introducing some correspondences for which there is no other warrant in my analysis, e.g. <a> alone spelling /eə/ in *vicarious*. For more detail see section A.8 in Appendix A.

TABLE 3.2: FULL LIST OF /r/-LINKING CATEGORIES.

| Phoneme before /r/-linking | Grapheme spelling that phoneme | /r/-linking grapheme | Example(s) | Notes |
|---|---|---|---|---|
| /ə/ | <ar> | <r> | polarise | |
| | | | familiarity, hilarity, peculiarity, polarity, vulgarity | Stress shifts to last syllable of stem, the vowel there shifts to /æ/ and is spelt only by <a>, and <r> spells only /r/ |
| | | | vicarious | Stress shifts to last syllable of stem, and the vowel there shifts to /eə/ |
| | <er> | | ethereal, managerial | Stress shifts to last syllable of stem, and the vowel there shifts to /ɪə/ |
| | | | hyperintelligent, interagency, leverage, offering, sufferance | /ə/ may be elided – see section 6.10 |
| | <eur> | | amateurish | |
| | <er> | | foundress, hindrance, laundress, ogress, temptress, tigress, waitress, wardress, wintry | /ə/ is deleted, as shown by the disappearance of the penultimate <e> of the stem, and <r> spells only /r/ |
| | <or> | | actress, ambassadress, conductress, dominatrix, executrix | /ə/ is deleted, as shown by the disappearance of the penultimate <o> of the stem, and <r> spells only /r/ |
| | | | for instance, prioress, terrorist | |
| | | | authority | Stress shifts to last syllable of stem, the vowel there shifts to /ɒ/ and is spelt only by <o>, and <r> spells only /r/ |

## The phoneme-grapheme correspondences, 1: Consonants

| | | | | |
|---|---|---|---|---|
| /ə/ | <or> | <r> | authorial, dictatorial | Stress shifts to last syllable of stem, and the vowel there shifts to /ɔː/ |
| | | | favourite | /ə/ may be elided – see section 6.10 |
| | <our> | <r>, plus deletion of <u> from final syllable of stem | glamorise, rigorous, vigorous | |
| | <re> | | central, fibrous, lustr-al/ous, metrical, spectral | /ə/ is deleted (as shown by disappearance of <e>), and <r> spells only /r/ |
| | | | mediocrity, sepulchral, theatrical | /ə/ is deleted (as shown by disappearance of <e>), stress shifts to syllable before suffix if not already there, vowel there shifts to /ɒ, ʌ, æ/, and <r> spells only /r/ |
| | | <r> following <e>-deletion | calibration | /ə/ is deleted (as shown by disappearance of <e>), stress shifts to first syllable of suffix, and <r> spells only /r/ |
| | | | acreage, massacreing, ochreous, ogreish /ˈeɪkərɪdʒ, ˈmæsəkərɪŋ, ˈəʊkərəs, ˈəʊɡərɪʃ/ | /ə/ is **not** deleted (as shown by retention of <e>), and <r> spells only /r/, but the schwa and /r/ seem to be spelt by the <e> and <r> in reverse order |
| | <ure> | | injurious | Stress shifts to 2nd syllable of stem, and vowel there shifts to /jʊə/ |
| | | | adventurous, natural, naturist, procedural, treasury | /ə/ is spelt only by the <u> and may be elided, especially in derived adverbs – see section 6.10 – and <r> spells only /r/ |

TABLE 3.2: FULL LIST OF /r/-LINKING CATEGORIES, CONT.

| Phoneme before /r/-linking | Grapheme spelling that phoneme | /r/-linking grapheme | Example(s) | Notes |
|---|---|---|---|---|
| /ə/ | <ur> | <r> | murmuring | |
| | | | sulphuric | Stress shifts to last syllable of stem, and the vowel there shifts to /jʊə/ |
| | <er> | | conference, deference, preference | Stress shifts to first syllable, and last vowel phoneme of stem shifts to /ə/ (or may be elided – see section 6.10) |
| /ɜː/ | <err> | <rr> | errant | Preceding vowel shifts to /e/, and <rr> spells only /r/ |
| | <irr> | | whirring | |
| | <urr> | | purring | |
| | <er> | <rr> arising from consonant letter doubling (see section 4.2) | conferring, deferring, preferring, referral | |
| | <ur> | | furry, occurring | |
| | | | demurral | Preceding vowel shifts to /ʌ/, and <rr> spells only /r/ |
| /ɑː/ | <ar> | | sparring | |
| | <arre> | <rr> following <e>-deletion | bizarrery | |
| | <arrh> | <rrh> | catarrhal | |
| | <ar> | <r> | cigarette, czarina | Stress shifts to suffix, and in *cigarette* vowel phoneme preceding /r/ shifts to /ə/ |
| /wɑː/ | <oir> | | memoirist | |
| /eə/ | <heir> | <r> | inherit | Too complicated to analyse |
| | <air> | | repairing | |
| | <aire, heir> | | millionairess, heiress | Stress shifts to final syllable |
| | <ayor> | | mayoral, mayoress | In *mayoress*, stress shifts to final syllable |
| | <ear> | | wearing | |

| | | | | |
|---|---|---|---|---|
| /eə/ | <ere> | <re> | *thereupon* | |
| | | <r> following <e>-deletion | *wherever, compering* | |
| | <are> | | *staring* | |
| | | | *preparedness* | |
| /aɪə/ | <ire> | <r> following <e>-deletion | *entirety* | 2nd <e> surfaces as /ɪ/ – see section 7.2 |
| | | | *wiring* | |
| | | | *inspiration* | Stress shifts to first syllable of suffix, vowel in last syllable of stem shifts to /ɪ/ or /ə/ and is spelt only by the <i>, and <r> spells only /r/ |
| | | | *satirical* | Stress shifts to last syllable of stem, the vowel there shifts to /ɪ/ and is spelt only by the <i>, and <r> spells only /r/ |
| | <yre> | | *lyrical* | Vowel in stem shifts to /ɪ/ and is spelt only by the <i>, and <r> spells only /r/ |
| | | | *pyromaniac* | |
| /ʊə/ | <ure> | | *enduring, surety* | |
| | <oor, our> | <r> | *boorish, touring* | |
| /ɔː/ | <ar> | <rr> arising from consonant letter doubling (see section 4.2) | *warring* | |
| | <or> | | *abhorrent* | Preceding vowel shifts to /ɒ/ and is spelt only by <o>, and <rr> spells only /r/ |
| | <or, oar, oor, our> | <r> | *mentoring, hoary, flooring, pouring* | |
| /ɔː/ | <ore> | <r> following <e> deletion | *boring* | |
| /ɪə/ | <ere> | | *interfering* | |
| | | | *sincerity* | Preceding vowel shifts to /e/ and is spelt only by <e>, and <r> spells only /r/ |
| | <ear, eer, ier> | <r> | *dearer, hearing, cheering, tiering* | |
| /aʊə/ | <our, ower> | | *devouring, towering* | |

An even fuller analysis would also mention cases of /r/-linking occurring where an intervening consonant phoneme has been dropped, as in the place- and surname *Wareham* /ˈweərəm/ (where the /h/ of the Anglo-Saxon placename element *ham* was dropped many centuries ago) and the British Tommy's adage about medals: 'Win 'em and wear 'em' – here the end of the sentence is also pronounced /ˈweərəm/, the /ð/ phoneme of RP /ˈweə ðəm/ (with no /r/) having been elided. But this book is not about placenames, surnames or accents other than RP.

Sometimes /r/-linking is overgeneralised to words which do not have a letter <r> in the written form (and never had, and still do not have, a /r/ phoneme in any accent of English when pronounced in isolation): the best-known example is *law and order* pronounced /ˈlɔːrəˈnɔːdə/ ('Laura Norder') with 'intrusive /r/', rather than /ˈlɔːwəˈnɔːdə/. (But this phrase never seems to be pronounced /ˈlɔːrəˈndɔːdə/ ('Lauren Dawder'), with the <d> of *and* made explicit.) An example that occurs in children's speech is *drawing* pronounced /ˈdrɔːrɪŋ/ rather than /ˈdrɔːɪŋ/. Cruttenden (2014: 316) provides several more examples.

On the other hand, /r/-linking is sometimes avoided where the spelling suggests it would be natural. For example, the recorded announcers at Sheffield railway station say /ˈplætfɔːm fɔː ˈeɪ, ˈmæntʃɪstə ˈeəpɔːt, ˈmæntʃɪstə ˈɒksfəd ˈrəʊd, ˈʃaɪə əʊks/ rather than /ˈplætfɔːm fɔːˈreɪ, ˈmæntʃɪstəˈreəpɔːt, ˈmæntʃɪstəˈrɒksfəd ˈrəʊd, ˈʃaɪərəʊks/ for 'Platform 4A', 'Manchester Airport', 'Manchester Oxford Road', 'Shireoaks'.

Almost all instances of /r/-linking are also examples of what I call dual-functioning. That is, after linking, the <r>, etc., continues to function as part of the grapheme spelling the pre-linking phoneme while also spelling /r/ in its own right. Exceptions shown in Table 3.2 where an <r> ceases to function as part of the grapheme spelling the pre-suffixation phoneme and therefore only spells /r/ after suffixation are: *familiarity, hilarity, peculiarity, polarity, vulgarity, foundress, laundress, ogress, temptress, tigress, waitress, wardress, actress, ambassadress, conductress, dominatrix, executrix, protrectress, authority, mediocrity, sepulchral, theatrical, central, fibrous, lustr-al/ous, metrical, spectral, calibration, demurral, inspiration, satirical, lyrical, abhorrent, sincerity.*

For other categories of dual-functioning see section 7.1.

For cases in which /ə/ may be elided after /r/-linking see also section 6.10.

For 'linking /w/' and 'linking /j/' see sections 3.8.7-8. Like /r/-linking, both occur frequently between a stem word and a suffix or a following word beginning with a vowel phoneme. However, there are two key differences: (1) in /w/- and /j/-linking, the quality of the glide between stem and suffix or next word is entirely predictable from the stem-final phoneme, whereas /r/-linking never is (in RP), and can be explained only historically - it occurs where once there was a postvocalic /r/; (2) similar /w/- and /j/-glides occur **within** many stem words where there is no indication of them in the spelling - /r/-linking never occurs within stem words.

## 3.7 Consonants with doubled spellings which are regular at the end of one-syllable words after a short vowel spelt with one letter: /k tʃ f dʒ l s v z/

In addition to their frequency in stem words, the doubled spellings of /k f l s/ occasionally arise from suffixation, e.g. *picnicking, iffy, modelling, gassing* (see sections 4.2 and 4.3.1).

### 3.7.1 /k/ as in *coo*

#### THE MAIN SYSTEM

For all these categories see Notes and Table 3.3.

*Basic grapheme*    \<c\>    59%    e.g. *cat*

Regular in all positions **except** (1) before \<e, i, y\>, where the regular spelling is \<k\> (2) before final /əl/ spelt \<-le\> after a short vowel spelt with one letter, where the regular spelling is \<ck\> (3) word-finally in one-syllable words, where the regular spelling is \<ck\> after a short vowel spelt with one letter, otherwise \<k\> For other exceptions see below

| | | | |
|---|---|---|---|
| *Other frequent grapheme* | <k> | 21% | regular before <e, i, y>, e.g. *kelp, kit, sky*, including word-finally within split digraphs, e.g. *like, make*; also word-finally in one-syllable words except those where <ck> is regular. Only exceptions: *ache, Celt, Celtic, sceptic* and one pronunciation of words beginning *encephal-*; *arc, chic, disc*, and a few more words |
| *Doubled spelling* | <ck> | 6% | regular in word-final position in one-syllable words after a short vowel spelt with one letter, e.g. *crack*; also before final /əl/ spelt <-le> after a short vowel spelt with one letter, e.g. *heckle* – see section 4.3.3; for other occurrences medially in stem words see Table 3.3; there are several word-final occurrences in polysyllables, e.g. *derrick, dunnock, haddock, hammock, hummock, slummock* |
| *Frequent 2-phoneme grapheme* | /ks/ spelt <x> | 5% | word-initially, only in the Greek letter-name *xi* pronounced /ksaɪ/; regular medially, e.g. *buxom, maxim, next* (for exceptions see below); also finally where the /s/ is part of the stem, e.g. *box* (only exception: *aurochs*) |
| *Rare grapheme* | <q> | 3% | e.g. *quick* See <cq, cqu, qu, que> within the Oddities, below, and Notes |

## THE REST

| | | |
|---|---|---|
| *Doubled spelling + <e>* | | (does not occur) |
| *Oddities* | | 6% in total |
| | <cc> spells /k/ | – before <e, i, y>: only in *baccy, biccy, recce* /ˈrekiː/ (short for *reconnoitre*), *soccer, speccy, streptococci* <br> – where the next letter is **not** <e, i, y>: in about 45 words mainly of Latin origin, namely *acclaim, acclimatise, accolade, accommodate, accompany, accomplice, accomplish, accord, accost, account,* |

*accoutrement, accredit, accrete, accrue, acculturate, accumulate, accurate, accursed, accuse, accustom, desiccate, occasion, occlude, occult, occupy, occur, succour, succubus, succulent, succumb.*
Words of non-Latin origin in this group are *broccoli, buccaneer, ecclesiastic, felucca, hiccup, mecca, moccasin, peccadillo, peccary, piccolo, raccoon, scirocco, staccato, stucco, tobacco, toccata, Wicca, yucca*
See Notes for the complementary value of <cc> before <e, i, y>, and on why <cc> is not the doubled spelling of /k/

<cch>  only in *bacchanal, Bacchante, bacchic, ecchymosis, gnocchi, saccharide, saccharine, zucchini*. In *bacchanal, Bacchante, ecchymosis, saccharide, saccharine*, the <h> could be deleted without altering the English pronunciation – see just above; but in *bacchic, gnocchi, zucchini* this change might make them look as if they were pronounced with /ks/

<ch>  mainly in words of Greek origin, e.g. *amphibrach, anarchy, anchor, archaic* and every other word beginning /aːk/ (except *arc, ark*), *brachial, brachycephalic, bronchi(-al/tis), catechis-e/m, chalcedony, chameleon, chaos, character, charisma, chasm, chemical, chemist, chiasma, chimera, chiropody* (also pronounced with initial /ʃ/), *chlamydia, chloride, chlorine, choir, cholesterol, cholera, choral, chord, choreograph(-er/y), chorus, chrism, Christian, Christmas, Chris(topher), chrome, chromosome, chronic* and every other word beginning /krɒn-/, *chrysalis, chrysanth(emum), chyle, chyme, cochlea, diptych, distich, drachma, echo, epoch, eschatology, eucharist, eunuch, hierarch(y)* and every other polysyllabic non-compound word ending /aːk(iː)/ (except *aardvark*), *hypochondriac, ichor, lichen* pronounced /ˈlaɪkən/ (also pronounced /ˈlɪtʃən/), *machination, malachite, mechani-c/sm, melanchol-y/ic, monarch(-y/ic), ochlocracy, ochre, orchestra, orchid, pachyderm, parochial, pentateuch, psyche* and all its derivatives, *scheme, schizo* and all its derivatives, *scholar, scholastic, school, stochastic, stomach, strychnine,*

synchronise, synecdoche, technical, technique, trachea, triptych, trochee.
Words of non-Greek origin in this group are *ache, aurochs, baldachin, chianti, chiaroscuro, cromlech, Czech, lachrymose, masochist, Michael, mocha, oche, pinochle, pulchritude, scherzo, schooner, sepulchre*; also *broch, loch, pibroch, Sassenach* when pronounced with /k/ rather than Scots /x/ (for this symbol see section 2.3)

&lt;cq&gt;  only in *acquaint, acquiesce, acquire, acquisitive, acquit*

&lt;cqu&gt;  spells only /k/ (not /kw/) only in *lacquer, picquet, racquet*

&lt;cu&gt;  only in *biscuit, circuit* (contrast '*circuitous*' where the &lt;u&gt; 'surfaces' – see section 7.2.2); cf. &lt;bu&gt; under /b/, section 3.5.1, and &lt;gu&gt; under /g/, section 3.5.3

&lt;g&gt;  only in *length, lengthen, strength, strengthen* pronounced /leŋkθ, 'leŋkθən, streŋkθ, 'streŋkθən/ (for their alternative pronunciations see under /n/, section 3.5.5) – for the rationale of this analysis see Notes under /ŋ/, section 3.8.2 – and in *angst* /æŋkst/, *disguise* /dɪs'kaɪz/, *disgust* pronounced /dɪs'kʌst/, i.e. identically to *discussed*; *disguise, disgust* are also pronounced /dɪz'ɡaɪz, dɪz'ɡʌst/, i.e. with both medial consonants voiced rather than voiceless

&lt;gh&gt;  only in *hough*

&lt;ke&gt;  only in *Berkeley, burke*

&lt;kh&gt;  only in *astrakhan, gurkha, gymkhana, khaki, khan, khazi, khedive, sheikh, Sikh*

&lt;kk&gt;  only in *chukker, dekko, pukka* and inflected forms of *trek*, e.g. *trekkie*

&lt;qu&gt;  as a digraph spelling only /k/ (not /kw/) occurs initially or medially (never finally – cf. next paragraph) in about 50 words mainly of French origin, namely *bouquet, conquer* (/w/ surfaces in *conquest* – see section 7.2), *coquette, croquet, croquette, etiquette, exchequer, liqueur, liquor, liquorice, maquis, mannequin, marquee, marquetry, masquerade, mosquito, parquet, piquant, quatrefoil, quay, quenelle, quiche, so(u)briquet, tourniquet*, and, in conservative RP-speakers' accents, *questionnaire, quoits*; also medially in *applique, communique,*

*The phoneme-grapheme correspondences, 1: Consonants*   51

|  |  |
|---|---|
|  | *manque, risque* – see next paragraph; also phonemically but not orthographically word-final in *opaque*; *claque, plaque*; *basque, casque, masque*; *antique, bezique, boutique, clique, critique, mystique, oblique, physique, pique, technique, unique*; *bisque, odalisque*; *toque*; *peruque*; *brusque* pronounced /bruːsk/, and a few more rare words where the final written <e> is part of a split digraph with a preceding vowel letter spelling variously /eɪ, aː, iː, əʊ, uː/. The words *basque, casque, masque, bisque, odalisque* and *brusque* pronounced /bruːsk/, where there is also an <s> before the <qu>, cause a special extension to the definition of a split digraph – see section A.6 in Appendix A and the Notes under <a.e, i.e, u.e>, sections 10.4/24/38 |
| <que> as a trigraph spelling only /k/ (not /kw/ plus vowel) | occurs word-initially only in *queue* and medially only in *milquetoast* (where it is nevertheless stem-final in a compound word); otherwise only word-finally and only in about 18 words mainly of French origin, namely: <br>(1) with a preceding consonant letter such that <que> could be replaced by <k> without changing the pronunciation: *arabesque, barque, basque, brusque* pronounced /brʌsk/ (also pronounced /bruːsk/), *burlesque, casque, catafalque, grotesque, marque, masque, mosque, torque* and the derived forms *picturesque, romanesque, statuesque*. However, in this group *barque, basque, casque, marque, masque, torque* are kept visually distinct from *bark, bask, cask, mark, mask, torc* <br>(2) with a preceding vowel letter such that <que> could be replaced by <ck> without changing the pronunciation: *baroque, cheque* (cf. US *check*), *monocoque, plaque* pronounced /plæk/ (also pronounced /plaːk/) |
| <x> spells /k/ (not /ks/, etc.) | only in *coxswain* and before /s/ spelt <c> in a small group of words of Latin origin, namely *exceed, excel(lent), except, excerpt, excess, excise, excite* |
| Other 2-phoneme graphemes | See also Notes |
| /kʃ/ |  |
| (1) spelt <x> | only in *flexure, luxury, sexual* /ˈflekʃə, ˈlʌkʃəriː, ˈsekʃ(uːw)əl/ |

52  Dictionary of the British English Spelling System

|   |   | (2)<br>spelt <xi> | only in *anxious, complexion, connexion* (also spelt *connection*), *crucifixion, fluxion, (ob)noxious* |
|---|---|---|---|
|   |   | /ks/ |   |
|   |   | (1)<br>spelt <xe> | only in *annexe, axe, deluxe, (River) Exe*. The <e> in *axe* is redundant, as the US spelling *ax* shows (but cf. the 'Three-Letter Rule', section 4.3.2). The <e> in *annexe* /ˈæneks/ ('addition to building or document') is also phonologically redundant (and mainly omitted in US spelling) but, where used, differentiates this word visually from *annex* /əˈneks/ ('take over territory'). Similarly, deleting the final <e> from the French spelling of *de luxe* would get too close to soap and washing powder |
|   |   | (2)<br>spelt <xh> | only in *exhibition, exhortation, exhumation* – for *exhibit, exhort, exhume* see under /g/, section 3.5.3 |
| 3-phoneme<br>grapheme |   | /eks/<br>spelt <x> | only in *X-ray*, etc. One of only two 3-phoneme graphemes in the whole language |

## NOTES

For adverbs with the unstressed ending /ɪkliː/ spelt <-ically> see section 6.10.

It is unphonological but true that it is easier to state the main correspondences of /k/ in terms of following **letters** rather than following **phonemes**. (For an attempt to do it phonologically see Carney, 1994: 217).

<k> is used to spell /k/ mainly before the letters <e, i, y>, that is, just where <c> would usually spell /s/ – see below. There are very few exceptions:

1) where /k/ is spelt <c> despite being before <e, i>: *Celt, Celtic, sceptic*, all of which have alternative spellings with <k> (and the Glasgow football club is in any case /ˈseltɪk/), *arced, arcing, synced, syncing* (which means that the spelling *synch* for this verb is better); also several words beginning *encephal-*, all of which have two pronunciations, with /s/ (where the spelling with <c> is regular) or /k/ (where it is irregular), e.g. *encephalitis* /enˈsefəlaɪtəs, eŋˈkefəlaɪtəs/ – note too the alternation between /n, ŋ/ in the first syllable. Also, in July 2006 the derived form *chicest* /ˈʃiːkɪst/ appeared on a magazine cover, and in May 2010 *ad hocery* appeared in the *Guardian*. There seem to be no exceptions with /k/ spelt <c> before <y>

2) where /k/ is spelt <k> despite **not** being before <e, i, y>: *alkali, askance, blitzkrieg, hokum, kale, kangaroo, kaolin, kappa, kapok, kaput, klaxon,*

*kleptomaniac, koala, kohl, kopek, Koran, kosher, krypton, kwashiorkor* (twice), *leukaemia, mazurka, oakum, okay, okra, paprika, polka, sauerkraut, shako, skate, skulk, skull, skunk, sudoku, tektite, ukulele.*

<k> is also the regular spelling of /k/ at the end of one-syllable words where the preceding phoneme is NOT a short vowel, e.g. *bark* (only exception: *burke*); also in two-syllable words after a consonant letter and before final /əl/ spelt <-le> – but there are very few words in this set, namely *ankle, crinkle, rankle, sparkle, sprinkle, tinkle, twinkle, winkle, wrinkle* (exceptions: *circle, uncle*).

<q> is almost always used to spell /k/ when followed by /w/, which in this context is always spelt <u>. For exceptional spellings of /kw/, see /w/, section 3.8.7.

In addition to its single-grapheme spelling, <x>, /ks/ has several 2-grapheme spellings. There are none in initial position (where /ks/ perhaps occurs only in *xi* anyway). Word-finally, where the /s/ is not part of the stem the regular spelling in one-syllable words after a short vowel is <cks>, and <ks> in other one-syllable words; <cs> is regular in polysyllables – for exceptions to all of these see Table 3.3. Medially, there are three 2-grapheme spellings of /ks/: <xc> is rare – see the last entry among the Oddities above; <cs> is even rarer – it seems to occur only in *ecstasy, ecstatic, facsimile, frolicsome, tocsin* (contrast *toxin*); <cc> occurs in a few words mainly of Latin or French origin where the following letter is <e, i, y>, namely *accede, accelerate, accent, accept, access, accident, accidie, coccyx, eccentric, flaccid* pronounced /'flæksɪd/ (also pronounced /'flæsɪd/), *occident, occiput, Occitan(e), succeed, success, succinct* pronounced /sək'sɪŋkt/ (also pronounced /sə'sɪŋkt/), *vaccine.*

It is because <c> before <e, i, y> almost always spells /s/ that <cc> can not function as the doubled spelling of /k/ – before a suffix beginning with <e, i, y> the second <c> would represent /s/ (as in the group of words just listed). So when a suffix beginning with a vowel letter is added to words ending in /k/ spelt <c>, the <c> is usually doubled to <ck>, e.g. *bivouacked, picnicking, trafficked* – but the principle of avoiding <c> spelling /k/ before <e, i, y> is not applied to *arced, arcing, chicest* (cf. above and section 4.2). <cc> also has the very rare pronunciation /tʃ/ only in *bocce, cappuccino* (see next section).

/kʃ/ has scarcely any 2-grapheme spellings, but cf. *baksheesh.*

The word *ache* is one of the few where the split grapheme <a.e> has two consonant letters in its midst (it could equally well be spelt *°ake*).

As Carney says (p.216), '/k/ is the most divergent of the consonants'. For this reason, a further analysis of the major spellings of /k/ is given in Table 3.3.

TABLE 3.3: THE DISTRIBUTION OF <c, ck, k, x> IN SPELLINGS OF /k, ks/.

In each main box below, the regular spelling is stated at the top or above the relevant set of words. (For exceptions besides those in the Table, see the 2- and 3-phoneme graphemes and Oddities above).

|  | initial | medial | final |
|---|---|---|---|
| /k/ before <e, i, y> | <k>, e.g. *kelp, kit, kyle* Exceptions: *Celt, Celtic* | <k>, e.g. *sketch, skit, sky* Exceptions: *sceptic*; *lichen* pronounced /ˈlaɪkən/ (also pro-nounced /ˈlɪtʃən/); *chicken, cricket, jacket, mackerel, pernickety, pickerel, pocket, rocket, sprocket; mackintosh; finicky* Words ending in <-c> usually add <k> when a suffix beginning with a vowel letter is added, e.g. *bivouacked, picnicking, trafficked* (but *arced, arcing, chicest* do not) | <k> Occurs only within split digraphs, e.g. *cake, eke, bike, poke, rebuke, fluke, tyke* Exception: *ache* |
| /k/ **not** before <e, i, y> | <c>, e.g. *cake, close, coal, cross, cute* Exceptions: *kagoul* (also spelt *cagoule*), *kale, kangaroo, kaolin, kappa, kapok, kaput, kayak, klaxon, klepto-maniac, koala, kohl, kopek, Koran, kosher, krypton* | <c>, e.g. *scale, eclogue, scorch, across, acute* Exceptions: With <ck>: between short vowel spelt with one letter and final /əl/ spelt <-le>, e.g. *crackle* (see section 4.3.3), plus *beckon, buckaroo, buckshee, chickadee, cockatoo, cockaigne, cockatrice, cockney, gecko, hackney, hickory-dickory, huckster, jackanapes, lackadaisical, reckon, rucksack, sackbut* With <k>: in two-syllable words after a consonant letter and before final /əl/ spelt <-le>, namely *ankle, crinkle, rankle, sparkle, sprinkle, tinkle, twinkle, winkle, wrinkle* (exceptions: *circle, uncle*), plus *alkali, askance, blitzkrieg, hokum, leukaemia, mazurka, oakum, okay, okra, paprika, periwinkle, polka, sauerkraut, shako, skate, skulk, skull, skunk, sudoku,* | In one-syllable words after a short vowel spelt with one letter: <ck>, e.g. *back, beck, trick, clock, duck* Exceptions: *bloc, choc, doc, hic, mac, roc, sac, sic, spec, tec, tic; flak, suk, trek, yak* In other one-syllable words: <k>, e.g. *ark, bank, brook, freak* Exceptions: *arc, chic, disc, franc, orc, talc, torc, torque, zinc* In polysyllables: <c>, e.g. *politic* Exceptions: With <ck>: *alack, attack, bailiwick, bannock, barrack, bollock, bullock, burdock, buttock, cassock, Cossack, derrick, dunnock, fetlock, fossick, gimcrack, gimmick, haddock, hammock, hassock, haversack, hemlock, hillock, hollyhock, hummock, limerick,* |

|  |  | *tektite, ukase, ukulele*<br>With <x> spelling only /k/ because the following <c, sw> spells /s/: *exceed, excel, excellent, except, excerpt, excess, excise, excite; coxswain* | *mattock, maverick, niblick, paddock, pollack, ransack, rollick, rollock, rowlock, rucksack, shamrock, slummock, tussock, warlock*<br>With <k>: *aardvark, asterisk, basilisk, batik, bergomask, berserk, Bolshevik, bulwark, damask, kopek, mountebank, muzak, obelisk, Slovak, sputnik, springbok, tamarisk, tomahawk, yashmak* |
|---|---|---|---|
| /ks/ | Very rare – perhaps occurs only in Greek letter name *xi* pro-nounced /ksaɪ/ | <x>, e.g. *maxim, next, toxin*<br>Exceptions:<br>– where <x> occurs but spells only /k/ (see box above): *exceed, excel, excellent, except, excerpt, excess, excise, excite; coxswain*;<br>– others: *accede, accelerate, accent, accept, access, accident, accidie, coccyx, eccentric, flaccid, occident, occiput, Occitan, succeed, success, succinct, vaccine; ecstasy, ecstatic, facsimile, frolicsome, tocsin* | Where /s/ is part of stem:<br><x>, e.g. *fax, perplex, six, box, influx, pyx*<br>Only exception: *aurochs*<br>Where /s/ is not part of stem, = is a suffix: all the non-suffixed forms of such words belong in the two boxes above, and in all these cases, when suffixed, /ks/ is spelt with the non-suffixed grapheme plus <s> |

## 3.7.2 /tʃ/ as in *chew*

### THE MAIN SYSTEM

For all these categories see Notes

| Basic grapheme | <ch> | 65% | regular initially except before /uː/, e.g. *chin, church*; also finally (except in one-syllable words after a short vowel spelt with one letter), e.g. *church* (exceptions: *despatch, dispatch, eldritch*); rare medially, but cf. *bachelor, duchess* |
|---|---|---|---|
| Other frequent grapheme | <t> | 25% | regular medially, e.g. *actual, intuition*; also initially before /uː/ spelt <u, u.e>, e.g. *tulip, tune*; never word-final |

| | | | |
|---|---|---|---|
| Doubled spelling | <tch> | 10% | word-initially, only in *Tchaikovsky*; rare medially – does NOT occur before final /əl/ spelt <-le> – but there are a few examples, e.g. *butcher, crotchet, hatchet, ketchup, kitchen, patchouli, pitcher, ratchet, satchel, (e)scutcheon, tetchy, wretched*; regular in word-final position in one-syllable words after a short vowel spelt with one letter, e.g. *match*; exceptions: *much, rich, such, which, niche* pronounced /nɪtʃ/, *kitsch, putsch*; also (irregularly after a diphthong/long vowel) in *aitch, retch* |

## THE REST

| | | |
|---|---|---|
| Doubled spelling + <e> | | (does not occur) |
| Oddities | | <1% in total |
| | <c> | only in *cellist, cello, cicerone* (twice), *concerto* (second <c>) |
| | <cc> | only in *bocce, cappuccino* |
| | <che> | only in *niche* pronounced /nɪtʃ/, which could be spelt *\*nitch*; *niche* is also pronounced /niːʃ/ |
| | <ci> | only in *ancient, ciabatta* |
| | <cz> | only in *czardas* /ˈtʃɑːdæʃ/, *Czech* /tʃek/ |
| | <te> | only in *righteous* |
| | <th> | only in *posthumous* |
| | <ti> | only in *con/di/indi/in/sug-gestion, question, rumbustious* and the derived forms *combustion, exhaustion*. In words like *nation, lotion, equation* I count the <i> as part of a digraph with the preceding consonant letter – see /ʃ, ʒ/, sections 3.8.3-4 |
| | <tsch> | only in *kitsch, putsch* |
| 2-phoneme graphemes | (none) | |

## NOTES

Because /tʃ/ is a sibilant consonant, adding any of the suffixes regular noun plural and third person singular person tense verb (spelt <es> – for an exception see next sentence) and regular singular and irregular plural possessive (spelt <'s>) to a stem ending in /tʃ/ adds a syllable /ɪz/ as well as a morpheme: *matches, detaches, (the) Church's (mission)*. The only word ending in /tʃ/ where the stem already ends in <e> appears to be *niche* pronounced /nɪtʃ/; in this case the ending is just <s>. See also /z/, section 3.7.8, and /ɪ/, section 5.4.3.

The regular spellings of /tʃ/ are:
- initially, <t> before /uː/, otherwise <ch>
- medially, <t>
- finally, <tch> in one-syllable words after a short vowel spelt with one letter, otherwise <ch>.

Examples:
- initial <t> before /uː/: *tuba, tube, tuber, Tuesday* /'tʃuːzdiː/, *tuition* /tʃuː'ɪʃən/, *tulip, tumour, tumult(uous), tumulus, tuna, tune* pronounced /'tʃuːn/, *tunic, tureen, tutor*
- initial <ch> otherwise: *chin, church*
- medial <t>:
- a small set of words ending in /tʃən, tʃəs/ spelt <-tian, -tion, -tious>: *Christian, combustion, con/di/indi/in/sug-gestion, exhaustion, question, rumbustious*
- many nouns ending in /tʃə/, which is mostly spelt <-ture>, e.g. *adventure, capture, creature, culture, picture*
- a set of adjectives ending in /tʃuːwəs/, which are all spelt <-tuous>, e.g. *tortuous, virtuous*
- a small set of nouns in <-tuary>: *actuary, estuary, mortuary, obituary, sanctuary, statuary, voluptuary*, whether pronounced with /tʃuːwəriː/ or /tʃəriː/. For the elision of the <u> see section 6.10
- a larger set of adjectives in <-tual>: *accentual, actual, conceptual, contractual, effectual, eventual, factual, habitual, intellectual, mutual, perpetual, punctual, ritual, spiritual, textual, virtual,* etc., whether pronounced with /tʃuːwəl/ or /tʃəl/. For the elision of the <u> see again section 6.10. The elision seems even more prevalent in the derived adverbs in <-tually>
- a small set of words where /tʃ/ is spelt <t> and a following medial /ə/ (always in the penultimate syllable, with the stress on the antepenultimate syllable) is spelt <u>: *century, congratulate, fistula, flatulen-ce/t, fortunate, petulan-t/ce, postulant, postulate, saturate, spatula, titular*

- a ragbag of words with /tʃ/ spelt <t> followed by /uː/ spelt <u, u.e> (occasionally in word-final position as <ue>), e.g. *impromptu; gargantuan, perpetuate; attitude, multitude, solitude; habitué; statue, virtue; intuition, pituitary; costume; fortune, importune, opportune; virtuoso; obtuse; de/in/pro/sub-stitute, de/in/pro/re/sub-stitution*
- just two words where the stress falls on the syllable following /tʃ/ spelt <t> and that syllable contains <ur(e)> spelling /ʊə/: *centurion, mature*. In all the other words with medial /t/ spelt /tʃ/ listed above the stress falls on an earlier syllable.
- final <tch> after a short vowel spelt with one letter in monosyllables: *match, sketch, pitch, botch, hutch, butch*
- final <ch> otherwise: *attach, arch, church*.

Exceptions (other than those listed under Oddities):
- initial <t> other than before /uː/: none
- initial <ch> before /uː/: only *chew, choose*
- initial spellings other than <t, ch>: <tch> only in *Tchaikovsky*
- medial spellings other than <t>: only *archer, bachelor, cochineal, duchess, duchy, lecher, lichen* pronounced /ˈlɪtʃən/ (also pronounced /ˈlaɪkən/), *macho, treacher-y/ous; butcher, crotchet, hatchet, ketchup, kitchen, patchouli, pitcher, ratchet, satchel, (e)scutcheon, tetchy, wretched* as stem words, but there are also many derived forms, e.g. *lurcher, marcher, matching, preacher, righteous, (re)searcher, teacher*; also the words in <ti> listed in the Oddities
- final <tch> in monosyllables after a diphthong or long vowel: only *aitch, retch* pronounced /riːtʃ/ (also pronounced /retʃ/, where <tch> is regular)
- final <tch> in polysyllables: only *despatch, dispatch, eldritch*
- final <ch> in monosyllables after a short vowel: only *much, rich, such, which*
- final spellings other than <tch, ch>: see Oddities.

As a spelling of /tʃ/, <ti> is rare and occurs only at the beginning of the final syllable of a stem word and immediately after a stressed syllable ending in /s/ spelt <s>, e.g. *question*.

All the words in which /tʃ/ is spelt <t> were formerly pronounced with the sequence /tj/, and conservative RP-speakers may still pronounce them that way (or imagine that they do). Pronunciations with /tj/ would require an analysis with the /t/ spelt <t> and the /j/-glide either spelt <i> (where that is the next letter) or subsumed into the spelling of a 2-phoneme sequence with the following vowel. However, I think that in current RP the process of affricating /tj/ to /tʃ/ is virtually complete (as Cruttenden, 2014: 83 says), and has eliminated pronunciations with /tj/, which I have therefore ignored. An English friend who once did a year's teaching exchange in a primary school in the United States would ask the pupils every day, 'What day is it?' and on Mondays, Wednesdays, Thursdays and Fridays they would answer. But on Tuesdays they would insist she give the name of the day, and would then delightedly point out, 'You say Choozdee /'tʃuːzdiː/!' (as opposed to their /'tuːzdiː/ 'Toozdee', where the /j/-glide has been dropped without affricating the /t/, or perhaps was never present).

For the parallel affrication of /dj/ to /dʒ/ see section 3.7.4, and see also section 5.4.7.

## 3.7.3 /f/ as in *few*

### THE MAIN SYSTEM

| | | | |
|---|---|---|---|
| Basic grapheme | <f> | 84% | e.g. *fish* |
| Other frequent grapheme | <ph> | 11% | in many words of Greek origin, e.g. *philosophy*. See Notes |
| Doubled spelling | <ff> | 4% | regular in word-final position in one-syllable words after /aː/ spelt <a>, e.g. *staff*, and after a short vowel spelt with one letter, e.g. *gaff, cliff, off, gruff*; cf. section 4.3.5 and /aː/, section 5.5.1; for *off* see also section 4.3.2 (exceptions: *graph, gaffe, chef, clef, if, strafe* is not an exception because it has /uː/ spelt <a.e>); also regular medially before final /əl/ spelt <-le> after a short vowel spelt with one letter, e.g. *duffle* – see section 4.3.3; there are also some independent medial examples, e.g. *affray, buffet* (both pronunciations and meanings), *chiffon, offer, proffer, ruffian, soffit, suffer* – see section 4.3.5. Also see Notes |

## THE REST

| | | |
|---|---|---|
| Doubled spelling + <e> | <ffe> | only in *gaffe, giraffe, pouffe*; also in usual pronunciation of *difference, different, sufferance* – for the elided vowel see section 6.10 (but not in *afferent, efferent*) |
| Oddities | | 1% in total |
| | <fe> | only in *carafe, housewife* ('sewing kit' pronounced /ˈhʌzɪf/) and, in rapid speech, *conference, deference, preference, reference* – for the elided vowel see section 6.10 |
| | <ft> | only in *often, soften* pronounced /ˈɒfən, ˈsɒfən/ |
| | <gh> | medially, only in *draught* and derived forms of the following words; otherwise only word-final and only in *chough, cough, enough, laugh, rough, slough* ('shed skin'), *sough, tough, trough* |
| | <pph> | only in *sapphic, sapphire, Sappho* /ˈsæfɪk, ˈsæfaɪə, ˈsæfəʊ/ |
| | <v> | only in *kvetch, svelte, svengali, veldt* |
| 2-phoneme graphemes | (none) | |

## NOTES

In monosyllables, the default spelling is <f>, except where <ff> is regular as defined above. There are a few exceptions with the Greek <ph> spelling: *graph, lymph, morph, phase, phone, phrase*.

In polysyllabic stem words, there are the following tendencies in the distribution of the three main spellings of /f/:

- <ph> occurs almost solely in words of Greek origin, and <f, ff> in other words – but how (unless you have studied Classical Greek, as I did, or know modern Greek) can you tell which words are of Greek origin? Though few people could answer this explicitly, many internalise the word-elements which have that origin and require the <ph> spelling, e.g. *graph, lymph, morph, phag, phall, pharmac, pharyng, phase, pheno, phleb, phil(e/o), phob(e), phon(e/ic/o-), phor(e), phosph, photo, phrase, phren, phyll, phys, phyt(e/o), soph, spher, taph*. As Carney (1994: 229) points out, there is further guidance towards <ph> in polysyllabic words if other Greek word-elements are present, e.g. *anthrop, apo, chloro, chron, crypto, dia, dys, epi, eu, geo, hiero, hydro, hyper, hypo, lexi, macro, meta, micro, oid, ology, ortho, peri, scop, syn, tele*, thus aiding correct spelling of, e.g., *apocrypha(l)*, *chlorophyll*, *cryptographer*, *diaphragm*, *euphemism*, *euphoria*, *hieroglyphics*, *metaphor*, *psephology*.

Words with the element /fænt/ were all once spelt with <ph> and most still are (e.g. *phantasm*, *phantom*) but, awkwardly, three of the commonest are now spelt with <f>: *fantasise*, *fantastic*, *fantasy*.

The Greek elements *neo*, *para* may be misleading; they have taken on lives of their own in modern English (e.g. *neocon*, *paramedic*, where the second element in each word has a Latin origin) and might therefore mislead writers into, e.g., *°neofite*, *°paraprophessional*.

Beyond this, one can only list some of the commoner of the other words containing <ph>: *alpha, aphid, aphrodisiac, asphyxiate, blaspheme, cenotaph, dolphin, elephant, hyphen, lymph, nymph, orphan, phalanx, pheasant, phenol, phial, philistine, phloem, phoenix, siphon/syphon, sphinx, sylph, trophy, zephyr*, and four words where the pronunciation varies between /f/ and /p/: *diphtheria, diphthong, naphtha, ophthalmic*. Words of non-Greek origin in this set are: *caliph, cipher/cypher, nephew* (also pronounced with /v/), *pamphlet, pharaoh, Pharisee, phwoar!, samphire, seraph, triumph*.

Nothing but a source of confusion would be lost if all these words with /f/ spelt <ph> were instead spelt with <f>, as the cognate words are in Italian and Spanish.

- <ff>
    1) For 2-syllable words ending in /əl/ spelt <-le> and with a short vowel spelt with one letter in the first syllable, see above.
    2) There is a strong tendency for /f/ to be written <ff> in the middle of two-syllable words where the immediately preceding vowel phoneme is short and written with a single letter, e.g. *offer*. For examples and exceptions, see section 4.3.5.
    3) There is also a strong tendency for /f/ to be written <ff> rather than <f> at the end of the third from last syllable of a word /f/ is an exception to a wider rule in this respect. For examples and exceptions, see section 4.4.5.
    4) Word-finally in polysyllables not of Greek origin <ff> predominates: *bailiff, caitiff, chiffchaff, dandruff, distaff, handcuff, mastiff, midriff, plaintiff, pontiff, rebuff, riffraff, sheriff, tariff*, plus *fisticuffs*; contrast *belief, (hand)kerchief, mischief, relief, caliph, seraph, triumph*.

5) In the few remaining words not of Greek origin, <ff> again predominates: *affidavit, affiliate, affinity, effeminate, efficacious, effrontery, paraffin, ragamuffin*; contrast *cafeteria, defeasible, deferential, defibrillate, defoliant, nefarious*.

- <f> is the default spelling. The only generalisation, however, is that it is regular in consonant clusters in words not of Greek origin, e.g. *afraid, after, deflate, deflect, defray, defrock, kaftan*; exceptions include *affray, effrontery*.

## 3.7.4 /ʤ/ as in *jaw*

**THE MAIN SYSTEM**

For all these categories see also Notes.

| | | | |
|---|---|---|---|
| Basic grapheme | <j> | 29% | never word-final; regular initially (e.g. *jet*), and medially when not followed by <e, i, y>, e.g. *ajar, banjo, cajole, conjugal, enjoy, juju, major, (maha)rajah, sojourn*. On this basis, the initial <j> in *jujitsu* is regular, but the medial one is not |
| Other frequent graphemes | <g> | 51% | never word-final (except *Reg, veg*); regular medially before <e, i, y> |
| | <ge> | 10% | word-initial only in *geograph-er/y, geomet-er/ry, Geordie, George, Georgia(n), georgic*; rare medially, but cf. *burgeon, dungeon, gorgeous, hydrangea, pageant, pigeon, sergeant, sturgeon, surgeon, vengeance* where the following /ə/ (or /ɪ/ in *pigeon*) is spelt <a, o, ou>; also *dangerous, vegetable* if <e> is elided – see section 6.10; also in the derived forms *singeing, swingeing* to prevent confusion with *singing, swinging*, and *bingeing, spongeing, whingeing* to avoid the misapprehension that there might be verbs *to \*bing, to \*spong, to \*whing* (but *fringing, impinging* never retain the <e>); mostly word-final, e.g. *binge, blancmange, change, disparage, flange, fringe, garage* |

pronounced /ˈgærɪdʒ/, *haemorrhage, hinge, image, language, lounge, mortgage, orange, impinge, scavenge, singe, sponge, village, whinge* and hundreds of words ending in <-age> where the <e> is also part of the split digraph <a.e>, e.g. *age, rage, stage*. See section 7.1 for dual-functioning, section 10.4 for<a.e>, and section A.6 in Appendix A for the rarity of other split digraphs with included <g>

| | | | |
|---|---|---|---|
| *Doubled spellings* | <dge> | 5% (with <dg>) | never word-initial or medial; regular in word-final position in one-syllable words after a short vowel spelt with one letter, e.g. *bridge, judge*. See next paragraph, and section 6.4 on when <e>-deletion does and does not occur before suffixes beginning with a vowel letter |
| | <dg> | | never word-initial or -final; medially, does NOT occur before final /əl/ spelt <-le>, and most occurrences arise from deleting <e> from <dge> before suffixes beginning with a vowel letter, e.g. *bridging*. However, there are a few words with independent medial /dʒ/ spelt <dg>: *badger, budgerigar, budget, budgie, codger, cudgel, didgeridoo, dodgem, fidget, gadget, kedgeree, ledger, midget, podgy, smidgen, smidgin, todger, widget*; also, as more obviously belonging to this set than to a set with medial <dge>, provided <eo> is recognised as a spelling of /ə/ (see p.155), *bludgeon, curmudgeon, dudgeon, gudgeon, smidgeon, widgeon* |

## THE REST

| | |
|---|---|
| *Doubled spelling + <e>* | (cannot occur because unsuffixed word-final doubled spelling already ends in <e>) |
| *Oddities* | 5% in total |

| | | |
|---|---|---|
| | <ch> | only in *ostrich, sandwich, spinach* pronounced /ˈɒstrɪdʒ, ˈsæmwɪdʒ, ˈspɪnɪdʒ/ |
| | <d> | never word-final; frequent initially and medially before /uː, ə, ʊə/ spelt with various graphemes involving letter <u>, namely <eu, eur, ew, u, ua, ue, u.e, ur, ure>, e.g. (initially) *deuce* (cf. the homophone *juice*), various words beginning with (Greek) *deuter-*; *dew, due* (which are homophones, and cf. the further homophone *Jew*); *dual/ duel* (cf. the homophone *jewel*), *duet, duty, dune, dupe; durable, duration, duress, during;* (*medially*) *grandeur; arduous, assiduous, (in)credulous, deciduous, education, fraudulen-ce/t, graduate* pronounced either /ˈɡrædʒuːwət/ (noun) or /ˈɡrædʒuːweɪt/ (verb), *glandular, modul-e/ar, nodul-e/ar, pendulum, sedulous; gradual, individual, residual* whether pronounced with /dʒuːwəl/ or /dʒəl/ (for the eliding of the <u> see section 6.10); *endure, procedure, verdure* (cf. the homophone *verger*). /r/-linking occurs in the derived forms *endurance, procedural* – see section 3.6. See also Notes |
| | <di> | only in *cordial* pronounced /ˈkɔːdʒəl/ (also pronounced /ˈkɔːdiːjəl/), *incendiary, intermediary, stipendiary, subsidiary* pronounced with /-dʒəriː/, *soldier* |
| | <dj> | only in about 10 words of Latin origin: *adjacent, adjective, adjoin, adjourn, adjudge, adjudicate, adjunct, adjure, adjust, adjutant,* plus *djinn* |
| | <gg> | only in *arpeggio, exaggerate, loggia, suggest* and the derived forms *Reggie, veggie, vegging*. The last three words appear to be the only examples of <gg> spelling /dʒ/ arising from consonant-doubling before a suffix – see section 4.2 |
| | <gi> | only in *allegiance, contagio-n/us, egregious, legion, litigious, plagiaris-e/m, region, religio-n/us* and the derived forms *collegial, prestigious, vestigial* |
| | <jj> | only in *hajj* |
| 2-phoneme graphemes | (none) | |

## NOTES

The words *geograph-er/y, geomet-er/ry* could alternatively be analysed as having initial /dʒ/ spelt <g> and the following /ə/ spelt <eo>, but this would entail a counter-intuitive analysis of *Geordie, George, Georgia(n), georgic* as having /ɔː/ spelt <eor>, so I have retained the analysis of *geograph-er/y, geomet-er/ry* as having initial /dʒ/ spelt <ge> and the following /ə/ spelt <o>.

Because /dʒ/ is a sibilant consonant, addition of any of the suffixes regular noun plural and third person singular person tense verb (both spelt <s> where the stem ends in <e>, otherwise <es>) and regular singular and irregular plural possessive (spelt <'s>) to a stem ending in /dʒ/ adds a syllable /ɪz/ as well as a morpheme: *languages, sandwiches, (the) bridge's (collapse)*. See also /z/, section 3.7.8, and /ɪ/, section 5.4.3.

To summarise, the regular spellings of /dʒ/ are:
- in word-initial position: <j> (73% of spellings in that position)
- in medial position before <e, i, y>: <g>
- in medial position otherwise: <j>
- in stem-final position in unsuffixed one-syllable words after a short vowel spelt with one letter: <dge>
- in stem-final position when <dge> loses the <e> before a suffix beginning with a vowel letter (see section 6.4): <dg>
- otherwise in word-final position (including dual-functioning of the <g> within split digraphs): <ge>.

Exceptions (in addition to the Oddities):
- initial <g> (27% of spellings in that position): *gaol, gee, gel* (/dʒel/ 'viscous liquid'; contrast *gel* pronounced /gel/, 'posh' version of *girl*), *gelatin, gelignite, gem, geminate, Gemini, Gemma, gen, gender, gene, general, generate, generic, generous, genial, genie, genital, genitive, genius, gent, gentle, genuflect, genuine, genus*, most words beginning with (Greek) *geo* 'earth', e.g. *geographic* (but not those listed above as having initial /dʒ/ spelt <ge>), *Geoff(rey), geranium, gerbil, geriatric, germ, German, gerrymander* (also spelt with <j>), *gerund, gestate, gesture, giant, gibber, gibbet, gibe, giblets, gigantic, gigolo, gill* (/dʒɪl/ 'quarter of a pint'; contrast *gill* /gɪl/ 'lung of fish'), *Gillingham* /ˈdʒɪlɪŋəm/ in Kent (but /ˈgɪlɪŋəm/ in Dorset and Norfolk), *gimbal(s)* (also pronounced with /g/), *gimcrack, gin, ginger(ly), ginseng, gipsy, giraffe, giro, gist, gym(nas-t/ium), gyp, gypsum, gypsy, gyrate*, various words beginning with (Greek) *gyro-, gyves*

- medial <j> before <e, i>: only in *jujitsu, majest-y/ic* and words with the Latin element <ject> ('throw'), namely *ab/de/e/in(ter)/ob/pro/re/sub-ject, conjecture, trajectory* (no exceptions before <y>)
- medial <g> not before <e, i, y>: only in *margarine* (also pronounced with /g/), second <g> in *mortgagor*
- medial <dg>: see list above
- medial <ge>: see list above
- final <g>: only in *Reg, veg*
- final <dge> in words of more than one syllable: only in *abridge, cartridge, (ac)knowledge, partridge, porridge.*

All the words in which /dʒ/ is spelt <d> were formerly pronounced with the sequence /dj/, and conservative RP-speakers may still pronounce them that way (or imagine that they do). Pronunciations with /dj/ would require an analysis with the /d/ spelt <d> and the /j/-glide subsumed into the spelling of a 2-phoneme sequence with the following vowel. However, I think that in current RP the process of affricating /dj/ to /dʒ/ is virtually complete (as Cruttenden, 2014: 83 says) and has eliminated pronunciations with /dj/, which I have therefore ignored.

For the parallel affrication of /tj/ to /tʃ/ see section 3.7.2, and see also section 5.4.7. In the case of /tʃ/ there are very few spellings competing with <t> in initial and medial positions before /uː/, etc., and <t> is therefore the regular spelling. However, for initial and medial /dʒ/ there are many words spelt with <j> before /uː/, etc., so that <d> cannot be considered the regular spelling in these circumstances, or 'promoted' to the main system. This also means that words in which /dʒ/ is spelt <d> cannot be predicted and just have to be learnt.

For the ending /ɪdʒ/ see also under /ɪ/, section 5.4.3.

## 3.7.5 /l/ as in *law*

**THE MAIN SYSTEM**

| | | | |
|---|---|---|---|
| Basic grapheme | <l> | 75% | e.g. *lift* |
| Doubled spelling | <ll> | 18% | e.g. *fill*. See Notes |
| Frequent 2-phoneme grapheme | /əl/ spelt <-le> | 8% | e.g. *dazzle, debacle, table, visible*. See Notes |

*THE REST*

| | | |
|---|---|---|
| *Doubled spelling + <e>* | <lle> | medially, only in *decollet-age*/e; otherwise only final. Regular in the ending *-ville*, e.g. *vaudeville*; also in *bagatelle, belle, braille, chanterelle, espadrille, fontanelle, gazelle, grille, pastille, nacelle, quadrille* (but not *reveille, tagliatelle* where the <e> spells /iː/). In *chenille, tulle* I analyse /l/ as spelt <ll> and <i.e, u.e> as split digraphs spelling /iː, uː/ - see sections 5.7.2, 5.7.6, A.6 - and medially in *guillemot* <lle> spells /liː/ |
| *Oddities* | | <1% |
| | <gl> | only in a few Italian loanwords, e.g. *imbroglio, intaglio, seraglio, tagliatelle* |
| | <le> | except in *Charles*, only word-final and only in *aisle, cagoule, clientele, gargoyle, joule, isle, lisle, voile.* On *isle, lisle* see also /aɪ/ spelt <is>, section 5.7.3 |
| | <lh> | only in *philharmonic, silhouette* |
| *Other 2-phoneme graphemes* | /əl/ spelt <l> | only word-final and only in *axolotl, dirndl, shtetl* |
| | /lj/ spelt <ll> | only in *carillon* |

*NOTES*

At 18%, <ll> has the highest frequency of all the doubled consonant spellings (at least in stem words, i.e. discounting consonant-doubling before suffixes):

- It occurs in the two exceptional word-initial doubled consonant spellings *llama, llano*.
- It is regular in word-final position in one-syllable words after /ɔː/ spelt <a>, e.g. *all*, and after a short vowel spelt with one letter, e.g. *shall, ell, ill, moll, cull, bull*. Exceptions: *col, gal, gel* (both /gel/, posh pronunciation of *girl*, and /dʒel/ 'lotion'), *mil* (abbreviation of *millimetre*), *nil, pal; gal, pal* would otherwise look identical to *gall, pall* and be pronounced with /ɔː/. For *all, ell, ill* see also section 4.3.2.

- There is a strong tendency for /l/ to be spelt <ll> in the middle of two-syllable words where the immediately preceding vowel phoneme is short and written with a single letter. For examples and exceptions, see sections 4.3.4 and 4.4.6.
- There is also a preference for /l/ to be spelt <ll> rather than <l> at the end of the third from last syllable of a word. /l/ is an exception to a wider rule in this respect. For examples and exceptions, see section 4.4.5.
- There appear to be only a few polysyllabic non-compound words ending in <ll>: *chlorophyll* and some rare words in *-phyll, idyll, plimsoll* (also spelt *plimsole*). All other non-compound polysyllables end in <l>, except those listed above under <lle>.
- Similarly, there appear to be only three three-syllable words with <ll> at the end of the second syllable/beginning of the last syllable: *embellish, intellect, parallel*.
- In words of more than three syllables, no generalisation seems possible, so here is a list of such words which have <ll>: *allegory* (3 syllables if the <o> is elided), *alleviate, alligator, alliterate,* various words beginning with (Greek) *allo-, ballerina, calligraphy, camellia, collaborate, collateral, fallopian, hallelujah, hallucinate, hullabaloo, illegible, illegitimate, illiberal, illimitable, illiterate, illuminate, mellifluous. Alleviate, alliterate* and all those just listed beginning <coll-> and <ill-> belong to the (to most people, meaningless) category of words with Latin roots and assimilated Latin prefixes - see section 4.3.1.

On reducing <ll> to <l> in compound words see section 4.4.7.

In non-final positions, the 2-phoneme sequence /əl/ only has straight (non-reversed) 2-grapheme spellings, e.g. *allowed, aloud*. But in final position, although the reversed spelling <-le> predominates, there is considerable variation between that and several non-reversed spellings. The situation is too complex to summarise at this point; see sections 4.3.3 and 4.4.2-3.

For 2-grapheme spellings of /lj/ see under /j/, section 3.8.8.

For <lle> in *chancellery, jewellery* see section 6.10.

## 3.7.6 /s/ as in *sue*

### THE MAIN SYSTEM

For all these categories see Notes and Tables 3.4–5.

| | | | |
|---|---|---|---|
| *Basic grapheme* | <s> | 79% (with <se, ss>) | e.g. *sat, persuade, bias* Regular (1) initially and medially where the next letter is **not** <e, i, y>; (2) in most unstressed final syllables of polysyllables; (3) in various suffixes and contracted forms after a non-sibilant voiceless consonant; (4) within split digraph <o.e> |
| *Other frequent graphemes* | <c> | 15% (with <ce>) | e.g. *city, decide* Regular initially and medially where the next letter IS <e, i, y>. Never word-final |
| | <ce> | | e.g. *fence, mice* Except in a few suffixed forms (see section 6.4), only word-final, where it is regular after /n/ and when the <e> is also part of split digraphs <a.e, i.e, u.e, y.e>, e.g. *ace, ice, puce, syce* (for dual-functioning see section 7.1, and for split digraphs section A.6 in Appendix A), but is otherwise unpredictable |
| | <se> | | only word-final, where it is regular after /l, p/, after <r> forming part of a vowel di-/tri-graph, and after most vowel digraphs |

| | | |
|---|---|---|
| *Doubled spelling* | <ss> | regular word-finally in one-syllable words after /ɑː/ spelt <a> and after a short vowel spelt with one letter, e.g. *grass, fuss*; also in suffixes <-ess, -less, -ness> and in stressed final syllables of polysyllables |
| *Rare 2-phoneme grapheme* | /ks/ spelt <x> | see under /k/, section 3.7.1. Though rare as a correspondence for /s/, this counts as part of the main system because of its higher frequency as a correspondence for /k/ |

## THE REST

| | | |
|---|---|---|
| *Doubled spelling + <e>* | <sse> | except in *divertissement*, only word-final, e.g. *bouillabaisse, crevasse, duchesse, finesse, fosse, impasse, lacrosse, largesse* (also spelt *largess*), *mousse, noblesse, palliasse, wrasse* and a few more rare words |
| *Oddities* | | 6% in total |
| | <cc> | only in *flaccid, succinct* pronounced /ˈflæsɪd, səˈsɪŋkt/ (also pronounced with /ks/) |
| | <ps> | only word-initial and only in some words of mainly Greek origin, e.g. *psalm, psalter, psephology, pseud(o)* and many compounds, *psionic, psittacosis, psoriasis, psych(e/o)* and many compounds, and a few more very rare words. /p/ surfaces in *metempsychosis* – see section 7.2 |
| | <sc> | only in *abscess, abscissa, adolescen-t/ce, ascend, ascertain, ascetic, corpuscle, crescent* (also pronounced with /z/), *descend, discern, disciple, fascicle, fascinate, isosceles, lascivious, miscellany, muscle, (re)nascent, obscene, omniscient, oscillate, plebiscite, prescient, proboscis, proscenium, rescind, resuscitate, scenario, scene, scent, sceptre, sciatic(a), science, scimitar, scintilla, scion, scissors,* |

*The phoneme-grapheme correspondences, 1: Consonants* 71

*scythe, susceptible, transcend, viscera(l), viscid* and a few more rare words, plus suffixed derivatives of next group. /k/ surfaces in *corpuscular, muscular* – see section 7.2

<sce>  only in stressed final syllables of verbs ending /es/ spelt <-esce>, e.g. *acquiesce, coalesce, convalesce, deliquesce, effervesce, evanesce* and some other very rare words, plus *reminisce*

<sch>  only in *schism* pronounced /ˈsɪzəm/

<st>  only medial.
Between a short vowel spelt with one letter and final /əl/ spelt <-le>, <st> is the regular spelling of /s/, but this is a small set: *pestle, trestle, bristle, Entwistle, epistle, gristle, thistle, Thistlethwaite, Twistleton, whistle, apostle, jostle, Postlethwaite, throstle, bustle, hustle, rustle* and the derived forms *nestle, wrestle* (exceptions: *hassle* (but I once received an email with this word spelt *hastle*, showing the power of this sub-rule), *tassel, corpuscle, muscle, tussle*) (/t/ surfaces in *apostolic, castellan, castellated, epistolary* – see section 7.2); also, with a preceding long vowel (in RP), *castle*; also occurs before final /ən/ spelt <-en>, but this is an even smaller set: *glisten, listen* and the derived form *christen* with preceding short vowels, *fasten* with a preceding long vowel (in RP), and the derived forms *chasten, hasten, moisten* with preceding long vowels or diphthongs.
The only other examples of medial /s/ spelt <st> within stem words appear to be *forecastle* in either of its pronunciations /ˈfouksəl, ˈfɔːkaːsəl/, *mistletoe, ostler*. In *nestle, wrestle, christen, chasten, hasten, moisten, fasten,* /t/ has been lost at a morpheme boundary. Other examples of compounds with lost /t/ so that <st> spells /s/ are *chestnut, Christmas, durstn't, dustbin, dustman, mustn't, waistcoat* /ˈweɪskəut/ and sometimes *ghastly*.

72  Dictionary of the British English Spelling System

|  |  | This loss of /t/ at a morpheme boundary is one small aspect of a very frequent process which is too widespread and complicated to tackle in this book, focused as it mainly is on citation forms of stem words – see Appendix A, section A.1 |
|---|---|---|
|  | <sth> | only in *asthma, isthmus* if pronounced without /θ/ |
|  | <sw> | only in *answer, coxswain, sword* /ˈɑːnsə, ˈkɒksən, sɔːd/ and *boatswain* pronounced /ˈbəʊsən/ (also pronounced /ˈbəʊtsweɪn/) |
|  | <t> | only the penultimate <t> in about 10 words ending in <-tiation>, e.g. *differentiation, initiation, negotiation, propitiation, transubstantiation*, and only for RP-speakers who avoid having two occurrences of medial /ʃ/ in such words (see Notes under /ʃ/, section 3.8.3). In French, on the other hand, <t> is one of the most frequent correspondences for /s/ |
|  | <z> | only in *blitz(krieg), chintz, ersatz, glitz, howitzer, kibbutz, kibitz, klutz, lutz, pretzel, quartz, ritz, schmaltz, schnitzel, seltzer, spritz(er), Switzerland, waltz, wurlitzer* |
| *Other 2-phoneme graphemes* | /ts/ spelt <z, zz> | see under /t/, section 3.5.7 |
|  | /ks/ spelt <xe> | only in *annexe, axe*. See comments under /k/, section 3.7.1 |
|  | /ks/ spelt <xh> | only in *exhibition, exhortation, exhumation* – for *exhibit, exhort, exhume* see under /g/, section 3.5.3 |
| *3-phoneme grapheme* | /eks/ spelt <x> | see under /k/, section 3.7.1 |

## NOTES

For the very few occasions when <ss> is reduced to <s> in compound words see section 4.4.7.

/s/ is the phonological realisation of various grammatical suffixes (regular noun plural and third person singular person tense verb (both spelt <s> where the stem ends in <e>, otherwise <es>), regular singular and irregular plural possessive (spelt <'s>)), and of *is, has* when contracted (also spelt <'s>), after any voiceless non-sibilant consonant (/p t k f θ/). As just shown, in all these cases the spelling contains <s>.

However, because /s/ itself is a sibilant consonant, adding any of the suffixes just listed to a stem ending in /s/ adds a syllable /ɪz/ as well as a morpheme: *horses, fusses, Brooks's*. On this and the topic of the previous paragraph see also /z/, section 3.7.8, and /ɪ/, section 5.4.3.

Because /s/ is almost as divergent as /k/, a further analysis of the major spellings of /s/ is given in Tables 3.4-5. As with /k/, it is unphonological but true that it's easier to state all the initial and medial correspondences of /s/, and some of the stem-final ones, in terms of following **letters** rather than following **phonemes**. (For an attempt to do it phonologically see Carney, 1994: 234-6).

There are several words in <-se> in which the <e> appears redundant since the <s> alone would spell /s/ and the <e> is not part of a split digraph, namely *carcase* (also spelt *carcass*), *purchase; mortise* (also spelt *mortice*), *practise, premise* (also spelt *premiss*), *promise, treatise* (cf. *thesis*); *purpose; porpoise, tortoise; apocalypse, apse, collapse, eclipse, elapse, ellipse, glimpse, prolapse, relapse, traipse*. In *copse, corpse, lapse* the <e> is equally redundant phonographically but serves to differentiate these words visually from *cops, corps, laps*.

The virtual non-existence of <-oce> and the rarity of <-oss> as spellings for word-final /əʊs/ mean that <-ose> is almost entirely predictable as the spelling of this stem-word ending. However, this seems to be one of very few examples where a pattern of this sort is more reliable than predictions from the separate phonemes. On this see also section A.7 in Appendix A.

For the medial /s/ in *eczema* see section 6.10.

TABLE 3.4: THE DISTRIBUTION OF <c, s, ss> IN INITIAL AND MEDIAL SPELLINGS OF /s/ OTHER THAN IN /ks/ (FOR /ks/ SEE ABOVE AND UNDER /k/, SECTION 3.7.1).

In each main box below, the regular spelling is stated at the top in **bold**.

For other exceptions see the 2- and 3-phoneme graphemes and Oddities above.

|  | Initial | medial |
|---|---|---|
| /s/ not before <e>, <i>, <y> | <s>, e.g. *sale, scale, skull, slime, smooth, snake, soap, spill, still, suave, swede*<br>Exceptions (all with <c>): *caecum, caesium, caesura, coelacanth, coelenterate, coeliac, coelom, coenobite, coenocyte* (there are none where the next phoneme/ letter is a consonant) | <s>, e.g. *descant, askance, asleep, dismiss, consonant, dyspnoea, disaster* (second <s>), *persuade, aswill*<br>Exceptions (there are none where the next **letter** is a consonant, but those in capitals in this list are exceptions where the next **phoneme** is a consonant): *apercu, facade* (lacking French cedillas); *ambassador, assail, assassin* (first <ss>), *assault, assay, cassava, commissar, dissatisfy, essay, massacre, pessary, reconnaissance, renaissance*; *hassle, tussle*; *associate, assonance, assorted, bassoon, blossom, caisson, dissociate, dissolute, dissonant, lasso, lesson, lissom, voussoir; alyssum, ASSUAGE, assume* pronounced /əsˈjuːm/, *DISSUADE*; also *EMISSARY, NECESSARY, PROMISSORY* with elided vowels (see section 6.10) |
| /s/ before <e>, <i>, <y> | <c>, e.g. *ceiling, city, cyclic*<br>Exceptions (all with <s>): *sea, seal, seam, seance, sear, search, season, seat, sebaceous, sebum, secant, sec-ateurs, secede, seclude, second, secret(e), secretary, sect(ion), secular, secure, sedan, sedate, sedentary, sedge, sediment, sedition, seduce, see, seed, seek, seem, seep, seethe, segment, segregate, segue, self, sell, semantic, semaphore, semblance, semen, semi, seminar, semiotics, semite, semolina, senate, send, senile, senior, sense, sensual, sent-ence, sentient, sentiment, sentinel, sentry,* | <c>, e.g. *accept, decide, bicycle*<br>Exceptions:<br>Words ending in /sɪs/ are spelt <-sis>, e.g. *Sis* (abbreviation of *sister*), *thesis* (only exception: *diocese*)<br>Words ending in /sɪtiː/ preceded by a consonant letter or by /ɒ/ spelt <o> are spelt <-sity>, e.g. *adversity, density, diversity, falsity, immensity, intensity, pervers-ity, propensity, sparsity, university, varsity; animosity, curiosity, generosity, impetuosity, verbosity, virtuosity, viscosity* (exceptions: *scarcity; atrocity, ferocity, precocity, reciprocity, velocity;* and cf. *city* itself) |

*sepal, separate, sept, septic, sepulchre, sequel, sequence, sequester, sequin, seraph, serenade, serene, serf, serge, sergeant, serial, series, serious, sermon, serpent, serrated, serum, serve, sesame, session, set, settle, seven, sever, severe, sew, sewer* (in both pronun-ciations and meanings), *sex; sibilant, sibling, sibyl, sick, side, sidereal, sidle, siege, siesta, sieve, sift, sigh, sight, sign, Sikh, silage, silent, silica, silk, sill, silly, silo, silt, silver, simian, similar, simmer, simper, simple, simultaneous, sin, since, sincere, sine, sinew, sing, singe, single, sinister, sink, sinuous, sip, siphon, sir, sire, siren, sisal, sister, sit, sitar, site, situation, six, size, sizzle; sybarite, sycamore, syce, sycophant, syllable, syllogism, sylph, symbiosis, symbol, symmetry, sympathy, symphony, symposium, symptom, synaesthesia, synagogue, synapse, synch(ro-), synergy, synod, synonym, synopsis, syntax, synthesis, syphilis, syphon, syringe, syrup, system, syzygy* | Words ending in /sɪv/: if preceded by a short vowel spelt with one letter they are spelt <-ssive> (e.g. *massive*), otherwise <-sive> (e.g. *adhesive*) (but N.B. *sieve* itself)
Other exceptions:
with <s>: *abseil, absent, arsenal, arsenic, beseech, consecutive, consensus, consent, consequen-ce/t, corset, counsel, desecrate, disembark, dysentery, insect, morsel, prosecute, transept; basin, consist, disinfect, disinherit, misinform, misinterpret, parasite, transit; asylum; apostasy, argosy, controversy, courtesy, ecstasy, fantasy, greasy, heresy, hypocrisy, idiosyncrasy, jealousy, leprosy, minstrelsy, pleurisy, prophesy* (verb, pronounced /ˈprɒfɪsaɪ/ – the noun *prophecy*, pronounced /ˈprɒfɪsiː/, has regular <c>); *autopsy; biopsy, catalepsy, curtsy, dropsy, epilepsy, gipsy, narcolepsy, necropsy, tipsy*
with <ss>: *antimacassar, assegai, assemble, assent, assert, assess, asset, casserole, cassette, connoisseur, cussed* ('stubborn'), *delicatessen, dissect, dissemble, disseminate, dissension, dissent, dissertation, disservice, essence, essential, fricassee, lessen, masseu-r/se, mussel, necessity, trousseau; admissible, assassin* (second <ss>), *assiduous, assign, assimilate, assist, assize, brassica, bassinet, chassis, classic, classify, dissident, dissimilar, dissipate, fossil, gossip, jurassic, lassitude, messiah, permissible,* (im)*possible, potassium, prussic, triassic; embassy, hussy*

TABLE 3.5: THE DISTRIBUTION OF <c, ce, s, se, ss> IN STEM-FINAL SPELLINGS OF /s/ OTHER THAN IN /ks/ (ALSO EXCLUDING GRAMMATICAL SUFFIXES).

For /ks/ see above and under /k/, section 3.7.1. For /s/ as a grammatical suffix, see above.

Categories listed in the left-hand column below apply to both monosyllables and polysyllables except where stated.

For exceptions besides those in the Table, see the 2- and 3-phoneme graphemes and Oddities above.

| In mono-syllables after /aː/ spelt <a> and after a short vowel spelt with one letter: <ss> | Examples: *brass, class, glass, grass, pass; ass, bass* (/bæs/ 'fish'), *crass, lass, mass; bless, cess, chess, cress, dress, guess, less, mess, ness, press, stress, tress; bliss, hiss, kiss, miss, p*ss; boss, cross, doss, dross, floss, loss, moss; buss, cuss, fuss, muss, truss; puss*. Exceptions: *gas, yes, Sis* (abbreviation of *sister*), *this, bus, plus, pus, thus, us* Extension: There appears to be only one other one-syllable stem word in which a long vowel/diphthong is spelt with a single letter before word-final /s/: *bass* (/beɪs/ '(player of) large stringed instrument'/'(singer with) low-pitched voice') |
|---|---|
| After /n/: <ce> | Examples: (monosyllables) *dance, chance, glance, lance, prance, stance, trance; fence, hence, pence, thence, whence; mince, prince, quince, since, wince; nonce, once, sconce; bounce, flounce, ounce, pounce, trounce; dunce;* (polysyllables) *abundance, evidence* and hundreds of other words ending <-ance/-ence>, *convince, evince, province, ensconce, an/de/(mis)pro-nounce* Exceptions: (monosyllables) *manse; dense, sense, tense; rinse;* (polysyllables) *expanse; condense, dispense, expense, immense, incense* (noun and verb), *intense, license, nonsense, recompense, suspense; response* |
| After /l, p/: <se> | Examples: (monosyllables) *dulse, else, false, pulse; apse, copse, corpse, glimpse, lapse, traipse;* (polysyllables) *convulse, impulse, repulse; apocalypse, eclipse, ellipse, col/e/pro/re-lapse* Exceptions: (none) |
| After <r> forming part of a vowel di-/tri-graph: <se> | Examples: (monosyllables) *arse, coarse, course, curse, Erse, gorse, hearse, hoarse, horse, morse, Norse, nurse, purse, sparse, terse, verse, worse;* (polysyllables) *adverse, averse, concourse, converse, discourse, disburse, disperse, diverse, endorse, immerse, intercourse, intersperse, inverse, obverse, recourse, rehearse, reimburse, remorse, reverse, traverse, transverse, universe* Exceptions: (monosyllables) *farce, fierce, force, pierce, scarce, source, tierce;* (polysyllables) *commerce, divorce, enforce, reinforce, perforce, resource* |

| | |
|---|---|
| After other vowel digraphs: <se> | Examples: (monosyllables) *cease, crease, grease, lease, geese, goose, loose, moose, noose, douse, grouse, house* (noun), *louse, mouse*; (polysyllables) *decease, de/in-crease, release, porpoise, tortoise, caboose, papoose, vamoose*<br>Exceptions: (monosyllables) *sauce, peace, fleece, deuce, niece, piece, choice, voice, juice, sluice; gneiss*; (polysyllables) *invoice, rejoice* |
| In words ending /əʊs/: <s> within split digraph <o.e> spelling /əʊ/ (see also Notes above Table) | Examples: (monosyllables) *close* (adjective/noun), *dose*; (polysyllables) the 'sugar' words *dextrose, glucose, lactose, sucrose* (all of which have alternative pronunciations in /əʊz/), and adjectives *comatose, lachrymose, morose, verbose* and dozens of others (see also section A.7 in Appendix A)<br>Only exceptions: *Croce* (rare surname); *gross, engross* |
| Where any other long vowel, diphthong or /juː/ is spelt with a split digraph: <ce>, such that the <e> functions as part of both graphemes (for dual-functioning see section 7.1) | Examples: (monosyllables) *ace, brace, dace, face, lace, grace, mace, pace, place, race, space, trace; dice, ice, lice, mice, nice, price, rice, slice, spice, splice, thrice, trice, twice, vice; puce, spruce, truce, syce;* (polysyllables) *apace, de/ef/out/re-face, disgrace, embrace, en/inter-lace, dis/mis/re-place, retrace; advice, caprice, device, entice, police, sacrifice, suffice; ad/com/de/e/in(tro)/(re)pro/re/se/tra-duce, prepuce*<br>Exceptions: (monosyllables) *base, case, chase; use* (noun); (polysyllables) *a/de-base, encase; obese; concise, paradise, precise; abstruse, obtuse, recluse;* also *merchandise, abuse, excuse, refuse* as nouns and *diffuse* as an adjective |
| In stressed final syllables of polysyllables: <ss> | Examples: *abyss, address, amiss, assess, caress, confess, discuss, dismiss, distress, duress, excess, express, impress, morass, possess, process* (verb), *profess, progress* (verb), *prowess, recess, redress, repress, remiss, success*<br>Exceptions: none (?) |
| In polysyllables ending in unstressed /sɪs/: <s> | Examples (from many that could be given): *(anti/meta/syn-)thesis, catharsis*<br>Only exception: *diocese* |
| In other cases of final unstressed /ɪs/ in polysyllables: <ce> | Examples (from many that could be given): *apprentice, auspice, chalice, justice, practice*<br>Exceptions: *axis, cannabis, marquis, metropolis, pelvis; practise, premise, promise, treatise; premiss*<br>N.B.: *mortice, mortise* has both spellings, and cf. Latin (*rigor*) *mortis* ('(stiffness) of death') |

TABLE 3.5: THE DISTRIBUTION OF <c, ce, s, se, ss> IN STEM-FINAL SPELLINGS OF /s/ OTHER THAN IN /ks/ (ALSO EXCLUDING GRAMMATICAL SUFFIXES), CONT.

| In other unstressed final syllables of polysyllables: <s> | Examples (from many that could be given): *bias, canvas, corpus, cosmos, fabulous, horrendous, rickets, syllabus, tonsilitis, virus*<br>Exceptions:<br><se> only in *carcase, purchase, purpose*<br><ss> in *abscess, access, albatross, blunderbuss, buttress, canvass, carcass, compass, congress, cutlass, egress, embarrass, empress, harass, ingress, isinglass, mattress*, all the compounds of *press, process* (noun), *progress* (noun), *trespass, windlass* |
|---|---|

## 3.7.7 /v/ as in *view*

**THE MAIN SYSTEM**

| | | | |
|---|---|---|---|
| Basic grapheme | <v> | 98% | e.g. *oven* |
| Other frequent grapheme | <f> | | only in *of*, and *roofs* pronounced /ruːvz/ (neither counted in percentages) |
| Doubled spelling | <ve> | 2% | regular in word-final position, e.g. *give, have, positive*. Exceptions: *bruv, chav, derv, gov, guv, lav, leitmotiv, of, rev, satnav, shiv, Slav, sov, spiv*; <ve> also spells /v/ in *average, deliverable, evening* (noun, 'late part of day', pronounced /ˈiːvnɪŋ/, as distinct from the verb of the same spelling, 'levelling', pronounced /ˈiːvənɪŋ/), *every, leverage, several, sovereign* – cf. section 6.10 – but is very rare medially in stem words (but see Notes) and never occurs initially |

**THE REST**

| | |
|---|---|
| Doubled spelling + <e> | (cannot occur because doubled spelling already ends in <e>) |

| Oddities | | <1% in total |
|---|---|---|
| | <bv> | only in *obvious* pronounced /ˈɒviːjəs/ |
| | <ph> | only in *nephew* pronounced /ˈnevjuː/ (also pronounced /ˈnefjuː/), *Stephen* (also spelt *Steven*) |
| | <vv> | only medial and only in *bevvy, bovver, chavvy, chivvy, civvy, divvy, flivver, lavvy, luvv-ie/y, navvy, revving, savvy, skivvy, spivvery, spivvy* |
| 2-phoneme graphemes | (none) | |

## NOTES

<vv> is very rare (it occurs only in the words just listed, most of which are slang), and in word-final position <ve> functions in its place as the doubled spelling of /v/ (see next paragraph).

English spelling has a tacit rule that words must not end in <v>, except for a few slang and foreign words and modern abbreviations (see above under 'Doubled spelling'). Word-finally, therefore, the regular spelling of /v/ is <ve>, which occurs in at least 1,000 words. At least 700 of these are polysyllabic adjectives and nouns ending in unstressed /ɪv/ spelt <-ive>, e.g. *adjective, endive, expletive, gerundive, massive, narrative, olive, relative*. (A century ago Dewey tried, but failed, to have the phonographically redundant final <e> removed from the US spelling of these words; it is equally redundant in all the non-split digraph categories mentioned below, but is probably even more resistant to change there. He might have had more success if he had advocated removal of the redundant final <e> in words ending in <-ate, -ite> where the <e> is also not part of a split digraph – for these words see sections 3.5.7 and 9.34 – or any of the other graphemes with redundant final <e>, of which there are many).

Among the small number of remaining polysyllables are the preposition *above*, the noun *octave*, and groups of words with:
1) /l/ spelt <l> preceding <ve>, e.g. *dissolve, evolve*
2) vowel digraphs preceding <ve>, e.g. *bereave; receive* and several other words in <-ceive>; *deserve; achieve, believe, relieve, reprieve, retrieve*
3) split digraphs where the <e> is part of both the digraph and <ve>, e.g. *behave, conclave, forgave; alive, archive, arrive, deprive, naive, ogive, recitative, revive, survive; alcove, mangrove*.

Among monosyllables with final /v/ spelt <ve> are those with

1) a short vowel phoneme immediately preceding <ve>, namely *have; give, live* (verb, /lɪv/); *dove, glove, love, shove*; and – with its unusual digraph spelling of a short vowel – *sieve*
2) /l/ spelt <l> preceding <ve>, e.g. *salve* pronounced /sælv/), *valve; delve, shelve, twelve; solve*
3) vowel digraphs preceding <ve>, e.g. *waive; calve, halve, salve* pronounced /sɑːv/; *carve, starve; mauve; greave, heave, leave; sleeve; nerve, serve; grieve, thieve; groove; curve*
4) split digraphs where the <e> is part of both the digraph and <ve>, e.g. *gave, shave, suave, wave; breve, eve; drive, five, hive, jive, live* (adjective, /laɪv/), *swive, wive; cove, drove, move, prove; gyve*.

The point of this long analysis has been to show in how few words ending in a single vowel letter plus <ve> the <e> forms digraphs both with the <v> and with the vowel letter (for dual-functioning see section 7.1). In this respect <ve> is very unlike the other principal word-final consonant digraphs formed with <e>, namely <ce, ge, se>.

Medially, <ve> occurs in:
- the few words mentioned above under 'Doubled spelling'
- a large number of regular plural nouns and singular verbs, e.g. *haves* (vs *have-nots*), *gives, grieves, initiatives, dissolves, lives* (verb), *loves, improves, preserves, mauves*
- a small number of irregular plural nouns ending in /vz/ spelt <-ves> where the singular forms have /f/ spelt <f>, namely *calves, dwarves, elves, halves, hooves, leaves, loaves, scarves, (our/your/them-)selves, sheaves, shelves, thieves, turves, wharves, (were)wolves*. On 4/1/15 the form *behalves* appeared in the *Observer*; various websites decry this form as obsolete or unnecessary
- a very few similar words where the <f> in the singular is within the split digraph <i.e>: *knives, lives* (/laɪvz/; the singular verb of the same spelling is pronounced /lɪvz/), *(ale/good/house/mid-)wives* (but if *housewife* 'sewing kit' pronounced /ˈhʌzɪf/ has a plural it is presumably pronounced /ˈhʌzɪfs/).

Why the irregular words in the third category in this list with no <e> in the singular have an <e> in the plural is unclear (i.e. they could be spelt *elvs, *leavs, etc.), unless verbs like *calve, halve, leave, salve, shelve, thieve* and their singular forms *calves, halves, leaves, salves, shelves, thieves* influence the plural nouns, or the strong prohibition on word-final <v> (see above) extends to stem-final position in plurals.

A couple of the nouns just listed have alternative, regular plurals: *dwarfs, turfs*, and the only plural of *lowlife* is said to be *lowlifes* (though I have seen the form *lowlives* in print).

Conversely, *roofs*, which (officially) has only that regular plural spelling, has both the regular pronunciation /ruːfs/ and the irregular pronunciation /ruːvz/, but the latter pronunciation is hardly ever recognised in the spelling as *rooves (though this form has been printed twice in *The Guardian*: (1) 18 July 2009, main section, p.39 (in a puzzle); (2) 26 September 2009, Review section, p.7 (in a poem); internet exploration revealed various people wondering if *rooves or *roofs* was the plural spelling because they say /ruːvz/). This pronunciation and the spelling *roofs* provide the only other example, besides *of*, of /v/ spelt <f>.

## 3.7.8 /z/ as in *zoo*

### THE MAIN SYSTEM

For all these categories see Notes.

*Basic grapheme* <z>  5%  regular in word-initial position,
(with   e.g. *zoo* (only exceptions: *sorbet*
<ze> –  pronounced /ˈzɔːbeɪ/ (also
for this,  pronounced /ˈsɔːbeɪ/), *sauerkraut*
see below  if pronounced with German /z/, and
under   the words in <x–> listed below);
Oddities)  medially, only in *amazon, azyme, bazooka, bedizen, benz-ene/ol, bezel, bezique, blazer, bombazine, bonanza, brazen, cadenza, chimpanzee, coryza, crazy, denizen, enzyme, extravaganza, frozen, gazebo, gazump, gizmo, (hap)hazard, hetero-/mono-zygous, influenza, lazy, lizard, magazine, mazurka, muzak, ozone, phizog, plaza, protozoa, razor, samizdat, schnauzer, spermatozoon, stanza, teazel/teazle* (also spelt *teasel*), *trapez-ium/oid, vizard, vizier, vizor* (also spelt with <s>), *wizard, wizen(ed), zigzag*;

word-finally without a following <e> only in *fez, phiz, quiz, topaz, whiz*, the abbreviated compound word *showbiz* and a few other very rare words; phonemically word-final within split digraphs, only in *amaze, blaze, craze, daze, gaze, glaze, graze, haze, laze, maze, raze; trapeze; cloze, doze, froze*, plus the four nouns ending in /aɪz/ always spelt <-ize> (*assize, capsize, prize, size*) and the large number of verbs ending in /aɪz/ spelt <-ize> (almost all of which have alternative spellings in <-ise>)

| | | | |
|---|---|---|---|
| *Other frequent graphemes* | <s> | 93% (with <se>) | word-initial only in *sorbet* if pronounced /ˈzɔːbeɪ/ and *sauerkraut* if pronounced with German /z/ Regular (1) in medial position, e.g. *chisel, preside, seismic, talisman*; (2) word-finally (see above for exceptions with <z>, and below for all other exceptions); (3) in various suffixes and contracted forms after a vowel or non-sibilant voiced consonant – see Notes |
| | <se> | | never word-initial or -medial (except medially in compound words, e.g. *gooseberry* /ˈgʊzbriː/), *housewife* 'sewing kit', pronounced /ˈhʌzɪf/; also in *miserable* if pronounced /ˈmɪzrəbəl/ – see section 6.10); regular word-finally in content words after a long vowel or diphthong spelt with a digraph, e.g. *blouse, bruise, cause, chauffeuse, cheese, choose, drowse, noise, parse, please, raise* |

| | | | |
|---|---|---|---|
| Doubled spelling | <zz> | <1% | regular at the end of one-syllable words after a short vowel spelt with one letter – but see Notes; also regular before word-final /əl/ spelt <-le> after a short vowel spelt with one letter, e.g. *dazzle* (see section 4.3.3); otherwise only in *blizzard, buzzard, dizzy, fizzog, gizzard, grizzly, mizzen, muezzin, muzzy, pizzazz, razzmatazz, scuzzy, snazzy, tizzy, wazzock*. For <zz> arising from consonant-doubling before a suffix see section 4.2 |

## THE REST

| | | |
|---|---|---|
| Doubled spelling + <e> | | (does not occur) |
| Oddities | | 2% in total |
| | <cz> | only in *czar(ina)* |
| | <sc> | only in *crescent* pronounced /ˈkrezənt/ (also pronounced /ˈkresənt/) |
| | <ss> | only medially and only in *Aussie, brassiere, dessert, dissolve, hussar, Missouri, possess, scissors* |
| | <ts> | only in *tsar* |
| | <x> | word-initially, only in some words of Greek origin, namely *xanthine, xanthoma, xanthophyll, xenon, xenophobia* and several other words beginning *xeno-*, *Xerox* and several other words beginning *xero-*, *xylem, xylene, xylophone* and several other words beginning *xylo-*. Medially, only in *anxiety* pronounced /æŋˈzaɪjɪtiː/ (also pronounced /æŋˈgzaɪjɪtiː/). French loanwords ending in <-eau> are sometimes in the plural written French-style with /z/ spelt <x> rather than <s>, e.g. *beau-s/x, bureau-s/x, flambeau-s/x, gateau-s/x, plateau-s/x, portmanteau-s/x, trousseau-s/x;* |

|  |  |  |
|---|---|---|
|  |  | indeed, my dictionary gives only the <x> form in *bandeaux, chateaux, rondeaux, tableaux*. In my opinion the <x> form is outmoded and unnecessary |
|  | <ze> | only word-final and only in *adze, bronze* after consonant phonemes, plus *baize, booze, breeze, freeze, frieze, furze, gauze, maize, ooze, schmooze, seize, sleaze, sneeze, snooze, squeeze, wheeze* after long vowels or diphthongs spelt by digraphs – in all these words the <e> is phonographically redundant but spellings without it would look odd. In the hundreds of verbs ending /aɪz/ which may or must be spelt with <-ize>, plus the few other stem words where <z> appears within split digraphs (see above), it is unnecessary to analyse the <z> as also being part of digraph <ze> because the <z> spells /z/ without the <e> – but see Notes |
| *2-phoneme graphemes* /gz/ spelt <x, xh> |  | <1% see under /g/, section 3.5.3 |
|  | /ɪz/ spelt <s> | only, following an apostrophe, in regular singular and irregular plural possessive forms ending in a sibilant consonant (/s, z, ʃ, ʒ, tʃ, dʒ/), e.g. *Brooks's (book), jazz's (appeal), Bush's (government), (the) mirage's (appearance), (the) Church's (mission), (the) village's (centre), (the) geese's (cackling)*. See Notes |

## NOTES

/z/ is the phonological realisation of various grammatical suffixes (regular noun plural and third person singular person tense verb (both spelt <s> where the stem ends in <e>, otherwise <es>), regular singular and irregular plural possessive (spelt <'s>)), and of *is, has* when contracted (also spelt <'s>), after any vowel or voiced non-sibilant consonant (/b d g l m n ŋ v ð/). As just shown, in all these cases the spelling contains <s>.

However, because /z/ itself is a sibilant consonant, adding any of the suffixes just listed to a stem ending in /z/ adds a syllable /ɪz/ as well as a morpheme: *fuses, quizzes, jazz's*. On this and the topic of the previous paragraph see also /s/, section 3.7.6, and /ɪ/, section 5.4.3.

<zz> is regular word-finally in one-syllable words after a short vowel spelt with one letter, but there are only seven words in this set (*buzz, fizz, frizz, fuzz, jazz, tizz, whizz*, plus two polysyllables: *pizzazz, razzmatazz*) and there are 10 counter-examples (*as, fez, has, his, is, phiz, quiz, was, whiz* and *cos*, the abbreviation of *because*; *cos*, the lettuce and the abbreviation of *cosine*, vary in pronunciation between /kɒz/ and /kɒs/) - but three of the counter-examples (*has, is, was*) are verbs following the rule that grammatical endings in /z/ are spelt <s>.

<zz> is also regular before word-final /əl/ spelt <-le> after a short vowel spelt with one letter (see section 4.3.3), and very rare other than in this and the context mentioned in the preceding paragraph.

<z> is regular in word-initial position, and very rare elsewhere, except in one class of verb stem endings. In British English, almost all the verbs whose stems end in /aɪz/ can be spelt with either <-ise> or <-ize>, e.g. *atomise/atomize*. There are a few which can only be spelt with <-ize>, namely *capsize, prize, size*, and a larger group which can only be spelt with <-ise>, namely *advertise, advise, apprise, chastise, circumcise, comprise, compromise, despise, devise, enterprise, excise, exercise, franchise, improvise, incise, merchandise, premise* (/prɪˈmaɪz/ 'base argument upon'), *prise, realise, revise, rise, supervise, surmise, surprise, televise.*

Exceptions to the <-ise/-ize> choice are a few verbs which are mainly spelt with <-yse> in British English (though US spellings in <-yze> are becoming commoner): *analyse, breathalyse, catalyse, dialyse, electrolyse, paralyse*. And plural nouns and singular verbs whose stems end in /aɪ/ and which therefore end in /aɪz/ when suffixed (e.g. *dies, dyes, lies, vies*) follow different rules.

Of the 15 words ending /eɪz/ spelt with a split digraph, 11 are spelt with <-aze> (*amaze, blaze, craze, daze, gaze, glaze, graze, haze, laze, maze, raze*), and 4 with <-ase> (*erase, phase, phrase, ukase*). *Vase* appears to be the only word ending in /ɑːz/ (in RP).

The only word in which word-final /iːz/ is spelt <-eze> is *trapeze*, and *cerise, chemise, expertise, reprise, valise* appear to be the only ones in which it is spelt <-ise>. Besides these spellings in which /iː/ is spelt by a split digraph (and in theory /z/ is spelt only by the <z>, though it is immaterial whether one instead recognises the <e> as part of digraph <ze> and therefore as dual-functioning), word-final /iːz/ has four further spellings in which /iː/ is spelt by a non-split digraph, and /z/ definitely by either <ze> (*breeze, freeze, sneeze, squeeze, wheeze; frieze*) or <se> (*appease,* (dis)ease, (dis)please, heartsease, pease, tease; cheese). In all other cases, of which there are dozens, especially nationality/language words, plus these, word-final /iːz/ is spelt <-ese>. This may seem to be one of the few cases where the spelling of a final /VC/ pattern is more predictable as a unit than from correspondences for its two phonemes, but actually it is predictable from them: the regular spelling of /iː/ in closed final syllables of polysyllables is <e.e> (see section 5.7.2), and the regular spelling of phonemically word-final /z/ is <s>. See also section A.7 in Appendix A.

There are only 2 words ending /əʊz/ spelt <-oze>: doze, froze; the rest are spelt with <-ose>, e.g. chose, close (verb), hose, pose, prose, rose, those.

There are no words ending /(j)uːz/ spelt <-uze>, and only 1 spelt <-ose>: lose; the rest are spelt with <-use>, e.g. abuse (verb), accuse, amuse, bemuse, excuse (verb), enthuse, (con/dif/ef/in/suf-)fuse, hypotenuse, muse, peruse, refuse (verb), ruse, use (verb).

In all cases other than those listed, the regular spelling of medial and final /z/ is <s>, including the grammatical suffixes mentioned above.

## 3.8 Consonants without doubled spellings: /h ŋ ʃ ʒ θ ð w j/

### 3.8.1 /h/ as in *who*

Occurs only before a vowel phoneme, therefore never word-finally.

**THE MAIN SYSTEM**

| Basic grapheme | <h> | 97% | e.g. *behave, have* |
| Other frequent graphemes | (none) | | |

**THE REST**

| Oddities | <j> | | only in *fajita, jojoba* (twice), *marijuana, mojito, Navajo* |
| | <wh> | | 3% – only in *who, whom, whose, whole, whoop(er/ing), whore* |
| 2-phoneme graphemes | (none) | | |

## NOTES

/h/ is rare medially, but cf. *adhere, behave, behind, bohemian, cahoots, clerihew, cohere, cohort, enhance, inhabit, inherit, mayhem, perhaps* pronounced /pəˈhæps/ rather than /præps/, *prehensile, shanghai,* and compound words such as *anyhow, meathook, mishap, mishit, peahen, poorhouse, prehistoric, sawhorse, sunhat, warhead, warhorse.*

Because Carney (1994) did not include function words such as *who, whom, whose* in his frequency counts, his percentage for /h/ spelt <wh> is distinctly lower than if he had included them.

## 3.8.2 /ŋ/ as in *ring*

Occurs only post-vocalically, and therefore never word-initially (in English). Also, except in very rare cases such as *spraing*, occurs only after short vowel phonemes (and even then never after /ʊ/ (in RP); also very rare after /e, ə/ – see Notes)

### THE MAIN SYSTEM

| | | | |
|---|---|---|---|
| Basic grapheme | <ng> | 75% | e.g. *bang, sing, zing, long, lung* |
| Other frequent grapheme | <n> | 25% | before /k, g/, however spelt, e.g. *sink, zinc, anxious, conquer, ankle, uncle, length; longer, kangaroo, anxiety.* See Notes |

### THE REST

| | | |
|---|---|---|
| Oddities | <nc> | only in *charabanc* /ˈʃærəbæŋ/ |
| | <nd> | only in *handcuffs, handkerchief* /ˈhæŋkʌfs, ˈhæŋkətʃɪf/ |
| | <ngh> | only in *dinghy, gingham, Singhalese* /ˈdɪŋiː, ˈgɪŋəm, sɪŋəˈliːz/ (contrast *shanghai* /ʃæŋˈhaɪ/) |
| | <ngu> | only in a very few suffixed forms of words in next category, namely *haranguing, tonguing*. See also end of section 6.4 |
| | <ngue> | only in *harangue, meringue, tongue* /həˈræŋ, məˈræŋ, tʌŋ/ (contrast *dengue* /ˈdeŋgeɪ/) |

*2-phoneme*                (none)
*graphemes*

## NOTES

The conclusion that /ŋ/ before /k/ is spelt <n> is based on words like *ankle* /'æŋkəl/, *carbuncle, crinkle, peduncle, periwinkle, rankle, sprinkle, tinkle, twinkle, uncle, winkle, wrinkle*, where /k/ is clearly spelt <k, c>, so that the preceding /ŋ/ must be represented by the <n>. Then the same analysis must apply to *angle* /'æŋgəl/, even though this means that here the letters <n, g> do not form the grapheme <ng> and do not jointly spell /ŋ/. The same applies to *finger* /'fɪŋgə/, but in *singer* /'sɪŋə/ there is no /g/ (in RP, though there is in Lancashire), so that here the letters <ng> **do** form a single grapheme representing /ŋ/.

The words *length, lengthen, strength, strengthen* pronounced /leŋkθ, 'leŋkθən, streŋkθ, 'streŋkθən/ (for their alternative pronunciations see under /n/, section 3.5.5) and *angst* /æŋkst/ appear to need an analysis in which /ŋ/ is spelt <n> and /k/ is spelt <g> – if so, these words and *disguise* /dɪsˈkaɪz/, *disgust* pronounced /dɪsˈkʌst/, i.e. identically to *discussed* (*disguise, disgust* are also pronounced /dɪzˈgaɪz, dɪzˈgʌst/, i.e. with both medial consonants voiced rather than voiceless) would be the only occurrences of /k/ spelt <g>, though the spelling of /ŋ/ with <n> in *angst, length, lengthen, strength, strengthen* conforms to the analysis of the many words with this correspondence just given (see also under /k/ in section 3.7.1).

The words *length, lengthen, strength, strengthen* are also among the very few in which /ŋ/ occurs after /e/. The only other examples seem to be *dengue, dreng* 'free tenant in ancient Northumbria', *enchiridion, enclave* pronounced /'eŋkleɪv/ (also pronounced /'ɒŋkleɪv/), *enkephalin, ginseng, nomenclature*, the abbreviation *SENCo* ('Special Educational Needs Coordinator') pronounced /'seŋkəʊ/, and words beginning *encephal-* when pronounced /enˈkefəl-/ (also pronounced /enˈsefəl-/). The only cases in which /ŋ/ follows /ə/ may be words like *concur(rent)* if pronounced /kəŋˈkɜː, kəŋˈkʌrənt/.

Although *long, strong, young* end in /ŋ/ (in RP) and are therefore to be analysed as containing /ŋ/ spelt <ng>, the comparative and superlative forms *longer, longest, stronger, strongest, younger, youngest* and the verb *elongate* all have medial /ŋg/, so here the /g/ has 'surfaced' and is represented by the <g> (see section 7.2), and the /ŋ/ is spelt <n>. Similarly with *diphthongise, prolongation*, which gain a /g/ relative to unsuffixed *diphthong, prolong*. By contrast, in *longevity* /lɒnˈdʒevɪtiː/ the surfacing phoneme is /dʒ/.

The word *anxiety* has two pronunciations: /æŋˈgzaɪɪtiː, æŋˈzaɪɪtiː/, where the second lacks /g/. Both are rarities: the first is the only instance of /ŋg/ where the /g/ is not spelt <g>; the second is the only case where /ŋ/ is spelt <n> without a following /k, g/.

## 3.8.3 /ʃ/ as in *fission*

**THE MAIN SYSTEM**

| | | | |
|---|---|---|---|
| *Basic grapheme* | <sh> | 37% | e.g. *ship, fish*; regular in initial and final positions; rare medially, but cf. *ashet, baksheesh, banshee, bishop, buckshee, Bolshevik, bolshie, bushel, cashier, cashmere, cushion, dasheen, dishevel, fashion, geisha, kosher, kwashiorkor, marshal, pasha, pashmina, ramshackle, sashay, worship, yashmak* and words with the suffix *-ship*. For exceptions in initial and final positions see the Oddities, below. Also see Notes |
| *Other frequent graphemes* | All these graphemes occur only medially | | For all these categories see Notes and Table 3.6 |
| | <ti> | 55% (with <ci, si, ssi>) | regular medially, e.g. *nation*, but there are many exceptions |
| | <ci> | | e.g. *commercial, crucial, delicious, judicial, logician, magician, official, racial, social, special* |
| | <si> | | e.g. *aversion, emulsion, pension, repulsion, reversion, tension, torsion, version* |
| | <ssi> | | e.g. *accession, admission, discussion, emission, intercession, obsession, passion, percussion, permission, recession, remission, session* |

90  *Dictionary of the British English Spelling System*

| | | |
|---|---|---|
| *Rare grapheme* | <ce> | regular medially in /eɪʃəs/ spelt <-aceous>, e.g. *cretaceous, curvaceous, herbaceous, sebaceous* – see Notes and Table 3.6; otherwise only in *cetacean, crustacea(n), Echinacea, ocean, siliceous* |

## THE REST

*Oddities*  8% in total

*- in initial position*

| | | |
|---|---|---|
| | <ch> | only in 30+ words of mainly French origin, namely *chagrin, chaise, chalet, chamfer* pronounced /'ʃæmfə/ (also pronounced /'tʃæmfə/), *chamois* (whether pronounced /'ʃæmiː/ or /'ʃæmwaː/), *champagne, chancre, chandelier, chaperone, charabanc, charade, chardonnay, charlatan, Charlotte, chassis, chateau, chauffeu-r/se, chauvinis-m/t, chef, chemise, chenille, cheroot, chevalier, chevron, chi-chi* (twice), *chic, chicane(ry), chiffon, chignon, chivalr-ic/ous/y, chute* |
| | <s> | only in *sugar, sure* and (German pronunciations of) *spiel, stein, strafe, stumm* |
| | <sch> | only in *schedule* (also pronounced with /sk/), *schemozzle, schist, schistosomiasis, schlemiel, schlep, schlock, schmaltz, schmo(e), schmooze, schnapps, schnauzer, schnitzel, schnozzle, schuss, schwa* |
| | <sj> | only in *sjambok* |

*- in medial position*

| | | |
|---|---|---|
| | <c> | e.g. *officiate, speciality, specie(s), superficiality* and sometimes *ap/de-preciate, associate*. See Notes |
| | <ch> | only in about 20 words of mainly French origin, namely *attaché, brochure, cachet, cachou, cliché, crochet, duchesse, echelon, embouchure, Eustachian, machete, machicolation, machine, marchioness, nonchalant, parachute, pistachio, recherché* (twice), *ricochet, ruching, sachet*; also sometimes in (Greek) *chiropody* (hence the punning shop name *Shuropody*) |
| | <che> | only in *rapprochement* |

|  |  |  |
|---|---|---|
|  | <chs> | only in *fuchsia* |
|  | <s> | only in *asphalt* pronounced /'æʃfelt/ (also pronounced /'æsfælt/), *censure, commensurate, ensure, insure, tonsure* |
|  | <sc> | only in *conscie, conscientious, crescendo, fascis-m/t*. See Notes |
|  | <sch> | only in *maraschino, meerschaum, seneschal* |
|  | <sci> | only in *conscience, conscious, fascia, luscious*. See Notes |
|  | <se> | only in *gaseous* pronounced /'geɪʃəs/ (also pronounced /'gæsi:jəs/). See Notes |
|  | <ss> | only in *assure, fissure, issue, pressure, tissue* |
|  | <t> | mainly before <-iate> with the <i> spelling /i:/ (and with 'invisible' /j/-glide), e.g. *differentiate, expatiate, ingratiate, initiate, negotiate, propitiate, satiate, substantiate, vitiate,* plus *minutiae, otiose* pronounced /'əʊʃi:jəʊs, 'əʊʃi:jəʊz/ (also pronounced /'əʊti:jəʊs, 'əʊti:jəʊz/), *partiality, ratio*; also *novitiate* pronounced /nə'vɪʃi:jət/ (also pronounced /nə'vɪʃət/). See Notes |

- *in final position*

|  |  |  |
|---|---|---|
|  | <ce> | only in *liquorice* pronounced /'lɪkərɪʃ/ |
|  | <ch> | only in *Welch* and, in phonemically word-final position, *fiche, gouache, moustache, niche* pronounced /ni:ʃ/, *pastiche, quiche, ruche*, where the <e> is part of the split digraphs <a.e, i.e, u.e> spelling /ɑ:, i:, u:/ |
|  | <che> | only in about 12 words of mainly French origin, namely *avalanche, barouche, brioche, cache, cartouche, cloche, creche, douche, farouche, gauche, louche, panache* |

*2-phoneme graphemes* /kʃ/

|  |  |  |
|---|---|---|
|  | (1) spelt <x> | only in *flexure, luxury, sexual* /'flekʃə, 'lʌkʃəri:, 'sekʃ(u:w)əl/ |
|  | (2) spelt <xi> | e.g. *anxious*: see under /k/, section 3.7.1 |

## NOTES

Because /ʃ/ is a sibilant consonant, adding any of the suffixes regular noun plural and third person singular person tense verb (both spelt <s> where the stem ends in <e>, otherwise <es>) and regular singular and irregular plural possessive (spelt <'s>) to a stem ending in /ʃ/ adds a syllable /ɪz/ as well as a morpheme: *quiches, fishes, Bush's*. See also /z/, section 3.7.8, and /ɪ/, section 5.4.3.

Some rules could probably be given for when <sh> is regular medially, but these would be more complicated than giving the list of examples, above.

As spellings of medial /ʃ/ in **stem** words, <ti, ce, ci, sci, se, si, ssi> occur only at the beginning of the final syllable of a word and immediately after the stressed syllable, and the final syllable is always one of /əl, ən, əs/ or (very rarely) /əm/ (*consortium* pronounced /kən'sɔːʃəm/ (usually pronounced /kən'sɔːtiːjəm/), *nasturtium*), /əns/ (*conscience*) or just /ə/ (e.g. *consortia* pronounced /kən'sɔːʃə/ (usually pronounced /kən'sɔːtiːjə/), *fascia, militia*); and <si> is always preceded by a consonant **letter** (except in *Asian*). Exceptions with these features but other spellings of medial /ʃ/: *bushel, marshal, seneschal; cushion, Eustachian, fashion; fissure, fuchsia, geisha, pressure*.

The default spelling of medial /ʃ/ is <ti>; for example, it is regular in words ending in /eɪʃən, eɪʃəl, iːʃən, əʊʃən, (j)uːʃən/, e.g. *nation, spatial, accretion, lotion, evolution, pollution* (exceptions: *Asian, racial, cetacean, crustacean, Grecian, ocean, Confucian, Rosicrucian*). However, because medial /ʃ/ has so many other spellings, the major patterns are set out in Table 3.6. What does not come over particularly clearly even then is that the only case where there is substantial three-way confusion is over final /ɪʃən/: the majority spelling is <-ition>, e.g. *volition*, but there is competition (!) from <-ician, -ission> - see the top right-hand and bottom left-hand boxes of the Table (and beware of *Titian*).

TABLE 3.6: THE DISTRIBUTION OF <ti, ce, ci, si, ssi> AS SPELLINGS OF MEDIAL /ʃ/.

| Default spelling: <ti> | Exceptions (in addition to those in <sh> listed under the basic grapheme and those listed among Oddities above or under Subpatterns and Sub-exceptions below):<br><ci>: *facial, glacial* pronounced /ˈgleɪʃəl/ (also pronounced /ˈgleɪsiːjəl/), *racial, (e)special, financial, provincial, social, commercial, crucial; Grecian; academician, electrician, logician, magician, mathematician, mortician, musician, obstetrician, optician, patrician, phonetician, physician, politician, statistician, tactician* (N.B. most words in <-ician> are occupations); *suspicion; Confucian, Rosicrucian; precious, specious; siliceous; auspicious, avaricious, capricious, delicious, judicious, malicious, meretricious, officious, suspicious, vicious; atrocious, ferocious, precocious* and various other rare words<br><si>: *controversial, torsion*<br><ssi>: *fission* |
|---|---|
| Each of the subpatterns below is an exception to the rule that the default spelling is <ti>, and each subpattern has its own sub-exceptions (some of which revert to <ti>) ||
| **Subpattern** | **Sub-exceptions** |
| For /eɪʃəs/ the regular spelling is <-aceous>, e.g. *cretaceous, curvaceous, herbaceous, sebaceous* plus about 100 other words, mostly scientific and all very rare | *audacious, capacious, contumacious, efficacious, fallacious, gracious, loquacious, mendacious, perspicacious, pertinacious, pugnacious, rapacious, sagacious, tenacious, vivacious, voracious; gaseous, spatious, Ignatius* |
| For /ɪʃəl/ the regular spelling is <-icial>, e.g. *artificial, beneficial, (pre)judicial, official, sacrificial, superficial* (but this is a very small set) | *initial* plus 4 other rare words in <-itial> |
| For /ʃən/ preceded by /ɜː/ spelt <er, ur> or by /l, n/ spelt <l, n>, the regular spelling is <-sion>, e.g. *(a/re-)version, excursion, emulsion, expulsion, pension, tension* | *Cistercian, coercion* (also pronounced with /ʒ/), *exertion, Persian* (also pronounced with /ʒ/), *tertian; gentian* |
| For /ʃən/ preceded by /æ, e, mɪ, ʌ/ spelt <a, e, mi, u>, the regular spelling is <-ssion>, e.g. *(com)passion; (ac/con/inter/pro/re/se/suc)cession, con/pro-fession, ag/di/e/in/pro/re/retro/trans-gression, com/de/ex/im/op/re/sup-pression, session* and all its compounds; *(ad/com/e/inter/intro/manu/per/re/sub/trans)mission; con/dis/(re)per-cussion* | *national, ration, (ir)rational;*<br><br><br><br><br><br>*Prussian, Russian* |

Spellings of medial /ʃ/ with <c, sc, t> always have a following <i(e)>, but the <i(e)> is a separate grapheme spelling /iː/. Some of the relevant words have alternative pronunciations with /s/, e.g. *appreciate* /əˈpriːʃiːjeɪt, əˈpriːsiːjeɪt/, *negotiate* /nɪˈgəʊʃiːjeɪt, nɪˈgəʊsiːjeɪt/, *species* /ˈspiːʃiːz, ˈspiːsiːz/.

And then there seems to be a phonological constraint in many RP-speakers' accents against medial /ʃ/ occurring twice in words ending in /iːjeɪt/ which already have one medial /ʃ/ and then would acquire another if suffixed to end in /iːˈjeɪʃən/. For example *appreciation* and *negotiation* are mainly pronounced /əpriːsiːˈjeɪʃən, nɪgəʊsiːˈjeɪʃən/, not /əpriːʃiːˈjeɪʃən, nɪgəʊʃiːˈjeɪʃən/. But this in turn does not apply in words which do not end in /eɪʃən/ spelt <-ation>: *conscientious* is always pronounced with two occurrences of medial /ʃ/: /kɒnʃiːˈjenʃəs/, and *recherché* obviously has two: /rəˈʃeəʃeɪ/. The constraint also clearly does not apply to words with the *-ship* suffix, e.g. *relationship* /rɪˈleɪʃənʃɪp/.

## 3.8.4 /ʒ/ as in *vision*

The least frequent phoneme in spoken English.

### THE MAIN SYSTEM

For all three categories see also Notes.

| | | | |
|---|---|---|---|
| *Basic grapheme* | <si> | 91% (with <s>) | e.g. *freesia, vision*. Only medial |
| *Rare graphemes* | <s> | | only medial before <u> and only in *casual, usual, visual*; (*dis/en/fore-*) *closure, composure, embrasure, erasure, exposure, leisure, measure, pleasure, treasure, treasury, usur-er/y/ious* |
| | <ge> | 4% | never initial; medially, only in *bourgeois(ie), mange-tout*; regular in word-final position, where it occurs only in about 25 words of mainly French origin, namely *beige, cortege, concierge, liege, melange,* |

*rouge* and, with the <e> also forming part of the split digraphs <a.e, i.e, u.e> (for dual-functioning see section 7.1), in *badinage, barrage, camouflage, collage, corsage, decalage, décolletage, dressage, entourage, espionage, fuselage, garage* pronounced /ˈgæraːʒ/, *massage, mirage, montage, triage, sabotage; prestige; luge;* only exception in word-final position is *raj* /raːʒ/

## THE REST

*Oddities* — 5% in total

<ci> — only, exceptionally but increasingly, in *coercion* pronounced /kəʊˈwɜːʒən/ (usually pronounced /kəʊˈwɜːʃən/)

<g> — initially, only in *genre, gilet;* medially, only in *aubergine, conge, dirigiste, largesse, negligee, protege, regime, tagine* and *lingerie* pronounced /ˈlænʒəriː/ (also pronounced /ˈlɒndʒəreɪ/); never word-final

<j> — only in *jihad, raj* and some rare French loanwords, e.g. *bijou, goujon, jabot, jalousie, jupe*

<se> — only in *nausea, nauseous* pronounced /ˈnɔːʒə(s)/ (also pronounced /ˈnɔziːjə(s)/)

<ti> — only in *equation* /ɪˈkweɪʒən/

<z> — only in *azure* pronounced /ˈæʒə, ˈeɪʒə/ (also pronounced /ˈæzj(ʊ)ə, ˈeɪzj(ʊ)ə/), *seizure* /ˈsiːʒə/

<zi> — only in *brazier, crozier, glazier* pronounced /ˈbreɪʒə, ˈkrəʊʒə, ˈgleɪʒə/ (also pronounced /ˈbreɪziːjə, ˈkrəʊziːjə, ˈgleɪziːjə/)

*2-phoneme grapheme* — /gʒ/ spelt <x> — see under /g/, section 3.5.3

## NOTES

Because /ʒ/ is a sibilant consonant, adding any of the suffixes regular noun plural and third person singular person tense verb (both spelt <s> where the stem ends in <e>, otherwise <es>) and regular singular and irregular plural possessive (spelt <'s>) to a stem ending in /ʒ/ adds a syllable /ɪz/ as well as a morpheme: *massages*, (*the*) *Raj's* (*collapse*). See also /z/, section 3.7.8, and /ɪ/, section 5.4.3.

As spellings of /ʒ/, <si, s> occur only medially and immediately after the stressed syllable, and are preceded by a vowel, and <s> is always followed by <u>. Almost all spellings with <si> are followed by <-on>, e.g. *vision*, but there are a few others, namely *crosier, hosier(y), osier*.

Although Carney gives 91% for <si, s> combined, it is clear that the great majority of these must be <si> spellings, since there are rather few words with /ʒ/ spelt <s> and a large number with /ʒ/ spelt <si>. This is why I have classified /ʒ/ spelt <s> as a rare grapheme.

Treating <ge> as the regular spelling of word-final /ʒ/ is justified by the first six words of French origin listed above: here the preceding vowel phonemes (plus the /n/ in *melange*) are represented without the aid of the word-final <e>. In the other 19 words <ge> is clearly still spelling /ʒ/, but it is necessary (and parallels other parts of the analysis) to analyse the <e> as also forming part of the split digraphs <a.e, i.e, u.e> spelling /ɑː, iː, uː/ (even though the last two correspondences have only one instance with included <g> each) – for dual-functioning see section 7.1. Then I analyse the /e/ in *cortege* as spelt only by the first <e> because it is a short vowel and no short vowels (in my analysis) are spelt by split digraphs – see section A.6 in Appendix A. Then <g> has to be recognised as a grapheme spelling /ʒ/ separate from <ge> because of the few words listed where this correspondence occurs initially and medially and the following vowel letters are obviously (involved in) separate graphemes.

The spelling <zh> is also used to represent /ʒ/, but because this occurs only in transcriptions of Russian names, e.g. *Zhivago, Zhores*, I have not added it to the inventory of graphemes.

## 3.8.5 /θ/ as in *thigh*

### THE MAIN SYSTEM

*Basic grapheme*          <th>     100%

*Other frequent graphemes*    (none)

*The phoneme-grapheme correspondences, 1: Consonants* 97

### THE REST

| | | |
|---|---|---|
| *Oddities* | <phth> | only in *apophthegm* /'æpəθem/, *phthalate* /'θæleɪt/ |
| | <the> | only in *Catherine* with first <e> elided (see section 6.10), *saithe* (/seɪθ/, 'fish of cod family') |
| *2-phoneme grapheme* | /tθ/ spelt <th> | see under /t/, section 3.5.7 |

### NOTES

In the rare word *saithe*, the only function of the <e> seems to be to keep this word visually distinct from *saith* (/seθ/, archaic form of *says*) with the rare spelling <ai> for /e/.

See also the Notes under /ð/, next.

## 3.8.6 /ð/ as in *thy*

### THE MAIN SYSTEM

| | | |
|---|---|---|
| *Basic grapheme* | <th> | 100% |
| *Other frequent graphemes* | (none) | |

### THE REST

| | | | |
|---|---|---|---|
| *Oddity* | <the> | <1% | only word-final and only in *breathe, loathe, seethe, sheathe, soothe, staithe, teethe, wreathe*. See Notes |
| *2-phoneme graphemes* | (none) | | |

### NOTES

In all the words listed under Oddity, the vowel digraphs preceding <-the> spell a long vowel or diphthong, and there is therefore no need to analyse the final <e> as part of complex split graphemes <ea.e>, etc. However, in *bathe, lathe, unscathed* (the free form *scathe* meaning 'to harm' does not occur, but underlies both *unscathed* and *scathing*), *swathe, blithe, lithe, tithe, writhe, clothe, hythe, scythe,* the final <e> is part of the split digraphs <a.e, i.e, o.e, y.e> spelling /eɪ, aɪ, əʊ, aɪ/, so here /ð/ is again spelt <th>. The final <e> keeps *breathe, loathe, seethe, sheathe, soothe, teethe, wreathe, bathe, lathe, swathe, clothe* visually distinct from *breath, loath* (also spelt *loth*), *seeth* (/ˈsiːjɪθ/, archaic third person singular present tense form of *see*), *sheath, sooth, teeth, wreath, bath, lath, swath, cloth*. For the few minimal pairs differing only in having /θ/ or /ð/ see section 9.36.

The fact that both /θ/ and /ð/ are spelt <th> is useful in writing: people whose accents have different distributions of the two phonemes nevertheless spell the relevant words identically. This is particularly the case with some plural nouns, e.g. *baths* pronounced /bɑːðz/ in RP but /bæθs/ by many people from the North of England; the singular has /θ/ in both cases. But this does not help people trying to read unfamiliar words containing <th> – though again see section 9.36.

## 3.8.7 /w/ as in *well*

Occurs only before a vowel phoneme, and therefore never word-finally

**THE MAIN SYSTEM**

For all these categories, and /w/ not represented at all, see Notes.

| | | | |
|---|---|---|---|
| *Basic grapheme* | <w> | 64% | e.g. *word*. regular initially, rare medially |
| *Other frequent graphemes* | <u> | 31%, of which 27 percentage points are occurrences of /kw/ spelt <qu> | e.g. *quick, language*. Never initial, regular medially |
| | <wh> | 5% | medially, only in *erstwhile, meanwhile, narwhal, over-/under-whelm*; otherwise only initial and only in *whack, whale, wham(my), whang, wharf, what, wheat, wheedle, wheel, wheeze, whelk, whelp, when, whence, where, wherry, whet,* |

*whether, whey, whiff, whiffle, Whig, which, while, whim, whimper, whimsical, whimsy, whin, whine, whinge, whinny, whip, whippersnapper, whippet, whippoorwill, whirl, whir(r), whisk, whisker, whisk(e)y, whisper, whist, whistle, whit, white, whither, whitlow, Whitsun, whittle, Whitworth, whiz(z), whoa, whomp, whoopee, whoops, whoosh, whop, whump, whup, why, whydah* and a very few other rare words (e.g. *whilom*)

## THE REST

| | | |
|---|---|---|
| Oddities | | <1% in total |
| | <hu> | only in *chihuahua* (twice) |
| | <ou> | only in *Ouija* |
| | <ww> | only in *bowwow, glowworm, powwow, skew(-)whiff, slowworm* |
| 2-phoneme graphemes | /wʌ/ spelt <o> | only in *once, one* – unless you prefer to consider the /w/ as not being represented in the spelling at all – see Notes and section 9.0 |
| | /wɑː/ | See also Notes |
| | (1) spelt <oi> | only in a few words more recently borrowed from French, e.g. *bourgeoisie, coiffeu-r/se, coiffure, pointe, soiree, toilette* |
| | (2) spelt <oir> | mainly word-final and only in a very few words more recently borrowed from French, namely *abattoir, avoirdupois, boudoir, memoir, noir, reservoir, soiree, voussoir*. /r/-linking occurs in *memoirist, noirish* – see section 3.6 |

|   |   |   |
|---|---|---|
| | (3) spelt <oire> | only word-final and only in a very few words more recently borrowed from French, namely *aide-memoire, conservatoire, escritoire, grimoire, repertoire* |
| | (4) spelt <ois> | only word-final and only in a very few words more recently borrowed from French, namely *avoirdupois, bourgeois, chamois* (the animal, pronounced /ˈʃæmwaː/, as opposed to the leather made from its skin, pronounced /ˈʃæmiː/, the latter also being spelt *shammy*), *patois* (contrast *fatwa*). /z/ surfaces in *bourgeoisie* – see section 7.2 |
| | /waɪ/ spelt <oy> | only in *foyer* pronounced /ˈfwaɪjeɪ/, *voyeur*. Here the <y> is both part of the digraph <oy> spelling /waɪ/ and also a single-letter grapheme spelling /j/. For dual-functioning see section 7.1 |
| 3-phoneme grapheme | /ˈwaɪə/ | spelt with a single grapheme <oir> only in *choir* – one of only two 3-phoneme graphemes in the entire language |

## NOTES

If we follow Crystal (2012: 131–2), 'more recently' in terms of loanwords from French means after the Great Vowel Shift, which ended about AD 1600.

Although phoneme /w/ never occurs at the end of an English stem word, letter <w> is very frequent in word-final position, where it always follows a vowel letter with which it forms a digraph spelling a vocalic sound. See also 'linking /w/' later in these Notes.

The 2-phoneme sequences /kw, gw/ are almost always spelt <qu, gu> respectively.

<u> spelling /w/ occurs not only in the familiar /kw/ spelt <qu>, e.g. *quick, squash*, but also in a few words after /k, g, s, z/ spelt <c, g, s, ss, z>, e.g. *cuirass, cuisine, cuisssr; anguish, distinguish, extinguish, guacamole, guano, guava, iguana* pronounced /ɪˈgwaːnə/, *language, languish, linguist, penguin, sanguine, segue, unguent; persuade, pueblo, puissan-ce/t, pursuivant, suave, suede, suite; assuage, dissuade; Venezuela* (usually pronounced with /z/) and some very rare words; otherwise perhaps only in *ennui, etui* /ɒnˈwiː, eˈtwiː/. In these contexts <u> is clearly a consonant letter, though it is very rarely taught as having (like <y>) both vowel and consonant functions.

In linguistic terms it is unnecessary to analyse /kw/ as a single phonetic unit since in all words containing /kw/ (those where it is spelt <qu>, plus the Oddities *acquaint, acquiesce, acquire, acquisitive, acquit* (in these five words /k/ is spelt <cq>), *awkward, coiffeur, coiffeuse, coiffure, cuisine, kwashiorkor* and even *choir*) the /k/ is spelt separately, as it is also in compounds like *backward*. However, for teaching purposes many authors treat /kw/ and <qu> as units in close correspondence. Even though this ignores not only the (admittedly few) words just listed where /kw/ is not spelt <qu> (including *acquaint, acquiesce, acquire, acquisitive, acquit*) but also the 60+ words where <cqu, qu, que> are not pronounced /kw/ (see under /k/, section 3.7.1), this pragmatic approach to /kw/ spelt <qu> seems justified by the high frequency of this correspondence.

The frequency of <wh> is actually higher than 5% because Carney (1994: 253) did not count the function words *what, when, whence, where, whether, which, while, whither, why*. Scots and others who have the phoneme /ʍ/ (think 'hw') in their accent presumably have little difficulty in knowing which words to spell with <wh>, but the rest of us just have to learn them.

/wʌ/ also has 2-grapheme spellings, e.g. <wo> in *wonder*. /waː/ has the 2-grapheme spellings <oi> in *coiffeur, coiffeuse, coiffure*, <ua> in *guacamole, guano, guava, iguana, suave*, and <wa> in *kwashiorkor*. /waɪə/ has the 2-grapheme spellings <wire> in *wire* and <uire> in *acquire, quire, require*.

Medial /w/ spelt <w> is quite rare in stem words. The only words in which a medial <w> has only the function of spelling /w/ seem to be *awkward* (second <w>), *fatwa, kiwi, kwashiorkor*. There are rather more examples in which the <w> is both a grapheme in its own right spelling /w/ and part of one of the digraphs <ew> spelling /(j)uː/, e.g. in *ewer, jewel, newel, sewer* (/'suːwə/, 'foul drain'), *skewer, steward*, or <ow> spelling /əʊ/ – in stem words this occurs only in *bowie, rowan* (in its English pronunciation /'rəʊwən/) – or /aʊ/ in *bowel, dowel, rowel, towel, trowel, vowel; bower, cower, dower, flower, glower, power, shower, tower, coward, dowager, howitzer, prowess*, plus the Scottish pronunciation of *rowan* /'raʊwən/. For words containing /əʊ, aʊ/ see also sections 5.7.4, 5.6.2, and for dual-functioning section 7.1.

There are also various stem words where medial /w/ occurs in the pronunciation as a glide between /(j)uː, əʊ, aʊ/ and a following vowel phoneme but has no representation in the spelling, for example:

- after /(j)uː/: *altruism, bruin, casual, cruel, cruet, doing, dual, duel, duet, duo, fluid, genuine, gruel(ling), iguana* pronounced /ɪgjuːˈwaːnə/, *pirouette, ruin, silhouette, suet, toing, truant, (in)tuition, usual, zoology, zoomorphic*

- after /əʊ/: *coerce, coincide, coition, coitus, co-op, cooperate, co-opt, coordinate, co-own, egoism, froing, going, heroic, heroin(e), jingoism, Noel, no-one, oboist, phloem, poem, soloist, spermatozoon, stoic(al)*
- after /aʊ/: *devour, flour, hour, lour, our, scour, sour* and *dour* pronounced /'daʊwə/, all of which end in /'aʊwə/, plus the stray medial example of *sauerkraut*.

This pattern of representing or not representing medial /w/ after /(j)uː, əʊ, aʊ/ before a following vowel phoneme is paralleled when stem words ending in those phonemes have a suffix beginning with a vowel phoneme added. In all such cases there is a 'linking /w/' glide between the stem and the suffix (see Cruttenden, 2014: 152), but this is represented in the spelling only if the stem word already ends in <w>, otherwise not. If there is a <w> it continues to function as part of the spelling of the stem-final vowel while also now spelling /w/ – the familiar dual-functioning (see section 7.1). If the stem does not end in <w> the spelling simply ignores the /w/-glide. For examples of both categories see Table 3.7.

TABLE 3.7: EXAMPLES OF /w/ REPRESENTED OR NOT BETWEEN A STEM WORD ENDING IN /(j)uː, əʊ, aʊ/ AND A SUFFIX BEGINNING WITH A VOWEL PHONEME

| Preceding phoneme(s) | /w/ represented in spelling by <w> | /w/ not represented in spelling |
|---|---|---|
| /(j)uː/ | *brew-er/ing, chewing, few-er/est, hewer, Jewish, leeward* pronounced /'luːwəd/ (also pronounced /'liːwəd/), *mewing, new-er/est, renewer, sinew-ous/y, stewing, (inter/re-)view-er/ing* | *do-er/ing, lassoing, toing (and froing); canoeing, shoeing; mooing, shampooing, shooing, tattoo-ing/ist; rendezvousing; accru-al/ing, argu-able/ing, continu-al/ance/ing/ous, gluing, issu-able/ing, pursu-ance/ing, rescuable, subduable, statuesque, su-able/ing, virtuous* |
| /aʊ/ | *allow-ance/ing, avowal, bowing* ('inclining the head'), *miaowing* | *Maoist; plough-er/ing* |
| /əʊ/ | *sewer* (/'səʊwə/, 'one who sews'), *sewing; blowing, bowing* ('playing stringed instrument'), *follow-er/ing, owing, shadowing, showing, sow-er/ing, willowy.* N.B. Where the <ow> is not stressed, not only does linking /w/ occur but the vowel is often reduced to /ə/ and is therefore spelt simply by the <o>, e.g. *widower*. | *plateauing; hoeing, toeing; (toing and) froing, going* |

And this pattern also occurs when stem words ending in /(j)uː, əʊ, aʊ/ are followed by a word beginning with a vowel phoneme. In all such cases there is a 'linking /w/' glide between the two words, but again this is represented in the spelling only if the first word already ends in <w>, otherwise not. Since this book is mainly concerned with stem words and their derivatives, only a few examples of inter-word /w/-glides not represented in the spelling will be given: *to estimate* /tuˈwestɪmeɪt/, *go away* /ˈɡəʊwəˈweɪ/, *slough of despond* /ˈslaʊwəvdɪsˈpɒnd/.

See also the parallel phenomenon of 'linking /j/' (next section), and the subtly different one of /r/-linking (section 3.6).

## 3.8.8 /j/ as in *yell, union*

Occurs only before a vowel phoneme, and therefore never word-finally.

For all these categories, the percentages, and /j/ not represented at all, see Notes.

### THE MAIN SYSTEM

| | | | |
|---|---|---|---|
| *Basic word-initial grapheme* | <y> | 19% | e.g. *yellow*. Regular (very few exceptions) initially except before /uː, ʊə/; rare medially |
| *Other frequent grapheme* | <i> | c.5% | e.g. *onion*. Only medial |
| *Frequent 2-phoneme graphemes* | /juː/ | | See also the main entry for /juː/, section 5.7.5 |
| | (1) spelt <u, u.e> | 62% | e.g. *union, illusion, cute*. Regular as spellings of /juː/ in non-final and closed final syllables respectively; <u> word-final only in *coypu, menu, ormolu* |
| | (2) spelt <ew> | 11% | e.g. *few*. Regular as spelling of /juː/ word-finally in monosyllables |
| *Rare 2-phoneme grapheme* | /juː/ spelt <ue> | for percentage see below | regular as spelling of /juː/ word-finally in polysyllables, e.g. *pursue* |

## THE REST

| | | |
|---|---|---|
| *Oddities* | All medial | <1% in total |
| | <h> | only in a very few words between 2 vowels, namely *annihilate, vehement, vehicle, vehicular* |
| | <j> | only in *hallelujah* and *majolica* pronounced /maɪˈjɒlɪkə/ (also pronounced /məˈdʒɒlɪkə/) |
| | <ll> | only in French-like pronunciations of *bouillabaisse* /buːjaːˈbes/ and *marseillaise* /maːseɪˈjez/ and Latin American Spanish-like pronunciation of *tortilla* /tɔːˈtiːjaː/ |
| *Other 2-phoneme graphemes* | | 3% in total |
| | /juː/ spelt <eau, eu, ewe, ui, ut, uu> (with <ue>, 3% of spellings of /juː/) | see under /juː/, section 5.7.5 |
| | /jʊə/ spelt <eur, ur, ure> | see Notes below and under /ʊə/, section 5.6.5 |
| | /jə/ spelt <eu, u, ua, ure> | see under /ə/, section 5.4.7 |
| | /lj/ spelt <ll> | only in *carillon*. Most occurrences of /lj/ (all medial) have one of the 2-grapheme spellings <li, lli> – see the groups of words in the Notes beginning *battalion, civilian*. The sequence /lj/ also occurs in *halyard, failure* but in both the /l/ is spelt <l>; in *halyard* the /j/ is spelt separately as <y>, but in *failure* is subsumed with the final /ə/ in <ure> |
| | /nj/ spelt <gn> | only in *chignon, cognac, gnocchi, lasagne, lorgnette, mignonette, monsignor, poignant, seigneur, soigné, vignette* |

## NOTES

Although /j/ never occurs at the end of an English stem word when pronounced alone or before a word beginning with a consonant phoneme, letter <y> is very frequent in word-final position, where it always spells a vocalic sound, either singly or as part of a digraph. See also 'linking /j/' later in these Notes, and section 11.5.

The correspondences for initial /j/ are fairly straightforward:
- if the word is a monosyllable /j/ is spelt <y>, e.g. *yacht, yolk*. Only exceptions: *ewe, Ewell* (contrast *yew, you, Yule*), *uke, Ure, use* (both the noun /juːs/ and the verb /juːz/ and their derived forms)
- if the word is a polysyllable and the next phoneme is /uː/, the /j/ is usually subsumed into <u> spelling the 2-phoneme sequence /juː/, e.g. *union, university* (exceptions: *eucalyptus, eucharist, euchre, eugenic, eulogy, eunuch, euphemism, euphorbia, euphoria, Eustachian, euthanasia, ewer* with /j/ subsumed instead into <eu, ew>; *Yucatan, Yugoslav, Yupik* with /j/ explicitly represented as <y>)
- if the word is a polysyllable and the next phoneme is /ʊə/, the /j/ is usually subsumed into <ur> spelling the 2-phoneme sequence /jʊə/ – but this category includes mainly *urea* and various words derived from it, e.g. *urethra, urine, urology* (exceptions: *eureka, eurhythmic*)
- otherwise, that is in polysyllables where the next phoneme is **not** /uː, ʊə/, initial /j/ is almost always spelt <y>, e.g. *yellow*, etc.

In medial positions, large numbers of instances of /j/ are subsumed into 2-phoneme spellings of /jə, jʊə, juː/, and lists of these can be found in sections 5.4.7, 5.6.5 and 5.7.5 respectively. There are also a very few instances of other 2-phoneme spellings – see above. Otherwise, where a consonant phoneme precedes /j/ the predominant spelling appears to be <i>, e.g. in:
- a group of words ending /jən/ spelt <-ion> after a stressed syllable: *battalion, billion, bunion, champion, companion, dominion, million, minion, onion, opinion, pavilion, pinion, union, vermilion*
- a small group of words ending /jəriː/ spelt <-iary> after a stressed syllable: *apiary, auxiliary, aviary, breviary, domiciliary, pecuniary, topiary* (contrast *January* with final /jəriː/ spelt <-uary> and requiring /je/ to be analysed as spelt <ua>) (but for *incendiary, intermediary, stipendiary, subsidiary* pronounced with /dʒəriː/, i.e. with /dj/ affricated to /dʒ/, see section 3.7.4)
- a further ragbag: (with /lj/ spelt <(l)li>) *civilian* (3rd <i>), *colliery, milieu*, plus, in rapid speech, *brilliant* (2nd <i>); (others) *behaviour, envious, piano, pronunciation* (1st <i>), *spaniel*, (*inter-/re-)view*, etc.

In these cases after a consonant <i> is clearly a consonant letter, though even more rarely than <u> is it taught as having (like <y>) both vowel and consonant functions. There are a few exceptions with <y>: *banyan* /ˈbænjæn/, *biryani, canyon* /ˈkænjən/, *halyard, lanyard, vineyard*.

Otherwise, i.e. in situations not yet covered and where /j/ is both preceded and followed by vowel phonemes, the predominant spelling of medial /j/ is probably zero, i.e. it is not represented at all. There are a few exceptions among the Oddities above, plus just three with <i> (*alleluia, onomatopoeia, pharmacopoeia*, where the <i> can be taken to represent /j/ since the preceding <u, oe> spell /uː, iː/), and rather more with <y>:

- *beyond, bowyer* /ˈbəʊjə/, *lawyer, sawyer, yoyo*, where <y> spells only /j/, plus *bayonet, cayenne, crayon, mayonnaise, rayon*, which can be economically analysed as having /eɪ/ in their non-final syllables spelt (regularly – see sections 5.7.1, 6.3) just by the <a>, so that /j/ is spelt just by the <y>
- *abeyance*, where /j/ is spelt <y> but the <y> is also part of <ey> spelling /eɪ/
- *arroyo, doyenne* pronounced /dɔɪˈjen/, *foyer* pronounced /ˈfɔɪjə/, *loyal* /ˈlɔɪjəl/, *Oyer* (and *Terminer*), *royal* /ˈrɔɪjəl/, *soya*, where /j/ is spelt <y> but the <y> is also part of <oy> spelling /ɔɪ/
- *coyote* /kaɪˈjəʊtiː/, *doyen* and *doyenne* both pronounced /dwaɪˈjen/, *foyer* pronounced /ˈfwaɪjeɪ/, *kayak* /ˈkaɪjæk/, *papaya, voyeur* /vwaɪˈjɜː/, where /j/ is spelt <y> but the <y> is also part of <ay, oy> spelling /aɪ/.

(For dual-functioning see section 7.1).

A list of words in which /j/ is not represented at all in medial positions could go on for pages. A few examples (illustrating the range of spellings within which /j/ is invisible) are: (with final /ə/) *bacteria, cochlear, idea, linear, meteor, senior* (all these words and many others would be analysed by Carney as ending in /ɪə/, whereas I assign them to /iːjə/); (others) *aphrodisiac, appreciate, archaic, audience, axiom, caviar, chaos, chariot, create, creole, dais, deify, diary, dossier, foliage, genius, hilarious, jovial, lenient, mosaic, museum, odious, pantheon, period, radii, radio, reinforce, ruffian, serviette, simultaneous, society, soviet, spontaneity, stallion, tedium, triangle, triage, video*.

This pattern of representing or not representing medial /j/ between two vowel phonemes is paralleled when stem words ending in /aɪ, eɪ, ɔɪ, iː/ have a suffix beginning with a vowel phoneme added. In all such cases there is a linking /j/-glide between the stem and the suffix, but this is represented in the spelling only if the stem word ends in a digraph ending in <y>, otherwise not. If there is such a digraph the <y> continues to function as part of the spelling of the stem-final vowel while now also spelling /j/ – the familiar dual-functioning (see section 7.1). If the stem does not end in a digraph ending in <y> the spelling simply ignores the /j/-glide. For examples of both categories see Table 3.8.

TABLE 3.8: EXAMPLES OF /j/ REPRESENTED OR NOT BETWEEN A STEM WORD ENDING IN /aɪ, eɪ, ɔɪ, iː/ AND A SUFFIX BEGINNING WITH A VOWEL PHONEME.

| Preceding phoneme | /j/ represented in spelling by a digraph ending in <y> | /j/ not represented in spelling |
|---|---|---|
| /aɪ/ | | *shanghaiing; higher, highest, sighing; beautifying, defying, dryer, dyer, flyer, fryer, supplying,* plus:<br>– some words obeying the <y>-replacement rule (section 6.5), e.g. *alliance, amplifier, defiance, drier, flier;*<br>– the four words which obey the <ie>-replacement rule (section 6.6): *dying, lying, tying, vying;*<br>– two Oddities: *dyeing, eyeing.*<br>See also paragraph below Table |
| /eɪ/ | *betrayal, conveyance, layer, layette, obeying, playing, prayer* pronounced /ˈpreɪjə/ ('one who prays'), *preying, purveying, surveying* | *crocheting, inveighing, laity, neighing, ricocheting, segueing, weighing* |
| /ɔɪ/ | *annoyance, boyish, buoyant, cloying, destroyer, enjoying, joyous, toying* | |
| /iː/ | *jockeying, moneyer, volleying* | *absenteeism, agreeing, beauteous, fleeing, fre-er/est, liar, nauseous* pronounced /ˈnɔːziːjəs/, *orgiastic, precising, seeing, leylandii, fasciitis, skiing, taxiing,* plus many words obeying the <y>-replacement rule (section 6.5), e.g. *acrimonious, bolshi-er/est, calumniate, carrier, centurion, comedian, dalliance, dutiable, enviable, historian, industrial, luxuriance, melodious, memorial, remedial, studious, twentieth, thirtieth,* etc., *variable, variance* |

The words with stems ending in <y> which I've placed under '/j/ not represented in spelling' opposite /aɪ/ in Table 3.8 may seem not to belong there but in the other column. The <y> here could be analysed as representing both the /aɪ/ and the /j/, but this would be the only example in my entire analysis of a letter having two single-letter functions – in all other cases the dual-functioning letter's first function is as part of a di- or trigraph (see section 7.1). Also, none of the other words in this box would support such an analysis, and as it happens none of the digraphs ending in <y> which spell /aɪ/ occur word-finally (see section 5.7.3); hence there are no words to put in the left-hand box opposite /aɪ/.

Some further instances of 'invisible /j/' occur within suffixes, e.g. <-ial, -ian> /iːjəl, iːjən/ (though again Carney would assign these to /ɪə/).

And this pattern also occurs when stem words ending in /aɪ, eɪ, ɔɪ, iː/ are followed in running speech by a word beginning with a vowel phoneme. In all such cases there is a 'linking /j/' glide between the two words (see Cruttenden, 2014: 152), but again this is represented in the spelling only if the first word already ends in a digraph ending in <y>, otherwise not. Since this book is mainly concerned with stem words and their derivatives, only a few examples of inter-word /j/-glides not represented in the spelling will be given: *I understand* /aɪjʌndəˈstænd/, *inveigh against* /ɪnˈveɪjəˈɡeɪnst/, *'hoi polloi' is Greek* /ˈhɔɪpəˈlɔɪjɪzˈɡriːk/, *free offer* /friːˈjɒfə/.

See also the parallel phenomenon of 'linking /w/' (previous section), and the subtly different one of /r/-linking (section 3.6).

The only percentage stated by Carney (p.256) is 19% for /j/ spelt <y>. In order to work out other percentages I have ignored non-represented /j/. For /j/ spelt <i> I deduced a percentage as follows: Mines *et al.* (1978, Table A-1, p.236) show that the ratio of initial to medial /j/ is about 4:1. Since /j/ spelt <y> is very rare medially, and the Oddities and the 2-phoneme graphemes spelling sequences other than /juː/ are negligible, it is safe to take the 'junior partner' in this ratio as medial /j/ spelt <i>. Hence the figure of c.5% as the percentage for this spelling of /j/.

- It follows that 2-phoneme spellings of /juː/ constitute most of the remaining 76%. Carney (p.201) states that <u, u.e> are 82% of spellings of /juː/, hence {82% x 76%} = 62% of the spellings of /j/, and that <ew> is 15% of spellings of /juː/, hence {15% x 76%} = 11% of spellings of /j/. The remaining {100%−(19%+5%+62%+15%)} = 3% of spellings of /j/ are mainly the minority 2-phoneme spellings of /juː/, plus spellings of /jə, jʊə/.

# 4. How do you know when to write a consonant letter double?

For some people one of the main bugbears of English spelling is remembering to write, for example,
*accommodation* not *accomodation*
*occurred* not *occured*.

In a national survey of adults' spelling in England and Wales in 1995 using just 15 words, *accommodation* produced the most errors; 68% of the people in the survey got it wrong (see Basic Skills Agency, 1996).

Doubled consonant letters are a bugbear even though the doubled consonant spelling with the highest frequency for its phoneme is <ll> at only 18% of occurrences of /l/, and most other doubled consonant spellings are much less frequent. So in this chapter I provide some guidance on this – but be warned: the guidance does not and can not cover every word, so I end up saying 'The rest you just have to remember, or check in a dictionary'.

## 4.1 The easy bits

### 4.1.1 Consonant letters are never doubled at the beginning of a word

Well, hardly ever. There is *llama* (the animal, as opposed to *lama*, a Tibetan monk), and *llano* meaning a South American, treeless, grassy plain or steppe; also Welsh names like *Ffestiniog* and *Lloyd* – but I'm dealing with English, and not with names.

## 4.1.2 Some consonant letters are never or almost never written double: <h, j, q, v, w, x, y>

The rule that these seven letters are rarely doubled applies to the whole of the rest of this chapter, but I will mention it again where necessary. Almost all the exceptions occur in compound words, for example *bathhouse, beachhead, fishhook, hitchhiker, witchhunt* and *withhold*, where the first <h> is always part of a digraph or trigraph ending the first element of the compound word; also *bowwow, glowworm, powwow, skew(-)whiff* (usually spelt with the hyphen, however) and *slowworm*. There are also a few slang words with <vv>: *bevvy, bovver, chivvy* (also spelt *chivy*), *civvy, divvy, flivver, luvv-y/ie, navvy, revving, savvy, skivvy, spivv(er)y*. Some brandnames deliberately flout this rule, e.g. *Exxon*.

## 4.1.3 Doubled consonant letters are very rare after long vowels and diphthongs

– in stem words, that is, though they do of course arise from compounding and suffixation, e.g. *glowworm, keenness, preferring, really, referral, slowworm, warring*. Perhaps the only **classes** of exception are monosyllables ending in /ɑːf, ɑːs, ɔːl/ (the first two of these apply in RP but in few other accents), which are mainly spelt <-aff, -ass, -all>, e.g. *chaff, class, ball* (see /f, s, l/, sections 3.7.3, 3.7.6, 3.7.5). There are also stray individual exceptions, e.g. *bouffant, chauffeu-r/se, coiffeu-r/se, coiffure, feoffee, feoffment, pouffe, souffle; droll, plimsoll, poll, roll, scroll, stroll, toll; braille, camellia, chenille, Ewell, marseillaise, raillery, surveillance, thralldom* (also spelt *thraldom*), *tulle; arrhythmia* if pronounced with initial /eɪ/, *potpourri; caisson* if pronounced /ˈkeɪsən/ (also pronounced /kəˈsuːn/), *croissant, mousse, pelisse, renaissance* if pronounced /rəˈneɪsɒns/, *trousseau, voussoir; aitch, retch* if pronounced /riːtʃ/; *pizza*. Words with final <rr, rre, rred, rrh> (*charr, parr, err, chirr, shirr, skirr, whirr, burr, purr, barre, bizarre, parterre; abhorred, preferred, referred; catarrh, myrrh*) may look like exceptions too, but here <rr>, etc., are part of the spellings of the long vowel or diphthong (see /r/, section 3.5.8).

This rule also implies its converse, namely that single-letter spellings of consonant phonemes are regular after long vowels and diphthongs.

However, unfortunately the counterparts to these rules are very unreliable: after short vowels both single and double consonant letters occur with great frequency, and much of the rest of this chapter is an attempt to grapple with that.

For all four circumstances see Table 4.1, and for the grapheme–phoneme direction see Table 10.4 in section 10.42. Also, for an extended historical explanation of why both single and doubled consonant spellings occur after short vowels, see Crystal (2012), chapters 7 and 8.

TABLE 4.1: SINGLE AND DOUBLE CONSONANT SPELLINGS AFTER SHORT AND LONG VOWELS

|  | After long vowel/diphthong | After short vowel |
|---|---|---|
| **Single consonant letter** | Regular | Both occur, and doubled spellings are sometimes predictable but mostly not – see the rest of this chapter |
| **Doubled consonant spelling** | Very rare | |

## 4.2 The main consonant-doubling rule (Part 1 of 'double, drop or swop' – see sections 6.4-5)

[Acknowledgments: I owe the terms 'consonant-doubling', '<e>-deletion' and '<y>-replacement' largely to John Mountford, and the mnemonic 'double, drop or swop' for them (though I may have re-ordered it) to Jennifer Chew. I also owe the following insight to John Mountford.]

The three rules 'double, drop or swop' are mutually exclusive: no more than one of them can be applied to the same word at the same point (though a word with more than one suffix may exhibit more than one of them).

The consonant-doubling rule applies only to single stem-final consonant letters and when they double before suffixes beginning with a vowel letter. For this rule, word-final <y> counts as a vowel letter but still obeys the restriction that it never doubles, but medial <u> spelling /w/ (after <q>; there seem to be no instances relevant here after <g>) counts as a consonant letter. The rule mostly involves the verb endings <-ed, -ing>, but also applies to:

- the adjective suffixes <-able, -est, -y>, as in *regrettable, saddest, gassy, runny, starry*
- the noun suffixes <-age, ance, -ation>, as in *cribbage, scrummage, slippage, stoppage, tonnage; admittance, remittance, riddance; cancellation*; (with medial <u> = /w/) *quittance*
- the verb suffix <-en>, in *fatten, flatten, gladden, madden, redden, sadden*

- the noun and adjective suffix <-er>, as in *plodder, sadder*
- the noun and adjective suffix <-ery>, as in *cattery, jewellery, jobbery, lottery, nunnery, piggery, shrubbery, slippery, snobbery, tannery, thuggery*
- the noun suffix <-ess>, in *goddess* (only)
- the adjective suffix <-ous>, in *libellous, marvellous* (only).

To state the main consonant-doubling rule neatly we need the convention that <C> means 'any **single** consonant letter', <C*> means 'any consonant letter except those that never double' and <V> means 'any **single** vowel letter'.

So then **the main consonant-doubling rule** is:
1) In one-syllable words ending <CVC*>, double the final consonant letter before any suffix beginning with a vowel letter;
2) In two-syllable **verbs** ending <CVC*>, double the final consonant letter before any suffix beginning with a vowel letter if the last syllable of the stem is stressed or if (in British but not US spelling) the last letter of the stem is <l>.
3) Otherwise, do not double the final consonant letter.

The second part of the rule applies where the **stem** is a two-syllable verb, regardless of what part of speech the suffixed form is.

Examples:
- words formed from one-syllable nouns and adjectives: *clubbable, fitter, furry, gassy, goddess, mannish, matting, sadder, saddest, skittish, starry, trekkie*; (with medial <u> = /w/) *quizzable, quizzical* (even though the doubling makes these words break two other rules – see sections 4.4.5-6), *quiddity, squaddie*

    Extension: *pittance* has <tt> despite being derived not from a one-syllable English word but, via French, from the Latin noun *pietas*; at no stage before entering English did it have <tt>.

    Exception: *ladette*, which by the main consonant-doubling rule should be *laddette – but perhaps the shift of stress to the last syllable makes the difference.

- words formed from one-syllable verbs: *banned, biddable, fitted, hopping, penned, plodder, riddance, riggable* (of sails or an election), *rotten, running, runny, slippage, slippery, starring, stoppage, swimmable, whammy*; (with medial <u> = /w/) *quipped, quittance, squatter*

    Partial exception: Although the plural of the noun *bus* can only be spelt *buses*, the late 20th-century conversion of this word into a verb caused confusion over what its derived forms should be, so that dictionaries now show both *buses, busing, bused* and *busses, bussing, bussed*. The first set look as though the stem vowel might be pronounced /juː/ rather than /ʌ/, but the second set are all forms of the archaic verb *to buss* meaning 'to kiss' – take your pick.

- two-syllable verbs formed from one-syllable adjectives by adding <-en>: *fatten, flatten, gladden, madden, redden, sadden*
  Extension: Several past participles of irregular ('strong') one-syllable verbs are also formed this way: *bitten, (for)bidden, ((mis)be/for/ill-)gotten, hidden, ridden, smitten, written*. In all of these except *(for)bidden* the stem vowel phoneme changes. On the two-syllable verb forms in this bullet point and the previous one see also section 4.3.5.
- two-syllable verbs with stress on last syllable: *abetted, abhorrence, admittance, allotted, beginning, committal, debarred, demurring, deterrence, forgetting, interred, occurred, recurrence, regrettable, transmittable*; (with medial <u> = /w/) *acquittal, equipped, equipping*
  Contrast two-syllable verbs with stress on first syllable: *coveted, focusing, focused, laundered, marketing, merited, targeted* – some prefer the spellings *focussing, *focussed* but the second <s> is unnecessary, since it is unlikely in this case (given that the stress is on the first syllable) that the spellings with <s> would suggest pronunciations with /juː/ rather than /ə/. Also contrast *benefited* (where again the doubling in *benefitted* is unnecessary).
- two-syllable verbs ending in *-fer* stressed on last syllable: *conferring, deferring, preferred, referral*
  Contrast two-syllable verbs ending in *-fer* stressed on first syllable: *differed, offering, proffered, sufferance*.
  In this category, if the suffix constitutes a separate syllable (<-al, -ance, -ing>), whether the <r> doubles or not, /r/-linking occurs – see section 3.6 – and the <rr, r> is both a grapheme in its own right spelling /r/ and part of a larger grapheme <err, er> spelling /ɜː, ə/ respectively. For dual-functioning see section 7.1.
- two-syllable verbs ending in <l>, British spelling:
  (stress on first syllable) *cancellation, counsellor, cudgelling, gambolled, labelled, leveller, libellous, marvellous, pedalling, quarrelling, signalling, traveller*
  (stress on second syllable) *(un)controllable, compelled, enrolled, excelled, fulfilling, propellor, rebellion*

Compare US spelling:
(stress on first syllable) *cancelation, counselor, cudgeling, gamboled, labeled, leveler, libelous, marvelous, pedaling, quarreling, signaling, traveler*
(stress on second syllable) *(un)controllable, compelled, enrolled, excelled, fulfilling, propellor, rebellion.*
Also contrast three-syllable verbs: *(un)paralleled*.
Extension: The two-syllable verbs *dial, trial* and the three-syllable verb *initial* double the <l> in British spelling, despite having a vowel letter and not a consonant letter before the <a>: *dialling, trialled, initialled* (cf. US *dialing, trialed, initialed*).
Other extensions:

- *diagrammatic, programmatic* have <mm>, for (Greek) etymological reasons
- *caravanner, caravanning, wainscotting* have <nn, tt>, presumably to prevent the third <a> or the <o> in the stems appearing to be pronounced /eɪ, əʊ/
- *questionnaire* has <nn> – but *millionaire* has <n>. No explanation of the difference suggests itself

• Two-syllable verbs that end in the single consonant letter <c> after a vowel letter mostly double it to <ck> before <-ed, -ing>: *frolicking, mimicking, panicking, picnicked, shellacked*. This also applies to the three-syllable verb *bivouacked* and, by further extension, to the adjectives *panicky, rheumaticky* (*finicky* appears to be a stem word). On 11 March 2013 in a column for the *Guardian* a Kenyan denied that his country would be '*banana-republicked*'. But the principle is not extended to the one-syllable verb *arc*, which has the forms *arced, arcing*, not *\*arcked, \*arcking*. If the verb *spec* meaning 'draw up a specification' has derived forms they might also be *speced, specing* rather than *\*specked, \*specking* (since these might derive from *speck*). And *speccy* ('derogatory name for a person who wears spectacles') belongs to a different group of exceptions (see under /k/ spelt <cc> in section 3.7.1).
Exceptions: *conference, deference, preference, reference* do not have <rr> because the stress has shifted to the first syllable (and the vowel in <fer> may be elided – see section 6.10); contrast *conferring, deferring, preferred, referral*; and compare *referee*, with stress shifted to the final syllable, and <r>

- the verbs *infer, transfer* do not double the <r> before <-able>: *inferable, transferable*, presumably because there is variation in which syllable is stressed: /traːnsˈfɜːrəbəl/ vs /ˈtraːnsfrəbəl/ – for the elided vowel in the latter pronunciation see section 6.10
- where a two-syllable compound verb has a monosyllabic verb as its last element, consonant-doubling occurs even if the stress is on the first syllable: *inputting, leapfrogged*
- some two-syllable verbs with stress on the first syllable double the final consonant to avoid the vowel in the last syllable of the stem looking as if it should be pronounced long: *formatted, hobnobbing, kidnapped, worshipper*.

Oddities: The independent noun *chancellor*, the noun *tranquillity* and verb *tranquillise* which are based on a two-syllable adjective, the noun *teetotaller* which is based on a three-syllable adjective, and the seven words *coralline, crystalline, crystallise, panellist, pupillage, rascally, sibylline* which are based on two-syllable nouns (so none of these words are based on two-syllable verbs), nevertheless have <ll> before endings beginning with a vowel letter in British spelling (but not in US spelling: *chancelor, tranquility, coraline, crystaline, crystalize, panelist, pupilage, rascaly, sibyline*) for no reason that I can find, except perhaps a mistaken analogy with words based on two-syllable verbs. Also, the adjective *woollen* has <ll> in British spelling (but the US spelling is *woolen*), and *woolly* has <ll> in both systems. And the British spelling of the adjective *weaselly* has <ll> (US spelling allows both *weaselly* and *weasely*).

## 4.3 Other hints for writing a consonant letter double

### 4.3.1 Where the two parts of a compound word, or an affix and a stem, have adjacent identical consonant letters, the consonant letter is written double

- If the second part of a compound word begins with the same consonant letter as the first part ends in, the consonant letter is written double: *bathhouse, beachhead, fishhook, glowworm, headdress, hitchhiker, penname, slowworm, stepparent, still-life, withhold*. As already noted, this list contains some of the few examples where letters which are rarely written double do occur double. There are various exceptions, the most frequent being *grandad* which in my opinion should be spelt *granddad*. For others, see section 4.4.7.

- If a suffix begins with the same consonant letter as the stem ends in, the consonant letter is written double: *actually, keenness, soulless*.
- If a prefix ends in the same consonant letter as the stem begins with, the consonant letter is written double, for example *dissatisfy, illegible, immature, innate, irreplaceable, misspell, overrun, pellucid, subbranch, transsonic, unnatural*. The problem here is knowing which word-beginnings are prefixes (this is clear enough with <mis-, over-, sub-, trans-, un->, although there are few words beginning *miss-, overr-, subb-, transs-* or *unn-*) but otherwise often needs etymological knowledge. For example, in *announce* and *assimilate*, the doubled consonant letters arise historically from assimilation of the Latin prefix *ad-* to the first consonant of the stem, and in *pellucid* from assimilation of the Latin prefix *per-*, but this is not much help – mostly you just have to remember, that is develop a feel for the pattern of, which words have a doubled consonant letter in this position and which do not.

## 4.3.2 Monosyllabic content words with /VC/ structure have a double consonant letter: the Three-Letter Rule

The entire list of words to which this 'rule' applies is *add, all, ass, ebb, egg, ell, ill, inn, odd, off* (contrast the function words *as, in, of*), and the name *Ann*, and within this list the doubling in *all, ass, ell, ill, off* is regular anyway. In terms of spelling, this rule also applies to *err* (contrast the filler word *er*) even though its pronunciation is a single long vowel and contains no consonant (in RP). In all, however, where consonant-doubling is concerned, this rule seems to apply only to the 12 three-letter words just listed.

Exceptions: *ad* (advert(isement)), *el, em, en* (old-fashioned printers' terms for sizes of spaces), *id*.

This is part of a general tendency in English that content words must be spelt with at least three letters, even if they contain only one or two phonemes and therefore could be spelt with fewer than three letters. Other examples are:

- (one-phoneme words) *awe, aye, eye, ore, owe* (contrast the function words *I, oh, or*)
- (two-phoneme words) *bee, buy, bye, hie, high, hoe, low, know, sew, sow, wee* (contrast the function words *be, by, Hi!, ho* (exclamation of surprise), *lo, no, so, we*), plus *ate* pronounced /et/, *bow, car* (cf. the vehicle name *Ka*), *chi* (and this Greek letter name does indeed have the alternative spelling *ki*), *die, doe* (but the spelling *do* is pre-empted), *dough, dye, ewe, far, fee, feo, fie, foe* (contrast *Fo*, as in *Fee, Fie, ..., Fum* – but is *Fo* a word?), *guy, joe, key, knee, lea, lee, lie, lye, mow, nigh, pea, pee, pie, poh, quay, roe, row, sea, see, sigh, tea, tee, toe* (but the spelling *to* is pre-empted), *tow, rue, rye, vie, whoa, woe, yew*.

Some of the positional spelling constraints of English help to maintain the three-letter rule. For example, if it were generally acceptable to spell word-final /dʒ/ with <j> then *edge* could be spelt *ej*. This spelling would observe the rule against doubling <j>; *ejj* would be an even odder spelling (the <jj> in *hajj*, now the accepted spelling of the word for the Muslim pilgrimage, reflects the doubled pronunciation of the final consonant in Arabic). Some of the common digraphs also help to maintain the three-letter rule; for example, *ash* would consist of two letters if English had a one-letter grapheme for /ʃ/.

Three-phoneme content words containing /ks/ are mostly written with two letters, using <x>; *ax* (in US spelling; contrast British *axe*), *ex* (contrast the river-name *Exe*), *ox* and the Greek letter name *xi*. However, the examples just cited appear to be the only 3-phoneme words in the language containing the sequence /ks/. There are about 15 three-phoneme words containing /juː/, which can be spelt <u>, and these words could therefore also in theory be written with two letters. However, only the Greek letter names *mu* and *nu* are written this way, and all the rest are written with at least three letters: *cue, dew, due, few, hew, hue, lieu, mew* (homophone of *mu*), *gnu, knew, new* (these last three being homophones of *nu*), *pew, queue, view*. And neither *ewe* nor *you* would ever be written *u or *yu (cep wen txtng, fcors).

Other function words spelt with fewer than three letters are *a, ah, am, an, as, at, er, he, I, if, in, is, it, me, my, of, on, so, to, up, us, we, ye*. *Do* and *go*, despite often being content words, make do with two letters because of their other use as auxiliary verbs; in contrast, the function word *are* has three letters even though it could be spelt *ar* like the filler word (but this would make the contracted forms *they'r, *we'r, *you'r look very odd).

Other content words which are spelt with two letters (and are therefore exceptions to the three-letter rule) are *ma, pa, pi* (the Greek letter name and numerical constant; contrast *pie*), *ta* ('thanks'; contrast *tar*), and the musical terms *do, re, mi, fa, so, la, ti*.

## 4.3.3 Consonant phonemes /b d f g k p t z/ are almost always spelt with double letters before final /əl/ spelt <-le> where the immediately preceding vowel phoneme is short, stressed and spelt with a single letter

Examples:
*babble, dabble, gabble, rabble, scrabble, pebble, dibble, dribble, nibble, scribble, bobble, cobble, gobble, hobble, nobble, wobble, bubble, rubble, stubble;*
*addle, skedaddle, paddle, saddle, staddle, straddle, swaddle, twaddle, waddle, meddle, peddle, Biddle, diddle, fiddle, griddle, middle, piddle, riddle, twiddle, widdle, coddle, doddle, noddle, toddle, cuddle, (be)fuddle, huddle, muddle, puddle;*
*baffle, raffle, snaffle, waffle, piffle, riffle, skiffle, sniffle, whiffle, duffle, kerfuffle, muffle, ruffle, scuffle, shuffle, snuffle, truffle;*
*(be)draggle, gaggle, haggle, raggle-taggle, snaggle, straggle, waggle, giggle, jiggle, niggle, wiggle, wriggle, boggle, boondoggle, goggle, hornswoggle, joggle, toggle, woggle, juggle, muggle, smuggle, snuggle, struggle;*
*cackle, crackle, hackle, (ram)shackle, tackle; freckle, heckle, speckle; fickle, mickle, pickle, prickle, sickle, stickle, tickle, trickle; cockle; buckle, chuckle, knuckle, muckle, suckle, truckle;*
*apple, dapple, grapple, cripple, nipple, ripple, stipple, tipple, topple, supple; (em)battle, cattle, prattle, rattle, tattle, wattle, fettle, kettle, mettle, nettle, settle, brittle, little, skittle, spittle, tittle, whittle, bottle, dottle, mottle, pottle, throttle, cuttlefish, scuttle, shuttle, Suttle;*
*(be)dazzle, frazzle, razzle-dazzle, embezzle, drizzle, fizzle, frizzle, grizzle, mizzle, sizzle, swizzle, nozzle, s(c)hemozzle, schnozzle, guzzle, muzzle, nuzzle, puzzle.*

Also *squabble, quibble, squiggle* if the <u> in these words is counted (as it should be) as a consonant letter.

Most of the words in this list belong to the less formal/more Anglo-Saxon part of the vocabulary. This rule is one of the only two situations in which <zz> is the regular spelling of /z/, since /z/ is never spelt <s, ss, z> in this position.

Exceptions: *chattel, subtle, treble, triple* (if these words followed this rule they would be spelt *°chattle, °suttle, °trebble, °tripple* – and, as shown above, there is a surname spelt *Suttle*).

Extensions (1): Where the consonant between the vowel and <-le> is /s/ it is mainly spelt <st> (see section 3.7.6): *nestle, pestle, trestle, wrestle; bristle, epistle, gristle, mistle thrush* (also spelt *missel thrush*), *thistle, Thistlethwaite, Twistleton, whistle; apostle, jostle, Postlethwaite, throstle; bustle, hustle, rustle.* This extension also applies to *mistletoe* even though the <-le> is not word-final. Sub-exceptions: *hassle* (but I once received an email with this word spelt *°hastle*, showing the power of the <st> sub-rule), *tussle* which conform to the main rule above, plus *muscle*, which conforms to neither the main rule nor this sub-rule about medial /s/ (nor does *corpuscle*, but since it is stressed on the first syllable it does not fall under the main rule), and *missel thrush* in that spelling.

Extensions (2): There are also a few words where the other conditions are met (consonant preceding final /əl/ not in the set /l, m, n, r/ or in the set which never double, vowel preceding that stressed, short and spelt with one letter) but the final /əl/ is not spelt <-le> which nevertheless have the consonant spelt double: *chattel, cudgel, duffel, estoppel, fossil, glottal, jackal, missal, missel thrush* in that spelling, *mussel, nickel, offal, rebuttal, satchel, tassel, vassal, vessel, wittol* and a few words in <-ittal> which are derived forms obeying the main consonant-doubling rule: *(ac)quittal, committal, remittal.* This list contains the only words, apparently, in the entire language with final /əl/ preceded by /dʒ, tʃ/ spelt double as <dg, tch>: *cudgel, satchel.*

There are no words following this pattern in which the consonant phoneme before the /əl/ is /m, n, r/, that is, none spelt <*-mmle, *-nnle, *-rrle> (for a possible reason see the end of section 4.4.3) – contrast *mammal, pommel, pummel, trammel; channel, flannel, fennel, kennel, funnel, runnel, tunnel; barrel, sorrel;* also *quarrel, squirrel* if the <u> in these words too is counted as a consonant letter. Also, it would be odd if the consonant phoneme before the /əl/ were /l/ – the only word with a short, stressed vowel followed by /l/ followed by /əl/ appears to be the obsolete word *fallal* ('trinket'). And by definition this rule cannot apply to <h, j, q, v, w, x, y> even though, for example, *axle, hovel* could in theory be spelt *°axxle, °hovvle.*

For the converse of this rule, see sections 4.4.2–3 below.

The sets of consonant phonemes to which this rule does or does not apply cut across those which are mainly written double or single at the end of one-syllable words after a short vowel spelt with one letter – see Table 4.2.

TABLE 4.2: NON-EQUIVALENCE OF SETS OF CONSONANT PHONEMES SPELT DOUBLE IN TWO SITUATIONS

|  | Consonant phonemes which are mainly written double at the end of one-syllable words after a short vowel spelt with one letter | Consonant phonemes which are mainly written single at the end of one-syllable words after a short vowel spelt with one letter |
|---|---|---|
| Consonant phonemes which are mainly written double between a stressed short vowel spelt with one letter and word-final /əl/ spelt <-le> | /k f s* z/ | /b d g p t/ |
| Consonant phonemes to which the rule above does not apply | /tʃ dʒ l v/ | /m n/ |

*/s/ is mainly spelt <ss> word-finally and <st> medially in these circumstances.

Consonant phonemes to which both rules are irrelevant: /h r w j/ because they do not occur word-finally, and /ŋ ʃ ʒ θ ð/ because they have no one-letter word-final spelling.

## 4.3.4 More generally, consonant letters are mostly written double in the middle of two-syllable words where the immediately preceding vowel phoneme is short and written with a single letter

Unlike the previous rule, this one applies only to two-syllable words, but regardless of which syllable is stressed. Examples and exceptions (none of which have final /əl/ because of the preceding section) are listed in Table 4.3, grouped in order of the phonemes in Table 2.1.

As Table 4.3 shows, /v/ is the only phoneme in this position for which one-letter spellings are in the majority – see also section 4.4.3.

TABLE 4.3: EXAMPLES OF AND EXCEPTIONS TO THE RULE THAT TWO-SYLLABLE WORDS HAVE MEDIAL CONSONANT LETTERS WRITTEN DOUBLE AFTER A SHORT VOWEL PHONEME WRITTEN WITH A SINGLE LETTER

| Phoneme | Examples | Exceptions |
|---|---|---|
| /b/ | abbey, abbot, bobbin, cabbage, gibbous, hobbit, hobby, hubbub, rabbit, ribbon, robber, rubber, rubbish, Sabbath, stubborn | abet, cabin, robin, suburb |
| /d/ | adduce, buddy, haddock, judder, midden, sodden, sudden | adit, edit |
| /g/ | beggar, dagger, haggis, jagged, maggot, nugget, ragged, rugged, rugger, sluggish, trigger | vigour |
| /m/ | ammo, command, commend, commie, commit, common, commute, gammon, grammar, hammock, hummock, immense, immerse, lemma, mummy, slummock, stammer, summer, summit, summon(s) | amuse, camel, comet, damage, famine, gamut, lemon, premise, promise |
| /n/ | annex(e), announce, annoy, banner, bonnet, cannon, channel, connect, dinner, fennel, flannel, funnel, ginnel, innate, kennel, penny, runnel, tenner, tunnel | banish, canard, canon, enough, menace, money, onyx, penance, planet, punish, tenor |
| /p/ | appal, appeal, appear, apply, approve, copper, happy, hippy, oppose, puppet, supper, tappet | epic |
| /t/ | attack, attempt, attend, attract, better, butter, button, buttress, ghetto, glitter, jitter(s), latter, letter, mattress, rattan, rotten, scatter, tattoo, tittup, written | atom |
| /r/ | arrange, arrest, barrow, berry, borrow, burrow, carriage, carrot, carry, cherry, correct, derrick, garrotte, herring, horrid, hurry, lorry, marriage, mirror, morrow, parrot, porridge, quarry, serrate, sorrow, sorry, squirrel, stirrup, terrine, terror, warrant, wherry, worrit, worry | cherish, cherub, larynx, tarot |
| /z/ | none spelt with <zz>, but cf. dessert, dissolve, hussar, possess, scissors | none spelt with <z>, but cf. bosom, busy, closet, risen |
| /k/ | account, hiccup, occur, peccary, soccer, speccy | decade, vacuum |

TABLE 4.3: EXAMPLES AND EXCEPTIONS OF THE RULE THAT TWO-SYLLABLE WORDS HAVE MEDIAL CONSONANT LETTERS WRITTEN DOUBLE AFTER A SHORT VOWEL PHONEME WRITTEN WITH A SINGLE LETTER, CONT.

| Phoneme | Examples | Exceptions |
|---|---|---|
| /f/ | affair, affect, affirm, affix, afflict, afford, affray, affright, affront, buffer, boffin, buffoon, caffeine, chaffinch, chiffchaff, chiffon, coffee, coffer, coffin, differ, diffuse, efface, effect, effete, effort, gaffer, griffin, guffaw, jiffy, muffin, offal, offend, offer, office, proffer, puffin, riffraff, saffron, scaffold, suffer, suffice, suffix, suffrage, suffuse, tiffin, toffee. Also, with long vowel in first syllable, chauffeu-r/se, coiffure, souffle | before, default, defeat, defect, defence, defend, defer, defile, defunct – but all of these are regular because of the prefixes. Also, with long vowel in first syllable, gofer, tofu, tufa, wafer |
| /l/ | allay, allege, allot, allow, alloy, allude, allure, ally, ballet, balloon, billet, bullet, bully, callous, callow, challenge, collage, collapse, collar, collate, colleague, collect, college, collide, collie, collude, ellipse, fellow, follow, pallet, pallor, pillar, pollute, shallot, silly, swallow, trellis, wallet; also billion, brilliant, colliery, million if pronounced with two syllables | balance, chalet, choler, colour, column, felon, lily, malice, olive, palace, palate, police, salad, salon, scholar, solemn, talent |
| /s/ | assent, assert, assess, assume, blossom, cosset, cussed (/'kʌsɪd/ 'stubborn'), gossip, massive, missive, posset | |
| /v/ | bevvy, bovver, chivvy (also spelt chivy), civvy, divvy, flivver, luvvy/ie, navvy, revving, savvy, skivvy | bevel, carvel, cavil, chervil, chivy (also spelt chivvy), civil, clever, coven, covet, devil, ever, evil, frivol, gavel, govern, gravel, grovel, hovel, larval, level, marvel, naval, navel, never, novel, oval, prevent, serval, travel, ravel, revel, shovel, shrivel, snivel, swivel |

Many more double consonants in two-syllable words result from affixation and the main consonant-doubling rule, e.g. *misspelt, misspent, sub-branch; fitter, fully, furry, goddess, mannish, matting, sadder, saddest, starry; fitted, hopping, plodder, riddance, running, starring; fatten, flatten, gladden, madden, redden, sadden, gotten, bitten, hidden, ridden, smitten, written.*

Extension: This pattern also applies not only to /k/ spelt <ck>, e.g. *beckon, chicken, cricket, gecko, jacket, pocket, reckon, rocket, sprocket,* but also to /dʒ, tʃ/ spelt <dg, tch>, e.g. *badger, bludgeon, budget, budgie, codger, fidget, gadget, ledger, midget, todger, widget; butcher, crotchet, hatchet, ketchup, kitchen, ratchet, scutcheon, wretched.*

However, most two-syllable words ending in <-ic, -id, -it, -ule> do not obey this rule – see section 4.4.6. And by definition this rule too cannot apply to <h, j, q, w, x, y>.

For the converse of this rule, see section 4.4.4 below.

## 4.3.5 At the end of one-syllable words where the preceding vowel phoneme is short and spelt with a single letter the following consonant phonemes are mostly written double: /k tʃ f dʒ l s z v/

This generalisation brings together the rules for these consonants stated individually in sections 3.7.1–8.

Examples: *back, hick, quick, rock, sack, sick, tick, hutch, itch, match, duff, off, badge, bodge, fill, full, shall, buss, fuss, puss, jazz, dove, shove*

Exceptions: *hic, roc, sac, sic, tic, much, rich, such, chef, clef, deaf, if, veg, Czech, flak, suk, trek, yak, col, gal, gel* (both pronunciations and meanings), *mil, nil, pal, bus, gas, plus, pus, this, thus, us, yes, as, cos* (in both pronunciations /kɒz, kɒs/), *has, his, is, was, gov, guv, lav, of, rev, shiv, sov, spiv*

# 4.4 Hints for *not* writing consonant letters double

## 4.4.1 At the end of one-syllable words where the preceding vowel phoneme is short and spelt with a single letter the following consonant phonemes are mostly written single: /b d g m n p t/

This generalisation brings together the rules for these consonants stated individually in sections 3.5.1–7.

Examples: *rob, bad, dog, jam, run, lap, put*

Exceptions: *ebb, add, odd, rudd, Sudd, egg, Ann, inn, Lapp, bott, butt, matt, mitt, mutt, putt, watt.*

There appear to be no exceptions ending <-mm>. Six of the exception words obey the /VC/ part of the 'Three-Letter Rule' – see section 4.3.2.

## 4.4.2 When do you not write consonant phonemes /b d f g k p t z/ with double letters before final /əl/ spelt <-le>?

In other words, when does the rule in 4.3.3 above not apply? When any of the conditions mentioned there is missing, namely:

- where the immediately preceding vowel is unstressed, e.g. *laughable, visible* and all the other words ending in /əbəl/ (see section 6.6), plus *article, carbuncle, multiple, principle, tubercle, ventricle*
- where the preceding vowel is short and stressed but spelt with more than one letter, namely *couple, double, treadle, trouble*. These are the only exceptions in this category; if they followed the main 'stressed short vowel + single consonant phoneme + /əl/' pattern they would be spelt *cupple, *dubble, *treddle, *trubble
- where the preceding vowel is stressed but long, e.g. *able, bamboozle, bauble, beadle, beagle, beetle, bible, boodle, bridle, bugle, burble, chortle, circle, cradle, curdle, cycle, dawdle, disciple, doodle, eagle, fable, feeble, foible, garble, gargle, gurgle, hurtle, idle, inveigle, kirtle, ladle, maple, marble, myrtle, needle, noodle, noble, ogle, people, poodle, purple, rifle, rouble, scruple, sidle, sparkle, staple, startle, steeple, stifle, table, title, tousle, treacle, trifle, turtle, warble, wheedle*
- where there are two consonant phonemes between the stressed, short vowel and the /əl/, e.g. *amble, ample, assemble, bramble, brindle, bumble, bundle, candle, cantle, crumble, crumple, dandle, dimple, dissemble, dwindle, ensemble, example, fondle, fumble, gamble, gentle, grumble, handle, humble, jumble, kindle, mantle, mumble, nimble, pimple, ramble, resemble, ramble, rumble, rumple, sample, scramble, shamble(s), simple, spindle, stumble, swindle, temple, thimble, trample, tremble, trundle, tumble, uncle, wimple*; also the group in /ŋgəl/ spelt <-ngle>: *angle, bangle, bungle, dangle, dingle, jangle, jingle, jungle, mangle, mingle, shingle, single, spangle, strangle, tangle, tingle, wangle, wrangle.*

But note (for its relevance to the next section) that all these categories of exception still spell final /əl/ with <-le>.

The rule in section 4.3.3 also mostly does not apply (but see the words listed towards the end of section 4.3.3) where the /əl/ ending is not written <-le>, e.g. *pedal, rebel, shekel*.

## 4.4.3 Digression: When do you not spell final /əl/ as <-le>?

Strictly speaking this section does not belong in a chapter on doubled and single consonant spellings (logically it belongs under /ə/ in section 5.4.7), but its relevance will become apparent at the end of this section; and it arises pretty directly out of the last paragraph in the previous section, where spellings of word-final /əl/ other than <-le> are mentioned.

Three categories where final /əl/ is not spelt <-le> have already been mentioned:

- The words listed at the end of section 4.3.3 where the preceding consonant is spelt double even though the final /əl/ is not spelt <-le>
- Words with the 'short vowel + single consonant phoneme + /əl/' pattern in which the consonant phoneme is /m, n, r/. These are almost all spelt with <-el> even though the consonant is spelt double: *pommel, pummel, trammel; channel, flannel, fennel, kennel, funnel, runnel, tunnel; barrel, quarrel, sorrel, squirrel*. Exception: *mammal*
- Words where the medial consonant is /v/ (this list expands on those above): *anvil, approval* and several other nouns ending in /uːvəl/ spelt <-oval>, *(ar)rival* and many other nouns and adjectives ending in /aɪvəl/ spelt <-ival>, *bevel, carnival, carvel, cavil, chervil, civil, coeval* and various other words ending in <-eval>, *devil, dishevel, drivel, estival, evil, festival, frivol, gavel, gingival, gravel, grovel, hovel, interval, larval, level, marvel, naval, navel, novel, oval, (un)ravel, retrieval, revel, serval, shovel, shrivel, snivel, swivel, travel, upheaval, valval, weevil*.

This list of words with medial /v/ illustrates very clearly most of the range of other spellings for final /əl/: <-al, -el, -il, -ol>. (The only ones not illustrated are <-ul, -yl>, which are very rare and do not occur with medial /v/.) But it also raises the question: can any rules be given for when to use each of these six possible spellings of final /əl/ other than <-le>?

(Here I ignore the words where final /əl/ is spelt <l>, since there are only three words in this set: *axolotl, dirndl, shtetl*).

Carney (1994: 346) points out that the following three categories mainly have <-al>:

- nouns formed from verbs: *appraisal, approval, arousal, avowal, betrothal, dispersal, disposal, espousal, perusal, proposal, recital, refusal, renewal, reversal, withdrawal*
- adjectives formed from nouns: *basal, bridal, brutal, causal, central, colloidal, digital, fatal, formal, fugal, homicidal, modal, orbital, oriental, primal, spinal, spiral, thermal, tidal, tonal, triumphal, universal*
- adjectives based on bound forms: *conjugal, dental, final, frugal, fungal, glottal, legal, marital, mental, municipal, mural, natal, nominal, ordinal, papal, principal, regal, renal, skeletal, vital.*

He also points out that words ending in /əkəl, ɪkəl/ may be spelt <-acle, -icle, -ical> – for all of these see section 4.4.6.

Beyond this the contexts become so specific and any 'rules' so complicated that it seems simpler to give lists:
- words ending in <-al>: *admiral, animal, arsenal, cannibal, caracal, coral, crystal, cymbal, dental, dismal, floral, gimbal, hospital, hymnal, (im)partial, initial, jackal, journal, legal, lethal, local, madrigal, mammal, marshal, martial, medal* (cf. *meddle*), *memorial, metal* (cf. *mettle*), *missal, narwhal, nuptial, offal, opal, parental, pedal* (cf. *peddle*), *petal, plural, rascal, sacral, sandal, scandal, sepal, several, signal, sisal, spatial, substantial, total, vandal, vassal, ventral, vocal*
- words ending in <-el>: *angel, apparel, babel, betel, bezel, brothel, bushel, calomel, camel, cancel, caramel, carpel, chancel, chapel, charnel, chisel, cockerel, colonel, corbel, counsel, damsel, diesel, doggerel, easel, enamel, evangel, gospel, grapnel, hazel, hostel, kernel, label, laurel, libel, lintel, mackerel, mantel, minstrel, model, mongrel, morsel, nickel, panel, parcel, pastel, petrel, rebel* (noun and verb), *scalpel, scoundrel, sentinel, shekel, shrapnel, snorkel, sorrel, spandrel, timbrel, tinsel, wastrel, weasel, yodel, yokel*
- words ending in <-il>: *April, basil, council, fossil, gerbil, lentil, nostril, pencil, pupil, stencil, tonsil*
- words ending in <-ol>: *carol, gambol, idol, Mongol, petrol, symbol*
- words ending in <-ul>: *consul, mogul*
- words ending in <-yl>: *beryl, (ptero)dactyl, sibyl.*

Some of the words listed in this section ending in <-il, -yl> may be pronounced with /ɪl/ rather than /əl/, but very few have this pronunciation consistently. Reflecting on my own accent I think I have /ɪl/ only in *anvil, gerbil, nostril* and *(ptero)dactyl*; also in *idyll* and the few compound words ending in *-phyll*.

Why is there such a contrast in the spellings of final /əl/ between those with <-le> and those with <a, e, i, o, u, y> followed by <l>? I think the prime reason for this variation is whether the stem word, when suffixed with an ending which begins with a vowel phoneme and adds a syllable, retains a schwa vowel before the /l/ or not: where /ə/ is not retained, the spelling is <-le>, otherwise one of the other possibilities. Consider Table 4.4, which is certainly not definitive and where <l>-doubling (in British spelling) is ignored, but to which I have yet to find any exceptions.

TABLE 4.4: SOME CASES WHERE STEM WORDS ENDING IN /əl/ DO OR DO NOT RETAIN /ə/ BEFORE A SUFFIX BEGINNING WITH A VOWEL PHONEME

| with /ə/ when suffixed – none spelt with <-le> before suffixation | without /ə/ when suffixed - all spelt with <-le> before suffixation |
|---|---|
| cannibalism, hospitalise, journalese, mammalian, medallion, metallic, pedalling, rascally, scandalous, signalling, vandalism; angelic, cancelling, caramelise, channelling, chiselling, cudgelling, evangelise, flannelling, pummelling, quarrelling, rebellion, squirrelling, tunnelling, yodelling; councillor, fossilise, pupillage; carolling, gambolling, idolatry, symbolism; consulate; beryllium, sibylline | angling, assemblage, babbling, baffling, beagling, bottling, bristling, burglar, chaplain, chortling, coddling, crackling, cuddling, doubly, drizzling, dwindling, embezzler, fiddling, gambling, heckler, jangling, jostling, meddling, muddler, muffler, multiply (verb or adverb), nestling, niggling, peddling, rattling, rippling, rustling, saddler, smuggler, startling, straggler, tattler, trickling, trifling, visibly, whistling, wrestling |

A tiny piece of evidence in favour of my theory might be this. Consider the words *gambol, gamble; pedal, peddle*. As stem words these form two pairs of homophones pronounced /ˈgæmbəl, ˈpedəl/, but when suffixed with /ɪŋ/ they become (in my accent) two minimal pairs:

*gambolling* /ˈgæmbəlɪŋ/ v. /ˈgæmblɪŋ/ *gambling*
*pedalling* /ˈpedəlɪŋ/ v. /ˈpedlɪŋ/ *peddling*

and the schwa is elided (see section 6.10) only in the words which have final /əl/ spelt <-le> – or, to put this more phonologically, the <-le> spelling occurs only where the schwa is elided.

## 4.4.4 When do you not write doublable consonant letters double in the middle of two-syllable words (other than those ending in /əl/)?

In other words, when does the rule in 4.3.4 above not apply? When either of the conditions mentioned there is missing, namely:
- where the preceding vowel is long, e.g. *auburn, phoneme, pony* – this category is very large; *bouffant* and other polysyllables listed in section 4.1.3 are sub-exceptions, having a preceding long vowel, yet having their medial consonants spelt double
- where the preceding vowel is short but spelt with more than one letter, namely *breeches, courage, cousin, flourish, heifer, jealous, meadow, nourish, peasant, pheasant, pleasant, ready, steady, weapon, woofer* pronounced /ˈwʊfə/, *zeal-ot/ous* – this category is very small, probably containing only these 16 words; *Aussie* is a sub-exception, having its preceding short vowel spelt with two letters, yet having its medial consonant spelt double. Possible additions might seem to be *heaven, heavy, leaven* but medial /v/ is hardly ever spelt <vv>.

## 4.4.5 The third syllable from the end of a word rarely ends in a doubled consonant letter

Examples and exceptions not arising from affixation (none of which have final /əl/ because of section 4.4.3) are listed in Table 4.5, grouped in order of the phonemes in Table 2.1.

TABLE 4.5: EXAMPLES OF THE RULE THAT THE THIRD SYLLABLE FROM THE END OF A WORD RARELY ENDS IN A DOUBLED CONSONANT LETTER, WITH EXCEPTIONS NOT ARISING FROM AFFIXATION

Many other words could be listed, including almost all of those ending in <-ical> (see next section) and all those ending in <-ology>.

| Phoneme | Examples | Exceptions not arising from affixation |
|---|---|---|
| /b/ | *abusive, cabaret, (de-)liberate, ebony, liberal, liberty, probable, tribunal* | *shibboleth* |
| /d/ | *badinage, judicial, prodigal, tradition* | |
| /g/ | *bigamy, exogamy, trigamy* and many others | *aggregate, aggressive, doggerel, ziggurat* |

### How do you know when to write a consonant letter double?

| | | |
|---|---|---|
| /m/ | *amateur, criminal, family, nemesis, ominous, similar* and many others | *accommodate, ((un)in)flammable, dia/pro-grammatic, immodest* |
| /n/ | *analyse, benefit, denizen, draconian, economic, general, genital, manacle, manager, manifest, minimal, minimum, minister, obscenity, penalise, plenary, sanity* | *binnacle, cannibal, perennial, pinnacle, tinnitus, zinnia* |
| /p/ | *capital, popular, supersede* and many others | *apparel, apparent, apprehend, frippery, opposite, opponent* |
| /t/ | *cataract, gratitude, platitude, strategy* and many others | *attention, attraction, attribute, battery, petticoat, smattering* |
| /r/ | *arena, caravan, character, chariot, clarify, clarion, coracle, heresy, heroin(e), irony, miracle, oracle, origin, serious, spiracle* | *arroyo, carrion, corridor, erratic, horrendous, horrible, horrific, horrify, hurricane, interrogate, scurrilous, serrated, terrible, terrific* |
| /z/ | *hesitate, misery, visible* and many others | *brassiere, razzmatazz* |
| /k/ | *executive, faculty* and many others | *accomplice, accomplish, cockerel, impeccable, mackerel, occupy, pickerel* |
| /f/ | *defeasance, defecate, defensive, deference, defiance, deficient, deficit, definite, mafia, safari* and a few others | *affable, afferent, affiance, affluent, buffalo, daffodil, difficult, diffident, effable, effendi, efferent, effervesce, efficient, effigy, effloresce, effluent, effulgent, effusive, graffiti, ineffable, offensive, official, raffia, ruffian, suffocate, suffragan, taffeta, tiffany* |
| /l/ | *celery, element, elephant, holiday, military* (pronounced /ˈmɪlɪtriː/, with three syllables – see section 6.10), *pelican, quality, relevant, solitude, telephone, vilify* | *allegiance, allergy, allocate, allusion, ballistic, ballyhoo, bellicose, beryllium, bullion, bulletin, celluloid, collier, collision, colloquy, ebullient, fallacy, fallible, gallery, galleon, gallivant, gullible, illegal, illicit, illusion, illustrate, intelligent, lollilop, metallurgic, metallurgy, miscellany, mullion, palliate, pellucid, pillion, pillory, postillion, raillery, scallywag, scullery, scullion, stallion, syllable, syllabic, syllabub, syllabus, sylloge;* also *billion, brilliant, million* if pronounced with three syllables |

TABLE 4.5: EXAMPLES OF THE RULE THAT THE THIRD SYLLABLE FROM THE END OF A WORD RARELY ENDS IN A DOUBLED CONSONANT LETTER, WITH EXCEPTIONS NOT ARISING FROM AFFIXATION, CONT.

| Phoneme | Examples | Exceptions not arising from affixation |
|---|---|---|
| /s/ | *complicity, ferocity* and dozens of other words listed in Table 3.4 | *ambassador, assemble, dissemble, dissension, dissipate, dissolute, dissonance, essential, tessellate* |
| /v/ | *cavity, evidence, government, levity, poverty, privacy, trivial* | (none) |

These lists appear to show that for /f, l/ the balance is the other way – doubled spellings outnumber one-letter spellings in this position.

Some other exceptions do arise from suffixation, e.g. *rabbinic, robbery, shrubbery; addiction, addictive; communist; settlement; diffusion, officer; alliance, hellenic, medallion.*

## 4.4.6 Doubled consonant letters are very rare immediately before the endings <-ic(al), -id, -it, -ule>

Examples: *acidic, acoustic, acrobatic, agaric, aquatic, arabic, catholic, choleric, clinic(al), comic(al), diagrammatic, ecliptic, economic(al), elliptic(al), erratic, etymological, fanatic, genetic, graphemic, heroic, historic(al), horrific, lunatic, lyric(al), medical, metallurgic(al), mimic, phonemic, politic(al/s), programmatic, rabbinic(al), radical, rhetoric(al), sonic, sporadic, strategic, syllabic, terrific, topic(al), typical, volcanic; acid, arid, avid, fetid, florid, frigid, intrepid, placid, rabid, rapid, rigid, solid, stolid, tepid, timid, valid, vapid, vivid; credit, davit, deposit, emit, habit, (il)licit, limit, omit, profit, spirit, visit, vomit; globule, module, schedule.*

Exceptions: *attic, britannic, classic(al), cyrillic, ferric, gallic, idyllic, jurassic, metallic, phallic, philippic, prussic, quizzical, tannic, traffic, triassic, tyrannical; flaccid, horrid, pallid, torrid, triffid; commit, hobbit, rabbit, soffit, summit, whodunnit, worrit; cellule, ferrule, floccule, gemmule, pinnule.*

Most of the exceptions are instead obeying the rule that preceding short vowels in two-syllable words are followed by doubled consonant letters (section 4.3.4).

Though most words ending /ɪkəl/ where the ending is unstressed are spelt <-ical>, there are a few exceptions: *article, canticle, cubicle, chronicle, clavicle, conventicle, curricle, cuticle, fascicle, follicle, icicle, particle, testicle, vehicle, ventricle*. And where the /ɪ/ in /'ɪkəl/ is stressed this ending is spelt <-ickle> – see section 4.3.3. (See section 6.10 for words ending in /ɪkliː/ spelt <-ically>.) For the few polysyllabic words in which the ending /ɪk/ is not spelt <-ic> see Table 3.3.

There is also a group of words ending in /əkəl/ spelt <-acle> which need to be mentioned here: *barnacle, binnacle, coracle, manacle, miracle, obstacle, oracle, pinnacle, receptacle, spectacle, spiracle, tentacle, tabernacle*. None seem to have pronunciations in /ɪkəl/, and only *binnacle, pinnacle* are exceptions to the rarity of doubled letters before such endings.

## 4.4.7 When do you reduce <ll> to <l>?

There are some stem words which have <ll> when they stand alone, but sometimes <l> when they do not. As far as I can tell, this affects only the few adjectives ending in <ll>, adjectives ending in <-ble> when suffixed to become adverbs, and the words *all, chill, fill, full, null, pall, roll, skill, stall, still, thrall, till* (preposition) and *will*:

- adjectives ending in <ll> lose an <l> before the adverbial ending <-ly>: *drolly, dully, fully, shrilly* (see also section 4.6.1)
- similarly, adjectives ending in <-ble>, when combining with <-ly> to form adverbs, first lose the <e>, then lose an <l>, e.g. *probably, visibly* and not *probablely, *visiblely or even *probablly, *visiblly
- *all* sometimes loses an <l> when it is a prefix: *albeit, almighty, almost, already, although, altogether, always* (but not usually *alright)
- *till* loses an <l> in *until*
- *chill* loses an <l> in *chilblain* (but not in *windchill*)
- *skill, will* lose an <l> before *-ful*: *skilful, wilful*
- *full* loses an <l> in the compound verb *fulfil* and the derived noun *fulfilment*, and in all the adjectives and nouns ending in *-ful*, e.g. *beautiful, handful* (but not in *craw-full*). The noun *ful(l)ness* has two spellings
- *fill* also loses an <l> in the compound verb *fulfil* and the derived noun *fulfilment*, but because *fulfil* is a two-syllable verb with stress on the second syllable AND ending in <l>, it has <ll> before suffixes beginning with a vowel letter (and then is the same in British and US spelling): *fulfilling, fulfilled* (but contrast *infill, refill*)
- five of the other six stems behave like *fill* when forming prefixed or suffixed verbs and nouns derived from them: *annul, annulment, appal, enrol, enrolment, instil, instilment* (a rare but real word), *enthral,*

- *enthralment, thraldom* (also spelt *thralldom*, for which see also section 10.42)
- *stall* loses an <l> only in *instalment* and not in *forestall, install, installation*. The spelling *instal*, for example, would suggest the pronunciation /ˈɪnstəl/, not /ɪnˈstɔːl/.

Most of the words listed above lose an <l> in both British and US spelling, but in a few cases the single <l>'s listed above (usually) remain double in US spelling: *skillful, willful, fulfill, fulfillment, fullness, appall, enroll, enrollment, instill, instillment, enthrall, enthrallment, installment*.

Extensions (1): Given ... *sixth, seventh*, ... *sixteen, seventeen* ... and *sixty, seventy* ..., one might have expected *eightth, *eightteen, *eightty, but these are always reduced to *eighth, eighteen, eighty*.

Extensions (2): In *dispirit-ed/ing, pastime, transpire*, <ss> becomes <s>, and several compounds of *mass* ('religious service') end in *-mas*: *Candlemas, Christmas, Lammas, Martinmas, Michaelmas*. But *less* always retains its full spelling as a suffix, e.g. *hopeless, useless*.

Extensions (3): The word meaning 'male grandparent' should, logically, be spelt *Granddad* but is almost always simplified (incorrectly, in my opinion) to *Grandad* (cf. sections 3.5.5, 9.23 on *Granma*), and on 22/4/14 I came across *grandaughter* on a birthday card website.

## 4.5 Learn the rest

There are other more detailed tendencies and quasi-regularities. But they are complicated to state, and some require knowledge of etymology or very close attention to pronunciation; and all have exceptions. So other words (and there are many of them) you just have to learn. And, sadly, *accommodation*, with <cc> and <mm> (but <d>), and *necessary*, with <ss> (but <c>), are two of them.

## 4.6 Consolation prizes

### 4.6.1 Consonant letters are never written triple

Well, almost never; the only words in English containing three consecutive identical consonant letters are said to be *Invernessshire* and *Rossshire* (though there is also *still-life*, which has to have the hyphen to make it conform to the rule). What this rule is really saying is that (for instance) when adjectives ending in <ll> have *-ly* added, the resulting adverb is written with <ll>, not *<lll>: e.g. *drolly, fully*, not *drollly, *fullly*. This ensures that the separate word *fully* looks the same as the ending of adverbs derived from adjectives in *-ful*, e.g. *beautifully*. (In Estonian, which is said to have triple consonant phonemes, they are still written with double letters).

## 4.6.2 Final <CC> + <e>

And there is another pattern which is pretty reliable. Where a word ends in a short vowel phoneme plus a consonant phoneme and then is written with a final <e>, the consonant letter is usually written double. Final /short vowel/+<CC+e> is admittedly rare. It occurs mainly in words more recently borrowed from French (i.e. after the Great Vowel Shift), with a few imports from elsewhere, for example *gaffe, bagatelle, fontanelle, gazelle, grille, vaudeville, programme, comedienne, grippe, steppe, finesse, impasse, largesse, etiquette, gazette, lorgnette, mignonette, omelette, palette, toilette, vignette*, plus all the recent coinages ending <-ette> or <-ville>, e.g. *ladette, launderette, dullsville*. *Braille, giraffe, pouffe* and *mousse* can be considered as extensions to the pattern – the preceding vowel phonemes are long (in RP) – and *carafe* is a clear exception, with <f>. It is also noticeable that most of the polysyllables in this category have final-syllable stress – some exceptions are *dullsville, etiquette, omelette, palette, programme, vaudeville*, all with initial-syllable stress.

The written pattern <-CC+e> occurs also in *barre* and *bizarre*, but here, since these words do not end in a /r/ phoneme (in RP), <arre> is a four-letter grapheme spelling the long vowel /ɑː/. Similarly, in *parterre*, <erre> is a four-letter grapheme spelling the diphthong /eə/. But all three words conform to the spelling pattern of final <-VCCe>, and the two disyllables have final-syllable stress.

# 5. The phoneme-grapheme correspondences of English, 2: Vowels

## 5.1 The general picture: the principal spellings of English vowel phonemes

This chapter can be summed up by saying that only five of the vowel phonemes of RP /æ, e, ɒ, aʊ, juː/ have highly regular spellings (80%+) wherever they occur, while none of the other 15 has a spelling accounting for more than 60% of its occurrences (though see section 5.4.3 for the possibility that /ɪ/ may also belong in the highly regular group).

The main regularities for all 20 vowel phonemes, plus /juː/, are summarised in Table 5.1, by position in the word. The letter-name vowels /eɪ, iː, aɪ, əʊ, juː/, plus /uː/, need to be analysed according to position within non-final vs final **syllables** (and then, within final syllables, according to two further, crossed dichotomies; see also sections 6.2 and 6.3), whereas all the rest need to be analysed according to position as initial, medial or final **phoneme**. The phonemes are therefore classified into short pure vowels, long pure vowels other than /iː, uː/, diphthongs other than /eɪ, aɪ, əʊ/, and the letter-name vowels plus /uː/.

Amidst the clutter of Table 5.1 various generalisations can be discerned:
- five of the short pure vowels have a predominant spelling in initial position (/ʊ/ does not occur in this position, in RP)
- the letter-name vowels and /uː/ have remarkable consistency in non-final syllables (with the notable exception of /iː/ in unstressed syllables)

- the letter-name vowels and /uː/ mostly have split digraph spellings in closed final syllables (with the notable exceptions of /iː, uː/ in monosyllables)
- there is a minor and scattered pattern before consonant clusters: in closed monosyllables the long vowel /ɑː/ and the letter-name vowels /aɪ, əʊ/ are spelt with the single letters <a, i, o> and the letter-name vowel /eɪ/ is spelt <ai> before /nt/; for /ɑː, eɪ/ this pattern extends to closed final syllables of polysyllables
- digraphs with <-y> (<ay, oy>) tend to occur word-finally and to alternate with digraphs with <i> (<ai, oi>) elsewhere
- similarly, digraphs with <-w> (<aw, ew, ow>) tend to occur word-finally and to alternate with digraphs with <u> (<au, eu, ou>) elsewhere
- the biggest muddle is /ɔː/.

TABLE 5.1: MAIN SPELLINGS OF THE 20 VOWEL PHONEMES, PLUS /juː/, BY WORD POSITION.

| VOWELS OTHER THAN THE LETTER-NAME VOWELS AND /uː/ | | | |
|---|---|---|---|
| Vowel | Position | | |
| | Initial phoneme | Medial phoneme | Final phoneme |
| **Short pure vowels** | | | |
| /æ/ | <a> | | (does not occur) |
| /e/ | <e> | | (does not occur) |
| /ɪ/ | <i>, but frequently <e> in unstressed syllables | <i>, but <a> in word-final unstressed /ɪdʒ/, and frequently <e> in other unstressed syllables | (does not occur) |
| /ɒ/ | <o> | <o>, but mainly <a> after /w/ | (does not occur) |
| /ʌ/ | <u>, but there are many examples with <o> | | (does not occur) |
| /ʊ/ | (does not occur) | <oo> in monosyllables ending in /d, k/, <u> elsewhere | (does not occur) |
| /ə/ | <a>, with few exceptions | <a>, with many exceptions | <er>, with many exceptions |
| **Long pure vowels other than /iː, uː/** | | | |
| /ɑː/ | <ar>, but <a> before consonant clusters | | (nothing predominates) |
| /ɜː/ | (very rare) | <er>, but <or> after initial /w/ | <er> |

| /ɔː/ | <au, or>, but mainly <a> before /l/ | <au, aw, or, ore>, but mainly <a> after /w/ and before /l/ | | <aw, or, ore> | |

**Diphthongs other than** /eɪ, aɪ, əʊ/

| /ɔɪ/ | <oi> | | | <oy> | |
|---|---|---|---|---|---|
| /aʊ/ | <ou> | <ou>, but <ow> before /l, n/ and vowel letters | | <ow> | |
| /eə/ | <air> | <ar> | | <are> | |
| /ɪə/ | (very rare) | <er> | | <ear> | |
| /ʊə/ | (so rare and diverse that no generalisations are worthwhile) | | | | |

**THE LETTER-NAME VOWELS, PLUS /uː/**

| Vowel | In non-final syllables | In final syllables | | | |
|---|---|---|---|---|---|
| | | Closed | | Open | |
| | | In polysyllables | In monosyllables | In polysyllables | In monosyllables |
| /eɪ/ | <a> | <ai> before /nt/, otherwise <a.e>, with many exceptions with <ai> | | <ay> | |
| /iː/ | mainly <e>; many exceptions with <i> in unstressed syllables | <e.e>, with many exceptions | <ee>, with many exceptions | <y>, with many exceptions | <ee>, with some exceptions |
| /aɪ/ | <i> | <i.e> | <i> before consonant clusters, <igh> before /t/, otherwise <i.e> | <y>, with a few exceptions, mostly with <i> | <y>, with more exceptions than examples |
| /əʊ/ | <o> | <o.e> | <o> before consonant clusters, otherwise <o.e> | <ow> in two-syllable words after /l, r/, otherwise <o> | <ow> |
| /juː/ | <u> | <u.e> | | <ue> | <ew> |
| /uː/ | <u> | <oo> in stressed final /ˈuːn/, otherwise <u.e> | <oo> | <oo> | <ew> |

## 5.2 Order of description

In sections 5.4-7 I set out the vocalic phoneme-grapheme correspondences between RP and British spelling, under the vowel phonemes listed in the order in which they appear in Table 5.1. Section 5.4 covers short pure vowels, section 5.5 long pure vowels other than /iː, uː/, section 5.6 diphthongs other than /eɪ, aɪ, əʊ/, and section 5.7 the letter-name vowels plus /uː/.

Under each vowel phoneme I deal with the spellings in this order:
1) The basic grapheme. In my opinion, each of the 20 vowel phonemes of English, plus /juː/, has a basic grapheme, the one which is most frequent and/or seems most natural as its spelling.
2) Other graphemes which are used to spell that phoneme with reasonable frequency.
3) Oddities, graphemes which are used to spell that phoneme only rarely.
4) Any 2-phoneme graphemes in which the phoneme occurs. (Almost all the 2-phoneme graphemes are also Oddities, but a few belong to the main system and are included there).
5) Any 3-phoneme grapheme in which the phoneme occurs. Both 3-phoneme graphemes are definitely Oddities.

Most entries end with Notes, and some have Tables.

By reasonable frequency here I usually mean at least 9% of the occurrences of that phoneme in running text. The reason for setting a generally higher criterion for vowel spellings than for consonant spellings (see section 3.2) is that vowel spellings are so much more varied. For the choice of 9% see in particular /ɔː/ spelt <au, aw> and /uː/ spelt <ew> (sections 5.5.3, 5.7.6), which definitely have to be considered parts of the main system of English spelling; and contrast (at 8%) /ʌ/ spelt <ou>, /ɜː/ spelt <ear> and /ɔː/ spelt <our> (sections 5.4.5, 5.5.2, 5.5.3), which equally certainly are Oddities and not parts of the main system. However, as with consonant phonemes, the dividing line cannot be absolute. I have 'promoted' four infrequent correspondences, /ɒ/ spelt <a> at 6%, /ɪə/ spelt <eer> at 8%, /juː/ spelt <ue> - percentage unknown, but clearly very low, and /uː/ spelt <ue> at <1% (sections 5.4.4, 5.6.4, 5.7.5-6), to the main system, where they obviously belong. In the case of /uː/ spelt <ue> this is largely because in the grapheme-phoneme direction the correspondences of <ue> are highly regular - see section 10.37.

Again, the frequencies are Carney's text frequencies (see section 3.2), but for /ɪ, ɪə/ I take issue with them, and for /iː/ I dispense with them completely - see sections 5.4.3, 5.6.4, 5.7.2.

## 5.3 The main system and the rest

As for the consonant phonemes, under each vowel phoneme I separate the correspondences with graphemes into what I consider to be the main system and the rest. The correspondences I include in the main system are those which seem to me to operate as part of larger regularities, even though pretty rarely as absolute rules. For instance, there is a strong tendency in English spelling for the letter-name vowel phonemes /eɪ, iː, aɪ, əʊ, juː/, plus /uː/, to be written with the single vowel letters <a, e, i, o, u> in non-final syllables. Within the main system I include only the correspondences which seem to me to form part of these larger regularities. For the vowel phonemes these comprise the basic correspondences and the correspondences which have reasonable frequency as I've defined it above, plus a few with lower frequencies which have to be in the main system, but not the 2-phoneme graphemes (with a few exceptions), or the 3-phoneme graphemes and Oddities. Correspondences which have reasonable frequency are shown in 9-point type, the rest in 7.5-point.

## 5.4 Short pure vowels: /æ e ɪ ɒ ʌ ʊ ə/

N.B. Six of the seven short pure vowels do not occur word-finally, but /ə/ is frequent in that position.

### 5.4.1 /æ/ as in *ash*

Does not occur word-finally.

**THE MAIN SYSTEM**

| | | | |
|---|---|---|---|
| Basic grapheme | <a> | 99% | e.g. *cat* |
| Other frequent graphemes | (none) | | |

**THE REST**

| | | |
|---|---|---|
| Oddities | | 1% in total |
| | <ae> | only in *Gaelic* pronounced /ˈgælɪk/ |
| | <ai> | only in *Laing, plaid, plait* |
| | <al> | only in *salmon* |

140  *Dictionary of the British English Spelling System*

                                                                                                                                                                                

|  |  |  |
|---|---|---|
|  | <ei> | only in *reveille* |
|  | <i> | only in *absinthe, impasse, ingenu(e), lingerie* pronounced /ˈlænʒəriː/ (also pronounced /ˈlɒndʒəreɪ/), *meringue, pince-nez, timbale, timbre* |
| *2-phoneme graphemes* | (none) |  |

## 5.4.2 /e/ as in *end*

Does not occur word-finally, and is rare before /ŋ/ – see section 3.8.2.

### THE MAIN SYSTEM

| *Basic grapheme* | <e> | 84% | e.g. *pet* |
|---|---|---|---|
| *Other frequent graphemes* | (none) |  |  |

### THE REST

| *Oddities* |  | 16% in total |
|---|---|---|
|  | <a> | only in *any, ate* pronounced /et/ (also pronounced /eɪt/), *many, Thames*, first <a> in *secretaria-l/t*, second <a> in *asphalt* pronounced /ˈæʃfelt/ (also pronounced /ˈæsfælt/), and |
|  |  | – a few words ending <-ary> with the stress two syllables before the <a>, e.g. *necessary, secretary*, pronounced /ˈnesəseriː, ˈsekrəteriː/ (also pronounced /ˈnesəsriː, ˈsekrətriː/ with no vowel phoneme corresponding to the <a> – for the elided vowels in this and the next three paragraphs see section 6.10) |
|  |  | – a few adverbs ending <-arily>, e.g. *militarily, necessarily, primarily, voluntarily* pronounced /mɪlɪˈterɪliː, nesəˈserɪliː, praɪˈmerɪliː, vɒlənˈterɪliː/ with the <a> stressed (also pronounced either /mɪlɪˈteərɪliː, nesəˈseərɪliː, praɪˈmeərɪliː, vɒlənˈteərɪliː/ with /eə/ spelt <ar> and the <r> also a grapheme in its own right spelling /r/ – for dual-functioning see |

*The phoneme-grapheme correspondences, 2: Vowels* 141

section 7.1 – or reduced to four syllables as /ˈmɪlɪtrəliː, ˈnesəsrəliː, ˈpraɪmrəliː, ˈvɒləntrəliː/ with stress shifted one or two syllables forward, again no vowel phoneme corresponding to the <a>, and the vowel before /liː/ changed from /ɪ/ to /ə/)

– *temporary* pronounced /ˈtempəreriː/ (also pronounced /ˈtemprəriː/ with no vowel phoneme corresponding to the <o> and the <a> now spelling /ə/)

– *temporarily* pronounced /tempəˈrerɪliː/ (also pronounced either /tempəˈreərɪliː/ with /eə/ spelt <ar> and the <r> also a grapheme in its own right spelling /r/ – for dual-functioning see section 7.1 – or reduced to three syllables as /ˈtemprəliː/ with no vowel phonemes corresponding to the <o> or the <a> and the two /r/ phonemes reduced to one)

| | | |
|---|---|---|
| | <ae> | only in *aesthetic* pronounced /esˈθetɪk/ (also pronounced /iːsˈθetɪk/), *haemorrhage*, *haemorrhoid* |
| | <ai> | only in *bouillabaisse*, *said*, *saith* and (usually, nowadays) *again(st)* |
| | <ay> | only in *says* |
| | <ea> | 6% in about 60 words – see Note |
| | <ei> | only in *heifer*, *leisure*, *seigneur* |
| | <eo> | only in *Geoff(rey)*, *jeopardy*, *Leonard*, *leopard* |
| | <ie> | only in *friend* |
| | <u> | only in *burial*, *bury* |
| 2-phoneme graphemes | (none) | |
| 3-phoneme grapheme | /eks/ spelt <x> | only in *X-ray*, etc. |

## NOTES

There are only about 60 stem words in which /e/ is spelt <ea>, but no rule can be given to identify them, so here is a list: *Beaconsfield; treacher-ous/y;*

*bread, breadth, dead, dread, (a)head, lead* (the metal, plus derivatives *leaded, leading*), *meadow, read* (past tense and participle), *Reading* (Berkshire), *(al)ready, spread, (in)stead, steadfast, steady, thread, tread(le); deaf, breakfast; dealt, health, jealous, realm, stealth, wealth, zeal-ot/ous; dreamt, seamstress; cleanly* (adjective, plus derivative *cleanliness*), *cleanse, leant, meant; leapt, weapon; (a)breast; peasant, pheasant, pleasant; measure, pleasure, treasure; sweat, threat(en); breath, death; feather, heather, leather, weather; endeavour, heaven, heavy, leaven* and other derivatives not listed. In my opinion very little would be lost if all these words were instead spelt with <e> – indeed, one spelling reform proposal is that the first change should be to spell all occurrences of /e/ with <e> and nothing else – but:

- this might be difficult for some of the Oddities above
- *bred, led, red, lent, wether* would become homonyms of the words already so spelt
- various words would have to acquire unfamiliar letters to conform to other rules: *\*tretcher-ous/y, \*bredded, \*bredding, \*dredded, \*dredding, \*hedded, \*hedding, \*ledded, \*ledding, Redding* (so spelt in first map, 1611), *\*(al)reddy, \*reddying, \*reddied, \*reddies, \*deff, \*breckfast, \*jellous, \*zell-ot/ous, \*weppon, \*swetted, \*swetting, \*thretten(ed/ing)*.

## 5.4.3 /ɪ/ as in *ink*

Does not occur word-finally, in my opinion/version of RP. For doubts about the percentages see Notes.

### THE MAIN SYSTEM

For all these categories see Notes.

| | | |  |
|---|---|---|---|
| *Basic grapheme* | <i> | only 61% if word-final /ɪ/ spelt <y> is allowed, but a lot more otherwise | e.g. *sit*. Regular in initial and medial positions |
| *Other frequent graphemes* | <y> | 20% if word-final /ɪ/ spelt <y> is allowed, but a lot less otherwise | e.g. *bicycle, crystal* |

| | | |
|---|---|---|
| <e> | only 16% if word-final /ɪ/ spelt <y> is allowed, but a lot more otherwise | e.g. *diocese* (first <e>), *England, English, enough, entirety* (both <e>'s), *extreme* (first <e>), *pretty, scavenge* (first <e>), *stupefy, variety*. Regular in certain suffixes |

## THE REST

*Oddities*      at least 4% in total

- *in stressed syllables*

| | |
|---|---|
| <ee> | only in *breeches* /ˈbrɪtʃɪz/ |
| <hea> | only in *forehead* pronounced /ˈfɒrɪd/ |
| <ie> | only in *sieve* |
| <o> | only in *women* |
| <u> | only in *business, busy* |

- *in unstressed syllables*

| | |
|---|---|
| <a> | in about 250 words ending in unstressed word-final /ɪdʒ/, which is mainly spelt <-age>, e.g. *village*, plus *furnace, menace, necklace, octave, orange, signature, surface, spinach* pronounced /ˈspɪnɪdʒ/ and second <a> in *character, palace*. See Notes |
| <ai> | only in *bargain, captain, chamberlain, chaplain, fountain, mountain, porcelain* |
| <ee> | only in *been* when unstressed, *cheerio* /bɪn, tʃɪriːˈjəʊ/ |
| <ei> | only in *counterfeit* pronounced /ˈkaʊntəfɪt/ (also pronounced /ˈkaʊntəfiːt/), *forfeit, sovereign, surfeit* |
| <ia> | only in *carriage, marriage* |
| <ie> | only in *(hand/nec)kerchief, mischief, mischievous* |
| <o> | only in *pigeon* (taking <ge> as spelling /dʒ/; compare *pidgin*) |
| <u> | only in *lettuce, minute* (noun /ˈmɪnɪt/, '60 seconds'), *missus* |

|  |  |  |
|---|---|---|
|  | <wi> | only in *housewife* ('sewing kit', pronounced /ˈhʌzɪf/) |
| 2-phoneme grapheme | /ɪz/ spelt <s> | only, following an apostrophe, in regular singular and irregular plural possessive forms ending in a sibilant consonant (/s, z, ʃ, ʒ, tʃ, dʒ/), e.g. *Brooks's* (*book*), *jazz's* (*appeal*), *Bush's* (*government*), (*the*) *mirage's* (*appearance*), (*the*) *Church's* (*mission*), (*the*) *village's* (*centre*), (*the*) *geese's* (*cackling*). See /z/, section 3.7.8 |

## NOTES

Carney (1994: 135, 139, 161, 380, 430) states that, in the version of RP which he analysed (and which he and many other phoneticians prefer to call SBS, Southern British Standard, and Cruttenden (2014) now dubs GB, General British), /ɪ/ does occur word-finally and in that position is mainly spelt <y>. His percentages for the spellings of /ɪ/ are based on that analysis. But he also points out (especially on pp.134-5, 380) that many (especially younger) RP-speakers do not have word-final /ɪ/ in their accents, but (a short version of) /iː/ instead. And on page xxii he says that /ɪ/ does not occur in final open syllables, thus contradicting most of his other statements on this (cf. also his p.56).

Cruttenden (2014: 97; and cf. p.84), on the other hand, says: 'Word-final unaccented /ɪ/ has now been replaced in all but the oldest GB speakers by /iː/ ..., e.g. in *copy*'. I agree, and think that children learning to spell English are more likely to hear the final phoneme of, say, *city* as /iː/ rather than /ɪ/, and different from the definite /ɪ/ in the first syllable. Similarly, Mines *et al.* (1978, Table A-2, p.237) show that only about 1% of occurrences of /ɪ/ in their analysis were word-final (admittedly in the General American accent, but here the point is applicable to RP as well). I have therefore not followed Carney's analysis, but Cruttenden's, and count /ɪ/ as occurring only in initial and medial positions. This does mean, unfortunately, that I have not been able to use Carney's percentages (which, oddly, Cruttenden, 2014: 113) retains) without reservation, and he does not provide enough information to re-calculate them (this would require knowing what proportion of <y>-spellings are word-final). This difference in analysing /ɪ/ also entails differences in the analysis of and percentages for /iː/ - see section 5.7.2.

<i> is regular in initial and medial position in both stressed and unstressed syllables.

Exceptions with <e>: The only words in which /ɪ/ is spelt <e> in **stressed** syllables are *England*, *English*, *pretty* and *Cecily* pronounced /ˈsɪsɪliː/ and

therefore as a homophone of *Sicily* (*Cecily* is also pronounced /ˈsesɪliː/).
Categories where <e> is the **regular** spelling of **un**stressed /ɪ/ are:
- the past tense and past participle verb ending <-ed> spelling /ɪd/ after /t, d/, e.g. *ousted, decided*. N.B. Carney (1994: 135) says this ending is not included in his percentages
- a few adjectives which are derived from or resemble past participles but have /ɪd/ rather than the expected /d, t/, but often with a different meaning, e.g. *accursed, aged* (/ˈeɪdʒɪd/ 'elderly' vs /eɪdʒd/ 'having x years'), *beloved* (/bɪˈlʌvɪd/ 'the loved one' vs /bɪˈlʌvd/ 'adored'), *blessed* (/ˈblesɪd/ 'holy' vs /blest/ 'consecrated'), *cragged, crooked* (/ˈkrʊkɪd/ 'untrustworthy' vs /krʊkt/ 'at an angle'), *Crutched* (*Friars*), *cursed* (/ˈkɜːsɪd/ 'damnable' vs /kɜːst/ 'swore badly/put a hex on'), *cussed* (/ˈkʌsɪd/ 'stubborn' vs /kʌst/ 'swore mildly'), *deuced, dogged* (/ˈdɒgɪd/ 'persistent' vs /dɒgd/ 'followed'), *fixed* (/ˈfɪksɪd/ 'persistent' vs /fɪkst/ 'mended'), *horned* (*owl*), *jagged* (/ˈdʒægɪd/ 'with sharp points' vs /dʒægd/ past tense of *jag*), *learned* (/ˈlɜːnɪd/ 'wise' vs /lɜːnd/ regular past tense of *learn*), (*bow/one-*)*legged, naked, ragged* (/ˈrægɪd/ 'torn, exhausted' vs /rægd/ past tense of *rag*), *rugged, sacred, supposed* (/səˈpəʊzɪd/ 'apparent' vs /səˈpəʊzd/ past tense of *suppose*), *wicked, wretched*. In (*ac*)*cursed, blessed, crooked, Crutched, cussed, deuced, fixed, wretched*, not only does the /ɪ/ surface (see section 7.2) but the /t/ voices to /d/
- the past participle verb ending <-ed> spelling /ɪd/ before adverbial <-ly>, e.g. *advisedly, allegedly, assuredly, barefacedly, composedly, confusedly, deservedly, determinedly, fixedly, markedly, relaxedly, (un)reservedly, supposedly, unabashedly, unashamedly, undisguisedly, unrestrainedly*. Again, in *barefacedly, fixedly, markedly, relaxedly*, not only does the /ɪ/ surface (see section 7.2) but the /t/ voices to /d/
- the <ed> element in a very few nouns in <-ness> formed from past participles, e.g. *preparedness*, where not only does the /ɪ/ surface (see section 7.2) but also /r/-linking occurs (see section 3.6) and the <r> is both part of the grapheme <are> spelling /eə/ and a grapheme in its own right spelling /r/. For dual-functioning see section 7.1
- the superlative adjective ending <-est>, e.g. *biggest, grandest*
- the archaic second and third person singular verb endings <-est, -eth>, e.g. *gavest, goeth*
- the noun plural and third person singular present tense verb endings /ɪz/ sometimes spelt <-es> after /s, z, ʃ, ʒ, tʃ, dʒ/ – see the entries for those consonants in sections 3.6.6, 3.6.8, 3.7.3, 3.7.4, 3.6.2,

3.6.4. N.B. Carney (1994: 135) says this ending is not included in his percentages either
- the unstressed noun suffixes /ɪs, lɪs, lɪt, nɪs/ spelt <-ess, -less, -let, -ness>, e.g. *goddess, listless, booklet, madness*. There are many nouns ending in unstressed /ɪs/ when it is not a suffix and is therefore not spelt <-ess>, e.g. *furnace, menace, palace* (all of which have alternative pronunciations in /əs/), *diocese* (which is exceptional in various ways – see under /iː/, section 5.7.2), *justice, practice, mortice/mortise, practise, premise/premiss, promise, treatise* and all nouns ending in /sɪs/, e.g. *crisis*. The set of words ending in stressed /ɪs/, all but one spelt with <-iss>, is very small: *amiss, bliss, dismiss, diss, hiss, kiss, miss, p*ss, remiss, Swiss* (exception: *abyss*)
- the unstressed prefixes (Germanic) /bɪ/ and (Latin) /dɪ, ɪ, ɪks/ɪgz, prɪ, rɪ/ spelt <be-, de-, e-, ex-, pre-, re->, e.g. *before, beholden, decline, deliver, effective, efficient, extreme, examine, precede, predict, regale, reject*
- the ending /ɪtiː/ when the previous letter is <i>, i.e. in *anxiety, dubiety, gaiety, moiety, notoriety, (im)piety, (im)propriety, sobriety, society, variety,* plus *entirety, naivety, nicety, surety*. The last four words are exceptions to the general rule that the ending /ɪtiː/ is spelt <-ety> only when the previous letter is <i>, otherwise <-ity>, e.g. *nullity, paucity*, including cases where this involves <e>-deletion or <y>-replacement or -deletion (e.g. *scarcity, laity* – see sections 6.4-6); but the more regular spellings *entirity, *naivity, *nicity, *surity would look odd, as would *layity. In *entirety, surety*, /r/-linking occurs (see section 3.6) and then the <r> is both part of the graphemes <ir, ur> spelling /aɪə, ʊə/ and a grapheme in its own right spelling /r/. For dual-functioning see section 7.1. The spelling of the ending /ɪtiː/ with <e> when the previous letter is <i> is one of the ways in which English spelling avoids the sequence <ii>, which appears to be tolerated only in *alibiing, fasciitis, leylandii* (and probably many other biological species names), *Pompeii, radii, shanghaiing, Shiite, skiing, taxiing* (all of which have an automatic intervening /j/-glide).

Then there are groups of words with /ɪ/ spelt <e> where no rule can be given:
- the ending /ɪt/ is normally spelt <-it> (e.g. *rabbit* and about 200 other words) but is spelt <-et> in, e.g., *ashet, brisket, budget, buffet* ('strike'), *dulcet, facet, fillet, gannet, gullet, nugget, plummet, punnet, russet, secret, valet* (also pronounced with /eɪ/) and about 150 other words, so all words with both endings just have to be learnt

- the ending /ɪfaɪ(d)/ is spelt with <e> rather than <i> in just four words: *liquefy, putrefy, rarefied, stupefy*. These endings are normally spelt <-if-y/ied> (e.g. *nullify, pacified*), including cases where this involves <e>-deletion or <y>-replacement (e.g. *amplify, jollify* – see sections 6.4–5); *liquefy* has the alternative spelling *liquify*, but the more regular spellings *\*putrify, \*rarified, \*stupify* would look odd
- a ragbag of other words, e.g. *allegation, employ, forest, hallelujah, integral* (when pronounced /ˈɪntɪɡrəl/, with stress on first syllable; also pronounced /ɪnˈteɡrəl/, with stress on second syllable), *kitchen, mannequin, regalia, subject* (noun /ˈsʌbdʒɪkt/, with stress on first syllable; the verb is pronounced /səbˈdʒekt/), *vinegar*; first <e> in *anecdote, antelope, barometer* and all the instruments ending in <-ometer> (but not *kilometre* or other compounds of *metre*), *celebrity, consecrate, eccentric, ellipse, elope, enamel, integrate, negate, neglect, scavenge, sequential*; second <e> in *elegant, elephant, elevate, peregrine*, and many others.

Initial /ɪ/ spelt <y> is extremely rare, occurring only in the archaic word *yclept* ('named'), and the names of the plant and essential oil *ylang-ylang* (also spelt *ilang-ilang*), the type of boat *yngling*, and the elements *ytterbium, yttrium* and the names *Yvette, Yvonne*. Only in *yngling, yttrium* is it stressed.

Other exceptions with /ɪ/ spelt <y> are all medial and mainly of Greek origin. No generalisations seem possible about contexts in which medial /ɪ/ is spelt <y> rather than <i>, so here is a list: *abyss, acetylene, acronym, amethyst, analysis, analytic, aneurysm* (also spelt *aneurism*), *antonym, apocalypse, apocrypha(l), asphyxiate, beryl, bi/tri-cycle, calyx, cataclysm, catalyst, chlamydia, chlorophyll* and a few other words ending in *-phyll, coccyx, cotyledon, crypt(ic), crystal, cyclamen, cygnet, cylinder, cymbal, cynic, cyst, (ptero)dactyl, di/tri-ptych, dynasty* (first syllable), *eponym, etymology* (second syllable), *eucalyptus, glycerine, gryphon, gymkhana, gym(nast/ium), gyp, gypsum, gypsy* (first syllable), *hieroglyph, hydroxyl* (last syllable), *hymn, hypnosis, hypnotise, hypocrisy* (first syllable), *hypocrite, idyll, larynx, lymph, lynch, myriad, metempsychosis, nymph, onyx, oryx, oxygen, paralysis, paralytic, paroxysm, pharynx, phylactery* (first syllable), *physics, polygamy* (second syllable), *polymer, polyp, pygmy* (first syllable), *pyx, rhythm, salicylic, sibyl, strychnine, sybarite, sycamore, sycophant, syllabic, syllable, syllabub, syllabus, sylloge, symbol, sympathy, syndicate, synonym* (first and last syllables), *syntax, synthetic, syphilis, tryst, tyranny* (first syllable). In my opinion, nothing but a source of confusion would be lost if all such words were spelt with <i>.

There are fairly clear rules for spelling word-final /ɪdʒ/. When stressed, its regular spelling is <-idge> and there appear to be no exceptions, but there are very few words in this set: (a)*bridge, fridge, midge, ridge*. When unstressed, the regular spelling is <-age>, e.g. *cabbage, disparage, garage* pronounced /ˈgærɪdʒ/, *image, mortgage, village* and about 250 other words. However, here there are several exceptions, with various spellings: *carriage, college, (ac)knowledge, marriage, ostrich, privilege, sacrilege, sandwich* pronounced /ˈsæmwɪdʒ/ (and many other placenames with this ending – but I'm not dealing with placenames), *selvedge, spinach* pronounced /ˈspɪnɪdʒ/, *vestige*, plus three words with, confusingly, the regular **stressed** spelling: *cartridge, partridge, porridge* (and the last of these is even more confusing because the alternative spelling *porage* has the regular **un**stressed ending).

## 5.4.4 /ɒ/ as in *ox*

Does not occur word-finally, or in US accents.

### THE MAIN SYSTEM

| | | | |
|---|---|---|---|
| Basic grapheme | <o> | 92% | e.g. *long* |
| Other frequent grapheme | <a> | 6% | e.g. *squash, wash, what*. See Notes |

### THE REST

| | | |
|---|---|---|
| Oddities | | 2% in total |
| | <ach> | only in *yacht* |
| | <au> | only in *Aussie, Australia, Austria, because* (also increasingly pronounced, unusually, with stressed /ə/), *cauliflower, laurel, Laurence, sausage*, plus a few words also pronounced with /ɔː/: *auction, austere, caustic, claustrophobi-a/c, hydraulic, (bacca)laureate* |
| | <e> | in about 20 more recent French loanwords, e.g. (the relevant <e>'s are in caps) *ambiEnce, cliEntele, denouemEnt, détEnte, divertissemEnt, Embonpoint, Embouchure, En (suite), Enceinte* pronounced /ɒnˈsænt/ (also pronounced /enˈseɪnt/), *Enclave* pronounced |

*The phoneme-grapheme correspondences, 2: Vowels* 149

/ˈɒŋkleɪv/ (more often pronounced /ˈɒŋkleɪv/), *Encore, Ennui, EnsEmble, EntEnte, Entourage, Entracte, Entrepreneur, Entree, Envelope* pronounced /ˈɒnvələʊp/ (also pronounced /ˈenvələʊp/), *gEnre, rapprochemEnt, rEntier.* See Notes

<eau>  only in *bureaucracy, bureaucratise*

<ho>  only in *bonhomie, honest, honour* and derivatives

<i>  only in *lingerie* pronounced /ˈlɒndʒəreɪ/ (also pronounced /ˈlænʒəriː/)

<ou>  only in *cough, hough, lough, trough*

<ow>  only in *(ac)knowledge, rowlock*

2-phoneme graphemes  (none)

## NOTES

If we follow Crystal (2012: 131–2) and Upward and Davidson (2011: 176–9), 'more recent' in terms of loanwords from French means after the Great Vowel Shift, which began about AD1400 and was complete by about AD1600.

There is a reasonably strong tendency for /ɒ/ to be spelt <a> after /w/, however spelt – see Table 5.2, and cf. /ɔː/, section 5.4.3. The reason for putting this correspondence in the main system despite its percentage is that Carney will have excluded the two high-frequency function words *what, was,* and these are enough to make this a frequent correspondence.

TABLE 5.2: SPELLINGS OF /ɒ/ AS <a> AFTER /w/.

| after /w/ spelt <u><br>– always after /k/ spelt <q> | after /w/ spelt <w> | after /w/ spelt <wh> |
|---|---|---|
| *(e)quality, quad* and derivatives, *quadrille, quaff, quag(mire)* (also pronounced /ˈkwæɡ(-)/), *quagga* (also pronounced /ˈkwæɡə/), *qualify* and derivatives and associates, *quandary, quant* and derivatives, *quarantine, quarrel, quarry, quash, quatrain, squab(ble), squad* and derivatives, *squal-id/or, squander, squash, squat* | *swab, swaddle, swallow, swamp, swan, swap, swash(buckling), swastika, swat, swatch, twaddle, wad, waddle, waddy, wadi, waffle, waft* (also pronounced with /ɔː/), *wallah, wallet, wallop, wallow, wally, walrus* (also pronounced with /ɔː/), *wampum, wan, wand, wander, wannabe, want, wanton, warrant, warren, warrigal, warrior, was, wash, wasp, wassail, wast, watch, watt, wattle* | *what* |

TABLE 5.2: SPELLINGS OF /ɒ/ AS <a> AFTER /w/, CONT.

| Exceptions (words in which /ɒ/ is spelt <o> not <a> after /w/) | | |
|---|---|---|
| quod, quondam | swop, swot, wobble, wodge, wog, woggle, wok, wombat, wonk, wonton, wop, wot | whop(per) |

Other words in which /ɒ/ is spelt <a> are *ambience, bandeau, blancmange* (second <a>), *bouffant, chanterelle, confidant(e), debutante, diamante* (second <a>), *fiance(e), flambe, flambeau, insouciance, jalap* (first <a>), *mange-tout, moustache* (now mostly pronounced with /ɑː/ in RP), *nuance, scallop* (also pronounced /ˈskæləp/), *seance, stalwart* (first <a>), *wrath* pronounced /rɒθ/ (also pronounced /rɔːθ/). Elderly relatives of mine (born about 1880) would say /ˈɒlbət/ ('Olbat') when referring to Victoria's consort.

For more detail on the absence of /ɒ/ in US accents see Cruttenden (2014: 127) and Carney (1994: 59).

## 5.4.5 /ʌ/ as in *up*

Does not occur word-finally in RP, and does not occur at all in local accents of the north of England.

### THE MAIN SYSTEM

For both categories see Notes.

| | | | |
|---|---|---|---|
| Basic grapheme | <u> | 63% | e.g. *dulcimer, up* |
| Other frequent grapheme | <o> | 27% | e.g. *above, monk* |

### THE REST

Oddities     10% in total

<oe>    only in *does(n't)*

<oo>    only in *blood, flood*

<ou>    8% only in *chough, Colclough* pronounced /ˈkəʊklʌf/ (also pronounced /ˈkəʊkliː/), *country, couple, couplet, courage, cousin, double, doublet, enough, flourish,* *hiccough* (properly spelt *hiccup*), *housewife* ('sewing kit', pronounced /ˈhʌzɪf/), *nourish, rough, slough* ('shed skin'), *sough, souther-n/ly, touch, tough, trouble, young*

*The phoneme-grapheme correspondences, 2: Vowels* 151

| 2-phoneme grapheme | /wʌ/ spelt <o> | only in *once, one* |

## NOTES

Many people from the North of England do not have this phoneme in their accents, but retain the earlier /ʊ/ (see next section) in most of the words in which RP has /ʌ/. So far from simplifying their task, this presents them with three principal ways of spelling /ʊ/: <o, oo, u>. Also, in some northern accents some words in which RP has /ʌ/ are pronounced with /ɒ/, e.g. *one, among, nothing*.

For spelling RP /ʌ/ some regularities can be stated:

- <o> is regular before /θ, ð, v/: *doth, nothing* (is she sweet?); *brother, mother, other, smother; above, coven, covenant, (dis/re/un)cover, covert* pronounced /ˈkʌvɜːt/ (also pronounced /ˈkʊəvɜːt/), *covet(ous), covey, dove, glove, govern(or), lovage, lovat, love, Lovell, oven, plover, shove, shovel, slovenly, windhover* (exceptions: *southern, guv*)
- <u> is regular before /b, d, g, dʒ, k, p, ʃ, tʃ/: e.g. *club, hub, public; bud, mud, shudder; buggy, juggle, luggage; budget, cudgel, judge; buxom, duck, luxury; abrupt, cup, supper; blush, thrush, usher; clutch, duchess, much* (exceptions: *amok, Cadogan, conjure* ('do magic'), *pinochle, sojourn* (also pronounced with /ɒ/), *twopence, twopenny; country, couple, cousin, double(t), doubloon, touch, trouble*).

Since there are no other useful generalisations it seems best to give a list of other words with /ʌ/ spelt <o>: *accomplice, accomplish, become, borough, colour, colander* (also pronounced with /ɒ/), *Colombia* (second syllable), *come, comfort(able), comfrey, comfy, company, (en)compass, constable, coz, cozen, done, dost, dozen, dromedary, front, frontier, honey, London* (first syllable), *Monday, monetary, money, monger* and its compounds, *mongrel, monk, monkey, Monroe, Montgomery* (twice), *month, none, onion* (first syllable), *some, somersault, son, sponge, thorough, ton, tonne, tongue, won, wonder, worrit, worry*. Some words which used to have /ʌ/ in RP now have /ɒ/ instead, e.g. *combat, comrade, conduit, Coventry*.

/wʌ/ also has 2-grapheme spellings, e.g. <wo> in *wonder*.

## 5.4.6 /ʊ/ as in *pull*

Occurs only medially (in RP), and never before /ŋ/ (in RP).

## THE MAIN SYSTEM

For both these categories see Notes.

| | | | |
|---|---|---|---|
| Basic grapheme | <oo> | 64% | e.g. *hood, look* |
| Other frequent grapheme | <u> | 32% | e.g. *cushion, push* |

## THE REST

| | | |
|---|---|---|
| Oddities | | 4% in total (probably an underestimate because Carney will not have counted *could, should, would*) |
| | <o> | only in *bosom* (first <o>), *wol-f/ves, wolfram, wolverine, Wolverhampton, woman* |
| | <or> | only in *worsted* ('cloth') |
| | <ou> | only in *courier, pouffe* pronounced /pʊf/ (also pronounced /puːf/) |
| | <oul> | only in *could, should, would* |
| 2-phoneme graphemes | (none) | |

## NOTES

In RP (as distinct from local accents of the north of England, in which /ʊ/ is much more frequent) there are rather few words containing this phoneme, perhaps only about 80 stem words, plus a potentially much larger set of adjectives and nouns ending in /fʊl/ spelt <-ful>.

<oo> spelling /ʊ/ occurs in only about 28 stem words, namely four words which have alternative pronunciations with /uː/: *food* /fʊd, fuːd/, *hoodlum* /ˈhʊdləm, ˈhuːdləm/, *room* /rʊm, ruːm/, *woofer* /ˈwʊfə, ˈwuːfə/ (cf., as mentioned under Oddities, *pouffe*, though with a different grapheme), plus *Chinook, forsook, foot, gooseberry* /ˈgʊzbriː/, *hoof* (and its plural *hooves*), *poof(ter), soot, woof* (/wʊf/ 'barking'; contrast *woof* /wuːf/ 'weft'), *wool* and monosyllables ending in /d, k/: *good, hood* (plus its use as a suffix, e.g. *childhood* – but for *hoodlum* see above), *stood, wood* (and its derivative *woodbine*); *book, brook, cook, crook, hook, look, nook, rook, shook, took* (exceptions: *could, should, would; pud, suk*). The high percentage of <oo> spellings despite it occurring in so few words is due to some of those words having very high frequency.

<u> is regular everywhere except in the <oo> words and Oddities listed above. However, there are only about 57 stem words in this set in

RP: *ambush, Buddha, buffet* /ˈbʊfeɪ/ ('food'), *bulbul* (twice), *bull, bullace, bullet, bulletin, Bullingdon, bullion, bully, bulrush* (first <u>), *bulwark* (also pronounced with /ʌ/), *bush, bushel, butch, butcher* (but one of the teachers of English at my grammar school in the 1950s said /ˈbʌtʃə/), *cuckoo,* (*mea*) *culpa, cushion, cushty, cushy, ebullient* (also pronounced with /ʌ/), *fulcrum* (both <u>'s), *full, fulmar, fundi* (/ˈfʊndiː/ South and East African English for 'expert/skilled person'/in Britain, a member of the fundamentalist, uncompromising wing of the German Green Party; contrast *fundi* /ˈfʌndaɪ/, plural of *fundus* 'inner corner of organ'), *gerenuk, kaput, kibbutz, kukri, lungi, lutz, mullah, mush* (/mʊʃ/, slang for 'friend'), *muslim, Musulman* (twice), *pud, pudding, pull, pullet, pulpit, push, puss, put, putsch, schuss, s(c)htum, shufti, sputnik, sugar, suk, Sunni, thurible, thurifer, thruppence, tuk-tuk* (twice), *umlaut* (first <u>), *Zumba*, plus derivatives including *Buddhism, bullock, fulfil, fully, ful(l)ness, fulsome,* and the adjective/noun suffix /fʊl/ spelt <-ful> – there are at least 150 words so formed, e.g. *beautiful, handful*. Unstressed in that suffix and otherwise only in *ambush, fulcrum* (second syllable), *fulfil, gerenuk, tuk-tuk* (second syllable).

For elision of the /ʊ/ when /liː/ spelt <-ly> is added to adjectives in <-ful> to form adverbs see section 6.10.

## 5.4.7 /ə/ (the schwa vowel) as in the first sound in *about*

The most frequent phoneme in spoken English.

The only short vowel which does occur word-finally, in my opinion/ version of RP.

Occurs only in unstressed syllables, except in the increasingly frequent pronunciation of *because* as /bɪˈkəz/.

Rare before /ŋ/ – see section 3.8.2.

N.B. Where the schwa vowel is part of a diphthong it is dealt with elsewhere – see /eə, ɪə, ʊə, əʊ/, sections 5.6.3-5, 5.7.4. For the so-called 'triphthongs' /aɪə/ (which I analyse as a two-syllable sequence consisting of a diphthong plus schwa) and /aʊwə, ɔɪjə/ (which I analyse as two-syllable sequences consisting of a diphthong plus automatic intervening /w/- or /j/-glide plus schwa), see sections 5.7.3, 5.6.2 and 5.6.1 respectively. For this treatment of triphthongs, see also Cruttenden (2014: 153).

For all categories see also Notes, and for further guidance sections 6.7-9.

## THE MAIN SYSTEM

| | | | |
|---|---|---|---|
| *Basic grapheme* | <a> | 35% | e.g. *about*. Regular in initial and medial positions. Especially prevalent in initial position, where the only exceptions appear to be words formed from the Latin prefix *ob–* and its derivatives, e.g. *obscure, obtuse, occur, offend,* but medial position is much more variable |
| *Other frequent graphemes* | <o> | 19% | e.g. *Burton, obscure* |
| | <er> | 15% | e.g. *alter*. Regular in word–final position and in the prefixes *hyper-, inter-, per-, super-* when not stressed on <er>. All these prefixes permit /r/–linking (see section 3.6) before stems beginning with a vowel phoneme, e.g. *hyper-active, interactive, peroxide, supererogatory* |
| | <e> | 13% | e.g. *artery* |
| *Rare 2-phoneme grapheme* | /əl/ spelt <-le> | 6% | only word–final and only in this reversed spelling, e.g. *able, possible.* Though not very frequent as a correspondence for /ə/ this counts as part of the main system because of its higher frequency as a correspondence for /l/ – see section 3.6.5 |

## THE REST

| | | |
|---|---|---|
| *Oddities* | | 12% in total. Of all those listed, only <ar, or, ur> occur in both medial and final positions. None occur in initial position (see above under Basic grapheme, and Notes) |
| *- in medial position* | | |
| | <ai> | only in *certain, chieftain, coxswain, curtain, mainsail* (second syllable), *topsail, villain* |
| | <anc> | only in *blancmange* /bləˈmɒndʒ/ |

## The phoneme-grapheme correspondences, 2: Vowels 155

&lt;ar&gt;      regular in the suffixes /wəd(z)/ spelt &lt;-ward(s)&gt;, e.g. *afterwards, backward(s), downward(s), forward(s), froward, inward, leeward, onward, outward, windward*, and predominant in the ending /əd/ more generally – see Notes. Otherwise in an unpredictable ragbag of words, e.g. *anarchy, awkward, bastard, billiards, blackguard* pronounced /ˈblægəd/ (also pronounced /ˈblægɑːd/), *bombardier, bulwark, coward, custard, dotard, gabardine, halyard, innards, lanyard, monarch, mustard, niggardly, orchard, scabbard, stalwart, steward, vineyard, wizard*

&lt;eau&gt;      only in *bureaucrat(ic)*

&lt;ei&gt;      only in *foreign*

&lt;eo&gt;      only in *bludgeon, curmudgeon, dudgeon, dungeon, gudgeon, luncheon, puncheon, (e)scutcheon, smidgeon, sturgeon, surgeon, truncheon, widgeon*. See Notes

&lt;eu&gt;      only in *pasteurise* pronounced /ˈpɑːstʃəraɪz/

&lt;i&gt;      in a large number of adjectives ending in /əbəl/ spelt &lt;-ible&gt; where the stem without the /əbəl/ mostly does **not** sound like a real word, e.g. *possible*. See Basic grapheme &lt;a&gt; above, Notes and section 6.7. Also in a few adverbs ending &lt;-arily&gt; when not stressed on the &lt;a&gt;, which becomes elided (see section 6.10), so that the &lt;i&gt; in &lt;-ily&gt; spells /ə/, e.g. *necessarily, voluntarily* pronounced /ˈnesəsrəliː, ˈvɒləntrəliː/ (see also under /e/, section 5.4.2)

&lt;ia&gt;      only in *fuchsia, miniature, parliament*. In words like *crucial, initial* and in *Christian* I count the &lt;i&gt; as part of a digraph with the preceding consonant letter – see /ʃ, tʃ/, sections 3.8.3, 3.7.2

&lt;io&gt;      only in *cushion, fashion, marchioness, stanchion*. In words like *question, nation, lesion, vision, lotion, fusion* I count the &lt;i&gt; as part of a digraph with the preceding consonant letter – see /tʃ, ʃ, ʒ/, sections 3.7.2, 3.8.3-4

| | |
|---|---|
| <oar> | only in *cupboard, larboard, starboard* |
| <oi> | only in *connoisseur, porpoise, tortoise* |
| <or> | 2% regular medially in prefix /fə/ spelt <for->, e.g. *forbid, forget, forgive, forsake* (but this is a very small set); otherwise rare medially, but cf. *Deptford* (and many other placenames with this element), *Holborn, scissors, stubborn* |
| <ou> | regular in adjectives ending in /əs/ spelt <-ous>, e.g. *anxious, famous*. Otherwise only in *camouflage, doubloon, limousine, moustache, tambourine, vermouth* pronounced /ˈvɜːməθ/ (also pronounced /vəˈmuːθ/) |
| <ow> | only in *Meadowhall* (locally, in Sheffield), *sorrowful* |
| <u> | regular in unstressed prefix /səb/ spelt <sub->, e.g. *subdue, subject* (verb, pronounced /səbˈdʒekt/), *sublime, submerge, submit, subside, subsist, substantial*; also in nouns ending in unstressed /əs/ spelt <-us>. Otherwise in, e.g., *bogus, capitulate, cherub, commensurate, congratulate, conjugate, glandular, modular, naturist, petulan-t/ce, postulant, spatula* |
| <ua> | in nouns, only in *actuary, estuary, mortuary, obituary, sanctuary, statuary, voluptuary*, when pronounced with /tʃəriː/ rather than /tʃʊəriː/ (see also under /tʃ/, section 3.6.2), plus *casualty, February, victuals* /ˈkæʒəltiː, ˈfebrəriː, ˈvɪtəlz/; also often in rapid pronunciation of adjectives like *actual* (see again /tʃ/, section 3.6.2), *sexual* and especially adverbs derived from them (see also section 6.10 on elided vowels) |
| <ur> | perhaps usual only in *Saturday, surprise*, but there are several words which may have either /ɜː/ (see section 5.5.3) or /ə/, e.g. *liturgy, metallurgy, saturnine, surmise, surmount, surpass, survey* (verb), *survive* |
| <y> | only in *pyjama(s)* |

- *in final position*

    &lt;ah&gt;    only in *ayah, cheetah, fellah, haggadah, hallelujah, Hannah, loofah, messiah, moolah, mullah, mynah, pariah, purdah, (maha)rajah, Sarah, savannah, verandah, wallah* and some other very rare words

    &lt;ar&gt;    only in an unpredictable ragbag of words, e.g. *altar, beggar, briar, burglar, cedar, cellar, cochlear, collar, columnar, curricular, familiar, friar, fulmar, globular, jugular, liar, linear, lumbar, lunar, molar, nuclear, particular, peculiar, pedlar, peninsular, planar, polar, popular, regular, scalar, scapular, scholar, sugar, titular, vicar, vulgar*. Many such words permit /r/-linking, e.g. *polarise, polarity* – see section 3.6

    &lt;ere&gt;    only in *were* when unstressed

    &lt;eur&gt;    only in *amateur, chauffeur* (if stressed on first syllable and pronounced /ˈʃəʊfə/), *grandeur*. /r/-linking occurs in *amateurish* – see section 3.6

    &lt;or&gt;    regular in nouns formed from verbs in &lt;-ate&gt;, e.g. *administrator, agitator, alternator, commentator, creator, curator, dictator, elevator, incinerator, insulator, orator, spectator*, including cases where the verb is rare, e.g. *aviator*, plus groups ending in /ktə, esə, ɪtə/ spelt &lt;-ctor, -essor, -itor&gt;, e.g. *actor, conductor, constrictor, detector, reactor; aggressor, assessor, compressor, confessor, depressor, predecessor, possessor, professor, successor; capacitor, depositor, editor, inhibitor*. Otherwise only in an unpredictable ragbag of nouns, e.g. *advisor* (also spelt *adviser*), *camphor, conspirator, conqueror, contributor, conveyor, councillor, counsellor, distributor, donor, emperor, error, horror, incisor, inventor, languor, liquor, metaphor, pallor, pastor, phosphor, rotor, sailor, sponsor, squalor, stupor, suitor, survivor, terror, tormentor, torpor, traitor, tutor*, plus &lt;or&gt; in *rigor* only in the Latin phrase *rigor mortis*

| | |
|---|---|
| <ough> | only in *borough, thorough* |
| <our> | only in an unpredictable ragbag of words, e.g. *arbour, ardour, armour, behaviour, candour, clamour, clangour, colour, endeavour, favour, fervour, flavour, glamour, harbour, honour, humour, labour, neighbour, odour, parlour, rancour, rigour* (but <or> in the Latin phrase *rigor mortis*), *rumour, saviour, splendour, succour, tumour, valour, vapour, vigour*. In many of these words US spelling has <or> |
| <re> | only in an unpredictable ragbag of words, e.g. *accoutre, acre, calibre, centre, chancre, fibre, goitre, litre, louvre, lucre, lustre, manoeuvre, massacre, meagre* (contrast *eager*), *mediocre, metre* and its compounds, e.g. *kilometre* (contrast *meter* and its compounds, e.g. *barometer*), *mitre, ochre, ogre, reconnoitre, sabre, saltpetre, sceptre, sepulchre, sombre, spectre, theatre, timbre*. In many of these words US spelling has <er>. None of these words has a /r/ phoneme in the final syllable (in RP), but when a suffix beginning with a vowel is added, some lose /ə/ and have /r/-linking instead; e.g. *centre* /ˈsentə/ plus /əl/ becomes /ˈsentrəl/ (*central*) – see section 3.6. In *accoutrement* the schwa disappears and two phonemes surface: /r/ spelt <r> and /ɪ/ represented by the first <e> – see section 7.2. In *acreage, massacreing, ochreous, ogreish* /ˈeɪkərɪʤ, ˈmæsəkərɪŋ, ˈəʊkərəs, ˈəʊgərɪʃ/ /r/ also surfaces, but the schwa and /r/ seem to be represented by <e, r> in reverse order – see again section 7.2. Even more difficult to analyse is *manoeuvrer* if pronounced /məˈnuːvərə/, where no letter seems to spell the first schwa – but, as Gödel proved, no formal system can be both complete and consistent |
| <ur> | only in *augur, femur, langur, lemur, murmur* (second syllable), *sulphur* |
| <ure> | almost all examples of word-final /tʃə/ are spelt <-ture>, e.g. *architecture, capture, caricature, conjecture, creature* (contrast *preacher, teacher*), *culture, curvature, departure* (contrast *archer, marcher*), *expenditure, feature* (again |

*The phoneme-grapheme correspondences, 2: Vowels* 159

contrast *preacher, teacher*), *fixture, fracture, furniture, future, gesture, juncture, lecture, legislature, literature, manufacture, miniature, mixture, moisture, nature, nurture* (contrast *lurcher, (re)searcher*), *pasture, picture* (contrast *pitcher*), *posture, puncture, rapture, rupture, scripture, sculpture, signature, stature, stricture, structure, temperature, texture, tincture, torture, (ad)venture, vulture.* Other examples of final /ə/ spelt <-ure> include *censure, conjure* ('do magic tricks') pronounced /ˈkʌndʒə/, *figure, injure, leisure, measure, perjure, pleasure, pressure, procedure, seizure, tonsure, treasure, verdure* (cf. *verger*); also in *azure* pronounced /ˈæʒə, ˈeɪʒə/ (also pronounced /ˈæzjə, ˈeɪzjə, ˈæzjʊə, ˈeɪzjʊə/). See Notes

|  |  |  |
|---|---|---|
|  | <yr> | only in *martyr, satyr, zephyr* |
| 2-phoneme graphemes | For /aɪə/ spelt <ir, ire, yr, yre> and /waɪə/ spelt <oir> | see under /aɪ/, section 5.7.3 |
|  | For /aʊwə/ spelt <hour, our> | see under /aʊ/, section 5.6.2 |
|  | For /ɔɪjə/ spelt <oir> | see under /ɔɪ/, section 5.6.1 |
|  | /əl/ spelt <l> | only in *axolotl, dirndl, shtetl.* See /l/, section 3.7.5 |
|  | /əm/ spelt <m> | see /m/, section 3.4.4 |
|  | /ən/ spelt <n> | see /n/, section 3.4.5 |
|  | /jə/ |  |
|  | (1) spelt <eu> | only in *aneurism/aneurysm, pasteurise* pronounced /ˈpɑːstjəraɪz/ (also pronounced /ˈpɑːstʃəraɪz/) |
|  | (2) spelt <u> | frequent in unstressed penultimate syllables of words of three or more syllables stressed on the antepenultimate syllable, e.g. *amulet, angular, argument, calculate, chasuble, coagulate, contributor, corpuscular, distributor, emulate, fabulous, garrulous, immunise, inaugural, incubus, insula-r/te, jugular, manipulate, muscular, nebulous, particular,* |

*penury, popul(o)us, querulous, regula-r/te, scapula(r), scroful-a/ous, scrupulous, stimulant/ate/us, succubus, succulent, tremulous, truculent, vernacular*; also in antepenultimate syllable of *copulation, population* with stress on following syllable. Where the preceding consonant is /d, t/ the sequences /dj, tj/ affricate to /dʒ, tʃ/ (see sections 3.7.4, 3.7.2 and cf. *pasteurise* above), e.g. in *(in)credulous, fraudulen-ce/t, glandular, modul-e/ar, nodul-e/ar, pendulum, sedulous; century, congratulate, fistula, flatulen-ce/t, fortunate, petulan-t/ce, postulant, postulate, saturate, spatula, titular*

(3) spelt <ua>   in my analysis, only in *January, valuable* – but see the discussion of words with <u, a> under <u>, section 10.36

(4) spelt <ure>   only in *failure, tenure* and *azure* pronounced /ˈæzjə, ˈeɪzjə/ (also pronounced /ˈæzjʊə, ˈeɪzjʊə, ˈæʒə, ˈeɪʒə/)

3-phoneme grapheme   /waɪə/ spelt with a single grapheme <oir>   only in *choir* – one of only two 3-phoneme graphemes in the entire language

## NOTES

Under /ɪə/ in section 5.6.4 you will see that I disagree with Carney's analysis of that phoneme and have therefore re-allocated a large number of words to /iː/ plus /j/-glide plus /ə/. However, this has not added any graphemes to the correspondences for /ə/. I have left Carney's percentages for /ə/ unchanged on the assumption that the distribution of its correspondences within his analysis of /ɪə/ is broadly similar to that within his analysis of /ə/.

The articles *a, the* are pronounced /ə, ðə/ before consonant phonemes in running speech, and sometimes also when pronounced as citation forms – and therefore stressed, thus also counting as partial exceptions to the rule that /ə/ occurs only in unstressed syllables. But they also have the alternative citation forms /eɪ, ðiː/, which are not exceptions. Other function words which have /ə/ in running speech, e.g. *to, was, were* pronounced /tə, wəz, wə/, are never so pronounced as citation forms, which are instead /tuː, wɒz, wɜː/.

The reason for the wide range of spellings for /ə/ is that any vowel, however spelt for its full pronunciation, can be reduced to the non-distinctive schwa in an unstressed syllable. The default spellings are <a> in initial and medial positions and <er> in final position, and some guidance can be given for a few major categories, but there are very many words that just have to be learnt – see the Oddities above and the various ragbag lists there and in these Notes.

### 1. Initial position
Here the hugely predominant spelling is <a>, and this applies both to the native English prefix *a-* (historically derived from *on*), e.g. in *abide, aboard, about, ahead, alight, aside, athwart, away,* and to derivatives of the Latin prefixes *ab-, ad-,* e.g. in *abrupt, abhor, abound, acclaim, accost, accuse, acquire, address, adhere, adopt, affirm, aggressive, allure, annul, appear, assure, attend, aver*; also in some words of other origins, e.g. (Greek) *anaemia, anathema, aroma*.

The only set of exceptions appears to be words with /ə/ spelt <o> in the Latin prefix *ob-* and its derivatives, e.g. *oblige, obscene, obscure, observe, obsess, obtain, occasion, occur, offend, official.*

### 2. Medial position
Again the default spelling is <a>, though less strongly than in initial position. Some patterning can be seen in initial and final word elements, but very little otherwise in medial position.

### 2.1 Medial position in prefixes/initial elements
A few guidelines can be given for when a schwa here is not spelt <a>:
- the prefixes /ˈhaɪpə, ˈɪntə, ˈsuːpə/ are almost always spelt <hyper-, inter-, super->
- the unstressed prefixes /kən (and related forms), prə, tə/ are spelt with <o>, e.g. *collect, collide, command, commit(tee), confess, connect, connive, connubial, contrast* (verb, pronounced /kənˈtrɑːst/), *corrode, corrupt; procure, produce, profane, profess(or), prolong; today, together, tomorrow*
- there are several words beginning <chloro-, micro-, mono-, phono-, photo-, saxo-> where the stress is on the first syllable and the schwa in the second syllable is spelt <o>.

### 2.2 Medial position in suffixes/endings/final syllables
The ending /ət/ in many nouns and adjectives is almost always spelt <-ate> – see the list of about 90 words under /t/ spelt <te>, section 3.4.7 (exceptions: *chariot, idiot, patriot*).

For those who say /ɪtɪv/ for words ending <-itive> the ending /ətɪv/ is always spelt <-ative>.

The adjectival ending /əbəl/ is mainly spelt <-able> in words where the unsuffixed form sounds like a real word, and mainly <-ible> where it doesn't, but there are numerous exceptions (see section 6.7).

The adjective-forming suffix /əl/ is usually spelt <-al>, e.g. *central, liberal, loyal, royal*; *(ar)boreal, cereal, corporeal, ethereal, funereal, marmoreal, sidereal, venereal*; *congenial, editorial, industrial, jovial, managerial, material, memorial, radial, remedial, serial* and about 450 others ending in <-ial>. For the various spellings of final /əl/ see also sections 4.4.3 and 4.4.2-3.

There are fairly clear rules for word-final /əm/:

- if preceded by /d/ the ending is usually the noun-forming suffix /dəm/ spelt <-dom>, e.g. *kingdom, thrall(l)dom, wisdom* (exceptions: *agendum, carborundum, macadam, madam, referendum, sedum, tandem*)
- if preceded by /z/ the spelling is almost always <sm> (only exception: *bosom*). See under /m/, section 3.4.4
- if preceded by /s/ the ending is usually adjectival /səm/ spelt <-some>, e.g. *handsome* (exceptions: *balsam, flotsam, jetsam; besom, blossom, buxom, hansom, lissom, ransom, transom*)
- otherwise word-final /əm/ is usually spelt <-um>, e.g. *atrium, bacterium, compendium, delirium, gymnasium, medium, opium, potassium, radium, stadium, tedium* and about 200 others ending in <-ium>, plus *album, colosseum, linoleum, lyceum, mausoleum, maximum, museum, petroleum, rectum* (exceptions: *algorithm, rhythm; amalgam, bantam, bedlam, buckram, gingham, marjoram; anthem, emblem, item, problem, stratagem, system, theorem, totem; atom, axiom, bottom, custom, fathom, idiom, maelstrom, phantom, pogrom, symptom, venom*).

There are fairly clear rules for word-final /əs/:

- in adjectives the spelling is almost always <-ous>, e.g. *famous* and at least 2000 others (only exceptions: *bogus, emeritus*)
- in nouns the spelling is almost always <-us>, e.g. *abacus, anus, bonus, cactus, campus, caucus, census, chorus, circus, citrus, corpus, crocus, discus, exodus, focus, fungus, genius, genus, hiatus, hippopotamus, isthmus, litmus, lotus, octopus, onus, nucleus, radius, rhombus, stimulus, surplus, syllabus, Taurus, terminus, tinnitus, virus* and

hundreds more (exceptions: (some of which are also pronounced with /ɪs/): *furnace, menace, necklace, palace, pinnace, populace, solace, surface, terrace; alias, bias, Candlemas, canvas, Christmas, Lammas, Martinmas, Michaelmas; carcase/carcass, purchase; canvass, trespass, windlass; purpose; porpoise, tortoise*)
- there seem to be only five pairs of adjective/noun homophones which differ only in the spelling of the /əs/ ending: *callous/callus, mucous/mucus, populous/populace, rufous/Rufus, venous/Venus*, though of course nouns which are rank-shifted to modifier position before other nouns retain the <-us> spelling: *chorus line, citrus fruit, litmus test*
- there seem to be only two words ending /əs/ which exist only as verbs: *embarrass, harass* (pronounced /ˈhærəs/ rather than the more recent /həˈræs/); the spellings of the other few verbs ending /əs/ are the same as the related nouns: *menace; bias; purchase; canvass, trespass; chorus, focus.*

The ending /əd/ is usually spelt <-ard>, e.g. *awkward, bastard, blackguard* pronounced /ˈblægəd/ (also pronounced /ˈblægɑːd/), *coward, custard, dotard, halyard, lanyard, mustard, orchard, scabbard, steward, vineyard, wizard* and see Oddities above for the suffixes /wəd(z)/ spelt <-ward(s)> (exceptions; *method, period, synod*).

The endings /ək, əp/ are usually spelt <-ock, -op>, e.g. *bollock, bullock, buttock, hassock, hillock, mattock, pillock, rowlock* (exception: *bulwark*); *bishop, gallop, wallop* (exceptions: *catsup, chirrup, ketchup, stirrup, syrup*).

In the suffix spelt <-ology>, the schwa after /l/ is always spelt <o>, e.g. *biology, chronology*.

In the suffix spelt <-ological>, the schwa before the first /l/ is always spelt <o>, e.g. *biological, chronological*, and the second one always <a>.

The ordinal numeral-forming suffix /əθ/ is always spelt <-eth> in *twentieth, ..., ninetieth*.

Beyond various words listed under the medial Oddities <al, el, eo, Io, or> there are some fairly clear rules for word-final /ən/:
- in the various endings pronounced /ʃən/, all words with <-si*n, -ti*n> have <o> for the schwa except *Asian, Persian, Prussian, Russian, gentian, Titian*; all words with <-ci*n> have <a> for the schwa except *coercion*
- the spelling <-on> otherwise occurs mainly in nouns, e.g. *bacon, Briton, button, carton, chameleon, cotton, galleon, halcyon, matron, melodeon, mutton, Odeon, person, piston, siphon/syphon, wanton,*

plus a set of words in <-ion>: *accordion, aphelion, bastion, battalion, billion, bullion, carrion, centurion, champion, clarion, collodion, companion, criterion, dominion, ganglion, medallion, million, mullion, minion, oblivion, onion, opinion, pavilion, perihelion, pinion, rebellion, scorpion, scullion, stallion, union*
- the irregular past participle ending /ən/ (that is, when the ending is pronounced as a full syllable, namely after a consonant phoneme) is spelt <en>, e.g. *(for)bidden, bitten, broken, chosen, eaten, fallen, forsaken, frozen, (for)given, hidden, (a)risen, spoken, stolen, swollen, (mis)taken, (a)woken, woven, written*, even in fossilised forms where the stem verb is now regular or its past participle is disused or used only adjectively, e.g. *beholden, bounden, brazen, cloven, drunken, graven, ((mis)be/ill-)gotten, laden, molten, proven, (bed)ridden, riven, rotten, (mis)shapen, shaven, shriven, shrunken, smitten, stricken, stridden, striven, thriven, (down)trodden*
- <en> also occurs in, e.g.; *alien, dozen, even, flaxen, garden, golden, happen, heaven, listen, open*
- <an> occurs in the noun/adjective ending /ən/ in *antipodean, caesarean, cyclopean, empyrean, epicurean, euclidean, European, galilean, Herculean, Jacobean, Linnaean, Manichaean, paean, pythagorean; plebeian; barbarian, comedian, grammarian, guardian, historian, pedestrian, reptilian, ruffian, thespian* and about 200 other words ending in <-ian>
- But the endings /ənt, əns, ənsiː/ have the variant spellings <- ant/-ent, -ance/ -ence, -ancy/-ency> – see section 6.8.

### 2.3 Otherwise in medial position
The default spelling is still <a>, e.g. sole <a> in *buffalo, dynamo, seraph, theatre*; first <a> in *banana, bravado, farrago, mama, palaver, papa, staccato*; second <a> in *archipelago, balaclava, ballast, breakfast*.
Exceptions:
- with <e> include *artery, bolero* (/ˈbɒlərəʊ/ 'garment'), *soviet*, first <e> in *coterie*;
- with <o> include *abdomen, acrobat, aphrodisiac, bolero* (/bəˈleərəʊ/, 'dance'), *cellophane, cenotaph, custody, daffodil, espionage, exodus, geographic, iodine, kaolin, lobelia, mandolin, mimeograph, parody, police, purpose, ricochet, second, theocratic, violate, vitriol*; first <o> in *creosote, stereophonic, tobacco*; second <o> in *broccoli, choreographic, colloquy, obloquy, rollocking*.

And see again the medial Oddities, above.

## 3. Final position

The default spelling is <-er>. Examples include: *amber, arbiter, auger, bitter, brother, cancer, character, chipper, chorister, clover, double-decker, eager, ember, knocker, ladder, laager, lager, lever, Londoner, lumber, mother, neuter, number, other, oyster, proper, slander, slender, sober, thunder, timber, tuber, water, yonder*; all comparative adjectives, e.g. *better, brighter, colder, dearer, easier, happier*; most agentive nouns formed from one-syllable verbs, e.g. *drinker, jumper, killer, roamer, runner, speller, viewer* (exceptions: *actor, sailor*); many longer agentive nouns where <e/y>-deletion (see sections 6.4, 6.6) applies, e.g. *astrologer, astronomer, biographer, commuter, diner, geographer, lover, philosopher, remembrancer, settler, subscriber*; also words with the suffix <-ometer> ('measuring device'), e.g. *barometer, thermometer* (contrast *kilometre* pronounced /ˈkɪləmiːtə/ to rhyme with *metre* and all its other compounds; however, *kilometre* is also pronounced /kɪˈlɒmɪtə/ to rhyme with all the words ending <-ometer>).

Exceptions (in addition to the Oddities, above):

- where the schwa vowel is spelt within a 2- or 3-phoneme grapheme: see those headings above
- spellings with <e>: *genre, macabre* (which appear to be the only two words where final <-re> is pronounced /rə/ rather than /ə/ – contrast the Oddities in <-re> listed above), *the* (unstressed before a word beginning with a consonant phoneme), *lasagne*. There seem to be very few words in this set
- spellings with <a>:
  1) *agenda, arcana, automata, bacteria, corrigenda, criteria, curricula, data, desiderata, ephemera, erotica, errata, esoterica, exotica, fauna, flora, fora, insignia, juvenilia, maxima, media, memorabilia, memoranda, militaria, millennia, miscellanea, minima, opera, phenomena, prolegomena, pudenda, referenda, schemata, stigmata, strata, trivia,* which etymologically are all Latin or Greek neuter plural nouns (though *agenda, opera* are now always singular in English, increasingly *data, media* are too, and *bacteria, criteria* are often used as singulars by people who don't know that their singulars are *bacterium, criterion*)
  2) also in a set of exotic loanwords of three or more syllables stressed on the penultimate syllable, e.g. *abscissa, alfalfa, alpaca, amenorrhoea, amoeba, anaconda, angina, angora, antenna, arena, aroma, aspidistra, aurora, balaclava, balalaika, ballerina,*

*banana, bandanna, belladonna, bonanza, bravura, cadenza, candelabra, carcinoma, cassava, cavatina, cedilla, chim(a)era, chinchilla, chorea, cicada, concertina, conjunctiva, corona, cyclorama, diarrhoea, dilemma, diploma, duenna, emphysema, enigma, eureka, extravaganza, farina, felucca, flotilla, glaucoma, gonorrhoea, gorilla, granadilla, guerrilla, gymkhana, hacienda, hegira, hosanna, hydrangea, hyena, idea, iguana, indaba, influenza, koala, lactorrhoea, lacuna, liana, logorrhoea, Madonna, magenta, mahatma, manila, mantilla, mazurka, madeira, miasma, mimosa, nirvana, (o)edema, ocarina, omega* pronounced /əʊˈmiːgə/, *operetta, pagoda, panacea, panatella, panorama, pashmina, patella, patina* pronounced /pəˈtiːnə/, *penumbra, persona, pharmacopoeia, pianola, placenta, propaganda, protozoa, pyorrhoea, regatta, rotunda, rubella, saliva, sarcoma, savanna, scintilla, semolina, siesta, sonata, sultana, syringa, tapioca, tiara, toccata, tombola, trachea, umbrella, urea, urethra, vagina, Valhalla, vanilla, vendetta, veranda, verbena, verruca, viola* (/viːˈjəʊlə/ 'musical instrument')

3) also in a set of loanwords of two syllables stressed on the first syllable, e.g. *alpha, asthma, aura, china, cobra, coda, coma, comma, contra, copra, delta, diva, dogma, drama, eczema, era, extra, fatwa, gala, gamma, geisha, guava, gurkha, halma, henna, hydra, junta, karma, lama, lambda, lava, lemma, libra, llama, magma, manna, mantra, nova, okra, ouija, panda, pasha, plasma, plaza, polka, pukka, puma, pupa, quagga, quota, rhea, rota, saga, schema, skua, soda, sofa, stanza, stigma, tantra, toga, trauma, tuba, tufa, tuna, tundra, ultra, villa, visa, vista, viva, vodka, vulva, yoga, yucca, zebra, zeugma*

4) and a further ragbag of words which fit none of those categories, e.g. *algebra, ammonia, anaemia, anaphora, anathema, apnoea, area, azalea, begonia, camellia, camera, chlamydia, cholera, cinema, cithara, cochlea, copula, cornea, cupola, dyspnoea,* (en)*cyclopaedia, enema, formula, gondola, harmonica, hernia, hysteria, japonica, myopia, nausea, omega* pronounced /ˈəʊmɪgə/, *orchestra, parabola, patina* pronounced /ˈpætɪnə/, *peninsula, pergola, plethora, primula, replica, retina, salvia, scapula, sciatica, scrofula, sepia, stamina, swastika, taffeta, tarantula, tempera, utopia, vertebra, viola* (/ˈvaijələ/ 'flower/girl's name').

Any spelling for final /ə/ which ends in <r, re> allows /r/-linking, e.g. *central, ethereal, managerial, terrorist, authority, authorial, favourite, calibration, fibrous, leverage, polarise, cigarette* (with movement of the stress), *vicarious, vulgarity, dictatorial, rigorous* (with deletion of the <u> from the final syllable of the stem), *theatrical, sulphuric, injurious, adventurous* – see section 3.6.

## 5.5 Long pure vowels (other than /iː, uː/): /ɑː ɜː ɔː/

### 5.5.1 /ɑː/ as in *aardvark*

#### THE MAIN SYSTEM

| | | | |
|---|---|---|---|
| Basic grapheme | <ar> | 60% | e.g. *farther* |
| Other frequent grapheme | <a> | 34% | e.g. *father*. More frequent in RP than in other accents. Regular before consonant clusters, but also occurs elsewhere. See Notes |

#### THE REST

| | | |
|---|---|---|
| Oddities | | 6% in total |
| | <aa> | only in *baa, Baal, Graal, kraal, laager, naan, salaam* |
| | <aar> | only in *aardvark, aardwolf, bazaar, haar* |
| | <a.e> | only in final syllables and only in about 30 (mostly more recent French) loanwords, namely *ballade, charade, chorale, façade, gouache, grave* (/grɑːv/, 'French accent'), *locale, morale, moustache, promenade* (noun, 'seafront path'; the verb with the same spelling, 'walk at leisure', is pronounced with /eɪ/), *rationale, strafe, suave, timbale, vase*, plus a set of words ending in /ɑːʒ/ spelt <-age>, e.g. *badinage, barrage, camouflage, collage, corsage, decalage, décolletage, dressage, entourage, espionage, fuselage, garage* pronounced /ˈɡærɑːʒ/, *massage, menage, mirage, montage, triage, sabotage* (only exception to final /ɑːʒ/ spelt <-age>: *raj*). The <e> in *chorale, locale, morale, rationale* differentiates those words visually from *choral, local, moral, rational* |

|                      | <ah>   | only word-final and only in *ah, bah, hookah, hoorah, kabbalah, Shah, whydah* |
|---|---|---|
|                      | <al>   | only in *calf, half, calve(s), halve(s), salve(s)* (also pronounced /sælv(z)/); *almond, almoner, alms, balm, calm, embalm, malmsey, napalm, palm, psalm, qualm* |
|                      | <are>  | only in *are* when stressed |
|                      | <arr>  | only in *bizarrery, carr, charr, parr* |
|                      | <arre> | only in *barre, bizarre*. /r/-linking occurs in *bizarrery* – see section 3.6 |
|                      | <arrh> | only in *catarrh*. /r/-linking occurs in *catarrhal* – see section 3.6 |
|                      | <as>   | only in *fracas* |
|                      | <at>   | only in *eclat, entrechat, nougat* |
|                      | <au>   | only in *aunt, draught, laugh(ter)* |
|                      | <ear>  | only in *hearken* (also spelt, more regularly, *harken*), *heart, hearth* |
|                      | <er>   | only in *Berkeley* (the town in England), *Berkshire, Cherwell, clerk, derby, Derby, Ker* pronounced /kɑː/ (also pronounced /kɜː/), *sergeant* |
| 2-phoneme graphemes  | /wɑː/  | See also Notes |
|                      | (1) spelt <oi>   | only in a few words more recently borrowed from French, e.g. *bourgeoisie, coiffeu-r/se, coiffure, pointe, soiree, toilette* |
|                      | (2) spelt <oir>  | mainly word-final and only in a very few words more recently borrowed from French, namely *abattoir, boudoir, memoir, reservoir, voussoir*; non-finally, only in *avoirdupois*. /r/-linking occurs in *memoirist, noirish* – see section 3.6 |
|                      | (3) spelt <oire> | only word-final and only in a very few words more recently borrowed from French, namely *aide-memoire, conservatoire, escritoire, repertoire* |
|                      | (4) spelt <ois>  | only word-final and only in a very few words more recently borrowed from French, namely *avoirdupois, bourgeois* (/z/ surfaces in *bourgeoisie* – see section 7.2), *chamois* (the animal, pronounced /ˈʃæmwɑː/, as opposed to the leather made from its skin, pronounced /ˈʃæmiː/, the latter also being spelt *shammy*), *patois* (contrast *fatwa*) |

*NOTES*

If we follow Crystal (2012: 131–2) and Upward and Davidson (2011: 176–9), 'more recent' in terms of loanwords from French means after the Great Vowel Shift, which began about AD1400 and was complete by about AD1600.

In RP, <a> is regular before consonant clusters, e.g.
- (in monosyllables) *aft, craft, graft, haft, raft, shaft* (exception: *draught*); *chance, dance, glance, lance, prance, trance; ranch; can't, chant, grant, plant, shan't, slant* (exception: *aunt*); *ask, bask, cask, flask, mask, task; clasp, gasp, grasp, hasp, rasp; basque, masque; blast, cast, caste, fast, last, mast, past, vast* (other exception: *alms*);
- (in final syllables of polysyllables) *abaft, advance, enhance, avalanche, command, countermand, demand, remand, enchant, bergomask, aghast, contrast* (noun and verb);
- (in non-final syllables) *macabre; padre; after, rafter; example, sample; chancel, chancery; revanchis-m/t; commando, slander; answer; basket, casket; bastard, caster, castor, disaster, flabbergasted, ghastly, master, nasty, pasta* (also pronounced with /æ/), *pasteurise, pastime, pastor, pasture, plaster* (exceptions: *aardvark, aardwolf, laughter, malmsey*).

Otherwise, in non-rhotic accents such as RP no rules can be given for where /ɑː/ is spelt <a> rather than <ar>, so here are some lists of words where /ɑː/ spelt <a> occurs:
- several words before medial /ð/ spelt <th>, e.g. *father, lather, rather* (exception: *farther*), and before final /f, s, θ/ spelt <-ff(e)/-ph, -ss, -th>, e.g. *chaff, distaff, staff; giraffe; cenotaph*, and *graph* and all its unsuffixed compounds: *auto/cardio/ di/encephalo/epi/mimeo/para/photo/tele/tri-graph* (exceptions: *calf, half*); *brass, class, glass, grass, pass* (exception: *arse*); *bath, path* (exception: *hearth*)
- word-finally in *bra, hoopla, Libra, (grand)ma, mama, (grand)pa, papa, schwa, spa* (contrast several of the Oddities)
- a large set of words, many of them loanwords, but all ending in a vowel phoneme and with stressed /ɑː/ spelt <a> in the penultimate syllable, e.g. *armada, avocado, balaclava, banana, blasé* (sometimes stressed on last syllable), *bravado, bravo* (sometimes stressed on last syllable), *cadre, cantata, cascara, cassava, cicada, cinerama, cyclorama, desiderata, desperado, drama, farrago, finale, gala, Gestapo, guano, guava, gymkhana, iguana, incommunicado, karate, khaki, lager, lama, lava, legato, liana, literati, llama, llano, marijuana, mascara,*

*meccano, nazi, pajama, palaver, panorama, pastrami, plaza, praline, pro rata, pyjama, safari, saga, salami, schemata, sonata, soprano, staccato, stigmata, strata, sultana, tiara, toccata, tomato, tsunami, virago*

- a final ragbag: *adagio* (second <a>), *amen, banal* (second <a>), *castle, claque, corral, debacle, fasten, plaque, pajamas* (second <a>), *pyjamas* (first <a>).

Words in which final /ɑː/ is spelt <-ar> allow /r/-linking, e.g. *far away* /fɑːrəˈweɪ/, sometimes with <r>-doubling, e.g. *sparring* – see section 3.6.

/wɑː/ has the 2-grapheme spelling <ua> in *guacamole, guano, guava, iguana, suave*.

## 5.5.2 /ɜː/ as in *earl*

### THE MAIN SYSTEM

For all these categories see Notes.

| | | | |
|---|---|---|---|
| Basic grapheme | <er> | 38% | e.g. *berth, exert, herd, serf, sherd, tern, twerp; defer, infer, prefer, refer* |
| Other frequent graphemes | <ir> | 18% | e.g. *birth, fir, whirl* |
| | <or> | 17% | regular after initial /w/, e.g. *word* |
| | <ur> | 17% | e.g. *fur, gurgle, surf, turn, urn* |

### THE REST

| | | |
|---|---|---|
| Oddities | | 10% in total |
| | <ear> | 8% never word-final, and only in *dearth, earl, early, earn, earnest, earth, heard, hearse, learn, pearl, rehearse, (re)search, yearn* |
| | <ere> | only in *were* when stressed |
| | <err> | in stem words only in *err* (for which see also section 4.3.2), but frequent in consonant-doubling before suffixes, e.g. *preferred* (see section 4.2) |

| | | |
|---|---|---|
| | \<eu\> | only in *chauffeuse, coiffeuse, masseuse, milieu* |
| | \<eur\> | non-finally, only in *secateurs*; otherwise only word-final and only in about 12 recent loanwords of French origin, e.g. *chauffeur* (if stressed on second syllable, pronounced /ʃəʊˈfɜː/), *coiffeur, connoisseur, entrepreneur, hauteur, masseur, poseur, provocateur, raconteur, repetiteur, restaurateur, seigneur* and a few other rare words |
| | \<irr\> | only in *chirr, shirr, whirr* |
| | \<olo\> | only in *colonel* |
| | \<our\> | only medial, and only in *adjourn, bourbon* ('whiskey'), *courteous, courtesy, journal, journey, scourge,* and *tourney* pronounced /ˈtɜːniː/ (also pronounced /ˈtʊəniː) |
| | \<urr\> | in stem words only in *burr, purr,* but frequent in consonant-doubling before suffixes, e.g. *furry, demurring, occurred* (see section 4.2) |
| | \<yr\> | only in *gyrfalcon, myrmidon, myrtle* |
| | \<yrrh\> | only in *myrrh* |
| 2-phoneme graphemes | (none) | |

## NOTES

/ɜː/ is rare in initial position, and the dozen or so words in which it does occur are split between \<ear\> (*earl, early, earn, earnest, earth*), \<er\> (*ermine, ersatz, erstwhile*), \<err\> (only in *err*), \<ir\> (only in *irk*) and \<ur\> (*urban, urbane, urchin, urge, urgent, urn*).

\<er\> is the default spelling in medial and final positions. It is regular in *hyperbole, interpret, superfluous, superlative* and other words with initial /haɪˈpɜː, ɪntˈɜː, suːpˈɜː/ stressed on the second syllable and spelt \<hyper-, inter-, super-\>; *concern, discern, convert, revert* and other words with the (Latin) elements \<cern, vert\>; *confer, defer, prefer, refer* with the (Latin) element \<-fer\>. Other examples: *adverse, alert, averse, assert, berth, certain, commercial, conserve* and derivatives, *deserve, desert* (/dɪˈzɜːt/, 'abandon', as opposed to /ˈdezət/, 'arid area'), *dessert, determine, disperse, epergne, eternal, exertion, exterminate, ferment, germ, gherkin, herb, herd, hermit, immerse, inert(ia), jersey, kerchief, kernel, merge, mercenary, nerd, observe, perfect, perk, permanent, person, quern, reserve, reverse, serf, serpent, serve, submerge, swerve, tern, terse, thermal, thermos, twerp, universe, verger, verse, vertigo.*

<or> is regular after initial /w/ whether spelt <w> or <wh>: *whortle(berry), word, work, world, worm, worse(n), worship, worst, wort, worth(y)*; otherwise only in *attorney*. Exceptions: *were, whirl, whir(r)*.

<ir> is regular in the prefix /'sɜːkəm/ spelt <circum->, e.g. *circumflex, circumstance, circumvent*; also after /g, kw, θ/, as in *gird, gird(le), girder, girl, girn, girt, girth* (exceptions: *gherkin, gurgle, regurgitate*); *quirk, quirt, squirm, squirt; third, thirst, thirteen, thirty* (exceptions: *thermal, thermos, Thursday*). Otherwise <ir> occurs in an unpredictable set of words, e.g. *besmirch, birch, bird, birth, chirp, circle, circus, cirque, dirk, dirt, fir, firm, firmament, first, firth, flirt, hirsute, irk, kirtle, mirth, shirk, shirt, sir, skirl, skirmish, skirt, smirk, stir, swirl, twirl, Virgo, virtual, virtue, virtuoso, virtuous, whir, whirl, zircon.*

<ur> is regular:

1) in the (Latin) verb element <-cur> ('run') as in *concur, (dis)cursive, cursor, excursus, incur(sion), occur, recur* and more generally after /k/: *cur, curb, curd, curfew, curl, curlew, curse, curt, curtail, curtain, curtsey, curve, scurf, scurvy* (exceptions: *colonel, courteous, courtesy, kerchief, kernel, kersey, kirtle, skirl, skirmish, skirt*);

2) after /b, tʃ/ and after /s/ in initial syllables of polysyllables: *auburn, burble, burden, burdock, burgess, burgher, burglar, burgeon, burgoo, burgundy, burlap, burlesque, burly, burn, burnet, burnish, burp, bursar, burst, disburse, hamburger, laburnum, suburb; church, churl(ish), churn; surface, surfeit, surgeon, surly, surmise, surmount, surpass, surplice, surplus, surveillance, survey, survive* (exceptions: *berg, berth, birch, bird, birth; chirp, chirr, concerto* if pronounced with /ɜː/ rather than /eə/, *serpent*).

Otherwise <ur> occurs in an unpredictable set of words, e.g. *absurd, appurtenance, blur, blurt, demur, disturb, diurnal, expurgate, frankfurter, fur, (re)furbish, furl, furlong, furlough, furnace, furnish, furniture, further, furtive, furze, gurgle, hurdle, hurl, hurt, hurtle, insurgent, jodhpurs, liturgy-y/ical, lurch(er), lurk, metallurg-y/ical, murder, murky, murmur* (first syllable), *nasturtium, nocturnal, nurse, nurture, purblind, purchase, purgation, purgatory, purge, purl, purlieu, purloin, purport, purse, pursu-e/it, purvey, regurgitate, return, Saturn, saturnine, slur, splurge, spur, spurn, spurt, surd, surf, taciturn, Thursday, turban, turbid, turbine, turbot, turbulent, turd, turf/ves, turgid, turkey, turmoil, turn, turnip, turquoise, turtle, urban, urbane, urchin, urge, urgent, urn.* In some words where <ur> is not stressed it may be reuced to /ə/, e.g. *purport, pursu-e/it, surpass.*

Words in which final /ɜː/ is spelt with a grapheme which includes final <-r> allow /r/-linking (see section 3.6), e.g. *murmuring, whirring, purring,* sometimes with <r>-doubling (see section 4.2), e.g. *conferring, occurring, demurral.*

## 5.5.3 /ɔː/ as in *awe*

### THE MAIN SYSTEM

For all these categories see Notes.

| Basic grapheme | <or> | 25% (with <ore, ar>) | e.g. *order, afford, for.* See also Table 5.4 |
|---|---|---|---|
| Other frequent graphemes | <ore> | | only word-final, e.g. *before,* except in compounds of *fore-.* See also Table 5.4 |
| | <ar> | | regular medially after /w/, e.g. *ward.* See also Table 5.3 |
| | <a> | 29% | regular before /l/; otherwise only in *water, waft* pronounced /wɔːft/, *wrath* pronounced /rɔːθ/ |
| | <au> | 9% | e.g. *autumn, cause*; word-final only in *landau, Nassau.* See also Table 5.4 |
| | <aw> | 9% | never before /r/; e.g. *awful, crawl, paw.* See also Table 5.4 |

## THE REST

| | | |
|---|---|---|
| *Oddities* | | 28% in total |
| | \<al\> | 5% only in *balk, calk, chalk, falconer, stalk, talk, walk* |
| | \<augh\> | 2% only in *aught, caught, daughter, distraught, fraught, haughty, (Mc)Naught(on), naught, naughty, onslaught, slaughter, taught* |
| | \<aul\> | only in *baulk, caulk, haulm* |
| | \<aur\> | only in *bucentaur, centaur, dinosaur* (and the names of various dinosaur species, e.g. *pterosaur*), *minotaur* |
| | \<awe\> | only in *awe* and derivatives other than *awful* |
| | \<oa\> | only in *abroad, broad, broaden* |
| | \<oar\> | 2% only in *boar, board, coarse, hoar, hoard, hoarse, oar, roar, soar* |
| | \<oer\> | only in *Boer* pronounced /bɔː/ (also pronounced /bʊə/) |
| | \<oor\> | 3% only in *door, floor*; also *boor, moor, poor, spoor* if pronounced to rhyme with *door, floor* |
| | \<orp\> | only in *corps* (plural), pronounced /kɔːz/ |
| | \<orps\> | only in *corps* (singular), pronounced /kɔː/ |
| | \<orr\> | only in *abhorred* |
| | \<ort\> | only in *mortgage, rapport*. /t/ surfaces in *rapporteur* – see section 7.2 |
| | \<ough\> | 6% only in *bought, brought, fought, nought, ought, (be-)sought, thought, wrought* |
| | \<our\> | 8% only in *bourne, court(esan), course, four, mourn, pour, source, your(s)* |
| | \<ou're\> | only in *you're*. See section A.9 in Appendix A |
| *2-phoneme graphemes* | (none) | |

## NOTES

Generalisations for /ɔː/ are weak because it has so many spellings. However, some are possible for instances of /ɔː/ after /w/ and before /l/. \<ar\> is regular in medial position after /w/, however spelt – see Table 5.3 and cf. /ɒ/, section 5.4.4. There are no words in which /ɔː/ is spelt \<ar\> without a preceding /w/.

TABLE 5.3: SPELLINGS OF /ɔː/ AS <ar> AFTER /w/.

| after /w/ spelt <u> – always after /k/ spelt <q> | after /w/ spelt <w> | after /w/ spelt <wh> |
|---|---|---|
| quart(an/er/et/ic/ile/z); also, according to particle physicists, quark /kwɔːk/ (pronounced /kwɑːk/ by the rest of us) | award, dwar-f/ves, reward, sward, swarf, swarm, swart(hy), (a)thwart, towards, untoward, warble, ward, warden, warfarin, warlock, warm, warn, warp, wart; also war (only example in final position and therefore only one with potential /r/-linking (and concomitant <r>-doubling – see section 4.2), e.g. warring – see section 3.6) | whar-f/ves |
| Exceptions (words in which /ɔː/ is **not** spelt <ar> after /w/) | | |
| quorn, quorum, squaw, squawk | caterwaul, sworn, walk, wall, walnut, waltz, water, whorl, worn; also waft, walrus if pronounced with /ɔː/ rather than /ɒ/. wall, walnut, walrus, waltz instead follow the generalisation about /ɔː/ before /l/, next | |

<a> is regular in all positions before /l/:
- initial: *albeit, alder, alderman, all, almanac* (usually pronounced with /æ/), *almighty, almost, already, altar, alter, alternate* (with both stresses and meanings), *although, altogether, always* (only exception: *awl*, which is also pre-final – see below)
- medial (except before final /l/): *bald, balderdash, baldric, balsam(ic), balti, enthralment, falcon, false, falsetto, falter, halt, halter, instalment, malt, palfrey, palsy, paltry, psalter, salt, scald, thraldom* (also spelt *thralldom*), *walnut, walrus* (also pronounced with /ɒ/), *waltz* (exceptions: *assault, cauldron, fault, vault*)
- pre-final (= medial before final /l/; N.B. This is the only place in my entire analysis where I have found it useful to use the term 'pre-final'): *appal, ball, call, enthral, fall, gall, hall, pall, small, squall, (fore/in)stall, tall, thrall, wall* (exceptions: *caterwaul, haul, maul; awl, bawl, brawl, crawl, drawl, scrawl, shawl, sprawl, trawl, yawl; whorl*). As this list shows, here /l/ after <a> is mostly spelt <ll>, the only exceptions being *appal, enthral*. On variation between <l> and <ll> see also section 4.4.7.

The only words in which /ɔː/ is spelt <a> other than before /l/ are *waft* if pronounced /wɔːft/, *water*, and *wrath* if pronounced /rɔːθ/.

Beyond this it is simplest to list spellings of /ɔː/ in <au, aw, or, ore> - see Table 5.4.

Many other examples of medial /ɔː/ spelt <or> before /r/ arise from suffixation of words ending in <-ore> (e.g. *boring*), when /r/-linking occurs - see section 3.6. In all these suffixed cases and in all the cases where medial /ɔː/ spelt <or> occurs before a vowel, the <r> is both part of grapheme <or> spelling /ɔː/ and a grapheme in its own right spelling /r/ (for dual-functioning see section 7.1). However, dual-functioning does not apply to /ɔː/ spelt <au> before /r/ since <au> already spells /ɔː/ without the following <r>.

The only example of <r>-doubling in final /ɔː/ spelt <or> appears to be *abhorred*, where the stress in the stem word is on the last syllable and <rr> arises from the main consonant-doubling rule - see section 4.2. In *abhorrent* there is both <r>-doubling and /r/-linking (see section 3.6) but the preceding vowel changes to /ɒ/ and <rr> spells only /r/.

Although I have said above that /ɔː/ before /r/ is never spelt <aw>, we should remember the childish pronunciation of *drawing* as /ˈdrɔːrɪŋ/.

Words in which final /ɔː/ is spelt with other graphemes which include final <r> also allow /r/-linking, e.g. *hoary, flooring, pouring* - see again section 3.6.

TABLE 5.4: <au, aw, or, ore> AS SPELLINGS OF /ɔː/.

For other spellings of /ɔː/ see above.

|  | Initial | Medial | Final |
|---|---|---|---|
| <au> | (before /r/) *aura, aural* (also pronounced with /aʊ/), *aureole, aureomycin, auricle, auriferous, aurochs, aurora.* See notes above Table (not before /r/) *aubretia, auburn, auction* (also pronounced with /ɒ/), *audacious, audible, audience, audio, audit, auger, augment, augur, August, august, auk, aumbry, auspic-e/ious, austere, authentic,* | (before /r/) *apatosaurus* and many other dinosaur names, *saurian, sauropod, taurine, Taurus, thesaurus.* See notes above Table (not before /r/) *applaud, assault, astronaut, bauble, bauxite, caterwaul, caucus, caudal, cauldron, cause, caustic, cauterise, caution, clause, daub, daunt, debauch, exhaust, faucet, fault, faun, fauna, flaunt, flautist, fraud, gaudy, gaunt,* | only in *landau* |

## The phoneme-grapheme correspondences, 2: Vowels

| | | | |
|---|---|---|---|
| | author(ity), autis-m/tic, autograph, automatic, automobile, autonomy and many other compounds of <aut(o)->, autumn, auxiliary | gauntlet, gauze, glaucoma (also pronounced with /aʊ/), glaucous, haul, haunch, haunt, holocaust, hydraulic (also pronounced with /ɒ/), inaugurate, jaundice, jaunt, juggernaut, laud, launch, launder, laundry, marauder, maudlin, maul, mausoleum, nausea-a/ous, nautical, paucity, paunch, pauper, pause, plaudit, plausible, raucous, sauce, saucer, sauna, saunter, staunch, taunt, taut, vault, vaunt | |
| <aw> (never before /r/) | awful, awkward, awl, awning | bawd, bawl, brawl, brawn(y), crawl, dawdle, dawn, drawl, drawn, fawn, gawp, hawk, hawser, lawn, mawkish, pawn, prawn, scrawl, scrawny, shawl, shawm, spawn, sprawl, squawk, tawdry, tawny, tomahawk, trawl, trawler, yawl, yawn | caw, claw, draw, flaw, gnaw, guffaw, haw, jackdaw, jaw, law, lockjaw, macaw, maw, paw, raw, rickshaw, saw, seesaw, slaw, squaw, straw, thaw, yaw |
| <or> | (before /r/) oracy, oral, oration, orient (noun). See notes above Table | (before /r/) aurora, authorial, borax, chlorine, choral, chorus, corporeal (second syllable), decorum, dictatorial, editorial, euphoria, flora, floral (also pronounced with /ɒ/), forum, glory, memorial, oratorio (third syllable), quorum, variorum. See notes above Table | abhor, cantor, condor, corridor, cuspidor, décor, for, grantor, humidor, ichor, lessor, matador, mentor, mortgagor, nor, or, praetor, quaestor, realtor, tor, toreador, vendor |
| | (not before /r/) or, orb, orbit, orc, orchard, orchestra, orchid, ordain, ordeal, order, ordinary, ordnance, ordure, organ, organdie, organise, orgasm, orgy, ormolu, ornament, ornate, ornery, ornithology, orphan, orthodontist, orthodox and many other compounds of <ortho->, ortolan, orts | (not before /r/) abort(ion), absorb, absorption, adorn, afford, border, born(e), cavort, chord, chortle, cohort, consort, cord, cork, corm, corn, corner, cornice, corporal, corporeal (first syllable), corporation (first syllable), corpse, corset, corvette, disgorge, divorce, dork, dormitory, endorse, enormous, exorcise, extortion, | |

TABLE 5.4: <au, aw, or, ore> AS SPELLINGS OF /ɔː/. CONT.

| | Initial | Medial | Final |
|---|---|---|---|
| | | *force, forfeit, forge, fork, forlorn, form, forsythia, fort, forth, fortune, gorge, gormandise, gormless, gorse, horde, hormone, horn, hornet, horse, horticulture, important, inform, lord, lorgnette, morbid, mordant, morganatic, morgue, morning, morphine, morse, morsel, mortal, mortar, nork, normal, north(-ern/ly), perform, platform, porcelain, porch, porcupine, pork, porpoise, porphyry, portion, portico, portrait, record, remorse, report, resort, scorch, scorn, Scorpio, scorpion, shorn, short, snorkel, sorcerer, sordid, sorghum, sort, sport, stork, storm, suborn, support, sword, sworn, thorn, torc, torch, torment, torn, tornado, torpedo, torpid, torque, torsion, torso, tort, tortoise, torture, uniform, vortex, worn* | |
| <ore> | (occurs only in *ore*, which I classify as final) | only in compounds of *fore-*, of which there are 60+ | *adore, albacore, before, bore, carnivore, chore, claymore, commodore, core, deplore, encore, explore, fore, furore, galore, gore, herbivore, ignore, implore, lore, more, omnivore, ore, pinafore, pore, score, semaphore, shore, snore, sophomore, sore, spore, stevedore, store, swore, sycamore, therefore, tore, whore, wore, yore* |

# 5.6 Diphthongs (other than /eɪ, aɪ, əʊ/): /ɔɪ aʊ eə ɪə ʊə/

## 5.6.1 /ɔɪ/ as in *oyster*

**THE MAIN SYSTEM**

| | | | |
|---|---|---|---|
| Basic grapheme | <oi> | 61% | e.g. *boil*. Regular in initial and medial positions. Never word-final (except in the Greek phrase *hoi polloi*) |
| Other frequent grapheme | <oy> | 39% | e.g. *boy*. Regular in word-final position; rare elsewhere, but see Notes |

**THE REST**

| | | |
|---|---|---|
| Oddity | <aw> | only in *lawyer, sawyer* |
| 2-phoneme grapheme (counting the automatic /j/-glide as part of the first phoneme) | /ɔɪjə/ spelt <oir> | only in *coir* /ˈkɔɪjə/ |

**NOTES**

<oy> is regular in word-final position, <oi> elsewhere. Exceptions:
- <oi> word-finally: only in *hoi polloi*
- <oy> non-finally: only in *arroyo, boycott, coypu, foyer* pronounced /ˈfɔɪjə/ (also pronounced /ˈfwaɪjeɪ, ˈfɔɪjeɪ/), *gargoyle, groyne, hoyden, loyal, oyster* (only occurrence in initial position), *royal, soya, voyage*. In *arroyo, foyer* pronounced /ˈfɔɪjə/, *loyal, royal, soya, voyage* the <y> is both part of <oy> spelling /ɔɪ/ and also a grapheme in its own right spelling /j/. For dual-functioning see section 7.1.

*coir* is the only word in the language with /ɔɪjə/ spelt with the single grapheme <oir>. Word-final /ɔɪjə/ also has the 2-grapheme spellings <oya, oyer> only in *soya, foyer* pronounced /ˈfɔɪjə/, the first word of the name of the ancient court known as *Oyer and Terminer*, and *coyer*, comparative of *coy* ('Had we but world enough and time...'), and the 3-grapheme spelling <-awyer> only in *lawyer, sawyer* /ˈlɔɪjə, ˈsɔɪjə/. Effectively, therefore, all the example words mentioned so far in this paragraph rhyme. Medially, /ɔɪjə/ occurs in *loyal, royal* and their derivatives, and possibly nowhere else. It is also noticeable that within this (tiny) set of words, only *coir* itself does not contain <y>.

## 5.6.2 /aʊ/ as in *ouch*

**THE MAIN SYSTEM**

| | | | |
|---|---|---|---|
| Basic graphemes | <ou> | 93% (with word-final <ow>) | e.g. *about* |
| | word-final <ow> | | e.g. *allow* |
| Other frequent graphemes | (none) | | |

**THE REST**

| | | |
|---|---|---|
| Oddities | | 7% in total |
| | <aow> | only in *miaow* |
| | <au> | only in *ablaut, faustian, gaucho, gauleiter, glaucoma* pronounced /glaʊˈkəʊmə/ (also pronounced /glɔːˈkəʊmə/), *sauerkraut* (twice), *umlaut* and the Greek letter name *tau*; also in *aural* if pronounced /ˈaʊrəl/ to distinguish it from *oral* /ˈɔːrəl/ |
| | <ough> | only in *bough, doughty, drought, plough, slough* ('muddy place') |
| | pre-consonantal <ow> | 6% e.g. *brown* |
| 2-phoneme grapheme (counting the automatic /w/-glide as part of the first phoneme) | /aʊwə/ | |
| | (1) spelt <hour> | only in *hour* |
| | (2) spelt <our> | only in *devour, flour, lour, our, ours, scour, sour* and *dour* pronounced /ˈdaʊwə/ (which makes it a homophone of *dower*; *dour* is also pronounced /dʊə/). These words allow /r/-linking, e.g. *floury, scouring* – see section 3.6. Also see Notes |

## NOTES

<ow> is regular:
- in word-final position, e.g. *cow* (only exceptions: *thou* /ðaʊ/, archaic second person singular subject pronoun, *thou* /θaʊ/, 'one thousandth of an inch/a thousand pounds/dollars')
- before a schwa vowel spelt with a vowel letter or digraph, i.e. only in *bowel, dowel, rowel, towel, trowel, vowel; bower, cower, dower, flower, glower, power, shower, tower; coward, dowager* (no exceptions), plus *howitzer* with /ɪ/ and *prowess* with /e/; this would also cover *rowan* in its Scottish pronunciation /ˈraʊwən/ (/ˈrəʊwən/ in England)
- in most words ending in /aʊl/, namely *cowl, fowl, growl, howl, jowl, owl, prowl, scowl, yowl* (only exception to this sub-pattern: *foul*)
- in most words ending in /aʊn/, namely *brown, crown, down, drown, frown, gown, renown, town* (only exceptions to this sub-pattern: *(pro)noun*).

<ou> is regular everywhere else. Exceptions (in addition to the Oddities above and <ow> subpatterns just listed): *chowder, crowd, dowdy, powder, rowdy; cowrie, dowry; frowsty; blowsy* (contrast *blouse*), *bowser, browse, dowse, drowse, drowsy, frowsy*.

/aʊwə/ also has the 2-grapheme spellings <-ower> in *bower, cower, dower, flower, glower, power, shower, tower,* <owar> in *coward* and <owa> in *dowager*. All of these words except *coward* allow /r/-linking, e.g. *cowering, flowery* – see section 3.6.

In the words with medial <ow> followed by a vowel letter listed above, the <w> also represents a /w/-glide between /aʊ/ and the following schwa (or /ɪ/ or /e/). In these words, therefore, the <w> is both part of the digraph <ow> spelling /aʊ/ and a grapheme in its own right spelling /w/ (for dual-functioning see section 7.1). The words within this set ending in <-ower> form perfect rhymes with the words ending in <-our> listed above, and these too seem to me to have an automatic /w/-glide – but the /w/ is not represented in the spelling. So for the /w/-glide the alternative spellings mean 'Now you see it, now you don't '. For more on that, see sections 3.8.7 and 9.0.

## 5.6.3 /eə/ as in *air*

For the two sets of percentages see Notes.

## THE MAIN SYSTEM

| | | | |
|---|---|---|---|
| Basic grapheme | <are> | 59% (24%) (with <ar>) | only word-final, e.g. *bare, care, fare, flare, hare, pare, stare, tare, ware*. See Notes |
| Other frequent graphemes | <ar> | | initially, only in *area, Aries*; never word-final. Regular medially, especially where word-final <e> is deleted before a suffix beginning with a vowel letter, e.g. *caring*, but there are also independent examples, e.g. *adversarial, Aquarius, barium, commissariat, garish, gregarious, hilarious, malaria(l), multifarious, nefarious, parent, precarious, proletariat, Sagittarius, variegated, various, vary*, and a fairly large set of nouns/adjectives in <-arian>, e.g. *agrarian, barbarian* (2nd <ar>), *centenarian* and other age terms, *egalitarian, grammarian, librarian, proletarian, utilitarian, vegetarian*; in all these cases the <r> also spells /r/ (for dual-functioning see section 7.1). Medially before a consonant, only in *scarce, scarcity*. See Notes |
| | <air> | 28% (12%) | regular initially because of *air* and its compounds (see under <aer> below); medially, only in *fairy, prairie* (with dual-functioning <r> – see section 7.1) and (Scots) *bairn, cairn, laird*; otherwise only word-final and only in *affair, air* (again), *chair, corsair, debonair, despair, eclair, fair, flair, hair, impair, lair, mohair, pair, repair, stair* |

|  |  |  |
|---|---|---|
| | \<ear\> 10% (4%) | only word-final and only in *(for(e)-)bear, pear, swear, tear* ('rip'), *wear* |

## THE REST

*Oddities*        3% (60% !!) in total

- *non-final*

    \<aer\>    except in *anaerobic, faerie*, only initial and only in words where the morpheme *air* is followed by a vowel phoneme, namely several compounds of *aero-*, e.g. *aerobic, aerodrome, aeroplane, aerosol*, etc., plus *aerate, aerial*. In all these cases the \<r\> is both part of \<aer\> spelling /eə/ and a grapheme in its own right spelling /r/. For dual-functioning see section 7.1. Compounds with the spelling \<air\>, e.g. *aircraft, airmail*, are more numerous, and therefore (because there are so few other words beginning /eə/, namely *area, e'er*, and *heir* and its derivatives) \<air\> is the main word-initial spelling

    \<ao\>    only in *aorist*

    \<eir\>    only in *theirs*

    \<er\>    only in *bolero* (/bə'leərəʊ/, 'dance'), *concerto* pronounced /kən'tʃeətəʊ/ (also pronounced /kən'tʃɜːtəʊ/), *concierge, recherche, scherzo, sombrero*. In *bolero, sombrero* the \<r\> is both part of \<er\> spelling /eə/ and a grapheme in its own right spelling /r/. For dual-functioning see section 7.1

- *final*

    \<aire\>    only in a few polysyllabic recent loanwords of mainly French origin, namely *affaire, commissionaire, concessionaire, doctrinaire, laissez-faire, legionnaire, millionaire, questionnaire, secretaire, solitaire*. /r/-linking occurs in *millionairess* – see section 3.6

    \<ayer\>    only in *prayer* pronounced /preə/ ('religious formula'; contrast *prayer* pronounced /'preɪjə/, 'one who prays')

    \<ayor\>    only in *mayor* and derivatives. /r/-linking occurs in *mayoral, mayoress* – see section 3.6

    \<eah\>    only in *yeah*

    \<e'er\>    only in *e'er, ne'er, where'er* and a few other archaic contracted forms. See Section A.9 in Appendix A

    \<eir\>    not counted (22% !!) only in *their*

| | | |
|---|---|---|
| | <ere> | not counted (37% !!) (with <er>) only in *ere, there, (no)where* and a few polysyllabic recent loanwords of French origin, namely *ampere, brassiere, cafetiere, commere, compere, confrere, misere, premiere*. /r/-linking occurs in *thereupon, wherever, compering*, etc. – see section 3.6 |
| | <erre> | only in *parterre* |
| | <ey're> | only in *they're*. See Section A.9 in Appendix A |
| | <heir> | only in *heir*. There is /r/-linking in *heiress, inherit* – see section 3.6, and in *inherit* /h/ also surfaces – see section 7.2 |
| *2-phoneme graphemes* | (none) | |

## NOTES

If we follow Crystal (2012: 131–2) and Upward and Davidson (2011: 176–9), 'more recent' in terms of loanwords from French means after the Great Vowel Shift, which began about AD1400 and was complete by about AD1600.

<are> is regular word-finally (and would be more so if *there, where* were spelt *thare, *whare* – but that would destroy the parallelism with *here*), <air> initially, <ar> medially.

*Scarce, scarcity* are the only words in which /eə/ spelt <ar> occurs before a consonant and the <r> is only part of the grapheme <ar> (hence more logical spellings for them would be *scairce, *scaircity, on the model of *bairn, cairn, laird*); in all other cases <ar> occurs before a vowel and the <r> is both part of <ar> spelling /eə/ and a grapheme in its own right spelling /r/ – for dual-functioning see section 7.1.

Similarly, in all the patterns with word-final <r(e)> (which is every word-final pattern listed above except <eah>), there is potential /r/-linking (and dual-functioning) before a suffix beginning with a vowel phoneme (e.g. *staring, repairing, wearing*) or a following word beginning with a vowel phoneme – see section 3.6. Examples before a following word: *prayer of intercession, mayor of Sheffield, ne'er a hope in h*ll, misere ouverte, they're arriving, heir apparent*.

Carney (1994: 110–1) points out that text frequencies for /eə/ differ vastly according to whether function words are included or not: 'The three words *where, there* and *their* account for more than half the raw text frequency of /eə/'. In this book I have almost exclusively used his

*The phoneme-grapheme correspondences, 2: Vowels*   185

function-words-excluded frequencies, but at the head of this entry and against a couple of the Oddities I have shown, for interest, both those and (in brackets) the very different frequencies when function words are included.

## 5.6.4 /ɪə/ as in *ear*

For why the percentages are double Carney's see Notes.
For all medial and final occurrences see also Table 5.5.

**THE MAIN SYSTEM**

| Basic grapheme | <ear> | 56% | (except in *afeard, arrears, beard, bleary, weary* and the half-exception *ear*) only word-final, e.g. *appear, hear* |
| --- | --- | --- | --- |
| Other frequent graphemes | <ere> | 24% (with <er>) | only word-final, e.g. *interfere, mere, sincere.* Carney's (original) percentage excludes *here*, which would skew the figures (cf. /eə/, just above) |
| | <er> | | except in *era*, only medial, e.g. *hero, series.* In all cases the <r> functions also as the spelling of /r/ – see section 7.1 |
| | <eer> | 8% | except in *eerie* (where <r> functions also as the spelling of /r/ – see section 7.1), only word-final, e.g. *beer* |

**THE REST**

| Oddities | | 12% in total |
| --- | --- | --- |
| | <eir> | only in *weir, weird* |
| | <eyr> | only in *eyrie* (where <r> functions also as the spelling of /r/ – see section 7.1) |
| | <e're> | only in *we're*. See Section A.9 in Appendix A |
| | <ier> | never initial; medially, only in *fierce, pierce, tierce*; otherwise only final |

<ir>    only in *emir, fakir* (can be stressed on either syllable, and is also pronounced with /ə/), *kir, kirsch, nadir* pronounced /'neɪdɪə, næ'dɪə/ (also pronounced /'neɪdə/), *souvenir, tapir*

*2-phoneme graphemes*   (none)

## NOTES

Carney (1994: 190) posits two sources of this phoneme in RP:
1) cases where there used to be a /r/ consonant following an /iː/ vowel. A letter <r> remains in the spelling (usefully for speakers with rhotic accents), but in RP the /r/ has disappeared except when /r/-linking occurs (see section 3.6);
2) cases where there never was a /r/ phoneme but an /iː/ has combined with a following /ə/.

I accept the first category but not the second. Carney does say (ibid.) that the second category 'for some speakers may still represent disyllabic /iː/ plus /ə/', and I think this is the case in my accent and that of many other RP speakers. For example, on Carney's analysis the expression *Stay, dear* and the word *stadia* would both be analysed as pronounced /'steɪdɪə/, with two syllables, but I think only the former is so pronounced and that *stadia* is pronounced /'steɪdiːjə/, with three syllables (and an automatic /j/-glide before the final schwa – see section 3.8.8). I have therefore assigned almost all occurrences with <r> to /ɪə/ (for the exceptions see below), and all occurrences without <r> instead to /iːjə/.

Fortunately, unlike the situation with /ɪ, iː/, Carney provides just enough information to re-calculate the percentages for /ɪə/ without the second category, and the results (which are double the percentages given by Carney) are shown above.

<eer> may seem a more 'basic' spelling of /ɪə/ than <ear> but accounts for a much smaller percentage of its occurrences.

Curiously, Carney does not list <ier> or any of the words containing it in his treatment of /ɪə/, presumably because none occurred in his corpus.

The only words in which /ɪə/ occurs initially seem to be *ear* (where it is the whole word and therefore also final), *eerie, era* and *eyrie*.

Spellings with <r> which I believe belong to /iːjə/ rather than to /ɪə/ are few in number, and restricted to:
1) adjectives in <-ear, -iar>: *cochlear, linear, nuclear, familiar, peculiar*;
2) comparative adjectives in <-ier>, e.g. *easier, happier*.

In all these cases I believe the ending has two syllables.

A serendipitous outcome of my analysis of /ɪə/ is that all its occurrences in polysyllables are stressed, wherever in the word they occur, except that *fakir, frontier, nadir* can be stressed on either syllable and *belvedere* is often stressed on the first syllable.

Medially, the predominant spelling is <er>, and in polysyllables there are no exceptions; finally, the predominant spelling is probably <eer> in lexical frequency but definitely <ear> in text frequency because most of the words in which it occurs have high frequency. However, because no clear guidance can be given on which spelling of /ɪə/ occurs in which words in final position, lists for both medial and final positions are given in Table 5.5.

In all the patterns listed above which occur word-finally (which is all of them except <er, eyr>), there is potential /r/-linking before a suffix beginning with a vowel phoneme (e.g. *hearing, sincerity, beery*) or a following word beginning with a vowel phoneme – see section 3.6. Examples before a following word: *hear and obey, beer and skittles, we're off!*

TABLE 5.5: SPELLINGS OF /ɪə/ IN MEDIAL AND FINAL POSITIONS.

| medial | final |
|---|---|
| <ear> *afeared, beard* | <ear> *blear, clear, dear, drear, ear, fear, gear, hear, near, rear, sear, shear, smear, spear, tear* ('moisture from eye'), *year; appear, arrear* |
|  | <eer> *beer, cheer, deer, jeer, leer, peer, queer, seer, sheer, sneer, steer, veer; auctioneer, Brexiteer, career, charioteer, commandeer, domineer, electioneer, engineer, gazetteer, mountaineer, muleteer, musketeer, mutineer, pamphleteer, pioneer, privateer, profiteer, scrutineer, veneer, volunteer* |
| <eir> *weird* | <eir> *weir* |
| <er> *adherent, cereal, coherence, coherent, ethereal, funereal, hero, inherent, managerial, material, perseverance, serial, series, serious, serum, sidereal, venereal, zero*; also frequent when words in <-ere> are suffixed, e.g. *interfering* | <ere> *mere, sere, sphere; ad/co/in-here, austere, belvedere, cashmere, interfere, revere, severe, sincere* |
| <ier> *fierce, pierce, tierce* | <ier> *bier, pier, tier; bandolier, bombardier, brigadier, cashier, cavalier, chandelier, chevalier, clavier, corsetier, frontier, fusilier, gondolier, grenadier, halberdier, vizier* |

TABLE 5.5: SPELLINGS OF /ɪə/ IN MEDIAL AND FINAL POSITIONS, CONT.

| medial | final |
|---|---|
| <ir> *kirsch* | <ir> *fakir, kir, nadir, souvenir* |
| In all the words with <er> in this column the <r> is both a grapheme in its own right spelling /r/ and part of the grapheme <er> spelling /ɪə/. For dual-functioning see section 7.1. | All the words in this column have the potential for /r/-linking – see section 3.6, some with change of vowel, e.g. *sincerity*. |

## 5.6.5 /ʊə/ as in *rural*

This phoneme is so rare in RP that it would be futile to identify a basic grapheme, so I have just listed 1- and 2-phoneme graphemes. In all cases see Notes.

| 1-phoneme graphemes | <eur> | only in *pleurisy*, where the <r> also spells /r/. For dual-functioning see section 7.1 |
| | <oor> | only word-final and only in *boor, moor, poor, spoor* pronounced /bʊə, mʊə, pʊə, spʊə/ (also pronounced /bɔː, mɔː, pɔː, spɔː/). There is /r/-linking in, e.g., *boorish* – see section 3.6 |
| | <our> | only in *amour, bourbon* ('biscuit'), *bourgeois(ie), bourse, contour, detour, dour* pronounced /dʊə/ (also pronounced /ˈdaʊwə/), *entourage, gourd, gourmand, gourmet, houri, mourn* (e.g. in *mourning* pronounced /ˈmʊənɪŋ/ to distinguish it carefully from *morning* /ˈmɔːnɪŋ/), *potpourri* if we take the second <r> as spelling /r/, *tour, tourney* pronounced /ˈtʊəniː/ (also pronounced /ˈtɜːniː/), *tournament, tourniquet, troubadour, velour*. There is /r/-linking in, e.g., *touring* – see section 3.6 – and in *houri* the <r> is both part of grapheme <our> and a grapheme in its own right spelling /r/. For dual-functioning see section 7.1 |

|  |  |  |
|---|---|---|
|  | <ur> | never word-final; initially, only in *urtext*; otherwise only medial, e.g. *injurious, insurance, juror, jury, luxuriance, luxuriant, luxuriate, luxurious* (pronounced /lʌgˈʒʊəriːj-əns/ənt/eɪt/əs/), *prurien-t/ce, rural, usurious*; also *centurion, durable, (en)during, duress, maturity* pronounced /senˈtʃʊəriːjən, ˈdʒʊərəbəl, (ɪn)ˈdʒʊərɪŋ, dʒʊəˈres, məˈtʃʊərɪtiː/, i.e. with /tj, dj/ affricated to /tʃ, dʒ/. In all cases except *urtext* the <r> is both part of <ur> spelling /ʊə/ and a grapheme in its own right spelling /r/ – for dual-functioning see section 7.1 |
|  | <ure> | only word-final, e.g. *abjure, adjure, assure, brochure, caricature* (also pronounced with final /ə/), *conjure* /kənˈdʒʊə/ ('summon with an oath'), *cynosure, embouchure, endure* pronounced /ɪnˈdʒʊə/, *ensure, insure, mature* pronounced /məˈtʃʊə/, *overture* (if final syllable is pronounced /tʃʊə/ rather than /tʃə/), *sure* |
| 2-phoneme graphemes | /jʊə/ |  |
|  | (1) spelt <eur> | only in *Europe* (where the <r> is also a grapheme in its own right spelling /r/ – for dual-functioning see section 7.1) and *liqueur* pronounced /lɪˈkjʊə/ |
|  | (2) spelt <ur> | never word-final; initially, only in *urea* and various words derived from or cognate with it, e.g. *Uranus* pronounced /ˈjʊərənəs/ 'urine us' (also pronounced /jəˈreɪnəs/ 'your anus'), *urethra, uric, urine, urology*; medial examples are *bravura, curate* (both the noun 'junior cleric' pronounced /ˈkjʊərət/ and the verb 'mount an exhibition' pronounced /kjʊəˈreɪt/), *curie, curious,* |

|  |  |
|---|---|
|  | *furious, fury, mural, purify, purity, security, spurious*; also *centurion, durable, (en)during, duress, maturity* pronounced /sen'tjʊəriːjən, 'djʊərəbəl, (ɪn)'djʊərɪŋ, djʊə'res, mə'tjʊərɪtiː/, i.e. with /tj, dj/ NOT affricated to /tʃ, dʒ/. In all cases the <r> is both part of <ur> spelling /jʊə/ and a grapheme in its own right spelling /r/ – for dual-functioning see section 7.1 |
| (3) spelt <ure> | only word-final, e.g. *allure, coiffure, cure, demure, endure* pronounced /ɪn'djʊə/, *immure, inure, lure, manure, mature, ordure* pronounced /mə'tjʊə, ɔː'djʊə/, *overture* (if final syllable is pronounced /tjʊə/ rather than /tjə/), *photogravure, pure, secure, sinecure, Ure*; also in *azure* pronounced /'æzjʊə, 'eɪzjʊə/ (also pronounced /'æzjə, 'eɪzjə, 'æʒə, 'eɪʒə/) |
| Oddities | All the correspondences for this phoneme are Oddities |

**NOTES**

This phoneme is rare and getting rarer in RP, and may eventually disappear. Its rarity means percentages for graphemes would be misleading, as would treating /jʊə/ as a separate phoneme from /ʊə/ in parallel fashion to separating /juː/ from /uː/. Many words in which /ʊə/ used to occur now have /ɔː/ instead. For instance, the word *your* used to be pronounced /jʊə/ (and still is, in some accents), but in RP is now /jɔː/ – and *cure, liqueur, mature* and *pure* are now often heard as /kjɔː, lɪ'kjɔː, mə'tʃɔː, pjɔː/ in up-market accents. But words like *curious, fury, injurious, juror, jury, prurient, rural, spurious* seem to be resisting the change to /ɔː/. Check your own pronunciation of the words listed in this section.

Carney (1994: 194–5) also classifies as examples of /(j)ʊə/ many words in which letter <u> is followed by a spelling of /ə/ (e.g. *cruel, jewel, usual*). I analyse these instead as being pronounced with /(j)uː/ and /ə/ constituting a separate syllable (and an automatic intervening /w/-glide). It is noticeable that all these words end in a consonant phoneme.

*The phoneme-grapheme correspondences, 2: Vowels* 191

In phonologically similar words which end in a vowel phoneme (which here is always /ə/) it seems to be agreed that the ending is /'(j)uːwə/. Words in these (very small) groups are:
- (with /'uːwə/) *brewer*, *sewer* (/'suːwə/, 'foul drain', as opposed to *sewer* /'səʊwə/, 'one who sews'), *interviewer*, *viewer* (in the last two the /j/ glide is spelt <i> - contrast the next group);
- (with /'juːwə/) *ewer*, *fewer*, *hewer*, *newer*, *renewer*, *skewer* (cf. the homophone *skua*). A few derived forms also have /'uːwə/, e.g. *doer* ('one who does'), *two-er* ('conker which has broken two others').

In my analysis a few /(j)ʊə/ v. /'(j)uːwə/ minimal pairs seem possible, e.g. *Ure/ewer*, *dour/doer*, *tour/two-er* – but the phonological difference is minute (and some phoneticians would say non-existent).

## 5.7 Letter-name vowels: /eɪ iː aɪ əʊ juː/, plus /uː/

### 5.7.1 /eɪ/ as in *aim*

#### THE MAIN SYSTEM

For all these categories see Notes.

| | | | |
|---|---|---|---|
| *Basic grapheme* | <a.e> | 38% (76% in monosyllables) | regular in closed final syllables, e.g. *dilate, make, take, ache, champagne* |
| *Other frequent graphemes* | <a> | 27% | regular in non-final syllables of stem words, e.g. *agent, bacon, labour* |
| | <ay> | 18% | regular in open final syllables (= in word-final position), e.g. *chardonnay, day, display, way*; never initial; rare medially but cf. *always, claymore, mayhem, nowadays* |
| | <ai> | 12% | regular before /nt/, e.g. *paint* (only exceptions: *ain't* (sort of), *feint*); never word-final |

## THE REST

*Oddities*                        5% in total

         <ae>          only in *brae*, *Gaelic* pronounced /ˈgeɪlɪk/, *maelstrom*, *reggae*, *sundae*

         <ah>          only in *dahlia*

         <aigh>      only in *straight*

         <ais>         only in *palais*

         <ait>          only in *distrait*, *parfait*, and *trait* pronounced /treɪ/ (also pronounced /treɪt/)

         <alf>         only in *halfpence*, *halfpenny*

         <ao>          only in *gaol*

         <au>          only in *gauge*

         <aye>        only in *aye* ('ever')

         <e>           only in 60+ more recent loanwords mainly from French where French spelling has <é>, namely (in non-final position) *debris, debut, decor, eclair, ecru, elan, ingenu, precis*; first <e> in *debacle, debutante, decalage, decolletage, denouement, detente, elite, ingenue, menage, regime, seance*, (Greek) *heter/hom-ogeneity* pronounced /hetər/hɒm-əʊdʒɪˈneɪjɪtiː/ (usually pronounced /hetər/hɒm-əʊdʒɪˈniːjɪtiː/), (Old English) *thegn* and (Hawaian) *ukulele*; (word-finally) *abbe, attache, blase, cafe* (also pronounced with /iː/), *canape* (also pronounced with /iː/, hence the invitation I once received to a party with 'wine and canopies'), *cliche, communique, conge, consomme, coupe, diamante, fiance, flambe, frappe, glace, habitue, macrame* (derived from Turkish), *manque, outre, retrousse, risque, rose* ('pink wine'), *roue, saute, soigne, souffle, touche*, (Amerindian/Spanish) *abalone*, (Italian) *biennale, finale, latte*, (Greek) *agape* ('love feast'), (Spanish/Nahuatl) *guacamole*, (Japanese) *anime, kamikaze* and (Mexican Spanish) *tamale*; final <e> in (French) *emigre, expose, naivete, protege, recherche, resume* ('c.v.'), *retrousse* (KiSwahili/Spanish), *dengue* and (Turkish) *meze*.

*The phoneme-grapheme correspondences, 2: Vowels* 193

There is an increasing tendency to spell the French loanwords in this list, within English text, with <é>, thus signalling their status as not-yet-fully-assimilated loanwords (and my spell-checker keeps inserting <é> where I don't want it to) – but it could also be argued that this is yet another spelling complexity for native English speakers to cope with, especially since the Compact Oxford Dictionary recognises such forms as *flambés, flambéing, flambéed*, which on the other hand suggests that <é> is becoming a grapheme of English – if it does, where would it fit in the alphabet and therefore dictionaries?

<ea>    only in *break, great, steak, yea, Yeats*

<ee>    only word-final and only in about 13 more recent loanwords where French spelling has <ée>, namely *corvee, dragee* ('sugar-coated sweet') pronounced /ˈdrɑːʒeɪ/ (also pronounced /ˈdreɪdʒiː/), *entree, epee, fiancee, levee* ('reception or assembly', also pronounced with /iː/), *matinee, melee, nee, negligee, puree, soiree, toupee*. The tendency to use <é> is growing here too

<e.e>   only in *crepe, fete, renege, suede, Therese* /kreɪp, feɪt, rɪˈneɪg, sweɪd, təˈreɪz'/

<ei>    only in about 15 words, namely *abseil, apartheid, beige, deign, feign, feint, heinous* pronounced /ˈheɪnəs/ (also pronounced /ˈhiːnəs/), *lei* (only example in an open syllable), *obeisance, reign, rein, reindeer, seine, sheikh, skein, surveillance, veil, vein*

<eigh>  only in *eight, freight, heigh, inveigh, neigh, neighbour, sleigh, weigh, weight*

<er>    only word-final and only in a few more recent French loanwords, namely *atelier, croupier, dossier* pronounced /ˈdɒsliˌjeɪ/ (also pronounced /ˈdɒsiːjə/), *foyer* pronounced /ˈfwaɪjeɪ, ˈfɔɪjeɪ/ (also pronounced /ˈfɔɪjə/), *metier, rentier*

<es>    only in *demesne*

<et>    only word-final and only in about 20 more recent French loanwords, namely *ballet, beret, bidet, bouquet,*

|  |  |  |
|---|---|---|
|  |  | *buffet* ('food'), *cabaret, cabriolet, cachet, cassoulet, chalet, crochet, croquet, duvet, gilet, gourmet, parquet, piquet, ricochet, sachet, so(u)briquet, sorbet, tourniquet, valet* pronounced /ˈvæleɪ/ (also pronounced /ˈvælɪt/). /t/ surfaces (see section 7.2), always with change of preceding vowel, in *balletic* with /e/, *parquetry, valeting* with /ɪ/ |
|  | &lt;ey&gt; | never initial; medially, only in *abeyance, heyday*; word-finally, only in *bey, convey, fey, grey, hey, lamprey, obey, osprey, prey, purvey, survey, they, whey* |
|  | &lt;ez&gt; | only in *laissez-faire, pince-nez, rendezvous* |
| 2-phoneme graphemes | (none) |  |

## NOTES

If we follow Crystal (2012: 131-2) and Upward and Davidson (2011: 176-9), 'more recent' in terms of loanwords from French means after the Great Vowel Shift, which began about AD1400 and was complete by about AD1600.

&lt;a&gt; is regular in non-final syllables of stem words – see section 6.3. Exceptions (in addition to derived forms, e.g. *daily, gaily, playing*, and those listed among the Oddities above): *aileron, attainder, caitiff, complaisant, dainty, daisy, gaiter, liaison, maintain, plaintiff, plaintive, raillery, raisin, traitor, wainscot*, all with &lt;ai&gt;.

&lt;a.e&gt; is regular in closed final syllables, including not only the large number of mono- and polysyllables with a single final consonant phoneme spelt with a single letter, but also:

- five words with two consonant letters forming a digraph representing a single consonant phoneme separating &lt;a.e&gt;: *ache, champagne, bathe, lathe, swathe*
- the small group of words ending in /eɪndʒ/ spelt &lt;-ange&gt;: *arrange, change, grange, mange, range, (e)strange*, with two consonant phonemes separating &lt;a.e&gt; (no exceptions)
- the small group of words ending in /eɪst/ spelt &lt;-aste&gt;: *baste, chaste, haste, lambaste* (which has the variant form *lambast*, with /æ/), *paste, taste, waste*, still with two consonant phonemes separating &lt;a.e&gt; (exceptions: only *waist* as a stem word, but confusion is possible with a number of past-tense verbs, namely *based, chased, paced*).

The only monosyllable in which /eɪ/ is spelt just <a> without another vowel letter (and irregularly before a doubled spelling) is *bass* /beɪs/ '(player of) large stringed instrument'/'(singer with) low-pitched voice'.

<ay> is regular in word-final position in both mono- and polysyllabic stem words (for exceptions see the Oddities above), and rare elsewhere in stem words: the only medial examples seem to be *claymore, mayhem*, and there are none in initial position. However, medial <ay> spelling /eɪ/ does also occur in compound words, e.g. *always, hayfever, maybe, playground*, and frequently before suffixes, e.g. *playing*.

Fortunately, there are no occurrences of word-final /eɪ/ spelt <ai>, thus reducing the possibility of confusion with <ay>, but all words with /eɪ/ spelt <ai> are still exceptions, either to the prevalence of <a> in non-final syllables or to the prevalence of <a.e> in closed final syllables.

The only useful sub-rule is that <ai> is regular before /nt/, e.g. (in monosyllables) *faint, paint, plaint, quaint, saint, spraint, taint* (only exceptions: *ain't* (sort of), *feint*); (in polysyllables) *acquaint, attaint, complaint, con/di/re-straint*, plus *Aintree, dainty, maintain, maintenance, plaintiff, plaintive* (the last six words being apparently the only examples before /nt/ in non-final syllables of stem words), but it is not predictable by rule elsewhere. The rule that <ai> is regular before /nt/ is one of only two cases where the spelling of a rime/phonogram is more predictable as a unit than from the separate phonemes and there are enough instances to make the rule worth teaching – see section A.7 in Appendix A.

About half (by text frequency) of /eɪl, eɪn/ spellings in closed monosyllables have <-ail, -ain>, e.g. *ail, bail, fail, flail, frail, grail, mail, hail, jail, pail, quail, rail, sail, snail, tail, trail, wail* (also cf. *Braille*); *brain, chain, drain, fain, gain, grain, main, pain, plain, rain, sprain, stain, strain, swain, train, twain, vain, wain* and the irregular past participles *lain, slain* (see third paragraph below), but this means that these groups have maximum confusability with words in <-ale, -ane>, etc., e.g. (and listing just a few that are homophones of words in <-ail, -ain>) *ale, bale, male, hale, pale, sale, tale, whale; gaol; fane, lane, mane, pane, plane, vane, wane; feign, reign; rein, vein*, and all these words have to be learnt individually.

This is also true of:
1) polysyllables with <ail, ain(e)>: (in non-final syllables) *aileron, daily, gaily, raillery; attainder, wainscot*; (in final syllables) *assail, avail, curtail, detail, entail, entrails, prevail, retail, travail, wassail; ascertain,*

*chilblain, cocaine, contain, disdain, domain, entertain, explain, migraine, moraine, obtain, pertain, plantain, quatrain, remain, terrain*

2) the ragbag of other words (mono- and polysyllables) with <ai>, where there is also considerable potential for confusion: (in non-final syllables) *caitiff, complaisant, daisy, gaiter, lackadaisical, liaison, raisin, traitor;* (in final syllables) *afraid, aid, aide, aim, aitch, arraign, bait* (contrast *bate*), *baize* (contrast *bays*), *braid* (contrast *brayed*), *braise* (contrast *brays*), *campaign* (contrast *champagne*), *(de/ex/pro-)claim, cockaigne, faith, gait* (contrast *gate*), *liaise, maid* (contrast *made*), *maim, maize* (contrast *maze*), *malaise, mayonnaise, plaice* (contrast *place*), *praise, raid, raise* (contrast *raze*), *staid* (contrast *stayed*), *staithe, strait* (contrast *straight*), *traipse, waif, waist* (contrast *waste*), *wait* (contrast *weight*), *waive* (contrast *wave*), *wraith* and the irregularly-spelt (but not irregularly-pronounced) past tenses and participles *laid, paid* (see next paragraph).

As pointed out under /d/, section 3.5.2, the spellings *laid, paid* are irregular; the regular spellings would be *\*layed, \*payed*. But for the irregular past participles of *lie* ('be horizontal'), *slay* the spellings *lain, slain* seem preferable to *\*layn, \*layen, \*slayn, \*slayen*, and can perhaps be counted as extensions of the general <y>-replacement rule – see section 6.5.

There seem to be no words ending in /eɪ/ spelt <er> taking suffixes beginning with vowel letters, and therefore no /r/-linking (section 3.6). If so, this is the only such category.

## 5.7.2 /iː/ as in *eel*

For the absence of percentages see Notes.

### THE MAIN SYSTEM

For all these categories see Notes.

| | | |
|---|---|---|
| *Basic grapheme* | <ee> | e.g. *eel* (virtually the only occurrence in initial position), *beech, bee, see* |
| *Other frequent graphemes* | <e> | e.g. *ether, lever, be.* Regular in non-final syllables of stem words. In closed monosyllables, apparently only in *retch* |
| | <ea> | e.g. *each, beach, sea* |
| | <i> | e.g. *chic* (only example in a closed stem monosyllable), *alien, litre, ouija, safari* |

|  |  |  |
|---|---|---|
|  | \<y\> | almost entirely word-final, where it is the regular spelling in polysyllables, e.g. *city*, plus rare medial examples, e.g. *caryatid, embryo, halcyon, polysyllable* |
| Rare graphemes | \<e.e\> | rare in closed monosyllables; regular in closed final syllables of polysyllabic words, e.g. *complete, discrete, grapheme, phoneme* |
|  | \<ie\> | never initial. In non-final syllables only in *chieftain, diesel.* Otherwise only in final syllables: (closed monosyllables) *brief, chief, fief, field, fiend, frieze, grief, grieve, lief, liege, mien, niece, piece, priest, shield, shriek, siege, thief, thieve, wield, yield*; (open monosyllable) *brie* (only); (closed final syllables of polysyllables) *achieve, aggrieve, Aries, belief, believe, besiege, hygiene, relief, relieve, reprieve, retrieve, series, serried, species*; (open final syllables of polysyllables) *aerie, anomie, auntie, Aussie, birdie, bogie, bolshie, bonhomie, boogie, bookie, bourgeoisie, bowie, brassie, budgie, caddie, calorie, camaraderie, chappie, collie, commie, conscie, cookie, coolie, coterie, cowrie, curie, darkie, dearie, eerie, eyrie, gaucherie, genie, g(h)illie, girlie, goalie, hoodie, laddie, lassie, lingerie* pronounced /ˈlænʒəriː/ (also pronounced /ˈlɒndʒəreɪ/), *luvvie, menagerie, movie, nightie, organdie, pixie, prairie, reverie, rookie, quickie, specie, stymie, sweetie, talkie, zombie.* For '\<i\> before \<e\> except after \<c\>' see section 6.1 |

## THE REST

|  |  |  |
|---|---|---|
| Oddities | \<ae\> | only in (in non-final syllables) *aegis, aeon, aesthet e/ ic, anaemi-a/c* and other words ending /ˈiːmiːjə, ˈiːmɪk/ spelt \<-aemi-a/c\>, *anaesthetist, archaeolog-ical/ist/y, Caesar(ian), caesura, encyclopaedia, faeces,* |

*haemoglobin, Linnaean, Manichaean, mediaeval, naevus, paean, palaeolithic, praetor, quaestor.* Many of these words have alternative spellings in <e>, especially in US spelling; (in final syllables – always open; no examples in closed final syllables) *algae, alumnae, antennae, formulae, larvae, personae, pupae, vertebrae*

<ay>   only finally and only in *quay* and compounds of *day* (*birthday, holiday, Sunday, yesterday,* etc.), except *heyday, midday, nowadays, today, workaday,* which have /eɪ/, as does *holidaying*

<ei>   only medial and only in: (in non-final syllables) *ceiling, cuneiform, disseisin, (n)either* pronounced /ˈ(n)iːðə/ (also pronounced /ˈ(n)aiːðə/), *heinous* pronounced /ˈhiːnəs/ (also pronounced /ˈheɪnəs/), *inveigle, plebeian;* (in final syllables) *caffeine, casein, codeine, conceit, conceive, counterfeit* (also pronounced with /fɪt/), *deceit, deceive, perceive, protein, receipt, receive, seize.* For '<i> before <e> except after <c>' see section 6.1

<eo>   only in *feoffee, feoffment, people*

<ey>   except in *geyser* pronounced /ˈgiːzə/, only final and only in *abbey, alley, attorney, baloney, barley, blarney, blimey, cagey, chimney, chutney, cockney, comfrey, coney, donkey, dopey, flunkey, fogey, galley, gooey, hackney, hockey, homey, honey, jersey, jockey, journey, key, kidney, lackey, malarkey, matey, medley, money, monkey, motley, nosey, palfrey, parley, parsley, pokey, pulley, storey, tourney, turkey, valley, volley*

<i.e>  only in closed final syllables, but in at least 70 words – see Table 5.6 and the note below it

<is>   only finally and only in *chassis, commis* (*chef*), *coulis, debris, precis, verdigris* pronounced /ˈvɜːdɪgriː/ (also pronounced /ˈvɜːdɪgriːs/), *vis-à-vis* (last syllable)

<it>   only finally and only in *esprit, petit mal, wagon-lit*

<oe>   only in non-final syllables and only in *amenorrhoea, amoeba, apnoea, coelacanth, coelenterate, coeliac, coelom, coenobite, coenocyte, diarrhoea, dyspnoea, foetal, foetid, foetus, gonorrhoea, lactorrhoea, logorrhoea, oedema, oenology, oesophagus, oestrogen, oestrus, phoenix, pyrrhoea, subpoena,* plus

|  |  |
|---|---|
|  | *onomatopoeia, pharmacopoeia* if <ia> is taken as spelling /iːjə/. Many of these words have alternative spellings in <e>, especially in US spelling |
| <ois> | only in *chamois* (the leather, pronounced /ˈʃæmiː/ (also spelt *shammy*), as opposed to the animal from whose skin it is made, pronounced /ˈʃæmwaː/) |

*2-phoneme graphemes*   (none)

## NOTES

The reason for the absence of percentages here is my re-allocation of word-final <y> to /iː/ rather than /ɪ/ (see section 5.4.3), and of many of Carney's /ɪə/ words to /iːjə/ (see section 5.6.4). Carney doesn't give enough information on either set of words to calculate the effect of these re-allocations on the percentages for /iː/.

Unlike most of the split digraphs, <e.e> is not very frequent – in Carney's analysis (excluding final /iː/ spelt <y>) it accounts for only 3% of spellings of /iː/, and for only 27% even in monosyllables, and percentages counting in final /iː/ spelt <y> would be even lower. It is the second rarest of the split digraphs, the rarest being <y.e>.

The regular spellings of /iː/ are:
- in open and closed monosyllables: <ee>
- in open final syllables (= stem-finally) in polysyllables: <y>
- in closed final syllables of polysyllables: <e.e>
- in non-final syllables, especially of stem words: <e>, but there are large numbers of exceptions with <i>.

In open monosyllables the regular spelling is <ee>, as in *bee, fee, flee, free, gee, ghee, glee, knee, lee, pee, scree, see, spree, tee, thee, three, tree, twee, wee*. Exceptions: *be, he, me, she, the* (when stressed), *we, ye* – but these are all function words, which don't have to obey the Three-Letter Rule (see section 4.3.2); *flea, lea, pea, plea, sea, tea; key; ski; brie*.

In closed monosyllables Carney (1994: 157–8) lists 108 words with <ea>, 87 with <ee>, and 30 with minority spellings. However, those with <ee> seem more frequent, e.g. *beech, cheek, cheese, deep, feed, feek, feet, geese, green, keep, meet, need, seem, seen, sleep, sleeve, sneeze, speech, speed, street, week, wheel*. Also, analysing <ea> as the regular spelling here would seem odd, given that <ea> has several other correspondences, some of them with long lists of words, while <ee> has hardly any and they are all rare. I therefore take <ee> to be most regular spelling of /iː/ in closed monosyllables. For exceptions see Table 5.6, plus *chic, retch, seize*.

In open final syllables of polysyllables the regular spelling (in my analysis, as against Carney's) is <y>, e.g. *city, pretty*. Exceptions include:
- those listed under the rare grapheme <ie> and the Oddities <ae, ay, ey, is, it, ois> above
- *aborigine, acme, acne, adobe, anemone, apostrophe, bocce, catastrophe, coyote, dilettante, epitome, extempore, facsimile, (bona) fide, hebe, hyperbole, Lethe, machete, menarche, minke, nepenthe, oche, posse, psyche, recipe, reveille, sesame, simile, stele, strophe, tagliatelle, tsetse, ukulele, vigilante*
- a few words in <-e> where pronunciation of the final phoneme varies between /iː/ and /eɪ/: *abalone, cafe, canape, finale, forte, furore, guacamole, kamikaze, karate*
- one word in <-ea>: *guinea*
- all the words ending in <-ee> indicating 'person to whom something is done' (all with final stress), e.g. *addressee, amputee, appointee, assignee, conferee, debauchee, dedicatee, deportee, divorcee, draftee, employee, enrollee, examinee, grantee, inductee, internee, interviewee, invitee, legatee, lessee, licensee, mortgagee, nominee, parolee, patentee, payee, referee, trainee, transferee, trustee, vestee*
- a ragbag of other words ending in <-ee>, including: (with initial stress) *apogee, coffee, dragee* ('sugar-coated sweet') pronounced /ˈdreɪdʒiː/ (also pronounced /ˈdrɑːʒeɪ/), *filigree, fricassee, gee-gee, jubilee, kedgeree, levee* ('reception or assembly', also pronounced with /eɪ/), *lychee, manatee, pedigree, perigee, Pharisee, prithee, puttee, Sadducee, spondee, squeegee, standee, suttee, thuggee, toffee, trochee, yankee*; (with medial stress) *committee*; (with final stress) *absentee, agree, attendee, banshee, bargee, bootee, buckshee, chickadee, chimpanzee, decree, degree, devotee, dungaree, escapee, goatee, grandee, guarantee, jamboree, marquee, refugee, repartee, rupee, settee, truckee*
- a further ragbag of mostly foreign words ending in <i>: *anti, bikini, broccoli, chilli, confetti, deli, ennui, graffiti, khaki, kiwi, literati, macaroni, maxi, midi, mini, muesli, mufti, nazi, potpourri, safari, salami, scampi, spaghetti, sari, semi, shufti, stimuli, taxi, tsunami, umami, vermicelli, wiki, yeti, yogi.*

In closed final syllables of polysyllables the regular spelling is <e.e>. For exceptions in <ei> see the Oddities, and for those in <ea, ee, ie, i.e> see

Table 5.6. There are apparently just five exceptions with <i>: *ambergris, aperitif, batik, massif, motif*, and one with <e>: *harem*. There is also a small group with /iːz/ spelt <-es>, namely some plural nouns of Greek origin with the singular ending /ɪs/ spelt <-is>, e.g. *analyses* (/əˈnælɪsiːz/, the singular verb of the same spelling being pronounced /ˈænəlaɪzɪz/), *apotheoses, axes, bases* (/ˈæksiːz, ˈbeɪsiːz /, plurals of *axis, basis*; *axes, bases* as the plurals of *axe, base* are pronounced (regularly) /ˈæksɪz, ˈbeɪsɪz/), *crises, diagnoses, emphases, exegeses, nemeses, oases, periphrases, synopses, theses* and all its derivatives, plus (Greek singulars) *diabetes* (also pronounced with final /ɪs/), *herpes, litotes, pyrites*, (a stray Greek plural with singular in <-s>) *Cyclopes*, and (Latin plurals) *amanuenses, appendices, cicatrices, faeces, interstices, mores, Pisces, testes*.

A very odd word that is relevant here is *dioceses*. In its singular form *diocese*, pronounced /ˈdaɪjəsɪs/, each phoneme (except the automatic /j/-glide) can be related to a grapheme, provided the final /s/ is analysed as spelt <se>. But the plural has the two pronunciations /ˈdaɪjəsiːzɪz, ˈdaɪjəsiːz/. In the former, again each phoneme (except the /j/-glide) can be related straightforwardly to a grapheme, provided we accept that the first <e> spells /iː/, both <s>'s spell /z/ (the first being voiced despite being voiceless in the singular - cf. the other words of Greek origin just listed), and the second <e> spells /ɪ/. But in the second pronunciation it seems as though /iːz/ is spelt <-eses> and I am at a loss to know which letters to relate the two phonemes to - perhaps more rational spellings would be *˙diosis* (singular), *˙dioses* (plural), which would bring both forms into line with those listed above, and with all other words with final /sɪs/, which are all spelt <-sis>, despite neither *˙diosis* nor *˙dioses* having a genuine Greek etymology.

The five major possibilities in closed final syllables of polysyllables and in closed monosyllables are shown in Table 5.6. There appear to be no useful rules suggesting when spellings other than <e.e> in closed final syllables of polysyllables and <ee> in closed monosyllables occur - all the other words just have to be learnt.

In non-final syllables of stem words the letter-name spelling <e> (see section 6.3) predominates, especially in word-initial position, where the only exceptions appear to be *aegis, aeon, aesthete, eager, eagle, easel, Easter, easy, either* pronounced /ˈiːðə/, *oedema, oenology, oesophagus, oestrogen, oestrus*. In medial syllables <e> still predominates, e.g. *beauteous, completion, European, Jacobean, lever, phonemic, simultaneous, spontaneous* and thousands of others.

TABLE 5.6: <ea, ee, e.e, ie, i.e> AS SPELLINGS OF /iː/ IN CLOSED FINAL SYLLABLES.

| Regular spelling | In polysyllables: <e.e> | In monosyllables: <ee> on the basis of the argument above |
|---|---|---|
| Exceptions (in addition to those listed under the Oddities <ei, i, ie> and in the paragraphs above this Table) | | |
| <ea> | *impeach*; | *peace*; *beach, bleach, breach, each, leach, peach, pleach, preach, reach, teach* |
| | | *bead, knead, lead* (verb), *mead, plead, read* (present tense) |
| | | *leaf/ves, sheaf/ves* |
| | | *league* |
| | | *beak, bleak, creak, freak, leak, peak, sneak, speak, squeak, streak, teak, tweak, weak, wreak* |
| | *anneal, appeal, conceal, congeal, repeal, reveal;* | *deal, heal, leal, meal, peal, seal, squeal, steal, teal, veal, weal, zeal* |
| | | *beam, bream, cream, dream, gleam, ream, scream, seam, steam, stream, team* |
| | *demean;* | *bean, clean, dean, glean, jeans, lean, mean, quean, wean* |
| | | *cheap, heap, leap, neap, reap* |
| | *decease, decrease, increase, release;* | *cease, crease, grease, lease* |
| | *appease, disease;* | *ease, pease, please, tease* |
| | | *leash* |
| | | *beast, east, feast, least, yeast* |
| | *defeat, entreat, escheat, repeat, retreat;* | *beat, bleat, cheat, cleat, eat, feat, heat, leat, meat, neat, peat, pleat, seat, teat, treat, wheat* |
| | | *heath, sheath, wreath* |
| | | *breathe, sheathe, wreathe* |
| | *bereave* | *cleave, eave, greave, heave, leave, sheave, weave* |

*The phoneme-grapheme correspondences, 2: Vowels* 203

| <ee> | exceed, proceed, succeed; genteel; esteem, redeem; boreen, canteen, careen, colleen, dasheen, lateen, nanteen, sateen, tureen; discreet | (regular, e.g. *beef, deep, feed, green, seem, week*) |
|---|---|---|
| <e.e> | (regular, e.g. *complete, discrete, grapheme, phoneme*) | breve, cede, eke, eve, gene, glebe, grebe, meme, mete, Pete, rheme, scene, scheme, Steve, swede, Swede, theme, these |
| <ie> | achieve, aggrieve, belief, believe, besiege, hygiene, relief, relieve, reprieve, retrieve, series, species | brief, fief, field, fiend, frieze, grief, grieve, lief, liege, mien, niece, piece, priest, shield, shriek, siege, thief/ves, thieve, wield, yield |
| <i.e> | caprice, police; pastiche; prestige; fatigue, intrigue; automobile, imbecile; chenille; regime; benzine, brigantine, brilliantine, chlorine, cuisine, dentine, figurine, gabardine, guillotine, iodine, latrine, limousine, machine, magazine, margarine, marine, mezzanine, morphine, nicotine, opaline, phosphine, quarantine, quinine, ravine, routine, sardine, strychnine, submarine, tagine, tambourine, tangerine, terrine, trampoline, tyrosine, vaccine, wolverine; antique, boutique, critique, mystique, oblique, physique, technique, unique; cerise, chemise, expertise, valise; odalisque; pelisse; artiste, dirigiste, modiste; elite, marguerite, petite; naive, Khedive, recitative | fiche, niche, quiche; clique, pique; bisque; suite |

However, there are also at least a thousand exceptions – see under the Oddities <ae, ei, ey, oe> above, plus:
- with <i>:
    1) before <a> spelling /ə/ with automatic intervening /j/-glide (Carney would place these words under /ɪə/): *ammonia, anaemia, bacteria, begonia, camellia, chlamydia, (en)cyclopaedia, hernia, hysteria, media, myopia, salvia, sepia, utopia; amiable, dutiable, enviable, variable; congenial, jovial, managerial, material, memorial, radial, remedial, serial* and about 450 others ending in <-ial>; *barbarian, comedian, grammarian, guardian, pedestrian, ruffian, thespian* and about 200 others ending in <-ian>; *dalliance, luxuriance,*

*radiance, variance; suppliant, radiant, suppliant, variant; alien; audience, convenience, ebullience, experience, obedience, prurience, salience; expediency, leniency; convenient, ebullient, expedient, lenient, obedient, prescient, prurient, salient, sentient, subservient, transient; soviet; twentieth,* etc.; *period, sociological, axiom, accordion, bastion, battalion, bullion, carrion, centurion, clarion, collodion, ganglion, medallion, mullion, scorpion, scullion, stallion, chariot, patriot; commodious, compendious, curious, dubious, felonious, melodious, odious, previous, scabious, serious, studious, tedious* and about 100 others ending in <-ious>; *atrium, bacterium, compendium, gymnasium, medium, opium, potassium, radium, stadium, tedium* and about 200 others ending in <-ium>; *genius, radius;* also second <i> in *amphibious, bilious, billion, brilliancy, brilliant, criteri-a/on, delirium, editorial, fastidious, hilarious, historian, histrionic, idiom, idiot, industrial, juvenilia, memorabilia, millennia, oblivion, omniscience, omniscient, perfidious, perihelion, reptilian, resilience, resilient, trivia, vitriol,* third <i> in *incipient, initiate* (noun), *insidious, insignia, invidious, militaria;*

2) before other vowel phonemes with automatic intervening /j/-glide: *ap/de-preciate, associate* (verb), *audio, calumniate, caviar, foliage, luxuriate, medi(a)eval, negotiate, orient* (verb), *oubliette, patio, radio, ratio, serviette, studio, trio, verbiage, viola* (/viːˈjəʊlə/ 'musical instrument'); also first <i> in *conscientious, liais-e/on, orgiastic, partiality, psychiatric, speciality,* second <i> in *histrionic, inebriation, insomniac, officiate, superficiality, vitriolic,* third <i> in *initiate* (verb)

3) before a consonant phoneme other than /j/: *albino, ballerina, cappuccino, casino, cliché, concertina, farina, frisson, kilo, Libra, lido, litre, maraschino, merino, mosquito, ocarina, pinochle, piquant, scarlatina, semolina, visa;* also first <i> in *kiwi, martini, migraine, milieu,* second <i> in *bikini, incognito, libido;*

- with other main-system graphemes: *beacon, beadle, beagle, beaker, beaver, creature, deacon, feature, heathen, meagre, measles, queasy, reason, season, sleazy, squeamish, teasle, treacle, treason, weasel; beetle, cheetah, feeble, freesia, gee-gee, geezer, needle, squeegee, sweetie, teeter, wheedle; chieftain* and other compounds of *chief-, diesel; caryatid, embryo, halcyon, polyandry, polysyllable, polytechnic* and many others with *poly-.*

## 5.7.3 /aɪ/ as in *ice*

### THE MAIN SYSTEM

For all these categories see Notes.

| | | | |
|---|---|---|---|
| *Basic grapheme* | <i.e> | 40% (70% in monosyllables) | regular in closed final syllables (except in monosyllables before /t/ and consonant clusters; only other exception: *mic* /maɪk/, short for *microphone*), e.g. *bike, sublime* |
| *Other frequent graphemes* | <i> | 42% (with <ie (see Oddities), y>) | regular in non-final syllables, e.g. *item*, word-finally in polysyllables, e.g. *alkali*, and in monosyllables before consonant clusters, e.g. *child* |
| | <y> | | e.g. *beautify, by, cycle, psyche, sky*; regular word-finally |
| | <igh> | 13% | only in about 26 stem words (see section 10.25). Regular in monosyllables before /t/, e.g. *sight*. In non-final syllables, only in *blighty, righteous, sprightly*. Word-finally, only in *high, nigh, sigh, thigh* |

### THE REST

| | | | |
|---|---|---|---|
| *Oddities* | | | 5% in total |
| | <a> | | only in *majolica* pronounced /maɪˈjɒlɪkə/ (also pronounced /məˈdʒɒlɪkə/), *naif, naive, papaya* |
| | <ae> | | only in *maestro, minutiae* |

| | |
|---|---|
| <ai> | only in *ailuro-phile/phobe, assegai, balalaika, banzai, bonsai, caravanserai, Kaiser, naiad, samurai, shanghai* |
| <ais> | only in *aisle*. See Notes |
| <aye> | only in *aye* ('yes'), *aye-aye* |
| <ei> | only in *deictic, deixis, eider(down), eidetic, eirenic, either, Fahrenheit, feisty, gneiss, heist, kaleidoscope, meiosis, neither, poltergeist, seismic, stein* |
| <eigh> | only in *height, sleight* |
| <ey> | only in *geyser* pronounced /ˈgaɪzə/ (usually pronounced /ˈgiːzə/) |
| <eye> | only in *eye* |
| <ia> | only in *diamond* |
| <ie> | only word-final, e.g. *pie* (see Notes), except for suffixed forms after <y>-replacement (see section 6.5), e.g *allied, supplies* |
| <ir> | only in *iron* pronounced /ˈaɪjən/ (but the Scots pronunciation /ˈaɪrən/ has retained the /r/ and has more regular correspondences) |
| <is> | only in *island, isle(t), lisle, viscount*. See Notes |
| <oy> | only in *coyote* |
| <ui> | only in *duiker, Ruislip* |
| <ye> | only word-final and only in *bye, dye, lye, rye, Skye, stye* |
| <y.e> | only in final syllables and only in: (monosyllables) *byte, chyle, chyme, cyme, dyke, dyne, gybe, gyve, hythe, hype, rhyme, scythe, skype, style, syce, syne, thyme, tyke, type*; (polysyllables) *acolyte, analyse, anodyne, azyme, breathalyse, catalyse, coenocyte, condyle, dialyse, electrolyse, electrolyte, enzyme, formaldehyde, leucocyte, neophyte* and at least 14 other words ending in /faɪt/ spelt <-phyte>, *paralyse, phagocyte, proselyte, spondyle*, about 20 derivatives of *style*, *troglodyte*, and at least 20 derivatives of *type*. In my opinion, all these words (except *gyve*) could be spelt with <i.e> without loss |

| | | |
|---|---|---|
| 2-phoneme graphemes | /aɪə/ | |
| | (1) spelt <ir> | only medially and mainly where <-e> has been deleted from words in the next category, e.g. *aspiring, desirous, expiry, spiral, tiring*, but there are a few independent examples, e.g. *biro, giro, pirate, virus*. In all cases the <r> is both part of <ir> spelling /aɪə/ and a grapheme in its own right spelling /r/. For dual-functioning see section 7.1 |
| | (2) spelt <ire> | only word-final and only in *ac/in/re-quire, admire, a/con/in/per/re/tran-spire, attire, desire, dire, empire, entire, (expire, fire, hire, (be/quag-)mire, quire, saltire, samphire, sapphire, satire, shire, sire, spire, e)squire, tire, umpire, vampire, wire*. Many of these words allow /r/-linking, e.g. *inspiration, satirical, spiral, wiring* – see previous paragraph and section 3.6 |
| | (3) spelt <yr> | only medial and only in *empyrean, gyroscope, papyrus, pyrites, pyromaniac, thyroid, tyrant, tyro, tyrosine*. In all cases the <r> is both part of <yr> spelling /aɪə/ and a grapheme in its own right spelling /r/. For dual-functioning see section 7.1. Words in which <y, r> are separate graphemes include *dithyramb(ic), myriad, porphyr-y/ia, tyranny, syringa, syringe, syrup*, all with the relevant <y> spelling /ɪ/ |
| | (4) spelt <yre> | only word-final and only in *byre, gyre, lyre, pyre, tyre*. In my opinion these words could be spelt with <ire> without loss, as *tire* already is in US English. Some of these words allow /r/-linking – see section 3.6 – e.g. *pyromaniac*, and (with change of vowel and <r> spelling only /r/) *lyrical* |
| | /waɪ/ spelt <oy> | only in *foyer* pronounced /ˈfwaɪjeɪ/ (also pronounced /ˈfɔɪjeɪ, ˈfɔɪjə/), *voyeur* |
| 3-phoneme grapheme spelt with a single grapheme <oir> | /waɪə/ | only in *choir* – one of only two 3-phoneme graphemes in the entire language |

## NOTES

The regular spellings of /aɪ/ are:
- in non-final syllables, and in monosyllables before consonant clusters: <i>
- in monosyllables before /t/: <igh>
  in closed final syllables (except in monosyllables before consonant clusters and /t/): <i.e>
- word-finally: <y>.

<i> is regular in non-final syllables (see section 6.3), but for:
- exceptions listed under the Oddities <a, ae, ai, aye, ei, ey, ir, is, oy, ui> and the 2-phoneme grapheme /waɪ/ spelt <oy>, above, plus *Blighty, righteous, sprightly* (also spelt *spritely* because of its derivation from *sprite*)
- exceptions with <y>: *asylum, aureomycin, cryostat, cyanide, cycle, cyclone, cypress, (hama)dryad, dynamic, forsythia, glycogen, gynaecology, hyacinth, hyaline, hybrid, hydra, hydrangea, hydraulic, hydrofoil, hydrogen* and various other compounds of *hydro-, hyena, hygiene, hygrometer, hymen, hyperbole* and other compounds in *hyper-, hyphen, hypothesis* and other compounds in *hypo-, lychee, myopic, nylon, psyche* and almost all its derivatives (exception: *metempsychosis*, with /ɪ/), *pylon, stymie, thylacine, thymus, typhoid, typhoon, typhus, xylophone, zygote* and derivatives.

<i.e> is regular in closed final syllables of polysyllabic words, e.g. *alive, archive, capsize, combine, concise, decide, entice, exercise, oblige, senile, sublime*. Exceptions: see the Oddities listed above under <y.e>, plus *alight, behind, delight, Fahrenheit, fore/hind/in-sight, indict, paradigm, remind, uptight, watertight* and suffixed forms after <y>-replacement (section 6.5), e.g. *allied, supplies*.

In closed monosyllables:
- <i> on its own appears to be regular before consonant clusters: *child, Christ, mild, ninth, pint, whilst, wild* and the group with /aɪnd/ spelt <-ind>: *bind, blind, find, grind, hind, kind, mind, rind, wind* ('turn'). Possible extension: If the context were defined in terms of letters, *aisle, climb, isle, lisle* could be added. Exception under either definition: *heist*
- <igh> is regular before /t/: *bight, blight, bright, fight, flight, fright, hight, knight, light, might, night, plight, right, sight, slight, tight, wight, wright*. Exceptions: *height, sleight; bite, cite, kite, mite, rite, site, smite, spite, sprite, quite, white, write; byte*

- <i.e> is regular around other single consonant phonemes, e.g. *fine, hive, ice, knife, like, lime, mile, mine, pipe, prize, ride, rise*, including the small group with /ð/ spelt <th>: *blithe, lithe, tithe, writhe*. Exceptions: see the Oddities listed above under <y.e>, plus *aisle, climb, isle, lisle* (but for these four words see two paragraphs above), *mic, stein*.

In open final syllables of polysyllabic words <y> is regular, e.g. in 130+ words with the suffix <-fy>, e.g. *beautify*, and in *ally, ap/com/im/re/supply, defy, deny, descry, espy, July, multiply* (verb), *occupy, prophesy, rely*. Exceptions: *assegai, shanghai; aye-aye; a fortiori/posteriori/priori, alibi, alkali, alumni, alveoli, foci, fundi* (plural of *fundus*), *fungi, Gemini, gladioli, rabbi* and a few more rare words.

In open monosyllables the most frequent spelling is <y>: *by, cry, dry, fly, fry, my, ply, pry, scry, shy, sky, sly, spry, spy, sty, try, why, wry*, plus *buy, guy* (taking <bu, gu> to be digraphs spelling /b, g/); this set numbers 20 words. Exceptions (which number 24): *aye, eye, I; die, fie, hie, lie, pie, tie, vie; bye, dye, lye, rye, stye; high, nigh, sigh, thigh;* and the Greek letter names *chi, phi, pi, psi, xi*. A possible subrule might say that <ie> is regular after a single consonant **letter**, but this is a very small set, containing only the seven words *die, fie, hie, lie, pie, tie, vie*, and setting up this rule would cause problems for the grapheme-phoneme correspondences of <ie>.

The words *aisle, island, isle(t), lisle, viscount* are among the oddest in English spelling, with <(a)is> spelling /aɪ/ and the <s> having no consonantal value. *Isle, lisle* might have yielded to an analysis with /aɪ/ spelt <i.e> and the intervening <sl> spelling /l/ – but there is no other warrant for a grapheme <sl>, or for the 'split trigraph' <ai.e> which this analysis would have produced for *aisle* (whereas there is another warrant for the grapheme <ais>, in *palais* – see under /eɪ/, section 5.7.1). Also, this analysis would not have fitted the other words listed (or those with /iː/ spelt <is>, see section 5.7.2).

/waɪə/ also has the 2-grapheme spellings <wire> in *wire* and <-uire> in *(ac/re)quire*. And /aɪə/ has 2-grapheme spellings, e.g. <-iar> in *liar*, <-ier> in *drier*, <-yer> in *dryer, flyer*, <-igher> in *higher*. A possibly useful sub-rule is that word-initial /daɪə/ is always spelt <dia-> (derived from a Greek prefix) except in *dire* itself and *diocese*.

The <y> in *coyote, foyer, voyeur* is both part of the digraph <oy> spelling /(w)aɪ/ and also spells /j/ on its own. For dual-functioning see section 7.1.

## 5.7.4 /əʊ/ as in *oath*

**THE MAIN SYSTEM**

For all these categories see Notes.

| | | | |
|---|---|---|---|
| Basic grapheme | <o> | 59% | regular in non-final syllables, e.g. *focus*, finally in polysyllables (except in two-syllable words after /l, r/), and in closed monosyllables before a consonant cluster |
| Other frequent graphemes | <o.e> | 16% (72% in monosyllables) | regular in final closed syllables (except in closed mono-syllables before a consonant cluster), e.g. *bone, remote* |
| | <ow> | 18% | regular finally in two-syllable words after /l, r/ and in open monosyllables |

**THE REST**

| | | |
|---|---|---|
| Oddities | | 8% in total |
| | <aoh> | only in *pharaoh* |
| | <au> | only in *chauffeu-r/se, chauvinis-m/t, gauche, hauteur, mauve, saute, taupe* |
| | <eau> | only word-final and only in *bandeau, beau, bureau, chateau, flambeau, gateau, plateau, portmanteau, rondeau, tableau, trousseau* and a few other very rare words. For the plurals of these words see /z/, section 3.6.7, and <x>, section 9.41 |
| | <eo> | only in *Yeo, yeoman, Yeovil* |
| | <ew> | only in *sew, sewn, Shrewsbury* plus *shew(ed), shewn* (archaic spellings of *show(ed), shown*) |

| | | |
|---|---|---|
| | <oa> | only in (non-final syllables) *gloaming*; (closed final syllables of polysyllables) *approach, cockroach, encroach, reproach*; (closed monosyllables) *bloat, boast, boat, broach, cloak, coach, coal, coast, coat, coax, croak, float, foal, foam, gloat, goad, goal, goat, groan, groat, hoax, loach, load, loa-f/ves, loam, loan, loath, loathe, moan, moat, oaf, oak, oast, oat, oath, poach, roach, road, roam, roan, roast, shoal, soak, soap, stoat, throat, toad, toast, woad*; (finally) *cocoa, whoa* |
| | <oat> | only in *boatswain* pronounced /ˈbəʊsən/ (also pronounced /ˈbəʊtsweɪn/) |
| | <oe> | except in *throes*, only word-final and only in *aloe, doe, floe, foe, hoe, oboe, roe, schmoe, sloe, toe, woe*. See also sections 4.3.2 and 6.6 |
| | <oh> | only in *doh, kohl, Oh, ohm, soh* |
| | <ol> | only in *folk, Holborn, holm, yolk* and old-fashioned pronunciation of *golf* as /gəʊf/ |
| | <oo> | only in *brooch* |
| | <ore> | only in *forecastle* pronounced /ˈfəʊksəl/ (also pronounced /ˈfɔːkɑːsəl/) |
| | <os> | only in *apropos* |
| | <ot> | only in *argot, depot, entrepot, haricot, jabot, matelot, potpourri, sabot, tarot, tricot*. /t/ surfaces in *sabotage, saboteur* – see section 7.2 – where the <o> spells /ə/ |
| | <ou> | only in *boulder, bouquet* pronounced /bəʊˈkeɪ/ (also pronounced /buːˈkeɪ/), *mould, moult, poultice, poultry, shoulder, smoulder, soul* |
| | <ough> | only in *dough, furlough, (al)though* |
| | <owe> | only in *owe* |
| 2-phoneme graphemes | (none) | |

## NOTES

<o> is regular in non-final syllables, and the only exceptions I can find in stem words are *boulder, bouquet* pronounced /bəʊˈkeɪ/, *chauffeu-r/se, chauvinis-m/t, hauteur, gloaming, poultice, poultry, shoulder, smoulder, yeoman, Yeovil* – though there are many more in derived forms, e.g. *moulder/y, moult-ed/ing* – see section 6.3.

For nouns ending in <-o> which do or do not add <es> in the plural see section 6.6.

For 'linking /w/' and a few cases in which a preceding <o> reduces to /ə/ see section 3.8.7.

The group of stem monosyllables with final /əʊld/ spelt <-old> is one of only two cases where the spelling of the rime/phonogram is more predictable as a unit than from the correspondences of the separate phonemes, and there are enough instances to make the rule worth teaching; see section A.7 in Appendix A. The only monosyllabic stem word exception in British spelling is *mould*, and even that is spelt *mold* in the USA. The pattern generalises to the polysyllables listed above, plus *solder*. But this rule applies only to stem words, and they would have to be clearly distinguished from the past tenses/participles *doled, foaled, holed, poled, polled, rolled, tolled*.

For final syllables of stem words see Table 5.7.

TABLE 5.7: SPELLINGS OF /əʊ/ IN FINAL SYLLABLES OF STEM WORDS

N.B. The regular (default) spellings are shown in 9 point, exceptions in 7.5 point.

|  | In polysyllables | In monosyllables |
|---|---|---|
| Closed | <o.e>, e.g. *chromosome, remote*<br><br>Extension: Just one word with a 2-letter spelling of the word-final consonant phoneme, namely *cologne*<br><br>Exceptions: *approach, cockroach, encroach, reproach; control, enrol, extol, patrol; behold, cuckold, blind/mani-fold, marigold, scaffold, threshold* (see also paragraph below Table); *revolt; almost* | Before a consonant cluster: <o>, e.g. *bold, cold, fold, gold, hold, old, scold, sold, told, wold* (see also paragraph below Table); *bolt, colt, dolt, jolt, volt; don't, wont, won't; ghost, host, most, post*<br><br>Exceptions: *boast, coast, oast, roast, toast, mould* (hence the more consistent US spelling *mold*), *moult*. Also exceptions in phonetic (but not orthographic) terms are *coax, hoax*, but *cox*, *\*hox* or *\*coxe*, *\*hoxe* would not work, the first two because they would suggest the wrong vowel sound, the last two because <x> never occupies the 'dot' position in split digraphs – see section A.6 in appendix A.<br><br>Before a single consonant phoneme: <o.e>, e.g. *bone* (72% of spellings in monosyllables) |

|  |  |  | Extension: Five words with 2-letter spellings of the word-final consonant phoneme, namely *brogue, rogue, vogue, toque, clothe* |
|---|---|---|---|
|  |  |  | Exceptions: *gauche, mauve, taupe; sewn, shew-ed/n; bloat, boat, broach, cloak, coach, coal, coat, croak, float, foal, foam, gloat, goad, goal, goat, groan, groat, loach, load, loaf, loam, loan, loath, loathe, moan, moat, oaf, oak, oat, oath, poach, roach, road, roam, roan, shoal, soak, soap, stoat, throat, toad, woad* (for *coax, hoax* see above); *kohl, ohm; folk, yolk; boll, droll, poll, roll, scroll, stroll, toll; holm; comb; both, loth, quoth, sloth, troth; brooch; soul; bowl; blown, flown, grown, known, mown, own, show-ed/n, sown, thrown* |
| **Open** | In two-syllable words after /l, r/: <ow>, namely *bellow, below, billow, callow, fallow, fellow, follow, hallow, hollow, mallow, mellow, pillow, sallow, shallow, swallow, tallow, wallow, whitlow, willow, yellow; arrow, barrow, borrow, burrow, farrow, furrow, harrow, marrow, morrow, narrow, sorrow, sparrow, yarrow* |  | <ow>, namely *blow, bow* (goes with *arrow*), *crow, flow, glow, grow, know, low, mow, row* ('line, use oars'), *show, slow, snow, sow* ('plant seed'), *stow, throw, tow* |
|  | Exceptions: *aloe, cello, furlough, tableau; bureau, burro, pharaoh, tarot* |  | Exceptions: *beau; sew, shew; fro, go, lo, no, so; whoa; doe, floe, foe, hoe, roe, sloe, throe, toe, woe; doh, soh; dough, though; owe* |
|  | In longer words and other two-syllable words: <o>, e.g. *gecko, gizmo, Leo, manifesto, potato, Scorpio, tomato, Virgo* |  |  |
|  | Exceptions: *bandeau, chateau, flambeau, gateau, plateau, portmanteau, rondeau, trousseau; cocoa; oboe; apropos; argot, depot, sabot, tricot; although; bestow, bungalow, elbow, escrow, furbelow, meadow, minnow, shadow, widow, window, winnow* |  |  |

## 5.7.5 /juː/ as in *union*

The only 2-phoneme sequence to which I accord quasi-phonemic status – see sections 1.12 and 2.4.

### THE MAIN SYSTEM

| | | | |
|---|---|---|---|
| Basic graphemes | <u> | 82% (with <u.e>) | regular in non-final syllables, e.g. *pupil, union*; word-final only in *coypu, menu, ormolu, parvenu* |
| | <u.e> | | regular in closed final syllables, e.g. *attribute, mute, use* |
| Other frequent grapheme | <ew> | 15% | never initial; in non-final syllables, only in *newel, Newton, pewter, steward*; otherwise, only in final syllables and only in (closed) *hewn, lewd, mews, newt, thews*; (open) *clerihew, curfew, curlew, few, hew, Kew, knew, mew, mildew, nephew, new, pew, phew, sinew, skew, smew, spew, stew, view, yew*; from this (admittedly short) list, <ew> appears to be regular word-finally in monosyllables – see Notes |
| Rare grapheme | <ue> | percentage not known – see Oddities | appears to be regular word-finally in polysyllables – see Notes |

### THE REST

| | | |
|---|---|---|
| Oddities | | 3% in total (including <ue>) |
| | <eau> | only in *beauty* and derivatives |
| | <eu> | only in various words of Greek origin, e.g. *eucalyptus, eucharist, eudaemonic, eugenic, eulogy, eunuch, euphemism, euphorbia, euphoria, eureka, eurhythmic, euthanasia, leukaemia, neural, neurone, neurosis, Odysseus, Pentateuch, Perseus, pneumatic, pneumonia* and other words and names. |

*The phoneme-grapheme correspondences, 2: Vowels* 215

                        derived from Greek πνεῦμα *pneuma* ('breath') or πνεύμων *pneumon* ('lung'), *pseudo* and all its derivatives including (colloquial) *pseud, therapeutic, Theseus, zeugma*, plus various very rare words; plus (non-Greek) *deuce, euchre, Eustachian, feu, feud(al), neuter, neutr-al/on, teutonic*; only instances in monosyllables are *deuce, feu, feud, pseud*; word-final only in *feu*

           \<ewe\>      only in *ewe, Ewell, Ewelme*

           \<ui\>       only in *nuisance, pursuit*

           \<ut\>       only in *debut*. /t/ surfaces in *debutante* - see section 7.2

           \<uu\>      only in *vacuum* pronounced /'vækjuːm/

*2-phoneme graphemes*     All the graphemes in this section are 2-phoneme graphemes

## NOTES

All the spellings listed above are used to spell /juː/. \<eau, ewe, ut, uu\> are used **only** to spell /juː/, while the rest are used to spell both /juː/ and /uː/ - see next section.

   \<u\> is the regular spelling of /juː/ (and /uː/) in non-final syllables (see section 6.3), e.g. *pupil, union*. Exceptions: see the polysyllables listed under \<ew\> and the Oddities \<eau, eu, ui\> above.

   How can \<u\> function as the regular spelling of both /juː/ and /uː/ in non-final syllables without causing confusion? Because there are hardly any minimal pairs, words kept apart in meaning solely by the presence or absence of /j/. The only pairs I've been able to find in non-final syllables are *beauty/booty, bootie* (but not *bootee*, with stress on second syllable) and *pewter/Pooter* - and note that none of these words has \<u\> as the relevant spelling (and the last word is an invented surname). Similarly, I can find no minimal pairs separated only by the presence or absence of /j/ in the final syllables of polysyllables, and only a few such pairs/sets among monosyllables, namely *beaut* (Australian slang), *butte/boot; cue(d/s), queue(d/s), Kew/coo(ed/s); cute/coot; dew, due* when pronounced /djuː// *do; ewe, yew, you/Oo(h)!; feud/food; few/phoo; hew(s), hue(s), Hugh(es/'s)/ who(se); hewn/Hoon; Home* pronounced /hjuːm/, *Hu(l)me/whom; lewd/ looed; lieu/loo; mew/moo; mewed/mood; mews, muse/moos; mute/moot; pew(s), Pugh(s)/poo(s), Pooh('s); pseud/sued* (to me, these are /sjuːd, suːd/ respectively, though for many speakers they are homophones, in one pronunciation or the other); *puke/Pook*; *pule/pool*; *use* (verb)/*ooze*. Some people with Welsh accents distinguish *threw, through* as /θrjuː , θruː/, but for most speakers these are both /θruː/. Again, it is noticeable that none of these words has <u> as the relevant spelling, though some have <ue, u.e>.

The names *Hugh, Hughes, Lamplugh, Pugh* are the only words containing the grapheme <ugh> (the exclamation *ugh* contains two graphemes, <u, gh>), but because it occurs only in names I have not added <ugh> to the inventory of graphemes.

<u.e> is regular in closed final syllables of polysyllables, e.g. *attribute* (only exceptions: *pursuit, vacuum*) and in closed monosyllables, e.g. *mute, use* (exceptions: *deuce, feud; hewn, mews, newt, thews; Ewell, Ewelme*).

<ue> is only word-final and found only in (monosyllables) *cue, hue, queue*; (polysyllables) *ague, argue, avenue, barbecue, continue, curlicue, ensue, imbue, pursue, rescue, retinue, revenue, revue, value, venue*. Despite the shortness of the list just given, <ue> appears to be the regular spelling in word-final position in polysyllables (exceptions: *curfew, curlew, mildew, nephew; coypu, menu, ormolu*), and therefore qualifies as part of the main system. Also, as a grapheme <ue> has only two pronunciations (see section 10.37), and one of them is /juː/.

However, in word-final position in monosyllables <ew> appears to be regular (see the list above). Exceptions: *ewe; cue, hue, queue*.

/juː/ also has 2-grapheme spellings, e.g. in *adieu, view, yew, you* where /j/ is spelt <i, y> - see under /j/, section 3.7.8, and /uː/, next. But the 1-grapheme spellings listed above predominate, especially <u>. Here, /j/ is not spelt separately but subsumed in the 2-phoneme spelling.

## 5.7.6 /uː/ as in *ooze*

**THE MAIN SYSTEM**

For all these categories see Notes.

| | | | |
|---|---|---|---|
| *Basic grapheme* | <oo> | 39% | e.g. *ooze, booze, zoo*. Regular in closed monosyllables, e.g. *zoom* and about 80 other words; also regular in polysyllables both word-finally, e.g. *bamboo*, and in the stressed ending /'uːn/, e.g. *afternoon, baboon*; rare elsewhere |

*The phoneme-grapheme correspondences, 2: Vowels* 217

| | | | |
|---|---|---|---|
| *Other frequent graphemes* | \<u\> | 27% (with \<u.e\>) | regular in non-final syllables, e.g. *rudiments*, *super* |
| | \<u.e\> | | regular in closed final syllables of polysyllables, e.g. *intrude*, *recluse* |
| | \<o\> | 15% | only in 11 stem words and their derivatives – see Notes. Carney's percentage excludes *do*, *to*, *who*, which would distort the figures |
| | \<ew\> | 9% | regular word-finally in monosyllables, e.g. *blew* |
| *Rare grapheme* | \<ue\> | <1% | except for *gruesome*, *muesli* and *Tuesday* pronounced /ˈtʃuːzdiː/, only word-final and only in *accrue*, *blue*, *clue*, *construe*, *(resi/sub-)due*, *flue*, *glue*, *imbrue*, *issue*, *rue*, *slue*, *sprue*, *sue*, *tissue*, *true*. See Notes |
| *Frequent 2-phoneme sequence* | | /juː/, with 10 spellings – see previous section | |

## THE REST

| | | | |
|---|---|---|---|
| *Oddities* | | 10% in total | |
| | \<ee\> | only in *leeward* pronounced /ˈluːwəd/ (also pronounced /ˈliːwəd/) | |
| | \<eu\> | only in *rheum(ati-c/sm)*, *sleuth*, plus *adieu*, *lieu*, *purlieu* pronounced /əˈdjuː, ljuː, ˈpɜːljuː/ with \<i\> spelling /j/ (*lieu* is also pronounced /luː/) | |
| | \<ieu\> | only in *lieu* pronounced /luː/ (also pronounced /ljuː/) | |
| | \<oe\> | only in *canoe*, *hoopoe*, *shoe* | |
| | \<o.e\> | only in *combe*, *lose*, *move*, *prove*, *whose* /kuːm, luːz, muːv, pruːv, huːz/ and *gamboge* pronounced /gæmˈbuːʒ/, plus derived forms. See Notes | |
| | \<oeu\> | only in *manoeuvre* | |
| | \<ooh\> | only in *pooh* | |

218  *Dictionary of the British English Spelling System*

| | | |
|---|---|---|
| <ou> | 7% only in | |
| | (in non-final syllables) *accoutrement, acoustic, bivouac, boudoir, boulevard, bouquet, boutique, carousel, cougar, coupon, coulomb, coulter, coupe, coupon, croupier, crouton, embouchure, goujon, goulash, insouciance, louvre, moussaka, oubliette, outré, ouzo, pirouette, rouble, roulette, routine, silhouette, soubrette, soufflé, souvenir, toucan, toupee, troubadour, trousseau, voussoir* | |
| | (in closed final syllables) *ampoule, barouche, canteloupe, cartouche, (un)couth, croup, douche, ghoul, group, joule, mousse, recoup, rouge, route, soup, troupe, wound* ('harm') | |
| | (finally) *bayou, bijou, caribou, frou-frou, marabou, sou, you* | |
| <oue> | only in *denouement, moue* | |
| <ough> | only in *brougham, through* | |
| <oup> | only in *coup* | |
| <ous> | only in *rendezvous* | |
| <out> | only in *mange-tout, ragout, surtout* | |
| <oux> | only in *billet-doux, roux* | |
| <ui> | only in *bruise, bruit, cruise, fruit, juice, recruit, sluice, suit* | |
| <uu> | only in *muumuu* (twice) | |
| *Other 2-phoneme graphemes* | (none) | |

## NOTES

On <oo> see also Notes under /ʊ/, section 5.4.6.

All the spellings listed above are used to spell plain /uː/. Those beginning with <o> are used **only** to spell plain /uː/, while those beginning with <e, u> (except <ee>) are also used to spell /juː/ – see previous section.

No rules can be given for when /uː/ is spelt <o> because it occurs only in the following 11 stem words: (monosyllables) *do, to, tomb, two, who, womb*; (polysyllables) *caisson* pronounced /kəˈsuːn/, *canton* ('provide accommodation', pronounced /kænˈtuːn/), *catacomb, lasso, zoology*, plus derivatives including *cantonment, lassoing, whom*, derivatives of *zoology* with initial <zoo-> (Greek, 'living thing') forming two syllables pronounced

/zuːˈwɒ/ if the second syllable is stressed, otherwise /zuːwə/, derived forms of the very few words in which /uː/ is spelt <o.e> (see Oddities), e.g. *approval, movie, removal*, and the proper nouns *Aloysius* /æluːˈwɪʃəs/, *Romania, Wrotham* /ˈruːtəm/.

<u> is the regular spelling of /uː/ (and /juː/) in non-final syllables, e.g. *rudiments, super* – see section 6.3. Exceptions (in addition to derivatives of words with /uː/ spelt <o, o.e>, e.g. *cantonment, lassoing; ap/dis/im/re-prove, approval, movie, remove*, and among the Oddities above): *brewer, jewel, sewage, sewer* ('foul drain'); *bazooka, booby, boodle, boogie, boomerang, booty, canoodle, coolie, doodle(bug), googly, hoodoo, hoopoe, kookaburra, loony, moolah, noodle, oodles, oolong, poodle, voodoo*, plus *Aloysius, Romania, Wrotham*. For how <u> functions as the regular spelling of both <uː> and <juː> in non-final syllables, see previous section.

In closed final syllables of polysyllables:
- the stressed ending /uːn/ is mostly spelt <-oon>: *afternoon, baboon, bassoon, buffoon, cartoon, cocoon, doubloon, dragoon, festoon, harpoon, lagoon, lampoon, macaroon, maroon, monsoon, octaroon*. Exceptions: *caisson* pronounced /kəˈsuːn/ (also pronounced /ˈkeɪsən/), *canton* ('provide accommodation', pronounced /kænˈtuːn/)
- otherwise the regular spelling is <u.e>, namely in *include, intrude* and various other words in <-clude, -trude>, plus *peruque, abstruse, recluse, peruse, brusque* /bruːsk/ (also pronounced /brʌsk/), etc. For exceptions see Oddities, plus *vamoose*.

Exceptions to the rule that <oo> is the regular spelling in closed monosyllables are:
- with <u.e>: *spruce, truce; ruche; crude, prude, rude; luge; fluke; rule, tulle; brume, flume, plume; prune, rune; jupe; ruse; brute, chute, flute, jute, lute*
- others: *rheum, sleuth; shrewd, strewn; tomb, whom, womb; combe, lose, move, prove, whose; croup, douche, ghoul, group, joule, louche, mousse, rouge, route, soup, troupe, wound* ('harm'), *youth; ruth, truth; bruise, bruit, cruise, fruit, juice, sluice, suit*.

In word-final position the most frequent spellings are <-oo> in polysyllables, <-ew> in monosyllables:
- polysyllables: *ballyhoo, bamboo, buckaroo, cockatoo, cuckoo, didgeridoo, hoodoo, hullaballoo, kangaroo, kazoo, shampoo, taboo, tattoo, voodoo*. Exceptions: *adieu, purlieu; cashew, eschew, purview,*

*review; lasso; caribou, marabou; ecru, guru, jujitsu, juju, impromptu; accrue, construe, imbrue, issue, residue, subdue, statue, tissue, virtue*
- monosyllables: *brew, chew, crew, dew* pronounced /dʒuː/, *Jew, screw, shrew, strew, view, yew* and the irregular past tenses *blew, drew, flew, grew, slew, threw*. Exceptions: *lieu* (/luː/); *do, to, who; boo, coo, goo, loo, moo, shoo, too, poo, woo, zoo; sou, you; flu, gnu* (taking <gn> as spelling /nj/, though *gnu* could alternatively be analysed as having (like *gnat, gnaw*, etc.) /n/ spelt <gn> and /juː/ spelt <u> – take your pick); *blue, clue, due* pronounced /dʒuː/, *flue, glue, rue, sue, true*.

Despite the rarity of <ue> as a spelling of /uː/ it has to be counted as part of the main system because as a grapheme (see section 10.37) it has only two pronunciations, both frequent, and one of them is /uː/.

# 6. Some spelling rules for vowels

It is notoriously the case that English vowel spellings are much less predictable than consonant spellings (compare chapters 5 and 3), so in this chapter I provide some guidance on this – but be warned (again): the guidance doesn't and can't cover every word, so I end up saying 'The rest you just have to remember'. Such (relatively) easy bits as there are for vowel spellings are summarised at the beginning of chapter 5.

## 6.1 '<i> before <e> except after <c>'

This is the only spelling rule most British people can recite. Stated as baldly as that it is thoroughly misleading. A letter in *Times Higher Education* in the summer of 2008 (Lamb, 2008) provided a more nuanced formulation:

'<i> before <e> except after <c> if the vowel-sound rhymes with *bee*'.

The qualification 'if the vowel-sound rhymes with *bee*' (or similar) is hardly ever mentioned, perhaps because it is difficult to explain to children – but let us explore it.

In order to use the expanded rule, writers have first to realise that an /iː/ phoneme they wish to spell needs to be written with one of the graphemes <ei, ie> and not with any of the other possibilities – not necessarily an easy matter (a quick look at section 5.7.2 will reveal that there are 15 ways of spelling /iː/ in English besides <ie, ei>, some admittedly very rare). If they do realise they must choose between <ei> and <ie>, they will find that the expanded rule works pretty well for '<i> before <e>' (= not after <c>): there are at least 90 words with /iː/ spelt <ie>, and only two of these are exceptions to the rule: *specie, species*. But it works very poorly for '<e> before <i> after <c>': the only words that conform to it are *ceiling, conceit, conceive, deceit, deceive, perceive, receipt, receive*, and exceptions are more numerous: *caffeine, casein, codeine, cuneiform, disseisin, heinous, inveigle, Keith, plebeian, protein, seize*, plus *either, leisure, neither* in their US pronunciations, and *counterfeit* if you pronounce it to rhyme with *feet*.

I suppose you could count all these words together and say that the rule works for about 90 per cent of them – but the second half of the rule is weak, and writers are mostly left with no guidance on the myriad other words in which <ei> and <ie> occur without rhyming with *bee* – for examples see sections 10.12 and 10.23 (especially the set of words containing the sequence 'cie' which naïve spellers who forget the 'when the vowel-sound rhymes with *bee*' condition may well be confused about: *ancient, coefficient, conscience, conscientious, deficiency, deficient, efficiency, efficient, omniscience, omniscient, prescience, prescient, proficiency, proficient, science, scientific, society, sufficient, sufficiency*) – or in which /iː/ is not spelt either <ie> or <ei>. In my opinion, this rule should be consigned to oblivion.

## 6.2 'To spell the names of letters <a, i, o, u> in one-syllable words ending with a single consonant phoneme, write the vowel-name letter and the consonant letter and magic <e>'

This fact is well known, but not often expressed like this. Examples are too numerous and familiar to need listing. The rule holds good about three-quarters of the time for relevant monosyllables. There are about 60 'letter-name-vowel except /iː/ plus single consonant' endings in English monosyllables, and this rule works well for all but a handful of them. For example, the only word ending /əʊp/ and spelt with <-oap> is *soap* – all the rest are spelt with <-ope>, including *scope, slope*. The main exceptions are that /eɪl, eɪn/ are spelt <-ail, -ain> about as often as they are spelt <-ale, -ane> (see section 5.7.1), and that the principal spelling of /aɪt/ is <-ight> (see section 5.7.3).

The rule also applies, but less strongly, to the final syllables of polysyllabic words where the full letter-name sounds **including** /iː/ occur, and regardless of whether the syllable is stressed or unstressed.

There are two important limitations: it doesn't apply to phoneme /iː/ in monosyllables, and all words containing /aɪ/ spelt <y.e> (see section 5.7.3) are exceptions. So it could be stated more exactly (but less usefully for teaching purposes) as:

> 'In words ending in a single consonant phoneme, spell letter-name vowels (EXCEPT /iː/ in monosyllables) with their name letters plus the consonant letter plus magic <e> (and watch out for words spelt with <y> and magic <e>).'

In monosyllables ending in a consonant very few occurrences of /iː/ are spelt <e.e>, and the main spelling of /iː/ is <ee>, but there are many exceptions – and even more, numerically, in the final syllables of polysyllabic words even though there <e.e> is the most frequent pattern (see section 5.7.2).

## 6.3 'In non-final syllables of stem words, spell letter-name vowels with their name letters'

This is my generalisation of various regularities stated in sections 5.1 and 5.7: the letters <a, e, i, o, u> are the regular spellings of phonemes /eɪ, iː, aɪ, əʊ, juː/, plus /uː/, in non-final syllables, that is, outside one-syllable words and the final syllables of polysyllabic words. The rule applies to both stressed and unstressed syllables where the full letter-name sounds occur. Long lists of examples can be found in Wijk's *Rules of Pronunciation for the English Language*, especially pp.19-20, 22-26, 69, 73. A few representative examples (in stressed syllables before the semi-colons; in unstressed syllables after them) are:

- /eɪ/ spelt <a>: *agent, baby, bacon, capable, crustacean, danger, data, hazel, ingratiate, insatiable, labour, lady, loquacious, nation* and all the other words ending in /ˈeɪʃən/, *plagiarism, stranger, wastrel; fatalistic*
- /iː/ spelt <e>: *amenable, appreciable, decent, diabetes, European, frequent, idea, Leo, lever, medieval, museum, neon, oedema* (second syllable), *penalise, pleonasm, region, senior, sequence, species, theatre; abbreviation, area, galleon, geographic, hideous* and about 80 others ending in <-eous>, *nucleus, petroleum*
- /aɪ/ spelt <i>: *annihilate, bicycle, climate, dialogue, diaphragm, disciple, giant, hierarch, inviolable, liable, library, lion, rival, siphon, violence; criterion, diabetes, diarrhoea, gigantic, idea, iota*

- /əʊ/ spelt <o>: *diplomacy, focus, iota, lotion* and all the other words ending in /'əʊʃən/ (including *ocean* itself, despite the rest of its spelling), *molten, motor, negotiable, ocean, ochre, only, profile, rosy, sociable, swollen; coerce, cryostat, Eloise, grotesque, loquacious, obese*
- /juː/ spelt <u>: *alluvial* pronounced /əˈljuːviːjəl/, *computer, numerous, peculiar, reducible, stupid, unit; intuition* pronounced /ɪntjuːˈwɪʃən/
- /uː/ spelt <u>: *alluvial* pronounced /əˈluːviːjəl/, *inscrutable, judo, lunatic, scrutiny, suicide; fluorescent, intuition* pronounced /ɪntʃuːˈwɪʃən/, *judicial, superior.*

There are of course exceptions to all of these, e.g.

- /eɪ/ not spelt <a>: *Gaelic* pronounced /ˈgeɪlɪk/, *maelstrom; aileron, caitiff, complaisant, daisy, gaiter, liaison, maintain, maintenance, raillery, raisin, traitor, wainscot; bayonet, cayenne, crayon, layer, layette, maybe, mayonnaise, rayon; debacle, debris, debut(ante), decolletage, decor, denouement, detente, eclair, elan, elite, ingenu(e), menage, precis, regime, séance, ukulele; heinous* pronounced /ˈheɪnəs/, *obeisance, reindeer; neighbour; abeyance, heyday; laissez-faire, rendezvous*
- /iː/ not spelt <e>:

    1) Exceptions with <i> (there are at least 1000 words in this category – see under /iː/, section 5.7.2):

    (stressed) *albino, ballerina, casino, cliché, concertina, farina, kilo, lido, litre, maraschino, merino, mosquito, ocarina, piquant, scarlatina, semolina, visa;* first <i> in *kiwi, migraine;* second <i> in *bikini, incognito, libido*

    (unstressed) *ap/de-preciate, associate, audio, calumniate, caviar, foliage, luxuriate, mediaeval* (second syllable), *negotiate, orient, oubliette, patio, radio, ratio, serviette, studio, trio, verbiage;* also first <i> in *conscientious, liais-e/on, orgiastic, partiality, psychiatric, speciality,* second <i> in *inebriation, insomniac, officiate, superficiality, vitriolic,* third <i> in *initiate*

    2) Other exceptions: *aegis, aeon, aesthete, anaemi-a/c* and other words ending /ˈiːmɪə, ˈiːmɪk/ spelt <-aemi-a/c>, *anaesthetist, archaeology, Caesar, encyclopaedia* (fourth syllable), *faeces, haemoglobin, mediaeval* (third syllable), *naevus, praetor, quaestor; beacon, beadle, beagle, beaker, beaver, creature, deacon, eager, eagle, easel, Easter, easy, feature, heathen, meagre, measles, queasy, reason, season, sleazy, squeamish, teasle, treacle, treason,*

*weasel; beetle, cheetah, feeble, freesia, gee-gee, geezer, needle, squeegee, sweetie, teeter, wheedle; ceiling, cuneiform, heinous* pronounced /ˈhiːnəs/, *inveigle; feoffee, feoffment, people; geyser* pronounced /ˈgiːzə/; *amoeba, coelacanth, coelenterate, coeliac, coelom, foetal, foetid, foetus, oedema* (first syllable), *oenology, oesophagus, oestrogen, oestrus; phoenix, subpoena; caryatid, embryo(nic), halcyon, polyandry, polysyllable, polytechnic.* In US spelling many of the words just listed with <ae, oe> are instead spelt with <e>, thus conforming to the rule

- /aɪ/ not spelt <i>:
  1) Exceptions with <y>: *asylum, aureomycin, cryostat, cyanide, cycle, (hama)dryad, dynamic, forsythia, glycogen, gynaecology, hyacinth, hyaline, hybrid, hydra, hydrogen, hyena, hygiene, hygrometer, hymeneal, hyperbole* and other compounds in *hyper-, hyphen, hypothesis* and other compounds in *hypo-, lychee, myopic, nylon, psyche* and all its derivatives, *pylon, thylacine, thymus, typhoid, typhoon, typhus, xylophone, zygote* and derivatives
  2) Other exceptions: *naive, papaya; maestro; balalaika, Kaiser, naiad; aye-aye; deictic, deixis, eider, eidetic, eirenic, either, feisty, kaleidoscope, meiosis, neither, seismic; geyser* pronounced /ˈgaɪzə/; *blighty; iron; island, islet, viscount; coyote, foyer* pronounced /ˈfwaɪjeɪ/, *voyeur; duiker, Ruislip*
- /əʊ/ not spelt <o>: *chauffeu-r/se, chauvinis-m/t, hauteur; yeoman; gloaming; boulder* (contrast the comparative adjective *bolder*), *bouquet* pronounced /bəʊˈkeɪ/, *poultice, poultry, shoulder, smoulder*
- /juː/ not spelt <u>: *beauty; feudal, leukaemia, neurosis, pseudo; skewer; nuisance*
- /uː/ not spelt <u>: *leeward* pronounced /ˈluːwəd/; *pleurisy, rheumatism; brewer, jewel, sewage, sewer* ('foul drain'); *approval, movie* and other derivatives of words with /uː/ spelt <o.e>; *manoeuvre; bazooka, booby, boodle, boogie, boomerang, booty, canoodle, coolie, doodle(bug), googly, hoodoo, hoopoe, loony, moolah, noodle, oodles, poodle, voodoo; accoutrement, acoustic, boudoir, boulevard, bouquet, boutique, carousel, coulomb, cougar, coupon, croupier, goulash, insouciance, louvre, moussaka, oubliette, outré, ouzo, rouble, roulette, routine, silhouette, soubrette, soufflé, souvenir, toucan, toupee, troubadour, trousseau, voussoir; denouement; gruesome, muesli, Tuesday.*

But the generalisation seems mainly sound for stem words. It is particularly strong for /əʊ, juː/ spelt <o, u>; the only exceptions I've been able to find are the 13 and 7 respectively just listed. It's weakest for /iː/ spelt <e>, where there are over 1000 exceptions, and there are of course other instances in derived forms, e.g. (to name just a few) *mould-er/y, moult-ed/ing, fewer, hewer.*

For how the <e>-deletion rule makes many derived forms conform to this rule see the next section.

## 6.4 <e>-deletion (Part 2 of 'double, drop or swop')

For 'double, drop or swop' see also section 4.2 and the next section.

The main rule for dropping a word-final letter <e> when adding a suffix is easily stated:

In words which end in <e> preceded by a consonant letter, drop the <e> before suffixes beginning with a vowel letter.

Examples: *arousal, arrival, assemblage, baker, behaviour, chaplain, collegial, convalescent, debatable, drudgery, forcible, hated, muscly* (!), *revival, rousing, storage, surety, treasury, wiry, writing.*

Note that:
- when the suffix begins with <e> (past tense and participle <-ed>, agentive or comparative adjective-forming <-er>, superlative adjective-forming or archaic second person singular person tense ending <-est>, archaic third person singular person tense ending <-eth>, verb singular or noun plural <-es>, adjective-forming <-ent>, noun-forming <-ery, -ety>), technically the <e> of the stem is dropped and replaced by the <e> of the suffix, even though it looks simply as though <d, r, st, th, s, nt, ry, ty> has been added. A few quite odd words belong here, e.g. *bizarrery, freer, freest, weer, weest* (comparative and superlative forms of the adjectives *free, wee*), *freest, freeth, seest, seeth* (/ˈfriːjɪst, ˈfriːjɪθ, ˈsiːjɪst, ˈsiːjɪθ/, archaic second and third person singular present tense forms of the verbs *free, see*), *sightseer* /ˈsaɪtsiːjə/. In the words containing <e, e> those two letters, unusually, do not form a digraph;
- <e>-deletion makes many words in which it applies (including *arrival, collegial, debatable, hated, revival* and *writing*) conform to

the generalisation in the previous section about letter-name vowels in non-final syllables. Thus in the spelling *ageing*, now probably more frequent than *aging*, the <e> is strictly speaking unnecessary, as is the first <e> in *mileage* (also spelt *milage*);
- even more unnecessary is the <e> in *axeing*, which is starting to appear but should definitely be *axing*, the only possible form in US spelling where the unsuffixed form is *ax*; in 2012 I also noticed *apeing*, which should be *aping*. Similarly, the (US?) spelling *knowledgeable* strictly speaking has an unnecessary <e>, since *knowledgable* conforms better to the general <e>-deletion rule.

Exceptions: Where the consonant letter preceding word-final <e> is <c, g> forming a digraph with the <e> spelling /s, dʒ/ (whether or not the <e> is also part of a split digraph), the <e> is retained in order to show that <c, g> are not pronounced /k, g/, for example in *noticeable, peaceable, pronounceable, serviceable, traceable; advantageous, changeable, chargeable, damageable, manageable, marriageable, outrageous* (therefore not *\*noticable, \*peacable, \*pronouncable, \*servicable, \*tracable; \*advantagous, \*changable, \*chargable, \*damagable, \*managable, \*marriagable, \*outragous*). The <e> is also retained in *routeing, singeing, swingeing, whingeing* to avoid confusion with *routing* (from *rout*), *singing, swinging* and *winging*; also in *bingeing, cringeing, sponge-ing/y* to avoid suggesting the existence of stem words *\*to bing, \*to cring, \*to spong* – though there was of course *Bing* (*Crosby*), and *Spong* is a rare but real surname. Also, the <e> in *acreage, (a/un-)bridgeable, ogreish, ochreous, saleable, unshakeable* is never deleted. Conversely, when <-or> is added to *mortgage*, which should produce the spelling *\*mortgageor*, the result is instead *mortgagor*, thus both breaking what we might call the '<e>-retention' rule as it applies to words ending in /dʒ/ spelt <ge> and producing one of the few words in which <g> before <o> is pronounced /dʒ/ (see section 9.15). And the <e> of *more* is retained in *moreover*.

The past tense form *recceed* is very odd, not just visually (my spellchecker tried to change it to *recede*) or because of the irregular spelling of /k/ as <cc> before <e>, but also because the stem-final <e> isn't deleted before <-ed>. If it were, *\*recced* would look as though it was pronounced /rekt/, like *wrecked*. Similarly, the participle *recceing* also has to retain the <e> to spell /iː/.

The adjective *fiery* is always so spelt, and never *\*firey* or *\*firy*. There appear to be no words ending <irey>, but *\*firy* might seem a more logical

application of the <e>-replacement rule –perhaps there is a feeling that, because *fiery* is pronounced /ˈfaɪərɪː/, the schwa needs to be represented.
Extensions:
- Adjectives ending in <-able, -ible> drop the <e> and add <y> to form adverbs ending *-ly*, e.g. *probably, visibly*.
  (Almost all other adverbs add <-ly> but this would produce, e.g., *probablely, *visiblely which might suggest the presence of a non-existent schwa vowel corresponding to the <e>; and omitting the <e> from those forms would produce *probablly, *visiblly, which would go against the tendency to reduce <ll> to <l> - see section 4.4.7)
- *Whole* loses the <e> when <-ly> is added: *wholly* (though some dictionaries list the form *wholely*; contrast *solely*, which is never spelt *solly).
- A few words optionally lose the <e> before <-ment>: *abridg(e)ment, acknowledg(e)ment, judg(e)ment*, and *argument* always does.
- *Where* loses an <e> in *wherever* (but not in *whereas, whereat, whereupon*).
- *Nine* loses the <e> before <-th>, and *while* before <-st>: *ninth, whilst* (presumably so that they will not look as though they have two syllables, like archaic third or second person singular present tense verbs: *nineth, *whilest).
- One noun ending in <-ue> drops the <e> when adding <-ery> to form a derived noun: *demagoguery*.
- Adjectives ending in <-ue> drop the <e> when adding <-ly> to form adverbs: *duly, truly*; and *true* loses the <e> in *truism*, but *blueish* keeps it.
- A few verbs ending in <-ue> lose the <e> before <-able>: *arguable, issuable, rescuable, subduable, suable, valuable*. These six words (plus *changeable, debatable, saleable* and *serviceable*) all fit the generalisation about <-able> versus <-ible> (see section 6.7).

The extensions, noted in the last three bullet points above, of <e>-deletion to some suffixations of words ending in <-ue> never apply where the letter before the <e> is a vowel letter other than <u>, e.g. *hoeing*. Even where the preceding vowel letter **is** <u> some words can retain or drop the <e> before <-ing>, e.g. *cuing/cueing, queuing/ queueing*, but most other words with <ue> always drop the <e>, e.g. *arguing, burlesquing, issuing, rescued, subdued, suing, valued*.

However, where the stem ends in <-gue> the position is complicated. If the suffix begins with <e, i> AND the pronunciation of the <g> remains /g/ after suffixation only <e> is deleted, e.g. *catalogued, intriguing, voguish* (though I have also seen *vogueish* in print); but both letters <-ue> are deleted if either the pronunciation of the <g> changes to /dʒ/ after suffixing, e.g. *analogy, dialogic, ideological*, or the suffix begins with <a>, e.g. *fugal, vagary* (N.B. *\*vaguery* does not appear to exist). And then there is the group of 3 words ending in <-ngue> spelling /ŋ/: *harangue, meringue, tongue* retain the <u> in *haranguer, haranguing, meringued, tongued*, presumably to prevent the <ng> appearing to spell /ndʒ/: *\*haranger, \*haranging, \*meringed*; in the case of forms of *harangue*, also to prevent the second <a> looking as though it spells /eɪ/; and in the case of *tongue*, to avoid confusion with derivatives of *tong*, e.g. *tonged*.

## 6.5 <y>-replacement (Part 3 of 'double, drop or swop')

For 'double, drop or swop' see also sections 4.2 and 6.4.

The rule for replacing a word-final letter <y> with <i> when adding a suffix is more complicated than that for <e>-deletion:

> DON'T change the <y> if the preceding letter is a vowel letter, e.g. *playing*, or if the suffix is <-ing>, e.g. *crying*.
> Otherwise, in words which end in <y> preceded by a consonant letter:
> 1) change the <y> to <ie> before <-s>, e.g. *tries*;
> 2) change the <y> to <i> before other suffixes, e.g. *tried*.

Extensions and exceptions:

The 'multiples-of-ten' numerals from *twenty* to *ninety* change the <y> to <i> before <-eth>: *twentieth, thirtieth*, etc.

A few examples of <-y> changing to <i> before <-a> might be considered extensions, e.g. *porphyry, porphyria*.

There seems to be only one word where <y> after a vowel letter exceptionally is deleted before a suffix beginning with a vowel letter: *laity*.

There seem to be only four words where <y> changes exceptionally to <e>: *beauteous, duteous, piteous, plenteous*.

Where the preceding letter is a consonant letter, most words change <y> to <i> before <-ful, -fy, -hood, -less, -ly, -ment, -ness, -some,

-work>, e.g. *beautiful, bountiful, dutiful, fanciful, merciful, pitiful, plentiful; beautify, dandify, glorify, jollify, ladify, mummify, prettify; likelihood, livelihood; merciless, penniless; crazily, drily* (also spelt *dryly*), *greedily, wittily; accompaniment, embodiment, merriment; business* ('enterprise', pronounced /'bɪznɪs/), *foolhardiness, spiciness, weightiness; wearisome; handiwork*. But *bellyful, babyhood, shyly, slyly, wryly, busyness* ('state of being busy', pronounced /'bɪziːnɪs/), *dryness, shyness, slyness, wryness, bodywork* keep the <y>. Several other apparent exceptions to this paragraph (*joyful, playful, joyless, coyly, greyly, coyness, greyness, glueyness*) are obeying the part of the rule that says 'Don't change the <y> if the preceding letter is a vowel letter'. A great oddity is *multiplication*, which could be (mischievously) analysed as a derived form of the verb *multiply* with an otherwise unknown suffix <-cation> – in May 2009 I came across an instance of a child reported as writing *multiplycation*.

The adjective and adverb *daily*, the adverb *gaily*, the past tenses and participles *laid, paid* and the past participles *lain, slain* have <i> despite *day, gay, lay* (present tense of *laid*, past tense of *lie* 'be horizontal'), *pay, slay* having a vowel letter before the <y>; the regular spellings of *daily, gaily, laid, paid* would be *dayly, *gayly, *layed (and on 30 June 2010 I saw the form *overlayed in an exhibition caption at the British Library), *payed. The irregularity in *laid, paid* consists not just in changing <y> to <i> but also in omitting the <e> of the regular past tense and participle ending <-ed>. It is more difficult to work out what the 'regular' spellings of *lain, slain* would be. They are irregular past participles formed with the ending usually written <-en> (e.g. *broken, written*), but they also seem to be the only cases where this ending is added to stems ending in <-y>. The spellings *layen, *slayen would, however, look disyllabic even though the words are monosyllables – the few occurrences of medial /eɪ/ spelt <ay> are all in polysyllables, whether stem or compound words (see /eɪ/, section 5.7.1) – but on the other hand *layn, *slayn would spell medial /eɪ/ with <ay> when this correspondence never occurs in monosyllables. So perhaps *lain, slain* are logical after all.

The nouns *fryer* (as in *deep-fat-*) and *dyer* ('person who dyes') always have <y>. The noun meaning 'thing that dries' (as in *hair-, hand-, tumble-*) can be spelt *drier* or *dryer*, but the adjective meaning 'more dry' must be *drier*. The nouns meaning 'an aircraft pilot, a handbill', etc., can be either *flier* or *flyer*, but the adjective meaning 'more knowing and clever' is always *flyer* (and why this differs from the adjective *drier* escapes me).

## 6.6 <ie>-replacement, <y>-deletion and <e>-insertion

I've invented these terms to draw attention to three processes which contrast with those in the two previous sections. <ie>-replacement is regularly remarked upon, and <e>-insertion is a notorious source of confusion for some people, but <y>-deletion has hitherto apparently escaped notice.

<blockquote>
<ie>-replacement: There are just five verbs in which the opposite 'swop' to <y>-replacement occurs, that is, <ie> is changed to <y> before <-ing>, namely *belying, dying, lying, tying, vying*.
</blockquote>

What I have called '<y>-deletion' occurs where abstract nouns ending in <-y> correspond to 'agentive' nouns ending in <-er, -ist>, e.g. *astrolog-y/er, astronom-y/er, biograph-y/er, geograph-y/er, philosoph-y/er, botan-y/ist, chiropody-y/ist, geology-y/ist, misanthrop-y/ist, theor-y/ist*, etc. This might also cover the loss of <y> in *laity* relative to *lay* ('not clergy').

I've invented the term '<e>-insertion' to draw attention to the Oddity of some polysyllabic nouns which end in <-o> in the singular adding <e> before the plural ending <-s>, e.g. *heroes, potatoes, tomatoes*. This occurs only in nouns ending in <-o> (and in rare occurrences of such nouns being used as singular verbs, e.g. *The submarine torpedoes the battleship*), and never with other word-final single vowel letters: *bananas, clichés, rabbis, menus*, not *bananaes, *clichées, *rabbies, *menues. Carney (1994: 174) points out that there are a few clear rules here:

<blockquote>
'The <-oes> form is not found in decidedly Exotic words (*generalissimos, mulattos*) or in words where the plural is unusual (*indigos, impetigos*) or in words with the colloquial ending <-o> (*boyos, buckos, dipsos, winos*) ... [or] if there is a vowel before the final /əʊ/ ... (*radios, cameos*).'
</blockquote>

And to the last group one could add *patios, rodeos, studios*.

But otherwise one is reduced to listing words which:
- only have <-os>, e.g. *concertos, espressos, provisos, quartos, solos*
- only have <-oes>, e.g. *buboes, heroes, potatoes, tomatoes, torpedoes*
- can have either, e.g. *cargo(e)s, commando(e)s, halo(e)s, tornado(e)s*.

In my opinion, nothing but a source of confusion (for Dan Quayle, among others; this story re-appeared in the *Guardian* Education Section, 19 August 2008, p.3) would be lost if all such polysyllabic words were spelt only with <-os> (but monosyllables like *doe, floe* would still have plurals in <-oes>

because the <e> is there in the singular; *throes* would still need its <e> despite not having a singular form, *goes*, *noes* and the verb *does* would need to be exceptions, and past tenses would still need the <e>, e.g. *torpedoed*).

# 6.7 <-able/-ible>

These adjective endings are an awkward pair. The origins of the two spellings go back to Latin. (If the adjective's root is descended from a Latin verb of the 2nd, 3rd or 4th conjugation, the suffix is generally spelt <-ible>; otherwise, <-able> - and a fat lot of use that rule is to most people.) Pronunciation of the endings is no guide to which adjectives have which ending - both are pronounced /əbəl/, and there are almost no related forms in which the stress falls on the relevant syllable and gives the vowel its full value, thus removing the uncertainty. (The only exception seems to be *syllable* - *syllabic*, and here the <-able> word is a noun, not an adjective, and derived from Greek, not Latin).

However, there is a generalisation which is fairly reliable:

Try saying the adjective without the /əbəl/. If the result is a free-standing word, or ends in /k/ spelt <(c)c>, /g/ spelt <g> or /ʃ/ spelt <ci, ti>, spell the ending with <a>. Otherwise, spell it with <i>.

Examples: *biddable, suitable, walkable; amicable, applicable, despicable, educable, impeccable, implacable, irrevocable, practicable; navigable; appreciable, sociable, insatiable, negotiable*; (with retained <e>) *traceable, manageable; eligible, illegible, intelligible, susceptible*, plus the noun *crucible*.

Exceptions:
1) Where the root does not sound like a free-standing word but the ending has <a>: *abominable, admirable, affable, amenable, charitable, culpable, demonstrable, disreputable, equable, equitable, execrable, flammable, formidable, hospitable, impregnable, incalculable, ineffable, inestimable, inevitable, inexorable, inimitable, inscrutable, inseparable, interminable, inviolable, irritable, malleable, memorable, miserable, palpable, permeable, probable, tolerable, venerable.*
2) Where the root does sound like a free-standing word but the ending has <i>: *accessible, contemptible, convincible, defensible, discernible, flexible, forcible, gullible, reducible, responsible, sensible*; also *legible* and the noun *mandible* even though not derived from *ledge, manned*.

Curiously, the generalisation works for some <-able> words where the root sounds like a free-standing word but that word isn't related to the adjective ending in <-able>, for example *amiable, capable, liable, syllable, tenable, viable*, as though derived from *Amy, cape, lie, sill, ten, vie*. In some cases it is necessary to remove a prefix before the test works, e.g. (*un*)*palatable*.

## 6.8 <-ant/-ent, -ance/-ence, -ancy/-ency>

There are two useful generalisations for <-ant/-ent>:
1) The unstressed ending /mənt/ is almost always spelt <-ment>.
   Examples (N.B. when these words are nouns; when words of the same spelling are verbs or take the adjectival endings /əl, əriː/ spelt <-al, -ary> the <e> is traditionally pronounced /e/ (though this distinction is dying out), and this helps to indicate the <e> spelling): *complement, compliment, document, element, excrement, experiment, ferment, fragment, implement, increment, instrument, supplement*. Extension: The adjectives (*in*)*clement* also have /mənt/ spelt <-ment> but have no related verb.
   Exceptions: *adamant, claimant, clamant, dormant, informant*.
2) The ending /'esənt/ is always spelt <-escent>, e.g. *adolescent, convalescent*.

Otherwise all these paired endings are if anything even more awkward than <-able/-ible>. Again, the source of the spellings is Latin, and pronunciation is of little help - unless there's a related word in which the stress falls on the relevant syllable and the full sound of the vowel removes the uncertainty. For example:

>circumst*A*nce(*s*) - circumst*A*ntial
>
>compon*E*nt - compon*E*ntial
>
>confid*E*nce - confid*E*ntial
>
>consequ*E*nce - consequ*E*ntial
>
>differ*E*nce, differ*E*nt - differential
>
>domin*A*nt - domin*A*tion
>
>elem*E*nt - elem*E*ntal, elem*E*ntary
>
>eleph*A*nt - eleph*A*ntine
>
>influ*E*nce - influ*E*ntial

jubilAnt – jubilAtion
lubricAnt – lubricAtion
migrAnt – migrAtion
mutAnt – mutAtion
presidEncy, presidEnt – presidEntial
protestAnt – protestAtion
residEnce, residEnt – residEntial
substAnce – substAntial

# 6.9 Using related forms to spell schwa

Finding the full vowel in a related word is also the clue to spelling /ə/ in many other words. In the following examples, the words on the left have capitalised vowels spelling schwa whose spelling can be derived from the capitalised vowel letters in the words on the right:

abdOmen – abdOminal
AcadEmy – AcadEmic
acAdemic – acAdemy
adamAnt – adamAntine
advocAcy, advocAte (noun) – advocAte (verb)
anAlyse, anAlytic – anAlysis
Analysis – Analyse, Analytic
anARchy – anARchic
artEry – artErial
associAte (noun, adjective) – associAte (verb)
articulAcy, articulAte (adjective) – articulAte(d) (verb)
atOm – atOmic
Atomic – Atom
biOlogical – biOlogy
biolOgy – biolOgical

*canOn – canOnical*

*cAnonical – cAnon*

*cAtholicism – cAtholic*

*celEbrate – celEbrity*

*cElebrity – cElebrate*

*cOlloquial, cOlloquium – cOlloquy*

*collOquy – collOquial, collOquium*

*colUmn – colUmnar*

*cOlumnar – cOlumn*

*compOnential – compOnent*

*cOnfirm – cOnfirmation*

*cUstodial – cUstody*

*custOdy – custOdial*

*defInIte – fInIte*

*dramA – dramAtic*

*drAmatic – drAma*

*duplicAte* (noun/adjective) *– duplicAte* (verb)

*essEnce – essEntial*

*Essential – Essence*

*factOR – factORial*

*frequEnt* (adjective) *– frequEnt* (verb)

*grammAR – grammARian*

*grAmmarian, grAmmatical – grAmmar*

*infInIte – fInIte*

*majEsty – majEstic*

*mAjestic – mAjesty*

*medAl – medAllion*

*mEdallion – mEdal*

*memOry – memOrial*

mEmorial – mEmory
mentAl – mentAlity
methOd – methOdical
mEthodical – mEthod
monARch(y) – monARchical
mOnarchical – mOnarch(y)
Obligatory – Obligation
octAgon – octAgonal
orAcle – orAcular
Oracular – Oracle
palAce – palAtial
pAlatial – pAlace
pArabOla – pArabOlic
parAbolic – parAbola
patriOt – patriOtic
perfEct (adjective) – perfEct (verb)
photOgraph – photO, photOgrapher
phOtogrApher – phOtogrAph(ic)
populAR – populARity
prOcure – prOcurator
prOfessOR – prOfessORial
profEssorial – profEssor
psychiAtry – psychiAtric
regulAR – regulARity
separAte (adjective) – separAte (verb), separAtion
sepUlchre – sepUlchral
sObriety – sOber
sOciety – sOcial
sulphUR(ous) – sulphURic

*syllAble - syllAbic*

*telEgraph, telEgraphic - telEgraphy*

*telegrAphy - telegrAph, telegrAphic*

*theAtre - theatrical*

*variAnt - variAtion*

As the list shows, many pairs provide reciprocal guidance.

## 6.10 Elided vowels

Even more difficult for novice spellers and non-native learners may be words where a vowel letter appears in the written version that has no counterpart at all (not even schwa) in the spoken version. Five examples in common words are:

- *secondary* /ˈsekəndriː/ with no phoneme corresponding to <a>
- *different* /ˈdɪfrənt/ with no phoneme corresponding to <e>
- *business* /ˈbɪznɪs/ with no phoneme corresponding to <i>
- *category* /ˈkætəgriː/ with no phoneme corresponding to <o>
- *favourite* /ˈfeɪvrɪt/ with no phoneme corresponding to <ou>.

Even these few words show significant variability in the vowel grapheme that needs to be recovered and written. In this section I enclose many such elided vowel letters in round brackets - for this convention see Wijk (1966: 77-8). Vowel elision is one of four special processes which I have identified as operating in English spelling (for the others see section 3.6 and chapter 7), and has serious implications for any attempt to deduce the stress patterns of words from their written forms (see section A.10 in Appendix A).

The reason for this syncopation or telescoping phenomenon seems to be that English-speakers dislike having to say three syllables containing unstressed vowels consecutively, and tend to drop one where this would be the case. We even do it sometimes where there would be only two consecutive unstressed syllables. And it affects not just single words, but also strings of words in running speech, e.g. *I should have thought* can be telescoped into something like /aɪʃtəfˈθɔːt/, with three syllables rather than four. At the extreme this is the process which allowed W.S. Gilbert to create outrageous rhymes such as *monotony* rhyming with *got any*, that is, *monot'ny - got 'ny* /məˈnɒtniː - ˈgɒtniː/.

This trend towards eliding vowels seems to be due to the nature of English as a stressed-timed language. It is particularly strong in RP, so some non-native learners with experience of a wide range of the accents with which English is spoken might be helped by the US pronunciations of some words in this category:
- *secondary* /'sekəndeəriː/ with /eə/ corresponding to <a>
- *category* /'kætəgɔːriː/ with /ɔː/ corresponding to <o>.

But no helpful vowel phoneme surfaces in mid-Atlantic in *different*, so some such words will continue to pose problems.

Besides which, a great many native-speaking children learning to spell English will receive no such help from their own accents or those of people around them, and almost certainly won't notice the relevant details of different accents heard on television, video or DVD or at the cinema.

The largest category (that word again) of words with an elided vowel is those ending in /riː/ spelt <-ry> and with the main stress two syllables earlier and /ə/ or /ɪ/ in the syllable after the stress:
- with /ə/ in that syllable:

    *syllab(a)ry, apothec(a)ry, dromed(a)ry, legend(a)ry, second(a)ry, custom(a)ry, concession(a)ry, coron(a)ry, diction(a)ry, discretion(a)ry, legion(a)ry, mercen(a)ry, mission(a)ry, ordin(a)ry, precaution(a)ry, probation(a)ry, pulmon(a)ry, reaction(a)ry, revolution(a)ry, station(a)ry, urin(a)ry, vision(a)ry, advers(a)ry, emiss(a)ry, necess(a)ry, comment(a)ry, diet(a)ry, fragment(a)ry, moment(a)ry, necess(a)ry, propriet(a)ry, salut(a)ry, secret(a)ry, sedent(a)ry* (also pronounced with stress on the second syllable and with a schwa corresponding to <a>), *tribut(a)ry, volunt(a)ry*. In *extr(a)ordin(a)ry* /ɪkˈstrɔːdənriː/ the first <a> is also elided

    *cemet(e)ry, chancell(e)ry, confection(e)ry, dysent(e)ry, jewell(e)ry* (the alternative spelling *jewelry* avoids the problem), *monast(e)ry, station(e)ry*. In *confection(e)ry, jewell(e)ry, station(e)ry* the fact that <-y> is a suffix would help give the correct spelling

    *categ(o)ry, promiss(o)ry, amat(o)ry, conciliat(o)ry, conservat(o)ry, contribut(o)ry, declamat(o)ry, defamat(o)ry, desult(o)ry, dilat(o)ry, explanat(o)ry, explorat(o)ry, inflammat(o)ry, interrogat(o)ry, invent(o)ry* (also pronounced with stress on the second syllable and with a schwa corresponding to <o>), *laborat(o)ry, lavat(o)ry, mandat(o)ry, nugat(o)ry, obligat(o)ry, observat(o)ry, offert(o)ry, orat(o)ry, predat(o)ry, preparat(o)ry, promont(o)ry, purgat(o)ry, repert(o)ry, retaliat(o)ry, signat(o)ry, statut(o)ry*. Some words that fit this pattern in one pronunciation don't in another (even within RP, let alone the differences between RP and GA), e.g. *migratory* as either /ˈmaɪɡrətriː/ (three syllables, stress on first, <o> elided) or /maɪˈɡreɪtəriː/ (four syllables, stress on second, no elision).

- with /ɪ/ in that syllable:
*lapid(a)ry, vineg(a)ry, culin(a)ry, imagin(a)ry, prelimin(a)ry, budget(a)ry, dignit(a)ry, heredit(a)ry, milit(a)ry, monet(a)ry, pituit(a)ry, planet(a)ry, sanit(a)ry, solit(a)ry, unit(a)ry;*
*millin(e)ry, presbyt(e)ry*. In these words the fact that <-y> is a suffix would help give the correct spelling
*alleg(o)ry, audit(o)ry, de/ex/re/sup-posit(o)ry, dormit(o)ry, inhibit(o)ry, territ(o)ry, transit(o)ry*.

In many cases, where adjectives in the preceding lists add /liː/ spelt <-ly> to form adverbs the tendency to elide the vowel seems to me to be even stronger. A few examples would be *moment(a)rily, necess(a)rily, statut(o)rily, volunt(a)rily*, when stressed on the first syllable; those with <a> can alternatively be stressed on the <a>, in which case it is a full vowel pronounced /e/, e.g. *necessarily* pronounced /nesəˈserɪliː/ rather than /ˈnesəsrəliː/.

In a very few cases a related word with a surfacing vowel might help:

> *seminary – seminArian*
> *adversary – adversArial*
> *sanitary – sanitAtion*
> *dysentery – dysentEric*
> *presbytery – presbytErian*
> *allegory – allegOrical*
> *category – categOrical*
> *lavatory – lavatOrial*
> *oratory – oratOrical*
> *territory – territOrial*

But writers who already know the words in the right-hand column would surely already know the correct spellings of the words in the left-hand column; and in *secretary, secretarial* the pronunciation of the adjective might mislead uncertain spellers into writing *secretery, *secreterial (and I won't go into pronunciations such as /ˈsekətriː/ where the first /r/ is lost).

Extensions (1), where the ending is still /riː/ spelt <-ry> but the stress pattern is not as predictable:
- A few words where the stress is on the syllable immediately preceding the elided vowel: *gooseb(e)rry* /ˈgʊzbriː/, *raspb(e)rry* /ˈrɑːzbriː/, *strawb(e)rry* /ˈstrɔːbriː/), where in normal pronunciation there is no schwa vowel after the /b/; *annivers(a)ry, compuls(o)ry, element(a)ry, ev(e)ry, fact(o)ry, hist(o)ry, myst(e)ry, nurs(e)ry, vict(o)ry* pronounced /ˈevriː, ˈfæktriː, ˈhɪstriː, ˈmɪstriː, ˈvɪktriː/. Very rapid pronunciations of *February, diary, library, boundary* may also be contracted to two syllables /ˈfebriː, ˈdaɪriː, ˈlaɪbriː, ˈbaʊndriː/, but this is usually considered too colloquial
- *lit(e)rary* /ˈlɪtrəriː/, *(con)temp(o)rary* /(kən)ˈtemprəriː/, where the spoken ending is /rəriː/ and this is spelt <-rary>, so that the elided vowel is immediately after the stressed syllable. In *temporarily* pronounced /tempəˈrerɪliː/ there is a schwa in the relevant position but it gives no guide to the spelling, and the word may in any case be pronounced with three syllables: /ˈtemprəliː/; however, if it is pronounced /tempəˈreərɪliː/ this would guide the <a> spelling
- *vet(e)rin(a)ry*, which is usually pronounced (in RP) with only three syllables /ˈvetrɪnriː/, so that there are two elided vowels, needing to be spelt with the second <e> and the <a> (Mr Biggins, the farmer in *All Creatures Great and Small*, reduced it even further, to /ˈvetənrɪ/)
- a few nouns ending in <-tuary>: *act(u)ary, est(u)ary, mort(u)ary, obit(u)ary, sanct(u)ary, stat(u)ary, volupt(u)ary* which are normally pronounced with /tʃəriː/ rather than /tʃʊəriː/).

Extensions (2), where the ending is no longer /riː/ spelt <-ry> but the consonant after the elided vowel is still /r/:
- Words ending in /rəbəl, rətɪv, rətɪst/ spelt <-rable, -rative, -ratist>, where the preceding vowel always seems to be elided: *adm(i)rable, comp(a)rable, consid(e)rable, deliv(e)rable, fav(ou)rable, hon(ou)rable, inex(o)rable, mis(e)rable, op(e)rable, pref(e)rable, vuln(e)rable; dec(o)rative, fig(u)rative, gen(e)rative, op(e)rative; sep(a)ratist*. In some cases the unsuffixed stem will help: *consider, deliver, favour, honour, miser(y), prefer, décor, figure*
- Words where the vowel is sometimes elided, sometimes not, but the unsuffixed stem or a related word would normally guide the spelling:

*adv*ent(*u*)*rous, barb*(*a*)*rous* (cf. *barbarian*), *conf*(*e*)*rence, dang*(*e*)*rous, def*(*e*)*rence, diff*(*e*)*rence, diff*(*e*)*rent; ent*(*e*)*ring, fav*(*ou*)*rite, laund*(*e*)*rette* (the alternative spelling *laundrette* avoids the problem; in the spelling with three <e>'s this word is unusual in having the main stress on the syllable **after** the elided vowel), *lev*(*e*)*rage, nat*(*u*)*ral, off*(*e*)*ring, pref*(*e*)*rence, prosp*(*e*)*rous, suff*(*e*)*rance, temp*(*e*)*rament, utt*(*e*)*rance*

- Two adjective/verb pairs where a vowel is always or almost always elided in the adjective but a schwa in the verb may help to indicate where a corresponding vowel letter needs to be written: *delib*(*e*)*rate* (/dɪ'lɪbrət/ (adjective) with three syllables – contrast *deliberate* /dɪ'lɪbəreɪt/ (verb) with four syllables; *sep*(*a*)*rate* /'seprət/ (adjective) with two syllables – contrast *separate* /'sepəreɪt/ (verb) with three syllables, *separation*, where there is a schwa corresponding to the first <a>, though it is no guide to the correct spelling, so that *\*seperat-e/ion* are amongst the most frequent misspellings in English

- Words where the vowel is always or almost always elided and stems or related words do not help: *adm*(*i*)*ral, asp*(*i*)*rin, av*(*e*)*rage, cam*(*e*)*ra, Cath*(*e*)*rine, consid*(*e*)*rate* (if pronounced with three syllables), *corp*(*o*)*ral, corp*(*o*)*rate, desp*(*e*)*rate, em*(*e*)*rald, gen*(*e*)*ral, int*(*e*)*rest, lib*(*e*)*ral, lit*(*e*)*racy, lit*(*e*)*ral, lit*(*e*)*rature, op*(*e*)*ra, rest*(*au*)*rant, rhinoc*(*e*)*ros, sev*(*e*)*ral, sov*(*e*)*reign, temp*(*e*)*rament, temp*(*e*)*rature*; also *prim*(*a*)*rily* /'praɪmrəliː/ with 3 syllables, where the alternative 4-syllable pronunciation /praɪ'merɪliː/ would show that a vowel letter is needed after the <m> but the unusual correspondence of /e/ spelt <a> (see section 5.4.2) might mislead some writers into spelling the word *\*primerily*

- Words where the vowel might be elided in very rapid pronunciation but normal pronunciation would reveal the prefix: *hyp*(*e*)*ractive, hyp*(*e*)*rintelligent, int*(*e*)*ractive, int*(*e*)*ragency*

- the Latin phrase *et cet*(*e*)*ra*.

Extensions (3), where the consonant after the elided vowel is /l/:

- *cath*(*o*)*lic* pronounced /'kæθlɪk/ - contrast *cathOlicism; chanc*(*e*)*llor, choc*(*o*)*late, om*(*e*)*lette; origin*(*a*)*lly* /ə'rɪdʒɪnliː/; *p*(*o*)*liceman* pronounced /'pliːsmən/; *fam*(*i*)*ly* pronounced /'fæmliː/

- adverbs with the unstressed ending /ɪkliː/ which is almost always spelt <-ically>, e.g. *radic*(*a*)*lly*. Since all the corresponding adjectives end in /ɪkəl/ spelt <-ical> there should be no problem with spelling these adverbs, except when the pattern is overgeneralised to the few adverbs which are exceptions to it: *follicly* (*challenged*) (jocular form derived from *follicle*), *impoliticly, politicly* ('judiciously', stress on first syllable), *publicly*, not *follically (but this form seems to be gaining ground), *impolitically, *publically – but *politically* ('pertaining to government', stress on second syllable) does exist, as the adverb from *political*. Extensions: *equivoc(a)lly, unequivoc(a)lly*

- adjectives ending (in rapid speech) in /tʃəl/ spelt <-tual>: *accent(u)al, act(u)al, concept(u)al, contract(u)al, effect(u)al, event(u)al, fact(u)al, habit(u)al, intellect(u)al, mut(u)al, perpet(u)al, punct(u)al, rit(u)al, spirit(u)al, text(u)al, virt(u)al*. These words also have a slower pronunciation in /tʃuːwəl/ where the vowel is not elided and guides spelling
- adverbs derived from the adjectives just mentioned, e.g. *act(u)ally*, which seem to me to be pronounced with /tʃəliː/ more with often than /tʃuːwəliː/ but the spelling of the adjectives would guide the spelling of the adverbs
- some adverbs ending in <-fully> pronounced /fliː/, e.g. *beautif(u)lly, dutif(u)llyl*.

The next phoneme is also /l/ in a large set of words whose stems end in /əl/ spelt <-le>, where the schwa is lost when these words have a suffix added which adds a syllable, e.g. *peddle* /ˈpedəl/ v. *peddling* /ˈpedlɪŋ/, but these words do not add any consonant letter + elided vowel sequences to the inventory below because the <e> is deleted before the initial vowel letter of the suffix. For much more on this set of words see section 4.4.3.

Extensions (4), adverbs where the consonant after the elided vowel is /r/ and there is an ending /liː/ spelt <-ly>, e.g. *advent(u)rously, delib(e)rately, irrep(a)rably, pref(e)rably, nat(u)rally*. Here again I think that the tendency for the vowel to be elided is stronger than in the corresponding adjectives, but the spelling of the adjectives would guide the spelling of the adverbs.

Extensions (5), where the consonant after the elided vowel is /n/:
- *ars(e)nal, ars(e)nic, broad(e)ning, bus(i)ness, christ(e)ning, deep(e)ning, def(i)nitely, ev(e)ning, falc(o)ner, fash(io)nable, fresh(e)n-er/ing, fright(e)n-er/ing, gard(e)n-er/ing, laud(a)num, list(e)n-er/ing, nati(o)nal, nom(i)native, op(e)n-er/ing, pers(o)nal, prelim(i)nary, rati(o)nal, reas(o)nable, seas(o)ning, sharp(e)ner, sweet(e)n-er/ing, weak(e)ning, wid(e)ning* (for *opening* see also section 10.28)
- *twop(e)nny, halfp(e)nny* /ˈtʌpniː, ˈheɪpniː/ which no longer exist except in the memories of aging Brits like me, but where the ending was contracted to /pniː/.

*Some spelling rules for vowels* 243

For most of the words in this subcategory stems or related forms do help.
Extensions (6), a final ragbag:
- *caf(e)tiere* – contrast *café, cafeteria*
- *comf(or)table* – contrast *comfort*
- *ecz(e)ma* – contrast *eczematous*
- *forec(a)stle* pronounced /ˈfəʊksəl/
- *med(i)cine* – contrast *medicinal*
- *ramekin* pronounced /ˈræmkɪn/ (also pronounced /ˈræmɪkɪn/)
- *veg(e)table*.

In this section I have identified 49 consonant letter(s)-plus-elided vowel sequences (and there are probably others I've not noticed). Just 17 of these appear as consonant graphemes in chapter 3:
- <de> spelling /d/ is needed for *aide, horde*, etc., as well as for *considerable*
- <fe> spelling /f/ is needed for *carafe* as well as for *cafetiere, deference, preferably*, etc.
- <ffe> spelling /f/ is needed for *gaffe, giraffe, pouffe* as well as for *different*, etc.
- <ge> spelling /dʒ/ is needed for words like *image* as well as for *vegetable*
- <gi> spelling /dʒ/ is needed for words like *legion*
- <ke> spelling /k/ is needed for *Berkeley, burke* as well as for *weakening*
- <lle> spelling /l/ is needed for *bagatelle, vaudeville*, etc., as well as for *chancellery*
- <me> spelling /m/ is needed for *become, handsome*, etc., as well as for *camera, emerald, omelette, ramekin* pronounced /ˈræmkɪn/
- <ne> spelling /n/ is needed for *heroine*, etc., as well as for *confectionery, stationery*, etc.
- <pe> spelling /p/ is needed for *cantaloupe, troupe* as well as for *opera, operable, twopenny*, etc.
- <se> spelling /z/ is needed for *gooseberry* as well as *miserable*
- <si> is needed as the main correspondence for /ʒ/ in *vision*, etc., as well as for /z/ in *business*
- <(t)te> spelling /t/ are needed for words like *granite, route, gavotte, roulette*, as well as for *interest, literal, utterance*, etc.
- <the> is needed to spell /ð/ in words like *soothe* as well as /θ/ in *Catherine*

- <ve> spelling /v/ is needed for most words ending /v/ as well as for *every*, etc.
- <ze> is needed as a correspondence for word-final /z/ as well as for *eczema*.

The other 32 sequences are: <ba, ca, da, ga, ma, na, pa, ra, sa, ssa, ta, tau; be, she; fi, mi, pi, shio, tio; co, for, go, nou, po, so, sso, tho, to, vou, xo; fu, tu>. None of these are required by other parts of the analysis, so I have not added them to the inventory of graphemes. Even I find there are limits to the principle of accounting for every letter under the aegis of some phoneme or other (see section A.5 in Appendix A).

So for some of the words in this section you can rely on related forms; for the rest you have no guidance but your visual memory.

When the consonant letter-plus-elided vowel words are sorted alphabetically by the consonant letter, it becomes apparent that far and away the most common preceding letter is <t> – see the last paragraph of section 9.34.

# 7. Special processes

In this category I include processes which function outside the strict range of phoneme-grapheme correspondences but which are essential for understanding them. I have identified four:
- /r/-linking, which is dealt with in section 3.6
- elided vowels, which are dealt with just above in section 6.10
- dual-functioning
- surfacing sounds.

The last two have been referred to frequently in previous chapters and are drawn together in the next two sections.

## 7.1 Dual-functioning

I have invented this term to cover cases where, in my opinion, particular letters belong to two graphemes simultaneously. In my analysis this process affects only the letters <e, r, w, y>. For more background on this see section A.8 in Appendix A.

### 7.1.1 Letter <e>

Dual-functioning <e> occurs where the word-final consonant digraphs <ce, ge, ve> overlap with split vowel digraphs and the <e> belongs to both. For details see variously sections 3.7.4, 3.7.6 and 3.8.4 for <ce, ge, ve>, and sections 10.4/17/24/28/38/40 for the split digraphs. Conversely, see section 3.7.8 for why I never treat the <e> in <-ze> as part of a split digraph. I have also found it unnecessary to treat the <e> in <-se> as part of a split digraph.

## 7.1.2 Letter <r>

The major category of dual-functioning involving <r> is /r/-linking, or most of its instances – see Table 3.2 in section 3.6, where I point out which examples of /r/-linking do **not** count as instances of dual-functioning. Conversely, there are also cases of <r> having dual functions which are internal to stem words and therefore do not arise from /r/-linking. In all such cases the phoneme following the /r/ is a vowel:

- Words in which the word-initial morpheme *air* is followed by a vowel phoneme and is spelt <aer>, e.g. *aerate, aerial, aerobic, aerodrome, aeroplane, aerosol*. These all have the word-initial 2-phoneme sequence /eər/ in which /eə/ is spelt <aer> and the <r> also spells /r/
- Many cases of medial /eər/ spelt <ar> in which the <r> functions as part of <ar> spelling /eə/ and also spells /r/, e.g. *area, garish, gregarious, parent*
- Two cases of medial /eər/ spelt <er> in which the <r> functions as part of <er> spelling /eə/ and also spells /r/, namely *bolero* (/bə'leərəʊ/ 'dance'), *sombrero*
- Two cases of word-initial /ɪər/ in which the <r> functions as part of <eer, eyr> spelling /ɪə/ and also spells /r/, namely *eerie, eyrie*
- Words in which medial /ɪər/ is spelt <er> and the <r> functions as part of <er> spelling /ɪə/ and also spells /r/, e.g. *adherent, cereal, coherence, coherent, ethereal, funereal, hero, inherent, managerial, material, perseverance, serial, series, serious, serum, sidereal, venereal, zero*
- Words in which medial /aɪər/ is spelt <ir> and the <r> functions as part of <ir> spelling /aɪə/ and also spells /r/, e.g. *biro, giro, pirate, virus*
- One word (and derivatives) in which initial /jʊər/ is spelt <eur> and the <r> functions as part of <eur> spelling /jʊə/ and also spells /r/, namely *Europe*
- *urea* and many words derived from it in which initial /jʊər/ is spelt <ur> and the <r> functions as part of <ur> spelling /jʊə/ and also spells /r/
- Words in which medial /(j)ʊər/ are spelt <ur> and the <r> functions as part of <ur> spelling /(j)ʊə/ and also spells /r/, e.g. (with /ʊər/) *during* pronounced /'dʒʊərɪŋ/, *juror, jury, rural*; (with /jʊər/) *curate*

(pronounced both /ˈkjʊərət/ 'junior cleric' and /kjʊəˈreɪt/ 'mount an exhibition'), *curious*, *during* pronounced /ˈdjʊərɪŋ/, *fury*, *spurious*. For longer lists see section 5.6.5
- One word in which medial /ʊər/ is spelt <our> and the <r> functions as part of that grapheme spelling /ʊə/ and also spells /r/, namely *houri*. Contrast *potpourri*, in which, uniquely, /ʊə, r/ can be analysed (admittedly counter-intuitively, but there is no call for a grapheme <ourr>) as spelt separately as <our, r>
- Words in which initial or medial /ɔːr/ is spelt <or> and the <r> functions as part of <or> spelling /ɔː/ and also spells /r/, e.g. *aurora, authorial, borax, chlorine, choral, chorus, corporeal* (only the second <or> since the first is followed by a consonant), *decorum, dictatorial, editorial, euphoria, flora(l), forum, glory, memorial, oracy, oral, oration, oratorio* (only the medial occurrence - in my accent the initial phoneme is /ɒ/, not /ɔː/), *orient* (noun, pronounced /ˈɔːriːjənt/ - the verb of the same spelling is pronounced /ɒriːˈjent/), *quorum, variorum*.

## 7.1.3 Letter <w>

There are very few instances of dual-functioning <w>, and within stem words they are all medial and followed by a vowel phoneme:
- In *ewer, jewel, newel, skewer, steward*, <w> is both a single-letter grapheme spelling /w/ and part of the digraph <ew> spelling /(j)uː/
- In *bowie, rowan* (in its English pronunciation /ˈrəʊwən/), <w> is both a single-letter grapheme spelling /w/ and part of the digraph <ow> spelling /əʊ/
- In *bowel, dowel, rowel, towel, trowel, vowel; bower, cower, dower, flower, glower, power, shower, tower; coward, dowager, howitzer, prowess*, plus the Scottish pronunciation of *rowan* /ˈraʊwən/, <w> is both a single-letter grapheme spelling /w/ and part of the digraph <ow> spelling /aʊ/.

Other instances occur when words ending in <w>, which here is always part of a digraph spelling /(j)uː, əʊ, aʊ/, have a suffix beginning with a vowel phoneme added; also in running speech when such words are followed by a word beginning with a vowel phoneme. For examples and discussion of 'linking /w/' see Table 3.7 in section 3.8.7 and the paragraphs preceding and following it.

## 7.1.4 Letter <y>

Like <w>, there are very few instances of dual-functioning <y>, and within stem words they are all medial and followed by a vowel phoneme:
- In *abeyance*, /j/ is spelt <y> but the <y> is also part of <ey> spelling /eɪ/
- In *arroyo, doyenne* pronounced /dɔɪˈjen/, *foyer* pronounced /ˈfɔɪjeɪ, ˈfɔɪjə/, *loyal* /ˈlɔɪjəl/, *Oyer (and Terminer)*, *royal* /ˈrɔɪjəl/, *soya*, /j/ is spelt <y> but the <y> is also part of <oy> spelling /ɔɪ/
- In *coyote* /kaɪˈjəʊtiː/, *doyen* and *doyenne* pronounced /dwaɪˈjen/, *foyer* pronounced /ˈfwaɪjeɪ/, *kayak* /ˈkaɪjæk/, *papaya, voyeur* /ˌvwaɪˈjɜː/, /j/ is spelt <y> but the <y> is also part of <ay, oy> spelling /aɪ/.

Other instances occur when words ending in <y> forming part of a digraph spelling /eɪ, ɔɪ, iː/ have a suffix beginning with a vowel phoneme added; also in running speech when such words are followed by a word beginning with a vowel phoneme. See Table 3.8 in section 3.8.8 for examples and the paragraphs before and after it for discussion of 'linking /j/', including why I do not count <y> as a single-letter grapheme as having two functions in these circumstances.

## 7.2 Surfacing sounds

This is my term for phonemes which are absent in a stem word but present in one or more of its derived or associated forms. I have borrowed the term 'surfacing' from transformational-generative grammar of yesteryear (and probably misapplied it). The great majority of the examples involve **letters** in stem-final position or immediately before that which are 'silent' (as conventional terminology has it) in the stem but pronounced when the word is suffixed; but there are also a very few initial examples – there are some amongst related forms of words with elided vowels in section 6.10. Most examples involve consonants, but there are a few involving vowels in final position. Some cases require detailed etymological knowledge. Actually, linking /r, w, j/ could also count here, but I have already dealt with them.

### 7.2.1 Sounds which surface in stem-initial position

- In a few words with initial /n/ spelt <gn> the /g/ surfaces when the stem is prefixed: compare *Gnostic, gnosis* with *agnostic, diagnosis, prognosis*

*Special processes* 249

- In a couple of words with initial /n/ spelt <mn> the /m/ surfaces when the stem is prefixed: compare *mnemonic, mnemonist* with *amnesia, amnesty* (the etymological connection here is that all these words derive from the Greek word for 'memory')
- In one word with initial /s/ spelt <ps> the /p/ (and an etymologically related /m/) surface when the stem is prefixed: compare *psychosis* with *metempsychosis*
- Two of the few words with initial /t/ spelt <pt> are *pterodactyl, pterosaur*. The /p/ surfaces in *archaeopteryx, helicopter*
- In just one word where intial /n/ is spelt <kn> the <k>, assisted by an inserted <c>, surfaces as /k/: compare *knowledge* with *acknowledge*.

## 7.2.2 Sounds which surface in medial position

- Initial /t/ is spelt <tw> only in *two* and derivatives, e.g. *twopence, twopenny*, and the /w/ surfaces in *between, betwixt, twain, twelfth, twelve, twenty, twice, twilight, twilit, twin*. In this case it would probably be more accurate to speak of the /w/ in *two* being 'submerged' since it is present in all those other words and would have been pronounced in (much) older forms of English, as <w> still is pronounced /f/ in the related German words *zwei, zwo, zwanzig*
- There are three words in which <t> forms part of <st> spelling medial /s/ in the stem but /t/ surfaces in derivatives: compare *apostle, castle, epistle* with *apostolic, castellan, castellated, epistolary*. For the converse of this, i.e. words in which stem-final /st/ spelt <-st> becomes /s/ after suffixation, see /s/, section 3.6.6
- There are two words in which <c> forms part of <sc> spelling medial /s/ in the stem but /k/ surfaces in derivatives: compare *corpuscle, muscle* with *corpuscular, muscular*
- In a few words with medial or final /t/ spelt <bt> /b/ surfaces in related forms: compare *debt, doubt, subtle* with *debit, indubitable, subtility*
- In one word with medial /k/ spelt <cu> the <u> surfaces as /ju:/ in a derived form: compare *circuit* with *circuitous*
- In one word with medial /g/ spelt <gu> the <u> surfaces as /w/ in two related words: compare *languor* with *languid, languish*
- In one word with medial /k/ spelt <qu> the <u> surfaces as /w/ in a derived form: compare *conquer* with *conquest*

- In one word with final /t/ spelt <ct> /k/ surfaces in a derived form: compare *indict* with *indiction* (with change of vowel phoneme) – but not before inflectional suffixes in *indicts, indicting, indicted*
- In a few words with final /n/ spelt <gn> /g/ surfaces in derived or related forms: compare *impugn, malign, sign* with *pugnacious, repugnant, malignant, assignation, designation, resignation, signal, signature* (all with change of vowel phoneme) – but /g/ does not surface before inflectional suffixes, as in *impugns, impugning, impugned, maligns, maligning, maligned, signs, signing, signed*
- In three words with final /m/ spelt <gm> /g/ surfaces in derived or related forms: compare *paradigm, phlegm, syntagm* with *paradigmatic* (with change of vowel phoneme), *phlegmatic, syntagma(tic)* – but /g/ does not surface in *paradigms, phlegmy*
- There is only one word with final /t/ spelt <pt>, namely *receipt*, and /p/ surfaces in *reception, receptive* (with change of vowel phoneme)
- In adverbs ending <-edly> derived from past participles ending in <-ed> pronounced /d, t/, <ed> is nevertheless pronounced /ɪd/, so the <e> has surfaced as /ɪ/, e.g. *determinedly, markedly*. This also applies in a few nouns derived from such past participles, e.g. *preparedness*, and in a number of adjectives which are derived from or resemble past participles but have /ɪd/ rather than the expected /d, t/, but often with a different meaning, e.g. *aged* (/'eɪdʒɪd/ 'elderly' vs /eɪdʒd/ 'having ... years'), *dogged* (/'dɒgɪd/ 'persistent' vs /dɒgd/ 'pursued'). For many more examples see sections 5.4.3 and 10.15
- In *inherit* the /h, r/ of *heir* both surface – or is this taking things too far?

## 7.2.3 Sounds which surface in stem-final position

- In *acreage, ochreous, ogreish*, relative to the unsuffixed forms /r/ has surfaced in stem-final position, but /r/ and the preceding schwa seem to be represented by <r, e> in reverse order
- In *actress, ambassadress, ancestress, conductress, dominatrix, executrix, foundress, laundress, ogress, protrectress, temptress, tigress, wardress* (supposing any of these forms except *tigress* are still PC; if you want to see how many other 'feminine' forms in <-ess, -ix> are now disused and deservedly forgotten, take a look in *Walker's Rhyming Dictionary*), relative to *actor, ..., warder*, the schwas (and <e, o> which helped to spell them) have disappeared and /r/ has surfaced before the suffix

- In the one word *falsetto*, supposing the connection with *false* is clear, it could be considered that the <e> surfaces as /e/
- In *accoutrement* the final schwa of *accoutre* disappears and two phonemes surface: /r/ spelt <r> and /ɪ/ represented by the first <e>.
- In several words with final /m/ spelt <mn> /n/ surfaces before derivational suffixes: compare *autumn, column, condemn, damn, hymn, solemn* with *autumnal, columnar, columnist, condemnation, damnable, damnation, hymnal, solemnity* – but not before inflectional suffixes or adverbial <-ly>, e.g. *columns, condemned, damning, solemnly*
- In a few words with final /m/ spelt <mb> /b/ surfaces in derived or related forms: compare *dithyramb, bomb, rhomb, crumb* with *dithyrambic, bombard(ier), bombastic, rhomb-ic/us, crumble* and supposedly, according to some authorities, *thumb* with *thimble* – but not before inflectional suffixes, e.g. *bombs, bombing, crumbs*
- Although *long, strong, young* end in /ŋ/ (in RP) and are therefore to be analysed as containing /ŋ/ spelt <ng>, the comparative and superlative forms *longer, longest, stronger, strongest, younger, youngest* and the verb *elongate* all have medial /ŋg/, so here /g/ has surfaced and is represented by the <g>, and /ŋ/ is spelt <n>; similarly with *diphthong, prolong* when suffixed to *diphthongise, prolongation* – but /g/ does not surface before inflectional suffixes or adverbial <-ly>, e.g. *longing, strongly*
- But in *longevity* the surfacing phoneme is /dʒ/
- There are several French loanwords in which final vowel phonemes are spelt with graphemes containing final <t> and /t/ surfaces when the stem is suffixed: compare *ballet, debut, parquet, rapport, sabot, valet* (also pronounced with /ɪt/) with *balletic, debutante, parquetry, rapporteur, sabotage, saboteur, valeting*. In *balletic, parquetry, sabotage, saboteur* and (if the pre-suffixation ending is /eɪ/) *valeting*, the vowel phoneme also changes
- There is one French loanword in which final /waː/ is spelt <-ois> and the <s> surfaces as /z/ when the stem is suffixed: compare *bourgeois* with *bourgeoisie*.

# 8. The graphemes of written English

## 8.1 Choosing a written variety to analyse

To match my decision to analyse the RP accent, I have chosen British rather than US spelling as the written variety of English to analyse. In practice, this makes very little difference, since there is far less variation in the spelling of English than in its pronunciation. The differences between British and US spelling make almost no difference to the analysis of the graphemes of written English – the same graphemes are used in both systems, just with different correspondences.

## 8.2 How many graphemes, and how many correspondences?

More troublesome than the minor differences between British and US spelling are the wide differences in opinion between experts on how many graphemes there are in written English. Wijk (1966: 14) says that the 'sounds of the spoken [English] language are normally represented by 102 symbols in the written language', but a great many Oddities are concealed behind that 'normally'; also he does not count 15 doubled consonants, e.g. <bb, dd>.

At the other extreme, Mountford (1998: 109) says he will 'work with a combined set of some 235 consonant and vowel symbols', which on inspection of his tables on p.113 turns out to be more precisely 238 graphemes, which are involved in 407 correspondences. In his figure for graphemes Mountford includes many quite rare graphemes not counted by Wijk, but even Mountford admits that there are others which might be counted but which are so rare and marginal that they are not worth the bother. His example (p.112) is the possible grapheme <schsch> spelling the phoneme /ʃ/ only in the rare word *Eschscholtzia* (the California poppy).

Actually, both Wijk and Mountford are right, at different levels of analysis – the number of graphemes you recognise depends on how deep you go into the Oddities of the system (and on various technical decisions – I've summarised mine in Appendix A).

I am going to provide three estimates of the number of graphemes by counting:

1) all and only those which appear in what I've called the 'main system' in chapters 3 and 5;
2) the rest, including the minor patterns and Oddities;
3) both.

All the graphemes which appear in both the main system and the rest in chapters 3 and 5 are listed in Tables 8.1-2, which cover graphemes representing consonants and vowels respectively. Both contain relevant 2- and 3-phoneme graphemes; each of these appears more than once, either within the same Table or across the two. In both, the totals for correspondences show exactly how many entries there are in the relevant column, but those for graphemes show only the numbers of items which have not already appeared in the same column or a previous one. So in the 'Basic grapheme' columns, <th> is counted only once among consonant graphemes, and <a, o, oo, u> only once each among vowel graphemes. After those columns, for graphemes I've shown only the numbers of new items (indicated by + signs), with some subtotals.

TABLE 8.1: ALL THE CONSONANT GRAPHEMES OF WRITTEN ENGLISH, BY RP PHONEME.

The Table includes not only graphemes for single consonant phonemes, but also those for 2- and 3-phoneme sequences involving consonant phonemes. The consonant phonemes are listed in the same order as in chapter 3.

(For simplicity, almost all angled brackets indicating graphemes are omitted).

The graphemes of written English 255

TABLE 8.1: ALL THE CONSONANT GRAPHEMES OF WRITTEN ENGLISH, BY RP PHONEME.

| Phoneme | The main system | | | The rest | | | | | | 2- & 3-phoneme graphemes | |
|---|---|---|---|---|---|---|---|---|---|---|---|
| | Basic grapheme | Other frequent graphemes | Rare graphemes | Doubled spelling | Doubled spelling + \<e\> | Oddities, by number of letters | | | | Phoneme sequence | Graphemes |
| | | | | | | 1 | 2 | 3 | 4 | | |
| /b/ | b | – | – | bb | – | – | bh bu pb | – | – | – | – |
| /d/ | d | ed | – | dd | – | – | bd de dh | ddh | – | – | – |
| /g/ | g | – | – | gg | – | – | gh gu | gue | ckgu | /gz/ | x xh |
| | | | | | | | | | | /gʒ/ | x |
| /m/ | m | – | – | mm | mme | – | gm mb me mn nd | mbe | – | /əm/ | m |
| /n/ | n | – | – | nn | nne | – | gn kn mn nd ne ng nt nw pn | dne gne | – | /ən/ | n |
| | | | | | | | | | | /nj/ | gn |
| /p/ | p | – | – | pp | ppe | b | bp gh pe ph | – | – | – | – |
| /t/ | t | ed | – | tt | tte | – | bt ct dt pt te th tw | – | phth | /tθ/ | th |
| | | | | | | | | | | /ts/ | z zz |
| /r/ | r | – | – | rr | – | – | re rh wr | rrh | – | – | – |
| /k/ | c | k | q | ck | – | g | cc ch cq cu gh | cch | – | /eks/ | x |
| | | /ks/ spelt x | | | | x | ke kh kk qu | cqu que | – | /ks/ | xe xh |
| | | | | | | | | | | /kʃ/ | x xi |
| /tʃ/ | ch | t | – | tch | – | c | cc ci cz te th ti | che | tsch | – | – |
| /f/ | f | ph | – | ff | ffe | v | fe ft gh | pph | – | – | – |

256 *Dictionary of the British English Spelling System*

TABLE 8.1: ALL THE CONSONANT GRAPHEMES OF WRITTEN ENGLISH, BY RP PHONEME, CONT.

| Phoneme | The main system ||| The rest |||||| 2- & 3-phoneme graphemes ||
|---|---|---|---|---|---|---|---|---|---|---|---|
| | Basic grapheme | Other frequent graphemes | Rare graphemes | Doubled spelling | Doubled spelling + <e> | Oddities, by number of letters |||| Phoneme sequence | Graphemes |
| | | | | | | 1 | 2 | 3 | 4 | | |
| /dʒ/ | j | g ge | – | dg dge | – | d | ch di dj gg gi jj | – | – | – | – |
| /l/ | l | /əl/ spelt le | – | ll | lle | – | gl le lh | – | – | /əl/ /lj/ | – = |
| /s/ | s | c ce se | /ks/ spelt x | ss | sse | t z | cc ps sc st sw | sce sch sth | – | /ts/ /eks/ /ks/ | z zz x xe xh |
| /v/ | v | f | – | ve | – | – | bv ph vv | – | – | – | – |
| /z/ | z | s se | – | zz | – | x | cz sc ss ts ze | – | – | /gz/ /ɪz/ | x xh s |
| /h/ | h | – | – | n/a | n/a | j | wh | – | – | – | – |
| /ŋ/ | ng | n | – | n/a | n/a | – | nc nd | ngh ngu | ngue | – | – |
| /ʃ/ | sh | ci si ssi ti | ce | n/a | n/a | c s t | ch sc se sj ss | che chs sch sci | – | /kʃ/ | x xi |

# The graphemes of written English 257

| | | | ge s | n/a | g j z | ci se ti zi | – | – | | /ʒ/ | x |
|---|---|---|---|---|---|---|---|---|---|---|---|
| /ʒ/ | si | – | – | n/a | – | – | – | phth | | /tθ/ | th |
| /θ/ | th | – | – | n/a | – | – | the | – | | – | – |
| /ð/ | th | – | – | n/a | – | – | the | – | | /wɑ/ | o |
| /w/ | w | u wh | – | n/a | – | hu ou ww | – | – | | /wɑː/ | oi oir oire ois |
| | | | | | | | | | | /waɪ/ | oy |
| | | | | | | | | | | /waɪə/ | oir |
| /j/ | y | i /juː/ spelt ew, u, u.e | /juː/ spelt ue | n/a | h j | = | – | – | | /juː/ | eau eu ewe ui ut uu |
| | | | | | | | | | | /jʊə/ | eur ur ure |
| | | | | | | | | | | /jə/ | eu u ua ure |
| | | | | | | | | | | /lj/ | = |
| | | | | | | | | | | /nj/ | gn |
| graphemes | 23 | +16 | +2 | 7 | +0 | +59 | +19 | +4 | | | +19 =108 |
| correspondences | 24 | 26 | 6 | 7 | 18 | 92 | 22 | 5 | | | 36 =180 |

TABLE 8.2: ALL THE VOWEL GRAPHEMES OF WRITTEN ENGLISH, BY RP PHONEME PLUS /juː/.

The Table includes not only graphemes for pure vowel phonemes and diphthongs, but also those for 2- and 3-phoneme sequences involving vowel phonemes. The vowel phonemes are listed in the same order as in chapter 5 and, as there, the special 2-phoneme sequence /juː/ is included in the main list. (For simplicity, angled brackets indicating graphemes are omitted).

The graphemes of written English 259

TABLE 8.2: ALL THE VOWEL GRAPHEMES OF WRITTEN ENGLISH, BY RP PHONEME PLUS /juː/.

| Phoneme | The main system | | | The rest | | | | 2- & 3-phoneme graphemes | |
|---|---|---|---|---|---|---|---|---|---|
| | Basic grapheme | Other frequent graphemes | Rare graphemes | Oddities, by number of letters | | | | Phoneme sequence | Graphemes |
| | | | | 1 | 2 | 3 | 4 | | |
| /æ/ | a | – | – | i | ae ai al ei | | | – | – |
| /e/ | e | – | – | a u | ae ai ay ea ei eo ie | | | /eks/ | x |
| /ɪ/ | i | e y | – | | | | | /ɪz/ | s |
| /ɒ/ | o | a | – | a o u | ai ee ei ia ie wi | hea | | – | – |
| /ʌ/ | u | o | – | e i | au ho ou ow | ach eau | | /wʌ/ | o |
| /ʊ/ | oo | u | – | o | oe oo ou | | | – | – |
| /ə/ | a | e er o | /ə/ spelt le | o | or ou | oul | | /əl/ | l |
| | | | | i u y | ah ai ar ei eo eu ia io oi or ou ow re ua ur yr | anc ere eau eur oar our ure | ough | /əm/ | m |
| | | | | | | | | /ən/ | n |
| | | | | | | | | /je/ | eu u ua ure |
| | | | | | | | | /aɪə/ | ir ire yr yre |
| | | | | | | | | /aʊə/ | hour our |
| | | | | | | | | /ɔɪə, waɪə/ | oir |
| /ɑː/ | ar | a | – | | aa a.e ah al as at au er | aar are arr ear | arre arrh | /wɑː/ | oi oir oire ois |

260  *Dictionary of the British English Spelling System*

TABLE 8.2: ALL THE VOWEL GRAPHEMES OF WRITTEN ENGLISH, BY RP PHONEME PLUS /juː/, CONT.

| Phoneme | The main system | | The rest | | | | | 2- & 3-phoneme graphemes | |
|---|---|---|---|---|---|---|---|---|---|
| | Basic grapheme | Other frequent graphemes | Rare graphemes | Oddities, by number of letters | | | | Phoneme sequence | Graphemes |
| | | | | 1 | 2 | 3 | 4 | | |
| /ɜː/ | er | ir or ur | – | | eu yr | ear ere err eur irr olo our urr | yrrh | – | – |
| /ɔː/ | or | a ar au aw ore | – | | al oa | aul aur awe oar oer oor orp orr ort our | augh orps ough ou're | – | – |
| /ɔɪ/ | oi | oy | – | | | | | /ɔɪə/ | oir |
| /aʊ/ | ou | ow | – | | aw | aow | ough | /aʊə/ | hour our |
| /eə/ | are | air ar ear | – | | ao er | aer eah e'er eir ere | aire ayer ayor erre ey're heir | – | – |
| /ɪə/ | ear | eer er ere | – | | ir | eir eyr e're ier | | – | – |
| /ʊə/ | – | – | – | | ur | eur oor our ure | | /juə/ | eur ur ure |

| | | | | | | | | | |
|---|---|---|---|---|---|---|---|---|---|
| /eɪ/ | a.e | a ai ay | – | | e | ae ah ao au ea ee e.e ei er es et ey ez | ais ait alf aye | aigh eigh | – | – |
| /iː/ | ee | e ea y | e.e ie | | | ae ay ei eo ey i.e is it oe | – | | – | – |
| /aɪ/ | i.e | i igh y | – | | a | ae ai ei ey ia ie ir is oy ui ye y.e | ais aye eye | eigh | /aɪə/ /waɪ/ /waɪə/ | ir ire yr yre  oy  oir |
| /əʊ/ | o | o.e ow | – | | | au eo ew oa oe oh ol oo os ot ou | aoh eau oat ore owe | ough | – | – |
| /juː/ | u | ew u.e | ue | | | eu ui ut uu | eau ewe | | – | – |
| /uː/ | oo | ew o u u.e | ue | | | ee eu oe o.e ou ui uu | ieu oeu ooh oue oup ous out oux | ough | | |
| graphemes | 16 | +17 | +4  =37 | 0 | +34 | +116 | +49 | +15 | | +11  =109 |
| correspondences | 20 | 43 | 5  =68 | 14 | 116 | 70 | 70 | 20 | | 26  =246 |

Discounting duplicates (including those involving 2- and 3-phoneme graphemes), in Table 8.1 there are 58 graphemes and 73 correspondences in the main system, and 108 graphemes and 180 correspondences in the rest, making a total of 166 graphemes and 253 correspondences in which consonant phonemes are involved.

On the same basis, in Table 8.2 there are 37 graphemes and 68 correspondences in the main system, and 109 graphemes and 246 correspondences in the rest, making a total of 146 graphemes and 314 correspondences in which vowel phonemes are involved.

However, adding together the numbers in the two preceding paragraphs does not yield correct overall totals because several graphemes and correspondences appear in both Tables. Thus <i, u, y> occur as both consonant and vowel graphemes, and some 2-phoneme sequences and both 3-phoneme sequences represented by single graphemes contain both consonants and vowels. De-duplicating these complications reduces the number of graphemes by 28 (6 in the main system, 22 in the rest) and the number of correspondences by 24 (3 in the main system, 21 in the rest).

The full analysis therefore yields totals of:
- 89 graphemes and 138 correspondences in the main system
- 195 graphemes and 405 correspondences in the rest, and
- 284 graphemes and 543 correspondences overall.

Thus my analysis has led to distinctly higher totals even than Mountford's 238 graphemes and 407 correspondences. This is mainly because I have included a lot of correspondences found only in small numbers of more recent French loanwords which he did not include.

## 8.3 The graphemes of the main system and the rest

Alphabetical lists of the 89 graphemes of the main system and of the 195 others are provided in Tables 8.3 and 8.4 respectively. Theoretically it should be possible to spell any English word using just the 89 graphemes of the main system and their 138 main-system correspondences, since they cover all 44 phonemes and allow for different positions in the word and various other constraints. However, from my analysis and every other author's it is abundantly clear that the full system is much more complex – and, to give just one example, trying to spell schwa consistently as <er>

in stem-final position and <a> elsewhere would probably produce many confusing spellings.

Table 8.3 shows that there are, of course, 26 single-letter graphemes in English spelling; they all belong to the main system. The numbers of graphemes of all sizes in the main system and the rest are:

|  | main system | the rest | total |
|---|---|---|---|
| single letters | 26 | 0 | 26 |
| digraphs | 53 | 118 | 171 |
| trigraphs | 10 | 57 | 67 |
| four-letter graphemes | 0 | 20 | 20 |
| total | 89 | 195 | 284 |

Simplified versions of the tables of correspondences are provided in Appendix B: they are intended to be much more useful to teachers and to writers of early reading books than the comprehensive versions in Tables 8.1–2.

TABLE 8.3: ALPHABETICAL LIST OF THE 89 GRAPHEMES OF THE MAIN SYSTEM.

| a | a.e | ai | air | ar | are | au | aw | ay | |
|---|---|---|---|---|---|---|---|---|---|
| b | bb | | | | | | | | |
| c | ce | ch | ci | ck | | | | | |
| d | dd | dg | dge | | | | | | |
| e | ea | ear | ed | ee | e.e | eer | er | ere | ew |
| f | ff | | | | | | | | |
| g | ge | gg | | | | | | | |
| h | | | | | | | | | |
| i | ie | i.e | igh | ir | | | | | |
| j | | | | | | | | | |
| k | | | | | | | | | |
| l | le | ll | | | | | | | |
| m | mm | | | | | | | | |
| n | ng | nn | | | | | | | |
| o | o.e | oi | oo | or | ore | ou | ow | oy | |
| p | ph | pp | | | | | | | |
| q | | | | | | | | | |
| r | rr | | | | | | | | |
| s | se | sh | si | ss | ssi | | | | |
| t | tch | th | ti | tt | | | | | |
| u | ue | u.e | ur | | | | | | |
| v | ve | | | | | | | | |
| w | wh | | | | | | | | |
| x | | | | | | | | | |
| y | | | | | | | | | |
| z | zz | | | | | | | | |

*The graphemes of written English* 265

TABLE 8.4: ALPHABETICAL LIST OF THE OTHER 195 GRAPHEMES.

| aa | aar | ach | ae | aer | ah | aigh | aire | ais | ait | al | alf |
|---|---|---|---|---|---|---|---|---|---|---|---|
|  | anc | ao | aoh | aow | arr | arre | arrh | as | at | augh | aul |
|  | aur | awe | aye | ayer | ayor |  |  |  |  |  |  |
| bh | bd | bp | bt | bu | bv |  |  |  |  |  |  |
| cc | cch | che | chs | ckgu | cq | cqu | ct | cu | cz |  |  |
| de | ddh | dh | ddh | di | dj | dne | dt |  |  |  |  |
| eah | eau | e'er | ei | eigh | eir | eo | e're | err | erre | es | et |
|  | eu | eur | ewe | ey | eye | eyr | ey're | ez |  |  |  |
| fe | ffe | ft |  |  |  |  |  |  |  |  |  |
| gh | gi | gl | gm | gn | gne | gu | gue |  |  |  |  |
| hea | heir | ho | hour | hu |  |  |  |  |  |  |  |
| ia | ier | ieu | io | ire | irr | is | it |  |  |  |  |
| jj |  |  |  |  |  |  |  |  |  |  |  |
| ke | kh | kk | kn |  |  |  |  |  |  |  |  |
| lh | lle |  |  |  |  |  |  |  |  |  |  |
| mb | mbe | me | mme | mn |  |  |  |  |  |  |  |
| nc | nd | ne | ngh | ngu | ngue | nne | nt | nw |  |  |  |
| oa | oar | oat | oe | oer | oeu | oh | oir | oire | ois | ol | olo |
|  | ooh | oor | orp | orps | orr | ort | os | ot | oue | ough | oul |
|  | oup | our | ou're | ous | out | oux | owe |  |  |  |  |
| pb | pe | phth | pn | ppe | pph | ps | pt |  |  |  |  |
| qu | que |  |  |  |  |  |  |  |  |  |  |
| re | rh | rrh |  |  |  |  |  |  |  |  |  |
| sc | sce | sch | sci | sj | sse | st | sth | sw |  |  |  |
| te | the | ts | tsch | tte | tw |  |  |  |  |  |  |
| ua | ui | ure | urr | ut | uu |  |  |  |  |  |  |
| vv |  |  |  |  |  |  |  |  |  |  |  |
| wi | wr | ww |  |  |  |  |  |  |  |  |  |
| xe | xh | xi |  |  |  |  |  |  |  |  |  |
| ye | y.e | yr | yre | yrrh |  |  |  |  |  |  |  |
| ze | zi |  |  |  |  |  |  |  |  |  |  |

# 9. The grapheme-phoneme correspondences of English, 1: Graphemes beginning with consonant letters

A reminder: in chapters 9 and 10, the meanings of 'initial', 'medial' and 'final' referring to positions in words are different from their meanings in chapters 3-7, which deal with the phoneme–grapheme direction: here they refer to positions in **written** words, since these chapters deal with the grapheme–phoneme direction. So, for instance, here the 'magic <e>' in split digraphs is described as being in word-final position, and consonant letters enclosed within split digraphs are in medial position.

## 9.0 Unwritten consonant phonemes

This is the appropriate place to recall that some occurrences of medial and linking /w/ (and possibly two of initial /w/) and a great many occurrences of medial and linking /j/ are not represented in the spelling at all - see sections 3.8.7-8. Following linguistic convention, these instances can be described as spelt by zero, hence the numbering of this section. Necessarily, as far as these cases are concerned, the rest is silence.

## 9.1 General introduction to the grapheme-phoneme correspondences

In chapters 9 and 10 I present the grapheme-phoneme correspondences from British English spelling to RP using the inventory of 284 graphemes listed in chapter 8. This chapter covers graphemes beginning with consonant letters, chapter 10 those beginning with vowel letters; for this purpose <y> counts as a vowel letter. This arrangement is followed even with graphemes which begin with a letter of one category but always or mostly have correspondences with phonemes of the other category, e.g. <ed> in past verb forms, <le> in *table*, etc., and those which have both consonant and vowel pronunciations, especially <i, u, y>.

The distinction between the main system and the rest which was arrived at in chapters 3 and 5 is maintained here, in mirror-image. That is, the only graphemes which are treated as part of the main system are the 89 listed in Table 8.3, and the only grapheme-phoneme correspondences which are treated as part of the main system are the converses of the 138 phoneme-grapheme correspondences involving those graphemes in the 'main system' columns of Tables 8.1-2; this principle is maintained even for correspondences whose frequencies in this direction are low.

Other grapheme-phoneme correspondences which involve the 89 main-system graphemes are treated as exceptions to the main system (even where their correspondences in this direction have high frequencies). Because some correspondences which are frequent in the phoneme-grapheme direction are rare in the grapheme-phoneme direction, and *vice versa* (which indicates both a mismatch between the two directions and therefore a basic misdesign in the overall system), in chapters 9 and 10 I have abandoned the distinction between frequent and rare correspondences for the main-system graphemes. However, most minor correspondences are again treated as Oddities. (For exceptions to the last statement, see sections 9.5 and 10.2).

Across chapters 9 and 10 all 89 graphemes of the main system are covered. However, there are only 76 entries. This is mainly because of the 12 principal doubled consonant spellings which consist of two occurrences of the single letter which spells the same phoneme: <bb, dd, ff, gg, ll, mm, nn, pp, rr, ss, tt, zz> (the 13th is because <dg, dge> share an entry). Since these 'geminates' have hardly any pronunciations different from the basic one of the corresponding single letter, and their two letters hardly ever belong to separate graphemes (for the only exception I know of, see Notes to section 9.15), each is covered within a joint entry with the single letter.

Otherwise, in both chapters the graphemes of the main system are listed in alphabetical order, with cross-references to show where those consisting of more than one letter are not covered under their initial letter. Minor graphemes are listed under the appropriate main-system grapheme, e.g. <bd> under <b>, <ae> under <a>, <err> under <er>, etc.

[For compulsive counters: 2- and 3-phoneme graphemes are treated differently in these two chapters from chapters 3 and 5. There, each such grapheme was logged under each of the relevant phonemes. Here, each such grapheme is logged only once, under its initial letter. But the total number of correspondences remains the same.]

## 9.2 When is a digraph not a digraph?

(Parallel questions apply to trigraphs and four-letter graphemes – see for example the competing possibilities for word-final <che> (section 9.9), the discussions of <gh> in the entry for <g, gg> (section 9.15), <ough> in the entry for <ou> (section 10.33), the discussion of vowel letters 'in hiatus' (section 10.42), and the paragraph beginning 'When is a split digraph not a split digraph?' in Appendix A, section A.6).

Some sequences of more than one letter which form main-system graphemes never or hardly ever occur except as those graphemes – a clear example is <ck>. Others have exceptions only at morpheme boundaries within words, e.g. <t, h> in a few words like *carthorse, meathook*, <o, o> in *cooperate, zoology*. Other main-system graphemes again occur only in restricted positions, so that all other occurrences of the same sequence of letters contain more than one grapheme – see for example <ce> (section 9.8). I attempt to give clear guidance related to each main-system grapheme (and in section 9.44 state a generalisation about the six graphemes other than <sh> which are pronounced /ʃ/), but in the end effectively have to assume that a human reader (as distinct from a computerised text-to-speech system) can recognise both morpheme boundaries within compound words and multi-letter graphemes within stem words. Carney (1994: 286-7) states the same assumption.

I also assume that readers of this book will realise that other occurrences of the sequences of letters which constitute minor multi-letter graphemes follow the general rules; therefore I do not waste space saying (for example) 'Occurrences of <p, s> other than word-initially consist of separate graphemes'. Conversely, where a correspondence for a single letter is said to be 'regular', this does not include cases where the letter forms part of another grapheme; for example, '<c> is pronounced /s/ before <e, i, y>' does not include its di/trigraphic occurrences in <ce, ci, sci>.

Both assumptions work better for graphemes beginning with consonant letters than for those beginning with vowel letters – but that is true of generalisations for the two sets of graphemes as a whole.

## 9.3 Frequencies

The frequencies in these chapters are derived from Gontijo *et al.* (2003). They used a corpus of 17.9 million words (the CELEX database, Version 2.5, Baayen *et al.*, 1995) in which both the British spelling and (a computerised version of) the RP pronunciation of every one of the 160,595 different words is represented. (The authors do, however, point out that 2,887 lines (1.8%) in the database contain multi-word expressions, of which the longest is *European Economic Community*, hence the number of lines with unique single words is actually 157,708.) Gontijo *et al.* based their graphemic analysis on that of Berndt *et al.* (1987), which was based on a corpus of only 17,000 words in US spelling, but adapted it for British spelling and expanded it to deal with rarer graphemes as their analysis proceeded. Ultimately, Gontijo *et al.*'s database contained a set of 195 graphemes and 461 grapheme-phoneme correspondences. While these numbers are rather smaller than my overall totals of 284 graphemes and 543 correspondences (see section 8.2), most of the 'missing' graphemes and correspondences are rare and would only be found by a total spelling nerd (= me).

As will be apparent, Gontijo *et al.* used a different corpus from Carney. Also, unlike Carney, they did not lemmatise their corpus (= remove suffixes and reduce words to their stem forms); nor did they ignore high-frequency words like *of, there, where*. However, they did relate the number of occurrences of a grapheme to the number of times each word appeared in the database – that is, they calculated text frequencies rather than lexical frequencies – see the discussion in section 3.3. Even so, their frequencies are not the mirror-image of Carney's. Producing mirror-image frequencies would require using exactly the same database, the same set of conventions (especially whether to lemmatise or not), and the same set of graphemes for the analyses in both directions. Such an analysis has yet to be undertaken.

Having established their sets of graphemes and correspondences, Gontijo *et al.* calculated the number of occurrences of each grapheme and its frequency within the whole database, and the frequency of every grapheme-phoneme correspondence as a subset of all the correspondences for the relevant grapheme For example, they calculated that:

- grapheme <a> accounted for 3,746,713 of the total of 67,590,620 grapheme occurrences
- <a> therefore represented 5.55% of all the grapheme occurrences in the database
- <a> pronounced /ə/ occurred 591,123 times, and that correspondence therefore represented 15.8% of the 3,746,713 correspondences for grapheme <a>.

To arrive at the percentages presented in chapters 9 and 10, I have modified Gontijo et al.'s results in various ways. To give just two examples:
1) The way they (and Mountford, 1998) analysed word-final <e> resulted in far too many split digraphs, trigraphs, etc.; e.g. they treated <a, e> in *collapse* as an example of <a.e>. In my opinion, <a, e> here are better analysed as <a> pronounced /æ/ and <e> as part of <se> pronounced /s/;
2) Their system recognised too few graphemes ending in <r>, e.g. <air> in *dairy* is split into <ai> pronounced /eə/ and <r> pronounced /r/, whereas my analysis posits that the <r> in such cases is not only a grapheme in its own right spelling /r/ but also part of <air> spelling /eə/ – see sections 5.6.3, 7.1 and 10.6, and section A.8 in Appendix A.

Rather than listing all the differences between my calculations and Gontijo et al.'s, let me just say that, where I could, I have re-allocated sets of words and correspondences in accordance with my analysis, and then re-calculated the frequencies of the correspondences within graphemes.

The outcomes are that:
- I give no percentages for a large number of minor graphemes, those which have only one pronunciation and for which it would be otiose to keep saying '100%'. This applies to 154 of the 195 minor graphemes across these two chapters
- for the 41 minor graphemes with more than one pronunciation I give percentages only in the few cases where Gontijo et al.'s data provide them, otherwise not
- I give separate percentages for the correspondences of as many main-system graphemes as possible, including (again, where Gontijo et al.'s data provide them) for the minor correspondences of such graphemes, e.g. under <ch>; for the main exceptions to this see the first paragraph of section 10.1.

## 9.4 The general picture: the regular pronunciations of English graphemes beginning with consonant letters

This chapter contains 38 main entries for graphemes beginning with consonant letters, in alphabetical order, even though Table 8.1 lists 58 graphemes spelling consonant phonemes in the main system. The reasons for the discrepancy are:
- as mentioned above, the 12 geminate spellings have joint entries with the single letters, and <dg, dge> have a joint entry

- all the correspondences for <ed, ew, i, u, ue, u.e, y>, consonantal, vocalic and 2-phoneme, are covered in chapter 10.

For the 51 main-system graphemes covered in this chapter, the general picture can be summed up as follows:

- The 21 graphemes listed in Table 9.1 have only one pronunciation each (except for one tiny exception under <b>):

TABLE 9.1: 21 MAIN-SYSTEM CONSONANT GRAPHEMES WITH ONLY ONE PRONUNCIATION EACH.

| These graphemes | |
|---|---|
| are always pronounced as | |
| | these phonemes |
| b, bb | /b/ |
| ck | /k/ |
| dd | /d/ |
| dg, dge | /dʒ/ |
| ff | /f/ |
| k | /k/ |
| mm | /m/ |
| nn | /n/ |
| p, pp | /p/ |
| q | /k/ |
| r, rr | /r/ |
| sh | /ʃ/ |
| ssi * | /ʃ/ |
| tch | /tʃ/ |
| tt | /t/ |
| ve * | /v/ |
| w | /w/ |

\* For these graphemes, the statement that they have only one pronunciation each involves defining the circumstances in which they constitute separate graphemes carefully; the rest are pronounced as shown in all positions in the word where they occur – this qualification is needed to recognise that several do not occur initially and others do not occur finally; all 21 occur medially.

- The 20 graphemes listed in Table 9.2 have only one frequent pronunciation each:

TABLE 9.2: 20 MAIN-SYSTEM CONSONANT GRAPHEMES WITH ONLY ONE FREQUENT PRONUNCIATION EACH.

| These graphemes | |
|---|---|
| are mostly pronounced as | |
|  | these phonemes |
| ch | /tʃ/ |
| ci * | /ʃ/ |
| d | /d/ |
| f (ignoring *of*) | /f/ |
| gg | /g/ |
| h | /h/ |
| j | /dʒ/ |
| l, ll | /l/ |
| le * | /əl/ |
| m | /m/ |
| ng | /ŋ/ |
| nn | /n/ |
| ph | /f/ |
| ss | /s/ |
| ti | /ʃ/ |
| v | /v/ |
| wh | /w/ |
| z, zz | /z/ |

\* For these graphemes, the statement that they have only one frequent pronunciation each involves defining the circumstances in which they constitute separate graphemes carefully; the rest are pronounced as shown in all positions in the word where they occur – this qualification is needed to recognise that several do not occur initially and others do not occur finally; all 20 occur medially.

- The nine graphemes listed in Table 9.3 have two main pronunciations each, and the circumstances in which the two pronunciations occur can be defined quite closely:

TABLE 9.3: NINE MAIN-SYSTEM CONSONANT GRAPHEMES WITH TWO REGULAR PRONUNCIATIONS EACH.

| This grapheme | has these two main pronunciations |
|---|---|
| c | /k, s/ |
| ce | /s, ʃ/ |
| g | /g, dʒ/ |
| n | /n, ŋ/ |
| se | /z, s/ |
| si | /ʒ, ʃ/ |
| t | /t, tʃ/ |
| th | /θ, ð/ |
| x | /ks, z/ |

<s> is the only main-system grapheme beginning with a consonant letter which is a major problem: it is mainly pronounced /s/ but has lots of exceptions (mainly where it is pronounced /z/) for which no rules can be stated, especially in medial position.

This means that 41 of these 51 graphemes have only one, or only one frequent, pronunciation, and the other 10 have only two main pronunciations each; none have more than two main-system pronunciations.

For completeness, it should also be noted that many minor consonant graphemes also have highly predictable pronunciations, e.g. word-final <que>. In fact, of the 107 graphemes beginning with consonant letters that are outside the main system, only 12 <cc che cz gh gn mn nd phth sc sch te xh> have more than one pronunciation. In any attempt (not made here) to estimate the overall regularity of the system this would need to be taken into account. However, many minor graphemes are so rare that they would not affect the regularity calculation unless they occur in high-frequency words.

To complete the picture for graphemes beginning with consonant letters, Table 9.4 lists all 51 of them and shows their main-system and

*The grapheme-phoneme correspondences, 1* 275

minor correspondences and numbers of Oddities. Table 9.4 is almost but not quite the mirror-image of Table 8.1 because:
- graphemes which begin with consonant letters but vowel phonemes (e.g. <ho> in *honest*) are included here;
- graphemes which begin with vowel letters but consonant phonemes (e.g. <ue> pronounced /juː/) are not included here but in Table 10.1.

TABLE 9.4: MAIN-SYSTEM GRAPHEMES BEGINNING WITH CONSONANT LETTERS, BY MAIN-SYSTEM AND MINOR CORRESPONDENCES AND NUMBERS OF ODDITIES.

| Grapheme | Main system | | The rest | |
| --- | --- | --- | --- | --- |
| | Basic phoneme | Other main-system correspondences | Exceptions to main system (minor correspondences) | Number of Oddities * which the grapheme 'leads' |
| b | /b/ | | /p/ | 6 |
| bb | /b/ | | | |
| c | /k/ | /s/ | /ʃ tʃ/ | 12 |
| ce | /s/ | /ʃ/ | | |
| ch | /tʃ/ | | /k ʃ dʒ/ | 3 |
| ci | /ʃ/ | | /tʃ ʒ/ | |
| ck | /k/ | | | 1 |
| d | /d/ | | /dʒ/ | 7 |
| dd | /d/ | | | 1 |
| dg | /dʒ/ | | | |
| dge | /dʒ/ | | | |
| f | /f/ | /v/ | | 2 |
| ff | /f/ | | | 1 |
| g | /g/ | /dʒ/ | /k ʒ/ | 12 |
| ge | /dʒ/ | /ʒ/ | | |
| gg | /g/ | | /dʒ/ | |
| h | /h/ | | /j/ | 5 |

\* including 2- and 3-phoneme pronunciations and doubled spellings which are not part of the main system.

TABLE 9.4: MAIN-SYSTEM GRAPHEMES BEGINNING WITH CONSONANT LETTERS, BY MAIN-SYSTEM AND MINOR CORRESPONDENCES AND NUMBERS OF ODDITIES, CONT.

| | Main system | | The rest | |
|---|---|---|---|---|
| Grapheme | Basic phoneme | Other main-system correspondences | Exceptions to main system (minor correspondences) | Number of Oddities * which the grapheme 'leads' |
| j | /dʒ/ | | /j ʒ h/ | 1 |
| k | /k/ | | | 4 |
| l | /l/ | | /əl/ | 1 |
| le | /əl/ | | /l/ | |
| ll | /l/ | | /j lj/ | 1 |
| m | /m/ | | /əm/ | 5 |
| mm | /m/ | | | 1 |
| n | /n/ | /ŋ/ | /ən/ | 7 |
| ng | /ŋ/ | | /n/ŋk/ | 3 |
| nn | /n/ | | | 1 |
| p | /p/ | | | 5 |
| ph | /f/ | | /p v/ | 2 |
| pp | /p/ | | | 2 |
| q | /k/ | | | 2 |
| r | /r/ | | | 3 |
| rr | /r/ | | | 2 |
| s | /s/ | /z ʒ/ | /ʃ/ | 12 |
| se | /s/ | /z/ | | 3 |
| sh | /ʃ/ | | | |
| si | /ʒ/ | /ʃ/ | /z/ | |
| ss | /s/ | | /ʃ z/ | 1 |
| ssi | /ʃ/ | | | |
| t | /t/ | /tʃ/ | /ʃ s/ | 5 |
| tch | /tʃ/ | | | |
| th | /ð/ | /θ/ | /t tʃ tθ/ | 2 |
| ti | /ʃ/ | | /tʃ ʒ/ | |
| tt | /t/ | | | 1 |
| v | /v/ | | /f/ | 1 |

| | | | | | |
|---|---|---|---|---|---|
| ve | /v/ | | | | |
| w | /w/ | | | | 2 |
| wh | /w/ | | /h/ | | |
| x | /ks/ | | /z k gz kʃ gʒ eks/ | | 4 |
| z | /z/ | | /s ʒ ts/ | | 2 |
| zz | /z/ | | /ts/ | | |
| Total | 51 | 12 | 49 | | 123 |
| 51 | | 63 | | 172 | |
| | Grand total of correspondences: 235 | | | | |

\* including 2- and 3-phoneme pronunciations and doubled spellings which are not part of the main system.

## 9.5 Order of description

In most of the 38 main entries in this chapter I list the items in this order:

1) The basic phoneme. In my opinion, each of these graphemes has a basic phoneme, the one that seems most natural as its pronunciation. Where the basic phoneme is the only pronunciation of the grapheme it is labelled 'Only phoneme'. Where a geminate spelling always or mostly has the same pronunciation as the single letter they are shown together. However, there are five geminate spellings which are minor graphemes: <cc, jj, kk, vv, ww> – these are listed under Oddities below the single letter. <hh> occurs too, but only at the morpheme boundary in compound words, e.g. *witchhunt*, and <q, x> appear doubled only in brand names or foreign words. These three are therefore mentioned only to exclude them.

2) Any other phoneme which counts as a main-system pronunciation of the grapheme, as defined above. Where there are no such phonemes this subheading is omitted.

These two categories constitute the main system for grapheme-phoneme correspondences for graphemes beginning with consonant letters. Correspondences in the main system are shown in 9-point type, the rest in smaller 7.5-point type.

3) Any doubled-letter grapheme which is not part of the main system (this sub-heading is also omitted where it is not relevant).

4) Exceptions to the main system, including any 2- or 3-phoneme correspondences for the main grapheme(s). The reason for listing

exceptions to the main system separately from the Oddities is that this is the clearest way of showing where the main rules break down.

5) The geminate spelling plus final <e>, if it occurs. Where it might but does not, I say so; elsewhere I omit this heading.

6) Oddities, minor graphemes which begin with the letter(s) of the main grapheme and occur only in restricted sets of words.

7) Any 2- or 3-phoneme graphemes which include, but do not have entirely the same spelling as, the main grapheme. Almost all the 2- and 3-phoneme graphemes are also Oddities, but a few belong to the main system and are included there.

Most entries end with Notes, and two (<s, se>) have Tables.

The only exceptions to this ordering are 15 of the graphemes which have only one pronunciation each: <b, bb, ck, dg, dge, k, p, pp, q, r, rr, sh, ssi, tch, ve>. Under each of these there is just one heading, 'Only phoneme', and it is automatically part of the main system without having to be so labelled; however, most of these entries have Notes. The other 6 graphemes which have only one pronunciation each (<dd, ff, mm, nn, tt, w>) have/are within more extended entries.

Where a grapheme cannot appear in all of initial, medial and final positions there is usually a note to this effect at the head of its entry, with this exception: because doubled consonant spellings never occur word-inirially (except <ll> in *llama, llano*), the headings where doubled spellings appear are not labelled to this effect.

## 9.6 <b, bb>

**THE MAIN SYSTEM**

Only phoneme (almost)   /b/   100%   e.g. *rabid, rabbit*

**THE REST**

|  |  | pronounced |  |
|---|---|---|---|
| Exception to main system | <b> | /p/ | only in *presbyterian* pronounced /prespɪˈtɪəriːjən/ (also pronounced /prezbɪˈtɪəriːjən/), where the <b> devoices to /p/ if the <s> is pronounced /s/ |

Word-final doubled letter + <e>   (does not occur)

| | | | |
|---|---|---|---|
| Oddities | <bd> | /d/ | only in *bdellium* /ˈdeliːjəm/ |
| | <bh> | /b/ | only in *abhor(red)* /əˈbɔː(d)/, *abhorrent* /əˈbɒrənt/, *bhaji*, *bhang(ra)*, *bhindi*, *Bhutan* and a few other rare words from the Indian sub-continent. <b, h> are usually separate graphemes at a morpheme boundary, as in *clubhouse*, *subheading* |
| | <bp> | /p/ | only in *subpoena* /səˈpiːnə/ |
| | <bt> | /t/ | only in *debt*, *doubt*, *subtle*. /b/ surfaces in *debit*, *indubitable*, *subtility* – see section 7.2 |
| | <bu> | /b/ | only in *build*, *buoy*, *buy* |
| | <bv> | /v/ | only in *obvious* pronounced /ˈɒviːjəs/ |
| 2-phoneme graphemes | (none) | | |

## NOTE

For <ba> in *syllabary*, and for <be> in *deliberate*, *gooseberry* /ˈgʊzbriː/), *liberal*, *raspberry* /ˈrɑːzbriː/), *strawberry* /ˈstrɔːbriː/), see section 6.10.

## 9.7 <c>

N.B. <ce, ch, ci, ck, tch> have separate entries.

### THE MAIN SYSTEM

| | | | |
|---|---|---|---|
| Basic phoneme | /k/ | 67% | e.g. *cat*. Regular before <a, o, u> and consonant letters |
| Other phoneme | /s/ | 30% | e.g. *city*. Regular before <e, i, y> |

### THE REST

| | | | |
|---|---|---|---|
| Exceptions to main system | | pronounced | 3% in total |
| | <c> | /k/ | before <e, i, y> only in *arced*, *arcing*, *Celt*, *Celtic* (but the Glasgow football team is /ˈseltɪk/), *sceptic*, *synced*, *syncing* |

(which means that the spelling *synch* for this verb is better), and words beginning *encephal*- pronounced /eŋkefəl-/ (also pronounced with /ensefəl-/). Also, in July 2006 the superlative adjective *chicest* /'ʃiːkɪst/ appeared on a magazine cover – the comparative would presumably be *chicer*

                                            <c>    /s/       other than before <e, i, y> only in *apercu*, *facade* (lacking their French cedillas)

                                              <c>    /ʃ/       only in *officiate*, *speciality*, *specie(s)*, *superficiality* and sometimes *ap/de-preciate*, *associate*. See Notes

                                              <c>    /tʃ/      only in *cellist*, *cello*, *cicerone* (twice), *concerto* (second <c>)

Word-final doubled letter + <e>    (does not occur; in *recce* <cc, e> are separate graphemes)

Oddities                            <cc>   /ks/      almost 100% before <e, i, y>, where (following the general rules for <c> above) the two letters are separate graphemes, e.g. *accent*, *occiput*, *coccyx*. This entry, with 2 graphemes corresponding separately to 2 phonemes, strictly speaking does not belong in this book based on correspondences to and from single graphemes, but it has to be included for clarity over the single-phoneme correspondences of <cc> in the next four paragraphs; <cc> pronounced /ks/ is not counted in the overall totals of correspondences

                                            <cc>   /tʃ/      before <e, i> only in *bocce*, *cappuccino*. There are no occurrences of <cc> pronounced /tʃ/ before <y>

_The grapheme-phoneme correspondences, 1_  281

| | | |
|---|---|---|
| <cc> | /s/ | before <i> only in *flaccid, succinct* pronounced /ˈflæsɪd, səˈsɪŋkt/ (also pronounced (regularly) /ˈflæksɪd, səkˈsɪŋkt/). There are no occurrences of <cc> pronounced /s/ before <e, y> |
| <cc> | /k/ | before <e, i, y> only in *baccy, biccy, recce* /ˈrekiː/ (short for *reconnoitre*), *soccer, speccy, streptococci* |
| <cc> | /k/ | 100% before <a, o, u>, e.g. *occasion, account, occur* |
| <cch> | /k/ | only in *bacchanal, Bacchante, bacchic, ecchymosis, gnocchi, saccharide, saccharine, zucchini* |
| <cq> | /k/ | only in *acquaint, acquiesce, acquire, acquisitive, acquit*, with the <u> being pronounced /w/ |
| <cqu> | /k/ | (not /kw/) only in *lacquer, picquet, racquet* |
| <ct> | /t/ | only in *Connecticut, indict, victualler, victuals*. /t/ surfaces in *indiction* – see section 7.2 |
| <cu> | /k/ | only in *biscuit, circuit* |
| <cz> | /tʃ/ | only in *czardas* /ˈtʃɑːdæʃ/, *Czech* /tʃek/ |
| <cz> | /z/ | only in *czar(ina)* /zɑː(ˈriːnə)/ |
| 2-phoneme graphemes | (none, but see <cc> pronounced /ks/ under Oddities) | |

## NOTES

Given the small numbers of words in which the major correspondences do **not** apply, those two correspondences stated context-sensitively mean that pronunciations of <c> as a single-letter grapheme are 97% predictable.

Medial <c> pronounced /ʃ/ is always followed by <i(e)>, but the <i(e)> is a separate grapheme pronounced /iː/. Some of the relevant words have alternative pronunciations with /s/, e.g. *appreciate* as /əˈpriːʃiːjeɪt/ or /əˈpriːsiːjeɪt/, *associate* as /əˈsəʊʃiːjeɪt/ or /əˈsəʊsiːjeɪt/ (taking *associate* as a verb; the noun of the same spelling ends in /ət/), *species* as /ˈspiːʃiːz/ or /ˈspiːsiːz/. However, when verbs ending in <-ciate> are nominalised with the suffix /ən/ spelt <-ion>, which compulsorily changes the final /t/ of the verb to medial /ʃ/, in many RP-speakers' accents a phonological constraint seems to operate against medial /ʃ/ occurring twice; for example *appreciation, association* are pronounced /əpriːsiːˈjeɪʃən, əˈsəusiːˈjeɪʃən/, not /əpriːʃiːˈjeɪʃən, əˈsəuʃiːˈjeɪʃən/.

For <ca> in adverbs ending <-ically>, which is always pronounced /ɪkliː/, *apothecary* and *forecastle* pronounced /ˈfəuksəl/, and for <co> in *chocolate, decorative,* see section 6.10.

## 9.8 <ce>

Never initial.

### THE MAIN SYSTEM

For both categories and for estimated percentages see Notes.

| | | |
|---|---|---|
| *Basic phoneme* | /s/ | except in a few suffixed forms (see section 6.4), only word-final, e.g. *fence, once, voice.* In final position there is only one exception |
| *Other phoneme* | /ʃ/ | never initial; word-finally only in *liquorice* pronounced /ˈlɪkərɪʃ/ (also pronounced /ˈlɪkərɪs/); otherwise only medial: regular in the ending <-aceous> pronounced /ˈeɪʃəs/, e.g. *cretaceous, curvaceous, herbaceous, sebaceous* and about 100 other words, mostly scientific and all very rare, plus *cetacean, crustacea(n), Echinacea, ocean, siliceous* |

### THE REST

| | | pronounced | |
|---|---|---|---|
| *Exception to main system* | word-final <ce> | /ʃ/, not /s/ | only in *liquorice* pronounced /ˈlɪkərɪʃ/ |
| *Oddities* | (none) | | |
| *2-phoneme graphemes* | (none) | | |

## NOTES

Gontijo *et al.* (2003) do not recognise word-final <ce> as a separate grapheme, so give data only for its medial occurrences. However, it is clear that in both of the very restricted circumstances where it is a separate grapheme <ce> is virtually 100% regular.

In all unsuffixed words with medial <ce> as a digraph the stress falls on the vowel preceding /s/ spelt <ce>, and that vowel is spelt with a single letter which has its letter-name pronunciation (only exception: *siliceous* /sɪˈlɪʃəs/).

In many words, word-final <e> after <c> following a single vowel letter is also part of a split digraph with the vowel letter; see the entries for the six split digraphs in chapter 10, sections 10.4/17/24/28/38/40. However, in some words the vowel letter preceding <ce> is a separate grapheme with its 'short' pronunciation, e.g. *practice*; for these exceptions also see the sections just cited.

In all cases other than those defined above, <c, e> are separate graphemes; in particular, note *oceanic* /əʊsiːˈjænɪk/, *panacea* /pænəˈsiːjə/. Word-final <c, e> are separate graphemes only in *fiance, glace* (now increasingly spelt even in English text with French <é>).

## 9.9 <ch>

N.B. <tch> has a separate entry.

### THE MAIN SYSTEM

*Basic phoneme*   /tʃ/   87%   e.g. *chew, detach*

### THE REST

|  |  | pronounced |  |
|---|---|---|---|
| Exceptions to main system | <ch> | /k/ | 10% regular (no exceptions) before a consonant letter, e.g. *aurochs, chlamydia, chloride, chlorine, chrism, Christ(ian(ity)), Christmas, Christopher, chrome, chromosome, chronic* and every other word beginning <chron->, *chrysalis, chrysanthemum, drachma, lachrymose,* |

*ochre, pinochle, pulchritude, sepulchre, strychnine, synchronise, technical, technique*; also in many words of Greek origin, e.g. *amphibrach, anarchy, anchor, archaic* and every other word beginning <arch-> where the next letter is a vowel letter (exceptions: *arch-enemy, archer*, with /tʃ/), *brachial, brachycephalic, bronchi(al/tis), catechis-e/m, chalcedony, chameleon, chaos, character, charisma, chasm, chemical, chemist, chiasma, chimera, chiropody* (also pronounced with initial /ʃ/), *choir, cholesterol, cholera, choral, chord, choreography, chorus, chyle, chyme, cochlea, diptych, distich, echo, epoch, eschatology, eucharist, eunuch, hierarch(y)* and every other polysyllabic non-compound word ending <-arch(y)>, *hypochondriac, ichor, lichen* pronounced /ˈlaɪkən/ (also pronounced /ˈlɪtʃən/), *machination, malachite, mechani-c/sm, melanchol-y/ic, orchestra, orchid, pachyderm, parochial, pentateuch, psyche* and all its derivatives, *scheme, schizo* and all its derivatives, *scholar, school, stochastic, stomach, synecdoche, trachea, triptych, trochee*. Words of non-Greek origin in this group are *ache, baldachin, chianti, chiaroscuro, cromlech, Czech, masochist, Michael, mocha, oche, scherzo, schooner*; also *broch, loch, pibroch, Sassenach* when pronounced with /k/ rather than Scots /x/. See Notes

&lt;ch&gt;    /ʃ/    2% phonemically and orthographically word-finally only in (Germanic) *milch, mulch, Welch*; otherwise only in about 50 words of mainly French origin, namely (initially) *chagrin, chaise, chalet, chamois, champagne, chancre, chandelier, chaperone, charabanc, charade, charlatan, Charlotte,*

*The grapheme-phoneme correspondences, 1*   285

|  |  |  |  |
|---|---|---|---|
|  |  |  | *chassis, chateau, chauffeu-r/se, chauvuinism, chef, chemise, chenille, cheroot, chevalier, chevron, Chicago, chi-chi* (twice), *chic(ane(ry)), chiffon, chignon, chivalr-ic/ous/y, chute*; also sometimes in (Greek) *chiropody* (hence the punning shop name *Shuropody*); (medially) *attache, brochure, cachet, cachou, cliche, crochet, duchesse, echelon, embouchure, Eustachian, machete, machicolation, machine, marchioness, nonchalant, parachute, pistachio, recherche* (twice), *ricochet, ruching, sachet, touche*; (phonemically but not orthographically word-finally) *fiche, gouache, moustache, niche* pronounced /niːʃ/ (also pronounced /nɪtʃ/), *pastiche, quiche, ruche.* Contrast word-final <che> pronounced /ʃ/ and word-final <ch, e> as separate graphemes, below |
|  | <ch> | /dʒ/ | 1% only in *ostrich, sandwich, spinach* pronounced /ˈɒstrɪdʒ, ˈsæmwɪdʒ, ˈspɪnɪdʒ/ |
| Oddities | <che> | /ʃ/ | only in *barouche* and about 13 words of French origin, namely (medially) only *rapprochement*; (finally) *avalanche, blanche, brioche, cache, cartouche, cloche, creche, douche, farouche, gauche, louche, panache.* In all these words the final <e> is irrelevant to the pronunciation of the preceding vowel grapheme. Contrast the words where word-final <e> after <ch> is instead part of a split digraph (*ache* and *fiche ... ruche* two paragraphs above) and word-final <ch, e> as separate graphemes, below |
|  | <che> | /tʃ/ | only in *niche* pronounced /nɪtʃ/ (also pronounced /niːʃ/) |
|  | <chs> | /ʃ/ | only in *fuchsia* /ˈfjuːʃə/ |
| 2-phoneme graphemes | (none) |  |  |

## NOTES

There are a few cases in which word-final <ch, e> constitute two graphemes rather than one: *attache, cliche, recherche, touche* with /ʃeɪ/ (sometimes spelt even in English text with French <é>), *menarche, oche, psyche, synecdoche* with /kiː/, but there appear to be no cases at all in which <c, h> are separate graphemes.

<ch> is also sometimes pronounced /x/ as in Scots *broch, dreich, loch, Sassenach* and German-style pronunciations of names like *Schumacher*, but I have not included this correspondence in my analysis because /x/ is not a phoneme of RP.

## 9.10 <ci>

Only medial.

### THE MAIN SYSTEM

| | | | |
|---|---|---|---|
| Basic phoneme | /ʃ/ | 100% | regular when both preceded and followed by vowel letters, e.g. *audacious, magician, specious*. Extension: *commercial*, where the preceding <er> digraph nevertheless spells a (long) vowel phoneme. See also Notes |

### THE REST

| | | | |
|---|---|---|---|
| | | pronounced | |
| Exceptions to main system | <ci> | /tʃ/ | only in *ancient* /ˈeɪntʃənt/, *ciabatta* /tʃəˈætə/ |
| | <ci> | /ʒ/ | only, exceptionally but increasingly, in *coercion* pronounced /kəʊˈwɜːʒən/ (usually pronounced /kəʊˈwɜːʃən/) |
| Oddities | (none) | | |
| 2-phoneme graphemes | (none) | | |

## NOTES

In most cases the stress falls on the vowel preceding /ʃ/ spelt <ci>, and that vowel is spelt with a single letter which has its letter-name pronunciation. Exceptions: if the preceding vowel letter is <i> it is pronounced /ɪ/, e.g. *magician*; also *precious, special* with /e/.

In all other cases, <c, i> are separate graphemes.

# 9.11  <ck>

Never initial.

### THE MAIN SYSTEM

| Only phoneme | /k/ | 100% | e.g. *black* |

### THE REST

|  |  | pronounced |  |
|---|---|---|---|
| Exceptions to main system | (none) |  |  |
| Oddity | <ckgu> | /g/ | only in *blackguard* /ˈblægəd, ˈblægɑːd/ |
| 2-phoneme graphemes | (none) |  |  |

### NOTE

The only word in which <c, k> belong to separate morphemes and therefore graphemes seems to be *acknowledge*, and even there the phoneme is /k/. This counts as a curious 'surfacing' sound – see section 7.2.

# 9.12  <d, dd>

N.B. <dg, dge> have a separate entry. <ed>, as in past tense and participle verb forms, has a separate entry in chapter 10, section 10.15.

### THE MAIN SYSTEM

| Basic phoneme | /d/ | <d> 99%, e.g. *bud, buddy* |
|  |  | <dd> 100% |

## THE REST

|  |  | pronounced |  |
|---|---|---|---|
| Exceptions to main system | <d> | /dʒ/ | 1% of correspondences for <d>. Never word-final; regular initially and medially before <u> followed by another vowel letter or <r>, e.g. *arduous, assiduous, (in)credulous, deciduous, dual/duel* (cf. the homophone *jewel*), *due* (cf. the homophones *dew, Jew*), *duet, duke, dune, dupe, duty, education, graduate* pronounced either /'grædʒuːwət/ (noun) or /'grædʒuːweɪt/ (verb), *durable, duration, duress, during, endure, fraudulen-ce/t, glandular, modul-e/ar, nodul-e/ar, pendulum, sedulous, procedure, verdure* (cf. the homophone *verger*); also in *gradual, individual, residual* whether pronounced with /dʒuːwəl/ or /dʒəl/ (for the elision of the <u> see section 6.10). Also in a few words before <eu, ew>: *deuce* (cf. the homophone *juice*), various words beginning with (Greek) *deuter-, dew* (cf. the homophones *due, Jew*), *grandeur*. See Notes |
| Word-final doubled letter + <e> | (does not occur) |  |  |
| Oddities | <ddh> | /d/ | only in *Buddha* and derivatives, *saddhu* |
|  | <de> | /d/ | only in *aide, blende, blonde, horde* and in *bade, forbade* (past tenses of *bid, forbid*) pronounced /bæd, fə'bæd/ (also pronounced /beɪd, fə'beɪd/) |
|  | <dh> | /d/ | only in a few loanwords from the Indian subcontinent, e.g. *dhobi, dhoti, dhow, Gandhi, jodhpurs, sandhi, Sindh* |
|  | <di> | /dʒ/ | only in *cordial* pronounced /'kɔːdʒəl/ (also pronounced /'kɔːdiːjəl/), *incendiary, intermediary, stipendiary, subsidiary* pronounced with /dʒəriː/, *soldier* |
|  | <dj> | /dʒ/ | only in about 10 words containing the (Latin) prefix <ad->: *adjacent, adjective, adjoin, adjourn, adjudge, adjudicate, adjunct, adjure, adjust, adjutant*, plus *djinn* |
|  | <dne> | /n/ | only in *Wednesday* |

|  |  |  |  |
|---|---|---|---|
| | <dt> | /t/ | only in *veldt* |
| 2-phoneme graphemes | | | (none) |

## NOTES

For <da> in *dromedary, lapidary, laudanum, legendary, secondary,* <de> in *broadening, considerable, gardener, launderette, widening* and <di> in *medicine* see section 6.10.

All the words in which <d> is pronounced /dʒ/ were formerly pronounced with the sequence /dj/, and conservative RP-speakers may still pronounce them that way (or imagine they do). Pronunciations with /dj/ would require an analysis with the <d> pronounced /d/ and and the /j/-glide as part of the pronunciation of the <u> and following <r> or vowel letter. See <t>, section 9.33, for the largely parallel correspondence to voiceless /tʃ/, and <di> in the Oddities.

## 9.13 <dg, dge>

*Only phoneme* /dʒ/ 100% e.g. *badger, bridge, bridging, curmudgeon*

### NOTE

There seem to be no cases where <d, g(e)> are separate graphemes except at morpheme boundaries, e.g. *headgear*.

N.B. <ed> Though this grapheme has mainly consonant pronunciations, because it begins with a vowel letter it is covered in chapter 10, section 10.15.

## 9.14 <f, ff>

For percentages see Notes.

### THE MAIN SYSTEM

| | | | | |
|---|---|---|---|---|
| Basic phoneme | /f/ | <f> | e.g. *full.* 100% provided *of* is treated as a special case |
| | | <ff> | 100%. e.g. *cliff, staff* |
| Other phoneme for <f> | /v/ | | only in *of* and *roofs* pronounced /ruːvz/ |

## THE REST

|  |  | pronounced |  |
|---|---|---|---|
| Exceptions to main system | (none) |  |  |
| Word-final doubled letter + <e> | <ffe> | /f/ | only in *gaffe, giraffe, pouffe*; also in usual pronunciation of *different, difference, sufferance* (but not *afferent, efferent*) – see also section 6.10 |
| Oddities | <fe> | /f/ | only in *carafe* and some instances of elided vowels – see Notes |
|  | <ft> | /f/ | only in *often, soften* |
| 2-phoneme graphemes | (none) |  |  |

## NOTES

Gontijo *et al.* (2003) found that 88% of all occurrences of <f> in their database were <f> pronounced /v/ in *of*, and only 12% were <f> pronounced /f/ in other words, but this is thoroughly misleading. Provided <f> in *of* is recognised as a special case (and *roofs* pronounced /ruːvz/ is rare), all other graphemes beginning <f> are pronounced /f/, = 100% predictable.

For <(f)fe> in *cafetiere, conference, deference, difference, different; offering, preferable, preference, sufferance,* <fi> in *definitely,* <for> in *comfortable,* <fu> in *beautifully, dutifully* see section 6.10.

# 9.15 <g, gg>

N.B. <dg(e), ge, ng> have separate entries. The entry for <ng> also covers all the cases where <n> before <g> is a separate grapheme.

## THE MAIN SYSTEM

| Basic phoneme | /g/ | <g> 71%, <gg> 70% | e.g. *game, braggart, egg*. Regular except for <g> before <e, i, y>, but see the exceptions. Also see Notes |
|---|---|---|---|
| Other phoneme for <g> | /dʒ/ | 28% of correspondences for <g> | Regular before <e, i, y>. See Notes |

## THE REST

|  |  | pronounced |  |
|---|---|---|---|
| *Exceptions to main system* |  |  | exceptions for <g> are 1% of its correspondences in total |
|  | <g> | /g/ | before <e, i, y> in *auger, beget, bogie, bogey, conger, eager, finger, fogey, gear, gecko, geese, gel* (/gel/), conservative pronunciation of *girl*; contrast *gel* 'viscous liquid' pronounced /dʒel/), *geld, get, geyser, hegemon-y/ic, laager, lager, monger* and all its compounds, *renege* (for this word see also <e.e>, section 10.17, and Notes to next section), *target* (contrast *parget*, with regular /dʒ/), *tiger, together*; *anthropophagi, begin, giddy, gill* ('lung of fish'; contrast *gill* 'quarter of a pint' pronounced /dʒɪl/ and see Notes), *gillie* (also spelt *ghillie*), *gilt, gimbal(s)* (also pronounced with /g/), *gimlet, gimp, gird, girdle, girl, girn, girt, girth, give, gizzard, yogi* and first <g> in *gig, giggle, gingham, gynaecology* |
|  | <g> | /dʒ/ | not before <e, i, y> only in *gaol, margarine* (also pronounced with /g/), *Reg, veg*, and second <g> in *mortgagor* |
|  | <g> | /k/ | only in *length, lengthen, strength, strengthen* pronounced /leŋkθ, ˈleŋkθən, streŋkθ, ˈstreŋkθən/ (also pronounced /lenθ, ˈlenθən, strenθ, ˈstrenθən/) for the rationale of this analysis see Notes under /ŋ/, section 3.8.2 – and in *angst* /æŋkst/, *disguise* /dɪsˈkaɪz/, *disgust* pronounced /dɪsˈkʌst/, i.e. identically to *discussed*; *disguise, disgust* are also pronounced /dɪzˈgaɪz, dɪzˈgʌst/, i.e. with <s, g(u)> both voiced rather than voiceless |
|  | <g> | /ʒ/ | initially, only in *genre, gilet*; medially, only in *aubergine, conge, dirigiste, largesse, negligee, protege, regime, tagine* and *lingerie* pronounced /ˈlænʒriː/ (also pronounced /ˈlɒndʒəreɪ/) |

|  |  |  |  |
|---|---|---|---|
|  | <gg> | /dʒ/ | 30% of correspondences for <gg>, but occurs only in *arpeggio, exaggerate, loggia, Reggie, suggest, veggie, vegging*. See Notes |
| Word-final doubled letter + <e> | (does not occur) |  |  |
| Oddities | <gh> | /f/ | 75% of pronunciations for <gh>, but see Notes/. Medially, only in *draught, laughter*; otherwise only word-final and only in *chough, cough, enough, laugh, rough, slough* ('shed skin'), *sough, tough, trough* |
|  | <gh> | /g/ | 25% of pronunciations for <gh>, but see Notes. Word-final only in *ugh*; otherwise only in *afghan, aghast, burgher, ghastly, ghat, ghee, gherkin, ghetto, ghillie* (also spelt *gillie*), *ghost, ghoul, ogham, sorghum* and a few more rare words |
|  | <gh> | /k/ | only in *hough* /hɒk/ |
|  | <gh> | /p/ | only in misspelling of *hiccup* as \**hiccough* |
|  | <gi> | /dʒ/ | only in *allegiance, collegial, contagio-n/us, egregious, legion, litigious, plagiaris-e/m, prestigious, region, religio-n/us, vestigial* |
|  | <gl> | /l/ | only in a few Italian loan words, namely *imbroglio, intaglio, seraglio, tagliatelle* |
|  | <gm> | /m/ | only in *apophthegm, diaphragm, epiphragm, paradigm, phlegm, syntagm*. /g/ surfaces in *paradigmatic, phlegmatic, syntagma(tic)* – see section 7.2 |
|  | <gn> | /n/ | only in (initially) *gnarl, gnash, gnat, gnaw, gneiss, gnome, gnosis, Gnostic, gnu* (only exception: *gnocchi*, with /nj/, though *gnu* could also be analysed that way, with <gn> pronounced /nj/ and <u> pronounced /uː/ rather than /juː/ – take your pick); (medially) *cognisance* (also pronounced with /gn/), *physiognomy, recognise* pronounced /ˈrekənaɪz/ (usually pronounced /ˈrekəgnaɪz/); (finally) *align, arraign, assign, benign, campaign, coign, condign, consign, deign, design, ensign, feign, foreign, impugn* and a few other very rare words in *-pugn*, *malign, reign, resign, sign, sovereign, thegn*; |

also phonemically word-final in *champagne, cologne* where the final <e> is part of a split digraph with the letter before the <g>. /g/ surfaces in *agnostic, diagnosis, prognosis, malignant, pugnacious, repugnant, assignation, designation, resignation, signal, signature* – see section 7.2. For exceptions to <gn> pronounced /n/ see the 2-phoneme grapheme below

<gne>  /n/  only word-final and only in *cockaigne, epergne, frankalmoigne* /kəˈkeɪn, ɪˈpɜːn, ˈfræŋkælmɔɪn/. In *soigne* /swaːˈnjeɪ/ <gn, e> are separate graphemes

<gu>  /g/  only in (initially) *guarantee, guard, guerrilla, guess, guest, guide, guild, guilder, guile, guillemot, guillotine, guilt, guinea, guise, guitar, guy* and a few more rare words; (medially) *baguette, dengue, disguise* pronounced /dɪzˈgaɪz/ (also pronounced /dɪsˈkaɪz/), *languor* (the <u> surfaces as /w/ in *languid, languish* – see section 7.2) and suffixed forms of a few words in next category, e.g. *cataloguing, demagoguery*; (phonemically word-finally) *plague, vague; fatigue, intrigue; brogue, drogue, rogue, vogue; fugue* and a few more rare words; in this group the vowel letter before <g> and the final <e> form a split digraph – contrast *ague* /ˈeɪgjuː/ and *dengue* /ˈdeŋgeɪ/, and see <ngu, ngue> under <ng>. Also see Notes

<gue>  /g/  only word-final and only in *analogue, catalogue, colleague, decalogue, demagogue, dialogue, eclogue, epilogue, ideologue, league, monologue, morgue, pedagogue, prologue, prorogue, synagogue*, where the final <e> is irrelevant both to the 'short' pronunciation of <o> and to the 'long' pronunciations of <ea, or> preceding <gu>. In US spelling several of these words are spelt without the final <ue>

2-phoneme grapheme  <gn>  /nj/  only in *chignon, cognac, gnocchi, lasagne, lorgnette, mignonette, monsignor, poignant, seigneur, soigne, vignette* and possibly *gnu*

## NOTES

Given the small numbers of words in which the major correspondences for <g> do **not** apply, those two correspondences stated context-sensitively mean that pronunciations of <g> are 99% predictable. There are, however, a few homograph pairs with <g> pronounced /g/ in one and /dʒ/ in the other: *gel* /gel/ (posh pronunciation of *girl*) v. /dʒel/'hair lotion'; *gill* /'gɪl/ 'lung of fish' v. /dʒɪl/ 'quarter of pint', *Gillingham* /'gɪlɪŋəm/ in Dorset and Norfolk v. /'dʒɪlɪŋəm/ in Kent.

For words containg <n, g> before <e, i> in which the pronunciation of the <g> as /g/ is irregular see section 9.24.

Despite /dʒ/ being 30% of correspondences for <gg> I have not recognised it as a major correspondence because it occurs in so few words, and its high frequency seems to be almost entirely due to the two common words *exaggerate, suggest* – and *suggest*, pronounced /sə'dʒest/ in RP, has a different pronunciation in General American: /səg'dʒest/; here the <g>'s are separate graphemes representing separate phonemes – but this is no more 'regular' than the RP pronunciation because it is the only case where two consecutive <g>'s do not form a digraph – indeed, the only case of geminate consonant letters which would otherwise constitute a digraph not doing so.

The contexts in which <gh> is pronounced /g/ are easily defined – but so is the list of about a dozen words where this correspondence occurs. <gh> is also sometimes pronounced /x/ as in Irish *lough* and names like *McCullough, Naughtie*, but I have not included this correspondence in my analysis because /x/ is not a phoneme of RP.

<gh> is never a separate grapheme after <ai, ei> – see <aigh, eigh> under <ai, e>, sections 10.5, 10.12. However, no rule can be defined to distinguish the 10 or 11 words where <gh> is a separate grapheme pronounced /f/ after <au, ou> from those where <augh, ough> are four-letter graphemes, so these just have to be learnt. See also <augh> under <au>, section 10.9, and Notes to section 10.33 on <ough>.

<gu> mostly has 2-phoneme pronuncations, e.g. /gw/ in *anguish, distinguish, extinguish, guacamole, guano, guava, iguana, language, languish, linguist, penguin, sanguine, segue, unguent*; /gʌ/ in *gulf, gust*, etc.

For <ga> in *vinegary*, <go> in *allegory, category*, <gu> in *figurative*, see section 6.10.

# 9.16 <ge>

N.B. <dge> has a joint entry with <dg>.

## THE MAIN SYSTEM

For both categories and for absence of percentages see Notes.

*Basic phoneme* /dʒ/ word-initially, only in *geograph-er/y, geomet-er/ry, Geordie, George, Georgia(n), georgic*; rare medially, but cf. *burgeon, dungeon, gorgeous, hydrangea, pageant, sergeant, sturgeon, surgeon, vengeance* where the following vowel letter or digraph is pronounced /ə/, plus *pigeon* with /ɪ/; also *dangerous, vegetable* – see section 6.10; also *singeing, swingeing* (as distinct from *singing, swinging*), *whingeing*; word-finally, regular in hundreds of words ending <-age> pronounced /ɪdʒ/, e.g. *garage* pronounced /ˈgærɪdʒ/, *haemorrhage, image, language, mortgage, village* (for other words in <-age> see previous section); also in, e.g., *allege, blancmange, change, college, flange, hinge, lounge, orange, sacrilege, scavenge*

*Rare phoneme* /ʒ/ never initial; medially, only in *bourgeois(ie), mangetout*; word-finally, only in about 25 words of mainly French origin, namely *beige, cortege, concierge, liege, melange, rouge* and, with the <e> also forming part of the split digraphs <a.e, i.e, u.e> (for dual-functioning see section 7.1), in *badinage, barrage, camouflage, collage, corsage, decalage, décolletage, dressage, entourage, espionage, fuselage, garage* pronounced /ˈgærɑːʒ/, *massage, mirage, montage, triage, sabotage; prestige; luge*

## THE REST

(None).

## NOTES

Gontijo *et al.* (2003) do not recognise <ge> as a grapheme, so give no data for it. However, given that very few words have <ge> pronounced /ʒ/, the percentage for /dʒ/ would be high.

In many words, final <e> after <g> following <a> is part of a split digraph with the <a> – see section 10.4. There are also a very few examples ending <ege, ige, oge, uge> (sections 10.17/24/28/38) and none ending <yge> (section 10.40). On split digraphs see also section A.6, and for dual-functioning see section 7.1.

Except in the roughly 24 words listed under the basic phoneme, initial and medial <g, e> are always separate graphemes. Word-finally, the only such cases appear to be *conge, protege* with /ʒeɪ/ (sometimes spelt even within English text with French <é>), *sylloge* with /dʒiː/. In *renege* /rɪ'neɪg/ I analyse <e.e> as a split digraph pronounced /eɪ/ – see sections 10.17 and A.6 – and the <g> as a single-letter grapheme pronounced (uniquely in this position, and irregularly before <e>) /g/ (contrast *allege, college, sacrilege* with /dʒ/, *cortege* with /ʒ/).

N.B. For <gg> see under <g>.

## 9.17 <h>

Never occurs as a single-letter grapheme in word-final position.
N.B. <ch, ph, sh, tch, th, wh> have separate entries.

### THE MAIN SYSTEM

| Basic phoneme | /h/ | 100% | e.g. *cohort, have* |

### THE REST

|  |  | pronounced |  |
|---|---|---|---|
| Doubled letter |  |  | (<hh> occurs only in compound words, e.g. *bathhouse*, where the two letters belong to separate morphemes and graphemes) |
| Exceptions to main system |  |  | <1% |
|  | <h> | /j/ | only in a very few words between 2 vowels, namely *annihilate, vehement,* |

| | | | vehicle, vehicular /ə'naɪjɪleɪt, 'viːjəmənt, 'viːjɪkəl, viːˈjɪkjələ/ |
|---|---|---|---|
| Oddities | \<hea\> | /ɪ/ | only in *forehead* pronounced /ˈfɒrɪd/ |
| | \<heir\> | /eə/ | only in *heir* and derivatives (but there is /r/-linking in *heiress, inherit* – see section 3.6; and in *inherit* /h/ also surfaces; see section 7.2) |
| | \<ho\> | /ɒ/ | only in *bonhomie, honest, honour* and derivatives |
| | \<hu\> | /w/ | only in *chihuahua* (twice) |
| 2-phoneme grapheme | \<hour\> | /aʊwə/ | only in *hour* |

N.B. For \<i\> pronounced as the consonant phoneme /j/ see, nevertheless, the entry for \<i\> in chapter 10, section 10.22.

## 9.18 \<j\>

### THE MAIN SYSTEM

| Basic phoneme | /dʒ/ | 100% | e.g. *jet, majesty* |
|---|---|---|---|

### THE REST

| | | pronounced | |
|---|---|---|---|
| Doubled letter | \<jj\> | /dʒ/ | only in *hajj* |
| Exceptions to main system | | | <1% in total |
| | \<j\> | /j/ | only in *hallelujah* /hælɪˈluːjə/, and *majolica* pronounced /maɪˈjɒlɪkə/ (also pronounced /məˈdʒɒlɪkə/) |
| | \<j\> | /ʒ/ | only in *jihad, raj* and some rare French loanwords, e.g. *bijou, goujon, jabot, jalousie, jupe* |
| | \<j\> | /h/ | only in *fajita, jojoba* (twice), *marijuana, mojito, Navajo'* |
| Oddities | (none) | | |
| 2-phoneme graphemes | (none) | | |

## 9.19 <k>

N.B. <ck> has a separate entry.

### THE MAIN SYSTEM

| Only phoneme | /k/ | 100% | e.g. *kelp, kit, sky* |
|---|---|---|---|

### THE REST

| | | pronounced | |
|---|---|---|---|
| Doubled letter | <kk> | /k/ | only in *chukker, dekko, pukka* and inflected forms of *trek*, e.g. *trekkie* |
| Exceptions to main system | (none) | | |
| Word-final doubled letter + <e> | (does not occur) | | |
| Oddities | <ke> | /k/ | only in *Berkeley, burke* |
| | <kh> | /k/ | only in *astrakhan, gurkha, gymkhana, khaki, khan, khazi, khedive, sheikh, Sikh*. See Note |
| | <kn> | /n/ | only in *knack(er(s)), knap, knave, knead, knee, knell, knew, knick(er(s)), knickerbocker, knick-knack, knife, knight, knit, knob, knobbly, knock, knoll, knot, know(ledge), knuckle* and a few more very rare words. Contrast *Knesset*, with /kn/, and for *acknowledge* see section 7.2 |
| 2-phoneme graphemes | (none) | | |

### NOTE

<kh> also occurs in transcriptions of some Russian names, e.g. *Khrushchev, Mikhail*, where it is meant to represent the /x/ phoneme, like <ch> in Scots *loch* – but since (a) most English-speakers instead pronounce these names with /k/ (as in the words listed above under Oddities), and (b) the correspondence with /x/ occurs only in names, I have not included this correspondence in my analyses.

# 9.20 <l, ll>

N.B. <le> has a separate entry.

## THE MAIN SYSTEM

| | | | |
|---|---|---|---|
| Basic phoneme | /l/ | 100% | e.g. *lift, fill* |

## THE REST

| | | pronounced | |
|---|---|---|---|
| Exceptions to main system | <l> | as 2-phoneme sequence /əl/ | only in *axolotl, dirndl, shtetl* /'æksəlɒtəl, 'dɜːndəl, 'ʃtetəl/ |
| | <ll> | /j/ | only in French-/Spanish-like pronunciations of *bouillabaisse, marseillaise, tortilla* /buːjaː'bes, maːseɪ'jez, tɔː'tiːjaː/ |
| | <ll> | as 2-phoneme sequence /lj/ | only in *carillon* /kə'rɪljən/ |
| Word-final doubled letter + <e> | <lle> | /l/ | medially, only in *decollet-age/ee*; otherwise only final and only in the ending *-ville*, e.g. *vaudeville*, plus *bagatelle, belle, braille, chanterelle, espadrille, fontanelle, gazelle, grille, pastille, nacelle, quadrille* (but not *reveille, tagliatelle* where the <e> is pronounced /iː/). In *chenille, tulle* I analyse <ll> as pronounced /l/ and <i.e, u.e> as split digraphs pronounced /iː, uː/ – see sections 5.7.2, 5.7.6, A.6 – and medially in *guillemot* <lle> is pronounced /lː/ |
| Oddity | <lh> | /l/ | only in *philharmonic, silhouette* |
| 2-phoneme graphemes | (see above) | | |

## NOTE

For <lle> in *chancellery, jewellery* see section 6.10.

## 9.21 <le>

Only final.

### THE MAIN SYSTEM

| Basic pronunciation | /əl/ | 100% | only word-final after a consonant letter, e.g. *table*, *visible* |

### THE REST

| | | pronounced | |
| Exceptions to main system | <le> | /l/ | medially, only in *Charles*; otherwise only word-final and only in *aisle, cagoule, clientele, gargoyle, gunwale, joule, isle, lisle, voile*. See Notes |
| Oddities | (none) | | |
| 2-phoneme graphemes | (The basic pronunciation is a 2-phoneme sequence) | | |

### NOTES

In many words where final <le> follows a vowel letter and the main rule above therefore does not apply, word-final <e> after <l> following a single vowel letter is part of a split digraph with the vowel letter; see the entries for the six split digraphs in chapter 10, sections 10.4/17/24/28/38/40.

Initial and medial <l, e> are always two separate graphemes. Word-finally, the only such cases (i.e. the <e> is neither part of a split digraph nor part of a digraph with <l>) appear to be *souffle* (sometimes spelt even within English text with French <é>) with /leɪ/, *facsimile, hyperbole, ukulele* with /liː/, *biennale, finale, guacamole, tamale* with either.

The reason for picking out *aisle, cagoule, clientele, gargoyle, joule, isle, lisle, voile* as having word-final <le> is that the preceding vowel grapheme would be pronounced the same if the <e> were not present. Some of the spellings would then look even odder, but *cagoule* does have the alternative spelling *kagoul*.

N.B. For <ll> see under <l>.

## 9.22 <m, mm>

### THE MAIN SYSTEM

Basic phoneme    /m/    100%    e.g. *mum, sum, mummy, summit*

### THE REST

|  |  | pronounced |  |
|---|---|---|---|
| Exceptions to main system |  |  | <1% in total |
|  | <m> | as 2-phoneme sequence /əm/ | only word-finally, but regular in all the words ending in <-sm>, e.g. *chasm, enthusiasm, orgasm, phantasm, pleonasm, sarcasm, spasm,* several words ending in *-plasm* (e.g. *ectoplasm*), *chrism, prism, schism* and all the many other words ending in *-ism, macrocosm, microcosm, abysm, aneurysm* (also spelt *aneurism*), *cataclysm, paroxysm,* plus *algorithm, rhythm* and a few other very rare words; also *film* pronounced /'fɪləm/ in some Irish accents |
| Word-final doubled letter + <e> | <mme> | /m/ | now only in *oriflamme* and (non-computer) *programme* since *gram* and its derivatives are no longer spelt *\*gramme*, etc.; in *consomme* (sometimes spelt even within English text with French <é>), <mm, e> are separate graphemes |
| Oddities | <mb> | /m/ | only word-final and only in *dithyramb, lamb*; *climb, limb*; *aplomb, bomb, catacomb, comb, coomb, coxcomb, coulomb, hecatomb, rhomb, tomb, womb*; *crumb, dumb, numb, plumb, rhumb, succumb, thumb* and a few more very rare words. /b/ surfaces in *dithyrambic, bombard(ier), bombastic, rhomb-ic/us, crumble* and supposedly, according to some |

authorities, in *thimble* (from *thumb*) – see section 7.2. The word-form *number* has the two pronunciations /'nʌmbə/ ('amount, numeral') and /'nʌmə/ ('having less feeling', comparative form of the adjective *numb*)

&lt;mbe&gt;   /m/   only word-final and only in *buncombe* ('nonsense'; also spelt *bunkum*), *co(o)mbe* ('short valley'; also spelt *coomb*); contrast *flambe* /'flɒmbeɪ/ (sometimes spelt even within English text with French &lt;é&gt;), where &lt;m, b, e&gt; are all separate graphemes

&lt;me&gt;   /m/   never initial; mainly word-final and there only in *become, come, some, welcome* and the adjectival suffix /səm/ spelt &lt;-some&gt;, e.g. *handsome* (contrast *hansom*); medially only in *camera, emerald, omelette, ramekin* pronounced /'ræmkɪn/ (also pronounced /'ræmɪkɪn/) – see section 6.10 – and *Thames*

&lt;mn&gt;   /m/   100% of pronunciations of &lt;mn&gt; but see Notes. Only word-final and only in *autumn, column, condemn, contemn, damn, hymn, limn, solemn*. /n/ surfaces in *autumnal, columnar, columnist, condemnation, contemner, damnable, damnation, hymnal, hymnody, solemnity* – see section 7.2

&lt;mn&gt;   /n/   &lt;1% of pronunciations of &lt;mn&gt; but see Notes. Only in *mnemonic, mnemonist*. /m/ surfaces in *amnesia, amnesty* – see section 7.2

*2-phoneme grapheme* (see above)

## NOTES

Given the very different word positions of &lt;mn&gt; pronounced /m, n/ this grapheme is 100% predictable. Given that it never occurs medially it is also very easy to distinguish from instances of &lt;m, n&gt; as separate graphemes.

For <ma> in *customary*, <me> in *camera, emerald, omelette*, <mi> in *admirable, family* see section 6.10.

## 9.23 <n, nn>

N.B. <ng> has a separate entry, which also covers all the cases where <n> before <g> is a separate grapheme, including those mentioned here where the <n> is pronounced /ŋ/.

**THE MAIN SYSTEM**

| Basic phoneme /n/ | <n> 85%, <nn> 100% | e.g. *tin, tinny*. For <n>, /n/ is regular except before <c> pronounced /k/ and before <ch, g, k, q, x>. See Notes |
|---|---|---|
| Other phoneme /ŋ/ for <n> | 15% | regular before <c> pronounced /k/ and before <ch, g, k, q, x>, e.g. *concur* pronounced /kən'kɜː/, *uncle, zinc; anchor, synchronise; angle, England, fungus, language, langur, length* pronounced /leŋkθ/, *longevity, prolongation, single; ankle, sink, thanks; banquet, conquer; anxiety, anxious, larynx, lynx.* See Notes |

**THE REST**

| | | pronounced | |
|---|---|---|---|
| Exceptions to main system | | <1% | |
| | <n> | as 2-phoneme sequence /ən/ | only in *Haydn* (I mention him in memory of Chris Upward of the Simplified Spelling Society) and most contractions of *not* with auxiliary verbs, i.e. *isn't, wasn't, haven't, hasn't, hadn't, doesn't, didn't, couldn't, shouldn't, wouldn't, mayn't, mightn't, mustn't, oughtn't, usedn't,* some of which are rare to the point of disuse, plus *durstn't,* which is dialectal/comic; in all of these except *mayn't* the preceding phoneme |

is a consonant. Other contractions of *not* with auxiliary verbs (*ain't, aren't, can't, daren't, don't, shan't, weren't, won't*), i.e. all those with a preceding vowel phoneme (except *mayn't*) are monosyllabic (though some Scots say /ˈdeərənt/ with a preceding consonant and therefore two syllables, and also /r/-linking – see section 3.6). Curiously, *innit*, being a contraction of *isn't it*, reduces *isn't* to a single syllable

| | | | |
|---|---|---|---|
| Word-final doubled letter + \<e\> | \<nne\> | /n/ | only word-final and only in *cayenne, comedienne, cretonne, doyenne, tonne* and a few other rare words |
| Oddities | \<nc\> | /ŋ/ | only in *charabanc* /ˈʃærəbæŋ/ |
| | \<nd\> | /m/ | only in *sandwich* /ˈsæmwɪdʒ/ |
| | \<nd\> | /n/ | only in *grandfather*, *Grandma* (hence the frequent misspelling \**Granma* – cf. section 4.4.7 on *Gran(d)dad*), *handsome* (cf. *hansom* (*cab*)), *landscape* |
| | \<nd\> | /ŋ/ | only in *handcuffs, handkerchief* /ˈhæŋkʌfs, ˈhæŋkətʃɪf/ |
| | \<ne\> | /n/ | non-finally, only in *vineyard* (and even there it is stem-final within a compound word) and with an elided vowel (see section 6.10) in *confectionery, generative, stationery, vulnerable*; otherwise only word-final after a vowel letter and only in about 35 words, namely *bowline, Catherine, clandestine* pronounced /klænˈdestɪn/ (also pronounced /ˈklændəstaɪn/), *cocaine, compline, crinoline, demesne, (pre)destine, determine, discipline, done, engine, ermine, examine, famine, feminine, genuine, gone, groyne, heroine, hurricane* pronounced /ˈhʌrɪkən/ (also pronounced /ˈhʌrɪkeɪn/), *illumine, intestine, jasmine, marline, masculine, medicine, migraine, moraine, peregrine, ptomaine, saccharine, sanguine, scone* pronounced /skɒn/ (also pronounced |

/skəʊn/), *shone, urine, vaseline, wolverine*. In all but one of these words the <e> is phonographically redundant, in that its removal would not affect the pronunciation – the preceding vowel letter (if single) does not have its 'letter-name' pronunciation, and where there are two vowel letters they either form a digraph (*cocaine, groyne, migraine, moraine, ptomaine*) or are pronounced separately (*genuine*). The exception is *done*, which needs to be kept visually distinct from *don*, as *heroine* and *marline* ('rope') are from *heroin* and *marlin* ('fish'). The only words in which final <n, e> are separate graphemes are are *aborigine, acne, anemone*

<nt>  /n/  only in *denouement, divertissement, rapprochement*

<nw>  /n/  only in *gunwale*

2-phoneme grapheme  (see above)

## NOTES

Given the small numbers of words in which the major correspondences for <n> do **not** apply, those two correspondences stated context-sensitively mean that pronunciations of <n> are virtually 100% predictable. Actually, they occur even without being consciously noticed because of the phonological context.

Some words beginning *encephal-*, e.g. *encephalitis*, are pronounced either /ens-/, with the predominant pronunciation of <n> as /n/, or /eŋk-/, with the regular pronunciation of <n> as /ŋ/ before <c> pronounced /k/.

For <na> in *concessionary, coronary, culinary, discretionary, extraordinary* /ɪkˈstrɔːdənriː/, *imaginary, legionary, mercenary, missionary, ordinary, precautionary, preliminary, probationary, pulmonary, reactionary, revolutionary, stationary, urinary, veterinary* /ˈvetrɪnriː/, *visionary*, <ne> in *confectionery, general, generative, millinery, stationery*, <nou> in *honourable* see section 6.10.

## 9.24 <ng>

Never initial.

### THE MAIN SYSTEM

Basic phoneme /ŋ/ 100% e.g. *bang, sing, long, young, bung*. Regular word-finally, with no exceptions (in RP). /g/ surfaces in *long-er/est, strong-er/est, young-er/est, diphthongise, elongate, prolongation*, and /dʒ/ in *longevity* – see section 7.2. Medially in stem words, only in *clangour, hangar*, but there are thousands of occurrences in suffixed forms, e.g. *clangorous, clingy, hanger, ringer, singer, singing, stinger, swinging, wringer*. See Notes

### THE REST

| | | pronounced | |
|---|---|---|---|
| Exceptions to main system | | | <1% |
| | <ng> | /n/ or /ŋk/ | only in *length, lengthen, strength, strengthen*. See under /n, k, ŋ/, sections 3.4.5, 3.6.1, 3.7.2 |
| Oddities | <ngh> | /ŋ/ | only in *dinghy, gingham, Singhalese* /ˈdɪŋiː, ˈɡɪŋəm, sɪŋəˈliːz/ (contrast <ng, h> as separate graphemes in *shanghai* /ʃænˈhaɪ/) |
| | <ngu> | /ŋ/ | only in a very few suffixed forms of words in next category, e.g. *haranguing, tonguing*. See also end of section 6.4 |
| | <ngue> | /ŋ/ | only in *harangue, meringue, tongue* /həˈræŋ, məˈræŋ, tʌŋ/ (contrast <n, gu, e> as separate graphemes in *dengue* /ˈdeŋgeɪ/) |
| 2-phoneme graphemes | | See <ng> possibly pronounced /ŋk/, four rows above, and Notes | |

## NOTES

Medially in stem and compound words, the letters <n, g> are always separate graphemes representing separate phonemes except in the words listed under exceptions to the main system and Oddities above.

Before <e, i, y> the regular pronunciation of <n, g> is /ndʒ/ (e.g. *Abinger, angel, congeal, danger, dungeon, engender, ginger, harbinger, messenger, tangent; engine, ingenious, laryngitis; dingy, stingy*), i.e. <n, g> follow their main rules. Exceptions:

1) <n, g> pronounced /ŋg/ before <e, i> (there appear to be no such cases before <y>): *anger, conger, finger, hunger, linger, long-er/est, malinger, mangel, monger, strong-er/est, young-er/est; diphthongise, fungi* – here the <n> has its regular pronunciation before <g> – see previous section, but the pronunciation of the <g> as /g/ is the irregular one before <e, i>
2) <n, g> pronounced /nʒ/ before <e> (there appear to be no such cases before <i, y>): only in *ingenue, lingerie* pronounced /'lænʒəriː/ (also pronounced /'lɒndʒəreɪ/)
3) <n, g> pronounced /ndʒ/ before <e> (there appear to be no such cases before <i, y>): only in *longevity*
4) <ng> pronounced /ŋ/ before <e, i, y>): none in stem words, but as noted above there are hundreds of suffixed examples.

Before <a, o, u> and consonant letters the regular pronunciation is /ŋg/ (e.g. *angle, elongate, England, fungus, language, langur, prolongation, single*), i.e. the <n> has its regular pronunciation before <g> – see previous section, and the pronunciation of the <g> is also regular. Exceptions:

1) <ng> pronounced /ŋ/ before <a, o> (there appear to be no exceptions before <u>): only in *clangorous, clangour, hangar*
2) <ng> pronounced /n/ or /ŋk/ before a consonant letter: see *length*, etc., in the Oddities.

Word-finally, <n, ge> are always separate graphemes representing separate phonemes, with <n> always pronounced /n/ and <ge> usually pronounced /dʒ/ – but this is a small set: *arrange, change, grange, mange, range, strange; flange, orange, phalange; challenge, revenge, scavenge; cringe, fringe, hinge, singe, swinge, tinge, whinge; sponge; lounge, scrounge; lunge, plunge* To avoid confusion with *singing, swinging*, the verbs *singe, swinge* retain the <e> before <-ing>: *singeing, swingeing*, as does *spongeing* to avoid the mispronunciation that might arise from *sponging*. Exceptions:

1) with final <n, ge> pronounced /nʒ/: only in *melange*

2) with final <n, g, e> as three separate graphemes: only in *conge* /ˈkɒnʒeɪ/ (sometimes spelt even within English text with French <é>).

N.B. For *once, one* with their initial but unwritten /w/ see the entry for <o> in chapter 10, section 10.27; and for all the graphemes beginning <oi> which have correspondences beginning with consonant phoneme /w/ (<oi, oir, oire, ois>) see the entry for <oi> in chapter 10, section 10.29.

## 9.25 <p, pp>

N.B. <ph> has a separate entry.

### THE MAIN SYSTEM

| Only phoneme | /p/ | 100% | e.g. *apt, apple* |

### THE REST

|  |  | pronounced |  |
|---|---|---|---|
| Exceptions to main system | (none) |  |  |
| Word-final doubled letter + <e> | <ppe> | /p/ | only in *grippe, steppe* |
| Oddities | <pb> | /b/ | only in *Campbell, cupboard, raspberry* /ˈkæmbəl, ˈkʌbəd, ˈrɑːzbriː/ |
|  | <pe> | /p/ | only in *canteloupe, troupe* /ˈkæntəluːp, truːp/ (contrast *canape, recipe* /ˈkænəpeɪ, ˈresɪpiː/). See Notes |
|  | <pn> | /n/ | only word-initial and only in words derived from Greek πνεῦμα *pneuma* ('breath') or πνεύμων *pneumon* ('lung'), e.g. *pneumatic, pneumonia* |
|  | <pph> | /f/ | only in *sapphic, sapphire, Sappho* /ˈsæfɪk, ˈsæfaɪə, ˈsæfəʊ/ |
|  | <ps> | /s/ | only word-initial and only in some words of mainly Greek origin, e.g. *psalm, psalter, psephology, pseud(o)* and many compounds, *psionic, psittacosis, psoriasis, psych(e/o)* and many compounds, and a few more very rare words. /p/ surfaces in *metempsychosis* – see section 7.2 |

|  |  |  |
|---|---|---|
| <pt> | /t/ | only in *Deptford, ptarmigan, pterodactyl* (Greek, = 'wing finger'), *pterosaur* (Greek, = 'wing lizard'), *Ptolem-y/aic, ptomaine, receipt* and a few more very rare words. /p/ surfaces in *archaeopteryx, helicopter, reception, receptive* – see section 7.2 |

*2-phoneme graphemes* (none)

### NOTES

In the vast majority of cases of word-final <p, e> the <e> is part of a split digraph (except *canape* (sometimes spelt even within English text with French <é>), *recipe*) and the <p> is a separate grapheme (including in *canape, recipe*).

For <pa> in *comparable, separate* /ˈseprət/ (adjective), *separatist*, <pe> in *deepening, desperate, halfpenny, opening, operable, operative, prosperous, temperament, temperature, twopenny*, <pi> in *aspirin*, <po> in *corporal, corporate, policeman* pronounced /ˈpliːsmən/, *temporary* see section 6.10.

## 9.26 <ph>

### THE MAIN SYSTEM

| Basic phoneme | /f/ | 99% | e.g. *philosophy* and many other words mainly of Greek origin |
|---|---|---|---|

### THE REST

|  |  | pronounced |  |
|---|---|---|---|
| Exceptions to main system |  |  | <1% in total |
|  | <ph> | /p/ | only in *diphtheria, diphthong, naphtha, ophthalmic, shepherd*. The first four also have pronunciations with /f/ – e.g. /ˈdɪfθɒŋ/ versus /ˈdɪpθɒŋ/ |
|  | <ph> | /v/ | only in *nephew* pronounced /ˈnevjuː/ (also pronounced /ˈnefjuː/), *Stephen* |
| Oddities | <phth> | /t/ | only in *phthisic, phthisis* pronounced /ˈtaɪsɪk, ˈtaɪsɪs/ |

|  |  |  |
|---|---|---|
| | \<phth\> /θ/ | only in *apophthegm* /'æpəθem/, *phthalate* /'θæleɪt/ |
| 2-phoneme graphemes | (none) | |

## NOTE

<p, h> are separate graphemes only at morpheme boundaries in compound words, e.g. *cuphook*, *tophat*. And <ph, th> are separate graphemes in some of the words listed just above.

N.B. For <pp> see under <p>.

# 9.27 <q>

### THE MAIN SYSTEM

| Only phoneme | /k/ | 100% | e.g. *quick* |
|---|---|---|---|

### THE REST

|  |  | pronounced |  |
|---|---|---|---|
| Doubled letter | (does not occur) | | |
| Exceptions to main system | (none) | | |
| Oddities | | | For percentages see Note |
| | <qu> | only /k/ (not /kw/) | occurs initially or medially (never finally) in about 46 words mainly of French origin, namely *bouquet*, *conquer* (/w/ surfaces in *conquest* – see section 7.2), *coquette*, *croquet*, *croquette*, *etiquette*, *exchequer*, *liqueur*, *liquor*, *liquorice*, *maquis*, *mannequin*, *marquee*, *marquetry*, *masquerade*, *mosquito*, *parquet*, *piquant*, *quatrefoil*, *quay*, *quenelle*, *quiche*, *so(u)briquet*, *tourniquet*, and, in more conservative |

speakers' accents, *questionnaire, quoits*; medially also in *applique, communique, manque, risque* where the final <-e> is a separate grapheme (sometimes written even within English text as French <é>), unlike the words in the next paragraph; also phonemically but not orthographically word-final in *opaque*; *claque, plaque*; *antique, bezique, boutique, clique, critique, mystique, oblique, physique, pique, technique, unique*; *toque*; *peruque*; and a few more rare words where the final <e> is part of a split digraph with a preceding vowel letter spelling variously /eɪ, ɑː, iː, əʊ, uː/

<que>   as a trigraph pronounced only /k/ (not /kw/ plus vowel)

occurs word-initially only in *queue* and medially only in *milquetoast* (where it is nevertheless stem-final in a compound word); otherwise only word-finally and only in about 18 words mainly of French origin, namely:
(1) with a preceding consonant letter such that <que> could be replaced by <k> without changing the pronunciation: *arabesque, barque, basque, brusque* pronounced /brʌsk/ (also pronounced /bruːsk/), *burlesque, casque, catafalque, grotesque, marque, masque, mosque, picturesque, romanesque, statuesque, torque*. However, in this group *barque, basque, casque, marque, masque, torque* are kept visually distinct from *bark, bask, cask, mark, mask, torc*;
(2) with a preceding vowel letter with a short pronunciation such that <que> could be replaced by <ck> without changing the pronunciation: *baroque, cheque* (cf. US *check*), *monocoque, plaque* pronounced /plæk/ (also pronounced /plaːk/)

2-phoneme graphemes   (none)

## NOTE

Gontijo *et al.* (2003) do not recognise <que> as a separate grapheme. However, their calculations show that <qu, que> pronounced /k/ together constitute 9% of pronunciations of <qu> and that the other 91% of occurrences of <qu> are pronounced /kw/.

## 9.28 <r, rr>

Never word-final as separate graphemes.

### THE MAIN SYSTEM

| | | | |
|---|---|---|---|
| Only phoneme | /r/ | 100% | e.g. *very, berry* |

### THE REST

| | | pronounced | |
|---|---|---|---|
| Exceptions to main system | (none) | | |
| Word-final doubled letter + <e> | <rre> | /r/ | occurs only in *barre, bizarre, parterre*, where it forms part of the four-letter graphemes <arre, erre> and is not pronounced /r/ (except that <rr> represents /r/ after /r/-linking in *bizarrery* – see section 3.6) |
| Oddities | <re> | /ə/ | 100% of pronunciations of word-final <re>. Only word-final, and in that position almost entirely regular, e.g. *centre, mitre*. The only exceptions appear to be *genre, macabre* /ˈʒɒnrə, məˈkɑːbrə/, where <r, e> are separate graphemes representing separate phonemes |
| | <re> | /r/ | only in *forehead* pronounced /ˈfɒrɪd/ |
| | <rh> | /r/ | only in words of Greek origin, e.g. *rhinoceros, rhododendron*. There are some 2-phoneme exceptions at morpheme boundaries, e.g. *poorhouse, warhorse* |
| | <rrh> | /r/ | only medially and only in a few words of Greek origin, namely *amenorrhoea, arrhythmia, cirrhosis, diarrhoea,* |

*gonorrhoea, haemorrhage, haemorrhoid, lactorrhoea, pyorrhoea, pyrrhic.* N.B. In *catarrh, myrrh* <rrh> is not a separate grapheme, but forms part of the four-letter graphemes <arrh, yrrh> and is not pronounced /r/ (but in *catarrhal* /r/-linking occurs – see section 3.6)

| 2-phoneme graphemes | (none) |
|---|---|

## NOTE

For full treatment of /r/-linking, implying when stem-final <r> is and is not pronounced, see section 3.6.

## 9.29 <s, ss>

N.B. <se, sh, si, ssi> have separate entries.

### THE MAIN SYSTEM

| Basic phoneme | /s/ | <s> 56%, <ss> 89% | e.g. *cats, grass.* For <s>, except within split digraphs, /s/ is regular in all positions, including when <s> is a grammatical suffix or a contracted form after voiceless non-sibilant consonants. Only exceptions in word-initial position: *sorbet* (sometimes), *sugar, sure* and German pronunciations of *sauerkraut, spiel, stein, strafe, stumm.* For medial and final positions see Notes and Table 9.5. For <ss> see the exceptions to the main system, and <ssi>, section 9.32 |
|---|---|---|---|
| Other phonemes for <s> | /z/ | 43% | e.g. *dogs.* Never word-initial (except in *sorbet* pronounced /ˈzɔːbeɪ/ (also pronounced /ˈsɔːbeɪ/) and German pronunciation of *sauerkraut*). Regular within split digraphs, and when <s> is a grammatical suffix or a contracted form after stem-final vowels and |

/ʒ/  <1%   always preceded by a vowel letter and followed by <ua, ur>; only medial and only in *casual, sensual, usual, visual*; *(dis/en/fore-)closure, com/ex-posure, embrasure, erasure, leisure, measure, pleasure, treasure(r), treasury, usur-y/er/ious*. Despite its rarity in the grapheme–phoneme direction, this correspondence belongs in the main system because of its status as a main-system correspondence in the phoneme–grapheme direction – see section 3.8.4

## THE REST

| | | pronounced | |
|---|---|---|---|
| Exceptions to main system | | | See also Table 9.5 |
| | <s> | /ʃ/ | <1% of pronunciations of <s>. Only in (initially) *sugar, sure*, and German pronunciations of *spiel, stein, strafe, stumm*; (medially) *asphalt* pronounced /'æʃfelt/ (also pronounced /'æsfælt/), *censure, commensurate, ensure, insure, tonsure* |
| | <ss> | /ʃ/ | 7% of pronunciations of <ss>. Only in *assure, fissure, issue, pressure, tissue* |
| | <ss> | /z/ | 5% of pronunciations of <ss>. Only in *Aussie, brassiere, dessert, dissolve* (but contrast *dissolution*, with /s/), *hussar, Missouri, possess* (first <ss>), *scissors* |
| Word-final doubled letter + <e> | <sse> | /s/ | except in *divertissement*, only word-final, e.g. *bouillabaisse, crevasse, duchesse, finesse, fosse, impasse, lacrosse, largesse, mousse, noblesse, palliasse, wrasse* and a few more rare words (and contrast *retrousse* /rə'truːseɪ/, sometimes spelt even within English text with French <é>) |

## The grapheme-phoneme correspondences, 1   315

Oddities

        \<sc\> /s/     98% of pronunciations of \<sc\>, but see Notes. Regular before \<e, i, y\>, e.g. *ascend, disciple, scythe*. Irregularly, also in *corpuscle, muscle*; /k/ surfaces in *corpuscular, muscular* – see section 7.2. Exception: *sceptic*, with /sk/, which is also the regular pronunciation (following the general rules for \<s, c\>) before \<a, o, u\> (*corpuscle, muscle* appear to be the only occurrences of \<sc\> before a consonant letter). For other exceptions see next 2 paragraphs

        \<sc\> /ʃ/     1% of pronunciations of \<sc\>. Only in *conscie, conscientious, crescendo, fascis-m/t*

        \<sc\> /z/     <1% of pronunciations of \<sc\>. Only in *crescent* pronounced /ˈkrezənt/ (also pronounced /ˈkresənt/)

        \<sce\> /s/     only word-finally in verbs ending \<-esce\>, e.g. *acquiesce, coalesce, convalesce, deliquesce, effervesce, evanesce* and some other very rare words, plus *reminisce*. The final \<e\> surfaces as /ə/ in some suffixes, e.g. *convalescent* – see section 7.2

        \<sch\> /ʃ/     only in *maraschino, meerschaum, schedule, schemozzle, schist, schistosomiasis, schlemiel, schlep, schlock, schmaltz, schmo(e), schmooze, schnapps, schnauzer, schnitzel, schnozzle, schuss, schwa, seneschal*. Except in these words and *schism* (next paragraph) and in a few cases across a morpheme boundary (*discharge, escheat, eschew, mischance, mischief, mischievous*, with /stʃ/), \<s, ch\> is always pronounced /sk/, e.g. *school*. For absence of percentages here and in next paragraph see Notes

        \<sch\> /s/     only in *schism* pronounced /ˈsɪzəm/

        \<sci\> /ʃ/     only in *conscience, conscious, fascia, luscious* /ˈkɒnʃəns,ˈkɒnʃəs, ˈfeɪʃə, ˈlʌʃəs/

        \<sj\> /ʃ/     only in *sjambok* /ˈʃæmbʊk/

        \<st\> /s/     regular before final \<-en, -le\>, e.g. *chasten, christen, hasten, fasten, glisten, listen, moisten* (exception: *tungsten*); *castle, forecastle* (whether pronounced /ˈfəʊksəl/ or

|  |  |  | /ˈfɔːkɑːsəl/), nestle, pestle, trestle, wrestle, bristle, Entwistle, epistle, gristle, thistle, whistle, apostle, jostle, throstle, bustle, hustle, rustle; otherwise only in chestnut, Christmas, durstn't, dustbin, dustman, mistletoe, mustn't, ostler, Postlethwaite, Thistlethwaite, Twistleton, waistcoat pronounced /ˈweɪskəʊt/ and sometimes ghastly. /t/ surfaces in apostolic, epistolary – see section 7.2 |
|---|---|---|---|
|  | <sth> | /s/ | only in asthma, isthmus if pronounced without /θ/ |
|  | <sw> | /s/ | only in answer, coxswain, sword /ˈɑːnsə, ˈkɒksən, sɔːd/ and boatswain pronounced /ˈbəʊsən/ (also pronounced /ˈbəʊtsweɪn/) |
| 2-phoneme grapheme | <s> | /ɪz/ | only, following an apostrophe, in regular singular and irregular plural possessive forms after a sibilant consonant (/s, z, ʃ, ʒ, tʃ, dʒ/), e.g. Brooks's (book), jazz's (appeal), Bush's (government), (the) mirage's (appearance), (the) Church's (mission), (the) village's (centre), (the) geese's (cackling) |

## NOTES

Given that /s/ is the regular pronunciation of medial <s>, Table 9.5 lists categories where medial <s> is instead pronounced /z/, plus sub-exceptions with /s/ (and a very few sub-sub-exceptions with /z/).

And given that /s/ is the regular pronunciation of word-final <s> (including when it is a grammatical suffix or contracted form after a voiceless non-sibilant consonant), here is a list of categories where word-final <s> is instead pronounced:

- /z/
   1) regularly after vowels and voiced non-sibilant consonants when <s> is a grammatical suffix (regular noun plural and third person singular present tense verb and, following an apostrophe, regular singular and irregular plural possessive) or contracted from is, has. This includes plurals in <-es> pronounced /iːz/ of words of Greek and Latin origin which have singulars in <-is> pronounced /ɪs/, e.g. axes, crises, diagnoses, testes
   2) in a few function words: always, as, his, sans, and cos where this is the abbreviation of because

3) plus a few content words: *lens, missus,* and *series, species* (whether singular or plural), plus *cos*, the lettuce and the abbreviation of *cosine*, which vary in pronunciation between /kɒz/ and /kɒs/
• /ɪz/ – see the 2-phoneme pronunciation above.

For <(s)sa> in *adversary, emissary, necessary,* <(s)so> in *promissory, reasonable, seasoning,* <ste> in *christening, listener, listening* see section 6.10.

The percentages of /ʃ, z/ as pronunciations of <ss> are due solely to the high frequencies of a few words with these correspondences.

The percentages for <sc> depend on recognising it as a digraph rather than as two single-letter graphemes. However, the fact that it is mainly a digraph before <e, i, y> and hardly ever a digraph elsewhere helps with this.

Gontijo *et al.* (2003) state that /s/ accounts for 96% of pronunciations of <sch> and /ʃ/ for only 4% – but since <sch> pronounced /s/ occurs only in *schism* their corpus must have been very strange in this respect.

TABLE 9.5: MEDIAL <s> PRONOUNCED /z/, WITH SUB-EXCEPTIONS PRONOUNCED /s/ AND SUB-SUB-EXCEPTIONS PRONOUNCED /z/.

For other exceptions see above.

| Categories where medial <s> is exceptionally pronounced /z/ | Sub-exceptions where medial <s> is pronounced /s/ (with a few sub-sub-exceptions with /z/) |
|---|---|
| Almost always before <b> and always before <d, g, l, m>), but except before <m>, where there are hundreds of examples (e.g. *chasm, prism, seismic, talisman*), this is a small set: *asbestos, busby, husband, lesbian, presbyter, presbyterian* pronounced /prezbɪ'tɪəri:jən/, *raspberry* (taking <pb> to be a spelling of /b/); *Tuesday, Wednesday, Thursday, wisdom; phosgene; gosling, grisly, Islam, measles, measly, muslim, muslin, Oslo* (but the Norwegian pronunciation has /s/), *quisling* | only in *presbyterian* pronounced /prespɪ'tɪəri:jən/, where the <b> also devoices, unusually, to /p/ |
| Mostly after <m>, e.g. *crimson, flimsy, helmsman, whimsical, whimsy* | *hamster* |
| Mostly after <w>, e.g. *blowsy, drowsy, frowsy* | *frowsty* |

TABLE 9.5: MEDIAL <s> PRONOUNCED /z/, WITH SUB-EXCEPTIONS PRONOUNCED /s/ AND SUB-SUB-EXCEPTIONS PRONOUNCED /z/, CONT.

| Categories where medial <s> is exceptionally pronounced /z/ | Sub-exceptions where medial <s> is pronounced /s/ (with a few sub-sub-exceptions with /z/) |
|---|---|
| In the prefix <trans-> where the following phoneme is a vowel or a voiced consonant, e.g. *transact, transgress, transit(ion), translate, transmit, transmute* | *transitive, transom* |
| Mostly between vowel letters | Where the following letter is <e, i> followed by another vowel letter – see the main entries for <se, si>; <br> In compounds, e.g. *aforesaid, antiseptic, beside, research*; <br> Always in the endings <-osity, -sive, -some>; <br> Mostly in the ending <-sy> (sub-sub-exceptions with /z/: *busy, cosy, daisy, poesy, posy, queasy,* and derived forms such as *cheesy, easy, lousy* (despite the /s/ in *louse* – see Notes to next section), *noisy, nosy, prosy, rosy*); <br> In prefix <dis-> (sub-sub-exceptions with /z/: *disaster, disease*); <br> In prefix <mis->; <br> In a set of Greek words ending <-sis> in singular and <-ses> in plural: *analysis, basis, crisis, diagnosis, emphasis, oasis, prognosis, thesis*; <br> Plus *asylum, basin, bison, chrysalis, comparison, crusade, desecrate, desolate, desultory, dysentery, episode, gasoline, garrison, isolate, isosceles* and other words beginning <iso->, *kerosene, mason, nuisance, palisade, parasite, parasol, philosophy, prosecute, sausage, unison* and sometimes *venison* <br> In the 'sugar' words *dextrose, glucose, lactose, sucrose* the ending <-ose> can be pronounced /əʊs/ or /əʊz/ and this may also be true of many of the (mostly rare) adjectives ending in <-ose> – but *morose, verbose* (at least) have only /əʊs/ |
| In a few other odd words: *absolve, absorb, absorption, bowser, geyser, hawser, observe, palsy, pansy, tansy* | |

## 9.30 <se>

Never initial.

### THE MAIN SYSTEM

For both categories see Notes and Table 9.6. For the absence of percentages see Notes.

| | | |
|---|---|---|
| Basic phoneme | /s/ | only word-final. Regular after a consonant letter; otherwise unpredictable |
| Other phoneme | /z/ | only word-final. Regular (no exceptions) after <ai, au, ui>, but this covers only 10 words; otherwise unpredictable |

### THE REST

|  |  |  | pronounced |
|---|---|---|---|
| Exceptions to main system | (none) | | |
| Oddities | | | (N.B. All medial, therefore not classified as exceptions to main system) |
| | <se> | /ʃ/ | only in *gaseous* pronounced /ˈgeɪʃəs/ (also pronounced /ˈgæˈsiːjəs/) |
| | <se> | /z/ | only in *gooseberry* /ˈgʊzbriː/, *housewife* 'sewing kit' pronounced /ˈhʌzɪf/ |
| | <se> | /ʒ/ | only in *nausea, nauseous* pronounced /ˈnɔːʒə(s)/ (also pronounced /ˈnɔːziːjə(s)/) |
| 2-phoneme graphemes | (none) | | |

### NOTES

Gontijo et al. (2003) do not recognise <se> as a separate grapheme, hence the absence of percentages. I have based my choice of /s/ as the basic phoneme for <se> on its predominance in Table 9.6. This is admittedly a sort of lexical, rather than a text, frequency (see section 3.3).

Initial <s, e> and (except in the few Oddities listed) medial <s, e> always are/ belong to separate graphemes. Word-finally, the only words in which <s, e> are separate single-letter graphemes appear to be *tsetse*, usually pronounced /ˈtetsiː/ and the three French loanwords *blase, expose* ('report of scandal') and *rose* ('pink wine'), with /eɪ/ (increasingly spelt even within English text with French <é>). In almost all other cases of final <s, e> the <e> is part of a split digraph and the <s> is a single-letter grapheme – see previous section. Part of my definition of a split digraph (see section A.6 in Appendix A) is that the leading letter is not preceded by another vowel letter. This makes it easy to define and identify almost all the words ending <se> where these letters do form a digraph, namely those where <-se> is preceded by two vowel letters or a consonant letter: see again Table 9.6, which also distinguishes the relevant words according to /s, z/ pronunciations.

In the last row of the table are listed the only eight words in which the vowel letter before the <s> is a single vowel letter preceded in turn by a consonant letter, so that that vowel letter and the final <e> look as though they ought to form a split digraph, but do not; these are the only exceptions to my definition of grapheme <se> just above besides the four words listed earlier in the previous paragraph.

Given that the pronunciation of *house* as a verb is /haʊz/, the pronunciation of *houses* /ˈhaʊzɪz/ as a singular verb is regular, but as a plural noun shows a very rare irregularity: if it were regular it would be /ˈhaʊsɪz/ (the noun stem /haʊs/ plus the plural ending /ɪz/ which is regular after sibilant consonants). The voicing of the stem-final consonant is shared only with some words ending in /f/ in the singular but /vz/ in the plural, e.g. *leaf/leaves*, or in /θ/ in the singular but /ðz/ in the plural (in RP), e.g. *bath(s)*, plus *lousy* with /z/ from *louse* with /s/ (and contrast *mous(e)y* with /s/).

TABLE 9.6: /s, z/ AS PRONUNCIATIONS OF WORD-FINAL <se>.

|  | /s/ | /z/ |
| --- | --- | --- |
| After <ai, au, ui> | (none) | all, but this is a small set: *appraise, braise, chaise, praise; applause, cause, clause, pause; bruise, cruise* |
| After <ea, ee, oi, oo, ou, u> | *cease, crease, decease, decrease, grease, increase, lease, release; geese; porpoise, tortoise; goose, loose, moose, noose, vamoose; douse,* | *appease, ease, please, tease; cheese; noise, poise; choose; arouse, blouse, carouse, espouse, rouse,* plus *house* /haʊz/ as a verb and (suffixed) *houses* /ˈhaʊzɪz/ |

*The grapheme-phoneme correspondences, 1* 321

| | *grouse, louse, mouse, Scouse, souse, spouse,* plus *house* /haʊs/ as a singular noun (see Notes); *use* (noun) | as a plural noun and singular verb (see Notes); *fuse, muse, use* (verb) |
|---|---|---|
| After <r, w> (which here always form part of a vowel digraph) | all except those shown on right, including *dowse* (/daʊs/ 'splash with water', variant spelling of *douse*) | only in *parse; hawse, tawse; browse, dowse* (/daʊz/ 'detect water'), *drowse* |
| After any other consonant letter | all except *cleanse* | only in *cleanse* |
| After consonant + vowel, so looking as though there is a split digraph | all, but this is a small set because final <e> after <s> is normally part of a split digraph (see Notes above Table and previous section): *carcase, purchase; diocese* /ˈdaɪəsɪs/; *mortise, practise, premise, promise, treatise; purpose* | (none) |

For <se> in *arsenal, arsenic* see section 6.10.

## 9.31  <sh>

*Only phoneme*      /ʃ/      100%      e.g. *ship, fish*

**NOTE**

The only cases where, exceptionally, <s, h> do not form a digraph but belong to separate graphemes are at morpheme boundaries in compound words, e.g. *mishandle, mishap, mishit.* In *dishonest, dishonour,* however, there is no /h/ phoneme, so the letter <h> is (according to your analysis) either 'silent' or part of a grapheme <ho> pronounced /ɒ/. I prefer the latter analysis – see /ɒ/, section 5.4.4, and <h>, section 9.16.

## 9.32 <si>

Only medial.

### THE MAIN SYSTEM

| | | | |
|---|---|---|---|
| Basic phoneme | /ʒ/ | 55% | regular when both preceded and followed by vowel letters, e.g. *vision*. In all such words the stress falls on the vowel preceding /ʒ/ spelt <si>, and that vowel is always spelt with a single letter and has its letter-name pronunciation, e.g. *evasion, cohesion, erosion, collusion*, except that <i> is always short /ɪ/, e.g. *collision*. See Notes |
| Other phoneme | /ʃ/ | 45% | regular between a preceding consonant letter (which is always one of <l, n, r>) and a following vowel letter, e.g. *emulsion, repulsion; pension, tension; aversion, controversial, excursion, reversion, torsion, version*. In all these cases the stress falls on the vowel preceding <l, n, r>. Also, where the preceding consonant letter is <l, n> the preceding vowel is spelt with a single letter which has its 'short' pronunciation; where the consonant letter is <r> it forms a digraph with the vowel letter and the pronunciation is either /ɜː/ where the digraph is <er, ur> or /ɔː/ where it is <or> (there are no words ending <-arsion, -irsion>). See Notes |

## THE REST

|  | pronounced |  |
|---|---|---|
| Exception to main system | medial <si> /z/ | only in *business*. See also section 6.10 |
| Oddities | (none) |  |
| 2-phoneme graphemes | (none) |  |

## NOTES

<s, i> never form a digraph word-initially or -finally; medially they form a digraph only when followed by stem-final <-on>, plus *business, controversial*.

Given that the contexts in which the two pronunciations occur are almost entirely distinct, <si> is almost 100% predictable. The only exception is that *version* is now often pronounced /ˈvɜːʒən/ rather than /ˈvɜːʃən/.

N.B. For <ss> see under <s>.

# 9.33 <ssi>

Only medial.

| Only phoneme | /ʃ/ | 100% | regular when both preceded and followed by vowel letters, e.g. *accession, admission, discussion, fission, intercession, obsession, passion, percussion, permission, recession, remission*. Exception: *dossier*, in either pronunciation (/ˈdɒsiːjə, ˈdɒsiːjeɪ/). In all these cases, including *dossier*, the stress falls on the vowel preceding /ʃ/ spelt <ssi>, and that vowel is spelt with a single letter which has its 'short' pronunciation |
|---|---|---|---|

## NOTE

In all other cases, <ss, i> are/belong to separate graphemes, e.g. in *missile, passive*.

## 9.34 <t, tt>

N.B. <tch, th, ti> have separate entries.

| Basic phoneme | /t/ | <t> 94%, <tt> 100% | e.g. *rat, rattle* |
| Other phoneme for <t> | /tʃ/ | 2% of pronunciations of <t> | regular before <u> followed by either another vowel letter or a single consonant letter and then a vowel letter, e.g. (in initial position) *tuba, tube, tuber, Tuesday* pronounced /ˈtʃuːzdiː/, *tuition* pronounced /tʃuːˈwɪʃən/, *tulip, tumour, tumult, tumultuous, tumulus, tuna, tune* pronounced /ˈtʃuːn/, *tunic, tureen, tutor*; (medially) *impromptu; gargantuan, perpetuate; attitude, multitude, solitude; statue, virtue; habitue; intuition, pituitary; costume; fortunate, fortune, importune, opportune; capture, mature* and dozens of other words in <-ture> and derivatives such as *adventurous(ly), natural(ly); centurion, century, saturate; virtuoso; obtuse; de/in/pro/re/sub-stitution;* also in several groups where the stress is always on the syllable preceding /tʃ/ spelt <t>: *actual(ly), perpetual(ly), virtual(ly)* and several other words in <-tual(ly)>; *actuary, estuary, mortuary, obituary,* |

*The grapheme-phoneme correspondences, 1* 325

*sanctuary, statuary, voluptuary, congratulate, fistula, petulan-t/ ce, postulant, postulate, spatula, titular, contemptuous, fatuous, impetuous, tempestuous, tumultuous* (again) and several other words in <-tuous>. Though rare in this direction, this correspondence qualifies as part of the main system because of the high frequency and predictability of /tʃ/ spelt <t> – see section 3.7.2

## THE REST

|  |  | pronounced |  |
|---|---|---|---|
| *Exceptions to main system* | <t> | /ʃ/ | 5% of pronunciations of <t>. Mainly before <iat> with the <i> pronounced /iː/, e.g. *differentiate, expatiate, ingratiate, initiate, negotiate, propitiate, satiate, substantiate, vitiate,* plus *minutiae, otiose* pronounced /ˈəʊʃiːjəʊs, ˈəʊʃiːjəʊz/ (also pronounced /ˈəʊtiːjəʊs, ˈəʊtiːjəʊz/), *partiality, ratio.* Partial exceptions: *novitiate* can be pronounced with or without the /iː/: /nəˈvɪʃiːjət, nəˈvɪʃət/ and can therefore follow either this rule or the main rule for <ti>, see section 9.37; also, some of the words listed have alternative pronunciations with /s/, e.g. *negotiate, substantiate* as either /nɪˈɡəʊʃiːjeɪt, səbˈstænʃiːjeɪt/ or /nɪˈɡəʊsiːjeɪt, səbˈstænsiːjeɪt/. See also next paragraph |
|  | <t> | /s/ | <1% of pronunciations of <t>. Only the penultimate <t> in about 10 words ending in <-tiation>, e.g. *differentiation, initiation, negotiation,* |

*propitiation, transubstantiation*, and only for RP-speakers who avoid having two occurrences of medial /ʃ/ in such words (see Notes under /ʃ/, section 3.7.3), plus a few words where <t> is alternatively pronounced /ʃ/ – see previous paragraph. In French, on the other hand, /s/ is one of the most frequent correspondences for <t>

| | | | |
|---|---|---|---|
| Word-final doubled letter + <e> | <tte> | /t/ | only word-final, e.g. *cigarette, gavotte*. All such words have stress on the syllable ending in /t/ spelt <-tte> except *etiquette, omelette, palette*, which have stress on the first syllable. In *latte* <tt, e> are separate graphemes, as are <u.e, tt> in *butte* |
| Oddities | <te> | /t/ | mainly word-final and in that position in at least 120 words, namely |

– *Bacchante, composite, compote, confidante, cote, debutante, definite, detente, dirigiste, enceinte, entente, entracte, exquisite, favourite, granite, hypocrite, infinite, minute* ('sixtieth of an hour'), *opposite, perquisite, plebiscite, pointe, requisite, riposte, route, svelte*

– about 30 nouns/adjectives in <-ate> pronounced /ət/ where the verbs with the same spelling are pronounced with /eɪt/, e.g. *advocate, affiliate, aggregate, alternate* (here with also a difference in stress and vowel pattern: noun/adjective pronounced /ɔːlˈtɜːnət/, verb pronounced /ˈɔːltəneɪt/), *animate, appropriate, approximate, articulate, associate, certificate, coordinate, curate* (here with also a difference in meaning and stress: noun ('junior cleric') pronounced /ˈkjʊərət/, verb ('mount an exhibition') pronounced /kjʊəˈreɪt/), *degenerate, delegate, deliberate* (here with also a difference in syllable structure: adjective /dɪˈlɪbrət/ with three syllables

and an elided vowel – see section 6.10;
verb /dɪˈlɪbəreɪt/ with four syllables),
*designate, desolate, duplicate,
elaborate, estimate, expatriate,
graduate, initiate, intimate, legitimate,
moderate, pontificate* (here with
unrelated (?) meanings: noun ('pope's
reign') pronounced /pɒnˈtɪfɪkət/, verb
('speak pompously') pronounced
/pɒnˈtɪfɪkeɪt/), *precipitate* (but here
only the adjective has /ət/; the noun as
well as the verb has /eɪt/), *predicate,
separate* (here too with a difference in
syllable structure: adjective /ˈseprət/
with two syllables and an elided vowel
– see section 6.10; verb /ˈsepəreɪt/ with
three syllables), *subordinate, syndicate,
triplicate*. In the verbs and the many
other nouns and adjectives with this
ending pronounced /eɪt/, <e> is part
of the split digraph <a.e> pronounced
/eɪ/ and the <t> on its own is
pronounced /t/

– a further set of at least 60 nouns/
adjectives in <-ate> pronounced
/ət/ with no identically-spelt verb,
e.g. *accurate, adequate, agate,
appellate, celibate, climate, collegiate,
conglomerate, (in)considerate,
consulate, consummate, delicate,
desperate, (in)determinate, directorate,
disconsolate, doctorate, electorate,
episcopate, extortionate, fortunate,
illegitimate, immaculate, immediate,
inanimate, in(sub)ordinate, inspectorate,
intricate, inviolate, (bacca)laureate,
legate, (il)literate, novitiate, obdurate,
palate, particulate, (com/dis)passionate,
private, profligate, proletariate,
(dis)proportionate, protectorate,
proximate, roseate, senate, surrogate,
(in)temperate, triumvirate, ultimate,
(in)vertebrate* (a few of these words
have related verb forms with <-ate>

pronounced /eɪt/: *animate, legitimate, mediate, subordinate, violate*)
– possibly just one word where both noun and verb have <-ate> pronounced /ət/: *pirate*
–pronounced also occurs medially in a few words in rapid speech, e.g. *interest, literacy, literal, literary, literature, sweetener, veterinary* – see section 6.10.
In all cases where is pronounced the is phonographically redundant, but in a couple it makes the words visually distinct from words without the and with an unrelated meaning: *point, rout*. Exceptions where word-final <t, e> are separate graphemes: *coyote, dilettante, (piano)forte, karate, machete* /məˈʃetiː/, and the French loanwords *diamante, naivete, pate* ('paste'), *saute* (sometimes spelt even within English text with French <é>)

| | | |
|---|---|---|
| <te> | /tʃ/ | only in *righteous* |
| <ts> | /z/ | only in *tsar* |
| <tsch> | /tʃ/ | only in *kitsch, putsch* |
| <tw> | /t/ | only in *two* and derivatives, e.g. *twopence, twopenny*. /w/ surfaces in *between, betwixt, twain, twelfth, twelve, twenty, twice, twilight, twilit, twin* – see section 7.2 |

*2-phoneme graphemes*   (none)

## NOTES

For <ta> in *budgetary, commentary, dietary, dignitary, fragmentary, hereditary, military, momentary, monetary, pituitary, planetary, proprietary, salutary, sanitary, secretary* pronounced /ˈsekrətriː/, *sedentary* pronounced /ˈsedəntriː/ (also pronounced /sɪˈdentəriː/), *solitary, tributary, unitary, voluntary*, <tau> in *restaurant*, <(t)te> in *cemetery, dysentery, entering, et cetera, interest, literacy, literal, literature, literary* /ˈlɪtrəriː/, *monastery*, *mystery* /ˈmɪstriː/, *presbytery, sweetener, veterinary* /ˈvetrɪnriː/, *utterance*, <to> in *amatory, auditory, conciliatory, conservatory, contributory, declamatory, defamatory, de/ex/re/sup-pository, desultory, dilatory, dormitory, explanatory, exploratory, factory* /ˈfæktriː/, *history* /ˈhɪstriː/, *inflammatory, inhibitory, interrogatory, inventory* pronounced /ˈɪnvəntriː/ (also pronounced /ɪnˈventəriː/), *laboratory, lavatory, mandatory, nugatory, obligatory, observatory, offertory, oratory, predatory, preparatory, promontory, purgatory, repertory, retaliatory, signatory, statutory, territory, transitory, victory* /ˈvɪktriː/, <tu> in *accentual, actual(ly), actuary, adventurous(ly), conceptual, contractual, effectual, estuary, eventual, factual, habitual, intellectual, mortuary, mutual, natural(ly), obituary, perpetual, punctual, ritual, sanctuary, statuary, spiritual, textual, virtual, voluptuary* see section 6.10.

All the words in which <t> is pronounced /tʃ/ were formerly pronounced with the sequence /tj/, and conservative RP-speakers may still pronounce them that way (or imagine they do). Pronunciations with /tj/ would require an analysis with the <t> pronounced /t/ and and the /j/-glide as part of the pronunciation of the <u> and following <r> or vowel letter. See <d>, section 9.11, for the largely parallel correspondence to voiced /dʒ/, <di> in the Oddities there, and <ti>, section 9.37.

## 9.35 <tch>

| Only phoneme | /tʃ/ | 100% | e.g. *match* |

### NOTE

There appear to be no cases where <t, ch> are separate graphemes.

## 9.36 <th>

### THE MAIN SYSTEM

| Basic phoneme | /ð/ | 88% | in all (content and function) words ending in <-ther>, e.g. *brother, either*, except *anther, ether, panther*, and in all function words (except *both, through* and Scots *outwith*), i.e. *although, than, that, the*, |

thee, their, them, then, thence, there, these, they, thine, this, thither, those, thou (archaic second person singular pronoun), though, thus, thy, with, without; also in a very few other stem content words, namely *algorithm, bequeath, betroth* (but *troth* has /θ/), *booth, brethren, farthing, fathom, heathen* (but (unrelated) *heath* has /θ/), *mouth* /maʊð/ (verb), *oath* /əʊð/ (verb), *rhythm, smithereens, smooth, swarthy, withy* and derivatives, e.g. *betrothal*, plus some other derived forms: *earthen, loathsome, norther-n/ly, smithy, souther-n/ly, worthy*, even though their stems *earth, loath, north, smith, south, worth* have /θ/. Also, in RP, in plurals of some nouns which have /θ/ in the singular, e.g. *baths, oaths, paths, youths* /bɑːðz, əʊðz, pɑːðz, juːðz/

| Other phoneme | /θ/ | 12% | in three function words (*both, through* and Scots *outwith*) and in most content words, e.g. *anther, ether, methane, method, mouth* /maʊθ/ (noun), *oath* /əʊθ/ (noun), *panther, pith, thigh, thin, thou* (informal abbreviation meaning 'thousandth of an inch/thousand pounds/dollars'), *threw* |

## THE REST

pronounced

Exceptions to main system

<1% in total

| | <th> | /t/ | only in *Thai, thali, Thame, Thames, Therese, Thomas, thyme, Wrotham* /ˈruːtəm/ |
| | <th> | /tʃ/ | only in *posthumous* /ˈpɒstʃəməs/ |
| | <th> | as 2-phoneme sequence /tθ/ | only in *eighth* /eɪtθ/ |

| | | |
|---|---|---|
| Oddities | \<the\> /θ/ | only in *Catherine* with first \<e\> elided (see section 6.10), *saithe* (/seɪθ/, 'fish of cod family') |
| | \<the\> /ð/ | only word-final and only in *breathe, loathe, seethe, sheathe, soothe, staithe, teethe, wreathe*. Only exceptions: *absinthe* /æbˈsænt/, (the river) *Lethe* /ˈliːθiː/ (in Greek mythology), *nepenthe* /neˈpenθiː/ |
| 2-phoneme grapheme | (see above) | |

## NOTES

The communicative load of the /θ, ð/ distinction is very low – there are remarkably few minimal pairs differing strictly and only in these phonemes; even scraping the dictionary for rare words I have managed to identify only 10 such pairs. The only ones which are also identical in spelling appear to be *mouth, oath, thou* (for the distinctions in use/meaning see above), and the only pairs which are not identical in spelling appear to be *lo(a)th/loathe, sheath/sheathe, teeth/teethe, wreath/wreathe*, where the words in each pair are related in meaning, plus *ether/either* pronounced /ˈiːðə/ (also pronounced /ˈaɪðə/), *sooth/soothe, thigh/thy*, where they are not. Other pairs differing visually only in the absence or presence of final \<e\> (*bath/bathe, breath/breathe, cloth/clothe, lath/lathe, swath/swathe*) have a further phonological difference in the pronunciation of the preceding vowel grapheme; similarly, *seeth* (/ˈsiːjɪθ/, archaic 3rd person singular of *see*) differs from *seethe* /siːð/ in having two syllables rather than one.

The only cases where \<t, h\> do not form a digraph are at morpheme boundaries in compound words, e.g. *adulthood, bolthole, carthorse, coathook, goatherd, hothouse, meathook, pothole, warthog*.

For \<tho\> in *catholic* (as well as \<the\> in *Catherine*), see section 6.10.

## 9.37 \<ti\>

Only medial. For all categories see Notes.

### THE MAIN SYSTEM

| | | | |
|---|---|---|---|
| Basic phoneme | /ʃ/ | 94% | regular when followed by \<a, e, o\>, e.g. *confidential, inertia, infectious, nation, quotient*; cf. *Ignatius* |

## THE REST

|  |  | pronounced |  |
|---|---|---|---|
| Exceptions to main system | <ti> | /tʃ/ | 5% Regular when preceded by <s> and followed by <o>, but occurs only in *combustion, con/di/indi/in/sug-gestion, exhaustion, question, rumbustious,* plus *Christian* |
|  | <ti> | /ʒ/ | <1% only in *equation* |
| Oddities | (none) |  |  |
| 2-phoneme graphemes | (none) |  |  |

## NOTES

Given the different contexts in which /ʃ, tʃ/ occur, these pronunciations are almost 100% predictable.

In all cases other than those defined above, <t, i> are separate graphemes, e.g. in *consortium* pronounced /kənˈsɔːtiːjəm/ (also but less often pronounced /kənˈsɔːʃəm/), *till, native*; also in a few words which are exceptions to the main rule above: *cation* /ˈkætaɪən/, *consortia* pronounced /kənˈsɔːtiːjə/ (less often but, by the main rule above, more regularly pronounced /kənˈsɔːʃə/), *fortieth, otiose, pitiable*; and in two words which are sub-exceptions to <ti> pronounced /tʃ/, namely *bastion* /ˈbæstiːjən/, *Christianity* /krɪstiˈjænɪtiː/; also, the first <ti> is pronounced /siː/ in about 10 words ending in <-tiation>, e.g. *differentiation, initiation, negotiation, propitiation, transubstantiation*, but only by RP-speakers who avoid having two occurrences of medial /ʃ/ in a word of this sort. See also sections 3.7.3 and 9.35.

N.B. For <tt> see under <t>.

N.B. Though <u, u.e> have or are involved in various consonantal pronunciations see, nevertheless, the entries for <u, u.e> in chapter 10, sections 10.36, 10.38.

# 9.38 <v>

N.B. <ve> has a separate entry.

## THE MAIN SYSTEM

Basic phoneme   /v/   100%   e.g. *very, oven*

## THE REST

|  |  | pronounced |  |
|---|---|---|---|
| Exception to main system | <v> | /f/ | only in *kvetch, svelte, svengali, veldt* |
| Doubled letter | <vv> | /v/ | only in *bevvy, bovver, chavvy, chivvy, civvy, divvy, flivver, lavvy, luvv-y/ie, navvy, revving, savvy, skivvy, spivvery, spivvy* |
| Word-final doubled letter + <e> | (does not occur) |  |  |
| Oddities | (none) |  |  |
| 2-phoneme graphemes | (none) |  |  |

## NOTE

For <vou> in *favourable, favourite* see section 6.10.

# 9.39 <ve>

Only phoneme   /v/   never initial; for medial position see Notes; frequent word-finally

## NOTES

<ve> pronounced /v/ occurs medially in *average, deliverable, evening* (noun, 'late part of day', pronounced /ˈiːvnɪŋ/, as distinct from the verb of the same spelling, 'levelling', pronounced /ˈiːvənɪŋ/), *every, several, sovereign* (for these words see also section 6.10), and in a large number of regular plural nouns and singular verbs, e.g. *haves* (vs *have-nots*), *gives, grieves, initiatives, dissolves, lives* (verb), *loves, improves, stoves, preserves, mauves, gyves*; also in a small number of irregular plural nouns ending in <-ves> pronounced /vz/ where the singular forms have <-f> pronounced /f/, namely *calves, dwarves* (the form *dwarfs* also exists), *elves, halves, hooves, leaves, loaves, scarves, (our/your/them-)selves, sheaves, shelves, thieves, turves* (the form *turfs* also exists), *wharves, wolves*, plus a very few

nouns where the <f> in the singular is within the split digraph <i..e>: *knives, lives* (/laɪvz/; the singular verb of the same spelling is pronounced /lɪvz/), (*ale/good/house/mid-*)*wives* (but if *housewife* 'sewing kit' pronounced /ˈhʌzɪf/ has a plural it is presumably pronounced /ˈhʌzɪfs/).

In only 33 words, in my analysis (*behave, conclave, forgave, gave, shave, Khedive, suave, wave; breve, eve; alive, archive, arrive, deprive, drive, five, hive, jive, live* (adjective, /laɪv/), *naive, ogive, recitative, revive, survive, swive, wive; alcove, cove, drove, mangrove, move, prove; gyve*) is the <e> of final <ve> part not only of that digraph but also of a split digraph with a preceding single vowel letter. In practice this makes no difference – the word-final phoneme is /v/, so this aspect hardly needs analysing.

Gontijo *et al.* (2003) do not recognise <ve> as a separate grapheme. However, word-finally and medially before final <s>, <ve> always indicates /v/ regardless of whether it is so recognised, so is 100% predictable. Only the medial occurrences in *average, deliverable, evening* ('late part of day'), *every, several, sovereign* are problematic.

In other medial occurrences and all initial occurrences <v, e> are separate graphemes, e.g. *vest, oven*. The only word in which final <v, e> are separate graphemes appears to be *agave* /əˈɡɑːviː/.

# 9.40 <w>

N.B. (1) <wh> has a separate entry.
  (2) <aw, ew, ow> have separate entries in chapter 10, sections 10.10/21/34.

**THE MAIN SYSTEM**

| Basic phoneme | /w/ | 100% | e.g. *way* |
|---|---|---|---|

**THE REST**

| | | pronounced | |
|---|---|---|---|
| Exceptions to main system | (none) | | |
| Doubled letter | <ww> | /w/ | only in *bowwow, glowworm, powwow, slowworm* |

*The grapheme-phoneme correspondences, 1* 335

| Oddity | <wr> | /r/ | only in *awry* (only non-initial example), *wrap, wrasse, wreck, wren, wrench, wrest(le), wretch(ed), wriggle, wring, wrinkle, wrist, write, wrong, Wrotham* /ˈruːtəm/, *wrought, wry* and a few more rare words. The only words in which <w, r> do not form a digraph appear to be *cowrie, dowry* |
|---|---|---|---|
| 2-phoneme graphemes | (none) | | |

## 9.41 <wh>

### THE MAIN SYSTEM

| Basic phoneme | /w/ | 80% | e.g. *what, which.* See Notes |
|---|---|---|---|

### THE REST

| | | pronounced | |
|---|---|---|---|
| Exceptions to main system | <wh> | /h/ | 20% Only in *who, whom, whose, whole, whoop(ing), whooper, whore* |
| Oddities | (none) | | |
| 2-phoneme graphemes | (none) | | |

### NOTES

The high percentage for <wh> pronounced /h/ is due to the very high frequency of *who, whose, whole,* and recognition of the few words where this correspondence obtains should not be problematic.

Where <wh> is pronounced /w/ in RP, in many Scots accents it is pronounced /ʍ/, which is the voiceless counterpart of /w/ and sounds roughly like 'hw'; but because /ʍ/ is not a phoneme of RP this correspondence is not included in my analyses.

The very few cases where <w, h> do not form a digraph are at morpheme boundaries in compound words, e.g. *sawhorse.*

## 9.42 <x>

### THE MAIN SYSTEM

Basic pronunciation    /ks/    82%    e.g. *box, next, six*

### THE REST

Doubled letter    (does not occur)

                                    pronounced

*Exceptions to main system*                                    18% in total

<x>    /z/    regular in initial position, e.g. *xylophone* (except that some people pronounce the Greek letter name *xi* as /ksaɪ/); medial only in *anxiety* pronounced /æŋˈzaɪjɪtiː/ (also pronounced /æŋˈgzaɪjɪtiː/); rare word-finally. See Notes

<x>    /k/    only in *coxswain* /ˈkɒksən/ and before <c> pronounced /s/ in a small group of words of Latin origin, namely *exceed, excel(lent), except, excerpt, excess, excise, excite*

<x>    as 2-phoneme sequence /gz/    16% Only in some polysyllabic words of Latin origin, namely *anxiety* pronounced /æŋˈgzaɪjɪtiː/ (also pronounced /æŋˈzaɪjɪtiː/), *auxiliary, exact, exaggerate, exalt, exam(ine), example, exasperate, executive, executor, exemplar, exemplify, exempt, exert, exigency, exiguous, exile* pronounced /ˈegzaɪl/ rather than /ˈeksaɪl/, *exist, exonerate, exorbitant, exordium, exotic, exuberant, exude, exult* and a few more rare words; also in *Alexandra, Alexander* and becoming frequent in *exit* /ˈegzɪt/ (also pronounced /ˈeksɪt/). See Notes

|   |   |   |   |
|---|---|---|---|
| | \<x\> | as 2-phoneme sequence /kʃ/ | 1% Only in 3 words of Latin origin: *flexure, luxury, sexual* /'flekʃə, 'lʌkʃəriː, 'sekʃ(uːw)əl/ |
| | \<x\> | as 2-phoneme sequence /gʒ/ | only in *luxuriance, luxuriant, luxuriate, luxurious* /lʌg'ʒʊəriːj-əns/ənt/eɪt/əs/ |
| | \<x\> | as 3-phoneme sequence /eks/ | only in *X-ray*, etc. One of only two 3-phoneme graphemes in the whole language |
| Oddities | (none) | | |
| 2-phoneme sequences | (in addition to the basic pronunciation and three of the exceptions to the main system) | | |
| | \<xe\> | /ks/ | only in *annexe, axe, deluxe* |
| | \<xh\> | /gz/ | only in 7 polysyllabic words of Latin origin:*exhaust(ion), exhibit, exhilarat-e/ion, exhort, exhume* |
| | \<xh\> | /ks/ | only in 3 polysyllabic derivatives of words in the previous group: *exhibition, exhortation, exhumation* |
| | \<xi\> | /kʃ/ | only in *anxious, complexion, connexion* (also spelt *connection*), *crucifixion, fluxion, (ob)noxious* |
| 3-phoneme sequence | (see above) | | |

## NOTES

In almost all words beginning \<ex-\> followed by a vowel letter, if the stress is on the initial \<e\>, the \<x\> is pronounced /ks/, but if the stress is on the next vowel the \<x\> is pronounced /gz/. The only exceptions are *exile*, which is usually pronounced /'egzaɪl/, i.e. with initial stress but irregular /gz/ (though a regularised spelling pronunciation /'eksaɪl/ is sometimes heard); *exit*, which (conversely) is usually pronounced /'eksɪt/, i.e. with initial stress and regular /ks/, but is increasingly heard as (irregular) /'egzɪt/, perhaps under the influence of *exile*; and cf. *doxology, luxation, proximity* with /ks/ despite the stress being on the following vowel. This tendency to pronounce \<x\> as /gz/ before the stressed vowel applies also to the given names *Alexandra, Alexander*, but their abbreviated forms *Alexa, Alex* have /ks/ because the stress falls earlier.

<x> pronounced /z/ occurs word-initially only in some words of Greek origin, namely *xanthine, xanthoma, xanthophyll, xenon, xenophobia* and several other words beginning *xeno-, Xerox* and several other words beginning *xero-, xylem, xylene, xylophone* and several other words beginning *xylo-*. Word-finally, the plurals of some French loanwords ending in <-eau> are sometimes spelt French-style with <x> as well as <s>, e.g. *beau-s/x, bureau-s/x, flambeau-s/x, gateau-s/x, plateau-s/x, portmanteau-s/x, trousseau-s/x;* indeed, my dictionary gives only the <x> form in *bandeaux, chateaux, rondeaux, tableaux*. In all these cases <x> is also pronounced /z/. In my opinion the <x> form is outmoded and unnecessary.

For <xo> in *inexorable* see section 6.10.

## 9.43 <z, zz>

### THE MAIN SYSTEM

| Basic phoneme | /z/ | <z> 97%, | e.g. *zoo, dazzle, jazz* |
|---|---|---|---|
| | | <zz> 97% | |

### THE REST

| | | pronounced | |
|---|---|---|---|
| Exceptions to main system | | | 3% of pronunciations of both graphemes in total |
| | <z> | /s/ | only in *blitz(krieg), chintz, ersatz, glitz, howitzer, kibbutz, kibitz, klutz, lutz, pretzel, quartz, ritz, schmaltz, schnitzel, seltzer, spritz(er), Switzerland, waltz, wurlitzer* |
| | <z> | /ʒ/ | only in *azure* pronounced /ˈæʒə, ˈeɪʒə/ (also pronounced /ˈæzj(ʊ)ə, ˈeɪzj(ʊ)ə/), *seizure* /ˈsiːʒə/ |
| | <z> | as 2-phoneme sequence /ts/ | only in *Alzheimer's, bilharzia, nazi* (but Churchill said /ˈnɑːziː/), *scherzo, schizo(-)* |
| | <zz> | as 2-phoneme sequence /ts/ | only in *intermezzo, paparazzi, pizza, pizzicato* |

| Word-final doubled letter + <e> | (does not occur) | | |
|---|---|---|---|
| Oddities | <ze> | /z/ | only word-final. In other positions <z, e> are separate graphemes, e.g. in *zest*. The only word in which final <z, e> are separate graphemes is *kamikaze* |
| | <zi> | /ʒ/ | only in *brazier, crozier, glazier* pronounced /ˈbreɪʒə, ˈkrəʊʒə, ˈgleɪʒə/ (also pronounced /ˈbreɪziːjə, ˈkrəʊziːjə, ˈgleɪziːjə/) |
| 2-phoneme sequences | (see above) | | |

**NOTE**

The spelling <zh> is also used to represent /ʒ/, but because it occurs only in transcriptions of Russian names, e.g. *Zhivago, Zhores*, I have not added it to the inventory of graphemes.

## 9.44 Some useful generalisations about graphemes beginning with consonant letters

Almost all occurrences of geminate consonant letters are pronounced identically to the single letter. (Rule 28 in Clymer, 1963/1996 expresses this as 'When two of the same consonants are side by side, only one is heard.') To experienced users of English this may seem too obvious to state, but there are known instances (see, for example, Burton, 2007: 27) of adult literacy learners saying, when this was pointed out to them, 'Why did no-one ever tell me that? I thought there must be two sounds because there are two letters, and could never work them out'. And I have witnessed an 11-year-old boy having to be taught this by his catch-up scheme tutor.

There are minor exceptions under <gg, ll, ss, zz> among main-system graphemes (and a few more under geminate consonants among the rest), but the only major set of exceptions is words with <cc> pronounced /ks/ – and even here most instances exhibit regular correspondences: the first <c>

is pronounced regularly /k/ before a consonant letter, and the second <c> is pronounced regularly /s/ before <e, i, y>, e.g. *accent, occiput, coccyx*, so that here the real irregularities are the few words with <cc> pronounced /k/ before <e, i, y>: *baccy, biccy, recce* (short for *reconnoitre*), *soccer, speccy, streptococci*, and the two words with <cc> sometimes pronounced /s/ before <i>: *flaccid, succinct* – both have more regular pronunciations with /ks/, and there seem to be no such exceptions before <e, y>. This generalisation about geminate consonant letters is a very strong rule.

The five non-geminate doubled consonant graphemes (<ck, dg, dge, tch, ve>) and three of the four digraphs with <h> as the second letter (<ph, sh, th>) have virtually no irregular pronunciations, even though <th> has two major regular ones. <ch> is the exception, with several irregular pronunciations.

In addition, the lists in this chapter reveal two useful context-sensitive patterns:

- The six main-system graphemes other than <sh> which are pronounced /ʃ/, namely <ce, ci, sci, si, ssi, ti>, are fairly easy to distinguish from occurrences of these sequences which are not pronounced /ʃ/: these graphemes occur with this pronunciation only in medial position, and then mainly between two vowel letters, though <si> always has a consonant letter between it and the preceding vowel letter, and <ci, sci> sometimes have. Also, five of these graphemes (in these contexts) have only one pronunciation. (The exception is <ti>, where a few words have /tʃ/ instead, one (*equation*) has /ʒ/, and in a few words with two occurrences of <ti> before a vowel letter (e.g. *negotiation*) there is alternation between /ʃ/ and /s/.) This pattern, unlike the next one, would be difficult to formulate as a rule, and learners need to pick it up;
- The 'soft' pronunciations of <c, g> as /s, dʒ/ occur in similar contexts to each other (before <e, i, y>), and the 'hard' pronunciations /k, g/ correspondingly elsewhere.

The latter generalisation is simple enough to be taught as a rule, but teachers need to be alert to cases where learners may over-generalise it. It never applies to <ch, tch>, and learners will find various groups of (real or apparent) exceptions (some very rare):

1) exceptions to '<c> followed by <e, i, y> is pronounced /s/':
    - (with /k/) *arced, arcing, Celt, Celtic* (but the Glasgow football team is /ˈseltɪk/), *chicer, chicest, sceptic* (in British spelling) and words

beginning *encephal-* pronounced /eŋkefəl-/ (also pronounced with /ensefəl-/)
- (with /ʃ/) *cetacean, crustacea(n), Echinacea, liquorice, ocean, siliceous* and words ending in <-aceous> pronounced /'eɪʃəs/, e.g. *cretaceous, curvaceous, herbaceous, sebaceous* and about 100 others, mostly scientific and all very rare; also *officiate, speciality, specie(s), superficiality* and sometimes *ap/de-preciate, associate*
- (with /tʃ/) only *cellist, cello, concerto*
- (with <cc> pronounced /k/) *baccy, biccy, recce* (short for *reconnoitre*), *soccer, speccy, streptococci*;

2) exceptions to '<c> is pronounced /k/ everywhere else (except before <h>)':
- (with /s/): *apercu, facade*;

3) exceptions to '<g> followed by <e, i, y> is pronounced /dʒ/':
- (a fair number with /g/ (see section 9.15), some of them high-frequency words): *gear, get, give, tiger; giggle, girl, give*
- (with other but rare pronunciations): see section 9.15;

4) exceptions to '<g> is pronounced /g/ everywhere else':
- (with /dʒ/): *gaol, margarine, Reg, veg,* and second <g> in *mortgagor*
- (with other but mostly rare pronunciations): see section 9.15
- (with <gg> pronounced /dʒ/): *arpeggio, exaggerate, loggia, Reggie, suggest, veggie, vegging.*

For practical purposes with young learners, the rule about the 'soft' and 'hard' pronunciations of <c, g> can be considered 100% reliable, though they would probably need to be taught *liquorice* and *ocean*.

Inspection of the headings of sections 9.6–43 will show that about half give the percentage of the basic pronunciation as 100%, and several others are close to that. In quite a few other cases attention to the context will combine lower percentages into something over 90% or in the upper 80%'s. The only ones in the lower 80%'s are <wh, x>. Overall the predictability of the pronunciations of main-system graphemes beginning with consonant letters is probably over 90%. The two major exceptions are medial and final <s> and word-final <se>, both of which have the two main pronunciations /s, z/, and for which few useful generalisations can be given. Even so, the pronunciations of consonant graphemes are much more predictable than those of vowel graphemes, as is obvious from chapter 10.

# 10. The grapheme-phoneme correspondences of English, 2: Graphemes beginning with vowel letters

## 10.1 The general picture: the regular pronunciations of English graphemes beginning with vowel letters

All the introductory remarks in sections 9.1-3 also apply here, with one addition. Like Carney, Gontijo *et al.* (2003) analysed a variety of RP in which /ɪ/ does occur word-finally and is mainly spelt <y>, sometimes <i, ie>. As explained in sections 5.2, 5.4.3, 5.6.4 and 5.7.2, I disagree with this analysis, and instead, like Cruttenden (2014), posit that /ɪ/ does **not** occur word-finally. This meant that, in the phoneme-grapheme direction, I took issue with Carney's percentages for correspondences for /ɪ, ɪə/, and for /iː/ dispensed with them completely. The mirror-image situation is that for <ie> (section 10.23) I was able to re-calculate Gontijo *et al.*'s percentages, but could not do so for <i, y> (sections 10.22, 10.40), which therefore have no percentages.

This chapter contains 38 main entries, one for each of the 38 main-system graphemes beginning with a vowel letter. For those graphemes, the general picture can be summed up by saying that:

- just 4 have only one pronunciation: <air eer igh ore> (except for one tiny exception under <ore>)
- 18 have only one main-system pronunciation, but varying numbers of minor correspondences which are exceptions to the main system: <a.e ai are au aw ay ea ee e.e ere ie i.e ir o.e oi ou oy ur>

- 3 have only two main-system pronunciations (and no minor ones), and those two pronunciations occur in circumstances which can be fairly closely defined: <ed ue u.e>
- 6 have only two main-system pronunciations, which occur in circumstances which can be fairly closely defined (but varying numbers of minor correspondences): <ar ear ew oo or ow>
- 7 are moderately to highly variable: <a e er i o u y>. It is uncomfortable that this category includes all six of the vowel letters as single-letter graphemes.

And the lists just given still somewhat understate the case, since there are large numbers of Oddities – see Table 10.1.

Table 10.1 is almost but not quite the mirror-image of Table 8.2 because:
- graphemes which begin with vowel letters but consonant phonemes (e.g. <u> in *union*) are included here;
- graphemes which begin with consonant letters but vowel phonemes (e.g. <ho> in *honour*) are not included here but in Table 9.4.

For completeness, it should also be noted that many minor vowel graphemes have highly predictable pronunciations, e.g. <augh>. In fact, of the 105 graphemes beginning with vowel letters that are outside the main system, only 28 <ae ah al ao ais aye eau ei eigh eir eo eu eur ey ia is oa oar oe oir ois oor ough our ua ui ure yr> have more than one pronunciation. As with the minor consonant graphemes, in any attempt (not made here) to estimate the overall regularity of the system this would need to be taken into account; and again, many minor graphemes are so rare that they would not affect the regularity calculation unless they occur in high-frequency words.

TABLE 10.1: MAIN-SYSTEM GRAPHEMES BEGINNING WITH VOWEL LETTERS, BY MAIN-SYSTEM AND MINOR CORRESPONDENCES AND NUMBERS OF ODDITIES.

| | Main system | | The rest | |
|---|---|---|---|---|
| Grapheme | Basic phoneme | Other main-system correspondences | Exceptions to main system (minor correspondences) | Number of Oddities* which the grapheme 'leads' |
| a | /æ/ | /eɪ ɑː ɒ ɔː ə/ | /e ɪ aɪ/ | 22 |
| a.e | /eɪ/ | /ɑː/ | | |
| ai | /eɪ/ | | /æ e ɪ ə aɪ/ | 4 |
| air | /eə/ | | | 1 |
| ar | /ɑː/ | /eə ɔː/ | /ə/ | |
| are | /eə/ | | /ɑː/ | 3 |
| au | /ɔː/ | | /ɒ aʊ eɪ əʊ ɑː/ | 3 |

## The grapheme-phoneme correspondences, 2 345

| | | | | | |
|---|---|---|---|---|---|
| aw | /ɔː/ | | | /ɔɪ/ | 1 |
| ay | /eɪ/ | | | /e iː/ | 4 |
| e | /e/ | /iː ɪ ə/ | | /ɒ eɪ/ | 35 |
| ea | /iː/ | | | /e eɪ/ | 5 |
| ear | /ɪə/ | /eə/ | | /ɑː ɜː/ | |
| ed | /d/ | /t/ | | | |
| ee | /iː/ | | | /eɪ ɪ uː/ | |
| e.e | /iː/ | | | /eɪ/ | |
| eer | /ɪə/ | | | | |
| er | /ɜː/ | /ɪə ə/ | | /ɑː eə eɪ/ | 2 |
| ere | /ɪə/ | | | /eə ɜː/ | |
| ew | /uː/ | /juː/ | | /əʊ/ | 1 |
| i | /ɪ/ | /iː aɪ j/ | | /æ ɒ ə/ | 7 |
| ie | /iː/ | | | /e ɪ aɪ/ | 2 |
| i.e | /aɪ/ | /iː/ | | | |
| igh | /aɪ/ | | | | |
| ir | /ɜː/ | | | /ɪə aɪ aɪə/ | 2 |
| o | /ɒ/ | /ʌ uː əʊ ə/ | | /ɪ ʊ wʌ/ | 17 |
| o.e | /əʊ/ | /uː/ | | | |
| oi | /ɔɪ/ | | | /ə wɑː/ | 6 |
| oo | /ʊ/ | /uː/ | | /ʌ əʊ/ | 3 |
| or | /ɔː/ | /ɜː/ | | /ʊ ə/ | 4 |
| ore | /ɔː/ | | | /əʊ/ | |
| ou | /aʊ/ | | | /ɒ ʌ ʊ ə əʊ uː w/ | 18 |
| ow | /aʊ/ | /əʊ/ | | /ɒ ə/ | 1 |
| oy | /ɔɪ/ | | | /aɪ/ | 1 |
| u | /ʌ/ | /w ʊ uː juː/ | | /e ɪ ə jə/ | 8 |
| ue | /uː/ | /juː/ | | | |
| u.e | /uː/ | /juː/ | | | |
| ur | /ɜː/ | | | /ə ʊə jʊə/ | 5 |
| y | /j aɪ/ | /iː ɪ/ | | /ə/ | 7 |
| **Total** | 39 | 36 | | 71 | 162 |
| | 38 | | 75 | | 233 |
| | | Grand total of correspondences: 308 | | | |

\* including 2- and 3-phoneme pronunciations which are not part of the main system.

## 10.2 Order of description

In this chapter I deal in conventional alphabetical order with 33 of the 38 main-system graphemes of English which begin with vowel letters. The other main entries cover five of the six split digraphs. Three of these come immediately after the grapheme consisting of the same two letters not split, namely <e.e, i.e, u.e> after <ee, ie, ue> respectively. However, because <ae, oe> do not, in my analysis, belong to the main system and are dealt with under <a, o>, the sections dealing with <a.e, o.e> follow the sections dealing with <a, o>. The only split digraph which does not have a main entry is <y.e>, which is not part of the main system; it is dealt with under <y>, immediately after <ye>.

In most of the 38 main entries in this chapter I list the items in this order:
1) The basic phoneme. In my opinion, each of these graphemes has a basic phoneme, the one that seems most natural as its pronunciation.
2) Any other phonemes which are frequent pronunciations of the grapheme.
   - These two categories constitute the main system for grapheme-phoneme correspondences for graphemes beginning with vowel letters. Correspondences in the main system are shown in 9-point type, the rest in smaller 7.5-point type.
3) Exceptions to the main system, including any 2- or 3-phoneme correspondences for the main grapheme. The reason for listing exceptions to the main system separately from the Oddities is that this is the clearest way of showing where the main rules break down.
4) Oddities, minor graphemes which begin with the letter(s) of the main grapheme and occur only in restricted sets of words.
5) Any 2- and 3-phoneme graphemes which include, but do not have entirely the same spelling as, the main grapheme. Almost all of these are also Oddities, but a few belong to the main system and are included there.

Most entries end with Notes; none have Tables, but <i> (section 10.22) has a flowchart.

The only exceptions to this ordering are the four graphemes which have only one pronunciation each: <air, eer, igh, ore>. Under each of these there is usually just one heading, 'Only phoneme', and it is automatically part of the main system without having to be so labelled; however, the entries for <igh, ore> have Notes.

## 10.3 <a>

N.B. <a.e, ai, air, ar, are, au, aw, ay> have separate entries.

### THE MAIN SYSTEM

For all these categories see Notes.

| | | | |
|---|---|---|---|
| Basic phoneme | /æ/ | 50% | e.g. *cat, pasty* /'pæstiː/ ('pie') |
| Other phonemes | /ə/ | 16% | e.g. *about, dynamo, opera*. Regular when unstressed in all positions, including *a, an*, but see Exceptions and Notes in this section and Notes in the next section for unstressed <a> pronounced /e, ɪ, ɒ, ɔː, aɪ, ɑː/. Also see Notes in next section for words with final <-ate> pronounced /ət/ |
| | /ɑː/ | 9% | e.g. *blasé, father* |
| | /eɪ/ | 8% | e.g. *agent, bacon, pasty* /'peɪstiː/ ('whey–faced') |
| | /ɒ/ | 8% | e.g. *squash, was, what*. Regular after <qu, w> |
| | /ɔː/ | <1% | e.g. *always, bald, tall, water*. Regular in some circumstances |

### THE REST

| | | pronounced | |
|---|---|---|---|
| Exceptions to main system | <a> | /e/ | 1% only in:<br>– *any, ate* pronounced /et/ (also pronounced /eɪt/), *many, Thames*, first <a> in *secretaria-l/t*, second <a> in *asphalt* pronounced /'æʃfelt/ (also pronounced /'æsfælt/)<br>– a few words ending <-ary> with the stress two vowels before the <a>, e.g. *necessary, secretary* pronounced /'nesəseriː, 'sekrəteriː/ (also pronounced /'nesəsriː, 'sekrətriː/ with no vowel phoneme corresponding to the <a> – for |

the elided vowels in this and the next three paragraphs, see section 6.10) – a few adverbs ending <-arily>, e.g. *militarily, necessarily, primarily, voluntarily* pronounced /mɪlɪˈterɪliː, nesəˈserɪliː, praɪˈmerɪliː, vɒlənˈterɪliː/ with the <a> stressed (also pronounced /ˈmɪlɪtrəliː, ˈnesəsrəliː, ˈpraɪmrəliː, ˈvɒləntrəliː/ with stress shifted two vowels forward, again no vowel phoneme corresponding to the <a>, and the vowel before /liː/ changed from /ɪ/ to /ə/)
– *temporary* pronounced /ˈtempəreriː/ (also pronounced /ˈtemprəriː/ with no vowel phoneme corresponding to the <o>)
– *temporarily* pronounced /tempəˈrerɪliː/ (also pronounced either /tempəˈreərɪliː/ with <ar> pronounced /eə/ and the <r> also a grapheme in its own right pronounced /r/ – for dual-functioning see section 7.1 – or reduced to three syllables as /ˈtemprəliː/ with no vowel phonemes corresponding to the <o> or the <a> and the two /r/ phonemes reduced to one)

|          |        |       |                                                                                                                                                                                                                                                                                                                                          |
|----------|--------|-------|--------------------------------------------------------------------------------------------------------------------------------------------------------------------------------------------------------------------------------------------------------------------------------------------------------------------------------------------|
|          | <a>    | /ɪ/   | 1% only unstressed but in about 250 words ending in <-age>, which is mainly pronounced /ɪdʒ/, e.g. *village*, plus *furnace, menace, necklace, octave, orange, signature, surface, spinach* pronounced /ˈspɪnɪdʒ/ and second <a> in *character, palace*. For words where the ending <-age> is pronounced /eɪ, ɑːʒ/ see <a.e>, section 10.4 |
|          | <a>    | /aɪ/  | only in *majolica* pronounced /maɪˈjɒlɪkə/ (also pronounced /məˈdʒɒlɪkə/), *naif, naïve, papaya*                                                                                                                                                                                                                                            |
| Oddities | <aa>   | /ɑː/  | only in *baa, Baal, Graal, kraal, laager, naan, salaam*                                                                                                                                                                                                                                                                                    |
|          | <aar>  | /ɑː/  | only in *aardvark, aardwolf, bazaar, haar*                                                                                                                                                                                                                                                                                                 |
|          | <ach>  | /ɒ/   | only in *yacht*                                                                                                                                                                                                                                                                                                                            |
|          | <ae>   | /iː/  | is the usual correspondence, e.g. *aegis, aeon, aesthetic, algae, alumnae, antennae, archaeology, Caesar(ian), caesura, mediaeval, pupae, vertebrae*. For exceptions see next 3 rows                                                                                                                                                       |
|          | <ae>   | /e/   | only in *haemorrhage, haemorrhoid*                                                                                                                                                                                                                                                                                                         |

| | | |
|---|---|---|
| <ae> | /eɪ/ | only in *brae, Gaelic, maelstrom, reggae, sundae* |
| <ae> | /aɪ/ | only in *maestro, minutiae* |
| <aer> | /eə/ | only in *faerie* and compounds of *air* spelt <aer>, e.g. *aerial*. The <r> is also a grapheme in its own right pronounced /r/. For dual-functioning see section 7.1 |
| <ah> | /ə/ | only word-final and only in *ayah, cheetah, fellah, haggadah, Hannah, hallelujah, loofah, messiah, moolah, mullah, mynah, pariah, purdah, (maha)rajah, Sarah, savannah, verandah, wallah* and some other very rare words |
| <ah> | /ɑː/ | only word-final and only in *ah, bah, hookah, hoorah, kabbalah, Shah, whydah* |
| <ah> | /eɪ/ | only in *dahlia* |
| <al> | /ɑː/ | only in *calf, half; calve(s), halve(s), salve(s)* (also pronounced /sælv(z)/); *almond, almoner, alms, balm, calm, embalm, malmsey, napalm, palm, psalm, qualm* |
| <al> | /ɔː/ | only in *balk, calk, chalk, stalk, talk, walk*. See also <aul> under <au>, section 10.9 |
| <al> | /æ/ | only in *salmon* |
| <alf> | /eɪ/ | only in *halfpence, halfpenny* |
| <anc> | /ə/ | only in *blancmange* /bləˈmɒndʒ/ |
| <ao> | /eɪ/ | only in *gaol* |
| <ao> | /eə/ | only in *aorist* |
| <aoh> | /əʊ/ | only in *pharaoh* |
| <aow> | /aʊ/ | only in *miaow* |
| <as> | /ɑː/ | only in *fracas* |
| <at> | /ɑː/ | only in *eclat, entrechat, nougat* |
| 2-phoneme graphemes | (none) | |

## NOTES

For instances of <a> as an elided vowel see section 6.10.

\<a\> is the least predictable of the single-letter vowel graphemes. Its default pronunciation as a single-letter grapheme is /æ/, which occurs in many uncategorisable circumstances, but here are a few categories for guidance:
- regular before geminate and doubled consonant spellings, e.g. *flabbergasted* (first \<a\>), *back, cackle, add, addled, badge, badger, chaffinch, gaff, gaggle, ammo, annual, banns, apple, Lapp, arrow, classic(al), lass, match, satchel, battle, matt, jazz*, plus \<cc\> when the two letters are pronounced separately, e.g. *accent*. Extension: *gaffe*. Exceptions (in RP): *chaff, distaff, staff* and most words with final \<-ass\>, but this is a small set, namely *brass, class, glass, grass, pass*, with /ɑː/ (and there are four sub-exceptions with regular /æ/: *ass, bass* ('fish'), *lass, mass* and one, bizarrely, with /eɪ/: *bass* /beɪs/ '(player of) large stringed instrument'/'(singer with) low-pitched voice'), most words with final \<-all\> (see below), e.g. *all*, with /ɔː/ (sub-exceptions: *mall, shall* with regular /æ/), and several words with preceding \<w\>, namely *swaddle, swallow, twaddle, waddle, waddy, waffle, wallet, wallop, wallow, wally, wannabe, warrant, warren, warrigal, warrior, wassail, wattle*, plus *quaff, quagga* (also pronounced with /æ/), *quarrel, quarry, scallop, squabble*, all with /ɒ/
- regular in other words where \<a\> is the only or last vowel letter and is followed by at least one consonant letter (i.e. those without a geminate or doubled consonant spelling), e.g. *asphalt* pronounced /ˈæsfælt/ (also pronounced /ˈæʃfelt/), *bad, balderdash, bombast, cat, detract, gymnast, impact, lambast, pant*. Exceptions: see those with /ɑː, ɔː/ below
- in some words with \<a\> as the penultimate vowel letter followed by two or more consonant letters (or \<x\> and word-final \<e\>), other than those with \<-a.e\> pronounced /eɪ, ɑː/ (see the next section) and the long list of those with /ɑː/ (see below), e.g. *axe, collapse, flange*
- as the vowel letter before a consonant letter or cluster and the endings \<-ic(al)\>, e.g. *asthmatic, classic(al), drastic, dynastic, elastic, heraldic, mastic, peristaltic, plastic, spastic* (only exception: *aphasic*, with /eɪ/). The stress always falls on the relevant \<a\> except in *Árabic, lúnatic*, which are different from almost all other words in \<-aCic\> both in having the stress on the vowel two before the \<-ic\> and in having the \<a\> before the \<ic\> ending pronounced /ə/. There are also two relevant words with variant pronunciations: *(fly) agaric* /əˈgærɪk/

(regular) or /ˈægərɪk/ (exception), *chivalric* /ʃɪˈvælrɪk/ (regular) or /ˈʃɪvəlrɪk/ (exception); on *chivalric* the Oxford English Dictionary says 'The first pronunciation is that sanctioned by the poets'
- in some other words when <a> is at least the penultimate vowel letter (or, if the word-final letter is <e>, at least the antepenultimate vowel letter) and is followed by more than one consonant letter, e.g. *alto, altitude, altruism, bastion, chastise, formaldehyde, gasket, gather, mastiff, mastoid, pastel, pastern, pastille, pasty* ('pie'), *satchel,* and first <a> in *advantageous, asthmatic, asphalt* whether pronounced /ˈæsfælt/ or /ˈæʃfelt/, *bastinado, cantata, cascara, fantasia, maltreat, mascara*
- in a further ragbag of non-final occurrences, e.g. *acid, chariot, companion, habit, lavish, manioc, parish, patio, piano, placid, ration, vanish*; (first <a>) *avalanche, avocado, balaclava, basalt, caviar, marijuana, national, panorama, (ir)rational, valiant*; (first and second <a>'s) *alpaca*; (second <a>) *battalion*.

The task then is to define the circumstances in which <a> has other pronunciations. These can be summarised as follows.

For <a> pronounced /ɑː/ in RP (where it is much more frequent than in most other accents of English) Carney (1994: 291-4) gives a set of five rules, all of which have special conditions and exceptions. Instead, here is a set of categories with lists of examples (but with exceptions only for one category; for others they would be too numerous to list):
- word-finally: only in *bra, ma, pa, schwa, spa; grandma, grandpa, hoopla, mama, papa*
- often when <a> is the penultimate vowel letter and there is at least one earlier vowel letter in the word separated from it by at least one consonant letter and the relevant <a> is followed by a single consonant letter followed by word-final <a, i, o>: *armada, avocado, balaclava, banana, bastinado, cantata, cascara, cassava, cicada, cinerama, cyclorama, desiderata, desperado, farrago, Gestapo, gymkhana, iguana, incommunicado, karate, legato, liana, literati, marijuana, mascara, meccano, pajama, palaver, panorama, pastrami, pyjama, safari, salami, schemata, sonata, soprano, staccato, stigmata, sultana, svengali, tiara, toccata, tomato, tsunami, virago*. Extensions (1) with 'pronounced' final <e>: *biennale, blase, finale, karate, macrame* (contrast *sesame*, with /ə/); (2) a few words with no earlier vowel letter: *drama, gala, guano, guava* (in these two words <u> is a consonant

letter), *khaki, lager, lama, lava, llama, nazi, plaza, pro rata, saga, strata.* Exceptions: *alpaca, piano* with /æ/; *dado, data, halo, lumbago, potato, sago, tornado, volcano* with /eɪ/

- often before two consonant letters in words where <a> is the only vowel letter or the word-final letter is <e>: *chaff, staff, aft, craft, graft, haft, raft, shaft; hajj; chance, dance, glance, lance, prance, trance; blanch, branch, ranch; can't, chant, grant, plant, shan't, slant; graph; ask, bask, cask, flask, mask, task; clasp, gasp, grasp, hasp, rasp; basque, casque, masque; brass, class, glass, grass, pass; blast, cast, caste, fast, last, mast, vast; bath, lath* (also pronounced with /æ/), *path,* plus *tranche* with three consonant letters; probably none of these words would be pronounced with /ɑː/ in any accent other than RP
- in all the unsuffixed compounds of *graph: auto/cardio/choreo/di/ encephalo/epi/mimeo/para/photo/quad/tele/tri-graph,* where *-graph* is always unstressed; again, probably none of these words would be pronounced with /ɑː/ in any accent other than RP
- often before two or three consonant letters in words not covered in previous categories: *macabre; debacle; cadre, padre; distaff, giraffe; abaft, after, rafter; example, sample; advance, chancel, chancery, enhance; avalanche, revanchis-m/t; command, commando, countermand, demand, remand, slander; rascal* (first <a>); *answer; basket, bergomask, casket; aghast, caster, castle, castor, contrast* (verb and noun), *disaster, fasten, flabbergasted* (second <a>), *ghastly, master, nasty, pasta* (also pronounced with /æ/), *pasteurised, pastime, pastor, pasture, plaster; father, lather* (also pronounced with /æ/), *rather; latte.* Unstressed only in *distaff, avalanche, contrast* (/ˈkɒntrɑːst/, noun), *flabbergasted.* In this category, the first 4 words would probably be pronounced with /ɑː/ in all accents, the rest only in RP
- otherwise only in *amen* pronounced /ɑːˈmen/ (also pronounced /eɪˈmen/), *banal* (second <a>), *corral, praline, raj.*

(For <a.e> pronounced /ɑː/ see the next section).

<a> is pronounced /ɒ/ mainly after <qu, w> and only in the following groups of words:

- after <qu>, e.g. *quad* and all its derivatives, *quadrille, quaff, quag(mire)* (also pronounced /ˈkwæg(-)/), *quagga* (also pronounced /ˈkwægə/), *qualify* and all its derivatives and associates, *(e)quality, quandary, quant* and all its derivatives, *quarantine, quarrel, quarry, quash, quatrain, squab(ble), squad* and derivatives, *squal-id/or, squander, squash, squat.* Unstressed only in *quadrille.* Only exception, strictly speaking: *squall*, with /ɔː/. However, there are also fairly large sets of apparent exceptions which contain the <ar> digraph or the <are> trigraph – see sections 10.7–8

- after <w>, e.g. *swab, swaddle, swallow, swamp, swan, swap, swash(buckling), swastika, swat, swatch, twaddle, wad, waddle, waddy, wadi, waffle, waft* pronounced /wɒft/ (also pronounced /wɔːft/), *wallet, wallop, wallow, wally, walrus* pronounced /ˈwɒlrəs/ (also pronounced /ˈwɔːlrəs/), *wampum, wan, wand, wander, wannabe, want, wanton, warrant, warren, warrigal, warrior, was, wash, wasp, wassail, wast, watch, watt, wattle*; in all these words the <a> is stressed. Only exceptions, strictly speaking: *walk* (where <al> is in any case a digraph), *wall, water,* all with /ɔː/ – but see again the last sentence of the previous paragraph

- otherwise, only in *ambience, bandeau, bouffant, chanterelle, confidant(e), debutante, fiance(e), flambe, flambeau, insouciance, mange-tout, moustache* (now mostly pronounced with /ɑː/ in RP), *nuance, scallop, séance, wrath* pronounced /rɒθ/ (also pronounced /rɔːθ/), *what,* first <a> in *jalap, stalwart,* second <a> in *blancmange, diamante*; unstressed only in *bouffant, confidant(e), debutante, insouciance, nuance, seance.*

For a teaching rule based on the words with <qu, w, wh> followed by <a> see section 11.5.

<a> is pronounced /ɔː/:

1) in <al-> word-initially when it is a prefix reduced from *all: albeit, almighty, almost, already, although, altogether, always* and even in the mistaken spelling *ˣalright.* All unstressed except *almost, always*
2) before <ld, lt>: *alder, alderman, bald, balderdash, baldric, scald, thraldom* (also spelt *thralldom*), *altar, alter, alternate* (both pronunciations and meanings – see the next section), *although* (again), *altogether* (again), *balti, basalt, cobalt, exalt, falter, halt, halter, malt, paltry, salt*; unstressed only in *alternate* pronounced /ɔːlˈtɜːnət/ ('every other'), *although, altogether, basalt, cobalt.* Exceptions: *formaldehyde, heraldic, alto, altitude, altruism, maltreat, peristaltic* with /æ/; *asphalt* whether pronounced /ˈæsfælt/ or /ˈæʃfelt/; *contralto* with /ɑː/; *emerald, herald, ribald, loyalty, penalty, royalty, subaltern* with /ə/

3) before word-final <-ll>: *all, ball, call, fall, gall, hall, pall, small, squall, (in)stall, tall, thrall, wall* (but *mall, shall* have /æ/; *hallo*, though the <a> is not word-final, is the only other example of <a> before <ll> pronounced /æ/ (sometimes: the pronunciation of this word varies between /hæˈləʊ, heˈləʊ/ and /həˈləʊ/); and in *installation* the shifting of the stress because of the suffix reduces the <a> to /ə/, which is also the pronunciation of unstressed <a> before <ll> in, e.g., *balloon*). The <-all> pronounced /ɔːl/ group is one of only five cases where the pronunciation of a phonogram/rime is more predictable as a unit than from the correspondences of the separate graphemes, and there are enough instances to make the rule worth teaching; see section A.7 in Appendix A

4) otherwise only in *appal* (second <a>), *balsam* (first <a>), *falcon, enthral, instalment, palfrey, water*; also *waft, walrus, wrath* pronounced /wɔːft, ˈwɔːlrəs, rɔːθ/ (also pronounced /wɒft, ˈwɒlrəs, rɒθ/); in all these words the relevant <a> is stressed.

See also <al> pronounced /ɔː/ in the Oddities above, and <aul> under <au>, section 10.9.

<a> (as distinct from <a.e> - see next section) is pronounced /eɪ/ in just one word where it is the only vowel letter, namely *bass* /beɪs/ '(player of) large stringed instrument'/'(singer with) low-pitched voice'), and in four categories of longer words where a rule can be stated, plus a ragbag category where any rules would be too complex to be worth stating. <a> is pronounced /eɪ/ in:

1) large numbers of words where <-e> has been deleted before a suffix beginning with a vowel letter, e.g. *creation, navigating* - see sections 6.3 and especially 6.4. Exception: *orator* /ˈɒrətə/, where stress has shifted from *orate* /ɔːˈreɪt/

2) large numbers of words where <a> is followed by a single consonant letter other than <r> and then by:

- any of <ea, eou, ia, io, iou, iu> followed word-finally by a single consonant letter or none, e.g. *azalea; advantageous, cretaceous, herbaceous, instantaneous, subcutaneous; alias, facial, fantasia, regalia, labial, mania(c), palatial, racial; contagion, equation, evasion, invasion, occasion* and hundreds more ending in <-asion>, *nation* and thousands more ending in <-ation>, *radio, ratio; pugnacious; gymnasium, stadium, uranium*

- (<-ien-ce/t>, e.g. *patience; gradient, patient, salient*. Extension with two intervening consonant letters: *ancient*.

Exceptions: *battalion, caviar, chariot, companion, manioc, patio, ration, valiant*, plus *national*, which is a derivative of a word which obeys the rule, and *(ir)rational*, which are derivatives of a word which does not; all these words have /æ/.

In all these words (including the exceptions) the stress falls on the relevant <a>

3) a small group of words (and derivatives) where <a> is followed by a consonant letter and then <le, re>, e.g. *(dis/en-)able, cable, fable, gable, sable, (un)stable, table; cradle, ladle; maple, staple; sabre; acre, nacre* (but not *cadre, padre*, which have /ɑː/). Again, in all these words (including the exceptions) the stress falls on the <a>

4) almost all words in the ending <-ator>. Only exceptions: *consérvator, conspírator, órator, prédator, sénator*, which all have <a> pronounced /ə/ and stress on the vowel before that. All other words ending in <-ator> have the stress on the <a> if they have only one earlier vowel letter, e.g. *creátor, curátor, dictátor, spectátor*, otherwise on the vowel two before the <a>, e.g. *admínistrator, ágitator, áviator, cálculator, cómmentator, ínsulator*

5) in the following uncategorisable words: *aorta, apron, bacon, basal, bathos, blatant, blazon, cadence, canine, capon, chao-s/tic, fatal, favour, flavour, fragran-ce/t, kaolin, labour, lady, latent, mason, matron, nadir, nasal, natron, naval, pagan, papal, pastry, patent* ('obvious'; the word of the same spelling meaning 'registered design' can be pronounced with /eɪ/ or /æ/), *pathos, patron, planar, saline, savour, scalar, status, tapir, vacant, vagrant, vapour, wastrel*; (first <a>) *papacy, vacancy, vagary, vagrancy, wastrel*; also *creative, dative, native* – in all other adjectives ending <-ative> the <a> is unstressed and pronounced /ə/. The <a> is stressed in all these words except *aórta, chaótic*.

<a> is pronounced /ə/ only when unstressed. Even though this is the predominant pronunciation in unstressed syllables (which in any case cannot be deduced from the written forms of words – see section A.10 in Appendix A), virtually the only rule that can be given for where /ə/ occurs is that given in the second paragraph of these examples:

- word-initially: *abaft, about, advance, aghast, ago, appal, arrange, askance, askew, awry, azalea*
- medially in the endings <-able (in words where there is at least one earlier vowel letter), -al, -ance, -ancy, -ant, -ative, -iary>, e.g. *biddable, liable, syllable, valuable; actual, facial, fatal, labial, nasal, national, naval, normal, palatial, papal, (ir)rational, visual*;

- blatant, fragran-ce/t, vacan-cy/t, vagran-cy/t, valiant; causative, laxative, palliative (only exceptions: creative, dative, native – see just above); apiary, auxiliary, aviary, breviary, domiciliary, intermediary, pecuniary, stipendiary, subsidiary, topiary
- medially in some words ending in <-ate> – see next section
- medially also in thousands of unclassifiable words, e.g. archipelago, balloon, breakfast, buffalo, conservator, conspirator, dynamo, emerald, herald, loyalty, lunatic, orator, papa, penalty, predator, ribald, royalty, senator, subaltern; first <a> in battalion, blancmange, encephalogram, instantaneous, palatial; second <a> in alias, Arabic, avalanche, balaclava, ballast, balsam, damask, pagan, papacy, paragraph, vagary
- word-finally: aorta, armada, aroma, azalea, balaclava, banana, bravura, cantata, cascara, cassava, cicada, cinerama, cyclorama, data, desiderata, drama, fantasia, gala, guava, gymkhana, hosta, iguana, lama, lava, liana, llama, marijuana, mania, mascara, opera, pajama, panorama, pasta, plaza, pro rata, pyjama, regalia, saga, schemata, sonata, stigmata, strata, sultana, tiara, toccata.

# 10.4 <a.e>

Occurs only where the <e> is word-final.

See Notes for all categories and for how this split digraph is defined, and see section 11.4 for a teaching rule relevant to all split digraphs except <y.e>.

## THE MAIN SYSTEM

| Basic phoneme | /eɪ/ | 68% | regular in words where <a> is the only vowel letter other than the word-final <e>), e.g. make, take; in longer words, only in compounds plus assuage, engage, rampage |
|---|---|---|---|
| Other phoneme | /ɑː/ | 32% | only in about 40 mostly French loanwords, e.g. charade, mirage |

## THE REST

| Exceptions to main system | strictly speaking, none, but see Notes |
|---|---|
| Oddities | (none) |
| 2-phoneme graphemes | (none) |

## NOTES

The split digraph <a.e> is defined as covering words where word-final <e> is separated from the <a> by one consonant letter other than <r, w, x, y> and the <a> is not preceded by a vowel letter and the digraph is pronounced either /eɪ/ or /ɑː/. The definition covers both words where the intervening consonant letter is an independent grapheme and words where the <e> is also part of a consonant digraph <ce, ge, ve> – see sections 3.7.4, 3.7.6-7 and 3.8.4, and section 7.1 for dual-functioning.

The familiar /eɪ/ pronunciation occurs in many hundreds of words and does not need further illustration. The /ɑː/ pronunciation occurs only in about 40 (mostly French) loanwords; those which fit the main definition just given (for extensions see below) are *aubade, ballade, charade, chorale, façade, grave* (/grɑːv/, 'French accent'), *locale, morale, pavane, promenade* (noun, 'seafront path'; the verb with the same spelling, 'walk at leisure', is pronounced with /eɪ/), *rationale, rodomontade, roulade, soutane, strafe, suave* (where the <u> is a consonant letter), *timbale, vase*, plus a set of words ending in <-age> pronounced /ɑːʒ/, namely *badinage, barrage, camouflage, collage, corsage, decalage, décolletage, dressage, entourage, espionage, fuselage, garage* pronounced /ˈgæraːʒ/, *massage, menage, mirage, montage, triage, sabotage*.

The definition needs the following extensions:
- eight words in which two consonant letters forming a consonant digraph separate <a.e>: *ache, bathe, champagne, lathe, unscathed* (the free form *scathe meaning 'to harm' does not occur, but underlies both *unscathed* and *scathing*), *swathe* with /eɪ/, *gouache, moustache* with /ɑː/ (contrast *attache*, where the <a> is pronounced /æ/ and the <e> is a separate grapheme pronounced /eɪ/ and is increasingly written within English text as <é>; also contrast *cache, panache*, where the <a> is again pronounced /æ/, and <che> is a trigraph pronounced /ʃ/)
- five words in which <gu, qu> forming consonant digraphs separate <a.e>: *opaque, plague, vague* with /eɪ/, *claque, plaque* with /ɑː/
- eight words ending in <-ange> pronounced /eɪndʒ/ (i.e. <n, g> do **not** form a digraph): *arrange, (ex)change, grange, mange, range, (e)strange* (contrast the only other three words ending <-ange>, all with <e> as part of digraph <ge> pronounced /dʒ/ and <a> as a separate grapheme with varying pronunciations: *blancmange* with /ɒ/, *flange* with /æ/, *orange* with /ɪ/). Note that in the words with <-ange> pronounced /eɪndʒ/ the <e> is not only part of digraph <a.e> but also

forms part of digraph <ge> pronounced /dʒ/ – for dual-functioning see section 7.1
- seven words ending in <-aste> pronounced /eɪst/: *baste, chaste, haste, lambaste, paste, taste, waste*, and one with <-aste> pronounced /ɑːst/: *caste*.

For an attempt to justify this definition despite its circularity and fuzzy edges see Appendix A, section A.6.

In all cases where the <e> is not the last letter in the stem word, <a, e> with an intervening letter(s) are separate graphemes. This is also true of all words with <a> and word-final <e> separated by more than one consonant letter or by a consonant digraph, except the 29 words listed above.

Where <a> and word-final <e> are separated by just one consonant letter and the <a> is preceded by a consonant letter, the position is more complicated. Many such words **look** as if the <a, e> should constitute a split digraph – but they do not, according to my definition, because the vowel phoneme preceding the stem/final consonant phoneme is neither /eɪ/ nor /ɑː/. However, guidance is still needed on when words of this sort do not have either of the split digraph pronunciations, especially since there are pairs of words with identical spelling of which one does have <a.e> pronounced /eɪ/ and the other does not.

There are two groups of words in which unstressed <a> before stem-final <te> is not part of a digraph <a.e> pronounced /eɪ/ and is instead pronounced /ə/:
- at least 60 words (all nouns/adjectives) where this is the only pronunciation, e.g. *accurate, adequate, agate, appellate, celibate, chocolate, climate, collegiate, conglomerate, (in)considerate, consulate, consummate, delicate, desperate, (in)determinate, directorate, disconsolate, doctorate, electorate, episcopate, extortionate, fortunate, illegitimate, immaculate, immediate, inanimate, incarnate, in(sub)ordinate, inspectorate, intricate, inviolate, (bacca)laureate, legate, (il)literate, magistrate, novitiate, obdurate, palate, particulate, (com/dis)passionate, private, profligate, proletariate, (dis)proportionate, protectorate, proximate, roseate, senate, surrogate, (in)temperate, triumvirate, ultimate, (in)vertebrate*
- a further set of about 30 nouns/adjectives with final <-ate> pronounced /ət/ where the verbs with the same spelling have <-ate> pronounced /eɪt/, e.g. *advocate, affiliate, aggregate, alternate* (here with also a difference in stress and vowel pattern: noun/adjective

pronounced /ɔːlˈtɜːnət/, verb pronounced /ˈɔːltəneɪt/), *animate, appropriate, approximate, articulate, associate, certificate, coordinate, curate* (here with also a difference in meaning and stress: noun ('junior cleric') pronounced /ˈkjʊərət/, verb ('mount an exhibition') pronounced /kjʊəˈreɪt/), *degenerate, delegate, deliberate* (here with also a difference in syllable structure: adjective /dɪˈlɪbrət/ with three syllables and an elided vowel – see section 6.10; verb /dɪˈlɪbəreɪt/ with four syllables), *designate, desolate, duplicate, elaborate, estimate, expatriate, graduate, initiate, intimate, legitimate, moderate, pontificate* (here with unrelated (?) meanings: noun ('pope's reign') pronounced /pɒnˈtɪfɪkət/, verb ('speak pompously') pronounced /pɒnˈtɪfɪkeɪt/), *predicate, separate* (here too with a difference in syllable structure: adjective /ˈseprət/ with two syllables and an elided vowel – see section 6.10; verb /ˈsepəreɪt/ with three syllables), *subordinate, syndicate, triplicate*

There is no rule by which the words with <-ate> pronounced /ət/ can be distinguished from those with <-ate> pronounced /eɪt/ – they just have to be learnt. Where <-ate> is pronounced /ət/ the <e> is phonographically redundant.

There are hundreds of English words ending <-age>. In words where <a> is the only vowel letter) and their derivatives, e.g. *enrage, interstage*, plus *assuage, engage, rampage*, <a.e> is a digraph with the regular pronunciation /eɪ/. But in longer stem words (except the three just listed) <-age> is pronounced either /ɑːʒ/ or /ɪdʒ/:

- for the 18 words with /ɑːʒ/ (therefore containing the minority digraph pronunciation), see the the list above
- by far the most frequent pronunciation of stem-final <-age> in words with at least one earlier vowel letter before the <a>, e.g. *garage* pronounced /ˈɡærɪdʒ/, *image, mortgage, village* and about 250 other words) is therefore /ɪdʒ/. Here <a, e> do not form a digraph; <a> is a single-letter grapheme pronounced (peculiarly) /ɪ/ – see the previous section – and the <e> forms a digraph with the <g>. Again, there is no rule by which the other two groups of longer words ending <-age> (stressed pronounced /eɪdʒ/, stressed or unstressed pronounced /ɑːʒ/) can be distinguished from this group – they just have to be learnt.

An oddity here is the word *garage* with its two pronunciations (in RP), the more French-like /ˈɡærɑːʒ/ and anglicised /ˈɡærɪdʒ/ (see section A.6 in Appendix A).

Then there are just 14 words with <a> preceded by a consonant letter and separated from word-final <e> by one consonant letter in which the <e> is a separate grapheme pronounced /iː/ or /eɪ/ or sometimes either, namely six French loanwords increasingly spelt in English text with French <é>: *blase, cafe, canape, glace, macrame, pate* ('paste'), plus *agape* (/ˈægəpeɪ/, 'love feast' (from Greek), as opposed to /əˈgeɪp/, 'open-mouthed'), *biennale, curare, finale, kamikaze, karate, sesame, tamale.*

The only other exceptions to the rule that <-a.e> (with one intervening consonant letter) is a digraph are: *ate*, which is often pronounced /et/ rather than /eɪt/, *have* whether pronounced /hæv/ (stressed) or /əv/ (unstressed), and *furnace, menace, necklace, palace, pinnace, preface, solace, surface, terrace, carafe, gunwale, carcase, purchase, octave* with <-ace, -afe, -ale, -ase, -ave> pronounced variously /ɪs, æf, əl, əs, ɪv/.

# 10.5 <ai>

N.B. <air> has a separate entry. For the dual percentages see Notes.

**THE MAIN SYSTEM**

Basic phoneme   /eɪ/   43%/79%   e.g. *paint*

**THE REST**

|  |  | pronounced |  |
|---|---|---|---|
| Exceptions to main system | <ai> | /e/ | 46%/<1% only in *bouillabaisse, said, saith* and (usually, nowadays) *again(st)*. See Notes |
|  | <ai> | /ɪ/ | 8%/14% only in *bargain, captain, chamberlain, chaplain, fountain, mountain, porcelain* |
|  | <ai> | /ə/ | 4%/7% only in *certain, chieftain, coxswain, curtain, mainsail* (second <ai>), *topsail, villain* |
|  | <ai> | /æ/ | <1% only in *Laing, plaid, plait* |
|  | <ai> | /aɪ/ | <1% only in *ailuro-phile/phobe, assegai, balalaika, banzai, bonsai, caravanserai, Kaiser, naiad, samurai, shanghai* |

| Oddities | <aigh> | /eɪ/ | only in *straight* |
|---|---|---|---|
| | <ais> | /aɪ/ | only in *aisle* |
| | <ais> | /eɪ/ | only in *palais* |
| | <ait> | /eɪ/ | only in *distrait*, *parfait*, and *trait* pronounced /treɪ/ (also pronounced /treɪt/) |
| 2-phoneme graphemes | (none) | | |

## NOTES

Where two percentages are shown above, the first is that given by Gontijo *et al.* Among these, the percentage for <ai> pronounced /e/ has been completely distorted by the high frequency of *again*, *said*. I have therefore not promoted this correspondence to the main system, but I have re-calculated all the percentages for this grapheme omitting those two words. Where they differ from the originals, the revised percentages are shown second.

<a, i> are separate graphemes (with automatic intervening /j/-glide) in *algebraic, apotropaic, archaic, dais, formulaic, laity, mosaic, prosaic,* etc.

# 10.6 <air>

### THE MAIN SYSTEM

| Only phoneme | /eə/ | 100% | e.g. *pair*. Always stressed except in *corsair* (usually), *millionairess* (always), *mohair* (always) |
|---|---|---|---|

### THE REST

| | | pronounced | |
|---|---|---|---|
| Oddity | <aire> | /eə/ | only word-final and only in a few polysyllabic words of mainly French origin, namely *affaire, commissionaire, concessionaire, doctrinaire, laissez-faire, legionnaire, millionaire, questionnaire, secretaire, solitaire.* /r/-linking occurs in *millionairess* – see section 3.6 |

## 10.7 &lt;ar&gt;

N.B. &lt;are&gt; has a separate entry.

### THE MAIN SYSTEM

| | | | |
|---|---|---|---|
| Basic phoneme | /ɑː/ | 78% | regular in words where &lt;a&gt; is the only vowel letter (only exceptions: monosyllables in next paragraph); in longer words, regular before a consonant letter when stressed, e.g. *farther* (exceptions: see both paragraphs of Notes); also word-finally when stressed, e.g. *ajar, cigar, guitar, hussar* |
| Other phonemes | /ɔː/ | 8% | only in *athwart, award, dwar-f/ves, quark* pronounced /kwɔːk/ (also pronounced /kwɑːk/), *quart(an/er/ et/ic/ ile/z), reward, sward, swarf, swarm, swart, swarthy, thwart, towards, untoward, war, warble, ward, warden, warfarin, warlock, warm, warn, warp, wart, whar-f/ves* |
| | /eə/ | &lt;1% | initially, only in *area, Aries*; never word-final. Regular medially before a vowel letter other than word-final &lt;e&gt;, especially where &lt;-e&gt; has been deleted before a suffix beginning with a vowel letter, e.g. *caring*, but there are also independent examples, e.g. *parent* – see Note. Before a consonant letter, only in *scarce, scarcity* |

### THE REST

| | | pronounced | |
|---|---|---|---|
| Exception to main system | &lt;ar&gt; | /ə/ | 14% does not occur initially; medially, regular in the suffixes /-wəd(z)/ spelt &lt;-ward(s)&gt;, e.g. *afterwards, backward(s), downward(s),* |

*forward(s), forward, inward, leeward, onward, outward, windward* (exceptions: *towards, untoward* – see last but one paragraph); word-finally, regular when unstressed, e.g. *altar, peculiar, sugar* (exceptions: *antimacassar, ashlar, attar, avatar, cougar, dinar, lazar, samovar, sitar*). Otherwise only medial and only in an unpredictable ragbag of words, e.g. *anarchy, awkward, bastard, billiards, bombardier, bulwark, coward, custard, dotard, gabardine, halyard, innards, lanyard, monarch, mustard, scabbard, stalwart, steward, vineyard, wizard*

Oddities　　　(none)

2-phoneme　　(none)
graphemes

## NOTES

<ar> is always a digraph in the following circumstances (some of which overlap):
- word-finally, e.g. *car, cigar, war*;
- in words where <a> is the only vowel letter other than word-final <e>), e.g. *car, cart, scarce*;
- when the next letter is a consonant, e.g. *cart, carton, scarce, scarcity*;
- when the <e> of word-final <-are> has been deleted before a suffix beginning with a vowel letter, e.g. *caring* (though in these cases the <r> also functions as a grapheme in its own right – see section 7.1). But where the next letter is a vowel that is not part of a suffix, <ar> appears to be a digraph only in *adversarial, Aquarius, area, Aries, barium, commissariat, garish, gregarious, hilarious, malaria(l), multifarious, nefarious, parent, precarious, proletariat, Sagittarius, variegated, various, vary,* and a fairly large set of nouns/adjectives in <-arian>, e.g. *agrarian, barbarian* (2$^{nd}$ <ar>), *centenarian* and other age terms, *egalitarian, grammarian, librarian, proletarian, utilitarian, vegetarian*. In all these cases the <r> is both part of the digraph <ar> pronounced /eə/ and a grapheme in its own right pronounced /r/. For dual-functioning see section 7.1. Otherwise <a, r> are separate graphemes, e.g. *Arab, lariat, larynx, pharynx, scarab, scarify, variety*.

A few words have alternative pronunciations where one requires analysing <ar> as a digraph but the other does not, e.g. *secretariat*, where the first <a> and second <r> can be pronounced either /eər/ (with <ar> as a digraph and the <r> also a grapheme in its own right pronounced /r/) or /er/ (with the two letters functioning separately).

## 10.8  <are>

### THE MAIN SYSTEM

| Basic phoneme | /eə/ | 100% | only word-final, e.g. *care, pare* |
|---|---|---|---|

### THE REST

|  |  | pronounced |  |
|---|---|---|---|
| Exception to main system | <are> | /ɑː/ | <1% only in *are* when stressed (/ə/ when unstressed) |
| Oddities | <arr> | /ɑː/ | only in *bizarrery, carr, charr, parr* |
|  | <arre> | /ɑː/ | only in *barre, bizarre* (but /r/-linking occurs in *bizarrery* – see section 3.6) |
|  | <arrh> | /ɑː/ | only in *catarrh* (but /r/-linking occurs in *catarrhal* – see section 3.6) |
| 2-phoneme graphemes | (none) |  |  |

### NOTE

The only case where final <a, r, e> belong to separate graphemes is in *Hare Krishna*.

## 10.9  <au>

See Notes for dual percentages.

### THE MAIN SYSTEM

| Basic phoneme | /ɔː/ | 46%/80% | e.g. *aura, sauce, autumn, cause*; word-final only in *landau, Nassau* |
|---|---|---|---|

## THE REST

|  |  | pronounced |  |
|---|---|---|---|
| Exceptions to main system | <au> | /ɒ/ | 43%/1% only in *Aussie, Australia, Austria, because* (also increasingly pronounced, unusually, with stressed /ə/), *cauliflower, laurel, Laurence, sausage*, plus a few words also pronounced with /ɔː/: *auction, austere, caustic, claustrophobia/c, hydraulic, (bacca)laureate*. See Notes |
|  | <au> | /ɑː/ | 10%/17% only in *aunt, draught, laugh(ter)* |
|  | <au> | /əʊ/ | 1% only in a few more recent French loanwords, namely *chauffeu-r/se, chauvinis-m/t, gauche, hauteur, mauve, saute, taupe* |
|  | <au> | /aʊ/ | <1% only in *ablaut, Faustian, gaucho, gauleiter, glaucoma* (also pronounced with /ɔː/), *sauerkraut* (twice), *umlaut* and the Greek letter name *tau*; also in *aural* when pronounced /ˈaʊrəl/ to distinguish it from *oral* /ˈɔːrəl/ |
|  | <au> | /eɪ/ | only in *gauge* |
| Oddities | <augh> | /ɔː/ | only in *aught, caught, daughter, distraught, fraught, haughty, (Mc)Naught(on), naught, naughty, onslaught, slaughter, taught* (and contrast *draught, laugh(ter)* where <au, gh> are separate graphemes) |
|  | <aul> | /ɔː/ | only in *baulk, caulk, haulm*. See also <al> under <a>, section 10.3 |
|  | <aur> | /ɔː/ | only in *bucentaur, centaur, dinosaur* (and the names of various dinosaur species, e.g. *pterosaur*), *minotaur* |
| 2-phoneme graphemes | (none) |  |  |

## NOTES

If we follow Crystal (2012: 131–2), 'more recent' in terms of loanwords from French means after the Great Vowel Shift, which was complete by about AD 1600.

Where two percentages are shown above, the first is that given by Gontijo *et al.* (2003). Among these, the high percentage for /ɒ/ is almost entirely due to *because*. In this case, specifically because they show the number of occurrences of *because* in their database, Gontijo *et al.* provide enough information to re-calculate all the percentages for this grapheme omitting *because*. Where they differ from the originals, the revised percentages are shown second.

There appear to be no cases where <a, u> are separate graphemes.

For <au> as an elided vowel spelling in *restaurant* see section 6.10.

## 10.10 <aw>

### THE MAIN SYSTEM

| Basic phoneme | /ɔː/ | 100% | e.g. *awful, crawl, dawdle, paw* |

### THE REST

|  |  | pronounced |  |
|---|---|---|---|
| Exception to main system | <aw> | /ɔɪ/ | <1% only in *lawyer, sawyer* |
| Oddity | <awe> | /ɔː/ | only in *awe* and derivatives which retain <e> |
| 2-phoneme graphemes | (none) |  |  |

### NOTE

Where the next letter is a vowel (other than in a suffix) or a consonant digraph, <a, w> belong to separate graphemes, e.g. in *awake, award, aware, awry, awhile, caraway, megawatt.*

## 10.11 <ay>

### THE MAIN SYSTEM

| Basic phoneme | /eɪ/ | 91% | e.g. *day*. See Note |

### THE REST

|  |  | pronounced |  |
|---|---|---|---|
| Exceptions to main system | <ay> | /iː/ | 8% only finally and only in *quay* and compounds of *day: birthday,* |

|  |  |  | holiday, Sunday, yesterday, etc., except heyday, midday, nowadays, today, workaday, which retain /eɪ/, as does holidaying |
|---|---|---|---|
| Oddities | <ay> | /e/ | <1% only in says |
|  | <aye> | /eɪ/ | only in aye – the usual pronunciation for the meaning 'always, still' |
|  | <aye> | /aɪ/ | only in aye, aye-aye. Aye is always pronounced /aɪ/ when it means 'yes', sometimes also when it means 'always, still' |
|  | <ayer> | /eə/ | only in prayer pronounced /preə/ ('religious formula'; also pronounced /ˈpreɪjə/, 'one who prays') |
|  | <ayor> | /eə/ | only in mayor and derivitives (but there is /r/-linking in mayoral, mayoress – see section 3.6) |
| 2-phoneme graphemes | (none) |  |  |

## 10.12 <e>

N.B. <ea, ear, ed, ee, e.e, eer, er, ere, ew> have separate entries.

### THE MAIN SYSTEM

For all these categories see Notes.

| Basic phoneme | /e/ | 47% | e.g. bed, invent. Regular when it is the only or last vowel letter and is followed by at least one consonant letter, in earlier positions before consonant clusters, in stressed <ex->, and before <-Cic(al)> |
|---|---|---|---|
| Other phonemes | /ɪ/ | 39% | mainly when unstressed, e.g. corset; when stressed, only in England, English, pretty and Cecily pronounced /ˈsɪsɪliː/ and therefore as a homophone |

|  |  | of *Sicily* (*Cecily* is also pronounced /ˈsesɪliː/). Regular in some suffixes |
| --- | --- | --- |
| /iː/ | 8% | e.g. *be, decent, ether, psyche.* Regular with \<e\>-deletion, word-finally, and before or in certain endings |
| /ə/ | 5% | regular when unstressed, e.g. *the* (unstressed and before a consonant phoneme), *artery* |

## THE REST

|  | pronounced |  |
| --- | --- | --- |
| *Exceptions to main system* |  | 1% in total |
| \<e\> | /ɒ/ | in about 22 more recent French loanwords, e.g. (the relevant \<e\>'s are in caps) *ambiEnce, cliEntele, denouemEnt, détEnte, divertissemEnt, Embonpoint, Embouchure, En* (*suite*), *Enceinte* pronounced /ɒnˈsænt/ (also pronounced /enˈseɪnt/), *Enclave* pronounced /ˈɒŋkleɪv/ (more often pronounced /ˈeŋkleɪv/), *Encore, Ennui, EnsEmble, EntEnte, Entourage, Entracte, Entrepreneur, Entree, Envelope* pronounced /ˈɒnvələʊp/ (also pronounced /ˈenvələʊp/), *gEnre, rapprochemEnt, rEntier* |
| \<e\> | /eɪ/ | in words where \<e\> is the only vowel letter, only in *thegn*. Otherwise only in about 65 more recent loanwords mainly from French where French spelling has \<é\>, namely (in non-final positions) *debris, debut, decor, eclair, ecru, elan, ingenu, precis*; first \<e\> in *debacle, debutante, decalage, decolletage, denouement, detente, elite, ingenue, menage, regime, seance,* |

*The grapheme-phoneme correspondences, 2* 369

(Greek) *heter-/hom-ogeneity* pronounced /hetər-/hɒm-əʊdʒɪ'neɪjɪtiː/ (usually pronounced /hetər-/hɒm-əʊdʒɪ'niːjɪtiː/), (Hawaian) *ukulele* and (Turkish) *meze*; (word-finally) (French) *abbe, attache, blase, cafe* (also pronounced with /iː/), *canape* (also pronounced with /iː/, hence the invitation I once received to a party with 'wine and canopies'), *cliche, communique, conge, consomme, diamante, fiance, flambe, frappe, glace, habitue, macrame, manque, outre, pate* ('paste'), *retrousse, risque, rose* ('pink wine'), *roue, saute, soigne, souffle, touche,* (Amerindian/Spanish) *abalone,* (Greek) *agape* (/'ægəpeɪ/, 'love feast'), (Italian) *biennale, finale,* (Spanish/Nahuatl) *guacamole,* (Japanese) *anime, kamikaze* and (Mexican Spanish) *tamale*; final <e> in (French) *emigre, expose* ('report of scandal'), *naivete, protege, recherche, resume* ('c.v.'), *retrousse,* (KiSwahili/Spanish) *dengue* and (Turkish) *meze*. There is an increasing tendency to spell the French loanwords in this list, within English text, with <é>

| | | | |
|---|---|---|---|
| *Oddities* | <e'er> | /eə/ | only in *e'er, ne'er, where'er* and a few other archaic contracted forms. See section A.9 in Appendix A |
| | | | For '<i> before <e> except after <c>' see section 6.1 |
| | <ei> | /iː/ | 69% of pronunciations for <ei> only medial and only in *caffeine, casein, ceiling, codeine, conceit, conceive, counterfeit* pronounced /'kaʊntəfiːt/ (also pronounced /'kaʊntəfɪt/), *cuneiform, deceit, deceive, heinous* pronounced /'hiːnəs/ (also pronounced /'heinəs/), *inveigle, perceive, plebeian, protein, receipt, receive, seize* |

| | | |
|---|---|---|
| \<ei\> | /aɪ/ | 23% of pronunciations for \<ei\> only in *deictic, deixis, eider(down), eidetic, eirenic, either, Fahrenheit, feisty, gneiss, heist, kaleidoscope, meiosis, neither, poltergeist, seismic* and derivatives, *stein* |
| \<ei\> | /ə/ | 7% of pronunciations for \<ei\> only in *foreign* (which must therefore have been very frequent in Gontijo *et al.*'s (2003) database) |
| | | All other pronunciations of \<ei\> amount to <1% in total |
| \<ei\> | /eɪ/ | only in about 15 words, namely *abseil, apartheid, beige, deign, feign, feint, heinous* pronounced /ˈheɪnəs/ (also pronounced /ˈhiːnəs/), *lei* (only example in word-final position), *obeisance, reign, rein, reindeer, seine, sheikh, skein, surveillance, veil, vein* |
| \<ei\> | /ɪ/ | only in *counterfeit* pronounced /ˈkaʊntəfɪt/ (also pronounced /ˈkaʊntəfiːt/), *forfeit, sovereign, surfeit* |
| \<ei\> | /e/ | only in *heifer, leisure, seigneur* |
| \<ei\> | /æ/ | only in *reveille* |
| \<eigh\> | /eɪ/ | 89% of pronunciations for \<eigh\> only in *eight, freight, heigh, inveigh, neigh, neighbour, sleigh, weigh, weight* |
| \<eigh\> | /aɪ/ | 11% of pronunciations for \<eigh\> only in *height, sleight* |
| \<eir\> | /eə/ | only in *their(s)* and therefore virtually 100% |
| \<eir\> | /ɪə/ | only in *weir, weird* |
| \<eo\> | /ə/ | only in *bludgeon, curmudgeon, dudgeon, dungeon, gudgeon, luncheon, puncheon, (e)scutcheon, smidgeon, sturgeon, surgeon, truncheon, widgeon* |

| | | |
|---|---|---|
| &lt;eo&gt; | /e/ | only in *Geoff(rey)*, *jeopardy*, *Leonard*, *leopard* |
| &lt;eo&gt; | /iː/ | only in *feoffee*, *feoffment*, *people* |
| &lt;eo&gt; | /əʊ/ | only in *Yeo*, *yeoman*, *Yeovil* |
| &lt;es&gt; | /eɪ/ | only in *demesne* |
| &lt;et&gt; | /eɪ/ | only word-final and only in about 20 more recent French loanwords, namely *ballet*, *beret*, *bidet*, *bouquet*, *buffet* ('food'), *cabaret*, *cabriolet*, *cachet*, *cassoulet*, *chalet*, *crochet*, *croquet*, *duvet*, *gilet*, *gourmet*, *parquet*, *piquet*, *ricochet*, *sachet*, *so(u)briquet*, *sorbet*, *tourniquet*, *valet* pronounced /'væleɪ/ (also pronounced /'vælɪt/). /t/ surfaces in *balletic*, *parquetry*, *valeting* – see section 7.2. In these and all other cases &lt;e, t&gt; are separate graphemes – for examples see Notes |
| &lt;eu&gt; | /uː/ | only in *rheum(ati-c/sm)*, *sleuth*, plus *adieu*, *lieu* (also pronounced /luː/), *purlieu* if pronounced with /-juː/, in which case &lt;i&gt; is pronounced /j/ |
| &lt;eu&gt; | /ɜː/ | only in *chauffeuse*, *coiffeuse*, *masseuse*, *milieu* |
| &lt;eu&gt; | /ə/ | only in *pasteurise* pronounced /'paːstʃəraɪz/ (also pronounced /'paːstjəraɪz/ |
| &lt;eur&gt; | /ɜː/ | non-finally, only in *secateurs*; otherwise only word-final and only in about 12 more recent loanwords of French origin, e.g. *chauffeur* (if stressed on &lt;eur&gt;), *coiffeur*, *connoisseur*, *entrepreneur*, *hauteur*, *masseur*, *poseur*, *provocateur*, *raconteur*, *repetiteur*, *restaurateur*, *seigneur* and a few other rare words |
| &lt;eur&gt; | /ə/ | only in *amateur*, *chauffeur* (if stressed on &lt;au&gt;), *grandeur*. /r/-linking occurs in *amateurish* – see section 3.6 |

|  |  |  |  |
|---|---|---|---|
|  | <eur> | /ʊə/ | only in *pleurisy*; the <r> is also pronounced /r/. For dual-functioning see section 7.1. See section 5.6.5 for the increasing replacement of /ʊə/ by /ɔː/ |
|  | <ey> | /iː/ | except in *geyser* pronounced /'giːzə/, only final and only in *abbey, alley, attorney, baloney, barley, blarney, blimey, cagey, chimney, chutney, cockney, comfrey, coney, donkey, dopey, flunkey, fogey, galley, gooey, hackney, hockey, homey, honey, jersey, jockey, journey, key, kidney, lackey, malarkey, matey, medley, money, monkey, motley, nosey, palfrey, parley, parsley, pokey, pulley, storey, tourney, turkey, valley, volley* |
|  | <ey> | /eɪ/ | never initial; medially, only in *abeyance, heyday*; word-finally, only in *bey, convey, fey, grey, hey, lamprey, obey, osprey, prey, purvey, survey, they, whey* |
|  | <ey> | /aɪ/ | only in *geyser* pronounced /'gaɪzə/ (usually pronounced /'giːzə/) |
|  | <eye> | /aɪ/ | only in *eye* |
|  | <eyr> | /ɪə/ | only in *eyrie*; the <r> is also pronounced /r/. For dual-functioning see section 7.1 |
|  | <ey're> | /eə/ | only in *they're*. See section A.9 in Appendix A |
|  | <e're> | /ɪə/ | only in *we're*. See section A.9 in Appendix A |
|  | <ez> | /eɪ/ | only in *laissez-faire, pince-nez, rendezvous* |
| 2-phoneme graphemes | <eu> | as 2-phoneme sequence /juː/ | only in various words and names of Greek origin, e.g. *eucalyptus, eucharist, eudaemonic, eugenic, eulogy, eunuch, euphemism, euphorbia, euphoria, eurhythmic, euthanasia, leukaemia, neural, neurone, neurosis, Odysseus, Pentateuch, Perseus, pneumatic, pneumonia* |

*The grapheme-phoneme correspondences, 2* 373

|   |   | and other words derived from Greek πνεῦμα *pneuma* ('breath') or πνεύμων *pneumon* ('lung'), *pseud(o)* and all its derivatives, *therapeutic, Theseus, zeugma*, plus (non-Greek) *deuce, euchre, Eustachian, feu, feud(al), neuter, neutr-al/on, teutonic* and some other very rare words |
|---|---|---|
| \<eu\> | as 2-phoneme sequence /jə/ | only in *aneurism, pasteurise* pronounced /ˈpaːstjəraɪz/ (also pronounced /ˈpaːstʃəraɪz/) |
| \<eur\> | as 2-phoneme sequence /jʊə/ | only in *eureka, Europe* and derivatives (where the \<r\> is also pronounced /r/ – for dual-functioning see section 7.1) and *liqueur* pronounced /lɪˈkjʊə/ |

## NOTES

If we follow Crystal (2012: 131–2), 'more recent' in terms of loanwords from French means after the Great Vowel Shift, which was complete by about AD 1600.

Except in the cases noted in the Oddities, in \<eo, et, ez\> the \<e\> is a separate grapheme – cf. especially *someone*.

\<e, i\> are separate graphemes pronounced /iː, ɪ/ (with an intervening /j/-glide) in *albeit, atheis-m/t(ic), dei-fy/sm/st, hetero/homo-geneity, nucleic, pantheism, reify, reinforce, reinstate*.

\<e, u\> are separate graphemes pronounced /iː, ə/ (again with an intervening /j/-glide) in *coleus, linoleum, mausoleum, museum, nucleus, petroleum*.

For many examples of medial \<e, o\> as separate graphemes see below.

Percentages for \<eo, eu, eur, ey\> are not worth giving because so few words are involved.

For instances of \<e\> as an elided vowel see section 6.10.

The default pronunciation of \<e\> as a single-letter grapheme is /e/, but here are some categories for guidance:

- regular before geminate and doubled consonant spellings, e.g. *ebb, beck, speckled, cheddar, hedge(r), ineffable, egg, trekkie, bell, bellow, biennial, berry, blessed* /ˈblesɪd/, *stress, wretch(ed), sett, settle,*

*embezzle*. Extension: all the words ending <-ette>. Only exception: *retch* pronounced /riːtʃ/
- regular in other words where <e> is the only vowel letter and is followed by at least one consonant letter, e.g. *bed, phlegm, trek*. See section 11.3 for a teaching rule relevant to ..VC monosyllables
- regular before consonant clusters in words with at least one earlier vowel letter separated from the relevant <e> by at least one consonant letter, e.g. *accept, bedeck, except, inflect, reject, present* (verb), *prevent, repent, subject* /səbˈdʒekt/ (verb, with stress on <e>; the noun is pronounced /ˈsʌbdʒɪkt/). Extension: 3 words with <eCe> where <e.e> is not pronounced /iː, eɪ/ (for words where <e.e> is so pronounced see section 10.17): *allege, clientele, cortege*
- mostly when <e> is followed by more than one consonant letter and there is at least one later vowel letter, e.g. *better, bevvy, enter, freckle, pendulum, phlegmatic, splendid, terrible, terrify*
- when followed by a single consonant letter and the endings <-ic(al)>, e.g. *academic, aríthmétic* (adjective), *arithmetical, ascetic, athletic, atmospheric, genetic, heretical, parenthetical, pathetic*. Extension: *ethic-al/s*. Only exceptions: *acetic* (which is thus differentiated from *ascetic*), *emic, graphemic, phonemic, scenic*, with /iː/, *aríthmetic* (noun), *chóleric, climácteric, héretic*, with the relevant <e> pronounced /ə/. The stress always falls on the syllable spelt with the relevant <e> except in the four words just shown with different stresses
- in a few words (some very frequent) before <ver>, e.g. *beverage, clever, ever, every, never, reverend, several*. However, the exceptions are more numerous: *cantilever, fever, lever(age)* with /iː/; *persevere, revere, revers-e/al, severe* with /ɪ/
- in a further ragbag of non-final occurrences, e.g. first <e> in *celery, deference, element, emery, excellent, exile, exit, levee, machete, penance, preference, present* (noun, adjective), *president, reference, relevant, separate, seven, tether*; second <e> in *decrepit, presidential, replenish*; third <e> in *deferential, preferential, referential*; also *bevy, credit, debit, discretion, edit, fetish, heron, inherit, intrepid, lemon, leper, levy, medal, melon, merit, metal, pedal, pedant, perish, relish, special, tenant, tenon, tepid, very, xenon*.

The task then is to define the circumstances in which <e> has other pronunciations. These can be summarised as follows.

Word-final <e> is mainly 'silent', i.e. part of a digraph (split or not), trigraph or four-letter grapheme. It is 'pronounced':
1) as /eɪ/, only in the 42 words listed under the exception '<e> pronounced /eɪ/' above
2) as /iː/ in *be, he, me, she, the* (when stressed), *we, ye; aborigine, acme, acne, adobe, agave, anemone, apostrophe, bocce, catastrophe, coyote, dilettante, epitome, extempore, facsimile, (bona) fide, forte, furore, hebe, hyperbole, karate, machete, menarche, minke, nepenthe, oche, posse, psyche, recce, recipe, reveille, sesame, simile, stele, strophe, tagliatelle, tsetse, ukulele, vigilante*.

Non-final <e> is pronounced /iː/ in:
1) hundreds of words where the final <e> of <e.e> has been deleted before a suffix beginning with a vowel letter, e.g. *competing, schematic* – see sections 6.3 and especially 6.4
2) a number of words where <e> is followed by a single consonant letter other than <r> and then by
   - any of <eo, ia, io, iou, iu> followed word-finally by a single consonant letter or none, e.g. *chameleon* (first <e>), *meteor* (first <e>); *sepia; comedian, congenial, genial, Grecian, remedial* (second <e>); *cohesion, completion, lesion* and many more words ending in <-esion, -etion>, *senior, egregious* (second <e>), *facetious, ingenious, specious, tedious; genius, magnesium, medium, tedium*
   - <-ien-ce/cy/t>, e.g. *obedience, expediency* (second <e>), *leniency, convenient, expedient, ingredient*.

In all these words (and the first two exceptions listed next) the <e> in question is stressed. Exceptions: *discretion, special* with /e/, *dandelion, denial* with /ɪ/, *elegiac* with second <e> pronounced /ə/.

3) a very few words when unstressed before word-final <o(n/r)>: *galleon, Odeon, video*, second <e> in *chameleon, melodeon, meteor* (all with automatic intervening /j/-glide)
4) the ending <-eous> pronounced /iːjəs/, e.g. *aqueous, beauteous, courteous, (sub)cutaneous, erroneous, gaseous* pronounced /ˈgæsiːjəs/, *hideous, instantaneous, nauseous* pronounced /ˈnɔːziːjəs/, *simultaneous* and about 70 other words. But N.B. there are many words ending in <-eous> where the <e> is part of a digraph with the preceding letter, e.g. *advantageous, gaseous* pronounced /ˈgeɪjəs/, *gorgeous, nauseous* pronounced /ˈnɔːʒəs/, *righteous, siliceous* and a set of words in <-aceous> pronounced /ˈeɪʃəs/, e.g. *cretaceous, curvaceous,*

*herbaceous, sebaceous* and about 100 others, mostly scientific and all very rare

5) a number of words when stressed before a single consonant letter and word-final <a, o>, e.g. *beta, edema, ego* pronounced /'iːgəʊ/ (also pronounced /'egəʊ/), *emphysema, eta, hyena, magneto, schema, theta, torpedo, tuxedo, verbena, veto,* etc.

6) plurals of a few nouns with singular ending <-is> pronounced /ɪs/ and plural ending <-es> pronounced /iːz/, e.g. (Greek) *analyses* (/ə'nælɪsiːz/, the singular verb of the same spelling being pronounced /'ænəlaɪzɪz/), *apotheoses, axes, bases* (/'æksiːz, 'beɪsiːz/, plurals of *axis, basis*; *axes, bases* as the plurals of *axe, base* are pronounced (regularly) /'æksɪz, 'beɪsɪz/), *crises, diagnoses, emphases, exegeses, nemeses, oases, periphrases, synopses, (anti/hypo/meta/syn-)theses,* (Latin) *amanuenses, testes,* plus (Greek singulars) *diabetes, herpes, litotes, pyrites,* (a stray Greek plural with singular in <-s>) *Cyclopes,* and (other Latin plurals) *appendices, cicatrices, faeces, interstices, mores, Pisces*

7) the stressed prefixes <de-, e-, pre-, re-> pronounced /diː-, iː-, priː-, riː-/ in, e.g., *dethrone, egress, preschool, rephrase*

8) *alveolar, apotheosis, camellia, cathedral, cedar, choreograph, demon, ethos, femur, genus, harem, legal, lemur, leotard, lethal, mimeograph, negus, neon, osteopath, pecan, penal, penis, peony, pleonasm, rebus, regal, renal, retch* (pronounced /riːtʃ/ (also pronounced /retʃ/), *secant, theory, thesis* (but not its compounds), *venal, venial,* etc., (first <e> in) *abbreviate, appreciable, cotoneaster* /kə'təʊniːjæstə/, *creosote, decent, diabetes, egret, ether, febrile, feline, geodetic, heliotrope, immediate, inebriated, leonine, mediocre, meter, metre, recent, regent,* etc.

Carney would place all the words in categories 3 and 4, and those in category 8 where <e> is followed by a vowel grapheme pronounced /ə/, under /ɪə/.

The only words in which <e> is pronounced /ɪ/ in **stressed** syllables are *England, English, pretty* and *Cecily* pronounced /'sɪsɪliː/ and therefore as a homophone of *Sicily* (*Cecily* is also pronounced /'sesɪliː/). Categories where /ɪ/ is the **regular** pronunciation of **un**stressed <e> are:

- the unstressed prefixes <be-, de-, e-, ex-, pre-, re-> pronounced /bɪ, dɪ, ɪ, ɪks/ɪgz, prɪ, rɪ/ in, e.g., *before, beholden, decline, deliver, effective, efficient, extreme, examine, precede, predict, regale, reject*
- some occurrences of the ending <-ed> – see section 10.15

- the endings <-efy, -efied> pronounced /ɪfaɪ(d)/, which occur in just four words: *liquefy, putrefy, rarefied, stupefy*
- the ending <-ety> pronounced /ɪtiː/ in *anxiety, dubiety, entirety, gaiety, moiety, naivety, nicety, notoriety, (im)piety, (im)propriety, sobriety, society, surety, variety*
- the noun plural and third person singular present tense verb endings spelt <-es> and pronounced /ɪz/ after <c, ch, g, s, sh, z> pronounced variously /s, z, ʃ, ʒ, tʃ, dʒ/ – see the entries for those consonants in sections 3.6.6, 3.6.8, 3.7.3, 3.7.4, 3.6.2, 3.6.4 respectively. Exceptions: plurals of (Greek) nouns, etc., listed above
- the unstressed noun/adjective endings <-ess, -less, -let, -ness> pronounced /ɪs, lɪs, lɪt, nɪs/, e.g. *goddess, listless, booklet, madness*
- the superlative adjective ending <-est>, e.g. *biggest, grandest*
- the archaic second and third person singular verb endings <-est, -eth>, e.g. *gavest, goeth*
- mainly before final <t>, e.g. in *ashet, brisket, budget, buffet* ('strike'), *corset, dulcet, facet, fillet, gannet, gullet, nugget, plummet, punnet, russet, secret, tuffet, valet* (also pronounced with /eɪ/ and no /t/) and about 150 other words. For final <et> pronounced /eɪ/ see the Oddities.

There is also a ragbag of other words with non-final <e> pronounced /ɪ/, e.g. *allegation, employ, forest, hallelujah, integral* (when pronounced /ˈɪntɪɡrəl/; also pronounced /ɪnˈteɡrəl/), *kitchen, mannequin, regalia, subject* (noun /ˈsʌbdʒɪkt/, with stress on <u>; the verb is pronounced /səbˈdʒekt/), *vinegar, women*; first <e> in *anecdote, antelope, barometer* and all the instruments ending in <-ometer> (but not *kilometer* or other compounds of *meter*), *celebrity, consecrate, diocese, eccentric, ellipse, elope, enamel, integrate, negate, neglect, sequential*; second <e> in *elegant, elephant, peregrine*, and many others.

Examples of non-final <e> pronounced /ə/ include every unstressed final <-en> (e.g. *alien*) except in *women* (/ˈwɪmɪn/), plus *artery, bolero* (/ˈbɒlərəʊ/, 'garment'), *soviet*, first <e> in *coterie*; second <e> in *elevate*, the first <e> in the ending <-ence> in, e.g., *audience, conscience, convenience, ebullience, experience, omniscience, obedience, prurience, resilience, salience, science*; the <e> in the endings <-ency, -ent> in, e.g., *expediency, leniency; absent, (in)clement, convenient, ebullient, expedient, incipient, lenient, orient* (noun), *omniscient, obedient, prescient, present* (noun/adjective), *prurient, resident, resilient, salient, sentient, subservient, transient*; also, in nouns ending <-ment>, e.g. *complement, compliment, document, element* (note the second <e> too), *experiment, ferment, fragment, implement, increment, instrument* – on this last group see also section 6.8.

## 10.13 <ea>

N.B. <ear> has a separate entry.

### THE MAIN SYSTEM

Basic phoneme  /iː/   73%   e.g. *beach*

### THE REST

|  |  | pronounced |  |
|---|---|---|---|
| Exceptions to main system | <ea> | /e/ | 21% In about 60 words, namely: *Beaconsfield; treacher-ous/y; bread, breadth, dead, dread, (a)head, lead* (the metal, plus derivatives *leading, leaded), meadow, read* (past tense and participle), *Reading* (Berkshire, in first map (1611) spelt *Redding*), *(al)ready, spread, (in)stead, steadfast, steady, thread, tread(le); deaf, breakfast; dealt, health, jealous, realm, stealth, wealth, zealous, zealot; dreamt, seamstress; cleanly* (adjective, plus derivative *cleanliness), cleanse, leant, meant; leapt, weapon; (a)breast; peasant, pheasant, pleasant; measure, pleasure, treasure; sweat, threat(en); breath, death; feather, heather, leather, weather; endeavour, heaven, heavy, leaven* and other derivatives not listed |
|  | <ea> | /eɪ/ | 6% only in *break, great, steak, yea, Yeat(e)s* |
| Oddities | <eah> | /eə/ | only in *yeah* |
|  | <eau> | /ɒ/ | only in *bureaucracy, bureaucratise* |
|  | <eau> | /ə/ | only in *bureaucrat(ic)* |
|  | <eau> | /əʊ/ | only word-final and only in *bandeau, beau, bureau, chateau, flambeau, gateau, plateau, portmanteau, rondeau, tableau, trousseau* and a few other very rare words. For the plurals of these words see /z/, section 3.6.7, and <x>, section 9.42 |

| 2-phoneme grapheme | <eau> as 2-phoneme sequence /juː/ | only in *beauty* and derivatives |

## NOTES

The roughly 20 words listed above with <ead> pronounced /ed/ contrast with about 6 pronounced /iːd/: *bead, knead, lead* (verb), *mead, plead, read* (present tense). The <-ead> pronounced /ed/ group is one of only five cases where the pronunciation of a phonogram/rime is more predictable as a unit than from the correspondences of the separate graphemes, and there are enough instances to make the rule worth teaching; see section A.7 in Appendix A.

<e, a> are separate graphemes pronounced /iː, ɪ/ only in *lineage*; /iː, ə/ in *area, azalea, cereal, cornea, creativity, European, fealty, idea, Jacobean, (bacca)laureate, miscreant, nausea, panacea, theatre, urea*; /iː, æ/ in *beatitude, caveat, cotoneaster, deactivate, genealogy, meander, oleander, preamble, react, realign*; /iː, eɪ/ in *create, creation, delineate, nauseate, reagent*. In all these cases there is an automatic intervening /j/-glide.

<e, a> are/belong to separate graphemes also in a set of words in which <e> has not been deleted before suffixes beginning with a vowel letter, in order to mark <c, g> as pronounced /s, dʒ/ and not /k, g/, e.g. *noticeable, changeable* – for more detail see section 6.4.

## 10.14  <car>

### THE MAIN SYSTEM

| Basic phoneme /ɪə/ | 67% | medially only in *afeard, arrears, beard*, and (with <r> also a grapheme in its own right pronounced /r/ – for dual-functioning see section 7.1) *bleary, weary*; otherwise only word-final and only in *appear, arrear, blear, clear, dear, drear, ear, fear, gear, hear, near, rear, sear, shear, smear, spear, tear* ('moisture from eye'), *year* |

| | | | |
|---|---|---|---|
| Other phoneme /eə/ | | 1% | only word-final and only in (for(e)-) *bear, pear, swear, tear* ('rip'), *wear* |

### THE REST

| | | pronounced | |
|---|---|---|---|
| Exceptions to main system | \<ear\> | /ɜː/ | 29% never word-final, and only in *dearth, earl, early, earn, earnest, earth, heard, hearse, learn, pearl, rehearse, (re)search, yearn* |
| | \<ear\> | /ɑː/ | 4% only in *hearken* (also spelt, more regularly, *harken*), *heart, hearth* |
| Oddities | (none) | | |
| 2-phoneme graphemes | (none) | | |

### NOTES

All the words with final \<ear\> allow /r/-linking – see section 3.6.

Despite the percentage for \<ear\> pronounced /ɜː/ I have not promoted this correspondence to the main system because it occurs in so few words (though some have very high frequency).

\<e, ar\> are separate graphemes pronounced /iː, ə/ in *cochlear, linear, nuclear*; /iː, ɑː/ in *rearm*; (with \<a, r\> as separate graphemes) /iː, ə, r/ in *rearrange*. In all these cases there is an automatic intervening /j/-glide.

## 10.15 \<ed\>

### THE MAIN SYSTEM

| | | | |
|---|---|---|---|
| Basic phoneme /d/ | | 62% | in past tense and participle endings of regular verbs whose stems end in a vowel letter or in a consonant letter other than \<d\> |
| Other phoneme /t/ | | 38% | in past tense and participle endings of regular verbs whose stems end in a consonant letter other than \<t\> |

## THE REST

(None).

## NOTES

Where the stem of a regular verb ends in <(d)d, (t)t> pronounced /d, t/ the <-ed> ending is pronounced /ɪd/, e.g. *added, decided, matted, ousted*. This also applies in:

- a few adjectives which are derived from or resemble past participles but have /ɪd/ rather than the expected /d, t/, but often with a different meaning, e.g. *accursed, aged* (/ˈeɪdʒɪd/ 'elderly' vs /eɪdʒd/ 'having ... years'), *beloved* (/bɪˈlʌvɪd/ 'the loved one' vs /bɪˈlʌvd/ 'adored'), *blessed* (/ˈblesɪd/ 'holy' vs /blest/ 'consecrated'), *cragged, crooked* (/ˈkrʊkɪd/ 'untrustworthy' vs /krʊkt/ 'at an angle'), *Crutched (Friars), cursed* (/ˈkɜːsɪd/ 'damnable' vs /kɜːst/ 'swore badly/put a hex on'), *cussed* (/ˈkʌsɪd/ 'stubborn' vs /kʌst/ 'swore mildly'), *deuced, dogged* (/ˈdɒgɪd/ 'persistent' vs /dɒgd/ 'followed'), *fixed* (/ˈfɪksɪd/ 'persistent' vs /fɪkst/ 'mended'), *horned (owl), jagged* (/ˈdʒægɪd/ 'with sharp points' vs /dʒægd/ past tense of *jag*), *learned* (/ˈlɜːnɪd/ 'wise' vs /lɜːnd/ regular past tense of *learn*), *(bow/one/three-)legged, naked, ragged* (/ˈrægɪd/ 'torn, exhausted' vs /rægd/ past tense of *rag*), *rugged, sacred, supposed* (/səˈpəʊzɪd/ 'apparent' vs (/səˈpəʊzd/ past tense of *suppose*), *wicked, wretched*. In *(ac)cursed, blessed, crooked, Crutched, cussed, deuced, fixed, wretched*, not only does the /ɪ/ surface (see section 7.2) but the /t/ voices to /d/

- the past participle verb ending <-ed> pronounced /ɪd/ before adverbial <-ly>, e.g. *advisedly, allegedly, assuredly, barefacedly, composedly, confusedly, deservedly, determinedly, fixedly, markedly, relaxedly, (un)reservedly, supposedly, unabashedly, unashamedly, undisguisedly, unrestrainedly.* Again, in *barefacedly, fixedly, markedly, relaxedly*, not only does the /ɪ/ surface (see section 7.2) but the /t/ voices to /d/

- the <ed> element in a very few nouns in <-ness> formed from past participles, e.g. *determinedness, preparedness*. In *preparedness* not only does the /ɪ/ surface (see section 7.2) but also /r/-linking occurs (see section 3.6) and the <r> is both part of the grapheme <are> pronounced /eə/ and a grapheme in its own right pronounced /r/. For dual-functioning see section 7.1.

Given the phonological contexts, <ed> is 100% predictable.

Outside the verb endings listed, <e, d> are always separate graphemes, e.g. in *bed, biped, bred, led, quadruped, shed*.

## 10.16 <ee>

N.B. <e.e, eer> have separate entries.

### THE MAIN SYSTEM

| Basic phoneme | /iː/ | 100% | e.g. *beech, free, seen* |
|---|---|---|---|

### THE REST

|  |  | pronounced |  |
|---|---|---|---|
| Exceptions to main system |  |  | <1% in total |
|  | <ee> | /eɪ/ | only word-final and only in about 13 words where French spelling has <ée>, namely *corvee, dragee* ('sugar-coated sweet' pronounced /ˈdrɑːʒeɪ/; also pronounced /ˈdreɪdʒiː/), *entree, epee, fiancee, levee* ('reception or assembly', also pronounced with /iː/), *matinee, melee, nee, negligee, puree, soiree, toupee*. There is a growing tendency to spell these words in English with <ée> |
|  | <ee> | /ɪ/ | only in *been* when unstressed, *breeches, cheerio* /bɪn,ˈbrɪtʃɪz, tʃɪriːˈjəʊ/ |
|  | <ee> | /uː/ | only in *leeward* pronounced /ˈluːwəd/ (also pronounced /ˈliːwəd/) |
| Oddities | (none) |  |  |
| 2-phoneme graphemes | (none) |  |  |

### NOTE

<e, e> are separate graphemes only in a few unusual suffixed forms, e.g. *freer, freest, weer, weest* (comparative and superlative forms of the adjectives *free, wee*), *freest, freeth, seest, seeth* (/ˈfriːjɪst, ˈfriːjɪθ, ˈsiːjɪst, ˈsiːjɪθ/, archaic second and third person singular present tense forms of the verbs *free, see*),

*sightseer* /ˈsaɪtsiːjə/ (for more detail see section 6.4). There might then be a barely perceptible difference in pronunciation between two words spelt *seer*: disyllabic /ˈsiːjə/ 'person who sees' vs monosyllabic /sɪə/ 'person with second sight'.

## 10.17 <e.e>

Occurs only where the second <e> is word-final.

See Note for all categories and for how this split digraph is defined, and see section 11.4 for a teaching rule relevant to all split digraphs except <y.e>.

### THE MAIN SYSTEM

| | | | |
|---|---|---|---|
| Basic phoneme | /iː/ | 100% | e.g. *effete, grapheme, phoneme, scene, swede* |
| Other phoneme | /eɪ/ | <1% | only in *crepe, fete, renege, suede, Therese* /kreɪp, feɪt, rɪˈneɪg, sweɪd, təˈreɪz/ |

### THE REST

| | |
|---|---|
| Exceptions to main system | strictly speaking, none, but see Note |
| Oddities | (none) |
| 2-phoneme graphemes | (none) |

### NOTE

The split digraph <e.e> is defined as covering words where the word-final <e> is separated from the leading <e> by one consonant letter other than <r, w, x, y> and the leading <e> is not preceded by a vowel letter and the digraph is pronounced either /iː/ or /eɪ/. Unlike <a.e>, no extensions are needed. The definition covers both words where the intervening consonant letter is an independent grapheme and words where the <e> is also part of a digraph <ce, ge, ve> – see sections 3.7.4, 3.7.6-7 and 3.8.4, and section 7.1 for dual-functioning. Exceptions where the leading <e> is a separate grapheme and the word-final <e> only forms a digraph with the intervening consonant letter: *allege, annexe, clientele, cortege* with the penultimate <e> pronounced /e/ (cf. also *creche*), *college, privilege, sacrilege, sortilege* with the penultimate <e> pronounced /ɪ/. There are very few English words ending <-ege>, and the five just mentioned are most of them, apart from a few very obscure and obsolete terms, and *protegé*, which is increasingly spelt like that, with a French acute accent and the final <e> always pronounced separately: /'prɒtəʒeɪ/. The only other words in which <e, e> separated by a single consonant letter are separate graphemes appear to be *hebe, machete, naivete, stele, ukulele*. See also section A.6 in Appendix A.

## 10.18 <eer>

### THE MAIN SYSTEM

| | | | |
|---|---|---|---|
| Only phoneme | /ɪə/ | 100% | except in *eerie*, where <r> is also pronounced /r/ (for dual-functioning see section 7.1), only word-final, e.g. *beer*. Many words with this ending allow /r/-linking – see section 3.6 |

### NOTE

The only words in which <e, er> are separate graphemes appear to be *freer, weer* (comparatives of *free, wee*).

## 10.19 <er>

N.B. <ere> has a separate entry.

### THE MAIN SYSTEM

| | | | |
|---|---|---|---|
| Basic phoneme | /ɜː/ | 24% | regular medially when stressed before a consonant letter, e.g. *berth, exert, herd*; also word-finally when stressed, e.g. *aver, defer, deter, her, infer, inter, prefer, refer, transfer* |
| Other phonemes | /ə/ | 65% | regular word-finally when unstressed, e.g. *other, patter*; also in prefixes *hyper-, inter-, per-, super-* when not stressed on <er> |
| | /ɪə/ | <1% | never word-final; initially, only in *era*; regular medially before a vowel letter |

*The grapheme-phoneme correspondences, 2* 385

when stressed, e.g. *anterior, arterial, bacteria, cafeteria, criteri-a/on, deteriorate, diphtheria, experience, funereal, hero, imperial, inferior, material, mysterious, period, posterior, series, superior, ulterior, wisteria.* In all these words the <r> is both part of the digraph <er> pronounced /ɪə/ and a grapheme in its own right pronounced /r/ – for dual-functioning see section 7.1 – and the <er> is stressed. Also see Notes

## THE REST

| | | pronounced | |
|---|---|---|---|
| Exceptions to main system | <er> | /eə/ | 9% only in *bolero* ('dance'), *concierge, recherche, scherzo, sombrero.* In *bolero, sombrero* the <r> is both part of <er> spelling /eə/ and a grapheme in its own right pronounced /r/. This is also true of a few suffixed forms of words in the next section with <-ere> pronounced /eə/, e.g. *compering.* For dual-functioning see section 7.1 |
| | <er> | /eɪ/ | 1% only word-final and only in a few French loanwords, namely *atelier, croupier, dossier* pronounced /'dɒsiːjeɪ/ (also pronounced /'dɒsiːjə/), *foyer* pronounced /'fwaɪjeɪ, 'fɔɪjeɪ/ (also pronounced /'fɔɪjə/), *metier, rentier* |
| | <er> | /aː/ | <1% only in *Berkeley, Berkshire, Cherwell, clerk, derby, Ker* pronounced /kaː/ (also pronounced /kɜː/), *sergeant* |
| Oddities | <err> | /ɜː/ | in stem words only in *err*, but frequent in consonant-doubling before suffixes, e.g. *preferred.* All other occurrences of <e, rr> consist of two graphemes pronounced /e, r/, e.g. *terrible, terrier* |
| | <erre> | /eə/ | only in *parterre* |
| 2-phoneme graphemes | (none) | | |

## NOTES

Words ending <er> and the prefixes *hyper-, inter-, per-, super-* permit /r/-linking (see section 3.6) before following words/stems beginning with a vowel phoneme, e.g. *dearer and dearer* /ˈdɪərərənˈdɪərə/, *hyperactive, interactive, peroxide, supererogatory*.

In the case of medial <er> pronounced /ɪə/ plus /r/-linking there are also a few instances arising from suffixation of words belonging to the next section, e.g. *adherents, coherence, interfering, interferon, perseverance*. However, in other suffixed forms from words in the next section the pronunciation of the <e> changes and, although /r/-linking occurs, the <r> is a single-function grapheme pronounced /r/, e.g. *spherical, atmospheric, austerity, reverence, severity, (in)sincerity*; this is also true of *errant*, derived from *err*.

# 10.20 <ere>

For absence of percentages see Note.

## THE MAIN SYSTEM

| Basic phoneme | /ɪə/ | regular word-finally, e.g. *here, mere, sere, sphere; ad/co-here, atmosphere, austere, belvedere, cashmere, interfere, persevere, revere, severe, (in)sincere*. In *hereon* /r/-linking – see section 3.6 – occurs without <e>-deletion (which would produce *heron*) |

## THE REST

|  |  | pronounced |  |
|---|---|---|---|
| Exceptions to main system | <ere> | /eə/ | only word-final and only in *ere, there, where* and a few polysyllabic words of French origin, namely *ampere, brassiere, cafetiere, commere, compere, confrere, misere, premiere*. /r/-linking – see section 3.6 – occurs in *compering, wherever*, etc.; also in *thereupon* without <e>-deletion |
|  | <ere> | /ɜː/ | only in *were* when stressed |

| Oddities | (none) |
| 2-phoneme graphemes | (none) |

## NOTE

Gontijo *et al.* (2003) do not recognise /ɜː/ as a pronunciation of <ere>; presumably the version of RP they were using has *were* pronounced /weə/ and/or they analysed all its occurrences as unstressed /wə/. Because of this it was not possible to calculate percentages for <ere>.

# 10.21 <ew>

## THE MAIN SYSTEM

For both categories see Notes.

| Basic phoneme | /uː/ | 15% | e.g. *crew, shrewd, strewn, view, yew* |
| Frequent 2-phoneme sequence | /juː/ | 84% | e.g. *few, nephew, new, newt, steward* |

## THE REST

|  |  | pronounced |  |
|---|---|---|---|
| Exceptions to main system | <ew> | /əʊ/ | 1% only in *sew, sewn, Shrewsbury* plus *shew(ed), shewn* (archaic spellings of *show(ed), shown*) |
| Oddities | (none) | | |
| Other 2-phoneme grapheme | <ewe> | as 2-phoneme sequence /juː/ | only in *ewe, Ewell, Ewelme* |

## NOTES

<ew> pronounced /juː/ occurs medially only in *newel, Newton, pewter, steward*; otherwise, only where there is no further vowel letter and only in (closed) *hewn, lewd, mews, newt, thews*; (open) *clerihew, curfew, curlew, few, hew, knew, mew, mildew, nephew, new, pew, phew, sinew, skew, smew,*

*spew, stew*; also *dew* if pronounced /djuː/ rather than /dʒuː/. Except in these words and the few Oddities <ew> is always pronounced /uː/ – the high frequency of *few, knew, new* is presumably responsible for the few words with /juː/ having a much higher percentage of correspondences than those with /uː/. There seem to be no cases where <e, w> are separate graphemes.

N.B. For vocalic graphemes beginning with ('silent') <h> see section 9.17.

## 10.22 <i>

N.B. <ie, i.e, igh, ir> have separate entries.

### THE MAIN SYSTEM

For all these categories and the absence of percentages see Notes.

| | | |
|---|---|---|
| Basic phoneme | /ɪ/ | regular in initial position, e.g. *in, is, it,* and in medial position before a consonant letter (except where <e>-deletion has occurred), e.g. *his, live* (verb), *sit, this, with.* See section 11.3 for a teaching rule relevant to ..VC monosyllables |
| Other phonemes | /iː/ | regular word-finally, e.g. *kiwi, safari, spaghetti*; frequent medially (with /j/-glide), e.g. *ambience, alien, hernia, medial(ly)* |
| | /aɪ/ | regular medially where <e>-deletion has occurred, e.g. *writing*, and (with /j/-glide) where <i> is the first vowel letter in the word and is followed by another vowel letter, e.g. *bias* |
| | /j/ | only medially before a vowel letter, e.g. *adieu, behaviour, lieu, purlieu, saviour, union, (inter)view* |

### THE REST

| | | pronounced | |
|---|---|---|---|
| Exceptions to main system | <i> | /æ/ | only in *absinthe, impasse, ingenu(e), lingerie* pronounced /ˈlænʒəriː/ (also pronounced /ˈlɒndʒəreɪ/), *pince-nez, timbale, timbre* |

## The grapheme-phoneme correspondences, 2   389

| | | | |
|---|---|---|---|
| | <i> | /ɒ/ | only in *lingerie* pronounced /ˈlɒndʒəreɪ/ (also pronounced /ˈlænʒəriː/) |
| | <i> | /ə/ | in a large set of adjectives/adverbs ending in <-ibl-e/y> pronounced /-əbəl, -əbliː/, e.g. *possibl-e/y*, all of which can also be pronounced with /ɪ/. Also in a few adverbs ending <-arily> when not stressed on the <a>, which becomes elided (see section 6.10), so that the <i> in <-ily> is pronounced /ə/, e.g. *necessarily, voluntarily* pronounced /ˈnesəsrəliː, ˈvɒləntrəliː/ (also pronounced /nesəˈserɪliː, vɒlənˈterɪliː/ with <i> pronounced /ɪ/ and the preceding <a> stressed and pronounced /e/). Otherwise perhaps only in *Missouri* (second <i>) |
| Oddities | <ia> | /ɪ/ | only in *carriage, marriage* |
| | <ia> | /ə/ | only in *fuchsia, miniature, parliament, pharmacopoeia*. In words like *crucial, initial* I count the <i> as part of a digraph with the preceding consonant letter – see <ci, ti> in sections 9.10 and 9.36 |
| | <ia> | /aɪ/ | only in *diamond* |
| | <io> | /ə/ | only in *cushion, fashion, marchioness, stanchion*. In words like *nation, lesion, vision, lotion, fusion* I count the <i> as part of a digraph with the preceding consonant letter – see <si, ti> in sections 9.31 and 9.36. In all other cases <i, o> are separate single-letter graphemes – see many examples in the Notes |
| | <is> | /aɪ/ | only in *island, isle(t), lisle, viscount* |
| | <is> | /iː/ | only in *chassis, commis (chef), coulis, debris, precis, verdigris* pronounced /ˈvɜːdɪgriː/ (also pronounced /ˈvɜːdɪgriːs/), *vis-à-vis* (last <is>) |
| | <it> | /iː/ | only in *esprit, petit mal, wagon-lit* |
| 2-phoneme graphemes | (none) | | |

## NOTES

Gontijo *et al.* (2003) analyse a great many occurrences of medial <i> before another vowel letter as being pronounced /ɪ/, whereas I analyse them as being pronounced /iː/ + /j/-glide. Re-allocation proved impossible, hence the absence of percentages.

Except in the cases noted in the Oddities, in <ia, io, is, it> the <i> is the whole or part of a separate grapheme. In particular, for <i, a> see below.

For instances of <i> as an elided vowel see section 6.10.

The regular pronunciations of <i> as a single-letter grapheme are complicated, and best set out in a flowchart – see Figure 10.1 and the following numbered paragraphs keyed to it.

FIGURE 10.1: FLOWCHART TO DETERMINE THE REGULAR PRONUNCIATIONS OF <i> AS A SINGLE-LETTER GRAPHEME.

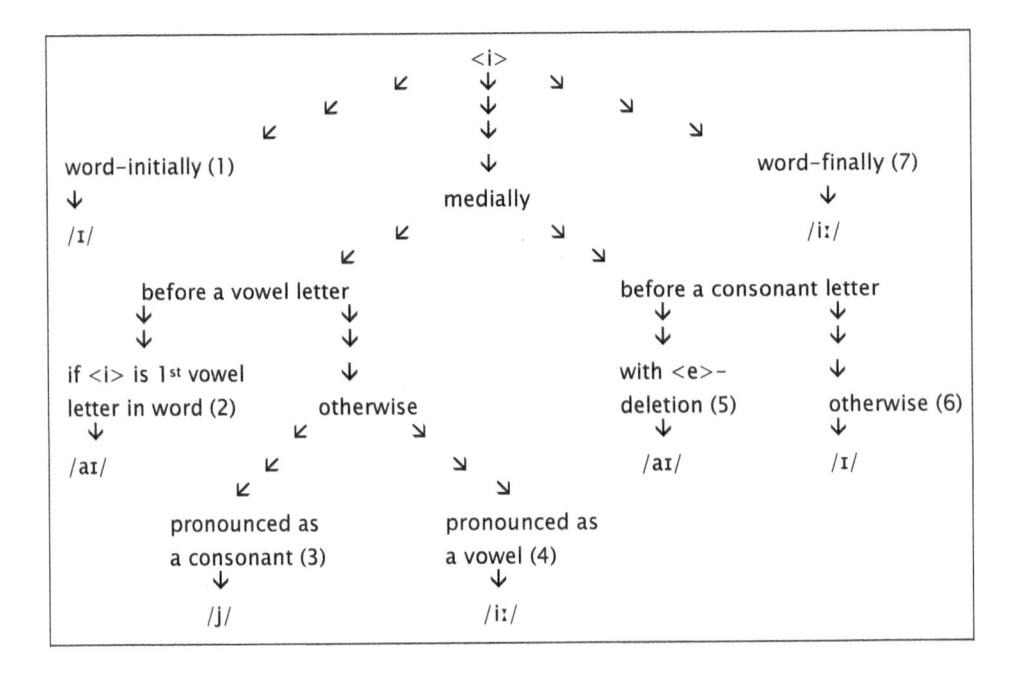

```
                              <i>
                   ↙           ↓           ↘
                  ↙            ↓            ↘
                 ↙             ↓             ↘
   word-initially (1)          ↓              word-finally (7)
        ↓                   medially                ↓
       /ɪ/              ↙            ↘             /iː/
              before a vowel letter    before a consonant letter
                        ↓                        ↓
                        ↓                        ↓
         if <i> is 1st vowel              with <e>-         otherwise (6)
         letter in word (2)   otherwise   deletion (5)           ↓
                ↓             ↙    ↘           ↓               /ɪ/
              /aɪ/           ↙      ↘         /aɪ/
                     pronounced as   pronounced as
                     a consonant (3)  a vowel (4)
                          ↓                ↓
                         /j/              /iː/
```

So the regular pronunciations of <i> as a single-letter grapheme are:
1) In initial position: /ɪ/, e.g. *iguana, ill, incognito, Indian, indigo, inn, innocent, irritate, is, it*. Exceptions, almost all with /aɪ/: *iambic, Iberian, ibex, ibis, ichor, icicle, icon, idea, identical, identity, ideology, idle, idol, iodine, ion, Ionic, iota, irate, iris, Irish, iron-y/ic, isinglass, isobar, isogloss, isosceles* and other compounds of (Greek) *iso-* ('equal'), *isolate*

(from Italian *isola* from Latin *insula* 'island'), *item, itinerary, ivory, ivy.* Only other exceptions: *impasse, ingenu(e)*, with /æ/

2) Medially where <i> is the **first** vowel letter in the word and is followed by another vowel letter: /aɪ/ (plus /j/-glide) in a large set of words, e.g. *bias, biology* and several other compounds beginning <bio->, *briar, client, diabolic* and several other compounds beginning <dia->, *friable, friar(y), giant, hiatus, liable, liar, lion, phial, pioneer, pliant, pliers, riot, sciatica, science, striation, triad, trial, triumph, viaduct, vial, violin*, etc. Exceptions (all with /iː/ plus /j/-glide): *clientele, fiancé(e), fiasco, fiord, kiosk, liais-e/on, liana, miasma, pianist, piano* (/piːˈjænəʊ/, with 3 syllables; in rapid speech also pronounced /ˈpjænəʊ/ with <i> pronounced as consonant /j/ and 2 syllables – cf. category (3) below), *piastre, trio, viola*

3-4) Medially where <i> is followed by another vowel letter but is **not** the first vowel letter in the word, it can be pronounced as a consonant or a vowel:

3) The consonantal pronunciation of <i> as /j/ occurs only medially before a vowel letter or digraph mostly pronounced /ə/ and almost always after the vowel bearing main stress:
   - in two groups of words: a group ending <-iary>: *apiary, auxiliary, aviary, breviary, domiciliary, incendiary, intermediary, pecuniary, stipendiary, subsidiary, topiary* (no exceptions, but this is a small set), and a group ending <-ion>: *battalion, billion, bunion, champion, companion, dominion, million, minion, onion, opinion, pavilion, pinion, union* (lots of exceptions – see category 4 below);
   - otherwise only in: *behaviour, brilliancy, colliery, junior, saviour, senior, spaniel*, plus (before a full vowel) *milieu* and, in rapid speech, *brilliant, envious* before /ə/ and (before a full vowel and, exceptionally, with the stress on the vowel after the <i>) *pronunciation*. In words like *brilliant, envious, million, pronunciation* (and cf. *piano* above), there is overlap with the next category because such words can be pronounced with consonant /j/ or vowel /iː/ plus /j/-glide, e.g. *million* as /ˈmɪljən/ (2 syllables) or /ˈmɪliːjən/ (3 syllables). Acoustically, the difference is very slight

4) The regular vocalic pronunciation of <i> as a single-letter grapheme in medial position (but not as the first vowel letter in the word – see (2) above) when followed by a vowel letter is /iː/ plus /j/-glide, e.g.
   - before <a, e, o, ou, u> pronounced /ə/ (Carney would place these words under /ɪə/): *ammonia, anaemia, bacteria, begonia, camellia,*

*chlamydia, (en)cyclopaedia, hernia, hysteria, media, myopia, salvia, sepia, utopia; amiable, dutiable, enviable, variable; myriad; aerial, congenial, jovial, managerial, material, memorial, radial, remedial, serial* and about 450 others ending in <-ial>; *barbarian, comedian, grammarian, guardian, pedestrian, ruffian, thespian* and about 200 others ending in <-ian>; *dalliance, luxuriance, radiance, variance; radiant, suppliant, variant; alias; alien; audience, convenience, ebullience, expedience, experience, obedience, prurience, salience; expediency, leniency, convenient, ebullient, expedient, lenient, obedient, orient* (/ˈɔːriːjənt/ noun), *pinochle, prescient, prurient, salient, sentient, subservient, transient; soviet; twentieth*, etc.; *period, sociological, axiom; accordion, bastion, battalion, billion, bullion, carrion, centurion, clarion, collodion, criterion, ganglion, medallion, mullion, oblivion, scorpion, scullion, stallion* (this group with <-ion> are rarely if ever pronounced with /j/, unlike similar words listed in (3) above); *chariot, patriot; commodious, compendious, curious, dubious, felonious, glorious, melodious, obvious, odious, previous, scabious, serious, studious, tedious* and about 100 others ending in <-ious>; *atrium, bacterium, barium, compendium, gymnasium, medium, opium, potassium, radium, stadium, tedium* and about 200 others ending in <-ium>; *genius, radius*; also second <i> in *amphibious, bilious, billiards, brilliant, criteria, delirium, editorial, fastidious, hilarious, historian, histrionic, idiom, idiot, industrial, juvenilia, memorabilia, millennia, omniscience, omniscient, perfidious, perihelion, reptilian, resilience, resilient, trivia(l), vitriol*, third <i> in *incipient, initiate* (noun), *insidious, insignia, invidious, militaria*;

- before <a, ae, a.e, ai, ar, e, o> pronounced as full vowel phonemes: *abbreviate, ap/de-preciate, associate, audio, calumniate, caviar, foliage, luxuriate, mediaeval, milliamp, negotiate, orient* (/ɒriːˈjent/, verb), *oubliette, patio, polio, radio, ratio, serviette, studio, verbiage*; also first <i> in *conscientious, orgiastic, partiality, psychiatric, speciality*, second <i> in *affiliate, bibliography, histrionic, inebriation, insomniac, officiate, superficiality, vitriolic*, third <i> in *initiate* (verb). In almost all these words (the only exceptions among those listed are *sociological, medi(a)eval, orient* (verb), *oubliette, serviette, bibliography, histrionic, inebriation, superficiality, vitriolic*) the main stress falls on the vowel before the relevant <i>. The consonant letter before the relevant <i> is hardly ever <c, s, sc, t> because <ci, si,

sci, ti> are almost always digraphs pronounced /ʃ/ or /ʒ/ (so the <i> is not pronounced separately) – see these graphemes' entries in chapter 9, and see also category (6) below – but in a few words the <i> is pronounced separately as /iː/ plus /j/-glide; examples among the words listed are *ap/de-preciate, associate, negotiate, patio, ratio, conscientious, partiality, speciality, initiate*

Exceptions with <i> not pronounced /iː/ (all with stressed <i> pronounced /aɪ/ plus /j/-glide): *alliance, certifiable, defiant, denial, elegiac, leviathan, verifiable; anxiety, dubiety, notoriety, (im)piety, (im)propriety, sobriety, society, variety*

5–6) Medially where <i> is followed by a consonant letter:

5) It is pronounced /aɪ/ in thousands of words where the final <e> of <i.e> has been deleted before a suffix beginning with a vowel letter – see sections 6.3 and especially 6.4, e.g. *bridal, cited, primal, riding, spinal, tribal, writing*. See also most exceptions to next category

6) Otherwise, mainly /ɪ/, e.g. *blink, divide* (first <i>), *piffle*. This is especially true:

   • before geminate and doubled consonant spellings, e.g. *pick, pickle, biddie, bridge, midget, difficult, higgledy-piggledy, pillow, cinnamon, tipple, mirror, kiss, missal, hitch, pitcher, little, skittle, skivvy, drizzle, fizz*. Extensions: all the words ending <-ville> and a few other words, e.g. *big, brink, province, wind* 'stiff breeze' (but see the group with /aɪ/ and those spelt <-ibl-e/y> below, plus other exceptions within the lists below)
   • in the endings <-ic(al), -ify>, e.g. *critic(al), parasitic, beautify*
   • before a single consonant letter follwed by the endings <-ic(al)>, e.g. *critic(al), parasitic*. In all such words except *impólitic, impóliticly* ('injudiciously'), *pólitic(s), pólaticly* ('judiciously'), the stress falls on the relevant <i>, but *political* follows the rule (more on this in the last paragraph of these Notes)
   • before the ending <-ly> in adverbs formed from adjectives in <-y>, e.g. *happily*. Note that addition of the suffix changes the stem-final vowel from /iː/ (in my analysis) to /ɪ/
   • before the endings <-cial, -cian, -cious, -ssion, -tion, -tious>, e.g. *beneficial, official, electrician, magician, auspicious, delicious, fission, mission, coition, fruition, fictitious, propitious*, plus *initial, provincial, siliceous, suspicion*. In all these words the stress falls on the <i> before the ending.

Exceptions:
- with /æ/: *absinthe, lingerie* pronounced /ˈlænʒəriː/ (also pronounced /ˈlɒndʒəreɪ/), *meringue, pince-nez, timbale, timbre*
- with /ə/: a large set of adjectives/adverbs ending in <-ibl-e/y> pronounced /əbəl, əbliː/, e.g. *possibl-e/y*, all of which can also be pronounced with /ɪ/. Also in a few adverbs ending <-arily> when not stressed on the syllable spelt with <a>, which becomes elided (see section 6.10), so that the <i> in <-ily> is pronounced /ə/, e.g. *necessarily, voluntarily* pronounced /ˈnesəsrəliː, ˈvɒləntrəliː/ (also pronounced /nesəˈserɪliː, vɒlənˈterɪliː/ with <i> pronounced /ɪ/ and stress on the preceding syllable spelt with <a> which is pronounced /e/)
- with /iː/: *albino, ambergris, amino, ballerina, batik, casino, chic, cliché, concertina, diva, farina, frisson, gilet, kilo, lido, litre, maraschino, marina, massif, merino, modiste, mosquito, motif, ocarina, piquan-t/cy, scarlatina, semolina, visa*; first <i> in *graffiti, kiwi, martini, migraine, milieu*, second <i> in *aperitif, bikini, incognito, libido*
- with /aɪ/ in a number of words before a single consonant letter and word-final <a, o>, e.g. *angina, giro, impetigo, lino, mica, proviso, rhino, saliva, silo, vagina, viva* (*voce*) ('oral exam'); otherwise only in *mic* /maɪk/. In all these words the syllable spelt with <i> is stressed
- with /aɪ/ in a number of words where <i> is the only or last vowel letter and is followed by more than one consonant letter: *child, Christ, indict, mild, ninth, paradigm, pint, whilst, wild* and the <-ign, -ind> groups: *align, assign, benign, consign, design, malign, resign, sign* (sub-exception: *ensign*, with /ə/); *behind, bind, blind, find, grind, hind, kind, (re)mind, rind, wind* pronounced /waɪnd/ ('turn'; contrast *wind* pronounced /wɪnd/ 'stiff breeze'). The <-ind> pronounced /aɪnd/ group is one of only five cases where the pronunciation of a phonogram/rime is more predictable as a unit than from the correspondences of the separate graphemes, and there are enough instances to make the rule worth teaching; see section A.7 in Appendix A
- with /aɪ/ in an unpredictable ragbag of other words, e.g. *binary, bison, finance, final*, first <i> in *finite* (but none of its derivatives), *library, licence, license, micron, migrant, minus, paradigmatic, piracy* pronounced /ˈpaɪrəsiː/ (also pronounced /ˈpɪrəsiː/), *primacy, primary, primate, primus, rival, silent, sinus, siphon, sisal, strident, tiger, trident, vibrant, vital*

7) The regular pronunciation of <i> as a single-letter grapheme in final position in words with at least one earlier vowel letter is /iː/, e.g. *anti*,

*bikini, graffiti, khaki, kiwi, muesli, spaghetti, svengali, wiki*. Exceptions (all with /aɪ/): *alibi, alkali,* (*anno*) *domini,* (*a*) *fortiori/ posteriori/priori,* (*lapis*) *lazuli, quasi, rabbi* and some Latin plurals, e.g. *alumni, bacilli, cacti, foci, fundi* (/'fʌndaɪ/, plural of *fundus* 'inner corner of organ'; contrast *fundi* pronounced /'fʊndiː/, either South and East African English for 'expert/skilled person', or a member of the fundamentalist, uncompromising wing of the German Green Party), *fungi, gladioli,* and lots of Latin biological terms with anglicised pronunciations, e.g. *leylandii*, plus Greek *bronchi, chi, phi, pi, psi, xi.*

There appear to be only nine words with <i> as the only vowel letter, and in word-final position; most have /aɪ/, namely the greeting *Hi!*, the pronoun *I*, and the Greek letter names (as pronounced in English) *chi, phi, pi, psi, xi*, but even this tiny set has two exceptions with /iː/: the musical term *mi*, and *ski*.

Almost all words ending /ɪk(əl/s) spelt <-ic(al/s)> have stress on the preceding syllable. Exceptions: *Árabic, aríthmetic* (noun), *ársenic* (noun, if pronounced /'ɑːsənɪk/ with three syllables), *bíopic* (pronounced /'baɪjəʊpɪk/ by those who recognise its origin as an abbreviation of 'biographical picture', = film), *cátholic* (if pronounced /'kæθəlɪk/, with three syllables), *cérvical* /'sɜːvɪkəl/ (as in *cérvical vertebrae*, in the neck – but see below), *chóleric, climácteric, héretic, impólitic(ly), lúnatic, pólitic(ly/s), rhétoric, túrmeric* – but *arithmétic* (adjective), *arithmétical, arsénic* (/ɑːˈsenɪk/, adjective), *herétical, polítical, rhetórical* follow the rule; so does *biópic* (pronounced /baɪˈjɒpɪk/ (rhymes with *myopic*) by those who apply the general 'stress the syllable before <ic>' rule, thus proving its psychological reality).

*Arsenic* (noun) and *catholic* pronounced with three syllables are exceptions, but both more often have the central written vowel elided (see section 6.10) and are pronounced /'ɑːsnɪk, 'kæθlɪk /, with two syllables. Phonologically, this makes them regular – they are stressed on the syllable preceding /ɪk/ spelt <ic>. However, in terms of predicting word stress from written forms, they are still exceptions – they are stressed on the syllable containing the second vowel letter before the <ic> instead of the first.

Other words with two pronunciations, but differing in stress, are (*fly*) *agaric* /əˈgærɪk/ (regular) or /ˈægərɪk/ (exception), *chivalric* /ʃɪˈvælrɪk/ (regular) or /ˈʃɪvəlrɪk/ (exception); on *chivalric* the Oxford English Dictionary says 'The first pronunciation is that sanctioned by the poets'. Extensions: Greek plurals such as *erótica*; the modern coinage *emóticon*. Also note the modern contrast in meaning between *cervical* /ˈsɜːvɪkəl/ in *cérvical vertebrae* (in the neck) and /sɜːˈvaɪkəl/ in *cervical cancer/smear* (in the cervix/entrance to the womb).

The vowel preceding <ic> always has a 'short' pronunciation (except in *aphasic* with /eɪ/, *acetic, emic, graphemic, phonemic, scenic* with /iː/, and *biopic* pronounced /ˈbaɪəʊpɪk/, *chromic, phobic* and all its compounds, with /əʊ/), as does the <i> in <ic>, except in *cervical* pronounced /sɜːˈvaɪkəl/.

# 10.23 <ie>

N.B. <i.e> has a separate entry. On the percentages see Notes.

## THE MAIN SYSTEM

| Basic phoneme | /iː/ | 73% | e.g. *brief, diesel, achieve, calorie* |

## THE REST

| | | pronounced | |
|---|---|---|---|
| Exceptions to main system | <ie> | /aɪ/ | 21% in a very small set of words in word-final position, namely *die, fie, hie, lie, pie, tie, vie* |
| | <ie> | /e/ | 6% only in *friend* |
| | <ie> | /ɪ/ | <1% only in *(hand/nec)kerchief, mischief, mischievous, sieve* |
| Oddities | <ier> | /ɪə/ | never initial; only in (medially) *fierce, pierce, tierce*; (word-finally) *bandolier, bier, bombardier, brigadier, cashier, cavalier, chandelier, chevalier, clavier, corsetier, frontier, fusilier, gondolier, grenadier, halberdier, pier, tier, vizier* and a few other very rare words. <ier> is always stressed, except that *frontier* is pronounced either /ˈfrʌntɪə/ or /frʌnˈtɪə/. In all other words ending <ier> the <i> and the <er> are/belong to separate graphemes and belong to separate syllables – see Notes |
| | <ieu> | /uː/ | only in *lieu* pronounced /luː/ (also pronounced /ljuː/) |
| 2-phoneme graphemes | (none) | | |

## NOTES

Even though Gontijo et al. (2003) analyse final <ie> in words where there is at least one earlier vowel letter as being pronounced /ɪ/ it was possible to re-allocate all such words to /iː/ and recalculate the percentages.

<i, e> are/belong to separate graphemes in *anxiety, convenient, leniency, science, twentieth* and all other words with those endings, plus *adieu, alien, client(ele), conscientious, diet, fiery, medieval, milieu, oubliette, quiet(us), serviette, spaniel, soviet, (inter/re-)view*. All have an intervening /j/-glide except *adieu, (inter/re-)view, spaniel*, where the <i> spells /j/ after a preceding consonant anyway.

<i, er> are, or belong to, separate graphemes in:
- all three-syllable comparative adjectives in <-ier> pronounced /iːjə/ formed from two-syllable adjectives ending in <-y>, e.g. *easier, happier*
- *barrier, espalier* with /iːjə/, *colliery* with /je/, *dossier* with /iːjə/ or /iːjeɪ/, *drier, flier, pliers* with /aɪə/
- a few words in which the <i> always or sometimes forms a digraph with the preceding consonant letter: *crosier, hosier, osier, brazier, crozier, glazier* sometimes pronounced with /ʒə/ (alternatively with /iːjə/); *soldier* with /dʒə/.

## 10.24 <i.e>

Occurs only where <e> is word-final.

See Notes for all categories and for how this split digraph is defined, and see section 11.4 for a teaching rule relevant to all split digraphs except <y.e>.

### THE MAIN SYSTEM

| Basic phoneme | /aɪ/ | 97% | e.g. *bike, live* (adjective), *time* |
| Other phoneme | /iː/ | 3% | only in about 88 mostly French loanwords, e.g. *police, quiche* |

### THE REST

| Exceptions to main system | strictly speaking, none, but see Notes |
| Oddities | (none) |
| 2-phoneme graphemes | (none) |

## NOTES

The split digraph <i.e> is defined as covering words where the <e> is separated from the <i> by one consonant letter other than <r> and the <i> is not preceded by a vowel letter and the digraph is pronounced either /aɪ/ or /iː/. The definition covers both words where the intervening consonant letter is an independent grapheme and words where the <e> is also part of a split digraph <ce, ge, ve> – see sections 3.7.4, 3.7.6-7 and 3.8.4, and section 7.1 for dual-functioning. See also section A.6 in Appendix A.

The familiar /aɪ/ pronunciation occurs in many hundreds of words and does not need further illustration. The /iː/ pronunciation occurs only in about 88 (mostly French) loanwords; those which fit the main definition just given (for extensions see below) are: *caprice, police; automobile, imbecile; centime, regime; beguine, benedictine* ('liqueur'), *benzine, bombazine, brigantine, brilliantine, chlorine, citrine, cuisine, dentine, figurine, gabardine, guillotine, iodine, latrine, libertine, limousine, machine, magazine, margarine, marine, mezzanine, morphine, nectarine, nicotine, opaline, phosphine, plasticine, pristine, quarantine, quinine, ravine, routine, sardine, sistine, strychnine, submarine, tagine, tambourine, tangerine, terrine, tontine, trampoline, tyrosine, undine, vaccine, vitrine, wolverine; anise, cerise, chemise, expertise, valise; elite, marguerite, petite, suite; naive, recitative.*

Extensions:
1) There are four words where <i.e> pronounced /aɪ/ is separated by two consonant letters forming a digraph: *blithe, lithe, tithe, writhe;*
2) There are 18 words where <i.e> pronounced /iː/ is separated by two letters forming a consonant digraph: *fiche, niche* pronounced /niːʃ/, *pastiche, quiche; fatigue, intrigue; chenille; antique, boutique, clique, critique, mystique, oblique, physique, pique, technique, unique; pelisse;*
3) There are three words where <i.e> pronounced /iː/ is separated by <s, t> pronounced separately: *artiste, dirigiste, modiste;*
4) There are two words where <i.e> pronounced /iː/ is separated by the three letters <squ> pronounced /sk/, with <qu> forming a consonant digraph: *bisque, odalisque.*

Exceptions (all words with at least one earlier vowel letter, except *give, live* (verb)) where the <i> is a separate grapheme pronounced /ɪ/ and the <e> forms a digraph with the intervening consonant letter:
- a set of words ending in <-ice> in which <-ce> is a digraph pronounced /s/: *accomplice, apprentice, armistice, artifice, auspice, avarice,*

*benefice, bodice, caddice, chalice, cicatrice* (but the plural *cicatrices* is pronounced /sɪkəˈtraɪsiːz/, *cockatrice, coppice, cornice, cowardice, crevice, dentifrice, edifice, hospice, jaundice, justice, lattice, malice, notice, novice, office, orifice, poultice, practice, precipice, prejudice, pumice, service, solstice, surplice*. All words in <-ice> with no earlier vowel letter are pronounced with /aɪs/, as are *advice, device, sacrifice, suffice* – and see above for *caprice, police*

- one word ending in <-ice> pronounced /ɪʃ/: *liquorice* (also pronounced with /s/)
- one word ending in <-ife> pronounced /ɪf/: *housewife* ('sewing kit'), pronounced /ˈhʌzɪf/
- a set of words ending in <-ine> in which <-ne> is a digraph pronounced /n/: *bowline, clandestine* pronounced /klænˈdestɪn/ (also pronounced /ˈklændəstaɪn/, in which case <i.e> is a split digraph), *compline, crinoline, (pre)destine, determine, discipline, doctrine, engine, ermine, examine, famine, feminine, genuine, heroine, illumine, imagine, intestine, jasmine, marline, masculine, medicine, peregrine, saccharine, sanguine, urine, vaseline*
- five words ending in <-ise> in which <-se> is a digraph pronounced /s/: *mortise, practise, premise, promise, treatise*
- several words in <-ite> in which <-te> is a digraph pronounced /t/: *composite, definite, exquisite, favourite, granite, hypocrite, infinite, opposite, perquisite, plebiscite, requisite*
- a large number of words ending in <-ive>, e.g. *adjective, massive*, all of which are pronounced with /ɪv/ except *naive, recitative*, which end in /iːv/ and therefore have the split digraph pronounced /iː/ and are so listed above; also *give, live* (verb) – most words in <-ive> with no earlier vowel letter have /aɪv/, e.g. *chive, dive, five, jive, live* (adjective), *shrive, strive, swive, thrive, wive*.

There are very few English words ending in <-ige>. The only two to which the regular pronunciation /aɪdʒ/ applies are *(dis)oblige* (both stressed on the <i> before <ge>). Otherwise there are only the two exceptions *vestige*, with unstressed /ɪdʒ/, and *prestige*, with stressed /iːʒ/.

The only words in which a final <e> after <i>+consonant is pronounced separately appear to be *anime* (from Japanese), *(bona) fide* (Latin) and *campanile* (from Italian).

# 10.25 <igh>

## THE MAIN SYSTEM

Only phoneme /aɪ/  100%  e.g. *sigh, sight*. Always follows a consonant letter, and is therefore never word-initial

## NOTES

In my analysis, there are no cases where <i, gh> are separate graphemes.

Provided that analysis is accepted, this is one of the very few rules without exceptions in the whole system. However, as far as I can ascertain (even digging around for rare and archaic words), there seem to be just 26 stem words in the entire language containing this grapheme: *high, nigh, sigh, thigh; bight, blight, bright, fight, flight, fright, hight, knight, light, might, night, plight, right, sight, slight, tight, wight, wright; alight* (in its 'descend from vehicle' sense; in its 'on fire' sense it is derived from *light* (a fire)), *delight; Blighty, sprightly* – some of which are of very high frequency – plus many derivatives. Perhaps the shortage of such words is why the rule is 100% reliable.

Clymer (1963/1996) cited two different supposed pronunciation rules that are relevant here:
11. When the letter *i* is followed by the letters *gh*, the *i* usually stands for its long sound and the *gh* is silent.
25. When *ght* is seen in a word, *gh* is silent.
He said rule 25 has 100% 'utility' (= reliability) and rule 11 only 71%.

Rule 25 really is 100% accurate in its own terms because it covers not only the 21 words listed above containing <ight> but also the only word containing <aight>: *straight*, and the only five words with <eight>: *eight, freight, height, sleight, weight*. However, the rule is unhelpful because (a) telling learners that some letters are 'silent' may be confusing (for more on that see section A.5 in Appendix A); (b) it seems to me much more logical to analyse the <gh> in all the relevant words as part of a vowel grapheme with the preceding vowel letter(s); (c) as it stands, the rule does not specify the pronunciation of the preceding vowel grapheme.

Rule 11 is also unhelpful on grounds (a) and (b). Also, as several commentators have pointed out, it fails to reach 100% reliability only because it is underspecified. If formulated as 'After a consonant letter, <igh> is always pronounced /aɪ/', it is 100% reliable and well worth teaching. The restriction 'after a consonant letter' is to exclude the six words with <aight/eight> listed in the previous paragraph, plus six with just <eigh>: *heigh, inveigh, neigh, neighbour, sleigh, weigh.*

For more about Clymer's rules see chapter 11.

# 10.26 <ir>

### THE MAIN SYSTEM

Basic phoneme    /ɜː/    100%    e.g. *fir*

### THE REST

| | | | pronounced | |
|---|---|---|---|---|
| Exceptions to main system | | | | <1% in total |
| | <ir> | /ɪə/ | | only in *emir, fakir, nadir* pronounced /ˈneɪdɪə, næˈdɪə/ (also pronounced /ˈneɪdə/), *kir, kirsch, souvenir, tapir* |
| | <ir> | /aɪ/ | | only in *iron* /ˈaɪən/ |
| | <ir> | as 2-phoneme sequence /aɪə/ | | only medially but always stressed and mainly where <-e> has been deleted from words in the following paragraph, e.g. *aspiring, desirous, expiry, spiral, tiring,* but there are a few independent examples, e.g. *biro, giro, pirate, virus.* In all cases the <r> is both part of <ir> and a grapheme in its own right pronounced /r/. For dual-functioning see section 7.1. In *deliri-ous/um,* by contrast, <i, r> are separate graphemes, the <i> is pronounced /ɪ/, and the <r> has only one function and is (of course) pronounced /r/ |
| Oddities | <ire> | as 2-phoneme sequence /aɪə/ | | only word-finally and only in *ac/in/re-quire, admire, a/con/in/per/re/tran-spire, attire, desire, dire, empire, entire, expire, fire, hire, (be/quag)mire, quire, saltire, samphire, sapphire, satire, shire, sire, spire, e)squire, tire, umpire, vampire, wire.* Many of these words allow /r/-linking, e.g. *aspiring, spiral* - see previous paragraph and section 3.6 |

|                          |        |      |                                                                                                                                                                                                                                                                                                                 |
|--------------------------|--------|------|------|
|                          | <irr>  | /ɜː/ | only in *chirr, shirr, whirr* and suffixed forms of verbs in <-ir>, e.g. *stirring*; otherwise <i, rr> are separate graphemes, e.g. in *irrigate, irritant*. In (e.g.) *stirring, whirring* there is /r/-linking (see section 3.5) and <rr> is both part of <irr> and a grapheme in its own right pronounced /r/. For dual-functioning see section 7.1 |
| *Other 2-phoneme graphemes* | (none) | | |

N.B. For word-final <l, le, m, n> involved in 2-phoneme sequences with /ə/ see sections 9.20–23.

## 10.27 <o>

N.B. <o.e, oi, oo, or, ore, ou, ow, oy> have separate entries.

### THE MAIN SYSTEM

For all these categories see Notes.

| *Basic phoneme* | /ɒ/  | 41% | predominant in words with no other vowel letter, e.g. *box, from, of, on, not, sock* |
|---|---|---|---|
| *Other phonemes* | /uː/ | 18% | only in *zoology* (first <o>) and derivatives and 10 other stem words – see Notes; several are very frequent |
| | /əʊ/ | 16% | e.g. *go, lotion, most, ocean, roving*. Regular where <e>-deletion has occurred, before some word-final consonant clusters, before some endings, word-finally, and in <-osis> |
| | /ə/  | 14% | e.g. *bishop, Briton, oblige, union* |
| | /ʌ/  | 9%  | only in a restricted set of words, e.g. *above, come, done, monk* |

## THE REST

|  |  | pronounced |  |
|---|---|---|---|
| Exceptions to main system |  |  | 2% in total |
|  | <o> | /ɪ/ | only in *pigeon* (taking <ge> as pronounced /dʒ/; compare *pidgin*), *women* |
|  | <o> | /ʊ/ | only in *bosom* (1st <o>), *wol-f/ves*, *wolfram*, *wolverine*, *Wolverhampton* (1st <o>), *woman* |
|  | <o> | as 2-phoneme sequence /wʌ/ | only in *once*, *one* |
| Oddities | <oa> | /əʊ/ | only in (initially) *oaf, oak, oast, oat, oath*; (medially) *approach, bloat, boast, boat, broach, cloak, coach, coal, coast, coat, coax, croak, encroach, float, foal, foam, gloaming, gloat, goad, goal, goat, groan, groat, hoax, loach, load, loaf, loam, loan, loath, loathe, moan, moat, poach, reproach, roach, road, roam, roan, roast, shoal, soak, soap, stoat, throat, toad, toast, woad*; (finally) *cocoa, whoa* |
|  | <oa> | /ɔː/ | only in *abroad, broad(en)* |
|  | <oar> | /ɔː/ | only in *boar, board, coarse, hoar, hoard, hoarse, oar, roar, soar* |
|  | <oar> | /ə/ | only in *cupboard, larboard, starboard* |
|  | <oat> | /əʊ/ | only in *boatswain* pronounced /ˈbəʊsən/ (also pronounced /ˈbəʊtsweɪn/) |
|  | <oe> | /iː/ | only in *amenorrhoea, amoeba, apnoea, coelacanth, coelenterate, coeliac, coelom, coenobite, coenocyte, diarrhoea, dyspnoea, foetal, foetid, foetus, gonorrhoea, logorrhoea, oedema, oenology, oesophagus, oestrogen, oestrus, pharmacopoeia, phoenix, pyorrhoea, subpoena*. Many of these words have alternative spellings in <e>, especially in US spelling |

| | | |
|---|---|---|
| <oe> | /əʊ/ | except in *throes*, only word-final and only in *aloe, doe, floe, foe, hoe, oboe, roe, schmoe, sloe, toe, woe* |
| <oe> | /uː/ | only in *canoe, hoopoe, shoe* |
| <oe> | /ʌ/ | only in *does(n't)* |
| <oer> | /ɔː, ʊə/ | only in *Boer* pronounced /bɔː, bʊə/ |
| <oeu> | /uː/ | only in *manoeuvre* |
| <oh> | /əʊ/ | only in *doh, kohl, Oh, ohm, soh* |
| <ol> | /əʊ/ | only in *folk, Holborn, holm, yolk* and old-fashioned pronunciation of *golf* as /gəʊf/ |
| <olo> | /ɜː/ | only in *colonel* |
| <os> | /əʊ/ | only in *apropos* |
| <ot> | /əʊ/ | only in *argot, depot, entrepot, haricot, jabot, matelot, potpourri, sabot, tarot, tricot*. /t/ surfaces in *sabotage, saboteur* – see section 7.2 |

Other 2-phoneme graphemes (none)

## NOTES

<o, a> (with intervening /w/-glide) belong to separate graphemes in *coagulate, coalesce, coalition, coaxial, Croatia, hypoallergenic, oasis, protozoa*, etc. For cases where <o, e> belong to separate graphemes see *coerce*, etc., below.

<ol, olo, os, ot> are single graphemes only in the Oddities listed.

For instances of <o> as an elided vowel see section 6.10.

The default pronunciation of <o> as a single-letter grapheme is /ɒ/, but here are some categories for guidance:
- regular in words with no other vowel letter, e.g. *bob, boll* (also pronounced with /əʊ/), *box, cod, crotch, dog, doll, from, knoll, lock, long, loll, loss, moll, odd, of, off, on, plonk, poll* ('parrot'), *troll, shop, yon*. Extensions: *begone, gone*. Exceptions: *boll* (sometimes), *droll, poll* ('head, vote'), *roll, scroll, stroll, toll* with /əʊ/, *wolf* with /ʊ/. See section 11.3 for a teaching rule relevant to ..VC monosyllables
- in a few words where <o> is the last vowel letter, e.g. *alcohol, belong, compost, methanol, micron, parasol, phenol, protocol*

- regular before geminate and doubled consonant spellings (in addition to relevant words in the previous category), e.g. *bobbin, cockle, locket, coddle, codger, lodge, coffee, toggle, atoll, dollop, holly, jolly, lolly, polly, topple, lorry, across, blossom, crotchet, bottle, s(c)hemozzle*, first <o> in *follow, connotation*. Extensions: *garrotte, gavotte*
- mostly before consonant clusters (in addition to relevant words in previous caregories), e.g. *confident, costume, doldrums, donkey, obstinate, ostensible, posterior, tonsils*, but there are quite a few exceptions – see later categories
- before a single consonant letter followed by the endings <-ic(al)>, e.g. *atomic, boric, carbolic, chaotic, exotic, frolic, harmonic, logic(al), phonic(s), tonic, topic(al)*. This includes all the words ending <-ological>, e.g. *biological, sociological*. Exceptions: *biopic* pronounced /ˈbaɪjəʊpɪk/, *chromic, phobic* and all its compounds, with /əʊ/
- in final <-ogue>, e.g. *analogue, catalogue, dialogue*, plus *baroque*
- as the first <o> in the suffix <-ology> pronounced /ˈɒlədʒiː/, e.g. *biology, chronology*, etc.
- in a few other non-final occurrences, e.g. *admonish, bother, demolish, grovel, homage, hovel, hover, moderate, modest, moral, novel, novice, olive, polish, poverty, project* (noun), *proper, provenance, proverb, robin, scholar, sovereign*, first <o> in *gondola, provocation*.

The task then is to try to define when <o> has other pronunciations.

<o> is pronounced /wʌ/ only in *once, one*.

No rules can be given for when <o> is pronounced /ʌ/, except that in stem words it never occurs word-finally, and initially it occurs only in *onion, other, oven*, so here is a list of its medial occurrences: *above, accomplice, accomplish, amok, become, borough, brother, Cadogan, colour, colander* (also pronounced with /ɒ/), *Colombia* (seond <o>), *come, comfort(able), comfrey, comfy, company, (en)compass, conjure* ('do magic tricks'), *constable, coven, covenant, (dis/re/un-)cover, covert* pronounced /ˈkʌvɜːt/ (also pronounced /ˈkʊəvɜːt/), *covet(ous), covey, coz, cozen, done, dost, doth, dove, dozen, dromedary, front, frontier, glove, govern, honey, London* (first <o>), *lovage, love, Lovell, Monday, monetary, money, monger* and its compounds, *mongrel, monk, monkey, Monroe, Montgomery* (twice), *month, mother, none, nothing, plover, shove, shovel, slovenly, smother, sojourn* (also pronounced with /ɒ/), *some, somersault, son, sponge, thorough, ton, tonne, tongue, twopence, twopenny, windhover, won, wonder, worrit, worry.* Some words which used to have /ʌ/ in RP now have /ɒ/ instead, e.g. *combat, comrade, conduit, Coventry.*

Similarly, no rules can be given for when <o> is pronounced /uː/, but it occurs only for the first <o> of *zoology* and derivatives with initial <zoo-> (Greek, 'living thing') spelling two syllables pronounced /zuːˈwɒ/ if the second syllable is stressed, otherwise /zuːwə/, and 10 other stem words: *caisson* pronounced /kəˈsuːn/, *canton* ('provide accommodation', pronounced /kænˈtuːn/), *catacomb, do, lasso, to, tomb, two, who, womb,* plus derivatives including *cantonment, lassoing, whom,* and a few from words in which <o.e> is a split digraph pronounced /uː/, e.g. *approval, movie, removal,* and the proper nouns *Aloysius* /æluːˈwɪʃəs/, *Romania, Wrotham* /ˈruːtəm/.

<o> is pronounced /əʊ/:
- in hundreds of words where final <e> has been deleted, e.g. *dosage, dotage, global, modal, polar, rosy, roving, tonal*
- regularly in word-final position, e.g. *albino, amino, audio, calico, casino, fiasco, fro, gecko, giro, go, incognito, indigo, impetigo, kilo, libido, lido, lino, kimono, manifesto, maraschino, merino, no, patio, piano, piccolo, polio, portico, potato, proviso, radio, ratio, rhino, scherzo, silo, studio, trio, tobacco, tomato, tremolo, video* (for exceptions with /uː/ see above)
- often before a consonant cluster, e.g. *behold, bold, cold, cuckold, (blind/mani-) fold, gold, hold, marigold, old, scaffold, scold, sold, threshold, told, wold; bolt, colt, dolt, jolt, revolt, volt; don't, wont, won't; almost, ghost, host, most, post; solder, soldier; bolster, holster; molten.* Word-final <-old> pronounced /əʊld/ group is one of only five cases where the pronunciation of a phonogram/rime is more predictable as a unit than from the correspondences of the separate graphemes, and there are enough instances to make the rule worth teaching; see section A.7 in Appendix A. Exceptions: *belong, font, cost, frost, lost* and most words where <o> is not the last vowel letter, e.g. *costume, foster, hostage, hostile,* all with /ɒ/, *scaffolding* with /ə/, *front* and others listed above with /ʌ/, *catacomb, tomb, womb* with /uː/
- in eight words before final <-ll>: *boll* (also pronounced with /ɒ/), *droll, plimsoll, poll* ('head, vote'), *roll, scroll, stroll, toll* (contrast *atoll, doll, knoll, loll, poll* ('parrot'), *troll,* all with /ɒ/), and in four words before final <-l>: *control, enrol, extol, patrol* (in these four words the syllable spelt with the relevant <o> is stressed)

- in a few other words with no other vowel letter: *both, comb, gross, loth, quoth, sloth, troth*
- in all the words in <-osis>, e.g. *diagnosis, neurosis*
- before a consonant letter other than <r> and word-final <a, o>, e.g. *aroma, diploma, iota, kimono, sofa* (in all these words the syllable spelt with the relevant <o> is stressed)
- (with intervening /w/-glide) in a few words before <e>: *coeducational, coerce, coexist, hydroelectric, phloem, poem, poetic* – but most examples of <oe> constitute a single grapheme; see the Oddities
- before endings <-ia(ge/l/n), -ion, -ious, -ium>: *ammonia, apologia, begonia, magnolia, foliage, ceremonial, colonial, social, custodian; corrosion, erosion, ex/im-plosion; devotion, lotion, (com/e/loco/ pro-)motion, notion, potion; acrimonious, atrocious, ceremonious, copious, euphonious, felonious, ferocious, harmonious, parsimonious, precocious, sanctimonious; chromium, opium, pandemonium, sodium, symposium* (in all these words the syllable spelt with the relevant <o> is stressed)
- in a ragbag of other words, e.g. *bogus, bohemian, bonus, bosun, brochure, bromide, cobra, cocoa, codeine, cogent, cohort, colon, crocus, focal, focus, grotesque, local, locus, lotus, molar, moment, (e)motive, nomad, notary, oval, potent, proton, robust, rodeo, rodent, romance, rosary, rotary, rotund, slogan, solar, sonar, total, betroth, vocal, votary, votive, yodel, yokel.*

/ə/ is the regular pronunciation of unstressed <o> in initial and medial positions. Word-initially, however, the pronunciation of <o> as /ə/ occurs only in the Latin prefix <ob-> and its derivatives, e.g. in *oblige, obscene, obscure, observe, obsess, obtain, occasion, occur, offend, official*. Medially, <o> is pronounced /ə/ in:
- the prefixes <con- (and related forms), pro-, to-> pronounced /kən (etc.), prə, tə/, e.g. *collect, collide, command, commit(tee), confess, connect, connive, connubial, consent, continue, contingency, contrast* (verb, pronounced /kən'trɑːst/), *corrode, corrupt; procure, produce, profane, profess(or), prolong; today, together, tomorrow*
- the end of the word-elements <bio-, chloro-, micro-, mono-, phono-, photo-, saxo-> when unstressed
- the very large set of words with word-final <-ion>, e.g. *coercion, vision, mission, nation, accordion, aphelion, bastion, battalion, billion, bullion, carrion, centurion, champion, clarion, collodion, companion, criterion, dominion, ganglion, ion, lion, medallion, million, mullion, minion, oblivion, onion, opinion, pavilion, perihelion, pinion, rebellion,*

- *scorpion, scullion, stallion, union* and even *anion, ion, cation* (no exceptions)
- the (much smaller) set of words with word-final <-eon>, namely *bludgeon, chameleon, curmudgeon, dudgeon, dungeon, galleon, gudgeon, melodeon, Odeon, smidgeon, sturgeon, surgeon, widgeon*. Only exception: *pigeon*, with /ɪ/
- another small set before word-final <m, n>: *axiom, bosom, bottom, custom; Briton, button, carton, cotton, iron, matron, pardon, siphon/syphon, summon, wanton*. Exception: *icon*, with /ɒ/
- a further small set where it occurs between a vowel letter and a single word-final consonant letter, e.g. *chariot, halcyon, idiot, idol, patriot, period, vitriol*
- the noun-forming ending <-dom> pronounced /dəm/, e.g. *kingdom, wisdom*
- the adjectival ending <-some> pronounced /səm/, e.g. *handsome*, and a few other words with the same-sounding ending; *besom, blossom, buxom, hansom, lissom, ransom, transom*
- the noun endings <-ock, -od, -op> pronounced /ək, əd, əp/, e.g. *bollock, bullock, buttock, hassock, hillock, mattock, pillock, rowlock; method, synod; bishop, gallop, wallop*
- the second <o> in the suffix <-ology> pronounced /ˈɒlədʒiː/, e.g. *biology, chronology*, etc.
- the first <o> in the suffix <-ological> pronounced /əˈlɒdʒɪkəl/, e.g. *biological, sociological*, etc.
- a ragbag of words including *abdomen, acrobat, agony, almoner, amphora, anemone, aphrodisiac, automobile* (twice), *carol, cellophane, cenotaph, cupola, custody, daffodil, ebony, espionage, exodus, geographic, iodine, irony, isobar, isogloss, isolate, ivory, kaolin, lobelia, mandolin, mimeograph, mutton, parabola, parody, pergola, petrol, piston, plethora, police, purpose, ricochet, second, sobriety, society, theocratic, violate, violin*; first <o> in *bolero* (/bəˈleərəʊ/, 'dance'), *creosote, piccolo, proprietor, stereophonic, tobacco, tremolo*; second <o> in *broccoli, choreographic, colloquy, gondola, obloquy, rollocking*.

## 10.28 <o.e>

Occurs only where the <e> is word-final.

See Notes for all categories and for how this split digraph is defined, and see section 11.4 for a teaching rule relevant to all split digraphs except <y.e>.

## THE MAIN SYSTEM

| | | | |
|---|---|---|---|
| Basic phoneme | /əʊ/ | 100% | e.g. *bone, chromosome, remote, cologne* |
| Other phoneme | /uː/ | <1% | only in *combe, lose, move, prove, whose* /kuːm, luːz, muːv, pruːv, huːz/ and *gamboge* pronounced /gæmˈbuːʒ/, plus the derived forms *ap/dis/im/re-prove, remove* |

## THE REST

| | |
|---|---|
| Exceptions to main system | strictly speaking, none, but see Notes |
| Oddities | (none) |
| 2-phoneme graphemes | (none) |

## NOTES

The split digraph <o.e> is defined as covering words where the <e> is separated from the <o> by one consonant letter other than <r, w> and the <o> is not preceded by a vowel letter and the digraph is pronounced /əʊ, uː/. The definition covers both words where the intervening consonant letter is an independent grapheme and words where the <e> is also part of a digraph <ce, ge (but see below), ve> – see sections 3.7.4, 3.7.6 and 3.8.4, and section 7.1 for dual-functioning.

The only extension needed is to cover *combe*, with two intervening letters forming a consonant digraph.

However, there are several words with <o, e> separated by a consonant letter(s) where the <o> is a separate grapheme and the <e> forms a di/trigraph with the consonant letter(s): *barcarole, compote, cote, (be)gone, scone, shone* with <o> pronounced /ɒ/, *above, become, come, done, dove, glove, love, none, shove, some, tonne* with /ʌ/, *purpose, welcome* and all the adjectives ending <-some> with /ə/. See also section A.6 in Appendix A.

There are very few English words ending <-oge>: *Doge* ('former chief magistrate of Venice'), which seems to be the only one in which the regular pronunciation of <o.e> as /əʊ/ always applies; *gamboge* pronounced /gæmˈbəʊʒ, gæmˈbuːʒ/; and a few even more obscure words derived from Greek or French. In *abalone, adobe, cicerone, coyote, expose* ('report of scandal'), *guacamole, sylloge* /ˈsɪlədʒiː/ <o, e> and the intervening consonant letter are all separate graphemes.

How should *opening* be analysed if it is pronounced not /ˈəʊpənɪŋ/ (where the <e> is pronounced /ə/) but /ˈəʊpnɪŋ/, with no medial schwa? Presumably not as the only instance of a non-word-final split digraph (/əʊ/ spelt <o.e>), but as another instance of an elided vowel – see section 6.10.

## 10.29 <oi>

### THE MAIN SYSTEM

Basic phoneme    /ɔɪ/    100%    e.g. *boil*

### THE REST

|  |  | pronounced |  |
|---|---|---|---|
| Exceptions to main system |  |  | <1% in total |
|  | <oi> | /ə/ | only in *connoisseur, porpoise, tortoise* |
|  | <oi> | as 2-phoneme sequence /waː/ | only in a few words more recently borrowed from French, e.g. *bourgeoisie, coiffeur/se, coiffure, croissant, pointe, soiree, toilette* |
| Oddity | <ois> | /iː/ | only in *chamois* (the leather, pronounced /ˈʃæmiː/ (also spelt *shammy*), as opposed to the animal from whose skin it is made, pronounced /ˈʃæmwaː/) |
| (Other) 2- and 3-phoneme graphemes |  |  |  |
|  | <oir> | as 2-phoneme sequence /ɔɪjə/ | only in *coir* |
|  | <oir> | as 2-phoneme sequence /waː/ | mainly word-final and only in a very few words more recently borrowed from French, namely *abattoir, boudoir, memoir, reservoir, voussoir*; non-finally, only in *avoirdupois*. /r/-linking occurs in *memoirist, noirish* – see section 3.6 |

| | | |
|---|---|---|
| <oir> | as 3-phoneme sequence /waɪə/ | only in *choir* |
| <oire> | as 2-phoneme sequence /waː/ | only word-finally and only in a very few words more recently borrowed from French, namely *aide-memoire, conservatoire, escritoire, grimoire, repertoire* |
| <ois> | as 2-phoneme sequence /waː/ | only word-finally and only in a very few words more recently borrowed from French, namely *avoirdupois, bourgeois* (/z/ surfaces in *bourgeoisie* – see section 7.2), *chamois* (the animal, pronounced /ˈʃæmwaː/, as opposed to the leather made from its skin, pronounced /ˈʃæmiː/, the latter also being spelt *shammy*), *patois* (contrast *fatwa*). Except in these words, <oi, s> are/belong to separate graphemes, e.g. in *noise, noisy* |

*NOTE*

If we follow Crystal (2012: 131–2), 'more recent' in terms of loanwords from French means after the Great Vowel Shift, which was complete by about AD 1600.

<o, i> (with automatic intervening /w/-glide) are separate graphemes in *coincide, coition, coitus, doing, echoic, echoing, egoism, Eloise, going, heroic, heroin(e), jingoism, Lois, oboist, soloist, stoic(al), toing* and *froing*.

## 10.30 <oo>

*THE MAIN SYSTEM*

For both categories see Notes.

| | | | |
|---|---|---|---|
| Basic phoneme | /ʊ/ | 51% | e.g. *book, good* |
| Other phoneme | /uː/ | 46% | e.g. *ooze, afternoon, baboon, booze, mood, snooker, bamboo, zoo, vamoose* |

## THE REST

|  |  | pronounced |  |
|---|---|---|---|
| Exceptions to main system | <oo> | /ʌ/ | 3% only in *blood, flood* |
|  | <oo> | /əʊ/ | <1% only in *brooch* |
| Oddities | <ooh> | /uː/ | only in *pooh* |
|  | <oor> | /ʊə/ | only in *boor, spoor*, and sometimes *moor, Moor, poor*. There is /r/-linking in, e.g., *boorish* – see section 3.6. See section 5.6.5 for the increasing replacement of /ʊə/ by /ɔː/ |
|  | <oor> | /ɔː/ | only in *door, floor*; also *moor, Moor, poor* if pronounced to rhyme with *door, floor*. There is /r/-linking in *Moorish* – see section 3.6. |
| 2-phoneme graphemes | (none) |  |  |

## NOTES

As the television series for teaching children to read used to say, 'Look out! OO is a double agent!' (sorry, James). That is, in RP <oo> is pronounced both /ʊ/ and /uː/ (never /juː/, however), the two pronunciations are fairly evenly balanced in frequency, and a few words can be pronounced with either phoneme, e.g. *food* /fʊd, fuːd/, *hoodlum* /ˈhʊdləm, ˈhuːdləm/, *room* /rʊm, ruːm/, *woofer* /ˈwʊfə, ˈwuːfə/ (and in some Scots accents there is no such distinction anyway).

<oo> pronounced /ʊ/ occurs in only about 28 stem words, namely the four words just listed plus *Chinook, forsook, foot, gooseberry* /ˈɡʊzbriː/, *hoof* (and its plural *hooves*), *poof(ter), soot, woof* (/wʊf/ 'barking'; contrast *woof* /wuːf/ 'weft'), *wool*, and most words ending in <d, k> with no earlier vowel letter: *good, hood* (plus its use as a suffix, e.g. *childhood), stood, wood* (and its derivative *woodbine); book, brook, cook, crook, hook, look, nook, rook, shook, took* (exceptions: *brood, mood, rood, snood; gook, snook, spook, stook* and the longer words *bazooka, gobbledegook, snooker*, all with /uː/).

The set of 12 words just listed with <-ook> pronounced /ʊk/ (against six with /uːk/) is one of only five cases where the pronunciation of a phonogram/ rime is more predictable as a unit than from the correspondences of the separate graphemes, and there are enough instances to make the rule worth teaching; see section A.7 in Appendix A.

In all words other than those pronounced with /ʊ/ and the three Oddities, <oo> is pronounced /uː/.

<o, o> (always with intervening /w/-glide, but not always with helpful hyphen) are separate graphemes in *co-op, cooperate, co-opt, coordinate, co-own, no-one, spermatozoon* and other words ending in <-zoon> ('living thing'), *zoology*.

## 10.31 <or>

N.B. <ore> has a separate entry.

### THE MAIN SYSTEM

| Basic phoneme | /ɔː/ | 72% | regular before a consonant letter (except another <r>), except in the following group and as noted under Oddities; for word-final position see the Exceptions, and for occurrences before a vowel letter see Notes |
|---|---|---|---|
| Other phoneme | /ɜː/ | 11% | regular after initial <w, wh> and before a consonant letter: *whortle(berry), word, work, world, worm, worse(n), worship, worst, wort, worth(y)* (exceptions: *worn* with /ɔː/, *worrit, worry* with /ʌ/, *worsted* 'cloth' with /ʊ/); otherwise only in *attorney* |

### THE REST

|  |  | pronounced |  |
|---|---|---|---|
| Exceptions to main system | <or> | /ə/ | 17% never initial; medially, regular in prefix <for-> pronounced /fə/, e.g. *forbid, forget, forgive, forsake* (but this is a very small set); otherwise rare medially, but cf. *Deptford* (and many other placenames with this element), *Holborn, scissors, stubborn*; regular word-finally, e.g. *error, horror, orator, sponsor*; exceptions (all with /ɔː/): *abhor, cantor, condor, corridor, cuspidor, décor, for* (when stressed), *grantor, humidor, ichor, lessor, matador, mentor, mortgagor, nor, or, praetor, quaestor, realtor, tor, toreador, vendor* |

|  |  |  |  |
|---|---|---|---|
|  | <or> | /ʊ/ | only in *worsted* ('cloth') pronounced /ˈwʊstɪd/ (when pronounced /ˈwɜːstɪd/ it means 'defeated') |
| Oddities | <orp> | /ɔː/ | only in *corps* (plural), pronounced /kɔːz/ |
|  | <orps> | /ɔː/ | only in *corps* (singular), pronounced /kɔː/ |
|  | <orr> | /ɔː/ | only in *abhorred* (in *abhorrent, borrow, horrible, horrid, torrid* <o, rr> are separate graphemes pronounced /ɒ, r/; and in *worrit, worry* <o, rr> are pronounced /ʌ, r) |
|  | <ort> | /ɔː/ | only in *mortgage, rapport*. /t/ surfaces in *rapporteur* – see section 7.2 |
| 2-phoneme graphemes | (none) |  |  |

### NOTE

Before a vowel letter, <or> is pronounced /ɔː/ only in *aurora, authorial, borax, chlorine, choral, chorus, corporeal, decorum, dictatorial, editorial, euphoria, flora(l), forum, glory, memorial, oracy, oral, oration, oratorio* (second <or>), *orient* (noun, 'The East', pronounced /ˈɔːriːjənt/), *quorum, variorum*. In all these words, the <r> is both part of the digraph <or> pronounced /ɔː/ and a grapheme in its own right pronounced /r/ (for dual-functioning see section 7.1), and the <or> is stressed (except in *oration* /ɔːˈreɪʃən/). Where the <or> is stem-final and the ending is a suffix, /r/-linking also occurs (see section 3.6), namely in *authorial, dictatorial, editorial, memorial*. In all other cases before a vowel letter, <o, r> are separate graphemes, e.g. in *corporation* (second <or>), *decorate, euphoric, florist, memory, orient* (verb, 'align correctly', pronounced /ɒriːˈjent/), first <or> in *orator, oratorio*. For <or> as an elided vowel spelling in *comfortable* see section 6.10.

## 10.32 <ore>

### THE MAIN SYSTEM

| Only phoneme (almost) | /ɔː/ | 100% | never initial; medially, only in compounds of *fore-*, of which there are 60+ (only exception: *forecastle* pronounced /ˈfəʊksəl/; also pronounced /ˈfɔːkɑːsəl/); regular word-finally, e.g. *carnivore, wore* |

## NOTE

In all other cases, <o, r, e> are separate graphemes, e.g. in *anorexia, forest*.

## 10.33 <ou>

### THE MAIN SYSTEM

| Basic phoneme | /aʊ/ | 48% | e.g. *about, out, pout, rout* |

### THE REST

|  |  | pronounced |  |
|---|---|---|---|
| Exceptions to main system | <ou> | /uː/ | 29% only in *accoutrement, acoustic, ampoule, barouche, bayou, bijou, bivouac, boudoir, boulevard, bouquet, boutique, canteloupe, caribou, carousel, cartouche, cougar, coulomb, coulter, coupe, coupon, (un)couth, croup, croupier, crouton, douche, embouchure, frou-frou, ghoul, goujon, goulash, group, insouciance, joule, louvre, marabou, moussaka, mousse, oubliette, outré, ouzo, pirouette, recoup, rouble, rouge, roulette, route, routine, silhouette, sou, soubrette, soufflé, soup, souvenir, toucan, toupee, troubadour, troupe, trousseau, vermouth* pronounced /vəˈmuːθ/ (also pronounced /ˈvɜːməθ/), *voussoir, you* |
|  | <ou> | /ə/ | 15% regular in the adjectival ending <-ous> pronounced /əs/, e.g. *anxious, famous*. Otherwise only in *camouflage, limousine, moustache, tambourine, vermouth* pronounced /ˈvɜːməθ/ (also pronounced /vəˈmuːθ/) |
|  | <ou> | /ʌ/ | 6% only in *chough, Colclough* pronounced /ˈkəʊlklʌf/ (also pronounced /ˈkəʊkliː/), *country, couple, couplet, courage, cousin, double, doublet, doubloon, enough, flourish, *hiccough* (properly spelt *hiccup*), *housewife* ('sewing kit', pronounced /ˈhʌzɪt/), *nourish, rough, slough* ('shed skin'), *sough, souther-n/ly, touch, tough, trouble, young* |

| | | | |
|---|---|---|---|
| | <ou> | /əʊ/ | 1% only in *boulder, bouquet* pronounced /bəʊˈkeɪ/ (also pronounced /buːˈkeɪ/), *mould(er/y), moult(ed/ing), poultice, poultry, shoulder, smoulder, soul* |
| | <ou> | /ɒ/ | only in *cough, hough, trough* |
| | <ou> | /ʊ/ | only in *courier, pouffe* pronounced /pʊf/ (also pronounced /puːf/) |
| | <ou> | /w/ | only in *ouija* |
| Oddities | <oue> | /uː/ | only in *denouement, moue* |
| | | | On all the <ough> categories see Notes |
| | <ough> | /ɔː/ | 42% of pronunciations of <ough> only in *bought, brought, fought, nought, ought, (be-)sought, thought, wrought* |
| | <ough> | /uː/ | 27% of pronunciations of <ough> only in *brougham, through* |
| | <ough> | /əʊ/ | 24% of pronunciations of <ough> only in *dough, furlough, (al)though* |
| | <ough> | /aʊ/ | 3% of pronunciations of <ough> only in *bough, doughty, drought, plough, slough* ('muddy place') |
| | <ough> | /ə/ | 2% of pronunciations of <ough> only in *borough, thorough* |
| | <ough> | /iː/ | only in *Colclough* pronounced /ˈkəʊkliː/ (also pronounced /ˈkəʊlklʌf/) |
| | <oul> | /ʊ/ | only in *could, should, would* (contrast *mould* /məʊld/ – another point in favour of the US spelling *mold*) |
| | <oup> | /uː/ | only in *coup* |
| | <our> | /ɔː/ | 67% of pronunciations of <our> only in *court(esan), course, four, mourn, pour, source, your(s)* |
| | <our> | /ə/ | 25% of pronunciations of <our> regular word-finally, e.g. *arbour, ardour, armour, behaviour, candour, clamour, clangour, colour, endeavour, favour, fervour, flavour, glamour, harbour, honour, humour, labour, neighbour, odour, parlour, rancour, rigour, rumour, saviour, splendour, succour, tumour,* |

*The grapheme-phoneme correspondences, 2* 417

|  |  |  |
|---|---|---|
|  |  | *valour, vapour, vigour*. In many of these words US spelling has <or>. For exceptions see next three paragraphs and the 2-phoneme sequence |
| <our> | /ɜː/ | 7% of pronunciations of <our> only medial, and only in *adjourn, bourbon* (/ˈbɜːbən/ 'whiskey'), *courteous, courtesy, journal, journey, scourge, sojourn* and *tourney* pronounced /ˈtɜːniː/ (also pronounced /ˈtʊəniː/) |
| <our> | /ʊə/ | 1% of pronunciations of <our> only in *amour, bourbon* (/ˈbʊəbɒn/ 'biscuit'), *bourgeois(ie), bourse, contour, detour, dour* pronounced /dʊə/ (also pronounced /ˈdaʊwə/), *entourage, gourd, gourmand, gourmet, houri, mourn* (e.g. in *mourning* pronounced /ˈmʊənɪŋ/ to distinguish it carefully from *morning* pronounced /ˈmɔːnɪŋ/), *potpourri* (if we take the second <r> as spelling /r/), *tour, tournament, tourney* pronounced /ˈtʊəniː/ (also pronounced /ˈtɜːniː/), *tourniquet, troubadour, velour*. There is /r/-linking in, e.g., *touring* - see section 3.6, and in *entourage, houri* the <r> is both part of grapheme <our> and a grapheme in its own right spelling /r/. For dual-functioning see section 7.1. See section 5.6.5 for the increasing replacement of /ʊə/ by /ɔː/. |
| <ou're> | /ɔː/ | only in *you're*. See section A.9 in Appendix A |
| <ous> | /uː/ | only in *rendezvous* |
| <out> | /uː/ | only in *mange-tout, ragout, surtout* |
| <oux> | /uː/ | only in *billet-doux, roux* |
| 2-phoneme grapheme | <our> as 2-phoneme sequence /aʊwə/ | in *devour, flour, lour, our, ours, scour, sour* and *dour* pronounced /ˈdaʊwə/ (also pronounced /dʊə/) |

## NOTES

<ou, r> are separate graphemes in *courage, flourish, nourish*.

For <ou> as an elided vowel spelling in *favourable, honourable* see section 6.10.

The six categories of <ough> listed above are those where it is a four-letter grapheme pronounced as a single phoneme, and the percentages given are for those circumstances. In other cases <ou, gh> are separate graphemes with separate pronunciations. For completeness the six 2-phoneme pronunciations of <ough> are listed here in the same manner as single-phoneme pronunciations:

<ough> pronounced /ɒf/ only in *cough, trough*
<ough> pronounced /ɒk/ only in *hough*
<ough> pronounced /ɒx/ only in (Irish) *lough* /lɒx/
<ough> pronounced /ʌf/ only in *chough, Colclough* pronounced /ˈkəʊlklʌf/, *enough, slough* ('shed skin'), *sough, tough*
<ough> pronounced /ʌp/ only in the (mis)spelling of *hiccup* as *hiccough*
<ough> pronounced /əx/ only in *McCullough* pronounced /məˈkʌləx/

Thus the 33 words containing <ough> have 12 pronunciations between them. The only semblance of a rule is that most of the words containing <-ought> (*bought, brought, fought, nought, ought, sought, thought, wrought*) are pronounced /ɔːt/, the only two exceptions being *doughty, drought* with /aʊt/. Note that two of the 2-phoneme pronuncations (/ɒx/ in *lough*, /əx/ in *McCullough*) do not occur in English stem words, and are therefore included here only for interest – they do not appear in my main lists of correspondences. See also Notes to section 9.15.

# 10.34 <ow>

### THE MAIN SYSTEM

| Basic phoneme | /aʊ/ | 45% | e.g. *allow, brown, cow, coward, how, owl* |
| Other phoneme | /əʊ/ | 44% | regular word-finally after <l, r>. See Note |

### THE REST

| | | pronounced | |
|---|---|---|---|
| Exceptions to main system | <ow> | /ɒ/ | 10% only in *(ac)knowledge, rowlock* |
| | <ow> | /ə/ | <1% only in *Meadowhall* (locally, in Sheffield), *sorrowful* |

| Oddity | <owe> /əʊ/ | only in *owe* |
|---|---|---|
| 2-phoneme graphemes | (none) | |

### NOTES

/əʊ/ is the regular pronunciation word-finally after <l, r>: *bellow, below, billow, blow, bungalow, callow, fallow, fellow, flow, follow, furbelow, glow, hallow, hollow, low, mallow, mellow, pillow, sallow, shallow, slow, swallow, tallow, wallow, whitlow, willow, yellow; arrow, barrow, borrow, burrow, crow, escrow, farrow, furrow, grow, harrow, marrow, morrow, narrow, row* /rəʊ/ ('line, use oars'), *sorrow, sparrow, throw, yarrow* (only exceptions: *allow* /əˈlaʊ/, *plow; brow, prow, row* /raʊ/ 'squabble'), *trow*).

Otherwise /əʊ/ occurs only in: (word-finally) *bestow, bow* (goes with *arrow;* contrast *bow* /baʊ/ 'incline deferentially'), *elbow, know, meadow, minnow, mow, shadow, show, snow, sow* ('plant seed'; contrast *sow* /saʊ/ 'female pig'), *stow, tow, widow, window, winnow;* (medially) *bowl, own* and the irregular past participles *blown, grown, thrown,* which derive from verbs listed above, plus *flown, known, mown, shown.*

All other occurrences of <ow> (bar the exceptions) are pronounced /aʊ/.

## 10.35 <oy>

### THE MAIN SYSTEM

| Basic phoneme | /ɔɪ/ | 100% | e.g. *boy* |
|---|---|---|---|

### THE REST

|  |  | pronounced |  |
|---|---|---|---|
| Exception to main system | <oy> | /aɪ/ | only in *coyote*. The <y> is both part of <oy> and a grapheme in its own right pronounced /j/. For dual-functioning see section 7.1 |
| Oddities | (none) | | |
| 2-phoneme grapheme | <oy> | as 2-phoneme sequence /waɪ/ | only in *foyer* pronounced /ˈfwaɪjeɪ/ (also pronounced /ˈfɔɪjeɪ, ˈfɔɪjə/), *voyeur* |

### NOTE

In medial examples of <oy> pronounced /ɔɪ/ before a vowel letter, namely in *arroyo, employee, foyer* pronounced /ˈfɔɪjeɪ, ˈfɔɪjə/, *loyal, royal, soya, voyage* and, I suppose, *coy-er/est*, comparative and superlative of *coy*, the <y> is both part of <oy> spelling /ɔɪ/ and a grapheme in its own right pronounced /j/. For dual-functioning see section 7.1.

## 10.36 <u>

N.B. <ue, u.e, ur> have separate entries.

### THE MAIN SYSTEM

On all these categories except /w/ see Notes.

| | | | |
|---|---|---|---|
| Basic phoneme | /ʌ/ | 44% | e.g. *but, up*; regular in prefix *un-* |
| Other phonemes | /ʊ/ | 6% | in RP, only in 50+ stem words, but many are very frequent; regular in suffix <-ful> |
| | /uː/ | 3% | e.g. *ruby* |
| | /w/ | <1% | regular after <q> pronounced /k/ (for exceptions, see under <cqu, qu, que> in sections 9.7, 9.27); also found in a few words after <c, g, s, ss, z>, namely *cuirass, cuisine, cuisse; anguish, distinguish, extinguish, guacamole, guano, guava, iguana* pronounced /ɪˈgwaːnə/, *language, languish, linguist, penguin, sanguine, segue, unguent; persuade, pueblo, puissan-ce/t, pursuivant, suave, suede, suite; assuage, dissuade; Venezuela* and some very rare words; otherwise perhaps only in *ennui, etui* /ɒnˈwiː, eˈtwiː/ |
| Frequent 2-phoneme sequence | /juː/ | 22% | e.g. *pupil, union*; word-final only in *coypu, menu, ormolu, parvenu* |

## THE REST

|  |  | pronounced |  |
|---|---|---|---|
| Exceptions to main system | <u> | /ə/ | 10% regular when unstressed. See Notes |
|  | <u> | /ɪ/ | 2% only in *busy, business, lettuce, minute* (noun /'mɪnɪt/, '60 seconds'), *missus* |
|  | <u> | /e/ | <1% only in *burial, bury* |
|  | <u> | as 2-phoneme sequence /jə/ | 14% in some words when unstressed See Notes |
| Oddities | <ua> | /ə/ | in nouns, only in *actuary, estuary, mortuary, obituary, sanctuary, statuary, voluptuary*, when pronounced with /tʃəriː/ rather than /tʃʊəriː/ (see also under /tʃ/, section 3.7.2), plus *casualty* /'kæʒəltiː/, *February* /'febrəriː/, *victuals* /'vɪtəlz/; also often in rapid pronunciation of adjectives like *actual* (see /tʃ/, section 3.7.2), *sexual* and especially adverbs derived from them. See Notes |
|  | <ui> | /uː/ | only in *bruise, bruit, cruise, fruit, juice, recruit, sluice, suit.* See Notes |
|  | <ui> | /aɪ/ | only in *duiker, Ruislip* |
|  | <uu> | /uː/ | only in *muumuu* (twice) |
| Other 2-phoneme graphemes | <ua> | as 2-phoneme sequence /jə/ | only in *January, valuable* |
|  | <ui> | as 2-phoneme sequence /juː/ | only in *nuisance, pursuit* |
|  | <ut> | as 2-phoneme sequence /juː/ | only in *debut.* /t/ surfaces in *debutante* – see section 7.2 |
|  | <uu> | as 2-phoneme sequence /juː/ | only in *vacuum* pronounced /'vækjuːm/ |

## NOTES

The consonantal pronunciation of <u> as /w/ is dealt with above. It is curious that the consonantal and vocalic pronunciations of <u> never occur adjacently, i.e. there are no instances of <uu> pronounced /wʌ wʊ wuː wə wɪ we/ or any of those with a /j/ glide between the two phonemes. This is despite the fact that at least one Latin word with such a sequence (*equus* /'ekwus/, 'horse') has various English derivatives – but they all have /e/ spelt <e> after /w/ spelt <u>. Where sequences such as /wʌ/ occur in English the /w/ is always spelt <w> and the vowel is rarely spelt <u> – the only words beginning <wu> appear to be *wunderkind, wuss* with <u> pronounced /ʊ/, and *Wurlitzer* with <ur> pronounced /ɜː/.

For instances of <u> as an elided vowel see section 6.10.

Except in the 10 words listed under Oddities, <u, i> always are/belong to separate graphemes, e.g. in several words listed under <u> pronounced /uː, juː/ below, including in particular *circuitous, fruition* (with intervening /w/-glide), plus words where <u> is part of a digraph with the preceding consonant letter: *biscuit, build, cataloguing* and a few more words with potential <e>-deletion from <-gue> before <-ing>, *circuit, guide, guild, guilder, guile, guillemot, guillotine, guilt, guinea, (dis)guise, guitar, suite.*

In RP (as distinct from local accents of the north of England, in which /ʊ/ is much more frequent), <u> is pronounced /ʊ/ in only about 57 stem words: *ambush, Buddha, buffet* /'bʊfeɪ/ ('food'), *bulbul* (twice), *bull, bullace, bullet, bulletin, Bullingdon, bullion, bullock, bully, bulrush* (first <u>), *bulwark* (also pronounced with /ʌ/), *bush, bushel, butch, butcher, cuckoo, (mea) culpa, cushion, cushty, cushy, ebullient* (also pronounced with /ʌ/), *fulcrum* (both <u>'s), *full, fulmar, fundi* (/'fʊndiː/ South and East African English for 'expert/skilled person'/in Britain, a member of the fundamentalist, uncompromising wing of the German Green Party), *gerenuk, kaput, kibbutz, kukri, lungi, lutz, mullah, mush* (/mʊʃ/, slang for 'friend'), *muslim, Musulman* (twice), *umlaut* (first <u>), *Zumba, pud, pudding, pull, pullet, pulpit, push, puss, put, putsch, schuss, s(c)htum, shufti, sputnik, sugar, suk, Sunni, thurible, thurifer, thruppence, tuk-tuk* (twice), plus derivatives including *Buddhism, bullock, fulfil, fully, ful(l)ness, fulsome,* and in the adjective/noun suffix <-ful> – there are at least 150 words so formed, e.g. *beautiful, handful.* Unstressed in that suffix but stressed in all other cases except *ambush, fulcrum* (second <u>), *fulfil, gerenuk, tuk-tuk* (second <u>).

In RP (as distinct from local accents of the north of England, in which /ʌ/ does not occur) <u> is pronounced /ʌ/:

- regularly before geminate and doubled consonant spellings, e.g. *bubble, bucket, duck, muddle, rudd, cudgel, judge, bluff, buffalo, muggle, gull, ullage, unnecessary, supper, curry, cussed* ('stubborn'), *fuss, hutch, (e)scutcheon, butter, putt, puzzle.* Exceptions: *bull, bullet, Bullingdon, bullion, bullock, butch, butcher, cuckoo, ebullient* (also pronounced with /ʌ/), *full, fully, mullah, pudding, pull,* both pronunciations of *stumm, puss, putsch, thruppence,* with /ʊ/

- regularly in other words where it is the only vowel letter and non-final, e.g. *bulk, brush, crux, dumb, dung, flux, hulk, just, mud, mush* ('squashy mess/command to husky'), *plump, sculpt, sulk, up*. See section 11.3 for a teaching rule relevant to ..VC monosyllables. Exceptions: *bush, mush* ('friend'), *pud, push* with /ʊ/, *ruth, truth* with /uː/ (for *brusque* see under <u.e>, section 10.38)
- in the prefix <sub-> when stressed, e.g. in *subject* (noun, pronounced /ˈsʌbdʒɪkt/), *sublimate, subterfuge*, etc.
- regularly where it is the last vowel letter in the word and non-final and stressed, e.g. *abrupt, adjust, annul, begun, robust, rotund*. Only exception: *impugn*, with /juː/
- mostly otherwise before two or more consonant letters or <x> where there is at least one later vowel letter, e.g. *blunder, butler, divulge, dungeon, fundi* (/ˈfʌndaɪ/, plural of *fundus* 'inner corner of organ'), *hundred, husband, inculcate, indulge, indulgence, presumption, promulgate, sunder, truncate, truncheon, tuxedo, ulterior*. Exceptions: *duplicate, duplicity, fuchsia, hubris, lubricate, lucrative, lucre, nutritious, putrid, rubric* and the prefix <supra->, with /(j)uː/
- in a ragbag of other stem words, e.g. *bunion, ketchup, punish, study, triumph, viaduct*
- in the native English prefix <un-> meaning 'not'.

Unlike the other vowel letters as single-letter graphemes, <u> is **not** pronounced short, i.e. /ʌ/, before a consonant and word-final <-ic(al)>. Instead it is pronounced /(j)uː/, e.g. *cubic, music, punic, runic, tunic* – see below.

A test for distinguishing the (Germanic) prefix <un-> 'not' pronounced /ʌn/ from the (Latin) initial element <un(i)-> 'one' pronounced /juːn(iː)/ which seems mainly reliable is this: Remove <un>. If what remains is a word, it is <un-> pronounced /ʌn/; if what remains is not a word, it is <un(i)-> pronounced /juːn(iː)/. For example, *uninformed* has /ʌn/; *uniformed* has /juːniː/. There appear to be only two words for which this does not work: *union, unit*, but neither is likely to be misunderstood, there being no words *un-ion* 'not an ion', *un-it* 'not an it'. However, based on *un(-)ion* is one of the longest homographs in English: *unionised*, which is either *union-ised* 'belonging to a trade union' or *un-ionised* 'not converted into ions'.

<u> is pronounced /uː/:
- word-finally, only in *ecru, flu, guru, impromptu, juju*, plus *gnu* if <gn> is analysed as pronounced /nj/
- in words where it is the only vowel letter and is followed by a consonant letter: only in *ruth, truth*

- in suffixed forms of stem words in <-u.e> pronounced /uː/ after <e>-deletion (sometimes with change of stem-final consonant), e.g. *brutal, crudity, inclusive, intrusion, reclusive, runic, secluded, trucial*, plus *truly* – in all these cases, the preceding letter is <l> or <r>
- in a small set of other words where there is at least one later vowel letter, mostly after <l, r>, e.g. *(af)fluent, alluvial, bruin, cruel, fluid, fluorescent, frugal, fruition, gluten, inscrutable, lucrative, lucre, ludicrous, luna-cy/tic, lunar, lupus, prudent, rubric, ruby, ruin, runic, scruple, scrutiny, solution, truant,* plus *judicial, judo, jujitsu, suicide, superior;* also in *casual, sexual, usual, visual* pronounced /ˈkæʒuːwəl, ˈsekʃuːwəl, ˈjuːʒuːwəl, ˈvɪʒuːwəl/. Where the letter following <u> is a vowel, the pronunciation has an intervening /w/-glide.

Wijk (1960: 15) points out that /uː/ is regular after /dʒ, r, ʃ, j/ (mainly spelt <j, r, ch/sh, y> and after /l/ spelt <l> after another consonant, both when <u> is a single-letter grapheme and in <u.e>. I would add that in current RP /uː/ is also regular after <d, t> pronounced /dʒ, tʃ/, e.g. in *arduous, assiduous, deciduous, dual, ducal, duel, duet, duly, duty, gradual, graduate, individual, residual; tuba, tuber, tulip, tumour, tumult(uous), tumulus, tuna, tunic, tureen, tutor; attitude, multitude, solitude; costume; fortune, importune, opportune; virtuoso; contemptuous, fatuous, impetuous, incestuous, perpetuate; spirituous, sumptuous, tempestuous, tortuous, tumultuous, unctuous, virtuous, voluptuous; obtuse; de/in/pro/re/sub-stitution. accentual, actual, conceptual, contractual, effectual, eventual, factual, habitual, intellectual, mutual, perpetual, punctual, ritual, spiritual, textual, virtual; actuary, estuary, mortuary, obituary, sanctuary, statuary, voluptuary.* Again, where the letter following <u> is a vowel, the pronunciation has an intervening /w/-glide.

<u> is pronounced /juː/:
- word-finally, only in *coypu, menu, ormolu, parvenu,* plus *gnu* if <gn> is analysed as pronounced /n/
- in words where it is the only vowel letter and is followed by a consonant letter: only in *impugn*
- mostly before a consonant letter and word-final <-ic(al)>, e.g. *cubic, music, punic, tunic* (exception: *runic*)
- in suffixed forms of stem words in <-u.e> pronounced /juː/ after <e>-deletion (sometimes with change of stem-final consonant), e.g. *accusation, allusion, at/con/dis/re-tribution, collusion, communal, community, computation, con/in-stitution, consuming, delusion,*

*disputacious, enthusiasm, elocution, evolution, execution, funeral, (con/dif/in/pro/trans-)fusion, (dis)illusion, nudity, persecution, pollution, prosecution, reducible, reputation, revolution, usage*
- in a large set of other words where there is at least one later vowel letter, e.g. *annual, computer, continuity, cubicle, cubit, duplicate, duplicity, fuchsia, fuel, genuine, hubris, human, humus, impecunious, ingenuity, lubricate, (pel)lucid, mucus, mutate, numerous, nutritious, peculiar, puny, putrid, student, stupid, tenuous,* the prefix <supra-> and many words with the (Latin) initial element <un(i)-> ('one'), e.g. *unanimous, unicorn, union, unison, unit, universe.* See above on distinguishing words with <un(i)-> from those with <un-> pronounced /ʌn/, the native English prefix meaning 'not'. Where the letter following <u> is a vowel, the pronunciation has an intervening /w/-glide.

<u> is pronounced /ə/:
- in a set of words containing <du, tu> pronounced /dʒə, tʃə/ when the <u> is the penultimate vowel grapheme in the word and unstressed, and separated from the next vowel letter by a single consonant letter, and the main stress is on the preceding syllable: *(in)credulous, educate, glandular, modular, nodular, pendulum, sedulous; century, congratulate, fistula, fortunate, naturist, petulant/ce, postulant, postulate, saturate, spatula, titular* and derivatives, e.g. *education, saturation* (cf. words with /jə/, below)
- in all occurrences of the endings <-ium, -ius> (with intervening /j/-glide), e.g. *atrium, bacterium, compendium, delirium, geranium, gymnasium, medium, opium, potassium, radium, stadium, tedium* and about 200 others ending in <-ium>; *genius, radius*
- in all occurrences of the endings <-um, -us> without a preceding <i>, e.g. *album, agendum, carborundum, colosseum, linoleum, lyceum, mausoleum, maximum, museum, petroleum, rectum, referendum; abacus, anus, bogus, bonus, cactus, campus, caucus, census, chorus, circus, citrus, corpus, crocus, discus, emeritus, exodus, focus, fungus, genus, hiatus, hippopotamus, isthmus, litmus, lotus, octopus, onus, nucleus, rhombus, stimulus, surplus, syllabus, Taurus, terminus, tinnitus, virus* and hundreds more
- in prefix <sub-> when unstressed, e.g. *subdue, subject* (verb, pronounced /səbˈdʒekt/), *sublime, submerge, submit, subside, subsist, substantial*
- otherwise in, e.g., *cherub, catsup, chirrup, stirrup, syrup.*

Also, in the entry for <ur>, section 10.39, reference is made to the long list in section 5.4.7 of nouns ending in <-ture> pronounced /tʃə/. In adjectives derived from nouns in that list, e.g. *adventurous* /əd'ventʃərəs/, *natural* /'nætʃərəl/), and especially in adverbs derived from those adjectives, e.g. *adventurously, naturally*, <u> may be pronounced /ə/ – or in rapid pronunciation the schwa may be absent (/æd'ventʃrəs(liː), 'nætʃrəl(iː)/), in which case the <u> is elided – see section 6.10. I think that the tendency for the vowel to disappear in rapid speech is stronger in the adverbs alluded to in this paragraph and listed in section 5.4.7 than in the adjectives.

<u> is pronounced /jə/ in several words where it is the penultimate vowel grapheme and unstressed, and separated from the next vowel letter by a single consonant letter, and main stress is on the preceding syllable, e.g. *amulet, angular* /'æŋgjələ/, *argument, calculate, chasuble, coagulate, contributor, corpuscular, distributor, emulate, fabulous, garrulous, immunise, inaugural, incubus, insula-r/te, jugular, manipulate, muscular, nebulous, particular, penury, popul(o)us, querulous, regula-r/te, scapula(r), scroful-a/ous, scrupulous, stimul-ant/ate/us, succubus, tremulous, truculent, vernacular*; also in, e.g. *glandular, spatula*, if pronounced with /djə, tjə/ rather than /dʒə, tʃə/ (see list above); also in the two words *copulation, population* where it is the antepenultimate vowel grapheme (and unstressed) and main stress is on the following syllable.

# 10.37 <ue>

N.B. <u.e> has a separate entry.

Does not occur initially. Except in *gruesome, muesli, Tuesday*, only word-final.

### THE MAIN SYSTEM

For both categories see Notes.

| Basic phoneme | /uː/ | 41% | e.g. *glue* |
| Frequent 2-phoneme sequence | /juː/ | 59% | e.g. *cue* |

### THE REST

(None).

## NOTES

This grapheme is not to be confused with word-final <-ue> in <gue, que>, where it is sometimes part of those graphemes – see sections 9.15, 9.27.

/uː/ is regular after <l, r>, namely in *blue, clue, flue, glue, slue; accrue, construe, gruesome, imbrue, rue, sprue, true,* and predominates after <d, t> (where older pronunciations with /juː/ are still sometimes heard): *due, residue, subdue; statue, Tuesday* pronounced /ˈtʃuːzdiː/, *virtue,* plus *issue, sue, tissue.* Only definite exception: *value,* with /juː/.

/juː/ is regular in almost all other cases, namely *ague, argue, avenue, barbecue, continue, cue, curlicue, ensue, hue, imbue, pursue, queue, rescue, retinue, revenue, revue, value, venue.* Exception: *muesli.*

Except in *gruesome, muesli, Tuesday,* <u, e> are always separate graphemes in medial position, e.g. *cruel* /ˈkruːəl/, *duel* /ˈdʒuːəl/ (homophonous with *jewel*), *duet* /dʒuːˈwet/ (words like these three have an intervening /w/-glide), *suede* /sweɪd/ (where <u> spells /w/ anyway). There is also one 2-grapheme exception in final position: *segue* /ˈsegweɪ/ (where <u> again spells /w/).

## 10.38 <u.e>

Occurs only where the <e> is word-final.

See Notes for both categories and for how this split digraph is defined, and see section 11.4 for a teaching rule relevant to all split digraphs except <y.e>.

### THE MAIN SYSTEM

For both categories see Notes.

| | | | |
|---|---|---|---|
| Basic phoneme | /uː/ | 11% | e.g. *rude* |
| Frequent 2-phoneme pronunciation | /juː/ | 89% | e.g. *cute* |

### THE REST

(None).

### NOTES

The split digraph <u.e> is defined as covering words where the <e> is separated from the <u> by one consonant letter other than <r, x> and the

<u> is not preceded by a vowel letter and the digraph is pronounced /uː/ or /juː/. The definition covers both words where the intervening consonant letter is an independent grapheme and words where the <e> is also part of a split digraph <ce, ge> – see sections 3.7.4, 3.7.6 and 3.8.4, and section 7.1 for dual-functioning.

The only extensions needed are to cover five words with two intervening letters forming consonant digraphs: *butte, fugue, peruque, ruche, tulle,* plus *brusque* pronounced /bruːsk/ (also pronounced /brʌsk/), with three intervening letters (including <qu> as a digraph) forming the consonant cluster /sk/. The only exceptions appear to be *lettuce, minute* (/ˈmɪnɪt/, '60 seconds'), with <u> pronounced /ɪ/ and <ce, te> forming digraphs pronounced /s, t/, and *deluxe* with <u> pronounced /ʌ/ and <xe> forming a 2-phoneme digraph pronounced /ks/. See also section A.6 in Appendix A.

/uː/ is regular after <ch, j, l, r>, namely in *(para)chute; June, jupe, jute; fluke, flume, flute, include* and various other words in <-clude>, *luge, lute, plume, recluse; abstruse, brume, brute, crude, intrude* and various other words in <-trude>, *peruque, peruse, prude, prune, ruche, rude, rule, rune, ruse, spruce, truce*, and predominates after <d, t> (where older pronunciations with /juː/ are still sometimes heard): *duke, dune* (homophonous with *June*), *introduce, reduce, module, nodule; tube, tulle, tune*. Exceptions: *delude, mameluke, pollute*, with /juː/.

/juː/ is regular in almost all other cases, e.g. *abuse, accuse, amuse, (at/con/dis-)tribute, centrifuge, commune* (noun and verb), *compute, consume, delude, deluge, dispute, enthuse, globule, huge, minute* /maɪˈnjuːt/ ('tiny'), *mule, mute, nude, perfume, pollute, refuge, repute, subterfuge, use* (noun and verb).

There are very few English words ending <-uge>: *centrifuge, deluge, huge, refuge, subterfuge* and a few more rarities, all with /juːdʒ/, plus *luge* with /uːʒ/ (there are none with /uːdʒ, juːʒ/).

The only word in which a final <e> after <u>+consonant is 'pronounced' rather than 'silent' appears to be *resume* ('c.v.').

## 10.39 <ur>

**THE MAIN SYSTEM**

*Basic phoneme*   /ɜː/   70%   e.g. *fur, occur, turn, urgent*. See Notes

*The grapheme-phoneme correspondences, 2* 429

## THE REST

|  |  | pronounced |  |
|---|---|---|---|
| Exceptions to main system | <ur> | /ə/ | 30% never initial; word-finally, only in *augur, femur, langur, lemur, murmur, sulphur*; medially, regular in prefixes *pur-, sur-* when unstressed, e.g. *purgation, purloin, purport, pursue, purvey; surmise, surmount, surpass, surprise, survey* (verb), *survive*; otherwise only in a few words, e.g. *auburn, expurgate, jodhpurs, liturgy, metallurgy, Saturday, saturnine*. See Notes |
|  | <ur> | /ʊə/ | <1% never word-final; initially, only in *urtext*; otherwise only medial and only in *centurion, durable, (en)during, duress, injurious, juror, jury, prurient/ ce, rural, usurious*, plus *luxuriance, luxuriant, luxuriate, luxurious* (/lʌgˈʒʊəriːj- əns/ənt/eɪt/əs/), *maturity, tureen* and derived forms of some words ending in <-ure> pronounced /ʊə/ (see below) after <e>-deletion, e.g. *insurance*. In all these medial cases the <r> is both part of <ur> and a grapheme in its own right pronounced r/. For dual-functioning see section 7.1. See also Notes |
|  | <ur> | as 2-phoneme sequence /jʊə/ | <1% never word-final; initially, only in *urea* and various words derived from it, e.g. *urethra, urine, urology*; otherwise only medial and only in *bravura, curate* (both the noun 'junior cleric' pronounced /ˈkjʊərət/ and the verb 'mount an exhibition' pronounced /kjʊəˈreɪt/), *curious, furore* whether pronounced /tjʊəˈrɔːreɪ/ or /ˈfjʊərɔː/, *furious, fury, lurid, mural, purify, purity, security, spurious* and derived forms of some words ending in <-ure> pronounced /jʊə/ (see below) after <e>-deletion, e.g. *manuring*. In all these medial cases the <r> is both part of <ur> and a grapheme in its own right pronounced /r/. For dual-functioning see section 7.1. See also Notes |

| | | | |
|---|---|---|---|
| Oddities | | | All word-final only in stem words |
| | <ure> | /ə/ | the regular pronunciation of <ure>, e.g. in *lecture, nature* and dozens of other words ending in unstressed <-ture> (for a long list see section 5.4.7), *censure, conjure* ('do magic tricks') pronounced /ˈkʌndʒə/, *figure, injure, leisure, measure, perjure, pleasure, pressure, procedure, tonsure, treasure, verdure* (cf. *verger*). For exceptions see the next paragraph and the 2-phoneme graphemes. Many of these words allow /r/-linking (see section 3.6), e.g. *natural, pleasurable, procedural* |
| | <ure> | /ʊə/ | only in *abjure, adjure, assure, brochure,* (also pronounced with final /ə/), *conjure* ('summon with an oath') pronounced /kənˈdʒʊə/, *cynosure, embouchure, ensure, insure, sure*; also *caricature, overture* if <-ture> is pronounced /tʃʊə/ rather than /tʃə/, and words like *endure, mature* if <-dure, -ture> are pronounced /dʒʊə, tʃʊə/ (see two paragraphs below and sections 9.12 and 9.33). Many of these words allow /r/-linking (see section 3.6), e.g. *assurance, maturity*. See also Notes |
| | <urr> | /ɜː/ | only in *burr, purr* and suffixed forms of words ending in <-ur>, e.g. *blurred, furry, demurring, occurred.* /r/-linking occurs in *furry, demurring* – see section 3.6. <u, rr> are separate graphemes pronounced /ʌ, r/ in, e.g., *demurral, furrier* pronounced /ˈfʌriːjə/ 'dealer in furs' (contrast the word of the same spelling pronounced /ˈfɜːriːjə/ 'more furry'), *hurry, scurrilous, scurry, slurry* |
| Other 2-phoneme pronunciations | <ure> | as 2-phoneme sequence /jə/ | only in *failure, tenure* and *azure* pronounced /ˈæzjə, ˈeɪzjə/ (also pronounced /ˈæzjʊə, ˈeɪzjʊə, ˈæʒə, ˈeɪʒə/); also possibly in words like *endure, mature* if <-dure, -ture> are pronounced conservatively with /dj, tj/ not yet affricated to /dʒ, tʃ/ (see two paragraphs above and sections 9.12 and 9.33). See also Notes |

|  |  |  |
|---|---|---|
| <ure> | as 2-phoneme sequence /jʊə/ | only in *coiffure, cure, demure, immure, inure, lure, manure, photogravure, pure, secure, sinecure.* See also Notes |

### NOTES

There are very few words with initial <ur->. Most are derivatives of *urea*, all with a following vowel letter and with <ur> pronounced /jʊə/ and <r> also pronounced /r/, i.e. dual-functioning (see section 7.1). There are only six words with a following consonant letter: *urbane, urchin, urge, urgent, urn* with regular /ɜː/ and *urtext* with /ʊə/. Except in *urtext, urea* and its derivatives, and the exceptions and the Oddity <urr> noted above, <ur> is always pronounced /ɜː/, and there appear to be no cases of <u, r> as separate graphemes.

Despite the high percentage for <ur> pronounced /ə/ I have not counted it as part of the main system because of the rarity of its converse – see section 5.4.7.

See section 5.6.5 for the increasing replacement of /(j)ʊə/ by /(j)ɔː/.

## 10.40 <y>

### THE MAIN SYSTEM

For all these categories and the absence of percentages see Notes, and for a teaching rule relevant to word-final <y> see section 11.6.

| | | |
|---|---|---|
| Basic word-initial phoneme | /j/ | e.g. *yellow, you, your*; never occurs word-finally; rare medially, where almost all occurrences are vocalic |
| Basic phoneme elsewhere | /aɪ/ | regular word-finally where it is the only vowel letter, in the suffix <-fy>, and medially after <e>-deletion, e.g. *fly, beautify, stylish* |
| Other phonemes | /iː/ | usual in prefix *poly-* and regular word-finally where there is at least one earlier vowel letter (except in the suffix <-fy>), e.g. *polytechnic, city, happy* |
| | /ɪ/ | never word-final; almost exclusively medial; occurs in many words of (mainly) Greek origin, |

e.g. *bicycle, crystal*; regular where it precedes a consonant letter and word-final <-ic(al)>, and mainly before consonant clusters

## THE REST

|  |  |  | pronounced |  |
|---|---|---|---|---|
| Exceptions to main system | <y> | /ə/ | | only in *pyjamas* |
| Oddities | <ye> | /aɪ/ | | only word-final, and only in *(good)bye, dye, lye, rye, Skye, stye* |
|  | <y.e> | /aɪ/ | | only where the <e> is word-final and only in: *acolyte, analyse, anodyne, azyme, breathalyse, byte, catalyse, chyle, chyme, coenocyte, condyle, dialyse, dyke, dyne, electrolyse, electrolyte, enzyme, formaldehyde, gybe, gyve, hythe, hype, leucocyte, neophyte* and at least 14 other words ending in <-phyte> pronounced /faɪt/, *paralyse, phagocyte, proselyte, rhyme, scythe, spondyle, style* and about 20 derivatives, *troglodyte, syce, thyme, tyke, type* and at least 20 derivatives; also alternative US spellings such as *analyze*. See Notes for how this split digraph is defined |
|  | <yr> | /ə/ | | only in *martyr, satyr, zephyr* |
|  | <yr> | /ɜː/ | | only in *gyrfalcon, myrmidon, myrtle* |
|  | <yrrh> | /ɜː/ | | only in *myrrh* |
| 2-phoneme graphemes | <yr> | as 2-phoneme sequence /aɪə/ | | only medial and only in *empyrean, gyroscope, papyrus, pyrites, pyromaniac, thyroid, tyrant, tyro, tyrosine*. In all cases the <r> is both part of the digraph <yr> pronounced /aɪə/ and a grapheme in its own right pronounced /r/. For dual-functioning see section 7.1. Words in which <y, r> are separate graphemes include *dithyramb(ic), myriad, porphyr-y/ia, syringa, syringe, syrup, tyranny*, all with the relevant <y> pronounced /ɪ/ |

| | | |
|---|---|---|
| <yre> | as 2-phoneme sequence /aɪə/ | only word-final and only in *byre, gyre, lyre, pyre, tyre*. Some of these allow /r/-linking – see section 3.6 – e.g. *pyromaniac* and (with change of vowel and <r> spelling only /r/) *lyrical* |

## NOTES

Gontijo *et al.* (2003) (like Carney – see section 5.4.3) analyse word-final <y> (except where it is the only vowel letter and in <-fy>) as pronounced /ɪ/. Because I instead analyse it as pronounced /iː/ and can not separate their final <y> pronounced /ɪ/ from medial <y> pronounced /ɪ/ I am unable to use their percentages for any of the correspondences of <y>.

Initial <y> is always pronounced /j/ before a vowel letter. Cases of initial <y> followed by a consonant letter are very rare, but in all of them <y> is pronounced /ɪ/, namely the archaic word *yclept* ('named'), the type of boat called *yngling*, and the names of the plant and essential oil *ylang-ylang* (also spelt *ilang-ilang*) and of the elements *ytterbium, yttrium* and the names *Yvette, Yvonne*.

Conversely, there are cases of medial <y> which are consonantal and are pronounced /j/. In a few, the <y> is solely a single-letter grapheme: *banyan* /'bænjæn/, *beyond, biryani, bowyer* /'bəʊjə/, *canyon* /'kænjən/, *halyard, lanyard, vineyard, yoyo*. In rather more the <y> functions both as a single-letter grapheme pronounced /j/ and as part of digraphs (for dual-functioning see section 7.1) with various pronunciations:
- eɪ/ in *abeyance, bayonet, cayenne, layer, layette, mayonnaise, prayer* pronounced /'preɪjə/ ('one who prays'), *rayon*; also in derived forms such as *betrayal, conveyance*
- /ɔɪ/ in *arroyo, buoyant* /'bɔɪjənt/, *doyen* pronounced /'dɔɪjən, dɔɪ'jen/, *doyenne* pronounced /dɔɪ'jen/, *foyer* pronounced /'fɔɪjeɪ, 'fɔɪjə/, *joyous, loyal, royal, soya*; also in derived forms such as *joyous*
- /aɪ/ in *coyote* /kaɪ'jəʊtiː/, *kayak* /'kaɪjæk/
- /waɪ/ in *doyen* and *doyenne* pronounced /dwaɪ'jen/, *foyer* pronounced /'fwaɪjeɪ/, *voyeur* /vwaɪ'jɜː/.

Consonantal <y> and initial vocalic <y> having been dealt with, the main question is how to predict the three main vocalic pronunciations in medial and final positions.

<y> is pronounced /aɪ/:
- word-finally where it is the only vowel letter, namely *by, cry, dry, fly, fry, my, ply, pry, scry, shy, sky, sly, spy, spry, sty, thy, try, why, wry,*

- plus *buy, guy* (taking <bu, gu> to be digraphs spelling /b, g/). No exceptions
- in the suffix <-fy>, e.g. *beautify, classify, notify*, including the three words with a preceding <e>: *liquefy, putrefy, stupefy*. The noun *salsify* ('root vegetable') is pronounced /'sælsɪfiː/ but is not a real exception because here <fy> is not a suffix
- word-finally also in a few other words where it is not the only vowel letter: *ally, ap/com/im/re/sup-ply, awry, defy, deny, descry, espy, July, multiply* (verb – contrast the adverb, with /iː/), *occupy, prophesy* (contrast *prophecy*, with /iː/), *rely*
- medially in hundreds of words where <e>-deletion has occurred, e.g. *stylish, typist*
- medially otherwise in an unpredictable ragbag of words, including *asylum, aureomycin, cryostat, cyanide, cycle, cyclone, cypress*, (*hama*)*dryad, dynamic, forsythia, glycogen, gynaecology, hyacinth, hyaline, hybrid, hydra, hydrangea, hydrant, hydraulic, hydrofoil, hydrogen* and various other compounds of *hydro-, hyena, hygiene, hygrometer, hymen, hyperbole* and other compounds in *hyper-, hyphen, hypothesis* and other compounds in *hypo-, lychee, myopic, nylon, psyche* and almost all its derivatives, *pylon, stymie, thylacine, thymus, typhoid, typhoon, typhus, xylophone, zygote* and derivatives.

<y> is pronounced /iː/:
- word-finally in most words where it is not the only vowel letter, e.g. *city, happy* and hundreds of others. For exceptions with /aɪ/ see above
- in the prefix *poly-* when the stress does not fall on the <y>, e.g. *polyandry* (with following /j/-glide), *polytechnic, polysyllable, polysyllabic* (exception: *polymer*, with /ɪ/). When the stress does fall on the <y> it is pronounced /ɪ/, e.g. in *polygamy*
- medially otherwise in very few words (with following /j/-glide), e.g. *caryatid, embryo(nic), halcyon*.

The only remaining occurrences of vocalic <y> are all medial and all pronounced /ɪ/:
- regular where it precedes at least one consonant letter and either of the endings <-ic(al)>, e.g. *cryptic, cyclic(al), cynic(al), paralytic, pyrrhic, salicylic, typical*. In this set *cyclic(al), typical* are exceptions (but apparently the only ones) to the rule (see above) that <e>-deletion before a suffix beginning with a vowel letter leaves a <y> from a previously split digraph pronounced /aɪ/

- regular in words where it is the only vowel letter and there is at least one following consonant letter, other than those with <-y.e>, but this is a small set: *crypt, cyst, gym, gyp, hymn, lymph, lynch, lynx, nymph, pyx, sylph, tryst*. Only exception: *psych*
- regular in where it is the last vowel letter and there is at least one following consonant letter, other than those with <-y.e>, e.g. *abyss, acronym, amethyst, aneurysm, antonym, apocalypse, beryl, calyx, cataclysm, catalyst, chlorophyll* and a few other words ending in *-phyll, coccyx, (ptero)dactyl, di/triptych, eponym, hieroglyph, hydroxyl* (second <y>), *idyll, larynx, onyx, oryx, pharynx, polyp, sibyl, synonym* (second <y>). No exceptions
- mostly predictable before two or more consonant letters or <x> where ther is at least one later vowel letter, e.g. *apocrypha(l), asphyxiate, bi/tricycle, cryptic, crystal, cyclamen, cygnet, cymbal, eucalyptus, gryphon, gymkhana, gymnast/ ium, gypsum, gypsy, hypnosis, hypnotise, metempsychosis, paroxysm, pygmy, rhythm, strychnine, syllable, syllabic, syllabub, syllabus, sylloge, symbol, sympathy, syndicate, syntax, synthetic, syphilis*. Exceptions, all with /aɪ/: *cycle, cyclone, cypress, forsythia, hybrid*, all the words beginning *hydr-, hygrometer, hyphen, lychee, psyche* and almost all its derivatives, *typhoid, typhoon, typhus*
- otherwise in an unpredictable ragbag of words, including *acetylene, analysis, analytic, chlamydia, cotyledon, cylinder, dithyramb(ic), eponym(ous), glycerine, hypocrite, metempsychosis, myriad, oxygen, paralysis, physics, polymer, porphyria, sybarite, sycamore, sycophant, synonym* (twice), *syringa, syringe, syrup* and first <y> in *dynasty, etymology, hypocrisy, polygamy, porphyry, tyranny*.

The split digraph <y.e> is defined as covering words where the <e> is separated from the <y> by one consonant letter other than <r> and the <y> is not preceded by a vowel letter and the digraph is pronounced /aɪ/. The definition covers both words where the intervening consonant letter is an independent grapheme and words where the <e> is also part of a split digraph <ce, ve> – see sections 3.7.6–7, and section 7.1 for dual-functioning. The only extension needed is to cover two words with two intervening consonant letters forming a digraph: *hythe, scythe*, and there appear to be no exceptions. See also section A.6 in Appendix A.

## 10.41 Correspondences of <a, e, i, o, u, y> (±word-final <e>) in content words with no other vowel letters (monosyllables)

There is more pattern to the correspondences of the vowel letters in monosyllabic content words than comes through in the relevant sections of this chapter above – see Table 10.2, the inspiration for which I owe to Irina Shcherbakova of Moscow. (Most monosyllabic function words are so often unstressed that their predominant vowel is /ə/.)

I have not included columns for the single vowel letters plus <w, y>, because over half the possible combinations do not occur, or for those sequences plus final <e>, because such words are rare. For <aw(e), ay(e), ew(e), ey(e), ow(e), oy> (<-oye> does not occur), see sections 10.10/11/21/12/34/35 respectively.

The comprehensiveness of Table 10.2 conceals the fact that, even where a cell does not say '(does not occur)', there may be very few instances. This is true of all the cells in the 'just the vowel letter' column (see below), and of words ending in <-ure>: *sure* is the only example in its cell, and the only companions for *cure* are *lure, pure*; *brae* is also an isolate.

Table 10.2 makes clear the parallelism in the correspondences of <i, y> in relevant words (though <y> is much rarer) – this is why I've put <y> next to <i>. Also, I've put <o, a> first because all the other vowel letter + <r> combinations are pronounced /ɜː/. Two more regularities are:
- Each vowel letter + <e> combination without an intervening consonant is pronounced the same as the corresponding split digraph;
- In word-final position <e, i, o> and sometimes <u> are pronounced like their letter-names (but <u> is sometimes /uː/, <a> is pronounced /aː/ and <y> is pronounced /aɪ/).

There are only about 19 exceptions to the regular short pronunciations before a single consonant letter: *raj* with /aː/, *quad, quag, squat, swab, swan, swat, wad, wan, was, what* with /ɒ/, *chic* with /iː/, *mic* with /aɪ/, *son, ton, won* with /ʌ/, *pud, put, suk* with /ʊ/.

The list of exceptions before geminate and other doubled spellings is longer, but still not extensive (the list would be shorter still in accents other than RP): *chaff, staff, hajj, brass, class, glass, grass, pass*, with /aː/; *bass* ('(player of) large stringed instrument'/'(singer with) low-pitched voice') with /eɪ/; *all, ball, call, fall, gall, hall, pall, small, squall, stall, tall, thrall, wall* with /ɔː/; *retch* pronounced /riːtʃ/; *boll* (sometimes), *droll, poll* ('head, vote'), *roll, scroll, stroll, toll* with /əʊ/.

**TABLE 10.2: REGULAR CORRESPONDENCES OF <a, e, i, o, u, y> (±WORD-FINAL <e>) IN MONOSYLLABIC CONTENT WORDS.**

| word ending in → | the vowel letter + any single consonant letter except <r, w, y> | the vowel letter + any geminate or doubled consonant spelling | just the vowel letter | the vowel letter + <e> | the vowel letter + any consonant letter (except <r, w, x, y>) + <e>, = split digraph | the vowel letter + <re> | the vowel letter + <r> |
|---|---|---|---|---|---|---|---|
| syllable type → | closed | closed | open | open | closed | open | open |
| vowel sound → <br><br> vowel letter ↓ | short | short | 'long', = letter name (except <a, y>, and <u> without /j/ glide) | 'long', = letter name (except <y>, and <u> without /j/ glide) | 'long', = letter name (except <y>, and <u> without /j/-glide) | r-coloured diphthong or 2-phoneme sequence (except <ore>) | long pure vowel |
| <o> | /ɒ/ <br> rod | /ɒ/ <br> lodge | /əʊ/ <br> go | /əʊ/ <br> roe | /əʊ/ <br> rode | /ɔː/ <br> fore | /ɔː/ <br> for |
| <a> | /æ/ <br> man | /æ/ <br> catch | /aː/ <br> pa | /eɪ/ <br> brae | /eɪ/ <br> name | /eə/ <br> care | /aː/ <br> car |
| <y> | /ɪ/ <br> gym | (does not occur) | /aɪ/ <br> sty | /aɪ/ <br> stye | /aɪ/ <br> style | /aɪə/ <br> pyre | (does not occur) |
| <i> | /ɪ/ <br> pin | /ɪ/ <br> brick | /aɪ/ <br> pi | /aɪ/ <br> pie | /aɪ/ <br> pine | /aɪə/ <br> fire | /ɜː/ <br> fir |
| <e> | /e/ <br> men | /e/ <br> bell | /iː/ <br> be | /iː/ <br> bee | /iː/ <br> scene | /ɪə/ <br> here | /ɜː/ <br> her |
| <u> without /j/ glide | /ʌ/ <br> cut | /ʌ/ <br> fuss | /uː/ <br> flu | /uː/ <br> flue | /uː/ <br> flute | /ʊə/* <br> sure | /ɜː/ <br> fur |
| <u> with /j/ glide | (does not occur) | (does not occur) | /juː/ <br> mu | /juː/ <br> cue | /juː/ <br> cute | /jʊə/* <br> cure | (does not occur) |

\* See section 5.6.5 for the increasing replacement of /(j)ʊə/ by /(j)ɔː/.

A further set arises from taking final <-ve> to be a doubled spelling. Although a few preceding single-letter vowels have the regular short pronunciation before <-ve>, namely *have, give, live* (verb, /lɪv/) (see sections 3.7.7 and 9.39), there are 18 words in which the <e> also forms a split digraph with the vowel letter, which therefore has a 'long' pronunciation (for dual-functioning see section 7.1): *gave, shave, suave, wave; breve, eve; drive, five, hive, jive, live* (adjective, /laɪv/), *swive, wive; cove, drove, move, prove; gyve* (see the parallel list for polysyllables in the next section), and four words with an irregular short pronunciation: *dove, glove, love, shove* with /ʌ/.

There are just nine words in the language in which the sole vowel letter is followed by word-final <rr>: *carr, charr, parr, err, chirr, shirr, whirr, burr, purr* – but in every case the three letters form a trigraph, and these are therefore not really exceptions to the doubled consonant spelling rules in Table 10.2. This applies even more strongly to *barre, bizarre, parterre, myrrh*.

There are only about 54 words with a single word-final vowel letter in the language, even when the dictionary is thoroughly scraped (and several function words are included); very few are exceptions – see Table 10.3.

TABLE 10.3: OPEN MONOSYLLABLES WITH A SINGLE VOWEL LETTER.

| Vowel letter | Words | Pronunciation |
|---|---|---|
| a | *bra, ma, pa, schwa, spa* | /ɑː/ |
| e | *be, he, me, she, the* (when stressed), *we, ye* | /iː/ |
| i | *Hi!*, the pronoun *I*, and Greek letter names *chi, phi, pi, psi, xi* (as pronounced in English) | /aɪ/ |
| | *mi, ti* (the musical terms), *ski* | /iː/ |
| o | *fro, go, lo, no* | /əʊ/ |
| | *do, to* (when stressed), *two, who* | /uː/ |
| u | *flu, gnu* if <gn> is analysed as pronounced /nj/ | /uː/ |
| | *gnu* if <gn> is analysed as pronounced /n/, and Greek letter names *mu, nu* (as pronounced in English) | /juː/ |
| y | *by, cry, dry, fly, fry, my, ply, pry, scry, shy, sky, sly, spy, spry, sty, thy, try, why, wry*, plus *buy, guy* (taking <bu, gu> to be digraphs spelling /b, g/) | /aɪ/ |

There appear to be only two exceptions for the vowel letter + <e> combinations (see sections 10.3/16/23/27/37/40), namely *nee* with /eɪ/ and *shoe* with /uː/ – but there are only about 40 such monosyllables in the entire language.

There are very few words which end in a vowel letter + consonant letter other than <r, w, x, y> + final <e> (and therefore like look monosyllables with split digraphs), but in which the <e> is 'pronounced' and the words are therefore disyllables and the vowel letter + <e> do not constitute a split digraph: *blase, cafe, glace, pate* ('paste'), *hebe, stele, (bona) fide*. (See also section 11.4).

There are also very few words which end in a vowel letter + <re> and have an irregular pronunciation: *are, ere, there, where, were* (all of which are function words), and the only two exceptions for vowel letter plus <r> are *war* with /ɔː/ and *kir* with /ɪə/.

## 10.42 Correspondences of <a, e, i, o, u, y> in words with at least one later vowel letter other than 'silent' <e> (polysyllables)

Only two columns in Table 10.2 can be generalised more or less straightforwardly to polysyllables, which can be defined for the purposes of this section as all those (huge numbers of) words which do not fit the definition of 'monosyllables' given in the heading of the previous section.

First, the single vowel letter graphemes are almost always pronounced 'short' (i.e. as /æ e ɪ ɒ ʌ ɪ/ respectively) before geminate and other doubled spellings in polysyllables as well as monosyllables – see Table 10.4, which is the mirror-image of Table 4.1.

TABLE 10.4: SHORT AND LONG PRONUNCIATIONS OF SINGLE-LETTER VOWEL GRAPHEMES BEFORE SINGLE AND DOUBLE CONSONANT SPELLINGS.

|  | Before doubled consonant spellings | Before other consonant clusters and single consonant letters |
|---|---|---|
| Short vowel pronunciation | Regular | Both occur, and long/short pronunciations are sometimes predictable but mostly not – see the rest of this section |
| Long vowel/diphthong pronunciation | Very rare |  |

There are very few exceptions to the rule that single-letter vowel graphemes before geminate and other doubled spellings are pronounced short in polysyllables. This even applies to various short pronunciations which are exceptions to the main one, e.g. words with <a> pronounced /ɒ/. The only exceptions I've been able to find are *camellia, pizza* with /iː/, *distaff* and sometimes *latte* with /ɑː/, *plimsoll* (also spelt *plimsole*, which would not be an exception) with /əʊ/, and *thralldom* (also spelt *thraldom*, which would not be an exception) with /ɔː/. The rule extends to consonant letter clusters which are or look like trigraphs (even though this not how I would analyse them): *arrhythmia* if pronounced with initial /eɪ/, *butte* with /juː/, *chenille, pelisse* with /iː/, *giraffe* with /ɑː/ and *ruche, tulle* with /uː/.

The largest (but still tiny) set of exceptions arises from analysing final <-ve> as a doubled spelling. Although most preceding single-letter vowel graphemes are pronounced short before <-ve> in polysyllables (see sections 3.7.7 and 9.39), there are 14 words in which the <e> also forms a split digraph with the vowel letter, which therefore has a 'long' pronunciation (for dual-functioning see section 7.1): *behave, conclave, forgave; alive, archive, arrive, deprive, naive, ogive, recitative, revive, survive; alcove, mangrove.*

The second column in Table 10.2 which generalises reasonably well to polysyllables concerns split digraphs. As can be seen in Table 11.3, there are only about 30 polysyllabic words in the language in which a word-final <e> separated from a preceding single vowel letter by a single consonant letter is 'pronounced' and therefore constitutes a separate syllable.

In most polysyllables which end in a vowel letter plus <e> with no intervening consonant letter the digraphs are pronounced as in the corresponding monosyllables. Thus almost all of those in <-ee> are pronounced /iː/, exceptions (all with /eɪ/) being *entree, epee, fiancee, matinee, melee, negligee, soiree* and a few other loanwords from French (see section 10.16), all of which are increasingly spelt in English with French <ée>.

Those in <-ie, -ye> are all pronounced with /aɪ/. Almost all those in <-oe> are pronounced with /əʊ/, the only exceptions being *canoe, hoopoe* with /uː/. However, most of those which end in <-ae> are Latinate (largely biological) terms with <ae> pronounced /iː/, and only *sundae, tenebrae* appear to have /eɪ/ like *brae*. Those in <-ue> fall into two subcategories: in most of those with <g, q> preceding <-ue> the three letters form a trigraph pronounced /g, k/, the only exceptions being *argue* with /juː/ and *dengue* with the <u> forming a digraph with the <g> pronounced /g/, and the <e> being pronounced /eɪ/ and constituting a separate syllable. All other words ending in <-ue> are pronounced with /(j)uː/.

The rest of this section is an attempt to find other 'rules' for the pronunciation of the vowel letters as single-letter graphemes in polysyllables. The rules below (which should probably be called 'generalisations') are listed in a logical order which gradually narrows down their scope; in this respect the organisation is quite different from that adopted in the sections above on the single vowel letters.

Some preliminaries:
- None of these rules apply to cases of consonantal <i, u, y>. However, I recognise that these are sometimes difficult to distinguish from cases where they have their vocalic pronunciations, and that some words slither between the two;
- None of these rules apply where the vowel letter forms a digraph with a following <l r w y>. However, again I recognise that these are sometimes difficult to distinguish from cases where the two letters are separate graphemes. In particular see <ar, er, ir, or, ur, yr>, sections 10.7/19/26/31/39/40;
- Where (vocalic) <y> is not mentioned there are either no cases or so few that no generalisation about them seems worthwhile;
- In several cases, the pronunciation of <u> has to be given as /(j)uː/ – that is, it is either /juː/ or /uː/ depending on other factors which are too complicated to include here – see section 10.36.

1) The predominant pronunciations of <a e o u> as single-letter graphemes when in 'hiatus', i.e. immediately before another pronounced vowel letter belonging to a separate syllable, are /eɪ iː/ (with following /j/-glide), /əʊ (j)uː/ (with following /w/-glide). A few examples are *aorta, archaic, chaos, chaotic, dais, kaolin, laity, prosaic; azalea, cameo, deity, erroneous, meteor, museum, neon, peony, petroleum, spontaneity; boa, heroic, poem, poetry, soloist, stoic; actual, annuity, bruin, continuity, cruel, cruet, dual, duel, fluid, genuine, gratuity, ruin, suicide, usual.* There seem to be few or no exceptions.

2) The predominant pronunciations of <i y> as single-letter graphemes when in hiatus appear to be /aɪ/ when stressed and /i:/ when unstressed (all with following /j/-glide), e.g. (stressed) *bias, client, dial, giant, psychiatry, science, society, triad, triangle, variety, viaduct, violent, violet; cryostat, cyanide, dryad, dyad, hyacinth, hyaline;* (unstressed) *alien, battalion, caviar, cheviot, comedian, delirious, dubious, fasciitis,*

*glacier, histrionic, lenient, medium, myriad, odious, odium, polio, premier, radii, radium, radius, retaliate, soviet, taxiing, valiant, caryatid, embryo, halcyon, polyandry*. Exceptions: *brio, Shiite, skiing, trio* with stressed <i> pronounced /iː/; *hyena, myopic* with unstressed <y> pronounced /aɪ/.

But the problem with both these categories is that some of the two-letter sequences involved function much more frequently as digraphs; this is particularly true of <ai ea ei eu oa oi ue>. Readers therefore just have to learn when these sequences are not digraphs – one bit of help here is that the second of two vowel letters in hiatus is never <y>.

3) The predominant pronunciations of <a i o y> when word-final in polysyllabic words and **un**stressed are /ə iː əʊ iː/. The absence of <e> here is due to the fact that word-final letter <e> is almost always part of a digraph and hardly ever constitutes a separate syllable (for the few exceptions see above and sections 10.12 and 11.4). <u> is also very rare in these circumstances and is not worth including in the rule. And all six vowel letters are so rarely **stressed** when functioning as word-final single-letter graphemes that no rule is worth giving for that situation (but see section A.10 in Appendix A).

All the following rules apply to cases where the vowel letter is followed by one or more consonant letters; this condition is stated only the first time.

4) The predominant pronunciation of <a e i o u> as single-letter graphemes when **un**stressed before a consonant letter(s) is /ə/, with a tendency for many instances of unstressed <e i> to be pronounced /ɪ/ – but this is circular and uninformative; there are few indications in the spelling of English words of when a syllable is unstressed (except by implication from the few rules which predict where the stressed syllable is – see Appendix A, section A.10), of when these graphemes have other pronunciations when unstressed (e.g. the first <u> in *museum*, the first <y> in *psychiatry*), or of when other graphemes are pronounced /ə/.

From here on, all the rules in this section refer to occurrences of the vowel letters **as single-letter graphemes when stressed**, so these conditions are stated only the first time.

5) The predominant pronunciations of <a e i o u y> **as single-letter graphemes when stressed** in the third (antepenultimate) and fourth syllables from the end of the word (that is, when the word continues (CV)CVCVC(silent <e>), where C can be one or more consonant letters) are /æ e ɪ ɒ (j)uː ɪ/. This applies to almost all words ending <-ical>, e.g.

*classical, heretical, political, logical, musical, lyrical*, and to many derived forms in which a suffix has lengthened a word and produced a change from a long to a short vowel sound, e.g. *national, profanity, serenity, divinity, wilderness*, the <e> in *egotism*. Other examples are *acrobat, agriculture, animal, antagonism, cameo, caviar, glacier, madrigal, sacrament, scarify, valiant, vocabulary*, and second <a> in *battalion; cheviot, decorative, democrat, deprecate, detriment, premier, secretary, specify, citizen, delirious, military, misery, crocodile, monument, oxygen, profligate* and *soviet* if pronounced with /ɒ/ (if pronounced with /əʊ/ it is an exception which instead obeys rule 10); *crucifix, cucumber, dubious, fugitive, funeral, impunity, lubricant, lucrative, ludicrous, mutilate, mutiny, nuclear, pugilist, scrupulous, scrutiny, cyclamen, myriad, polygamy, porphyria, syllable, syllabub, syllabus, sylloge, typical, tyranny*. For a major class of exceptions see rule 10. Other exceptions: *agency, favourite, decency, obesity, penalise, bribery, library, microscope, nitrogen, rivalry, motorist, notify, soloist, culinary, gluttony, jugular, truculent, hydrogen*. Some of these exceptions are derived forms retaining a letter-name vowel from the stem word.

A corollary here is that so few words are long enough to have syllables before the fourth from last that no rules are worth giving for these 'early syllables'.

6) The predominant pronunciations of <a e i o u> before two different consonant letters followed by word-final <-le, -re> in words with no earlier vowel letters are /æ e ɪ ɒ ʌ/, e.g. *angle, handle, tremble, uncle, muscle; centre, sceptre, spectre, lustre* and most of the <-stle> group (except *castle*) - see section 3.6.6.

7) The predominant pronunciations of <a e i o u y> before a consonant letter other than <l, r> followed by <l, r> where there is a later pronounced vowel letter (including the <e> of the 2-phoneme grapheme <-le>) are /eɪ iː aɪ əʊ (j)uː aɪ/. A few examples are *able, cradle, maple; bible, disciple, idle, title, trifle; noble; bugle, duplex, scruple; cycle, cyclone; acre, April, apron, flagrant, fragrant, sabre; fibre, mitre; cobra, ogre; lucre, putrid; cypress, hybrid*. Extension: *ochre*, where the first intervening consonant is represented by a digraph. Some exceptions: *establish, treble, triple, goblet, goblin, problem, publish; acrid, Avril, petrol, citr-ic/on/ous, copra*.

8) The predominant pronunciations of <a e i u> when followed by a single consonant letter and word-final <-ate, -et, -it, -ite, -ot, -ut, -ute> are

/æ e ɪ (j)uː/. A few examples are *gamut, granite, planet, tacit; legate, senate; rivet, limit, bigot, minute; unit.* I can find no examples with <o>. Some exceptions: *climate, pilot, private.*

9) The predominant pronunciations of <a e i o u> when followed by a single consonant letter and word-final <-ic, -id, -it, -ule> are /æ e ɪ ɒ (j)uː/. A few examples are *acid, rabid, squalid, tepid, frigid, timid, solid, stolid, cubic, humid, lucid, music, punic, putrid, runic, stupid, tunic.* Among the few exceptions are *acetic, fetid* pronounced /ˈfiːtɪd/ (also pronounced with /e/), *graphemic, phonemic, scenic, chromic,* and *phobic* and all its compounds.

10) The predominant pronunciations of <a e i o u> before a single consonant letter (except <r>) and an ending containing any of <ea eo eou eu ia ie io iou iu> are /eɪ iː ɪ əʊ (j)uː/, regardless of whether the ending contains two syllables or one. There are thousands of examples; a few are: (2-syllable ending, stress on antepenultimate – these words are exceptions to rule 5) *azalea, alien, radium; meteor, comedian, lenient, medium; erroneous, petroleum, polio, odious, odium; dubious;* (1-syllable ending, stress on penultimate) *courageous, facial, nation, spacious; cohesion, specious; delicious, magician; ocean, social, quotient; crucial, solution.* Exceptions: *companion, pageant, ration, spaniel* with /æ/; *discretion, precious, special* with /e/; *soviet* if pronounced with /ɒ/; *bunion, onion* with /ʌ/.

11) The predominant pronunciations of <a e i o u> as **stressed** single-letter graphemes before a single consonant letter and the endings <-al, -sive> are /eɪ iː aɪ əʊ (j)uː/, e.g. *fatal, naval; legal, regal, venal; arrival, final, reprisal, rival, spinal; local, modal, opal, oval, proposal, total, vocal; brutal, ducal, frugal, refusal, tribunal; evasive, adhesive, decisive, corrosive, explosive, abusive, conclusive, intrusive.* Exceptions: *medal, metal, pedal, petal* with /e/. Vowel letters preceding the ending <-ssive>, however, are 'short'.

Beyond this point, any further rules would apply to so few words that they are hardly worth stating, and, lamentably, there are large numbers of words which are not covered. The two largest gaps are probably (1) reduced pronunciations (/ə, ɪ/) of the single vowel letters when unstressed; (2) long and short pronunciations of the single vowel letters before single consonant letters in circumstances other than those covered above. These are the places where the pronunciation of single vowel letters is at its most unpredictable from the spelling in English and requires most effort to learn, and any attempt to show further regularities would be too complex to be useful because of the large numbers of exceptions.

The elephant in the room in this section is: how can you tell from the written forms of English words where the main stress falls, in order to work out where some of my 'rules' apply? For some discussion of this see section A.10 in Appendix A.

Inspection of the headings of sections 10.3-40 will show that rather more than might be expected (<air are aw ee e.e eer igh ir o.e oi ore oy>) give the percentage of the basic pronunciation as 100%, and two others (<ie i.e>) are close to that. But many of the rest are somewhat or considerably lower, and in three cases (<ere i y>) no useful figures can be given. Overall (but I have not (yet) done the calculation) I would guess that the predictability of the pronunciations of main-system graphemes beginning with vowel letters may be about 60%.

## 10.43 Consolation prize?

The only consolation prize is that almost all multi-letter graphemes beginning with vowel letters have far fewer correspondences and more regularity than the vowels letters as single-letter graphemes have - yet even here there is an egregious exception: <ou>, with 8 minor correspondences. As with various other aspects of the system, there is no choice but to learn the rest.

# 11. Evaluating some pronunciation rules for vowel graphemes

In this chapter I assess the reliability or otherwise of just five rules which purport to help children and others taking their first steps in reading to generate accurate pronunciations of vowel graphemes. For some rules covering the VC(C) part of CVC(C) monosyllables which could well be useful at a slightly later stage, see section A.7 in Appendix A.

## 11.1 Some history

There is a long tradition of teachers looking for rules for pronouncing vowel graphemes, and almost as long a tradition of finding most of them unhelpful. For example, McLeod (1961, cited in Carney, 1994: 70–74) reported 'the result of a survey to which 76 teachers in 28 Scottish schools contributed'. From 59 rules submitted McLeod set 32 aside 'since they merely grouped words according to common suffixes'. Of the other 27 only five are reading (grapheme-phoneme) rules, and only three of those concern vowel graphemes – they correspond to sections 11.2, 11.4 and 11.5 below. (The other two reading rules found by McLeod and discussed by Carney concern consonant graphemes, namely <wr> pronounced /r/ (see section 9.40) and <ch> allegedly pronounced /ʃ/ after <n>, which I have ignored. Except for a couple which cover very few words, all McLeod's spelling (phoneme–grapheme) rules are covered, without this being made explicit, in chapters 4 and 6).

© 2015 Greg Brooks, CC BY            http://dx.doi.org/10.11647/OBP.0053.11

The most famous article in this tradition is Clymer (1963, reprinted 1996). Of the 45 rules he discussed, five deal with syllabification, which is not relevant to this book, and six with word stress – see section A.10 in Appendix A. The other 34 rules all deal with grapheme-phoneme correspondences, 10 with consonant graphemes, 23 with vowel graphemes, and one with a mixture of the two. Many are trivial, or special cases of more general rules; when all of that and duplications are sorted out, the rules for vowel graphemes reduce to the five discussed in sections 11.2-6, of which four are useful and one (the best known) is not.

Johnston (2001) listed several replications of Clymer's study between 1967 and 1978; most arrived at similar conclusions. However, Gates (1983, 1986) re-formulated some generalisations to make them more reliable (as I have in some cases below), and Burmeister (1968) focused specifically on the best-known rule – see section 11.2. Johnston (2001) herself re-visited several of Clymer's rules for vowel graphemes without, in my opinion, adding anything of value.

## 11.2 'When there are two vowels side by side, the long sound of the first one is heard and the second is usually silent.'

Often popularly stated as: **'When two vowels go walking, the first does the talking.'**

This rule has long been popular in North America, despite having been blown to pieces by Clymer (1963/1996). It was meant to tell children which of two adjacent vowel letters indicates the pronunciation of a digraph, but it is unclear, or underspecified, in seven respects:

- It does not say (presumably assumes teachers and children know) which letters are 'vowels', but it seems clear that <a, e, i, o, u> are the intended vowel letters;
- It ignores the consonantal pronunciations of <i, u> when they precede other vowel letters, as in *onion, language* (see sections 10.22 and 10.36), presumably because these are not relevant to initial instruction;
- It does not say (presumably assumes teachers and children know) what the 'long sounds' (or 'talkings') of these vowel letters are, but again it seems clear that the 'letter-name' sounds /eɪ, iː, aɪ, əʊ, juː/ are meant;

*Evaluating some pronunciation rules for vowel graphemes* 449

- It is not clear why it says the second vowel letter is 'usually' silent – perhaps to allow for words like *dais, zoology* with two vowel letters which normally form a digraph but in particular words do not;
- It does not say whether sequences of two identical adjacent letters are to count as digraphs for this purpose, but I think the rule is meant to apply only to sequences of two different letters, so in what follows I have not looked at <aa, ee, ii (which never occurs as a digraph anyway), oo, uu (which only occurs in *muumuu, vacuum*)>, except for word-final <ee>;
- It doesn't say whether <w, y> are to count as vowel letters for this purpose. In her re-evaluation of the rule Johnston (2001) decided to include <aw, ew, ow, ay, ey, oy> (<iw, uw, iy, uy> never occur as digraphs), so I have followed this;
- It takes no account of <ye>, the only vowel digraph with <y> as first letter, but since this occurs in only seven words, it can be ignored.

There are two other possible sequences that never occur as digraphs: <iu, uo>. Assuming the 12 exclusions just mentioned (<aa, ee, ii, iu, iw, iy, oo, uo, uu, uw, uy, ye>), there are 23 relevant vowel digraphs consisting of adjacent vowel letters or a vowel letter plus <w, y>.

There is one set of words for which this rule holds true with few exceptions, namely monosyllables ending in <ae, ee, ie, oe, ue>, almost all of which (see Table 10.3) are pronounced with the letter-name sounds /eɪ, iː, aɪ, əʊ, juː/. Unfortunately (as Table 10.3 also shows), the total number of relevant words in the entire language is about 54.

Within the set of 23 relevant vowel digraphs, 12 belong to the main system and 11 are Oddities; they are all shown in Table 11.1 with their predominant pronunciations (except for <ae, ie, oe, ue> in word-final position in monosyllables), and relevant percentages of occurrence of those pronunciations derived or deduced from chapter 10.

From Table 11.1 is it clear that the rule only works for <ay, ea> and possibly <ai, ue> among main-system digraphs, plus four or five of the Oddities, a very poor result.

Because so few digraphs actually conform to the rule Burmeister (1968) advocated teaching them in groups, of which those which do conform would be one – but her other groups were entirely artificial because they supported no generalisations at all, and therefore failed to set digraphs which conform to the rule sufficiently apart.

Verdict: This rule should be consigned to oblivion, and digraphs should be taught individually.

TABLE 11.1: 'WHEN TWO VOWELS GO WALKING, THE FIRST DOES THE TALKING'

| | Digraph | Predominant pronunciation(s) | Conforms to the rule? |
|---|---|---|---|
| **Main system** | ai | /eɪ/ 43%<br>/e/ 46% | No, unless *said* is excluded |
| | au | /ɔː/ 46%<br>/ɒ/ 43% | No |
| | aw | /ɔː/ 100% | No |
| | ay | /eɪ/ 100% | Yes |
| | ea | /iː/ 73% | Yes |
| | ew | /juː/ 84% | No |
| | ie * | /iː/ 73% | No |
| | oi | /ɔɪ/ 100% | No |
| | ou | /aʊ/ 48%<br>/əʊ/ 1% | No |
| | ow | /aʊ/ 45%<br>/əʊ/ 44% | No |
| | oy | /ɔɪ/ 100% | No |
| | ue * | /juː/ 59%<br>/uː/ 41% | ? |
| **Oddities** | ae * | /iː/ 62% | No |
| | ao | /eɪ/ 69% | Yes |
| | ei | /iː/ 69% | Yes |
| | eo | /ə/ 70%<br>/iː/ only in *people* ** | No |
| | eu | /uː/ 58% | No |
| | ey | /iː/ 76% | Yes |
| | ia | /ə/ 57%<br>/aɪ/ only in *diamond* | No |
| | io | /ə/ 100% | No |
| | oa | /əʊ/ 96% | Yes |
| | oe * | /iː/ 65% | ? |
| | ua | /ə/ 100% | No |
| | ui | /uː/ 73% | No |

\* For monosyllables ending in these digraphs, the rule is largely true.
\*\* and two other very rare words – see section 10.12.

## 11.3 'When a written word has only one vowel letter, and that letter is followed by at least one consonant letter other than <r, w, y>, the vowel has its usual short pronunciation.'

A better-known version of the rule is 'When a word has only one vowel and that vowel is in the middle, it is usually short', but my formulation (above) is more accurate, partly because <a, o, u> have alternative pronunciations. Even though <r, w, y> in these circumstances after a vowel letter always form a vowel digraph with the vowel letter, for teaching purposes it would clearly be better to treat them here as consonant letters. The rule applies mainly or entirely to closed monosyllables, and regardless of the number of consonant letters following the vowel letter.

(English is rich in monosyllables – many years ago three American nerds compiled a list of 9,123 (Moser *et al.*, 1957), and there was once a competition to find or devise the longest one (Gardner, 1979), defined in terms of letters rather than phonemes; the competition was won by an American poet named William Harman, with *broughammed* ('travelled by brougham', which can be pronounced /bruːmd/ in General American but would have two syllables /ˈbruːwəmd/ in RP).

Most monosyllabic words in English are phonologically closed (end in a consonant phoneme(s)). Table 11.2 sets out the facts on my version of the rule, at least as far as the RP accent is concerned (it seems clear that <o> has no 'short' pronunciation at all in the General American accent – see Cruttenden (2014: 127) and Carney (1994: 59)).

TABLE 11.2: PRONUNCIATIONS OF VOWEL LETTERS IN WORDS WITH A SINGLE, NON-FINAL VOWEL LETTER FOLLOWED BY AT LEAST ONE CONSONANT LETTER OTHER THAN <r, w, y>.

| Vowel letter | Principal short pronunciation | Other short pronunciations | Long pronunciations |
|---|---|---|---|
| a | /æ/ | /ɒ/ in 25 words, e.g. *squash, was* | /ɔː/ in 26 words, e.g. *ball, salt, talk*; /ɑː/ in 18 words, e.g. *calm, half*; /eɪ/ only in *bass* (the musical term) |
| e | /e/ | – | /iː/ only in *retch* pronounced /riːtʃ/ |

TABLE 11.2: PRONUNCIATIONS OF VOWEL LETTERS IN WORDS WITH A SINGLE, NON-FINAL VOWEL LETTER FOLLOWED BY AT LEAST ONE CONSONANT LETTER OTHER THAN <r, w, y>, CONT.

| Vowel letter | Principal short pronunciation | Other short pronunciations | Long pronunciations |
|---|---|---|---|
| i | /ɪ/ | – | /aɪ/ in 18 words, e.g. *child, find, pint, sign*; /iː/ only in *chic* |
| o | /ɒ/ | /ʌ/ in 8 words, e.g. *son*; /ʊ/ only in *wolf* | /əʊ/ in 34 words, e.g. *both, colt, comb, don't, gross, post, roll, told*; /uː/ only in *tomb, whom, womb* |
| u | /ʌ/ | /ʊ/ in 14 words, e.g. *bull, push* | – |
| y | /ɪ/ | – | – |

Thus the total number of exceptions, even counting both categories, is no more than 150, some of which beginner readers are unlikely to encounter, and there are undoubtedly thousands of words which obey the rule. I therefore consider it to have high reliability, probably over 90%, and well worth teaching.

## 11.4 'When a final <e> is preceded by a consonant letter other than <r, w, x, y> and that consonant is preceded by a single vowel letter, the final <e> is silent and the other vowel letter has its letter-name ('long') sound.'

This is my attempt to formulate a rule for 'magic <e>'/split digraphs that is more accurate than some current formulations, e.g.
- 'The final <e> in a word is not pronounced'.
- '<e> at the end of a word makes the preceding vowel in the word long'.

Table 11.3 shows the relevant data.

TABLE 11.3: RELIABILITY OF RULES FOR SPLIT DIGRAPHS OR 'MAGIC <e>' WHERE THE INTERVENING LETTER IS NOT <r, w, x, y>.

| Split digraph | Predominant pronunciation | Alternative long pronunciation | Major exceptions | Words with 'pronounced' final <e> |
|---|---|---|---|---|
| a.e | /eɪ/ 68% | /ɑː/ 32%, e.g. *mirage* | Lots of words with <-age, -ate> pronounced /ɪdʒ, ət/, e.g. *village, accurate* | *agape* ('love feast'), *agave, biennale, blase, cafe, canape, curare, finale, glace, kamikaze, karate, macrame, pate* ('paste'), *sesame, tamale* |
| e.e | /iː/ 100% | – | – | *hebe, machete, meze, naivete, protege, stele, ukulele* |
| i.e | /aɪ/ 97% | /iː/ 3%, e.g. *police* | *bodice, give, live* (verb), lots of longer words with <-ive> pronounced /ɪv/, e.g. *massive*; various words with <-ine, -ite> pronounced /ɪn, ɪt/, e.g. *examine, definite* | *aborigine, anime, facsimile, (bona) fide, recipe, simile* |
| o.e | /əʊ/ 95% | – | *compote, gone, scone, shone* with /ɒ/, *above, become, come, done, dove, glove, love, none, shove, some* with /ʌ/, *welcome* and adjectives in <-some> with /ə/ | *abalone, adobe, anemone, coyote, epitome, extempore, expose* ('report of scandal'), *furore* pronounced /fjʊəˈrɔːreɪ/ (also pronounced /ˈfjʊərɔː/), *guacamole, hyperbole, sylloge* |
| u.e | /juː/ 89% | /uː/ 11%, e.g. *rude* | – | *resume* ('c.v.') |
| y.e | /aɪ/ 100% | – | – | – |

All the rules for split digraphs are predicated on the word-final <e> being 'silent', so the first necessity is to exclude polysyllables in which it is 'pronounced'. Table 11.3 shows that there are only about 39 words in the language in which a final <e> separated from a single preceding vowel letter by one consonant letter is 'pronounced', and three, *curare*, *extempore* and *furore* pronounced /fjʊəˈrɔːreɪ/, have the banned letter <r> intervening. Of the 39 words, only *cafe* is at all frequent.

The percentages shown were calculated without taking words with 'pronounced' final <e> or the major exception categories into account (but most of the words in those categories would again not feature in beginner readers' books), and this would reduce the strength of the main rules for <a.e, i.e, o.e>, but on the whole the 'magic <e>' rules hold good and are worth teaching. Most learners will, I think, acquire the /uː/ pronunciation of <u.e> without even noticing that they have, or that /uː/ is different from /juː/, and also learn without noticing it that <y.e> has the same pronunciation as <i.e> (most words with <y.e> are rare, so this digraph should present no problem for reading when encountered).

As it happens, the inclusion of <x> among the letters banned from the mid position in this rule excludes just three words in the entire language: *annexe*, *axe*, *deluxe*, so the rule could well be taught without <x>, and would then be parallel to the 'short vowel' rule in section 11.3. If consonant digraphs were admitted to the dot position for this analysis, other rare words would join the list with 'pronounced' final <e>, e.g. *antistrophe*, *oche*, *strophe*, *synecdoche*.

For more on split digraphs and their definition, see section A.6 in Appendix A.

## 11.5 'When <a> follows <qu, w, wh> and is not followed by <r>, or by any consonant letter plus <e>, it is pronounced /ɒ/.'

This rule is usually stated without the clause 'and is not followed by <r>, or by any consonant letter plus <e>', but this is essential to rule out the <ar> digraph and cases where 'magic <e>' would override (e.g. *quake*, *wade*, *whale*), and my version is therefore more accurate. There are 21 relevant words with <qua>, 42 with <wa>, and only *what* with <wha>. Of the 64 words, the only exceptions are *walk, wall, water,* all pronounced with /ɔː/, so this rule is highly reliable (95% if each word is given equal weighting). There are also seven words in which <a> is followed by <r(r)> but those letters do not form a di/trigraph and the <a> is pronounced /ɒ/: *quarantine, quarrel, quarry, warrant, warren, warrigal, warrior,* but these need to be taught separately because in the great majority of words in which <ar> follows <qu, w, wh> it is pronounced either /ɔː/ (e.g. *quart, ward, wharf*) or /ə/ (e.g. *steward, towards*).

## 11.6 'When <y> is the final letter in a word, it always has a vowel sound, either alone or in combination with a preceding <a, e, o>.'

Given that word-final <y> is never a consonant letter, this rule is 100% reliable. Formulated like this, it may seem entirely obvious to proficient readers, but may be helpful to learners. <ay, ey, oy> are also covered in section 11.2.

# Appendix A: Assumptions and technicalities

## A.1 Citation forms

This book is almost entirely concerned with the citation forms of words, that is, how they would be pronounced by people with RP accents who were asked to read them aloud from a list, and/or how the words' pronunciations are transcribed in broad IPA in the *Cambridge English Pronouncing Dictionary*. However, quite a few words have what Carney (1994) calls 'allegro' and 'lento' pronunciations, that is in more rapid and less rapid speech, and both may well feature in their citation forms if a sufficient sample of people is polled. I cover a few variants of this sort (see especially section 6.10), but it would be impossible to cover all of them.

## A.2 Phonemes

Phoneticians disagree profoundly about the **acoustic** existence of phonemes. However, for the purposes of analysing any alphabetic spelling system it seems to me that assuming the **psychological** reality of phonemes is inescapable, and I have proceeded on that assumption. One justification might be that there are no possible correlations between parts of letters and aspects of the acoustic signal. Another might be that otherwise it is difficult to imagine how alphabets came to be invented in the first place.

I have also assumed that long vowels take longer to pronounce than short vowels, even though the acoustic evidence shows this to be only partly true, if at all.

If phonemes are assumed to have some reality, how are they to be defined? The most basic definition is the one I offer in chapter 1: 'distinctive speech sounds', that is, differences in sound which make a difference to the meanings of words. Thus in English /b, p/ are phonemes because the words *bad, pad* (and many others) which differ in meaning differ in speech only in this respect. But a fuller definition would make it clear that phonemes exist in a dynamic system with others within (a particular variety of) a particular language.

So distinctions which are phonemic in English may not be in some other languages (e.g. /l, r/ are not separate phonemes in Japanese or Kikuyu), while distinctions that are not phonemic in English may be so elsewhere. For example, unaspirated and aspirated /k, k$^h$, p, p$^h$, t, t$^h$/ are not phonemic in English (and are therefore difficult for monolingual speakers of English to tell apart without training) because the unaspirated versions occur only after /s/ (try holding a hand in front of your mouth and saying *pin, spin* and notice the puff after the /p/ in *pin* and its absence in *spin*) - but are phonemic in many languages of the Indian sub-continent (and are thought to have been so in classical Greek, where the six phonemes were written κ, χ, π, φ, τ, θ respectively (in modern Greek χ, φ, θ represent /x (as in Scots *loch*), f, θ/ respectively - and this shows where the values of two IPA symbols have come from).

# A.3 Syllables

Though difficult to define rigorously, syllables are intuitively obvious - psycholinguists showed many decades ago that children can be taught very quickly how to count (or indicate by moving the right number of pebbles or other symbols) the syllables in words spoken to them by an experimenter - and that phonemes are much less intuitive and more difficult to count.

In strict linguistic terms, therefore, as just implied, only spoken words have syllables, and written words do not - but ordinary usage can be very confusing here since dividing and hyphenating words at line ends in print is called 'syllabification' (in Britain; 'syllabication' in North America). The word *extra* can be used to show the difference. If this word ever needed to be split between lines it would presumably appear as:

ex-

tra,

but its spoken syllables are /ˈek - strə/, with the two phonemes represented by the <x> belonging to separate syllables.

There are two reasons for insisting that only spoken words have syllables. First, imagining that written words have syllables further confounds already confused attempts to predict word stress from the written forms of words (see section A.10 below).

Secondly, even if it was thought useful to try to define syllables within written words, this would very quickly lead to problems. As the example of *extra* just demonstrated, it is often difficult, sometimes impossible, to say where the boundaries between written syllables are.

However, all of this poses a problem for the grapheme–phoneme sections of this book, chapters 9 and 10 – especially chapter 10 – because it is sometimes necessary even so to refer to syllables, and therefore (explicitly or by implication) to the spoken forms of words, including resorting to circumlocutions such as 'the syllable containing /s/ spelt <ce>'. Where this pinches most is in sections 10.41–42, where I attempt to give general rules for the pronunciation of the vowel letters as single-letter graphemes in monosyllables and polysyllables respectively, and in section A.10 below, where I summarise the difficulties involved in trying to predict where the stresses fall on English words, given only their written forms. For my attempt to get round some of this with clear definitions see the heading of section 10.41 and the first paragraph of section 10.42.

## A.4 Graphemes

The phoneme inventories of languages are mainly established by finding 'minimal pairs', spoken words which differ in only one sound segment but have different meanings; see again *bad/pad* above, and for another example (the few pairs of English words differing only in /θ/ v. /ð/ such as *wreath/wreathe*) see section 9.36. Some linguists try to establish the graphemes of an orthography similarly, that is by classifying all the letter shapes which differentiate written words with different meanings. For English, this would result in an inventory of about 50 graphemes – the upper- and lower-case versions of the 26 letters of the alphabet, plus 2 for the variant forms of lower-case <a, ɑ> and <g, ɡ> (unless those were called 'allographs' by analogy with the allophone variants of phonemes), possibly minus a few for letters with graphically similar upper- and lower-case forms <C, c; K, k; O, o; P, p; S, s; U, u; V, v; W, w; X, x; Y, y; Z, z>, possibly plus some for 'ligatures' (joined letters) which used to be used in print (e.g. <æ> in words like *ægis, Cæsar*), and possibly plus a few for common abbreviations and punctuation marks <& ! , . @ ? : ; ...> – but where would you stop? For example, are numerals graphemes? Also, this approach would signally fail to uncover any multi-letter graphemes, and by extension the feature I have labelled 'dual-functioning', both of which seem to me absolutely necessary in analysing English spelling.

I have instead taken the (to me) more common-sense approach of asking which letters and letter-combinations represent which phonemes (chapters 3 and 5), and then using the inventory of graphemes so established (chapter 8) to work back to phonemes (chapters 9 and 10).

## A.5 Every letter belongs to a grapheme (almost)

It is commonly believed that English spelling has lots of 'silent letters', 'magic <e>' being the classic example, along with the first letter in word-initial clusters such as <kn, wr>. Well yes, but every alphabetic script is composed entirely of silent letters, if you think about it. What is meant is letters which might as well not be there, since the spelling would represent the same word-sound without them, e.g.

| | | |
|---|---|---|
| *write* | which could be | *rite* (and is, in another meaning) |
| *honest* | which could be | *\*onest* |
| *friend* | which could be | *\*frend* |
| *beauty* | which could be | *\*buty* |

or letters which at their position in the written form of a word do not correspond to a phoneme at that position in the spoken form but may nevertheless affect its pronunciation, e.g. 'magic <e>'.

In my view the identification of silent letters is more a matter for spelling reformers than for teachers. Learners have to learn the current spellings, and have to develop ways of remembering non-obvious parts of the system – of which there are many more besides 'silent letters' (e.g. whether medial and linking /w/ and /j/ are represented in the spelling or not – see sections 3.8.7-8 and 9.0). It may be more helpful to learners to be asked 'How do we write /r/ at the beginning of *writing*?' and told '<wr> at the beginning of a word is pronounced /r/' than to be told 'The <w> at the beginning of *writing* is silent.'

In accordance with this idea I have adopted a 'principle of exhaustiveness' (first proposed by Albrow, 1972, and adopted by Carney, 1994): that is, as far as possible every letter in a word's spelling should be allocated to one of the phonemes in its spoken form. So you will find that I have analysed <wr> as one of the spellings of /r/, <ho> as one of the spellings of /ɒ/, <ie> as one of the spellings of /e/, <eau> as one of the spellings of the 2-phoneme sequence /juː/, <ps> as one of the spellings of /s/ (as in *psychology*), etc., etc.

On the whole, this works well. However, in section 6.10 you will find a whole set of elided vowels, cases where a vowel letter never corresponds to a phoneme, even in citation forms (or only in very conservative or artificial 'spelling guidance' pronunciations), and where I consider it would be over the top to add sequences consisting of those vowel letters and the preceding consonant letters to the inventory of graphemes. This does lead to a fuzzy boundary on the category of graphemes, but it seems to me that complete consistency is unattainable here.

The impossibility of completeness is particularly visible in the case of odd spellings of place- and personal names. For example, most of the letters in *Leicester, Worcester* can be assigned to phonemes in their spoken forms /ˈlestə, ˈwʊstə/ (as can all the letters in the alternative spellings *Lester, Wooster*), except <ce>: if the principle of exhaustiveness is to be maintained, these letters would, I think, have to be combined with the <s> as a new grapheme corresponding to /s/ – but there is no warrant for a grapheme <ces> in the main vocabulary, so I have not added it to the inventory or used *Leicester, Worcester* as examples of /e/ spelt <ei> or /ʊ/ spelt <or> respectively, even though these are in the inventory. And if you believe in *Cholmondeley-Featherstonhaugh* as a genuine spelling of a double-barrelled surname pronounced /ˈtʃʌmliːˈfænʃɔː/ you'd have to add /ʌ/ spelt <ol>, and puzzle over how to divide <onde> between /m, l/ with no principled way of allocating any of the letters to either phoneme. Worst of all, between the initial /f/ and final /ɔː/ of /ˈfænʃɔː/ I can see no way of getting the <s, n> to be part of the spellings of /n, ʃ/, which are in the opposite order to the letters.

# A.6 Split digraphs

The classic case of a so-called 'silent letter' which does influence the pronunciations of words and cannot be removed without altering them is the 'magic' <e> in split digraphs – but how should split digraphs be defined? A first and superficially appealing definition would be 'Cases of

<a, e, i, o, u, y> followed by a consonant letter and stem-final <e> where the <e> indicates the letter-name ('long') pronunciation of the vowel letter'. This will not work, because:
1) the pronunciation of <y.e> is /aɪ/, which is the name of <i> (and not /waɪ/, the name of <y>)
2) <u.e> is pronounced not only as <juː> but also as <uː>
3) all the other split digraphs except <y.e> also have pronunciations other than the 'letter-name' one.

For my separate definitions of the six split digraphs I recognise see sections 10.4/17/24/28/38/40. Here I attempt to generalise them in this formulation:

> A split digraph consists of stem-final <e> preceded by (usually) a single consonant letter (other than <h, j, q, r, w, x, y>) preceded by one of <a, e, i, o, u, y> where that letter is **not** preceded by a vowel letter and where the digraph is pronounced either as the name of the first letter of the digraph or as another long vowel or diphthong.

The last phrase covers the pronunciation of <y.e> and the /uː/ pronunciation of <u.e> as well as non-letter-name pronunciations of the other split digraphs.

The exclusion of <h, j, q> from occupying the 'dot' position in a split digraph is mentioned solely for completeness (and only here, and not in any of the relevant sections of chapter 10): there are not, and cannot be, any such sequences as <ahe, eje, iqe>, etc., in stem-final position. The exclusion of <r, w, x, y> from occupying the 'dot' position keeps out <are, ere, ire, ore, ure, yre; awe, ewe, owe; aye, eye> which need to be analysed as trigraphs to account for their correspondences, and <axe, exe> which need to be analysed as having <xe> as a digraph separate from the preceding vowel letter. (Other combinations, e.g. <iwe, oxe, uye>, do not occur).

Letter <g> as sole occupant of the 'dot' position is odd. There are no words ending <yge>, and very few ending <ege, ige, oge, uge> – see sections 10.17/24/28/38 – but there are hundreds ending <age>, many of which have neither of the split digraph pronunciations – see below, and see the entry for <a.e>, section 10.4, for the three competing pronunciations.

The restriction to one intervening consonant letter has to be relaxed to allow for words where there is clearly a split digraph according to the rest of the definition but there are two consonant letters or <gu, qu> forming a consonant digraph intervening. This extension covers varying numbers of words under <a.e, i.e, o.e, u.e, y.e> (and none under <e.e>), totalling about 64 in all. The full list of consonant digraphs which can occupy the dot position is <ch, gn, gu, ll, mb, qu, ss, th, tt>, and most words containing them are unusual. There are also just 13 stem words with <n, g> or <s, t> spelling separate phonemes intervening in <a.e> pronounced /eɪ/ which seem to me to fit the definition and which I have decided to include: *arrange, change, grange, mange, range, strange* (plus the derived forms *estrange, exchange)*; *baste, chaste, haste, lambaste, paste, taste, waste,* plus four oddities: *caste* with <a.e> pronounced /ɑː/ surrounding <st>, and three words with <squ> occupying the dot position: *bisque, odalisque* with surrounding <i.e> pronounced /iː/, and *brusque* pronounced /bruːsk/ (also pronounced /brʌsk/, which requires an analysis not involving a split digraph) with surrounding <u.e> pronounced /uː/. The dot position cannot be occupied by any other multi-letter sequence, in my analysis.

The stipulation that the leading letter in a split digraph must not be preceded by a vowel letter is needed to rule out vowel digraphs, etc., which do not need the final <e> to indicate their pronunciations. This differentiates my analysis from that of Mountford (1998), who recognises the following 12 'split trigraphs' with two vowel letters preceding the dot: <ai.e, au.e, ea.e, ee.e, ei.e, eu.e, ia.e, ie.e, oi.e, oo.e, ou.e, ui.e>, plus 10 more 'split trigraphs' with a consonant letter (counting not only <l. r> but also <w, y> as consonant letters) immediately preceding the dot: <al.e, ar.e, aw.e, er.e, ir.e, is.e, or.e, ow.e, oy.e, ur.e>, and even the following five 'split four-letter graphemes', all with two vowel letters and then a consonant letter preceding the dot: <ais.e, ear.e, ier.e, oar.e, our.e>. Some of these extended split graphemes were posited as far back as Cordts (1965). I have found none of them necessary in my analysis because all such cases yield instead to analyses with the letters before the dot forming graphemes in their own right, and the final <e> forming a di/trigraph with the preceding consonant letter(s).

The letter-name pronunciations of <a.e, e.e, i.e, o.e, u.e> as /eɪ, iː, aɪ, əʊ, juː/, plus <u.c, y.c> as /uː, aɪ/, then represent the obvious pronunciations of the split digraphs.

However, under <a.e, e.e, i.e, o.e> I have added /ɑː, eɪ, iː, uː/ respectively as alternative pronunciations to cover large numbers of words with <a.e> pronounced /ɑː/, just four stem words with <e.e> pronounced /eɪ/, a moderately large set of words with <i.e> pronounced /iː/, and just six with <o.e> pronounced /uː/. With these extensions, five of the six split digraphs have two pronunciations each, the exception being <y.e>, which is only pronounced /aɪ/. It seems to me that these extra correspondences of the split digraphs need to be analysed in this way and not, for example, as <a> in *massage*, etc., spelling /ɑː/ and the <e> only forming a digraph with <g>.

It is noticeable that for <a.e, e.e, i.e> these extra correspondences derive from French spelling conventions. As Crystal (2012) and especially Upward and Davidson (2011) document, French words which entered the English language before about 1600 became anglicised in pronunciation and followed English spelling conventions, such as they were (there had been some inconsistencies in Anglo-Saxon (Old English) spelling – in particular it had no consistent system for distinguishing long and short vowels – and after 1066 Norman French scribes introduced others). But what I have in several places called 'more recent' borrowings of French words (that is, those which arrived after the completion of the Great Vowel Shift in about 1600) in almost all cases retained their French spellings and (approximations to) their French pronunciations, despite the fact that this has introduced new correspondences for some vowel graphemes and increased the number of inconsistencies.

One of the very few words introduced after 1600 which did acquire an anglicised pronunciation is *blouse*: if it had behaved like other 'more recent' borrowings it would be pronounced closer to French as /bluːz/ rather than as anglicised /blaʊz/. The process of assimilation can be heard at work in *garage*, *mauve*, *doyen(ne)* and *foyer*:

- The General American pronunciation of *garage* as /ɡəˈrɑːʒ/ is closest to French, having only replaced /a/ with /ə/ in the first syllable and /ʁ/ with /r/ in the second. In RP, there are two pronunciations. In /ˈɡærɑːʒ/, the last two French phonemes have been retained, but the stress has shifted to the first syllable and the vowel in that syllable has shifted to /æ/. In /ˈɡærɪdʒ/, anglicisation is complete: the second syllable is now pronounced as in the great majority of polysyllabic words ending <-age>, and the only phoneme which is still pronounced as in French is the initial /ɡ/;
- In Britain, the pronunciation of *mauve* varies between French-like /məʊv/, with the English diphthong /əʊ/ replacing /o/, and /mɔːv/, with a fully anglicised vowel perhaps reflecting a 'spelling pronunciation' of <au>; the latter pronunciation is less usual;
- Both *doyen* and *doyenne* have a French-like pronunciation /dwaɪˈjen/ and a mid-way pronunciation /dɔɪˈjen/ where the French 2-phoneme sequence /waɪ/ has shifted to /ɔɪ/ but the stress has remained on the

second syllable; *doyen* (but not *doyenne*) also has the fully anglicised pronunciation /'dɔɪjən/ where the stress has moved to the first syllable;
• Similarly, *foyer* has three pronunciations: /'fwaɪjeɪ/ with the French pure vowels /a, e/ anglicised to diphthongs /aɪ, eɪ/ and the stress shifted to the first syllable, /'fɔɪjeɪ/ (which I first noticed in an RP speaker in November 2013) with the first diphthong further anglicised to /ɔɪ/, and /'fɔɪjə/ with the final vowel totally anglicised to schwa.

In large numbers of cases where the consonant in the dot position is <c, g>, and a small number where it is <v>, the <e> also forms a digraph with the consonant letter (for dual-functioning see section 7.1) spelling (and pronounced) /s, ʤ (or /ʒ/), v/ respectively. Traditionally, the <e> is said to 'mark' <c, g> as having their 'soft' pronunciations /s, ʤ/ (see also section A.8), and not their 'hard' pronunciations /k, g/. The alternative 'soft' pronunciation of <g> as /ʒ/ never seems to be noticed, but this is the least frequent phoneme in spoken English and its spellings are rarely taught explicitly. <ve> is different: the <v> would spell and be pronounced /v/ without the <e>, which is present purely as a strong spelling convention (see section 3.7.7) even when the <e> is not part of a split digraph.

When is a split digraph not a split digraph? Note the restriction to letter-names and alternative long vowels or diphthongs in my definition. There are also copious examples of words with final <e> preceded by a single consonant letter (other than <r, w, x, y>) preceded by <a, e, i, o, u> not preceded by another vowel letter where <a, e, i, o, u> have neither their letter-name pronunciations nor the alternative pronunciations listed above. For categories and lists see the exceptions mentioned under <a.e, e.e, i.e, o.e, u.e> in sections 10.4/17/24/28/38. (There are no such cases with <y.e>).

In general, these are words where what appear to be the 'leading' vowel letters in split digraphs are pronounced 'short'. In most cases the 'leading' vowel letter is pronounced /ə/ or /ɪ/, for example in *mortgage* (and lots of other words ending in unstressed <-age>), *purchase, accurate* (and lots of other words ending in <-ate>), *college, diocese, bodice* (and several other words ending in <-ice>), *engine* (and several other words ending in <-ine>), *mortise, practise, premise, promise, treatise, definite* (and several other words ending in <-ite>), *give, massive* (and thousands of other polysyllabic nouns and adjectives ending in <-ive>), *fulsome, handsome* (and all the other adjectives ending in <-some>), *welcome, purpose, lettuce, minute* (/'mɪnɪt/, '60 seconds'). Examples with other short vowel phonemes are *axe, have* (when stressed) with /æ/, *allege, annexe, clientele, cortege* with <e>, *compote, (be)gone, scone, shone* with /ɒ/, and *above, become, come, deluxe, done, dove, glove, love, none, shove, some* with /ʌ/. It seems to me that all such cases, unlike those involving long vowels, diphthongs or /juː/, are more economically analysed as having the relevant short vowel spelt variously <a, e, i, o, u> and the word-final <e> forming a digraph with the intervening consonant letter. All of this admittedly produces a fuzzy boundary around split digraphs, and a possible source of confusion over some words which might have a split digraph pronunciation, or not, but it seems to me that complete consistency is not attainable in this area either.

For an attempt at a pedagogical statement of the split digraph rule see section 11.4.

# A.7 Rhymes and phonograms (and rimes)

To keep this section simple to start with, let us define rhymes as those endings of one-syllable words which sound the same in more than one word, e.g. the /uːt/ sounds of *boot, coot, hoot, toot*, etc. Phonograms are the corresponding parts of written words, in this case <oot>; alternative terms for 'phonogram' are 'rime' (in that spelling) and '(word) body'. I do not use 'body' because it has more usual meanings in the language, and do not use 'rime' in this section because it is confusing to use homophonic terms for the corresponding parts of spoken and written words (and because there is already a word 'rime' meaning 'hoar frost').

There are claims (apparently first made by Adams, 1990: 85, but first systematically investigated by Treiman *et al.*, 1995) in the literature on teaching children to read and spell that many of the alternative spellings of vowel phonemes and the alternative pronunciations of vowel graphemes, considered to be unpredictable in isolation, are more predictable if phonograms and rhymes are considered as units. The claim was originally confined to monosyllables with CVC phonological structure, which led to monosyllables with no initial consonant, and therefore VC structure, and relevant polysyllables, being mostly overlooked. Although my analysis is focused almost entirely at the segmental (phoneme and grapheme) level, I have examined this claim (in its original version plus VCs and some polysyllables), and found it largely unconvincing.

In the spelling direction, it seems to me that there are no rhyme-phonogram correspondences in (C)VC monosyllables which would be worth teaching as units because all the 'families' of words are too small and/or have too many exceptions. However, in (C)VCC monosyllables there are just two that might be worth teaching:

/eɪnt/ spelt <-aint> in *faint, paint, plaint, quaint, saint, taint* (only exceptions: *ain't* (sort of), *feint*). Despite applying to only 6 monosyllables (against 2 exceptions), this is probably worth teaching because it generalises to the final syllables of 6 polysyllables: *acquaint, attaint, complaint, con/di/re-straint* and (despite possibly being split across syllable boundaries) to non-final syllables in at least 3 more: *maintain, plaintiff, plaintive*. Score: 6-2 in monosyllables, 15-2 overall.

/əʊld/ spelt <-old> in *bold, cold, fold, gold, hold, old, scold, sold, told, wold*, plus the final syllables in *behold, cuckold, blind/mani-fold, marigold, scaffold, threshold*. The only stem word exception is *mould* (and this is spelt *mold* in the US), but there is possible confusion with several past tenses/participles, some of which are homophones of the stem words: *bowled, doled, foaled, holed, poled, polled, rolled, soled, strolled, tolled*. Taking in non-final syllables of polysyllables appears to add just one example, *solder*, and one exception, *shoulder* (*soldier* does not qualify as either because here <old> spells /əʊldʒ/). Score: in monosyllables, 10-10 in UK, 11-9 in US; overall, 18-11 in UK, 19-10 in US. Despite the poor score in monosyllables, this would probably be worth teaching when children are clear about spelling regular past tenses and participles with <-ed>.

For a clear example of a phonogram whose spelling is entirely predictable at the segmental level, and therefore not worth teaching as a unit, see the discussion of /iːz/ under /z/, section 3.7.8.

Conversely, for the final syllable /zəm/ which is always unstressed (and is therefore not a rhyme) and almost always spelt <-sm> (only exception: *bosom*), see section 3.5.4. To the latter might be added words ending /əʊs/ (see section 3.7.6). There are only four monosyllables with this rhyme: *close* (adjective/noun), *dose, gross* and the very rare surname *Groce*, but dozens of polysyllables (the 'sugar' words *dextrose, glucose, lactose, sucrose* (all of which have alternative pronunciations in /əʊz/), and the adjectives *comatose, lachrymose, morose, verbose,* etc.), the only exception without <-ose> being the verb *engross*. So 'Word-final /əʊs/ is almost always spelt <-ose>' is a reliable generalisation – but probably of very limited use to young children and their teachers.

In the reading aloud direction, it seems to me that there are just five phonogram-rhyme correspondences which would be worth teaching as units, three applicable mainly to (phonologically) (C)VC monosyllables and two to (C)VCC monosyllables:

<-all> pronounced /ɔːl/ in *all, ball, call, fall, gall, hall, pall, small, squall, stall, tall, thrall, wall*. The only words which are exceptions in RP are *mall, shall*, with /æl/ – and *mall* is /mɔːl/ in General American. These final syllables would have to be clearly distinguished from non-final syllables with <all>, e.g. *alliance*. Score: 13-2 in RP, 14-1 in General American.

<-ead> pronounced /ed/ in *bread, dead, dread, head, lead* (the metal), *read* (past tense and participle), *spread, stead, thread, tread* (exceptions: *bead, knead, lead* (verb), *mead, plead, read* (present tense), with /iːd/). This pattern generalises to *breadth* if we are feeling generous, and to the final syllables of two polysyllables: *ahead, instead*. If we are feeling even more generous we can add some polysyllables with non-final <ead>, of which some but not all are derived forms of the relevant monosyllables: *already, meadow, Reading, ready, steadfast, steady, treadle* (contrast *reading, beadle*). Score: 11-6 in monosyllables, 20-8 overall.

<-ind> pronounced /aɪnd/ in *bind, blind, find, grind, hind, kind, mind, rind, wind* ('turn'), plus one stem polysyllable, *behind* (exceptions: *rescind, tamarind, wind* ('stiff breeze') with /ɪnd/). These final syllables would have to be clearly distinguished from non-final syllables with <ind>, e.g. *indicate*. Score: 9-1 in monosyllables, 10-3 overall.

<-old> pronounced /əʊld/ in *bold, cold, fold, gold, hold, old, scold, sold, told, wold*, plus *mold* in US spelling and the polysyllables *behold, cuckold, blind/mani-fold, marigold, scaffold, threshold* and (non-finally) *solder* (only exception: *soldier* with /əʊldʒ/). Score: in monosyllables, 10-0 in RP, 11-0 in General American; overall, 18-1 in RP, 19-1 in General American.

<-ook> pronounced /ʊk/ in *book, brook, cook, crook, hook, look, nook, rook, shook, took* plus polysyllables *Chinook, forsook* (exceptions: *gook, snook, spook, stook, gobbledegook*, all with /uːk/). Score: 10-4 in monosyllables, 12-5 overall.

This fairly meagre haul of reasonably reliable phonogram-rhyme correspondences would be worth adding to the similarly meagre haul of four reliable pronunciation rules for vowel graphemes analysed in chapter 11, but even together they fail to dent the importance of focusing almost all phonics teaching for reading on the segmental level. And phonics teaching for spelling should be even less influenced by the two possibly usable rhyme-phonogram correspondences listed above. For supporting evidence, see Solity and Vousden (2008: 490), who found that teaching onset-rimes would mean 'there would have to be a fourfold increase in the amount of information children would need to learn to read material aimed at children, and an eightfold increase to move on to adult-directed text'.

## A.8 Dual-functioning

In section 7.1 I deliberately sidestep an obvious question: why analyse any letters at all as belonging to more than one grapheme at the same time?

(Carney (1994: 37) was strongly opposed to 'overlapping' of graphemes, but did not analyse cases such as those I adduce here. However, he was rightly critical of Cordts (1965), who 'for reasons not explained' assigned some letters to two graphemes where this is not warranted, e.g. the <e> in *cake* to both <a.e>, which is essential, and to <ke> as a spelling of /k/, which is entirely unnecessary).

Well, if you do not assign some letters to more than one grapheme at the same time, the correspondences for some phonemes become even more complicated than they already are, and the results seem to me counter-intuitive. For example, it is clear that in *care* there are two graphemes <c, are> spelling the two phonemes /k, eə/. But how should derived forms such as *caring* be analysed? There are now five phonemes /k, eə, r, ɪ, ŋ/ of which /k, ɪ, ŋ/ are obviously spelt <c, i, ng>. The /r/ is also obviously spelt <r> – but does this mean that /eə/ is now spelt only <a>? If so, should this analysis be extended to independently-occurring medial examples such as *parent*? Here there are six phonemes /p, eə, r, ə, n, t/, of which four /p, ə, n, t/ are obviously spelt <p, e, n, t>, leaving <a, r> to spell /eə, r/. Both here and in *caring* we could analyse the <a> as spelling /eə/ and <r> as spelling /r/ and add /eə/ spelt <a> to the list of correspondences – but then in *scarce, scarcity* /eə/ can only be analysed as spelt <ar>, so /eə/ spelt <ar> has to stay in the inventory.

The problems just with /eə/ ramify when we look at words like *air*, *aeroplane*, *pair*, *pairing*, *mayor*, *mayoress*, *sombrero*, *scherzo*, *heir*, *heiress*: /eə/ spelt <air, ayor, er, heir> must be in the inventory to account for *air*, *pair*, *mayor*, *scherzo*, *heir*, but if we rule out dual-functioning we have to add /eə/ spelt <ae, ai, ayo, e, hei> to the list of correspondences (and delete only /eə/ spelt <aer>), and also add <ayo, hei> to the list of graphemes (and delete only <aer>) to account for *aeroplane*, *pairing*, *mayoress*, *sombrero*, *heiress*. Similar considerations apply to other phonemes spelt with graphemes ending in <e, r, w, y> where I posit dual-functioning. I therefore conclude that my analysis is actually conceptually neater, and keeps the lists of graphemes and correspondences from growing even more enormous.

Also, dual-functioning is an economical factor in English spelling in another sense – without it we would always have to spell various adjacent phonemes separately, and in many cases the system would have no well-motivated way of doing this. For example, *bolero*, *bowie*, *buoyant*, *hero*, *jury*, *parent* might have to be spelt *balairro, *boewie, *boiyant, *heerro, *joorry, *pairrant. And many other single-function spellings would probably be even stranger and more complicated.

My dual-functioning analysis solves a problem to which Venezky (1970: 53; in the following quotations I have edited Venezky's symbols into those used here) says 'no realistic solution is possible' without adopting his proposal for a set of graphemes he designates as 'markers'. These are, for example, the letter <e> in *clothe* and *pace*. He correctly notes that 'in each word [the <e>] marks two separate patterns. In *clothe* [it] marks the correspondences <o> → /əʊ/ and <th> → /ð/; in *pace* it marks <a> → /eɪ/ and <c> → /s/,' and goes on: 'The traditionalist is faced with a dilemma here; are the units <o.e/a.e> or <the/ce>? Or shall we take a fine razor and split <e> into two parts so that both alternatives can be taken?' This attempted reductio ad absurdum is proved meaningless once we accept that a letter can belong to two graphemes simultaneously.

# A.9 Graphemes containing apostrophes

There are four of these in my analysis: <ey're> spelling /eə/ in *they're*, <e'er> spelling /eə/ as a contracted form of *ever* either independently or in (e.g.) *ne'er*, *where'er*, <e're> spelling /ɪə/ in *we're*, and <ou're> spelling /ɔː/ in *you're*. Although these are all contracted forms and not stem words

I have included them because their pronunciations are distinctive, and unpredictable from the uncontracted forms.

Along the way I considered two other possible graphemes containing apostrophes for inclusion: <n'> spelling /ən/ as in *isn't*, etc., and <'s> as the regular singular and irregular plural possessive and the contraction of *is/has*. I decided against <n'> because it seemed neater to consider /ən/ in these contractions as spelt solely by the <n> (see section 3.5.5).

<'s> was in drafts of the book for a very long time, with three correspondences: /s/ after voiceless non-sibilant consonants, /z/ after vowels and voiced non-sibilant consonants, and /ɪz/ after sibilant consonants. It was the last of these that originally led me to include <'s>, on the grounds that it seemed a neat way of accounting for the 2-phoneme sequence /ɪz/ in this context; including this correspondence logically meant bringing in the other two. But I eventually took <'s> out on much the same grounds as for excluding <n'> - it seemed neater to consider /ɪz/ as spelt solely by the <s> (see section 3.7.8). Omitting this correspondence logically implied omitting the other two.

## A.10 Word stress

In the sections of chapter 10 devoted to the vowel letters <a, e, i, o, u> as single-letter graphemes I included /ə/ as one of their pronunciations, accompanied by the comment 'regular in unstressed syllables' or 'regular when unstressed', and the words 'stressed' and 'unstressed' occur in many other places in that chapter and this Appendix. In doing so, I evaded what might be considered a key issue in deriving the pronunciations of English words from their written forms: how can you tell which syllables are stressed and which are not?

The short answer is that this is a hugely complicated topic which could not fit in this book and would require a large, separate volume.

Some would say that that volume already exists, in the shape of Chomsky and Halle's (1968) famous study *The Sound Pattern of English*. But, technically, their rules for assigning stress, including and especially their Main Stress Rule, operate not on the written forms of English words but on abstract or 'deep' versions of them which, it is essential for present purposes to note, are **phonological**. Thus the entire analysis is strictly speaking irrelevant to the question of how to predict stress from **written** forms. Moreover, Chomsky and Halle's system is so complex that it is much too unwieldy for pedagogical purposes.

As far as I've been able to discover, there are just two authors who have tackled the question of how to predict word stress in English from **written** forms. Wijk (1966: 124) says:

> Though it is not possible to lay down any completely satisfactory rules for the stressing of English words, it should be emphasised that there are vast numbers of words which do not offer any difficulty at all in this respect.

and then proceeds (pp.125ff.) to present five principal categories of polysyllables for which he says it is possible to formulate a rule – but most do not seem well worked out, all except those I have adopted and numbered (1) and (2) below have copious exceptions, and all the rest tacitly assume that it is obvious how many syllables written English words have.

Dickerson (1978) cites several authors who have said, in effect, that it is impossible to predict the stress patterns of English words – but they were all referring to trying to predict the stress pattern from the **spoken** form, that is, from the sequence of full and reduced (schwa) vowels. (Rule 45 in Clymer, 1963/1996 'When the last syllable is the sound *r*' [assuming this means a General American retroflex ('r-coloured') version of /ə/] 'it is unaccented [=unstressed]' appears to be a confused statement of the obvious fact that in English /ə/ is almost never stressed, but is wrong to imply that this is true only in word-final position.) But if you already know the sequence of full and reduced vowels in English words you already know the stress pattern, and if you already know the stress pattern you already know the sequence of full and reduced vowels, so the argument is circular. Native speakers of English usually already know both, and do not need to be able to deduce the stress pattern from the written form, except perhaps when we encounter an unfamiliar word – and then we may well be in the same boat as foreign learners.

The serious implication here is that it can be difficult to work out from the spelling the pronunciation of a word you have never heard people say, especially if it is unusual, and easy to get some words wrong. For example, I have heard (or heard of) people pronouncing *cotoneaster* as /ˈkɒtəniːstə/ ('cotton-easter') rather than /kəˈtəʊniːjæstə/, *machete* as /məˈtʃiːt/ ('muh-cheat') rather than /məˈʃetiː/, *oesophagus* as /əʊˈwiːsəʊfægəs/ ('oh-wee-so-fag-us') rather than /iːˈsɒfəgəs/, *Yosemite* as /ˈjəʊzəmaɪt/

('yoh-zuh-might') rather than /jɒˈsemɪtiː/, and (possibly the most classic case) *misled* as /ˈmɪzəld/ (like the verb *mizzled*).

There are two words spelt *forestage*: the obvious two-syllable one pronounced /ˈfɔːsteɪdʒ/, 'the part of a theatrical performance area between the curtain and the orchestra pit', and with a morpheme boundary after *fore-*; and a three-syllable word from medieval English law with a morpheme boundary after *forest-*, pronounced /ˈfɒrɪstɪdʒ/ and meaning either 'a duty payable to the king's foresters' or 'a service paid by foresters to the king'. Similarly, *forestride*, with a morpheme boundary after *forest-* and therefore more often spelt as two words, pronounced /ˈfɒrɪstraɪd/ with three syllables, was briefly the name of a bus service in the Reading area; but it could be misread (and I did so misread it) as having a morpheme boundary after *fore-* and the two-syllable pronunciation /ˈfɔːstraɪd/, and as perhaps meaning a specially determined way of walking (but there is no trace of such a word in the dictionaries). All of this again illustrates the need, which I stated right at the start of this book, to look up the pronunciation of whole words in a good pronouncing dictionary (that is, one which uses IPA symbols).

Dickerson took what appeared to be a novel approach to the problem of deducing how English polysyllables are stressed from their written form. Unfortunately, I found it impossible to adopt. This is because he assumes that non-native learners of English know what a syllable is:

> To assign major stress to a word, only two syllables are relevant. One is called the Key Syllable, the other the Left Syllable, namely, the syllable immediately to the left of the Key.
>
> (Dickerson, 1978: 138)

This also assumes that learners know where syllables in **written** English words begin and end and (as with Wijk) how many syllables there are in written English words. These are huge assumptions and, as I found when I tried to work them through, very awkward to specify in detail, mainly because they covertly assume that the learner already knows the spoken form of the word – which is precisely what Dickerson says he is trying not to assume.

For example, it is true that the great majority of two-syllable words in English are stressed on the first syllable (as pointed out by Clymer, 1963/1996, rule 30) – but how is a reader who does not already know (for example) the words *blase*, *dais* to deduce from their **written** forms that they have two syllables when all other words ending <-ase> or containing <ai>

between two consonant letters are monosyllables? Even if that prediction were possible, trying to make a usable rule for stress on two-syllable words would still entail listing hundreds of such words which are instead stressed on the second syllable, including dozens of cases where verbs are stressed on the second syllable and identically-spelt nouns/adjectives are stressed on the first. Indeed, Hunnicutt (1976) showed that a computerised version of the Chomsky-Halle rules could not assign the correct stress to such pairs.

Another serious problem for any attempt to deduce the stress pattern of English words from their written forms arises from the existence of the elided vowels analysed in section 6.10 – it is hardly ever possible to deduce that a particular vowel letter in medial position (as opposed to stem-final 'silent' <e>) represents no phoneme at all and therefore isn't even a candidate for taking the stress. Consider, for example, *afferent* (three syllables, first <e> pronounced /ə/) and *different* (two syllables, first <e> elided). And in some words a particular vowel may be elided or not, often depending on accent, for example *migratory*, pronounced either as /ˈmaɪɡrətriː/ (three syllables, stress on first, <o> elided) or as /maɪˈɡreɪtəriː/ (four syllables, stress on second, no elision) or as /maɪɡrəˈtɔːriː/ (four syllables, stress on third, no elision).

So here I have merely stated a few useful rules for determining which syllable in polysyllables has main stress. The three most useful rules for predicting main stress are:

1) Virtually all words ending in <ea, eo, eou, eu, ia, io, iou, iu> followed by a single consonant letter or none and with at least one vowel letter earlier in the word have the stress on the syllable preceding <ea, eo, eou, eu, ia, io, iou, iu>, including all the hundreds of words ending <-tion> (as mentioned in rule 36 of Clymer, 1963/1996) and all those containing the five medial graphemes (other than <sh>) pronounced /ʃ/
2) Virtually all words ending in <-ience, -iency, -ient, -(s)sive>, have the stress on the preceding syllable
3) Virtually all words ending in <-ic(al)> have the stress on the preceding syllable. For exceptions see the last four paragraphs of section 10.22.

Otherwise, there are only rules covering small numbers of cases, such as:

4) Almost all words ending in <-ator> have the stress on the <a> if they have three syllables, e.g. *creátor, curátor, dictátor, spectátor*, otherwise on the syllable two before the <a>, e.g. *admínistrator, ágitator, áviator, cálculator, cómmentator, ínsulator*. Only exceptions: *consérvator,*

*conspírator, órator, prédator, sénator*, which all have <a> pronounced /ə/ and stress on the syllable before that

5) The grapheme <air> is always stressed in polysyllables except in *corsair* (usually stressed on first syllable), *millionairess* (where the feminine ending <-ess> is usually stressed instead), *mohair* (always stressed on first syllable)
6) All words ending in <-eer, -esce, -esque, -ique> have stress on the final syllable
7) The grapheme <ier> is always stressed in polysyllables, except that *frontier* can be stressed on either syllable (but there are lots of words where <i, er> are separate graphemes)
8) All words ending in <-tte> have stress on the final syllable except *etiquette, omelette, palette*, which have stress on the first syllable
9) Almost all words ending in <-oon> have stress on the final syllable except *forenoon, honeymoon, pantaloon*, which have stress on the first syllable, and those ending in <-zoon> ('living thing'), in which the ending has two syllables and is stressed on the first <o>.

There is also one helpful rule for where main stress does **not** fall:

10) The vowel letters as single-letter word-final graphemes in polysyllables are hardly ever stressed (Clymer, 1963/1996, rule 32 is a subset of this applying only to two-syllable words ending in a consonant letter followed by <y>). Strictly speaking this does not apply to word-final <e> as part of a split digraph, but that is of course never stressed either since there is no word-final vowel phoneme in such cases. There are very few exceptions, all of which are disyllables (and none at all with <i, u>): *mama, papa; blase* (which can also be stressed on the first syllable), *manque, outre, risque; lasso; ally* (if stressed on the second syllable, as the verb sometimes is), *ap/com/im/re/sup-ply, defy, deny, descry, espy, July, rely*. This rule implies that:
    - in all other two syllable words with a single vowel letter as the word final grapheme (that is, those with only one other vowel grapheme earlier in the word), the stress falls on that other vowel grapheme (= the first syllable)
    - a single-letter word-final vowel grapheme is never stressed in words of more than two syllables (except perhaps in unassimilated loanwords, e.g. Italian *omertà*), but this is of no help in predicting where the stress does fall in those longer words.

Similarly, Clymer's (1963/1996) rule 35 'when *ture* is the final syllable in a word, it is unaccented' (more accurately, 'when <-ture> is word-final, it is unstressed') is true, helpful if the word has only two syllables (e.g. *picture*), but useless for determining where the stress falls in longer words (e.g. *furniture*). And Clymer's rule 31 'If *a, in, re, ex, de*, or *be* is the first syllable in a word, it is usually unaccented [=unstressed]' poses huge problems. If it is meant to refer to prefixes, there is no way for anyone without deep etymological knowledge to tell when these word-beginnings are prefixes and when they are not. But if it is meant to refer to all words with these beginnings then it would be necessary to specify that each of them (except <ex-, in->) has to be followed by at least one consonant letter and all of them then by at least one vowel letter that is not 'magic <e>'; and even then a quick scan of a dictionary reveals that there are far too many exceptions for the rule to be useful.

So, beyond the few definitely or possibly useful rules given above, the task of predicting word stress from the written forms of English words also awaits another study. That study would have to avoid the assumption, which I have knowingly perpetrated/perpetuated in section 10.42 and in the 'rules' I have stated above, that readers can tell from the spelling of English words how many syllables their spoken forms contain.

# Appendix B: Pedagogically selected lists of phoneme-grapheme and grapheme-phoneme correspondences

These lists are intended to be much more useful to teachers and to writers of early reading books than the full lists of correspondences in chapter 8. Similar tables (also largely devised by me) appeared in the *Notes of Guidance* to *Letters and Sounds* (D*f*ES, 2007). As far as possible I have ensured that all words within the 1000 most frequent words in English whose correspondences are not covered by the major correspondences are listed in the right-hand columns of Tables B1-2 and in Tables B.6 and B.8. My source for the 1000 most frequent words was: http://en.wiktionary.org/w/index.php?title=Category:1000_English_basic_words&pagefrom=stamp#mw-pages [last accessed 20/8/2012].

For guidance on the phonetics underpinning the application of these lists in phonics teaching see Burton (2011), which also contains versions of these lists.

TABLE B.1: THE PHONEME-GRAPHEME CORRESPONDENCES OF BRITISH ENGLISH SPELLING, BY RP PHONEME, 1: CONSONANTS.

| Phoneme | Grapheme(s) | | As in ... | Common words with rare graphemes for the phoneme |
|---|---|---|---|---|
| | Basic | Other | | |
| /b/ | b | bb | bed rabbit | <bu> build buy |
| /k/ | c | ck k q ch | come back look queen Christmas | <cu> biscuit |
| /tʃ/ | ch | tch | children match | <t> nature picture <ti> question |
| /d/ | d | dd ed | dad teddy called | |

http://dx.doi.org/10.11647/OBP.0053.13

TABLE B.1: THE PHONEME–GRAPHEME CORRESPONDENCES OF BRITISH ENGLISH SPELLING, BY RP PHONEME, 1: CONSONANTS, CONT.

| Phoneme | Grapheme(s) Basic | Grapheme(s) Other | As in ... | Common words with rare graphemes for the phoneme |
|---|---|---|---|---|
| /f/ | f | ff ph | from off elephant | <ft> often soften <gh> cough enough laugh rough tough |
| /g/ | g | gg | get jogging | <gh> ghost <gu> guess guy |
| /h/ | h | | horse | <wh> who whole whose |
| /dʒ/ | j | dg dge g ge | just budgie bridge giant orange | |
| /m/ | m | mm | my mummy | <mb> climb lamb thumb <me> come some <mn> autumn column |
| /n/ | n | nn | now dinner | <gn> gnome sign <kn> knife knock knot know <ne> done engine none |
| /ŋ/ | ng | n | sing sink | <ngue> tongue |
| /p/ | p | pp | pen apple | <ph> shepherd |
| /r/ | r | rr | red berry | <rh> rgyme rhythm <wr> write wrong |
| /s/ | s | c ce se ss | sit city once horse grass | <sc> science scissors <st> castle Christmas listen whistle |
| /ʃ/ | sh | ti | ship station | <ch> machine <ci> special <s> sugar sure <ss> issue pressure tissue <ssi> permission |
| /ʒ/ | si | | vision | <s> measure pleasure treasure usual |
| /t/ | t | tt ed | but little looked | <pt> receipt <th> Thomas <tw> two |
| /θ/ | th | | thing | |
| /ð/ | th | | that | <the> breathe |
| /v/ | v | ve | very have | <bv> obvious <f> of |
| /w/ | w | u | went queen | <wh> what when (etc.) wheel whistle white /wʌ/ spelt <o> once one |
| /j/ | y | | yellow | <i> onion view |
| /z/ | z | s se ze zz | zoo is please sneeze puzzle | <si> business <ss> scissors |

Appendix B   479

TABLE B.2: THE PHONEME–GRAPHEME CORRESPONDENCES OF BRITISH ENGLISH SPELLING, BY RP PHONEME, 2: VOWELS.

| Phoneme | Grapheme(s) | | As in ... | Common words with rare graphemes for the phoneme |
|---|---|---|---|---|
| | Basic | Other | | |
| /æ/ | a | | and | |
| /ə/ | a | e er o | a the butter button | &lt;ar&gt; sugar &lt;i&gt; possible &lt;our&gt; colour favour honour &lt;re&gt; centre &lt;ure&gt; nature picture |
| /eɪ/ | a.e | a ai ay | came bacon paint day | &lt;aigh&gt; straight &lt;ea&gt; break great steak &lt;eigh&gt; eight &lt;ey&gt; they |
| /eə/ | air | are ar | fair fare parent | &lt;ear&gt; bear pear tear wear &lt;ere&gt; there where &lt;eir&gt; their |
| /ɑː/ | ar | a | far ask | &lt;al&gt; half &lt;are&gt; are &lt;au&gt; aunt laugh &lt;ear&gt; heart |
| /e/ | e | ea | went bread | &lt;a&gt; any many &lt;ai&gt; again(st) said &lt;ay&gt; says &lt;ie&gt; friend |
| /iː/ | ee | e ea ey ie y | see he beach key field city | &lt;e.e&gt; these &lt;eo&gt; people &lt;i.e&gt; police |
| /ɪə/ | eer | ear er ere | cheer hear hero here | &lt;ier&gt; fierce |
| /ɜː/ | er | ir or ur | her girl word fur | &lt;ear&gt; early earth heard learn &lt;ere&gt; were &lt;our&gt; journey |
| /ɪ/ | i | e y | is England gym | &lt;a&gt; language sausage &lt;o&gt; women &lt;u&gt; business minute |
| /aɪ/ | i.e | i igh y | like I night my | &lt;ei&gt; either &lt;eigh&gt; height &lt;eye&gt; eye &lt;ye&gt; goodbye /aɪə/ spelt &lt;ir, ire, yre&gt; biro fire wire tyre |
| /ɒ/ | o | a | not was | &lt;au&gt; because sausage &lt;ho&gt; honest honour &lt;ou&gt; cough |
| /əʊ/ | o | o.e ow | so bone blow | &lt;oa&gt; approach boat &lt;oh&gt; oh &lt;ough&gt; although |
| /ɔɪ/ | oi | oy | boil boy | |
| /ʊ/ | oo | u | book put | &lt;o&gt; woman &lt;oul&gt; could should would |
| /uː/ | oo | ew u u.e | too blew super rule | &lt;o&gt; do to two who &lt;oe&gt; shoe &lt;o.e&gt; lose move prove whose &lt;ou&gt; you &lt;ough&gt; through &lt;ue&gt; blue true &lt;ui&gt; fruit |

TABLE B.2: THE PHONEME-GRAPHEME CORRESPONDENCES OF BRITISH ENGLISH SPELLING, BY RP PHONEME, 2: VOWELS, CONT.

| Phoneme | Grapheme(s) | | As in ... | Common words with rare graphemes for the phoneme |
|---|---|---|---|---|
| | Basic | Other | | |
| /ʊə/ | oor | ure | poor sure | <our> tour |
| /ɔː/ | or | a ar au aw ore | for all warn sauce saw before | <augh> caught naughty <oar> board <oor> door floor <ough> bought brought fought ought thought <our> course four your |
| /aʊ/ | ou | ow | out down | /aʊə/ spelt <hour> hour /aʊə/ spelt <our, ower> flour flower |
| /ʌ/ | u | o | but some | <oo> blood flood <ou> country couple double encourage enough rough tough trouble young /wʌ/ spelt <o> once one |

TABLE B.3: THE PHONEME-GRAPHEME CORRESPONDENCES OF BRITISH ENGLISH SPELLING, 3: 2-PHONEME SEQUENCES FREQUENTLY SPELT WITH SINGLE GRAPHEMES.

| 2-phoneme sequence | Grapheme(s) | | As in ... | 2-grapheme spellings for same sequence |
|---|---|---|---|---|
| | Basic | Other | | |
| /əl/ (only word-final) | le | | little | animal label pencil carol beautiful |
| /juː/ | u | eau ew ue u.e | union beauty few argue cute | view you |
| /ks/ | x | | box | ban**ks** tri**cks** politi**cs** |

N.B. The 2-phoneme sequence /kw/ is almost always spelt <qu> and should also be taught as a unit.

TABLE B.4: THE GRAPHEME-PHONEME CORRESPONDENCES OF BRITISH ENGLISH SPELLING, 1: SINGLE GRAPHEMES FREQUENTLY PRONOUNCED AS 2-PHONEME SEQUENCES.

| Grapheme(s) | 2-phoneme sequence | Other phonemes | As in … |
|---|---|---|---|
| eau ew u ue u.e | /juː/ | (too many to list) | beauty few union argue cute |
| le (only word-final) | /əl/ | | little |
| x | /ks/ | | box |

N.B. The 2-grapheme sequence <qu> is almost always pronounced /kw/ and should be taught as a unit.

TABLE B.5: THE GRAPHEME-PHONEME CORRESPONDENCES OF BRITISH ENGLISH SPELLING, 2: MAJOR CORRESPONDENCES FOR CONSONANT GRAPHEMES.

| Grapheme(s) | Phoneme(s) | | As in … |
|---|---|---|---|
| | Basic | Other | |
| b bb | /b/ | | bed rabbit |
| c | /k/ | /s/ | come city |
| ce | /s/ | | once |
| ch | /tʃ/ | /k/ | children Christmas |
| ck | /k/ | | back |
| d dd | /d/ | | dad teddy |
| dg(e) | /dʒ/ | | budgie bridge |
| ed | /d/ | /t/ | called looked |
| f ff | /f/ | | from off |
| g | /g/ | /dʒ/ | get giant |
| ge | /dʒ/ | | orange |
| gg | /g/ | | jogging |
| h | /h/ | | horse |
| j | /dʒ/ | | just |
| k | /k/ | | look |
| l ll | /l/ | | leg ball |

TABLE B.5: THE GRAPHEME–PHONEME CORRESPONDENCES OF BRITISH ENGLISH SPELLING, 2: MAJOR CORRESPONDENCES FOR CONSONANT GRAPHEMES, CONT.

| Grapheme(s) | Phoneme(s) Basic | Phoneme(s) Other | As in ... |
|---|---|---|---|
| n | /n/ | /ŋ/ | now sink |
| ng | /ŋ/ | | sing |
| nn | /n/ | | dinner |
| p pp | /p/ | | pen apple |
| ph | /f/ | | elephant |
| q | /k/ | | queen |
| r rr | /r/ | | red berry |
| s se | /s/ | /z/ | sit is horse please |
| sh | /ʃ/ | | ship |
| si | /ʒ/ | | vision |
| ss | /s/ | | grass |
| t tt | /t/ | | but little |
| tch | /tʃ/ | | match |
| th | /θ/ | /ð/ | thing that |
| ti | /ʃ/ | /tʃ/ | station question |
| u | /w/ | | queen |
| v ve | /v/ | | very have |
| w | /w/ | | went |
| y | /j/ | | yellow |
| z ze zz | /z/ | | zoo sneeze puzzle |

TABLE B.6: THE GRAPHEME–PHONEME CORRESPONDENCES OF BRITISH ENGLISH SPELLING, 3: MINOR CORRESPONDENCES FOR CONSONANT GRAPHEMES.

| Grapheme(s) | Phoneme(s) | As in ... |
|---|---|---|
| bu | /b/ | build buy |
| bv | /v/ | obvious |
| ch ci | /ʃ/ | machine special |
| cu | /k/ | biscuit |
| f | /v/ | of |
| ft | /f/ | often soften |
| gh | /f g/ | cough enough laugh rough tough; ghost |
| gn | /n/ | gnome sign |
| gu | /g/ | guess guy |
| i | /j/ | onion view |
| kn | /n/ | knife knock knot know |
| mb me mn | /m/ | climb lamb thumb; come some; autumn column |
| ne | /n/ | done engine none |
| ngue | /ŋ/ | tongue |
| o | /wʌ/ | once one |
| ph | /p/ | shepherd |
| pt | /t/ | receipt |
| rh | /r/ | rhyme rhythm |
| s ssi | /ʃ/ | sugar sure; permission |
| s | /ʒ/ | measure pleasure treasure usual |
| sc | /s/ | science scissors |
| si | /z/ | business |
| ss | /ʃ z/ | issue pressure tissue, scissors |
| st | /s/ | castle Christmas listen whistle |
| t | /tʃ/ | nature picture |
| th tw | /t/ | Thomas two |
| the | /ð/ | breathe |
| wh | /h w/ | who whole whose; what when (etc.) wheel whistle white |
| wr | /r/ | write wrong |

TABLE B.7: THE GRAPHEME-PHONEME CORRESPONDENCES OF BRITISH ENGLISH SPELLING, 4: MAJOR CORRESPONDENCES FOR VOWEL GRAPHEMES.

| Grapheme(s) | Phoneme(s) Basic | Phoneme(s) Other | As in … |
|---|---|---|---|
| a | /æ/ | /eɪ ɑː ɒ ɔː ə/ | and bacon ask was all about |
| a.e ai ay | /eɪ/ | | came paint day |
| air are | /eə/ | | fair fare |
| ar | /ɑː/ | /eə ɔː/ | far parent warn |
| au aw | /ɔː/ | | sauce saw |
| e | /e/ | /iː ɪ ə/ | went he England the |
| ea | /iː/ | /e/ | beach bread |
| ear eer ere | /ɪə/ | | hear cheer here |
| ee ey | /iː/ | | see key |
| er | /ɜː/ | /ɪə ə/ | her hero butter |
| ew | /uː/ | | blew |
| i | /ɪ/ | /aɪ/ | is I |
| ie | /iː/ | | field |
| i.e igh | /aɪ/ | | like night |
| ir | /ɜː/ | | girl |
| o | /ɒ/ | /ʌ əʊ ə/ | not some so button |
| o.e | /əʊ/ | | bone |
| oi oy | /ɔɪ/ | | boil boy |
| oo | /uː/ | /ʊ/ | too book |
| oor | /ɔː/ | /ʊə/ | door poor |
| or | /ɔː/ | /ɜː/ | for worm |
| ore | /ɔː/ | | before |
| ou | /aʊ/ | | out |
| ow | /aʊ/ | /əʊ/ | down blow |
| u | /ʌ/ | /ʊ uː/ | but put super |
| u.e | /uː/ | | rule |
| ur | /ɜː/ | | fur |
| y | /aɪ/ | /ɪ iː/ | my gym city |

TABLE B.8: THE GRAPHEME-PHONEME CORRESPONDENCES OF BRITISH ENGLISH SPELLING, 5: MINOR CORRESPONDENCES FOR VOWEL GRAPHEMES.

| Grapheme(s) | Phoneme(s) | As in ... |
|---|---|---|
| a | /e ɪ/ | any many; language sausage |
| ai ay | /e/ | again(st) said says |
| aigh | /eɪ/ | straight |
| al are | /ɑː/ | half; are |
| ar | /ə/ | sugar |
| au | /ɑː ɒ/ | aunt laugh; because sausage |
| augh | /ɔː/ | caught naughty |
| ea ey | /eɪ/ | break great steak; they |
| ear | /eə ɑː ɜː/ | bear pear tear wear; heart; early earth heard learn |
| e.e eo | /iː/ | these; people |
| ei | /aɪ/ | either |
| eigh | /eɪ aɪ/ | eight; height |
| eir | /eə/ | their |
| ere | /eə ɜː/ | there where; were |
| eye | /aɪ/ | eye |
| ho | /ɒ/ | honest honour |
| hour | /aʊə/ | hour |
| i | /ə/ | possible |
| ie | /e/ | friend |
| i.e | /iː/ | police |
| ier | /ɪə/ | fierce |
| ir ire | /aɪə/ | biro fire wire |
| o | /ʊ ɪ wʌ/ | woman; women; once one |
| o oe o.e | /uː/ | do to two who; shoe; lose move prove whose |
| oa oh | /əʊ/ | approach boat oh |
| oar | /ɔː/ | board |
| oo | /ʌ/ | blood flood |
| oor | /ɔː/ | door floor |
| ou | /ɒ uː ʌ/ | cough; you; country couple double encourage enough rough tough trouble young |

TABLE B.8: THE GRAPHEME–PHONEME CORRESPONDENCES OF BRITISH ENGLISH SPELLING, 5: MINOR CORRESPONDENCES FOR VOWEL GRAPHEMES, CONT.

| Grapheme(s) | Phoneme(s) | As in ... |
|---|---|---|
| ough | /əʊ uː ɔː/ | although; through; bought brought fought ought thought |
| oul | /ʊ/ | could should would |
| our | /ə ɜː ʊə ɔː aʊə/ | colour favour honour; journey; tour; course four your; flour |
| ower | /aʊə/ | flower |
| re | /ə/ | centre |
| u | /ɪ/ | business minute |
| ue ui | /uː/ | blue true fruit |
| ure | /ə/ | nature picture |
| ye | /aɪ/ | goodbye |
| yre | /aɪə/ | tyre |

# References

Adams, Marilyn Jager, *Beginning to Read: Thinking and Learning about Print* (Cambridge, MA: MIT Press, 1990).

Albrow, Kenneth H., *The English Writing System: Notes towards a Description* (Schools Council Programme in Linguistics and English Teaching: Papers Series 11, volume 2) (London: Longman for the Schools Council, 1972).

Anon., *The Spelling Rulebook* (Wakefield: SEN Marketing, 2008).

Baayen, R.H., Piepenbrock, R. and Gulikers, L. *The CELEX Lexical Database* (Release 2, English version 2.5) [CD-ROM] (Philadelphia, PA: Linguistic Data Consortium, University of Pennsylvania, 1995, https://catalog.ldc.upenn.edu/docs/LDC96L14/celex.readme.html

Basic Skills Agency, *Writing Skills: A Survey of How Well People Can Spell and Punctuate* (London: Basic Skills Agency, 1996).

Bell, Masha, *Understanding English Spelling* (Cambridge: Pegasus Educational, 2004).

Brooks, Greg, *An Investigation into some Visual, Auditory and Articulatory Factors in Oral and Silent Reading of Children and Adults* (Unpublished PhD thesis, University of Leeds School of Education, February 1985). (British Library Lending Division microfilm no. D57713/85)

—, *Rationality and Phonics* (Professorial lecture, University of Sheffield, October 2007).

—, 'Using the International Phonetic Alphabet to Support Accurate Phonic Teachings', in Applied Linguistics and Primary School Teaching, Ellis, Sue and McCartney, Elspeth, eds. (Cambridge: Cambridge University Press, 2011), 25*8//8 http://bit.ly/1CTb6sq

—, Gorman, Thomas P., Kendall, Lesley, and Tate, Alison, *What Teachers in Training are Taught about Reading: A Summary Report to the Council for the Accreditation of Teacher Education* (Slough: NFER, 1991). Republished as Part B of CATE, *Training Teachers to Teach Reading: A Review* (London: Council for the Accreditation of Teacher Education, 1992).

—, Gorman, Thomas P., Kendall, Lesley, and Tate, Alison, *What Teachers in Training are Taught about Reading: The Working Papers* (Slough: NFER, 1992).

Brumfit, Christopher, ed., *Language in Teacher Education* (Southampton: National Congress on Language in Education, 1988). http://dx.doi.org/10.1017/s027226310001069x

Burmeister, L.E., 'Vowel Pairs', *The Reading Teacher*, 21 (1968), 445-62. http://dx.doi.org/10.2307/747098

Burton, Maxine, *Developing Adult Teaching and Learning: Practitioner Guides. Reading* (Leicester: National Institute of Adult Continuing Education, 2007).

—, *Phonetics for Phonics* (Leicester: National Institute of Adult Continuing Education, 2011).

—, and Brooks, Greg, *The Case for Using the International Phonetic Alphabet (IPA) in Teaching Teachers about Phonics. A Submission to the Rose Review of Best Practice in the Teaching of Reading* (Sheffield: authors, 2005) [mimeograph].

*Cambridge English Pronouncing Dictionary*, 18th Edition (Cambridge: Cambridge University Press, 2011).

Carney, Edward, *A Survey of English Spelling* (London: Routledge, 1994).

—, *English Spelling* (London: Routledge, 1997).

CATE, *Training Teachers to Teach Reading: A Review* (London: Council for the Accreditation of Teacher Education, 1992).

Chomsky, Noam, and Morris Halle, *The Sound Pattern of English* (New York: Harper and Row, 1968).

Clymer, T., 'The Utility of Phonic Generalizations in the Primary Grades', *The Reading Teacher*, 16 (1963), 252-58. Reprinted in *The Reading Teacher*, 50, 3 (November 1996), 182-87, http://joanwink.com/research/9706083317.pdf

Cook, Vivian, *The English Writing System* (London: Arnold, 2004).

Cordts, Anna D., *Phonics for the Reading Teacher* (New York: Holt, Rinehart and Winston, 1965).

Crystal, David, *Spell it Out: The Singular Story of English Spelling* (London: Profile Books, 2012).

Cruttenden, Alan, *Gimson's Pronunciation of English*, 8th edition (London: Routledge, 2014). http://dx.doi.org/10.4324/9780203784969

Dickerson, W.B., 'English Orthography: A Guide to Word Stress and Vowel Quality', *IRAL*, 16, 1-4 (1978), 127-47. http://dx.doi.org/10.1515/iral.1978.16.1-4.127

Gardner, M., 'Mathematical Games', *Scientific American*, 240, 1 (1979), 18-24. http://dx.doi.org/10.1038/scientificamerican0179-18

Gates, L., 'A Face Lift for the Silent *E*', *The Reading Teacher*, 37 (1983), 102-03.

—, 'The Consonant Generalizations Revisited', *Reading Horizons*, 26 (1986), 232-36.

Gontijo, Possi F.D., Gontijo, Ivair, and Shillcock, Richard, 'Grapheme-phoneme Probabilities in British English', *Behavior Research Methods, Instruments, and Computers*, 35, 1 (2003), 136-57. http://dx.doi.org/10.3758/bf03195506

Gorman, Thomas P., *What Teachers in Training Read about Reading* (Slough: NFER, 1989).

Haas, Walter, *Phono-Graphic Translation* (Manchester: Manchester University Press, 1970).

Hunnicutt, S., 'Phonological Rules for a Text-to-speech System', *American Journal of Computational Linguistics Microfiche*, 57 (1976), 1-72.

Johnston, F.P., 'The Utility of Phonic Generalizations: Let's Take another Look at Clymer's Conclusions', *The Reading Teacher*, 55, 2 (2001), 132-43.

Jones, Daniel, edited by Peter Roach, James Hartman, and Jane Setter, *Cambridge English Pronouncing Dictionary, 18th Edition* (Cambridge: Cambridge University Press, 2011).

Lamb, Bernard, 'Letter', *Times Higher Education*, 21 August (2008), p.28.

Lee, William R., *Spelling Irregularity and Reading Difficulty in English* (Slough: National Foundation for Educational Research, 1960).

MacLeod, M.E., 'Rules in the Teaching of Spelling', in Robbie, H.J.L., ed., *Studies in Spelling* (Publications of the Scottish Council for Research in Education XL) (London: University of London Press, 1961).

Mines, M. Ardussi, Hanson, Barbara F., and Shoup, June E., 'Frequency of Occurrence of Phonemes in Conversational English', *Language and Speech*, 21, 3 (1978), 221-41.

Moseley, David, *ACE Dictionary*, revised edn (Bayside NY: LDA Publishers, 1998).

Moser, H.M., Dreher, J.J. and Oyer, H.J., Technical Report No. 57. Ohio State University Research Foundation (1957). Cited in PMC Albert Ross Eckler, ed., 'Review: *English Monosyllables*'. *Word Ways: The Journal of Recreational Linguistics* (Indianapolis) 11-12 (1978), 118, http://en.wikipedia.org/wiki/List_of_the_longest_English_words_with_one_syllable

Mountford, John, *An Insight into English Spelling* (London: Hodder & Stoughton, 1998).

Department for Education and Skills Primary National Strategy, *Letters and Sounds: Principles and Practice of High Qality Phonics* (Norwich: D*f*ES Publications, 2007), http://www.smartkids.co.uk/docs/teacher_resources/Letters_Sounds_Manual/Notes_of_Guidance.pdf

Roach, Peter, *English Phonetics and Phonology: A Practical Course* (4th edn) (Cambridge: Cambridge University Press, 2009).

Rollings, Andrew G., *The Spelling Patterns of English* (Munich: LINCOM, 2004).

Shcherbakova, Irina F., 'Phonics: The Way We Do It' (Paper presented at 11th European Conference on Reading, Stavanger, Norway, July 1999).

Snowling, Margaret J. and Charles Hulme, eds, *The Science of Reading: A Handbook* (Oxford: Blackwell, 2005).

Treiman, Rebecca, Mullennix, John, Bijeljac-Babic, Ranka, and Richmond-Welty, E. Daylene, 'The Special Role of Rimes in the Description, Use, and Acquisition of English Orthography', *Journal of Experimental Psychology: General*, 124, 2, (1995), 107-36. http://dx.doi.org/10.1037/0096-3445.124.2.107

Solity, Jonathan and Vousden, Janet, 'Real books vs reading schemes: a new perspective from instructional psychology', *Educational Psychology*, 29, 4, (2009), 469-511.

Upward, Christopher and George Davidson, *The History of English Spelling* (Chichester: Wiley-Blackwell, 2011). 10.1002/9781444342994

Venezky, Richard L., *The Structure of English Orthography* (Janua linguarum, series minor, no. 82) (The Hague & Paris: De Gruyter Mouton, 1970). http://dx.doi.org/10.1515/9783110804478

Wijk, Axel, *Rules of Pronunciation for the English Language* (Oxford: Oxford University Press, 1966).

# This book need not end here...

At Open Book Publishers, we are changing the nature of the traditional academic book. The title you have just read will not be left on a library shelf, but will be accessed online by hundreds of readers each month across the globe. We make all our books free to read online so that students, researchers and members of the public who can't afford a printed edition can still have access to the same ideas as you.

Our digital publishing model also allows us to produce supplementary material online, including extra chapters, reviews, links and other digital resources. Find *Dictionary of the English Spelling System* on our website to access its online extras. Please check this page regularly for ongoing updates, and join the conversation by leaving your own comments:

http://www.openbookpublishers.com/isbn/9781783741076

If you enjoyed this book and feel that research like this should be available to all readers, regardless of their income, please think about donating to us. Our company is run entirely by academics, and our publishing decisions are based on intellectual merit and public value rather than on commercial viability. We do not operate for profit, and all donations, as with all other revenue we generate, will be used to finance new open access publications.

For further information about what we do, how to donate to OBP, additional digital material related to our titles or to order our books, please visit our website: www.openbookpublishers.com

OpenBook Publishers

Knowledge is for sharing

Printed in July 2021
by Rotomail Italia S.p.A., Vignate (MI) - Italy